The Diaries of
GEORGE WASHINGTON
Volume VI
January 1790–December 1799

ASSISTANT EDITORS

Beverly H. Runge, Frederick Hall Schmidt,
and Philander D. Chase

George H. Reese, CONSULTING EDITOR

Joan Paterson Kerr, PICTURE EDITOR

THE DIARIES OF
GEORGE
WASHINGTON

VOLUME VI

January 1790–December 1799

DONALD JACKSON AND DOROTHY TWOHIG
EDITORS

UNIVERSITY PRESS OF VIRGINIA

CHARLOTTESVILLE

This edition has been prepared by the staff of
The Papers of George Washington,
sponsored by
The Mount Vernon Ladies' Association of the Union
and the University of Virginia
with the support of
the National Endowment for the Humanities
and
the National Historical Publications
and Records Commission.

THE UNIVERSITY PRESS OF VIRGINIA

Copyright © 1979 by the Rector and Visitors
of the University of Virginia

First published 1979

Frontispiece: "Washington Reviewing the Western Army
at Fort Cumberland, Maryland,"
attributed to James Peale. (Metropolitan Museum of Art,
Gift of Col. and Mrs. Edgar William Garbisch, 1963) .

Library of Congress Cataloging in Publication Data (Revised)
Washington, George, Pres. U.S., 1732–1799.
The diaries of George Washington.
Includes bibliographies and indexes.
1. Washington, George, Pres. U.S., 1732–1799.
2. Presidents—United States—Biography.   I. Jackson,
Donald Dean, 1919–   II. Twohig, Dorothy.   III. Title
E312.8 1976 973.4'1'0924 [B] 75-41365
ISBN 0-8139-0807-8 (v. 6)

Printed in the United States of America

Contents

Maps

Illustrations

Illustrations

Acknowledgments

The editors wish to take this opportunity to acknowledge the contributions of the following staff members to volume VI of *The Diaries of George Washington:*

John Barnwell	Nancy H. Morris
Peter J. Carlton	Joanne Schehl
Bryson Clevenger	Karen Schwartz
Jeff Delahorne	Jessie Shelar
Joseph A. Guzinski	Matt Sutko
Beverly S. Kirsch	Kathleen Williams

Editorial Procedures and Symbols

Transcription of the diaries has remained as faithful as possible to the original manuscript. Because of the nature of GW's diary entries, absolute consistency in punctuation has been virtually impossible. Where feasible, the punctuation has generally been retained as written. However, in cases where sentences are separated by dashes, a common device in the eighteenth century, the dash has been changed to a period and the following word capitalized. Dashes which appear after periods have been dropped. Periods have been inserted at points which are clearly the ends of sentences. In many of the diaries, particularly those dealing with planting and the weather, entries consist of phrases separated by dashes rather than sentences. Generally if the phrase appears to stand alone, a period has been substituted for the dash.

Spelling of all words is retained as it appears in the manuscript. Errors in spelling of geographic locations and proper names have been corrected in notes or in brackets only if the spelling in the text makes the word incomprehensible. Washington occasionally, especially in the diaries, placed above an incorrectly written word a symbol sometimes resembling a tilde, sometimes an infinity sign, to indicate an error in orthography. When this device is used the editors have silently corrected the word.

The ampersand has been retained. The thorn has been transcribed as "th." The symbol for per has been written out. When a tilde is used to indicate either a double letter or missing letters, the correction has been made silently or the word has been transcribed as an abbreviation. Capitalization is retained as it appears in the manuscript; if the writer's intention is not clear, modern usage is followed.

Contractions and abbreviations are retained as written; a period is inserted after abbreviations. When an apostrophe has been used in contractions it is retained. Superscripts have been lowered, and if the word is an abbreviation a period has been added. When the meaning of an abbreviation is not obvious, it has been expanded in square brackets: H[unting] C[reek]; so[uther]ly.

Other editorial insertions or corrections in the text also appear in square brackets. Missing dates are supplied in square brackets in diary entries. Angle brackets ($<$ $>$) are used to indicate mutilated material. If it is clear from the context what word or words are missing, or missing material has been filled in from other sources, the words are inserted between the angle brackets.

A space left blank by Washington in the manuscript of the diaries is indicated by a square bracketed gap in the text. In cases where Washington has crossed out words or phrases, the deletions have not been noted. If a deletion contains substantive material it appears in a footnote. Words inadvertently repeated or repeated at the bottom of a page of manuscript have been dropped.

If the intended location of marginal notations is clear, they have been inserted in the proper place without comment; otherwise, insertions appear in footnotes.

In cases where the date is repeated for several entries on the same day, the repetitive date has been omitted and the succeeding entries have been paragraphed.

Because Washington used the blank pages of the *Virginia Almanack* or occasionally small notebooks to keep his diaries, lack of space sometimes forced him to make entries and memoranda out of order in the volume. The correct position of such entries is often open to question, and the editors have not always agreed with earlier editors of the diaries on this matter. Such divergence of opinion, however, has not been annotated.

Bibliographical references are cited by one or two words, usually the author's last name, in small capitals. If two or more works by authors with the same surname have been used, numbers are assigned: HARRISON [2]. Full publication information is included in the bibliography for each volume. The symbols used to identify repositories in the footnotes precede the bibliography.

Surveying notes and dated memoranda kept in diary form have not been included in this edition of Washington's diaries, although the information contained in them has often been used in annotation.

Individuals and places mentioned for the first time in this volume have been identified in the footnotes; those which have been identified in the first five volumes may be located by consulting the cumulative index at the end of this volume of the *Diaries.*

The Diaries of
GEORGE WASHINGTON
Volume VI
January 1790–December 1799

The Capital at New York

January–July 1790

January 1790

Friday first. The Vice-President, the Governor—the Senators, Members of the House of Representatives in Town—Foreign public characters and all the respectable Citizens came between the hours of 12 & 3 Oclock to pay the complimts. of the Season to me—and in the Afternoon a great number of Gentlemen & Ladies visited Mrs. Washington on the same occasion.

Abigail Adams noted that New Year's Day "in this state, & particularly in this city is celebrated with every mark of pleasure and satisfaction. The shops and publick offices are shut. There is not any market upon this day, but every person laying aside Buisness devote[s] this day to the social purpose of visiting & receiving visits" (Abigail Adams to Mary Cranch, 5 Jan. 1790, MITCHELL, 34).

Saturday 2d. Exercised in the Carriage with Mrs. Washington. Read the report of the Secretary of the Treasury respecting the State of his Department & proposed plans of Finance. Drank Tea at the Chief Justice's of the U. States.

REPORT OF THE SECRETARY OF THE TREASURY: In Sept. 1789 the House of Representatives, considering "an adequate provision for the support of the public credit, as a matter of high importance to the national honor and prosperity," had directed Alexander Hamilton to prepare a report on the state of public credit (HOUSE JOURNAL, 1:117). During the succeeding months Hamilton obtained extensive information on the current financial situation of the United States, but the final report went far beyond the original intentions of Congress. Drawing heavily upon precedent and writings on public finance, Hamilton included a sweeping and controversial plan for the re-establishment of public credit by providing for funding the public debt through an orderly system of collecting duties on imports and tonnage—implemented by duties on imported wines, spirits, coffee, and tea and on domestically distilled spirits. The plan also included federal assumption of debts contracted by the states during the Revolution. Hamilton's "Report Relative to a Provision for the Support of Public Credit," 9 Jan. 1790, was presented to the House of Representatives on 14 Jan. 1790 (HOUSE JOURNAL, 1:141). The report is in HAMILTON [2], 6:51–168.

Sunday 3d. Went to St. Pauls Chapel.

Monday 4th. Informed the President of the Senate, and Speaker the Ho. of Representatives that I had some Oral communications to make to Congress when each House had a Quoram, and desired to be informed thereof—and of the time & place they would receive them.

Walked round the Battery in the afternoon.

Received a Report from the Secretary at War respecting the State of the Frontiers and Indian Affairs, with other matters which I ordered to be laid before Congress as part of the Papers which will be referred to in my Speech to that body.

In the first line of this entry "Senate" reads "Sentate" in the MS.

A letterbook copy of GW's letter of this date to Congress is in DLC:GW. The second session of the First Congress had opened today, but the House of Representatives did not have a quorum until 7 Jan.; the Senate assembled a quorum on 6 Jan. On 6 and 7 Jan. the Senate and House appointed a committee "to wait on the President of the United States, and notify him that a quorum of the two Houses has assembled, and will be ready, in the senate-chamber, at such time as he shall appoint, to receive any communications which he may think proper to make" (DE PAUW, 1:213–14, 3:250–51). The "Oral communications" were GW's first annual message to Congress. REPORT: Knox's report, which included "a general statement of the Indian Department, and of the Southwestern frontiers," 4 Jan. 1790, is in ASP, INDIAN AFF., 1:59–80. GW sent it to the Senate and House of Representatives on 12 Jan. 1790.

Tuesday 5th.   Several Members of Congress called in the forenoon to pay their respects on their arrival in Town but though a respectable Levee at the usual hour, three Oclock the Visitors were not numerous.

Wednesday 6th.   Sat from half after 8 oclock till 10 for the Portrait Painter, Mr. Savage, to finish the Picture of me which he had begun for the University of Cambridge.

In the Afternoon walked round the Battery.

Miss Anne Brown stayed here on a visit to Mrs. Washington to a family dinner.

MR. SAVAGE: See entry for 21 Dec. 1789.

Thursday 7th.   About One Oclock recd. a Committee from both Houses of Congress informing me that each had made a House and would be ready at any time I should appoint to receive the Communications I had to make in the Senate Chamber. Named to morrow 11 oclock for this purpose.

The following Gentlemen dined here—viz.—Messrs. Langdon, Wingate, Strong and Few of the Senate—The Speaker, Genl. Muhlenberg and Scott of Pensylvania—Judge Livermore and

Foster of New Hampshire—Aimes & Thatcher & Goodhue of Massachusetts Mr. Burke of So. Carolina & Mr. Baldwin of Georgia.

COMMITTEE FROM BOTH HOUSES OF CONGRESS: See entry for 4 Jan. 1790. The committee consisted of Nicholas Gilman, Fisher Ames, and Joshua Seney from the House and Caleb Strong and Ralph Izard from the Senate (DE PAUW, 1:214–15).

Caleb Strong (1745–1819), a native of Northampton, Mass., graduated from Harvard in 1764 and was admitted to the Massachusetts bar in 1772. He was a member of the Constitutional Convention and the Massachusetts Ratifying Convention and was elected as a Federalist to the Senate in 1789.

THE SPEAKER: Frederick Augustus Conrad Muhlenberg (1750–1801), United States congressman from Pennsylvania, was speaker of the House of Representatives during the First and Third congresses. His brother, John Peter Gabriel Muhlenberg (1746–1807), who served as a brigadier general in the Continental Army 1777–83, had also been elected to Congress from Pennsylvania in 1789.

Thomas Scott (1739–1796) practiced law in Westmoreland County, Pa., and held a number of local offices in Pennsylvania before and during the Revolution. He was serving as justice of Washington County, Pa., when he was elected a member of the state's Ratifying Convention in 1787.

Samuel Livermore (1732–1803) was born in Waltham, Mass., graduated from Princeton in 1752, and was admitted to the Massachusetts bar in 1756. He moved to New Hampshire in 1758, where he held several local offices and was elected to the Continental Congress 1780–82, 1785. Livermore was a member of the New Hampshire Ratifying Convention in 1788. He was chief justice of the state supreme court from 1782 until 1789 when he was elected to the House of Representatives.

Abiel Foster (1735–1806) of New Hampshire was born in Andover, Mass., and graduated from Harvard in 1756. Foster was ordained a minister in 1761 and served as pastor of a church in Canterbury, N.H., from that year until 1779. From 1783 to 1785 he was a member of the Continental Congress and was judge of the court of common pleas, Rockingham County, N.H., 1784–88. He was elected to the First Congress in 1789.

Fisher Ames (1758–1808), one of the administration's principal supporters in Congress, was a native of Dedham, Mass., graduated from Harvard in 1774, and was admitted to the Massachusetts bar in 1781. In 1788 he was a member of the Massachusetts Ratifying Convention and in 1789 was elected as a Federalist to the First Congress.

George Thacher (1754–1824), a 1776 graduate of Harvard, was admitted to the Massachusetts bar in 1778 and began the practice of law in the District of Maine in the same year. He served in the Continental Congress in 1787 and was elected to the House of Representatives as a Federalist in 1789.

Aedanus Burke (1743–1802), a native of Ireland, was educated in France and immigrated to South Carolina before the Revolution. During the Revolution he held a number of military and legal positions under the state government and was a member of the state legislature 1779–87. He opposed adoption of the Constitution in the South Carolina Ratifying Convention and was an outspoken critic of the Society of the Cincinnati. A representative of

South Carolina backwoods democracy, he remained suspicious of the powers of the new government, particularly those of the executive.

Friday 8th. According to appointment, at 11 Oclock I set out for the City Hall in my Coach—preceeded by Colonel Humphreys and Majr. Jackson in Uniform (on my two White Horses) & followed by Mesr. Lear & Nelson in my Chariot & Mr. Lewis on Horse back following them. In their rear was the Chief Justice of the United States & Secretaries of the Treasury and War Departments in their respective Carriages and in the order they are named. At the outer door of the Hall I was met by the Doorkeepers of the Senate and House and conducted to the Door of the Senate Chamber; and passing from thence to the Chair through the Senate on the right, & House of representatives on the left, I took my Seat. The Gentlemen who attended me followed & took their stand behind the Senators; the whole rising as I entered. After being seated, at which time the members of both Houses also sat, I rose (as they also did) and made my Speech; delivering one Copy to the President of the Senate & another to the Speaker of the House of Representatives—after which, and being a few moments seated, I retired, bowing on each side to the Assembly (who stood) as I passed, and dessending to the lower Hall attended as before, I returned with them to my House.

In the Evening, a *great* number of Ladies, and many Gentlemen visited Mrs. Washington.

On this occasion I was dressed in a suit of Clothes made at the Woolen Manufactury at Hartford as the Buttons also were.

Robert Lewis was the son of Fielding Lewis and GW's sister Betty Washington Lewis. He was brought up at Kenmore, the Lewis home in Fredericksburg, and educated at the academy there. In Mar. 1789 GW wrote his sister: "Since you were speaking to me concerning your Son Bob, I have thought it probable that I may have occasion for a young person in my family of a good disposition, who writes a good hand. . . . If Bob is of opinion that this employment will suit his inclination, and he will take his chance for the allowance that will be made (which cannot be great) as there are hundreds who would be glad to come in, I should be very glad to give him the preference." The 19-year-old Robert accepted eagerly (GW to Betty Lewis, 15 Mar. 1789, DLC:GW; Robert Lewis to GW, 18 Mar. 1789, *Scribner's Monthly Mag.*, 14 [1877], 73). Since Mrs. Washington did not leave Mount Vernon for New York City until mid-May, Robert was instructed by his uncle to accompany her on her journey to the capital (GW to Lewis, 24 Mar. 1789, NN: Washington Collection; Robert Lewis's diary, "A Journey from Fredericksburg Virginia to New York," 13–20 May 1789, ViMtV). Lewis remained with GW as one of his secretaries until 1791 when he resigned to return to Fredericksburg and marry Judith Carter Browne (1773–1830), daughter of William Burnet and Judith Carter Browne of Elsing Green, King

William County (Lewis to GW, 10 Jan. 1791, ViHi). After his return to Virginia he acted as GW's agent in the management of portions of GW's western lands and served several terms as mayor of Fredericksburg (GW to Robert Lewis, 15 Oct. 1791, DLC:GW; SORLEY, 229–33).

A letterbook copy of GW's first annual address to Congress is in DLC:GW. See also WRITINGS, 30:491–95. William Maclay, who was present in the Senate chamber, noted: "All this morning nothing but bustle about the Senate chamber in hauling chairs and removing tables. The President was dressed in a second mourning, and read his speech well. The Senate, headed by their Vice-President, were on his right. The House of Representatives, with their Speaker, were on his left. His family with the heads of departments attended. The business was soon over and the Senate were left alone. The speech was committed rather too hastily, as Mr. [Pierce] Butler thought, who made some remarks on it, and was called to order by the Chair. He resented the call, and some altercation ensued" (MACLAY, 170). The *Pennsylvania Packet*, 13 Jan. 1790, noted that "the doors of the Senate Chamber were open, and many citizens admitted." SUIT OF CLOTHES: The *Pennsylvania Packet* for 14 Jan. 1790 noted: "The President of the United States, when he addressed the two Houses of Congress yesterday, was dressed in a crow-coloured suit of clothes, of American manufacture: The cloth appeared to be of the finest texture—the colour of that beautiful changeable blue, remarked in shades not quite black. This elegant fabric was from the manufactory in Hartford."

Saturday 9th.   Exercised with Mrs. Washington and the Children in the Coach the 14 Miles round.

In the Afternoon walked round the Battery.

For the fourteen miles round, see entry for 12 Dec. 1789.

Sunday 10th.   Went to St. Pauls Chapel in the forenoon. Wrote private letters in the Afternoon for the Southern Mail.

Monday 11th.   Sent my Instructions to the Commissioners (appointed to Negotiate a Treaty with the Creek Indians) with the report of their proceedings, to the Senate by the Secretary at War previous to their being laid before them and the other House in their Legislative Capacities.

Also communicated to both Houses, transcripts of the adoption & ratification of the New Constitution by the State of No. Carolina with Copies of the Letter from His Excellency Saml. Johnson President of the Convention, enclosing the same. These were sent by my private Secretary Mr. Lear.

For the commissioners appointed to negotiate with the Creek, see entries for 16 and 23 Nov. 1789. GW's letter to the Senate, 11 Jan. 1790, stating that he would instruct Knox to report on the results of the commissioners' negotiations, and his letter of 12 Jan. to the Senate and House enclosing Knox's report on the proceedings, with additional recommendations on Indian affairs in general, are in ASP, INDIAN AFF., 1:59–80.

The North Carolina Ratifying Convention met in the summer of 1789 and ratified the Constitution in November of that year. Copies of the letter dated 4 Dec. 1789 to GW from Samuel Johnston (1733–1816) and of North Carolina's instrument of ratification are in DNA: RG 46, Entry 5. Johnston had been elected as a Federalist to the United States Senate in 1789.

Tuesday 12th.   Exercised on Horse-back between 10 and 12, the riding bad.

Previous to this, I sent written Messages to both Houses of Congress informing them, that the Secretary at War would lay before them a full & complete Statement of the business as it respected the Negotiation with the Creek Indians—My Instructions to, and the Commissioners report of their proceedings with those People. The letters and other papers respecting depredations on the Western Frontiers of Virginia, & District of Kentucky All of which was for their *full* information, but communicated in confidence & under injunction that no Copies be taken, or communications made of such parts as ought to be kept secret.

About two Oclock a Committee of the Senate waited on me with a copy of their Address, in answr. to my Speech, and re-

Federal Hall and Wall Street, 1798; a watercolor by Archibald Robertson. (New-York Historical Society)

questing to know at what time and place it should be presented
I named my own House, and thursday next at 11 Oclock for
the purpose.

Just before Levee hour a Committee from the House of Representatives called upon me to know when & where they shd. deliver
their Address. I named Twelve oclock on thursday, but finding
it was there wish that it should be presented at the Federal hall,
and offering to surrender the Representatives Chamber for this
purpose by retiring into one of the Committee Rooms & there
waiting untill I was ready to receive it I would consider on the
place, and let them know my determination before the Houses
should sit tomorrow.

A respectable, though not a full Levee to day.

NEGOTIATION WITH THE CREEK INDIANS: See entry for 11 Jan. 1790. MY SPEECH:
See entry for 8 Jan. 1790.

Wednesday 13th.   After duly considering on the place for receiving the address of the House of Representatives, I concluded,
that it would be best to do it at my own House—first, because it
seems most consistent with usage & custom—2d. because there is
no 3d. place in the Fedl. Hall (*prepared*) to which I could call
them, & to go into either of the Chambers appropriated to the
Senate or Representatives, did not appear proper; and 3d. because
I had appointed my own House for the Senate to deliver theirs in
and, accordingly, appointed my own House to receive it.

Thursday 14th.   At the hours appointed, the Senate & House of
representatives presented their respective Addresses—The Members of both coming in Carriages and the latter with the Mace
preceeding the Speaker. The Address of the Senate was presented
by the Vice-President and that of the House by the Speaker
thereof.

The following Gentlemen dined here to day. viz.

Messrs. Henry & Maclay of the Senate and Messrs. Wadsworth,
Trumbull, Floyd, Boudinot, Wynkoop, Seney, Page, Lee, &
Mathews of the House of Representatives and Mr. John Trum-
bull.

John Henry (1750–1798), a Dorchester County, Md., lawyer, graduated from
Princeton in 1769 and studied law at the Middle Temple in London. Returning to Maryland in 1775, he served in the General Assembly and from
1778 to 1781 was a Maryland delegate to the Continental Congress where
he made a vigorous effort to secure supplies and recruits for the army. He
again served in the Continental Congress 1784–87 and was elected to the

United States Senate in 1789, serving until he resigned in 1797 to become governor of Maryland.

Sen. William Maclay described this dinner in his diary: "Dined this day with the President. It was a great dinner—all in the taste of high life. . . . The President is a cold, formal man; but I must declare that he treated me with great attention. I was the first person with whom he drank a glass of wine. I was often spoken to by him. Yet he knows how rigid a republican I am. I cannot think he considers it worth while to soften me" (MACLAY, 172–73). William Maclay (1737–1804), Antifederalist senator from Pennsylvania, served on the Forbes expedition during the French and Indian War and later studied law. Admitted to the Pennsylvania bar in 1760, he held a number of local positions during and after the Revolution. He was elected to the Senate in 1789 and served until Mar. 1791. During this time he became something of a gadfly; his journal records his outraged disapproval of what he considered the aristocratic pomp surrounding GW's administration.

GW's former aide-de-camp Jonathan Trumbull, Jr., was elected as a Federalist representative from Connecticut to the First Congress.

William Floyd (1734–1821), a native of Brookhaven, Long Island, N.Y., was a major general in the New York militia and a member of the New York legislature 1777–78, 1784–88. A signer of the Declaration of Independence, he served in the Continental Congress 1774–83.

Elias Boudinot (1740–1821), a member of a prominent colonial family, studied law and was admitted to the bar in 1760. One of New Jersey's leading lawyers, he was active in Patriot circles before and during the Revolution and was a member of the Continental Congress 1777, 1778, 1781–83, acting as president 1782–83. GW had frequent contacts with him while Boudinot was commissary of prisoners during the Revolution. He was an active supporter of the Constitution during the ratification process in New Jersey and after his election to Congress in 1789 became a stalwart supporter of most administration measures in the House of Representatives.

Henry Wynkoop (1737–1816) of Bucks County, Pa., a member of the Pennsylvania Assembly 1760–61, held a number of local judicial posts in Pennsylvania before and during the Revolution and served in the Continental Congress 1779–83. He was justice of the Pennsylvania High Court of Errors and Appeals from 1783 to 1789 and was elected to the First Congress from Pennsylvania in 1789.

Joshua Seney (1756–1798), a 1773 graduate of the University of Pennsylvania, practiced law in Queen Annes County, Md., and was a member of the Continental Congress 1787–88. He was elected to the First Congress from Maryland in 1789.

John Page of Rosewell was elected in 1789 as congressman from Virginia. Page, a noted amateur astronomer (see entry for 15 June 1774) served in the Virginia legislature during and after the Revolution and as governor of Virginia 1802–5. In 1789 Page married Margaret Lowther, daughter of William Lowther of Scotland. Richard Bland Lee had been elected from Virginia to the First Congress.

George Mathews (1739–1812), a native of Augusta County, Va., was colonel successively of the 9th and 3d Virginia regiments during the Revolution. After the war he settled in Oglethorpe County, Ga., and was elected governor of that state in 1787. He represented Georgia in Congress 1789–91 and was again governor of the state 1793–96.

John Trumbull (1756–1843) was the youngest son of Gov. Jonathan Trumbull of Connecticut and a brother of GW's former aide-de-camp Jonathan Trumbull, Jr. He showed a precocious ability in painting, but upon his father's insistence he attended Harvard, from which he graduated in 1773. At the outbreak of the Revolution Trumbull served as one of GW's aides but soon sought a more active command. He saw action as a major at Dorchester Heights and in June 1776 was appointed deputy adjutant to Horatio Gates. In 1778 he served as aide to John Sullivan in the Rhode Island campaign. In May 1780 he went to London where he studied painting briefly with Benjamin West. In Nov. 1780 he was arrested by British authorities under suspicion of treason but was soon released. He then went to France where he produced a painting of GW which was widely copied. Returning to the United States, he assisted his brother Joseph in supplying the army 1782–83. In 1783 he again went to Europe where he spent the next five years recording on canvas the events of the American Revolution. After returning to the United States in Dec. 1789, he began several portraits of GW and in Aug. 1790 wrote West: "I have several small portraits of the President . . . one in particular which I have done for Mrs. Washington a full length about 20 Inches hight . . . is thought very like—& I have Been tempted to disobey one of your injunctions & to attempt a large Portrait of him for this City which I am now finishing—the figure is near seven feet high compos'd with a Horse, & the back ground the evacuation of this Place by the British at the Peace:—the Harbour & Fleet with a Part of the fortifications & Ruins of the Town:—How I have succeeded I hardly dare judge: —the World have approved the resemblance" (TRUMBULL [2], 326).

Friday 15th. Snowing all day—but few Ladies and Gentlemen as visitors this Evening to Mrs. Washington.

Saturday 16th. Exercised in the Coach with Mrs. Washington & the two Children abt. 12 Oclock.

Sent the Report of the Post Master Genl. relative to the necessary changes in that Office to the Secretary of the Treasury that it may be laid before Congress—or such parts thereof as may be necessary for their Information.

The report of Postmaster General Samuel Osgood was probably a draft of Osgood's report on the state of the Post Office Department, including his suggestions for improvement of services and revenues. The final version was sent to Hamilton by Osgood, 20 Jan. 1790, and is in ASP, POST OFFICE, 5–7. The secretary of the treasury sent the report to the House of Representatives on 22 Jan. 1790 (DE PAUW, 3:270).

Sunday 17th. At home all day—not well.

Monday 18th. Still indisposed with an Aching tooth, and swelled and inflamed Gum.

Tuesday 19th. Not much company at the Levee to day—but the Visitors were respectable.

"Lady Washington's Reception," or "The Republican Court," painted in 1876 by Daniel Huntington. (Brooklyn Museum, gift of the Crescent-Hamilton Athletic Club)

Wednesday 20th. A Report from the Secretary at War, on the Subject of a National Militia altered agreeably to the ideas I had communicated to him was presented to me, in order to be laid before Congress.

See entries for 18 and 19 Dec. 1789. On 18 Jan. 1790 Knox submitted his completed report containing detailed plans and estimates of expenses for erecting a militia system "adequate to the probable exigencies of the United States, whether arising from internal or external causes." Knox's letter and report are in ASP, MILITARY AFF., 1:6–13. GW submitted it to Congress on 21 Jan. 1790 (DLC:GW).

Thursday 21st. The above report was accordingly transmitted to both houses of Congress by the Secretary at War in a written message from me.

The following Gentlemen dined here—viz.—Messrs. Elsworth, Patterson, Elmer Bassett and Hawkins of the Senate and Messrs. Sherman, Cadwalader, Clymer, Hartley, Heister, Smith (Maryland) & Jackson of the House of Representatives and Major Meridith, Treasurer of the United States.

William Paterson (1745–1806) was born in Ireland and came to America with his parents in 1747. The family settled first in Pennsylvania, moved to Connecticut, and then to New Jersey where William graduated from Princeton in 1763 and was admitted to the New Jersey bar in 1768. During the Revolution he held a number of state positions including that of attorney general 1776–83. He vigorously supported the making of the new Constitution at the Federal Convention in Philadelphia in 1787, while representing the interests of the small states. On 15 June 1787 he introduced the "New Jersey Plan," which provided for a unicameral legislature in which each state would have one vote. He was elected as a Federalist to the Senate from New Jersey in 1789, but upon the death of New Jersey Gov. William Livingston in 1790, Paterson was chosen to succeed him as governor of the state by the New Jersey legislature.

Jonathan Elmer (1745–1817) was born in Cedarville, N.J., graduated in medicine from the University of Pennsylvania in 1769, and set up a medical practice in Bridgeton, N.J. He served in the Continental Congress 1776–78, 1781–84, 1787–88 and in 1789 was elected as a Federalist to the United States Senate.

Richard Bassett (1745–1815) was born in Maryland, but after studying law and being admitted to the bar in Delaware he began the practice of law in that state. During the 1780s he served in the Delaware legislature and in 1787 was a member of the Constitutional Convention and the Delaware Ratifying Convention. He was United States senator from Delaware from 1789 to 1793.

Benjamin Hawkins (1754–1816) of North Carolina was attending Princeton when the Revolution began. It has frequently been suggested that young Hawkins's proficiency in French earned him a place on GW's staff, but this has not been substantiated (POUND, 5–6). His other military services during the Revolution are equally obscure, but by 1778 he was back in North Carolina acting as the state's commercial agent. In 1780 he was appointed one of the commissioners on North Carolina's newly formed board of trade. He was a member of the Continental Congress in 1781–84, 1786–87. In 1785 Hawkins was appointed by Congress as a commissioner to negotiate treaties with the southern Indians. He exhibited a flair for Indian diplomacy, and his adroitness resulted in the controversial Treaty of Hopewell with the Cherokee in 1785 and treaties with the Choctaw and Chickasaw in 1786. A staunch Federalist, he was elected senator from North Carolina in 1789 and during GW's administration was frequently relied upon for advice on Indian affairs.

Lambert Cadwalader (1742–1823), of Trenton, N.J., attended the University of Pennsylvania and was a member of the Pennsylvania constitutional convention in 1776. During the Revolution he was lieutenant colonel of the 3d Pennsylvania Battalion and colonel of the 4th Pennsylvania. Captured at Fort Washington, he was on parole until his resignation from the army in 1779. Cadwalader was a member of the Continental Congress 1784–87. He was elected congressman from New Jersey in 1789.

Thomas Hartley (1748–1800) was a native of Reading, Pa., and practiced law in York, Pa. During the Revolution he was a lieutenant colonel in the 6th Pennsylvania Battalion and colonel of the 11th Pennsylvania Regiment. In 1787 he was a member of the Pennsylvania Ratifying Convention. Hartley served in the House of Representatives from 1789 until his death.

Daniel Hiester (1747–1804), a Montgomery County, Pa., businessman, served in the Pennsylvania militia during the Revolution and as a member of the Supreme Executive Council of Pennsylvania, 1784–86. Hiester served as congressman from Pennsylvania from 1789 to 1796, when he moved to Hagerstown, Md. He was in 1801 again elected to Congress, this time from Maryland, serving until his death.

William Smith (1728–1814), Federalist representative from Maryland, was born in Pennsylvania and moved to Baltimore in 1761 where he established himself as a merchant. In 1774 he served on the city's committee of correspondence; in 1777–78 he was a member of the Continental Congress. Smith headed the committee of Baltimore merchants that presented GW with a miniature ship, the *Federalist,* in 1788 (see entry for 9 June 1788).

James Jackson (1757–1806), a leader of antiadministration forces in the House of Representatives, was born in Devonshire, Eng., and in 1772 immigrated to Savannah, Ga., where he was employed in a local law office. He held various state and local offices and served in the Georgia militia during the Revolution, seeing action at Savannah, Cowpens, and Augusta. In July 1782 he led the forces that occupied Savannah after the British evacuation. In 1788 he was elected governor of Georgia but declined to serve, and the next year he was elected to Congress from the eastern district of Georgia.

Friday 22d.   Exercised on Horse back in the forenoon.

Called in my ride on the Baron de Polnitz, to see the operation of his (Winlaws) threshing Machine. The effect was–the Heads of the Wheat being seperated from the Straw, as much of the first was run through the Mill in 15 minutes as made half a bushel of clean Wheat. Allowing 8 working hours in the 24. this would yield 16 Bushels pr. day. Two boys are sufficient to turn the Wheel, feed the Mill, and remove the Threshed grain after it has passed through it. Two men were unable, by winnowing to clean the wheat as it passed through the Mill, but a common dutch fan with the usual attendance would be *more* than sufficient to do it. The grain passes through without bruising and is well seperated from the Chaff. Womn. or boys of 12 or 14 years of age are fully adequate to the management of the Mill or threshing Machine. Upon the whole it appears to be an easier, more expeditious and much cleaner way of getting out Grain than by the usual mode of threshing; and vastly to be preferred to treading, which is hurtful to horses, filthy to the Wheat, & not more expeditious, considering the numbers that are employed in the process from the time the bed is begun to be formed until the grain has passed finally thro' the Fan.

Many, and respectable visitors to Mrs. Washington this Evening.

Friedrich, Baron von Poellnitz, occupied a farm of about 21 acres in the vicinity of Murray Hill on Manhattan, where he carried on a number of agricultural experiments. In 1790 he published an *Essay on Agriculture,* printed by Francis Childs and John Swaine. Later in the year he apparently sold his land to Capt. Robert Richard Randall and sometime before 1795 moved to Wraggtown, S.C. Poellnitz was an occasional correspondent of GW's on agricultural matters (see Poellnitz to GW, 26 Dec. 1789, 20 Mar. 1790, 28 July 1795, and GW to Poellnitz, 29 Dec. 1789, 23 Mar. 1790, DLC:GW; JANVIER, 123-24). In the late 1780s GW became greatly interested in Winlaw's thresher after reading "A Description of William Winlaw's Mill, for Separating the Grain from the Corn, in Place of Threshing," written by Winlaw himself and printed in Arthur Young's *Annals of Agriculture,* 6 (1786), 152-55. GW wrote Young, 1 Nov. 1787, that if the machine "possesses all the properties & advantages mentioned in the description, & you can, from your own knowledge, or such information as you can *entirely* rely on, recommend it as a useful machine, where labourers are scarce, I should be much obliged to you to procure one for me . . . provided it is so simple in its construction as to be worked by ignorant persons without danger of being spoiled (for such only will manage it here) & the price of it, does not exceed £15" (PPRF). Upon investigation, however, Young found the accounts of the thresher "too vague to be satisfactory; I have too many doubts about it to put you to the expence of purchase and freight" (Young to GW, 1 July 1788, DLC:GW). GW had continued to direct inquiries to American owners of the thresher (see GW to John Beale Bordley, 17 Aug. 1788, MHi: Waterston Papers). The Winlaw thresher was undoubtedly the "new invented threshing machine conducted by Baron Pollnitz and other Gentlemen farmers, in farmers' dresses, grinding and threshing grain" in the parade held in New York City in June 1788 to celebrate the ratification of the Constitution (DUER, 52).

Saturday 23d.   Went with Mrs. Washington in the Forenoon to see the Paintings of Mr. Jno. Trumbull.

Sunday 24th.   Went to St. Pauls Chapel in the forenoon. Writing private letters in the afternoon.

Monday 25.   A Mr. Francis Bailey—introduced by Messrs. Scott & Hartley of Pensylvania and Mr. White of Virginia offered a paper, in the nature of a Petition, setting forth a valuable discovery he had made of Marginal figures for Notes, Certificates, &ca. which could not by the ingenuity of Man be counterfeited—requesting I wd. appoint some person to hear and examine him on the Subject, that, if the facts stated by him should appear well founded, he might (being a Printer of Philadelphia) have the Printing of all that sort of the Public business for which this discovery should be found useful—and which he would do on as good terms as any other Printer independent of the discovery above mentioned all the advantage he should expect from which being to obtain a preference.

Read a letter from George Nicholas Esqr. of Kentucky to Mr. Madison which he put into my hands for information of the Sentiments of the People of that District.

The Sentiments are 2d. Novr.

That in the late Convention held in that District, the most important characters of that Party wch. has always been in favour of a Seperation, oppose the agreeing to it at this time upon a Supposition that the terms have been changed by Virginia so as to make them inadmissible in their present form. Their enemies say this cannot be their *true* reason: but, be them what they may, the scale is turned against the Seperation.

That he believes no late attempt has been made by either Spain or England to detach that District from the Union—but

That Spain is playing a game which, if not counteracted will depopulate that Country & carry most of the future emigrants to her Territory—That they have established a New Government, Independent of New Orleans at the Natches and sent thither a Man of character & abilities—who would not for *unimportant* purposes have accepted the appointment.

That this New Governor has put a stop to the reception of Tobacco from the Inhabitants of the United States—declaring that none shall be received in to the Kings Stores (where it used to be purchased and deposited) except from Spanish subjects and that these shall have ten dollars a hundred.

That other great advantages are held out to emigrants from the United States to settle in the Spanish Territory—such as a donation of Lands, and a certain sum in money for each family.

That the consequences of restriction on one hand, & encouragements to settlers on the other are obvious. The difference of Religion & government are all that can make any man hesitate in his choice and perfect liberty in both these the strongest assurances are given.

That the French Inhabitants of that Country, as well as future emigrants from the old States will certainly go there.

That persevering steadily in this conduct will drain the western Settlements.

That these considerations ought to make the Federal Government take (he thinks) the most decisive steps as to the right of Navigating the Missisipi, and induce it to pay particular attention to the gaining the affections of the Western people.

That the Steps hitherto taken with respect to them have had a contrary effect: No support havg. been given by the Genl. Government, and the regulation of Indian Affairs having been placed in hands who were interested in a continuance of their depredations on the Kentucky District.

That if a trade is not established with them on such a footing as to supply their wants that they will do this by plunder.

That the management of this business being in the hands of persons No. Wt. of the Ohio, it is inculcated on the Indians of the same side of the River that as the Kentuckians & they are seperate People, & in seperate Interests they may war with the first and not with them. That of this disposition and conduct there are sufficient proofs wherever it is found that the interests of the two sides clash.

That the Commissioners being always named from Persons livg. on that (No. Wt.) side of the River, and always holding the Treaties there contributes greatly to establish in the Indian Mind this opinion of their being a distinct people.

That the Kentucky District being 20 times as numerous as the Inhabitants of the other side, ought to have as great a share in the management of Indian Affairs as the people on the other side have.

That he is well convinced the bulk of the people in that District are strongly attached to the Union, & that characters might be found there better qualified to manage the business than those in whose hands it is now placed.

That if it is not the desire of the New Government to lose *all* its friends in that quarter a change must be made on this business. The Indians must be convinced that the Americans are all one people—that they shall never attack any part with impunity and that in future there real wants will be supplied in time of Peace. This is all they ask.

That they deny in positive terms, what the Officers on the No. Wt. side of the River assert—viz.—that hostilities are always commenced by the People of the Kentucky District. Expeditions have and will be carried on across the River in revenge for depredations of the Indians untill the Government takes up the matter effectually.

That Mr. Brown (to whom he has written) can inform in what light they are considered by the Officers on the other side of the Rivr.

That the want of money, he knows, prevents the Government from doing many things wch. otherwise would be undertaken, but that need not stop the necessary steps—because, if sanctioned by it they can raise any number of Men and furnish any quantity of provisions that may be wanting and will wait until their finances enable them to make satisfaction.

That he fears the Government have taken up an idea that that Country can be defended by a few Posts along the River. If so it is a most erroneous one for an Army would scarcely supply the Chain that would be necessary.

That the Post at the Mouth of Licking, is considered by many in the District of Kentucky as a check upon the said District. To this he can only say, if they are treated as fellow Citizens, checks are unnecessary but if it is intended to withhold from [them] all the benefits of good Government a little time will shew that, as heretofore they have found the troops useless and faithless as friends, so in future they shall despise them as enemies.

That upon the whole he shall close the subject with assurances that Government are deceived in the Accts. they have had from that Country—and that it is his opinion that the most serious consequences will follow from its persisting in the measures which have been pursued for sometime past.

Francis Bailey (c.1735–1815) was a Lancaster, Pa., printer and journalist. In 1771 he began publication of a long-lived series, the *Lancaster Almanac*. During the Revolution he published an edition of the Articles of Confederation and the fourth edition of Thomas Paine's *Common Sense* and in 1778 joined with Hugh Henry Brackenridge to publish the *United States Magazine*. In 1781 he became editor of the *Freeman's Journal or the North American Intelligencer* and acted as official printer to Congress and the state of Pennsylvania. The paper presented to GW today was undoubtedly a copy of Bailey's petition of 2 Feb. 1790, addressed to the Senate, requesting a Senate committee to examine his invention; GW's description corresponds with the wording of the petition (DNA: RG 46, Petitions and Memorials, Various Subjects). Bailey's petition, received in the Senate 2 Feb., was referred to a committee which recommended that the petition be referred to the secretary of the treasury. The House of Representatives, to which Bailey sent the petition on 29 Jan., also referred it to Hamilton (DE PAUW, 1:235, 245; HOUSE JOURNAL, 1:149, 151–52, 162, 164). Hamilton reported to the Senate, 23 Feb. 1790, that "it appears to him difficult to decide, to what extent that Invention will afford the Security against Counterfeiting, which is the Object of it," but "nevertheless he is of opinion, it will be likely to add to the difficulty of that pernicious practice, in a sufficient degree, to merit the countenance of Government, by securing to the Petitioner an exclusive right to the use of his Invention" (HAMILTON [2], 6:277).

George Nicholas's letter to James Madison, 2 Nov. 1789, is in DLC: Madison Papers. Nicholas (c.1749–1799), a graduate of the College of William and Mary and a lawyer, represented both Hanover and Albemarle counties in the Virginia Assembly in the 1780s. He was a member of the Virginia Ratifying Convention in 1788 where he vigorously supported the Constitution. He had close ties with Harry Innes and James Wilkinson, who were at this time deeply involved in land speculation in Kentucky and in the Mississippi trade. After the Ratifying Convention he moved to Kentucky and became a leader in the movement to separate Kentucky from Virginia. In 1792, when Kentucky achieved statehood, he helped draft the state constitution.

LATE CONVENTION: Nicholas is referring to the 8th Kentucky Convention, held in July 1789 to consider the question of impending statehood (see WATLINGTON, 182–85).

The new governor to whom Nicholas is referring is Manuel Gayoso de Lemos (1747–1799), who was born in Oporto, Portugal and educated in England. He entered the Spanish service in 1771 and in 1787 was appointed governor of the District of Natchez. Arriving in Natchez in June 1789 he served with distinction until he replaced the baron de Carondelet as governor general of Louisiana in 1797. Spain was attempting a new experiment in the district—designed to attract and assimilate non-Spanish immigrants to augment the district's sparse population. A proclamation of 20 April 1789 promised that new settlers would not be molested in religious matters, that they might bring in property without paying duty, and that they might expect generous grants of land (HOLMES [2], 34; NASATIR, 11). For the involved situation concerning tobacco in the Natchez district in 1789, see HOLMES [2], 91–94.

John Brown (1757–1837) attended Princeton and the College of William and Mary, served in the Revolution, studied law under Thomas Jefferson, and moved to Kentucky in 1783, settling first in Danville but soon moving to Frankfort. He served in the Continental Congress 1787–88 and in 1789 was elected to Congress as a Virginia representative from Kentucky. In 1792 he became United States senator from the state of Kentucky (WATLINGTON, 79–82). POST AT THE MOUTH OF LICKING: Fort Washington, established in 1789, near Cincinnati.

Tuesday 26th.   Exercised on Horse back in the forenoon.

The Visitors at the Levee to day were numerous and respectable—among whom was the Vice-President and the Speaker of the House of Representatives.

Read a letter handed to me by the Secretary of War, from a Colo. Danl. Smith of Miro Settlement in the State of No. Carolina in reply to one which was an answer to a letter recd. from the said Smith respecting Indian Affairs & State of the Frontier of that part of the Union and giving (as he was required to do) an Acct. of the Navigation of the river Tennessee & its waters—the Communications betwn. these & other Waters and the distances of places—as follow—viz.

The distance between the Settlements of white People South of the French Broad River (French broad is a branch of Holstein River, on the South Side, which is a branch of the Tennessee) and the Indians at and in the vicinity of Chota (a Cherokee Indian Town) is about 12 Miles.

He never passed down the Tennessee himself. That part of it

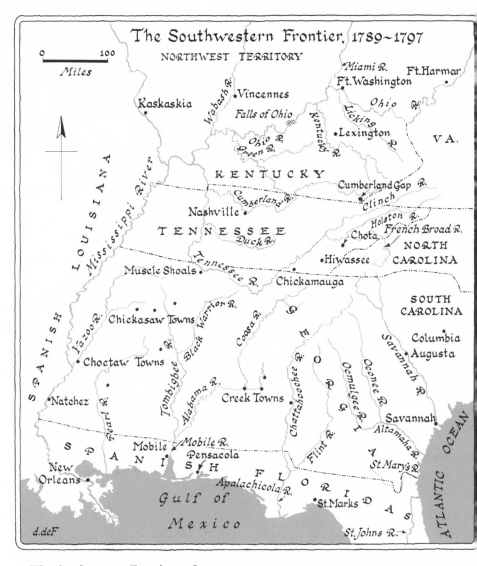

The Southwestern Frontier, 1789–1797

on which Chota stands, is a South Fork of the Holstein. Their Junction is about 20 Miles below Chota from which the whole River is called the Tennessee.

Boats of 7 or 8 tons burthen have frequently gone down the Holstein & the water is sufficient for those of greater burthen; but there is a place call'd the Suck, or boiling pot, where the River runs through the Cumberland Mountain that is somewhat difficult, occasioned by the narrowness of the water & suddeness of the turn that causes a rebound & kind of Whirl-pool, but many boats have passed it and he has not heard of damage to any of them nor has he been informed that there is any material difficulty in the Navigation more than is common in Rivers of that size where there is no tide.

Between the Suck, and the Muscle Shoals he is sure there is not.

Supposes the distance by Water from Chota to the last mentioned place is between 3 & 400 Miles. The width of the river is very unequal—generally about 500 yards except at the Suck where it is not half that width.

The Nature of the River, for the most part, is to have a bluff on one side and low grounds on the other (wch. is liable to be overflowed) alternately; the Banks are woody, and the low grounds thick with Cane.

The Cherokees may be classed into 3 divisions—The Valley settlements on the Tennessee above Chota, Eastward of the Iron Mountain—Those in the Neighbourhood of Chota and those in the neighbourhood of Chickamogga (which is a Creek running into the Tennessee on the South side a few Miles above Suck). They have detached villages besides—but the number of their Towns is unknown to him—nor can he say what number of Souls they may consist of but supposes of Warriors, there may be about 2000 or 2500 and of the three divisions the Chickamaggas are perhaps the most numerous.

Muscle Shoals, have different accts. given of them by people who have passed them. Some say they are 30 Miles, others not 15 in length—but all agree that the river *there* is about three Miles in width—very shallow and full of small Islands occasioned by drift wood lodging on the Rocks by wch. means Mud & Sand are accumulated. The lowest Shoal is accounted rather the worst. It is not possible for a large Boat to pass them in ascending the river at any Season, nor can they pass down them but in time of a flood.

Occhappo creek he had never heard of—nor has he understd. there was any Creek on the South side of the River near the Muscle Shoals that was navigable unless when the river was high.

Seven or 8 Miles below the Muscle Shoals, there was formerly a Cherokee Village at the Mouth of Cold water Creek but he never heard that it was Navigable. 15 or 20 Miles below this again is Bear Crk. on which a small tribe of Delawares live.

From the mouth of Cold Water Creek, or Bear Creek, to the highest Navigation of the Mobile he has heard it accounted 60 Miles but cannot say that it is so. The head waters of the Mobile may be about half that distance from the Tennessee.

Miro, is the name of the District on Cumberland that includes three Counties—Nashville the name of the Town where the Superior Court is held. From hence to the lower end of the Muscle Shoals is about 150 miles nearly South.

Duck river, a North branch of the Tennessee, where the path which leads from Nashville to the Chickasaw Nation crosses it is about 60 Miles from the Cumberland Settlemts.—About a South West course. About 100 miles further on the same direction is the nearest Chickasaw Towns. The Mouth of Duck River by water, he supposes may be near 200 miles below the Muscle shoals.

Cumberland Settlements are not very compact. They extend from the mouth of red River a No. branch of Cumberland River up to Bledsoes Creek being abt. 80 or 90 Miles. The strength of the Militia about 800 & increasing fast thinks they may be now, by the late emigrations 1000.

From Nashville to Lexington is, about 200, or 210 Miles by Land and from Nashville to the Falls of Ohio is abt. 140 Miles by Land.

From the Mouth of the Tennessee up to the Muscle Shoals the Navigation is good—equal to that of the Ohio below the Falls—the width of the River near half a Mile, in places almost double—the distance about 400 Miles.

Chickasaws have no towns on the Tennessee. The nighest they have to it is about 60 Miles from, or a little below Bear Creek. Their principal towns he has understood are on the heads of a Fork of the Mobile and on the head of the Yazoos. The number of their Warriors is about 800.

Choctaws lye farther to the Southward than the Chickasaws & are a numerous Nation. They are in alliance with the Chicasaws and he has heard their numbers estimated at 7 or 8000—at least equal to those of the Creeks—tho' not so well armed.

McGillivrays communications with the Cherokees he conceives has a constant tendency to excite them to War against the Frontiers of Georgia & No. Carolina—or at least cautioning them to be on their guard against the White People, & infusing suspicions into the minds of them. The Creeks have wanted them to join in a War against the White People but they have refused and would be glad to see them humbled for the Insolence with which they treat them.

It will be highly pleasing to his Settlement—Miro—to hear that Congress will protect it.

Daniel Smith (1748–1818), a native of Stafford County, Va., attended the College of William and Mary, held a number of surveying posts in Virginia before the Revolution, and was an active speculator in western lands. During the war he served as a colonel and, in 1779, as commissioner to survey the Virginia–North Carolina boundary. Around 1783 he moved to Sumner County, now in Tennessee but then part of North Carolina, where he became heavily involved in land speculation. In June 1790 GW appointed him secretary of the newly created Southwest Territory, which included the territory ceded by North Carolina upon its adoption of the Constitution (EXECUTIVE JOURNAL, 1:50; ABERNETHY, 29–30, 126; CARTER [4], 4:23, n.44). Smith's correspondence with Secretary of War Henry Knox has not been located.

MIRO SETTLEMENT: The Mero (Miro) District, along the Cumberland River, was formed by the North Carolina legislature in Aug. 1788 out of the counties of Davison, Sumner, and Tennessee. In 1790 its population consisted of 7,042 settlers and 1,151 slaves (MORSE [2]; ABERNETHY, 96–97). Chota, one of the major fortified Cherokee towns, was on the Little Tennessee River. THE SUCK, OR BOILING POT: sometimes called the Whirl, in the gorge of the Tennessee River, near Chattanooga. It is at the point where the river breaks through the Cumberland Mountains and narrows to about 70 yards. Below the Suck there were rapids for about 38 miles, and the river at this point was generally thought dangerous to navigation (WILLIAMS [3], 34; MORSE [2]). In this paragraph of the diary entry for 26 Jan. the word "damage" reads "dagage" in the MS.

The Muscle Shoals are at a point where the Tennessee River descends over 134 feet from a limestone plateau to the plain near present-day Florence, Ala. The rapids were sometimes called the Elk River Shoals (RAMSEY, 64). The Iron Mountains are a ridge of the Appalachians in northeast Tennessee and southern Virginia. OCCHAPPO CREEK: GW is referring to Occochappo Creek, below the Muscle Shoals (RAMSEY, 64). Coldwater Creek empties into the Tennessee River in present-day Alabama. The Indian town at the mouth of the creek was also called Coldwater by early settlers. BLEDSOES CREEK: probably Bledsoe Lick, "in the state of Tennessee . . . 32 miles from Big Salt Lick garrison, and 36 from Nashville" (MORSE [2]).

Wednesday 27th. Did business with the Secretaries of the Treasury & War—With the first respecting the appointment of Superintendants of the Light Houses, Buoys &ca. and for building one at Cape Henry—With the latter for nominating persons (named in a list submitted to me) for paying the Military Pensionrs. of the United States and the policy and advantages (which might be derived from the measure) of bringing Mr. Alexr. McGillivray Chief of the Creek Nation here being submitted to me for consideration I requested that a plan might be reported by which Governmt. might not appear to be the Agent in it, or suffer in its dignity if the attempt to get him here should not succeed.

TREASURY: "An Act for the establishment and support of Lighthouses, Beacons, Buoys, and Public Piers" (1 STAT. 53–54 [7 Aug. 1789]) provided for the upkeep of all lighthouses on United States territory for one year. Thereafter no expenses for lighthouse support would be defrayed unless the establishment was ceded to the federal government. Section 3 of the act provided for the erection of a lighthouse near the entrance of Chesapeake Bay, and in late 1789 Virginia ceded land for such a lighthouse at Cape Henry (Hamilton to Beverley Randolph, 10 Feb. 1790, HAMILTON [2], 6:261–62).

WAR: "An Act providing for the payment of the Invalid Pensioners of the United States" (1 STAT. 95 [29 Sept. 1789]) provided that the payment of military pensions granted by the states to invalid veterans of the Revolution should be continued by the United States. On 26 Jan. 1790 Knox wrote GW reporting that Hamilton had suggested that the responsibility for making payments should be relegated to the collectors of the customs appointed under the Treasury Department. A list of the collectors was enclosed in Knox's letter (DLC:GW). GW evidently agreed to this solution, for on 30 Jan. Hamilton wrote Jedediah Huntington, collector at New London, Conn., that in regard to invalid pensions, "the President having signified to me his pleasure, that the business in your state may be committed to your management; it remains for me to direct the necessary provision" (HAMILTON [2], 6:232–33).

CREEK NATION: The failure of the negotiations by David Humphreys, Cyrus Griffin, and Benjamin Lincoln with the Creek nation in late 1789 (see enry for 16 Nov.) left the problem of Indian depredations on the southern border still unsolved. It was suggested both in New York and on the frontier that the failure of the negotiations owed something to the ineptitude of the commissioners. Alexander McGillivray maintained that misunderstanding had arisen from "that puppy Humphries report to the president, it being a very unfavorable one and asserted that I would not treat on any terms whatever. . . . So I find that my different notes to them objecting to certain Stipulations were never produced to the president" (McGillivray to William Panton, 8 May 1790, CAUGHEY, 259–62).

On 15 Feb. 1790 Knox wrote to GW that he had conferred with Sen. Benjamin Hawkins of North Carolina, "who is well acquainted with the influential characters among the Creeks." It was Hawkins's opinion that McGillivray was anxious for a reasonable settlement with the United States and had indeed intimated to Hawkins that he might be persuaded to come to New York to open negotiations. Knox recommended that the experiment should be tried. The proposal "shall have the aspect of a private transaction, yet it shall have so much of the collateral countenance of government, as to convince Mr. McGillivray, that he may safely confide in the proposition as it relates to his own and the other Chiefs personal security until their return to their own Country. I have shown Mr. Hawkins the enclosed draft of a letter to Alexander McGillivray, it has received his approbation, and he is willing to copy and sign the same, adding thereto some circumstances relative

to a former correspondence on some philosophical enquiries" (DLC:GW).
Hawkins's letter to McGillivray, dated 6 Mar. 1790, is in CAUGHEY, 256–58.

Thursday 28th.   Sent a letter (with an Act of the Legislature of
the State of Rhode Island, for calling a Convention of that State to
decide on the Constitution of the Union) from Governor Collins,
to both Houses of Congress—to do which, was requested by the
Act, of the President.

The following Gentlemen dined here—viz.—The Vice Presi-
dent the Secretary of the Treasury—Messrs. Schuyler, Morris,
Izard Dalton and Butler of the Senate; and Messrs. Smith, (So.
Carolina) Stone, Schureman Fitzimmons, Sedgwick, Huger and
Madison of the House of Representatives.

RHODE ISLAND: Gov. John Collins's letter, enclosing the act of the Rhode
Island legislature authorizing a state ratifying convention, is dated 18 Jan.
1790. Collins expressed his pleasure at the legislature's decision but noted that
"The Operation of the Federal Government, according to the existing Laws,
will immediately prove greatly injurious to the Commercial Interests of this
State, unless a further Suspension of them can be obtained: I do therefore,
at the Request of the General Assembly, and in Behalf of the State, make
this application to the Congress of the United States, requesting a further
Suspension of the Acts of Congress subjecting the Citizens of this State to
the payment of foreign Tonnage, and foreign Duties, during the pleasure of
Congress" (DNA: RG 46, President's Messages, Entry 5).

James Schureman (1756–1824), a New Brunswick, N.J., merchant, graduated from Rutgers in 1775 and served in the Revolution. In 1783–85 and
1788 he was in the New Jersey legislature and in 1786–87 was a member of
the Continental Congress. In 1789 he was elected as a Federalist to the First
Congress.

Thomas Fitzsimons (1741–1811) was an Irishman who immigrated to Philadelphia as a young man. By the early 1760s he was well established as a
merchant in the West Indies trade. An active Patriot during the Revolution,
he served in the Continental Congress in 1782 and 1783, in the Pennsylvania
legislature 1786–87, and as a member of the Constitutional Convention in
1787. He was elected to the United States House of Representatives as a
Federalist in 1789 where he became a vigorous supporter of administration
measures.

Theodore Sedgwick (1746–1813) was born in West Hartford, Conn., and
educated at Yale. He began the practice of law in Great Barrington, Mass.,
in 1766 and then moved to Sheffield, Mass. During the Revolution he was a
member of the 1776 expedition against Canada and in 1780, 1782–85, and
1787–88 served in the Massachusetts legislature. Sedgwick was a member of
the Continental Congress 1785–88 and of the Massachusetts Ratifying Convention in 1788. In 1789 he was elected as a Federalist to the First Congress,
where he became a firm supporter of a strong executive and a spokesman for
the Washington administration's fiscal policies.

Daniel Huger (1742–1799), a member of a prominent South Carolina family, was born in Berkeley County, S.C., and educated in South Carolina and in England. He was a member of the state legislature in 1778–79, of the governor's council in 1780, and of the Continental Congress 1786–88 and was elected to the United States House of Representatives in 1789.

Friday 29th.   Exercised on horse back this forenn.; during my ride, Mr. Johnston, one of the Senators from No. Carolina who had just arrived came to pay his respects, as did Mr. Cushing, one of the Associate judges. The latter came again about 3 Oclock introduced by the Vice President.

Received from the Governor of No. Carolina, an Act of the Legislature of that State, authorising the Senators thereof, or one of the Senators and two of the Representatives, to make (on certain conditions) a Deed of Session of their Western Territory; described within certain Natural boundaries and requesting that the same should be laid before the Congress of the U. States.

Received also a letter from the Baron de Steuben, declarative of his distresses; occasioned by the Non-payment, or nonfulfilment of the Contract which was made with him by the Congress under the former Confederation and requesting my Official interference in his behalf. The delicacy of this case from the nature, and long labouring of it, requires consideration.

The Visitors to Mrs. Washington this Evening were numerous and respectable.

William Cushing (1732–1810), of Scituate, Mass., graduated from Harvard, studied law with Jeremiah Gridley of Boston, and was admitted to the Massachusetts bar in 1755. From 1760 to 1771 he practiced law in Pownalborough (Dresden) in the District of Maine; in 1772 he returned to Massachusetts to succeed his father as judge of the superior court. During the Revolution he adopted the Patriot cause and was retained by the state of Massachusetts as a justice on the Supreme Court. In 1779 he was a member of the Massachusetts state constitutional convention and in 1788 of the Massachusetts Ratifying Convention. GW appointed him an associate justice of the Supreme Court of the United States 24 Sept. 1789 (EXECUTIVE JOURNAL, 1:29).

Gov. Alexander Martin's letter to GW is dated 24 Dec. 1789 (DNA: RG 46, President's Messages). North Carolina originally passed an act of cession of its western lands to the Continental Congress in April 1784 but repealed it in October of that year. The state adopted the Constitution in Nov. 1789, and in December the legislature passed "An Act for the Purpose of Ceding to the United States of America, Certain Western Lands Therein Described" (N.C. STATE REC., 25:4–6). GW sent Martin's letter and the act of cession to the House and Senate on 1 Feb. (DE PAUW, 1:233, 3:281–82). The North Carolina deed of cession, 25 Feb. 1790, signed by North Carolina senators Samuel Johnston and Benjamin Hawkins, is in CARTER [4], 4:9–13. The

North Carolina cession, supplemented by a small grant from South Carolina, was constituted as the Territory Southwest of the River Ohio by Congress in May 1790 (1 STAT. 123 [26 May 1790]). The territory became the state of Tennessee in 1796.

When Baron von Steuben arrived in the United States in 1777, he had agreed verbally with a committee of Congress that he would join the army as a volunteer without rank or pay, but that if the United States succeeded in establishing independence his expenses incurred while in service would be paid. After the war Steuben repeatedly requested Congress to honor what he considered to be a binding contract. Congress delayed, not only from a lack of funds but from a persuasion that Steuben's appointment in May 1778 as a major general with the usual emoluments had abrogated the original agreement. On 14 Sept. 1789 a new petition from Steuben, requesting that his claims "for military services rendered during the late war, may be liquidated and satisfied," was presented to the House of Representatives. On 25 Sept. the committee on claims to which the petition had been referred sent it to the secretary of the treasury with instructions to report on it during the next session of Congress (DE PAUW, 3:206, 233). The petition and its supporting documents are in DNA: RG 46, Petitions and Memorials, Claims. Steuben's letter to GW, 29 Jan. 1790, requesting the president's support for his petition, is in DNA: RG 59, Misc. Letters. Hamilton reported favorably on Steuben's petition, 29 Mar. 1790, suggesting both an outright grant and an annuity, but Congress, probably in response to popular opposition to the petition, modified the sum. On 4 June the affair was settled, although not to the baron's satisfaction, by passage of "An Act for finally adjusting and satisfying the claims of Frederick William de Steuben," which granted him a lifetime annuity of $2,500 (6 STAT. 2; HAMILTON [2], 6:310–27; PALMER, 376–78).

Saturday 30.   Exercised with Mrs. Washington and the children in the coach, in the forenoon. Walked round the Battery in the Afternoon.

Sunday 31st.   Went to St. Pauls Chapel in the forenoon.

Mr. Wilson, one of the Associate Judges of the Supreme Court paid his respects to me after I returned from Church.

Spent the Afternoon in writing Letters to Mount Vernon.

James Wilson (1742–1798) was born in Scotland and educated at the universities of St. Andrews, Glasgow, and Edinburgh. He immigrated to America c.1765 and studied law in Philadelphia with John Dickinson. Admitted to the Pennsylvania bar in Nov. 1767, he began what was to be an outstanding legal career. He was elected to the Continental Congress 1775–76, 1782–83, and 1785–87. One of the signers of the Declaration of Independence, he was particularly adept in advancing legal justifications for independence. Wilson was a leading member of the Constitutional Convention and the Pennsylvania Ratifying Convention. In Sept. 1789 GW appointed him an associate justice of the Supreme Court although Wilson had earlier solicited the post of chief justice (Wilson to GW, 21 April 1789, PHi: Society Collection).

February 1790

Monday 1st.   Agreed on Saturday last to take Mr. McCombs House, lately occupied by the Minister of France for one year, from and after the first day of May next; and wd. go into it immediately, if Mr. Otto the present possesser could be accomodated and this day sent My Secretary to examine the rooms to see how my furniture cd. be adapted to the respective Apartments.

By the beginning of 1790 GW concluded that the house owned by Samuel Osgood which he had occupied since his arrival in New York City (see entry for 1 Oct. 1789) was no longer commodious enough to accommodate his family and staff and to maintain the dignity of the presidential office. In spite of the fact that it was expected that Congress might move the capital from New York City, GW decided to lease Alexander Macomb's mansion at Nos. 39–41 Broadway. "It was one of a block of three houses erected in 1787 and was four stories and an attic high, with a width of fifty-six feet. From the rear of the main rooms glass doors opened onto a balcony giving an uninterrupted view of the Hudson River. On entering, one found a large hall with a continuous flight of stairs to the top of the house. On each side of the hall were spacious, high-ceilinged rooms, used for the levees and dinners and always referred to by Washington as 'public rooms' " (DECATUR, 118, 148). Col. John May, who had visited the houses while they were still under construction in April 1788, noted "they are by far the grandest buildings I ever saw and are said to excel any on the continent. in one of the entry's I travelld up 5 flights of stairs" (MAY, 28). The Macomb house had been occupied by the comte de Moustier and, after his departure for France, by Louis Guillaume Otto, chargé d'affaires of the French embassy. Otto had served in the United States since 1779, and after his return to France in 1792 he was in charge of the political division of the department of foreign affairs until he lost his position with the fall of the Girondist regime. On 2 Feb. GW paid Samuel Osgood £253 10s. "for 3 quarter's Rent of the House & Tenements occupied by the President" and before he moved paid £665 16s. 6d. to purchase for the new house furniture and china left by Moustier (CtY: George Washington's Household Accounts, 68–74). GW requested that some alterations and additions be made to outside buildings (see Tobias Lear to Alexander Macomb, 4 Feb. 1790, owned by Mr. Sol Feinstone, Washington Crossing, Pa.). Preparations continued throughout the month, and the presidential household moved to the new residence on 23 Feb.

Tuesday 2d.   Exercised in the Carriage with Mrs. Washington.
    On my return found Mr. Blair one of the Associate Judges, The Attorney Genl. of the United States and Colo. Bland here.
    The Levee to day was much Crowded, and very respectable: among other Company, the District judge and Attorney, with the Marshall and all the Grand jurors of the Federal District Court (and a respectable body they were) attended.

First presidential residence, New York City. (New-York Historical Society)

Sent (yesterday) the Deed of Session of the Western Lands, by the State of No. Carolina to the United States to both Houses of Congress.

John Blair (1732–1800) was a member of a prominent Virginia family. He attended the College of William and Mary and in 1755 studied law at the Middle Temple. He was a member of the Virginia House of Burgesses 1766–70 and in the latter year became clerk of the council, serving at least until the mid-1770s. During the Revolution and the Confederation period, he held a number of judicial posts and became widely known in legal circles. As a member of the Constitutional Convention and the Virginia Ratifying Convention he vigorously supported the Constitution. GW appointed Blair an associate justice of the Supreme Court in Sept. 1789. Edmund Randolph had been appointed United States attorney general 25 Sept. 1789 but had remained in Virginia until the end of the session of the Virginia Assembly of which he was a member. He probably arrived in New York City at the end of January (REARDON, 179, 191). DISTRICT JUDGE: James Duane. DISTRICT . . . ATTORNEY: Richard Harison. THE MARSHALL: William Stephens Smith. DEED OF SESSION: See entry for 29 Jan. 1790.

Wednesday 3d.   Viewed the Apartments in the Ho. of Mr. Macombe—made a disposition of the Rooms—fixed on some furniture of the Ministers (which was to be sold & was well adapted to particular public rooms) and directed additional Stables to be built.

Thursday 4th.   Received from a Committee of both Houses of Congress, an Act, entitled "an Act for giving effect to the sevl. acts therein mentioned in respect to the State of North Carolina and other purposes."

The following company dined here, viz,—The Vice-President, the Chief Justice of the United States, Judges Cushing, Wilson, & Blair of the Supreme Court & Judge Duane of the District Court —The Attorney Genl. of the United States (Randolph) the Marshall, Attorney, & Clerk of the District viz. Smith, Harrison & Troup—Mr. Johnson & Mr. Hawkins of the Senate and the Secretaries of the Treasury & War Departmts. to wit Hamilton & Knox.

AN ACT: 1 STAT. 99–101 (8 Feb. 1790). This act extended the provisions of federal laws concerning import duties and tonnage to North Carolina, which had ratified the Constitution in Nov. 1789.

Robert Troup (1757–1832) studied law under John Jay and William Paterson and had a distinguished military career during the Revolution, earning a lieutenant colonelcy for his services in 1777 (JCC, 9:770). After serving on Horatio Gates's staff and participating in the Battles of Saratoga, he was appointed secretary of the newly formed Board of War in 1778. After the war he practiced law in Albany and New York City.

Friday 5th.   Received from Doctr. Williamson of No. Carolina a list of names whom he thought would be proper to fill the Revenue Offices in that State. Submitted the same to the Senators of that State for their Inspection and alteration.

Dr. Hugh Williamson (1735–1819) was born in Pennsylvania, graduated from the University of Pennsylvania in 1757, and after a brief career in the ministry, went to the University of Edinburgh to study medicine. After his return to America he practiced in Philadelphia until 1773. Around 1776 he established himself as a merchant in Edenton, N.C., and acted as surgeon general of North Carolina troops 1779–82. In 1782–85, 1787, and 1788 he served in the Continental Congress; at this time he was United States Representative from North Carolina. Williamson's letter to GW, 5 Feb. 1790, with enclosure, is in DLC:GW.

Saturday 6th.   Walked to my newly engaged lodgings to fix on a spot for a New Stable which I was about to build. Agreed with [   ] to erect one 30 feet sqr., 16 feet pitch, to contain 12 single stalls; a hay loft, Racks, mangers &ca.—Planked floor and underpinned with Stone with Windows between each stall for 65£.

The resignation of Mr. Harrison as an Associate Judge making a nomination of some other character to supply his place necessary I determined after contemplating every character which presented itself to my view to name Mr. Iredall of No. Carolina; because, in addition to the reputation he sustains for abilities, legal knowledge and respectability of character he is of a State of some importance in the Union that has given *No* character to a federal Office. In ascertaining the character of this Gentlemen I had recourse to every means of information in my power and found them all concurring in his favor.

On 28 Sept. 1789 GW had written Robert Hanson Harrison, one of his aides during the Revolution, offering him the post of an associate justice on the Supreme Court (DLC:GW). Harrison replied, 27 Oct., declining the post, partly because of the inconvenience of riding circuit, partly because of family responsibilities and reservations about his health (DNA: PCC, Item 59). On 25 Nov. GW again wrote Harrison, stating that there was a strong possibility that there would be changes in the Judicial Act which might make the post more attractive. "As the first Court will not sit until the first Monday in February, I have thought it proper to return your Commission, not for the sake of urging you to accept it contrary to your interest or convenience, but with a view of giving you a farther opportunity of informing yourself of the nature and probability of the change alluded to" (DLC:GW). Harrison again declined the post. He died in April 1790.

James Iredell (1751–1799) was born in Lewes, Eng., and in 1768 received a royal appointment as collector of the customs at Edenton, N.C. He quickly became a leading citizen of Edenton, studied law with Samuel Johnston, and in 1773 married Johnston's sister Hannah. Although a conservative, he supported the Patriot cause during the Revolution. His legal reputation in North Carolina grew during these years; he served briefly as a superior court judge in 1777 and from 1779 to 1781 he was state attorney general. In 1787 he served on the North Carolina Council of State and between 1787 and 1791 engaged in compiling a collection and revision of North Carolina statutes. GW's letter to Iredell, 13 Feb. 1790, offering him the post of associate justice, is in DLC:GW; Iredell's acceptance, 3 Mar. 1790, is in DNA: RG 59, Misc. Letters.

Sunday 7th.   Went to St. Pauls Chapel in the forenoon.

Monday 8th.   Nominated Officers for the Revenue department in No. Carolina—Mr. Iredall as an Associate Judge; and *all those* who had been temporarily appointed during the recess of the Senate to fill resigned Offices—likewise Majr. Saml. Shaw as Consul for Canton in China.

Sent the Bill which had been presented to me on Thursday last back to the House of Representatives with my approvg. Signature.

Samuel Shaw (1754–1794), of Massachusetts, served as a lieutenant and captain in the Revolution and saw action at Boston, Trenton, Princeton, Brandywine, Germantown, and Monmouth. For a time he served as aide-de-camp to Maj. Gen. Henry Knox. In 1784 he was offered the post of supercargo on the *Empress of China,* the first American vessel to sail to Canton. The experience he acquired in dealing with Chinese merchants resulted in his appointment by the Continental Congress in 1786 as American consul in Canton. He returned to the United States in Jan. 1789. On 2 Jan. 1790 he wrote GW informing him he was about to return to China and requesting that he be reappointed as consul (DLC:GW). Tobias Lear forwarded Shaw's commission on 13 Feb. 1790 (DNA: RG 59, Misc. Letters).

Tuesday 9th.   A good deal of Company at the Levee to day. Exercised on horse-back in the forenoon.

Wednesday 10th.   Sat from 9 until 11 Oclock for Mr. Trumbull to draw my picture in his Historical pieces.

Dispatched Commissions, and all the necessary Acts, to the Revenue Officers in No. Carolina.

Thursday 11th.   Exercised on horse-back in the forenoon.

The following Gentlemen dined here—viz.—Messrs. Leonard & Grout of Massachusetts—Huntington & Sturges of Connecticut—Silvester of New York Sinnickson of New Jersey—Gale of Maryland and Bland Parker and Moore of Virginia.

George Leonard (1729–1819) was born in Norton, Mass. After his graduation from Harvard in 1748 he held a number of judicial posts of increasing importance in his state and was judge of the common pleas court when he was elected to the First Congress. Jonathan Grout (1737–1807), a Petersham, Mass., lawyer, served in the Massachusetts House of Representatives 1781, 1784, 1787 and in the Senate 1788. An Antifederalist, he was elected to the First Congress in 1789. Benjamin Huntington (1736–1800), a Norwich, Conn., lawyer, graduated from Yale in 1761 and, before his election to the First Congress in 1789, served in the Massachusetts legislature and in the Continental Congress. From 1784 to 1796 he was mayor of Norwich. Jonathan Sturges (1740–1819), of Fairfield, Conn., graduated from Yale in 1759 and opened a law practice in Fairfield in 1772. He was a member of the state legislature 1772, 1773–84 and served in the Continental Congress 1774–87. Peter Silvester (1734–1808), a Kinderhook, N.Y., lawyer, was elected to the First Congress in 1789. Prior to his election he was a member of the First and Second Provincial Congresses 1775–76 and judge of the court of common pleas of Columbia County. Thomas Sinnickson (1744–1817), a Salem, N.J., merchant, held the rank of captain with New Jersey troops during the Revolution and was a member of the New Jersey legislature 1777, 1782, 1784–85, 1787–88.

George Gale (1756–1815), a native of Somerset County, Md., was a member of the Maryland Ratifying Convention in 1788. In Mar. 1791 GW appointed him supervisor of the revenue for Maryland. Josiah Parker (1751–1810) was a member of the 1775 Virginia Convention and served as colonel in the 5th Virginia Regiment during the Revolution. In 1780–81 he was in the Virginia

House of Delegates, and he served as naval officer for Portsmouth, Va., in 1786. Andrew Moore (1752–1821) was born near Fairfield, Rockbridge County, Va., studied at Augusta Academy (Washington and Lee), and was admitted to the Virginia bar in 1774. During the Revolution he served in the Continental Army 1776–78, and as a brigadier general in the Virginia militia. In 1780–83 and again in 1785–88 he was a member of the Virginia House of Delegates and in 1788 of the Virginia Ratifying Convention.

The *New-York Journal, and Weekly Register,* 18 Feb. 1790, noted that "the Birth-Day of the President of the United States was celebrated at Philadelphia the eleventh inst." In New York City, however, the Society of St. Tammany held an elaborate celebration on 22 Feb. and "Resolved, unanimously, That the 22d day of February (corresponding with the 11th Feb. old stile) be this day, and ever hereafter, commemorated by this Society as the BIRTH DAY of the Illustrious GEORGE WASHINGTON." Apparently this year the president's birthday was widely celebrated on 22 Feb. (*New-York Journal, and Weekly Register,* 25 Feb. 1790).

Friday 12th.   Sat from 9 Oclock untill 11 for Mr. John Trumbull for the purpose of Drawing my picture.

A good deal of Company (Gentlemen & Ladies) to visit Mrs. Washington this afternoon.

Saturday 13th.   Walked in the forenoon to the House to which I am about to remove—Gave directions for the arrangement of the furniture &ca. and had some of it put up.

Sunday 14th.   At home all day—writing private letters to Virginia.

Monday 15th.   Sat between 9 and 11 for Mr. John Trumbull.

Sent to both Houses of Congress a Letter from the President of New Hampshire, enclosing the adopted articles of amendments of the Constitution of the United States proposed by the latter at its last Session, to the States individually.

Perused two letters to Colo. Hawkins of the Senate, sent to me by the Secretary of War for my information—the one from a Lardin Clark dated Nashville, Warren County the 8th. of Septr. 1789—the other from Brigr. Genl. Joseph Martin dated Smiths River Jany. 1790. The first of these letters mentions that the loose and disorderly people that first settled the District in which he is remove as government (by means of the Superior Court) is extended amongst them and supplied by persons of better character & Morals—That the Spanish Governor of Louisiana is holding out every lure to envite the Citizens of the United States to settle under that Government—That a Doctor White who has been sometime at New Orleans does not seem to like the Government and discourages our Settlers from Migrating to it till it can at least be seen what measures the Government of the Union will take respecting the Navigation of the Mississippi—That Conventions which it had been proposed to hold in Kentucky, and other Districts of the Western Country for the purpose of addressing the old Congress on this subject had been proposed for the same reason—That there was no appearance of giving up the Post of the Natches to the U. States though it was within their Territory, on the Contrary Roman Catholick Churches were built there & provision made for newly arrived Priests—That the Spanish Governor has said that it is not want of Land that make them oppose our Settlements or which causes them to withhold the Navigation of the Missisipi from us, but because they do not like our advancing in such numbers, & so fast upon them—In short, they act under the operation of fear and Jealousy, though they will not acknowledge these to be the motives for their conduct—That it had been reported through the Western Settlements that Mr. Gardoqui had invited them to put themselves under the Spanish government with assurances of Peace & Trade as consequences of it and that Governor by Proclamation had invited them to become Inhabitants of Louisiana—That any person (he is informed) may take produce to New Orleans paying 15 pr. Ct.

George Washington peace medal, 1792. (Museum of the American Indian, Heye Foundation)

Duty to the King—That the Force (Military) in the two Floridas consist of two Regiments of 600 Men each and he is told a third is ordered to be raised to consist entirely of Spaniards by birth— That the District in which he is populates fast and will soon make a State—And as the Navigation of the Missisipi is essential to them, it must be obtained by treaty or by force, or they must connect themselves with the Spaniards—That it is not supposed, the two Floridas & Louisiana contain more than 20,000 Souls—That the distance from Nashville to New Orleans by Land (wch. he has travelled) is abt. 450 or 500 Miles and not a Mountain and hardly a hill in the way—That this year he supposes they will make 300 Hhds. of Tobacco—for wch. 3½d. only is given when the Spaniard gets 10 dollars pr. Hd. wt.

The other letter from Genl. Martin encloses the report of a Comee. of the Assembly of No. Carolina, which had been appointed to examine into a corrispondance between him and Mr. McGillivray, by which he stands acquitted of any intention to injure the U. States or any of them. Enforms him that from tolerable good information he has just heard that the Chicasaw Nation had made a stroke at the Chicamages Indians & were driving all before them—That several women & Children of the latter had run into the Inhabitants of little river for Refuge— That he shall set out for that County in a few days and as soon as the particulars can be known will give information of them. Wishes to know whether Congress approves of this War or not— thinks he can easily stop it if it does not meet their approbation —But adds their wars with one another may be the means of Peace to our frontiers—requests a hint on the subject by way of Richmond, directed to the care of the Postmaster there.

ARTICLES OF AMENDMENTS: Proposals for the amendments to the Constitution that were provided for by the fifth article of the Constitution and that were to become the Bill of Rights were introduced in Congress in May 1789. By Sept. 1789, 12 amendments had been agreed upon by the House and Senate, and on 24 Sept. the House resolved that "the President of the United States be requested to transmit to the executives of the several states which have ratified the Constitution, copies of the amendments proposed by Congress to be added thereto; and like copies to the executives of the states of Rhode-Island and North-Carolina" (DE PAUW, 3:84, 229). President of New Hampshire John Sullivan's letter to GW, 29 Jan. 1790, is in DNA: RG 46, President's Messages. Sullivan informed GW that New Hampshire had accepted all of the proposed amendments except the second, which provided that no "law vary[ing] the compensation for the services of the Senators and Representatives, shall take effect, until an election of Representatives shall have intervened" (DUMBAULD [2], 220). Of the 12 amendments originally submitted to the states, this article and the first article, which increased the representation in Congress after the first census had been taken, were not ratified by the states.

The letters submitted by Knox to GW have not been found. Lardner Clark was a leading Nashville merchant. Joseph Martin (1740–1808), of Albemarle County, Va., was a well-known figure on the frontier. He tried unsuccessfully to establish a settlement in Powell's Valley near the Cumberland Gap in 1769 and reoccupied the area in 1775. In 1777 he became Indian agent for Virginia to the Cherokee and established his headquarters on land that afterwards fell within North Carolina's boundaries. For many years he served as Patrick Henry's land agent on the frontier. In the mid-1780s Martin was involved in the proposals for the new State of Franklin, although he later opposed the project, and in the Muscle Shoals speculation. Martin attended the North Carolina Ratifying Convention in 1789 and served at various times in the North Carolina and Virginia legislatures. In June 1790 he became an active candidate for the post of governor of the newly created Southwest Territory (*Southern History Association Publications,* 4 [1900], 443–44; REDD, 113–18). At this time he was living in Henry County, Va., on Smith's River (Staunton River), the section of the Roanoke River above its confluence with the Dan River.

For the attempts of Esteban Miró, the Spanish governor of Louisiana, and Manuel Gayoso de Lemos, governor of Natchez, to attract American settlers, see entry for 25 Jan. 1790. Clark's reference to Don Diego de Gardoqui, the Spanish representative in the United States, concerns the plan devised by Gardoqui and Philadelphia speculator George Morgan (1743–1810) in 1789 to entice Americans to settle in Morgan's new settlement, developed under Spanish auspices, at New Madrid. Although at first a few westerners showed interest in moving to Spanish territory, these colonization schemes, and another sponsored by the South Carolina Yazoo Company at Nogales, were undermined by new and stringent economic policies of the Spanish government and by the extension of Spanish military control to the new settlements.

James White (1749–1809), a native of Philadelphia, had attended a Jesuit college in St. Omer, France, and studied medicine at the University of Pennsylvania. In 1785 he moved to Davidson County, N.C., and represented North Carolina in the Continental Congress 1786–88. While he was in Congress, White became deeply involved with Gardoqui in nebulous plans for persuading frontier areas to separate from the United States and accept Spanish protection. In 1786 White was chosen by Congress as Indian agent for the Southern Department and in the course of his service he traveled widely in the southwest, becoming involved in the so-called Spanish Conspiracy and in the creation of the State of Franklin.

The incident involving McGillivray referred to by Martin concerned a letter written by the latter from Tugaloe, N.C., to the Creek chief in Nov. 1788, enclosing resolves of the Continental Congress "by which you will see that Congress intends to deal out justice to the Cherokees, which gives me infinite pleasure." At the same time Martin expressed his wish that commissioners from Congress to the Creek would soon settle their differences with the United States and asked McGillivray's permission to lead some five hundred families from the United States to settle on Creek land (Martin to McGillivray, 8 Nov. 1788, N.C. STATE REC., 22:787–88). At the time the letter was written Martin was serving as an Indian commissioner for Congress. The letter was intercepted, apparently by members of the Georgia militia, and presented to the Georgia legislature. On 24 Jan. 1789 a committee of the legislature reported that Martin's action in "carrying on a correspondence of a private nature with Alexander McGilvary, yet, while this State is at war with the Creek nation, and the said Joseph Martin being in the service of the United States" was highly culpable and complaints should be made to Congress and to the governor of North Carolina (N.C. STATE REC., 21:1006). The report of the committee of the North Carolina Assembly appointed to investigate the matter exonerated Martin. The report was read in the assembly 15 Dec. 1789 and was enclosed by Martin in his letter to Benjamin Hawkins (N.C. STATE REC., 21:691).

Tuesday 16th.   Intended to have used exercise on Horse-back but the weather prevented my doing it. Rid to my intended habitation, and gave some directions respecting the arrangement of the furniture.

The Levee to day was thin. Received some papers from the Secretary at War respecting a corrispondence to be opened betwn. Colo. Hawkins of the Senate, and Mr. McGillivray of the Creek Nation for the purpose of getting the latter, with some other Chiefs of that Nation to this place as an expedient to avert a War with them. But, the Commissioning a Person to Negotiate this business with McGillivray without laying the matter before the Senate and the expence of the business appearing to bring in question the *Powers* of the President I requested to see & converse with the Secretary of War, tomorrow, on this Subject.

PAPERS FROM THE SECRETARY AT WAR: See entry for 27 Jan. 1790.

Wednesday 17th.   The Secretary attending; and reference being had to the Act constituting the Department of War, and the Act appropriating 20,000 dollrs. for the expence of Treating with the Southern Indians, seeming to remove (at least in a degree) the above doubts but not in an unequivocal manner, I desired him to take the opinion of the Chief Justice of the United States and that of the Secretary of the Treasury on these points and let me know the result.

"An Act to establish an Executive Department, to be denominated the Department of War" (1 STAT. 49–50 [7 Aug. 1789]) provided that the secretary of war could carry out such tasks regarding Indian affairs as might be entrusted to him by the president. "An Act providing for the Expenses which may attend Negotiations or Treaties with the Indian Tribes, and the appointment of Commissioners for managing the same" (1 STAT. 54 [20 Aug. 1789]) authorized expenditure of "a sum not exceeding twenty thousand dollars, arising from the duties on imports and tonnage" for the purpose of "defraying the expense of negotiating and treating with the Indian tribes."

Thursday 18th.   Sat for Mr. Trumbull from nine oclock till 10
—after which exercised in the Post Chaise with Mrs. Washington.
On our return home called on Mrs. Adams—Lady of the Vice-
Presidt.

The following company dined here to day—viz—Judge Cush-
ing and his Lady—The Post Master General & his Lady and
Messrs. Boudinot, Griffin, Coles, Gerry and White and their
Ladies.

Sent a Message to the Senate with the Copies of a Letter from
the Governor of Massachusetts and a resolve of the Assembly of
that State, respecting the disputed boundary between them and
the British of Nova Scotia.

THEIR LADIES: Mrs. William Cushing was Hannah Phillips Cushing (c.1754–
1834) of Middletown, Conn. Mrs. Samuel Osgood was Mary Bowne Franklin
Osgood, the widow of Walter Franklin (see entry for 1 Oct. 1789). Mrs.
Elias Boudinot was Hannah Stockton Boudinot (1736–1808), daughter of
John and Abigail Stockton of Princeton, N.J., and sister of Signer Richard
Stockton. She had married Boudinot in 1762. Mrs. Samuel Griffin was Betsy
Braxton Griffin (see entry for 10 Dec. 1789). Isaac Coles, United States
representative from Virginia, had married Catharine Thompson, daughter
of James Thompson, in Jan. 1790 (*Pa. Packet*, 7 Jan. 1790). Ann Thompson
(d. 1849), daughter of New York merchant James Thompson and Catherine
Walton Thompson, had married Elbridge Gerry in 1786. Mrs. Alexander
White (b. 1739) was Elizabeth Wood White, daughter of Col. James Wood,
founder of Winchester, Va.

The resolve of the Massachusetts legislature, 1 Feb. 1790, directed Gov.
John Hancock to write to the president "informing him that the subjects of
his Britannick Majesty have made and still continue to make encroachments
on the eastern boundary of this Commonwealth, in the opinion of the Legislature, contrary to the treaty of peace." Hancock wrote GW, 10 Feb. 1790,
transmitting a number of documents supporting the legislature's allegations.
GW transmitted the resolve of the Massachusetts legislature and Hancock's
letter to the Senate, 18 Feb. 1790 (DNA: RG 46, Entry 11). The enclosures
consisted of copies of some of the documents that had already been submitted
to the Senate by GW on 9 Feb. 1790, in a report to the Senate "relative to
differences with Great Britain respecting the Eastern Boundary" (see ASP,
FOREIGN RELATIONS, 1:90–99; DE PAUW, 2:359–87). The northeastern boundary
dispute concerned some 7,500 square miles of land between the United States
and New Brunswick; the boundary had been left unsettled at the Treaty of
Paris in 1783 because of uncertainty as to the location of the river St. Croix
which appeared on Mitchell's Map and was used as the boundary line by the
peace commissioners. Investigation in the area showed there was no St. Croix
River in the vicinity of the stream marked on Mitchell's Map. British ne-
gotiators held that the boundary line agreed upon at Paris was the Schoodiac
River while the United States maintained it was the Magaguadavic, east of
the Schoodiac (see MOORE [3], 1:5). The dispute on the location of the St.
Croix was settled by arbitration in 1798, a mixed commission agreeing that
the Schoodiac was the St. Croix on Mitchell's Map.

Friday 19th.   Exercised on horse-back about 9 oclock. Walked afterwards to my New House.

Received a Captn. Drew, Comr. of a British Sloop of War, sent Express to Sir John Temple Consul General of that Nation in the U. States.

The Visitors this Evening to Mrs. Washington were numerous and respectable.

Captain Drew, in command of the *Echo,* sailed on his return voyage to Plymouth 6 Mar. (*New-York Journal, and Weekly Register,* 11 Mar. 1790).

Saturday 20th.   Sat from nine until 11 for Mr. Trumbull. Walked afterwards to my New House—then rode a few miles with Mrs. Washington and the Children before dinner; after which I again visited my New House in my Coach (because it rained).

Sunday 21st.   Went to St. Pauls Chapel in the forenoon. Wrote letters respecting my domestic concerns afterwards.

The only private letter found for this day is GW to Samuel Powel, concerning the Philadelphia Society for Promoting Agriculture (DLC:GW).

Monday 22d.   Set seriously about removing my furniture to my New House. Two of the Gentlemen of the family had their Beds taken there and would sleep there to Night.

Tuesday 23d.   Few or no visiters at the Levee today, from the idea of my being on the move.

After dinner Mrs. Washington Myself & Children removed and lodged at our New habitation.

REMOVED: See entry for 1 Feb. 1790.

Wednesday 24th.   Employed in arranging matters about the House & fixing matters.

Thursday 25th.   Engaged as yesterday.

In the afternoon a Committee of Congress presented an Act for enumerating the Inhabitts. of the United States.

AN ACT: 1 STAT. 101 (1 Mar. 1790). This act provided for the taking of the first federal census.

Friday 26th.   A numerous company of Gentlemen & Ladies were here this Afternoon.

Exercised on Horse-back this forenoon.

Saturday 27th.   Sat for Mr. Trumbull this forenoon; after which exercised in the Coach with Mrs. Washington & the Children.

Sunday 28th.   Went to St. Pauls Chappel in the forenoon. Wrote letters on private business afterwards.

March 1790

Monday the First.   Exercised on horseback this forenoon, attended by Mr. John Trumbull who wanted to see me Mounted.

Informed the House of Representatives (where the Bill originated) that I had given my assent to the Act for taking a Census of the People.

Also communicated to both Houses the application from the field Officers of Harrison County (made through the County Lieutenant Colo. Duval) for Assistance as they apprehend the season was near at hand when Indian depredations would be commenced. With these, some other Papers respecting the western Frontiers were sent.

CENSUS: See entry for 25 Feb. 1790. John P. Duvall (Duval) was county lieutenant of Harrison County, Va. Henry Knox sent the application, together with other papers, to Congress (Knox to Congress, 2 Mar. 1790, and Knox to GW, 2 Mar. 1790, DLC:GW). Although Knox's letter to Congress is dated 2 Mar. in GW's letterbooks, the papers were apparently received in the House of Representatives by 1 Mar. (see DE PAUW, 3:310).

Tuesday 2d.   Much, and respectable company was at the Levy to day.

Caused a letter to be written to the Govr. of St. Jago respecting the Imprisonment of a Captn. Hammond.

On 20 Feb. 1790 Maria Hammond of New York City wrote GW complaining that her husband, Thomas Hammond, a sea captain, had been captured by the British frigate *Pomona* in Oct. 1789 "on the Coast of Africa, his Vessel and Cargo seized and sold, and himself and pilot put in Irons and in that situation delivered to the Portugueze Governor of the Island of St. Jago, where they are now closely confined, and in the most deplorable situation." Mrs. Hammond also enclosed a petition from her husband and the pilot of the ship, John Hilliard, complaining of their treatment. She requested GW's intervention with the Portuguese (DNA: RG 59, Misc. Letters). At the president's request Tobias Lear sent the petition to John Jay, 20 Feb., asking his opinion as to what procedures should be followed (DLC:GW). Jay apparently advised GW to make inquiries of Anseto Antone Freatz, the gover-

John Trumbull's historical painting "The Capture of the Hessians at Trenton." (Yale University Art Gallery)

nor of St. Jago, Cape Verde Islands, for on 1 Mar. 1790, Lear wrote to him, explaining the circumstances of the capture of Hammond and the sloop *Brothers* and stating "that the reason assigned for this seizure was, that dollars were found on board the Sloop, which dollars, they say, were taken from wrecks" near the island of Bonavista. "The President is desirous to be informed of the reasons which gave occasion to the treatment which these people have received; and in case your Excellency should not think it consistant with your duty to release them from Confinement, that you would direct them to be treated with such a degree of benevolence as the nature of the Offences with which they stand charged may permit" (DNA: RG 59, Misc. Letters).

Wednesday 3d.   Exercised on Horse-back between 9 and 11 Oclock.

Thursday 4th.   Sat from 9 until half after 10 Oclk. for Mr. Trumbull.
The following Gentlemen dined here to day—viz.—The Vice-Presidt. Messrs. Langdon, Wingate, Dalton, Strong, Ellsworth, Schuyler, King, Patterson, Morris, McClay, Bassett, Henry, Johnson, Hawkins, Izard, Butlar & Few all of the Senate.

According to an entry for this day in William Maclay's diary, "it was a dinner of dignity. All the Senators were present and the Vice-President. I looked often around the company to find the happiest faces. . . . The President seemed to bear in his countenance a settled aspect of melancholy. . . . At every interval of eating or drinking he played on the table with a fork or knife, like a drumstick" (MACLAY, 201).

Friday 5th.   A very numerous company of Ladies & Gentlemen here this Evening.

Saturday 6th.   Exercised in the Coach with Mrs. Washington and the Children and in the Afternoon walked round the Battery.
Received a letter from the Govr. of the Western Territory dated at the Rapids of Ohio giving an acct. of the State of Affairs in the Westn. Country.

Arthur St. Clair was appointed governor of the Northwest Territory in 1787. His letter to GW from "the Rapids of the Ohio," at present Louisville, Ky., has not been found. However, in a letter to GW, 1 May 1790, written from Cahokia in the Illinois Country, St. Clair stated: "In a Letter, which I had the honor to address to you from the Rapids of the Ohio, I mentioned the Information I had received respecting Mr. Morgan in that part of the Country" (DNA: RG 59, Territorial Papers, Northwest Territory). St. Clair's earlier letter concerned the activities of George Morgan (1743–1810), member of the former Philadelphia trading firm of Baynton, Wharton, & Morgan. In 1789 Morgan actively engaged, with Spanish representative Don

Washington's sketch for a cipher and crest
for his coach. (Library of Congress)

Diego de Gardoqui, in a scheme to develop the Spanish settlement of New
Madrid in what was then Spanish Louisiana and to entice Americans to
settle there.

Sunday 7th.   At home all day—writing letters on private business.

Monday 8th.   Sent to both Houses of Congress the Resolves of
the Delaware State to adopt and make part of the Constitution of
the United States the amendments proposed by the General Government except the first article of the said amendments the consideration of which they postponed.

A copy of Gov. Joshua Clayton's letter to GW, 19 Feb. 1790, enclosing the
resolution of the Delaware legislature, 28 Jan. 1790, is in DNA: RG 46,
President's Messages. For the amendments, see entry for 15 Feb. 1790.

Tuesday 9th.   A good many Gentlemen attended the Levy to
day; among whom were many members of Congress.

Wednesday 10th.   Exercised on Horse-back between 9 and 11
oclock. On my return had a long conversation with Colo. Willet,

who was engaged to go as a private Agent, but for public purposes, to Mr. McGillivray principal chief of the Creek Nation. In this conversation he was impressed with the critical situation of our Affairs with that Nation—the importance of getting him & some other chiefs to this City—the arguments justifiable for him to use to effect this—with such lures as respected McGillivray personally & might be held out to him. His (Colo. Willits) going, was not to have the appearance of a Governmental act. He & the business he went upon, would be introduced to McGillivray by Colo. Hawkins of the Senate (from No. Carolina) who was a correspondant of McGillivrays—but he would be provided with a Pass-port for him and other Indian chiefs if they inclined to make use of it; but not to part with it if they did not.

The letter from Colo. Hawkins to McGillivray was calculated to bring to his, & the view of the Crk. Nation the direful consequences of a rupture with the United States. The disposition of the General government to deal justly and honorably by them and the means by which they, the Creeks, may avert the calamities of War which must be brought on by the disorderly people of both nations, if a Treaty is not made & observed. His instructions relative to the principal points to be negotiated would be given to Colo. Willet in writing by the Secretary of War.

COLO. WILLET: For the government's earlier negotiations with the Creek, see entry for 16 Nov. 1789. In a letter to GW, 15 Feb. 1790, concerning the government's plan to bring Creek chief Alexander McGillivray to New York, Knox had suggested that a person be appointed to carry Sen. Benjamin Hawkins's letter of invitation to McGillivray (see entry for 27 Jan. 1790). "The bearer of the letter ought to be a man of real talents and judgment. Although the ostensible object of his mission should be the charge of the letter, yet the real object should be much more extensive. He should be capable of observing the effects of the proposition, on the mind of Mr. McGillivray and the other Chiefs. . . . The objects therefore of the mission require an important character who although not invested with any apparently dignified public commission ought to have such private powers and compensation as would be a sufficient inducement to a performance of the intended service" (DLC:GW). The choice as emissary fell on Marinus Willett (1740–1830), an Antifederalist New York merchant and veteran of the French and Indian War and the Revolution. Willett's mission proved successful. McGillivray found him "a Candid and Benevolent Character possessing abilitys but without Show or parade" and agreed to accompany him to New York (McGillivray to William Panton, 8 May 1790, CAUGHEY, 259–62).

Thursday 11th.   A Letter from Arthur Campbell Esqr. of Washington County Virginia to the Secretary at War was put into my hands by the latter containing the following information—the letter dated 6th. Feb. 90.

That half the Cherokee Nation wd. desire to remain Neutre in case of a war between the United States and the Creek Indians —viz.—Those in the Neighbourhood of Chota & all those which are called the Middle Settlements. The Towns on the Tennessee below Hiuassee, & those on the heads of the Caussa would aid the Creeks.

That from the Long Island in Holstein to the Junction of French Broad the Navigation is equal to that of Monongahela between the Mouth of Cheat & Pitsburgh. Below it it is exceeding good to where the River passes through Cumberland Mountain, a distance of about 150 Miles by Water. Here the River runs with great rapidity against a steep rock which forms its bank and makes a short turn & gives this place the name of the Whirl; the River here not being more than the 4th. of its common breadth above & below it is very deep but not dangerous with care.

That from this place the river moves with a gentle current Southerly near the foot of the Cumberland Mountn. on the West side for about 100 Miles (something Eastwardly of this distance the Mountain ends) then it begins to turn Northwardly 100 miles more to the upper end of the Muscle shoals.

That these Muscle shoals are gentle rapids for about 30 miles, and the difficulty lays in strangers missing the right Channel—the River being 2 Miles wide & full of small Islands.

That the Creek landing on the Tennessee, is about 80 Miles below the Whirl, from whence there is a good road to the Caussa, on the branches of which, and the Alibama river (both waters of the Mobile) most of the Upper Creeks live.

That below the Muscle shoals a Row boat of any size may ascend the river with almost the same facility it passes downwards.

That from Nashville to the lower settlements on Holstein the New road is computed 180 miles. Miro is the name of the District.

That from Nashville to the Muscle Shoals is 70 Miles.

That it is the upper Creeks *generally,* the Cherokees of the lower towns to wit Chickamaga, Nickgjack & Crows Town, that give annoyance to the Southern Settlements at Kentucky, the Path through the Wilderness, and the Holstein Settlements.

That the Miro District (which contains all the Cumberland Settlements) can raise 800 good Militia men—total number of Inhabitants may be abt. 4000 besides Slaves.

That Washington District in North Carolina contains 4000

Mila. and Washington District in Virginia about 2000 Do.—The two latter mostly in Holstein Valley.

That Kentucky District has betwn. Eight & 10,000 Men.

That in his opinion, a Regiment of Militia could be raised to go against the Southern Indians to serve one Campaign in Six weeks after the officers should receive orders for the purpose and that before the expiration of that time 560 Regular Troops could be enlisted to serve three years or better—call them Rangers. The light Infantry Companies & Troops of horse in the different western Counties might be ordered into Service agreeable to the existing Laws of Virga. Out of these a fine Ranging Regiment might be Enlisted.

That the Distances, as computed, from place to place are as follow—viz.

From Lexington in Kentucky

To Danville	30	Miles
Green River	60	
Big Barren River	60	
Red river Station	40	
Nashville on Cumbd.	25	
Muscle Shoals	70	
	285	

From Lexington to Crab Orchd.

From Lexington to Crab Orchd.	40
To Cumberland Gap	100
The Mouth of Hiwassee	70
Big Shoemac Town (Cherok.)	40
Creek Towns	60
	310

From Nashville to Holstein

To Bledsoes Lick	30
Big Salt lick (Cumberd.)	30
Junction of the Holstein & Tennessee	100
	160

From the Mouth of Holstein the direct way to the Creek Towns

To Hiwassee old Town (Cherokees)	40
Big Shoemac	30
Upper Creeks on Caussa Waters	60
	130

The following Gentlemen dined here to day—viz.

Mr. Read of the Senate, the Speaker, and following Gentlemen of the House of Representatives—viz.—Messrs. Gilman, Goodhue,

Aimes Wadsworth, Trumbull, Benson, Lawrence, Peter Muhlenberg, Wynkoop Vining, Carroll, Contee, Madison Page & Sumpter —also Judge Bedford and Mr. John Trumbull.

Arthur Campbell (1742–1811) was born in Augusta County, Va., and was active in Indian fighting on the Virginia frontier until c.1777 when he moved to North Carolina and settled near the Holston River in what is now Washington County, Tenn. He soon became a leading land speculator and spokesman for frontier interests and served frequently in the North Carolina Assembly. He was involved as early as 1782 in the movement to separate the western part of North Carolina from the state and in the mid-1780s became a leading proponent of the State of Franklin. His letter to Knox has not been found.

John Vining (1758–1802), a New Castle County, Del., attorney and a native of Dover, served in the Continental Congress 1784–86. Mr. Carroll is Daniel Carroll (1730–1796), cousin of Charles Carroll of Carrollton, who had been elected as a Federalist Representative to the First Congress. Benjamin Contee (1755–1815), a native of Prince George's County, Md., served in the 3d Maryland Battalion during the Revolution, in the Maryland House of Delegates 1785–87, and in the Continental Congress 1788–89. Thomas Sumter (1734–1832) was born near Charlottesville, Va., but moved in 1765 to the area of Eutaw Springs, S.C. He had a notable military career during the Revolution both in the Continental Army where he held the rank of colonel and as a brigadier general in the South Carolina militia, operating with considerable success against Banastre Tarleton and Lord Rawdon after the British invasion of South Carolina. After the Revolution he founded Stateburg, S.C., and became heavily involved in canal ventures and land speculation. Sumter was a member of the South Carolina Ratifying Convention and was elected from South Carolina to the First Congress where he became a spokesman for South Carolina Antifederalists. Gunning Bedford, Jr. (1747–1812), a native of Philadelphia, graduated from Princeton in 1771, studied law in Philadelphia with Joseph Reed, and moved to Delaware shortly before the Revolution. He served in the Continental Congress 1783–85 and as attorney general of Delaware 1784–89. Bedford was a delegate to the Constitutional Convention in 1787 and to the Delaware Ratifying Convention the same year. In 1789 GW appointed him federal judge for the district of Delaware.

Friday the 12th.   Exercised in the Post Chaise with Mrs. Washington from 10 Oclock till near 12.

Signed the Passport which was to be committed to Colo. Willet for Mr. McGillivray and other Chiefs of the Creek Nation of Indians, and other Papers necessary for his setting out on this business.

A Pretty numerous company of Visiters this evening to Mrs. Washington Levee.

Saturday 13th.   Exercised about 11 Oclock with Mrs. Washington & the Children, in the Coach.

Sunday 14th. Went to St. Pauls Chapel in the forenoon. Wrote letters on private business afterwards.

Monday 15th. Received an Address from the Roman Catholics of the United States presented by Mr. Carroll of the Senate, Mr. Carroll & Mr. Fitzimmons of the House of Representatives, and many others, Inhabitants of the City of New York.

Received a letter from the Executive of the State of Pensylvania, by the hands of a Mr. Ryerson one of the Representatives of that State in Assembly, respecting the exposed state of the County of Washington. This letter I sent to the Secretary of War to be laid before Congress.

I also received from the Speaker of the Assembly of Pensylvania, an Act, adopting the Amendments to the Constitution as proposed by Congress, except the first article thereof.

And Mr. Few, Senator from the State of Georgia, presented me with the Copy of an Address from that State requiring to knw. when it would be convenient for me to receive it in form. Finding it out of the usual style—State politics being blended there with, I informed Mr. Few that as soon as I could make it convenient to receive it He should have notice thereof.

ROMAN CATHOLICS: The undated complimentary address was signed by Bishop John Carroll, representing the Roman Catholic clergy, and by Charles Carroll of Carrollton, Daniel Carroll, Thomas Fitzsimons, and Dominick Lynch, in behalf of the Roman Catholic laity (DLC:GW). GW's reply, also undated, is in MdBAr. EXECUTIVE OF THE STATE OF PENSYLVANIA: Gov. Thomas Mifflin wrote GW "in Council" on 10 Mar. 1790, "transmitting to your Excellency a Letter which has been addressed to the Executive of this State by several very respectable Inhabitants of the County of Washington in Pennsylvania; in which they represent 'that many mischiefs have taken place in that County for several years past from the hostile incursions of the Indians, and that from the present aspect of Indian affairs in the western and South western Countries, the same are likely to continue' and request 'the interposition of Council with the President'" (DLC:GW). Knox delivered the letters to the House of Representatives on 16 Mar. 1790, where they were read and ordered to lie on the table (DE PAUW, 3:329). The letters were delivered to GW by Thomas Ryerson, who represented Washington County in the Pennsylvania Assembly. The act of the Pennsylvania legislature, 10 Mar. 1790, ratifying ten of the proposed amendments to the Constitution, is printed, with accompanying documents, in DE PAUW, 3:330–32. Pennsylvania failed to ratify the first two of the proposed amendments (see entry for 15 Feb. 1790). ADDRESS: Presumably this is the address to the president drafted in the Georgia General Assembly 22 Dec. 1789 (DLC:GW). After the usual compliments to GW, the assembly complained of Creek incursions on Georgia's frontiers. "On this subject we wish to be delicate; much has been already said—we have objected, and it has been contradicted; removed at a distance from the centre our actions have been liable to misrepresentation; but we trust that by this time, they are better explained. In the meantime while our population has been checked and our agriculture diminished—the blood of our citizens has been spilled, our public resources greatly exhausted; and our frontiers still open to fresh ravages. The failure of the late negociations for a peace with the Creek nation and the circumstances which attended the same, are the best evidence of the necessity of our measures, and a proof of the late hostile dispositions of these People. . . . Another circumstance of additional calamity attendant on our being the south frontier of the Union, is the facility of our black people crossing the spanish line, from whence we have never been able to reclaim them. . . . We take this occasion of bringing this business into view, with a perfect reliance, that you will cause such discussions to be made, as shall be necessary to bring about a remedy." Since Georgia was widely accused of provoking Indian retaliation by permitting settlement on Indian lands and by military excursions into Creek territory, GW's undated reply was carefully noncommittal, promising only to "make such use of the powers vested in me by the constitution as may appear to me best calculated to promote the public good" (DLC:GW).

Tuesday 16th.   Exercised on horseback between 10 & 12 Oclock. Previous to this, I was visited (having given permisn.) by a Mr. Warner Mifflin, one of the People called Quakers; active in pursuit of the Measures laid before Congress for emancipating the Slaves. After much general conversation, and an endeavor to remove the prejudices which he said had been entertained of the motives by which the attending deputation from their Society were actuated, he used Arguments to shew the immoralty—injustice and impolicy of keeping these people in a state of Slavery; with declarations, however, that he did not wish for more than a graduel abolition, or to see any infraction of the Constitution to effect it. To these I replied, that as it was a matter which might come before me for official decision I was not inclined to express any sentimts. on the merits of the question before this should happen.

The day being bad, not many Visiters attended the Levee. At it Mr. Smith of South Carolina presented the Copy of an Address from the Intendant and [   ] of the City of Charleston, and was told that I would receive it in form on Thursday at 11 Oclock.

Warner Mifflin (1745–1798), a prominent Quaker abolitionist, was born in Accomack County, Va. His father was a prosperous planter who held over 100 slaves; as a young man Mifflin became interested in the abolition movement and persuaded his father to free the family slaves. Although he generally eschewed political action, abstaining from voting on the ground that participation in government might be construed as support of slaveholding interests, he was instrumental in presenting a series of antislavery petitions to the Continental Congress during the Confederation (MIFFLIN; JONES [3], 326). The journal of the House of Representatives for 11 Feb. 1790 notes that "memorials of the people called Quakers, in their annual meetings, held at Philadelphia and New-York, in the year one thousand seven hundred and eighty-nine, were presented to the House and read, praying the attention of Congress in adopting measures for the abolition of the slave trade, and in particular in restraining vessels from being entered and cleared out, for the purposes of that trade." On 12 Feb. the memorial was referred to a committee, together with a memorial from the Quakers' New York meeting. The committee reported, 23 Mar., stating that Congress had no authority to interfere with the slave trade until 1808 when, as the Constitution provided, the trade would be abolished. Furthermore, the report continued, Congress had no authority to interfere with the states in matters concerning the slaves' welfare, although the members "have the fullest confidence in the wisdom and humanity of the Legislatures of the Several States, that they will revise their laws from time to time, when necessary, and promote the objects mentioned in the memorials, and every other measure that may tend to the happiness of slaves." The memorials and report met the fate of most other Quaker petitions on slavery; it was ordered that they "do lie on the table" (DE PAUW, 3:294–96, 316, 321, 333–37, 340–41). GW wrote David Stuart, 28 Mar., that the "memorial of the Quakers (and a very mal-apropos one it was) has at length been put to sleep, and will scarcely awake before the year 1808" (DLC:GW).

The document transmitted by Sen. William Loughton Smith was "The address of the Intendant [Thomas Jones] and Wardens of the city of Charleston, South-Carolina," dated in the city council 18 Feb. 1790, congratulating GW on his election as president (DLC:GW). GW's undated reply is also in DLC:GW.

Wednesday 17th.   Gave Mr. Few Notice that I would receive the Address of the Legislature of Georgia tomorrow at half after ten oclock.

Sent to both House[s] of Congress the Ratification of the State of Pennsylvania of the amendments proposed by Congress to the Constitution of the Union.

Thursday 18th.   At half past 10 I received the address of the Legislature of Georgia—presented by Mr. Few the Senator & the 3 representatives of the State in Congress.

At 11 Oclock the Address from the Intendent and Wardens of the City of Charleston was presented by Mr. Smith.

The following Gentlemen dined here—viz—Messrs. Livermore, Foster, Patridge, Thatcher, Shirman, Fitzimmons, Hartley, Seney, Lee, Burke, Tucker, Baldwin, Jackson & Mathews of the Representatives in Congress and Mr. Otis Secretary of the Senate, and Mr. Beckley Clerk of the House of Representatives.

In the Evening (about 8 Oclk.) I went with Mrs. Washington to the assembly where there were betwn. 60 & 70 Ladies & many Gentlemen.

March 1790

ADDRESS OF THE LEGISLATURE OF GEORGIA: See entry for 15 Mar. 1790. Georgia's three representatives were George Mathews, James Jackson, and Abraham Baldwin.

Friday 19th.   Exercised on Horseback betwn. 9 and 11 Oclock.

Information being given by Mr. Van Berkel, that Mr. Cazenove just arrived from Holland, and of a principal Mercantile House there had letters for me which he wished to deliver with his own hands and requesting to know when he might be presented for that purpose. It was thought, before this should be done, it might be proper to know whether they were of a public nature, and whether he was acting in a public character. If so, then to let them come to me through the Secretary of State—if not, then for him to send them, that the purport might be known before he was introduced, which might be at the next Levee when he might be received & treated agreeably to the consequence he might appear to derive from the testimonial of the letters. It being conceived that etiquette of this sort is essential with all foreigners to give respect to the Chief Majestrate and the dignity of the Government, which would be lessened if every person who could procure a letter of introduction should be presented otherwise than at Levee hours in a formal manner.

Theophile Cazenove (1740–1811) was born in Amsterdam and from 1763 to 1788 operated a leading brokerage firm in that city. Serious business reverses in the latter year led him to accept a commission as agent in the United States for a number of Dutch bankers, including Pieter Stadnitski & Son and Nicholaas and Jacob Van Staphorst, who were interested in the purchase of American securities and in investment in various American enterprises. In 1792 Cazenove was appointed agent in purchasing western lands for the six Dutch banking houses that banded together in 1796 as the Holland Land Company. Cazenove arrived in the United States early in 1790, carrying numerous letters of introduction to American financiers (see EVANS [3], 3–7).

Saturday 20th.   Exercised in the Coach with Mrs. Washington and the Children.

Sunday 21st.   Went to St. Pauls Chappel in the forenoon. Wrote private letters in the afternoon.

Received Mr. Jefferson, Minister of State about one Oclock.

Shortly after his return to the United States in 1789 (see entry for 7 Oct. 1789), Jefferson received GW's letter of 13 Oct. 1789 offering him the post of secretary of state (DLC: Jefferson Papers). Jefferson, who preferred to return to Paris, somewhat reluctantly indicated he was willing to serve, "but when I contemplate the extent of that office, embracing as it does the principal mass of domestic administration, together with the foreign, I cannot be in-

Thomas Jefferson, by Charles Willson Peale. (Independence National Historical Park Collection)

sensible of my inequality to it . . . my chief comfort will be to work under your eye, my only shelter the authority of your name, and the wisdom of measures to be dictated by you, and implicitly executed by me. . . . I do not see that the matters which have called me hither will permit me to shorten the stay I originally asked; that is to say, to set out on my journey Northward till the month of March. As early as possible in that month I shall have the honor of paying my respects to you in New York" (Jefferson to GW, 15 Dec. 1789, DLC:GW). For the circumstances of Jefferson's acceptance, see JEFFERSON [1], 16:169–70; GW to Jefferson, 21 Jan. 1790, DLC: Jefferson Papers; Jefferson to GW, 14 Feb. 1790, DNA: RG 59, Misc. Letters. Jefferson left Virginia early in March and arrived in New York today.

Monday 22d. Sat for Mr. Trumbell for my Picture in his Historical pieces—after which conversed for more than an hour with Mr. Jefferson on business relative to the duties of his office.

Tuesday 23d. A full, & very respectable Levee to day—previous to which I had a conversation with the Secretary of State on the following points, viz—

First, with respect to our Captives in Algiers, in which, after detailing their situation—the measures he had taken for their relief and the train in which the business was in by means of a Genl. [ ] who is at the head of a religious society in France whose practice it is to sollicit aids for the relief of the unfortunate Christians in captivity among the Barbarians, it was concluded betwn. us, that it had better remain in that train a while longer. This person had been authorised to go as far as about £150 Sterlg. each, for the ransom of our Captives; but the Algerines demanding a much larger sum it was conceived that acceding to it might establish a precedent which would always operate and be very burthensome if yielded to; and become a much stronger inducement to captivate our People than they now have, as it is more for the sake of the ransom than for the labour, that they make Slaves of the Prisoners. Mr. Short was to be written to on this Subject, and directed to make enquiry of this General [ ] what his expectations of redemption are at present.

Second—He is of opinion, that excepting the Court of France, there is no occasion to employ higher grades in the Diplomatic line than Chargé des affaires; and that these, by the respectibility of their appointments, had better be at the head of their grade, than Ministers Plenipotentiaries by low Salaries at the foot of theirs. The reason of the distinction, in favor of a Minister Plenipo at Versailles, is, that there are more Ambassadors at that Court than any other and therefore that we ought in some measure to approximate our Representative and besides, its being a Court with which we have much to do.

Third—With respect to the appointment of Consels he refers to a letter on the nature of this business—the places where necessary—and the characters best entitled to appointmts. which he had written on the Subject, while in France, to the Secretary of Foreign affairs.

Fourth—That it might be advisable to direct Mr. Charmichael to Sound the Spanish Ministry with respect to the obstacles which had hitherto impeded a Commercial Treaty to see if there was any disposition in them to relax in their Territorial claims & exclusive right to the Navigation of the River Missisipi.

FIRST: The Algerian captives were the 21 officers and men of two American ships—the *Maria* out of Boston and the *Dauphin* out of Philadelphia—that had been captured by Algerian corsairs off the coast of Africa in 1785. Fearing that the seamen, already held as slaves in Algiers, might be sold south into the interior of Africa, the United States government made several unsuccessful attempts to ransom them during the Confederation (ASP, FOREIGN RELATIONS, 1:100–104). By Dec. 1788 six of the captives were dead (Thomas Jefferson to Père Chauvier, 27 Dec. 1788, JEFFERSON [1], 14:395–97). Père Chauvier was the "Général et Grand Ministre" of the Order de La Sainte Trinité de la Redemption des Captifs, usually called the Mathurins. In 1786–88, while he was United States minister to France, Jefferson had discussed with members of the order the possibility that they might assist in redeeming the prisoners, and in Dec. 1788 he opened negotiations with Père Chauvier (JEFFERSON [1], 14:401–2). A recapitulation of Jefferson's efforts on behalf of the captives is in his "Report on American Captives in Algiers," 28 Dec. 1790 (JEFFERSON [1], 18:430–36).

William Short (1759–1849), a native of Surry County, Va., and a 1779 graduate of the College of William and Mary, accompanied Thomas Jefferson to Paris in 1784 where he served as his secretary and later as secretary of legation. When Jefferson returned to the United States, Short was left to represent the United States in France with the rank of chargé d'affaires (DE PAUW, 2:8–9).

SECOND: GW was undoubtedly concerned with Jefferson's opinion on diplomatic appointments because of discussion aroused by a bill for "providing the means of intercourse between the United States and foreign nations" (DE PAUW, 3:269). Introduced in Jan. 1790, the bill (House Bill No. 35) had engendered extensive and sometimes acrimonious debate on the appointment of American diplomats abroad and the manner in which they were to be paid. The bill involved constitutional questions as to whether the president should determine the rank and emoluments for diplomatic appointments or whether this was to be a function of Congress as had been the case during the Confederation (ANNALS OF CONGRESS, 1:1004–5, 1113, 1118–30, 2:1526; MACLAY, 248). On 31 Mar. 1790 "the committee to whom was re-committed the bill 'providing the means of intercourse between the United States and foreign nations,' presented an amendatory bill to the same effect, which was received and read the first time" (House Bill No. 52). See DE PAUW, 3:351. Debates in the House and Senate on the amended bill dragged on until the passage of "An Act providing the means of intercourse between the United States and foreign nations" (1 STAT. 128 [1 July 1790]).

THIRD: Jefferson's letter to John Jay, 14 Nov. 1788, detailed Jefferson's views on a consular establishment and suggested individuals who might fill consular posts in France (JEFFERSON [1], 14:56–66).

William Carmichael (c.1738–1795), of Queen's County, Md., served in the Continental Congress 1778–79 and as John Jay's secretary in Spain in 1779. In Sept. 1789 GW appointed him chargé d'affaires in Madrid.

Wednesday 24th.   Prevented from Riding by the unfavourableness of the Weather.

Thursday 25th.   Went in the forenoon to the Consecration of Trinity Church, where a Pew was constructed, and set apart for the President of the United Sts.

Received from the Senate their opinion and advice on the Papers which had been submitted to them respecting the Incroachments on the Eastern boundary of the United States, and the disputes consequent thereof.

And from a Comee. of Congress two Acts—one for establishing the mode for uniformity in Naturalization of Foreigners—the other Making appropriations for the support of Government for the year 1790. By this last was Grantd.

dollrs.	Cents	
141,492.73		for the Civil list
155,537.72		War Department
96,979.72		Invalid Pensions
10,000.		President—for Contingent Services of Governmt.
147,169.54		For demands enumerated by the Secrety. of the Treay. on wch. the light Ho. on Cape Henry is includd.
120.		To Jehoiakim McToksin
96.		James Mathers
96.		Gifford Dally.
551,491.71		Total amount.

The following Company dined here to day—viz—

The Chief Justice Jay & his Lady Genl. Schuyler & his Lady, the Secretary of the Treasury & his Lady, the Secretary of War & his Lady & Mrs. Greene The Secretary of State (Mr. Jefferson) Mr. Carroll & Mr. Henry of the Senate Judge Wilson, Messrs. Madison & Page of the Ho. of Representatives, and Colo. Smith Marshall of the District.

TRINITY CHURCH: See entry for 4 Oct. 1789. The Senate referred GW's letters of 9 and 18 Feb. (see entry for 18 Feb. 1790) concerning British encroachment on the northeast boundary of the United States to a Senate committee for consideration. The committee reported, 9 Mar., and on 24 Mar. the

Senate advised that steps be taken to settle the boundary line with Britain as soon as possible, that it should be suggested to the British court that if the dispute could not be otherwise settled, a joint commission should be appointed to consider the matter, and that testimony as to the location of the St. Croix River be collected in anticipation of discussions between the two powers (ANNALS OF CONGRESS, 1:983, 984–85, 989, 994). TWO ACTS: 1 STAT. 103–4 (26 Mar. 1790). Section 6 of the 1790 Appropriations Act provided the above sums for "Jehoiakim M'Toksin, in full compensation for his services as an interpreter and guide in the expedition commanded by Major-general Sullivan, in the year one thousand seven hundred and seventy-nine," and for Mathers and Dalley "for services during the late recess of Congress" (1 STAT. 104–6 [26 Mar. 1790]).

Friday 26th.   Had a further Conversation with the Secretary of State on the subject of Foreign appointments, and on the Provision which was necessary for Congress to make for them—the result of which was that under all circumstances it might be best to have Ministers Plenipy. at the Courts of France and England (if any advances from the latter should be made) And Chargés des Affaires in Spain & Portugal—Whether it might be necessary to send a Person in this character to Holland—one in the character of Resident—or simply a person well Skilled in commercial matters in any other character being questionable; nothing finally was decided—but it was concluded that the Secretary's information to a Committee of Congress with whom he was to converse on the subject of the Provision to be made, that the Salaries allowed to our Diplomatic characters was too low—that the Grades which wd. be fixed on, to transact our Affairs abroad would be as low as they cd. be made without giving umbrage that therefore, about 36,000 dollrs. might answer as a provision for the characters to the Courts before named—or that it might take forty nine or 50,000 dollars if it should be found that the lower grades will not answer.

The company this evening was thin, especially of Ladies.

FOREIGN APPOINTMENTS: See entry for 23 Mar. 1790.

Saturday 27th.   Exercised in the Coach with Mrs. Washington and the Children.

Sunday 28th.   Went to St. Pauls Chapel in the forenoon.

Monday 29th.   Exercised on Horseback in the forenoon and called at Colo. Walton Whites.

Tuesday 30th.   Exercised in the Post Chaise with Mrs. Washington.

The Company at the Levee to day was numerous & respectable.

Wednesday 31st.   Exercised on Horseback.

April 1790

Thursday the First.   Received from a Comee. of both Houses of Congress the following Acts. viz—"An Act to accept a Cession of the Claims of the State of No. Carolina to a certain District of Western Territory" and an "Act to prevent the exportation of Goods not duly inspected according to the Laws of the several States."

Communicated to both Houses of Congress a letter from the Govr. of So. Carolina, enclosing the adoption of the amendments by that State agreeably to the recommendation of Congress.

The following Company dined here to day. viz.

Governor Clinton, the Speakers of the Senate & House of Representatives of the State of New York Judge Duane, Baron de Steuben and Mr. Arthur Lee—Mr. King of the Senate, and the following Members of the House of Representatives—Mr. Leonard, Mr. Sedgwick, Mr. Grout, Mr. Van Rensalaer, Mr. Hathorn, Mr. Clymer, Mr. Heister, Mr. Stone, Mr. Williamson, Mr. Ash, and Mr. Huger.

ACTS: 1 STAT. 106–9 (2 April 1790); 1 STAT. 106 (2 April 1790). LETTER FROM THE GOVR.: Charles Pinckney to GW, 28 Jan. 1790, enclosed a resolution of the South Carolina legislature, 18 Jan. (DNA: RG 233, Journals, 1st Congress). GW sent the documents to the House 1 April (DE PAUW, 3:253).

The speaker of the New York Senate was Isaac Roosevelt. Gulian Verplanck was speaker of the legislature.

Arthur Lee was living at this time on his estate, Lansdowne, in Middlesex County, Va., and at Alexandria. He may have come to New York to see his brother Richard Henry Lee, now a member of Congress, who had been "brought near to my grave by a severe illness" (Richard Henry Lee to Arthur Lee, 19 May 1790, ViU: Lee Family Papers; BALLAGH, 2:510).

Jeremiah Van Rensselaer (1738–1810), representative to the First Congress from New York, graduated from Princeton in 1758 and served in the New York Assembly in 1789.

John Hathorn (1749–1825), a Federalist who also represented New York in the House of Representatives, served in the New York militia during the Revolution, in the New York Assembly in 1778–80, 1782–85, 1795, 1805, and in the New York Senate 1786–90, 1799–1803.

John Baptista Ashe (1748–1802) was born in Rocky Point, N.C. Ashe served as a colonel in the North Carolina militia during the Revolution and in the North Carolina House of Commons 1784–86. In 1787 he was a member of the Continental Congress and in 1789 was elected as a Federalist to the First Congress.

Friday 2d. Deposited the above Acts in the Secretary of States Office and informed the Houses of Congress thereof.

But a thin company this Evening, on acct. of the badness of the weather & its being good friday.

Saturday 3d. Exercised in the Coach with Mrs. Washington and the Children.

Gave notice to the Senate House of Congress that I had given my assent to the Act accepting the Cession of No. Carolina & to the other House that I had passed the Bill to prevent the exportation of Goods not duly inspected according to the Laws of the several States—these being the Houses in wch. they respectively originated.

Received from the Governor of the State of New York, three Acts of its Legislature—One adopting the Amendments (except the 2d.) proposed by Congress—another Ceding the Light House at the Hook to the United States and the third authorising & commanding the Goalers throughout the State to receive & safe keep Prisoners committed under the Authority of the United States.

GW's message assenting to "An Act to accept a cession of the claims of the State of North-Carolina to a certain district of Western territory" was read in the Senate on 3 April 1790 (DE PAUW, 1:274–75; see also entry for 29 Jan. and 1 April 1790). GW's message assenting to "An act to prevent the exportation of goods not duly inspected according to the laws of the several States" was read in the House on 3 April (DE PAUW, 3:355).

Gov. George Clinton's letter to GW, 2 April 1790, is in DNA: RG 46, Entry 5, President's Messages. It enclosed "An act declaring it to be the duty of the sheriffs of the several counties within this State to receive, and safe keep such prisoners as shall be committed under the authority of the United States," passed 20 Mar. 1790; "An act for vesting in the United States of America, the light-house, and lands thereunto belonging, at Sandy Hook," passed 26 Mar. 1790; and "An act ratifying certain articles in addition to, and amendment of the Constitution of the United States of America, proposed by Congress," passed 27 Mar. 1790. The letters and enclosures were read in the House of Representatives 5 April 1790 (DE PAUW, 3:346–47).

Sunday 4th. At home all day—unwell.

Monday 5th. Exercised with Mrs. Washington in the Post Chaize.

Sent duplicates of the Acts received (as above) from the Executive of New York to both Houses of Congress for their information; & deposited the originals in the Secretary of States Office.

Tuesday 6th.   Sat for Mr. Savage, at the request of the Vice-President, to have my Portrait drawn for him.

The Company at the Levee to day was thin. The day was bad.

The portrait for which GW sat today was painted by Edward Savage for John Adams and hung by the Adamses in their home in Quincy, Mass. (see EISEN, 2:458).

Wednesday 7th.   Exercised with Mrs. Washington in the Post Chaise.

Thursday 8th.   The following Company dined here viz—of the House of representatives—Mr. Gerry, Mr. Huntingdon, Mr. Cadwalader, Mr. Boudinot, Mr. Sinnickson, Mr. Scott, Mr. Gale, Mr. Parker, Mr. Moore, & Mr. Brown—of the Treasury Department, the Comptroller (Mr. Eveleigh) the Auditor (Mr. Wolcot), & the Register Mr. Nourse and of the Commissioners of Accts. Genl. Irvine and Mr. Kean—together with Mr. Gore, Attorney for the District of Massachusetts.

Nicholas Eveleigh (c.1748–1791), of Charleston, S.C., served in South Carolina regiments 1775–78 and in the South Carolina General Assembly in 1781. He was a delegate to the Continental Congress 1781–82 and served as comptroller of the treasury from 1789 to 1791.

Joseph Nourse (1754–1841) was born in England and immigrated to America with his parents, James Nourse (1731–1784) and Sarah Fouace Nourse (d. 1784) in 1769, settling on a plantation near Charles Town in what is now Berkeley County, W.Va. During the Revolution, Nourse served as aide to Maj. Gen. Charles Lee 1776 and clerk of the Board of War 1777–81. On 11 Sept. 1789 GW appointed him auditor of the Treasury (DE PAUW, 2:38–39, 552–53; LYLE, 199–202).

William Irvine (1741–1804), a native of Ireland and a graduate of Dublin University, served as a surgeon in the British navy before he immigrated to Pennsylvania in 1763, settling in Carlisle. During the Revolution he was a brigadier general in the Continental Army and after the war was a member of the Continental Congress 1786–88. John Kean (1756–1795), a Charleston, S.C., merchant, was a member of the Continental Congress 1785–87. On 9 Sept. 1788 Irvine was appointed by the Continental Congress one of three commissioners to settle state accounts with Congress under the terms of "An Ordinance for Settling the Accounts between the United States and the Individual States," 7 May 1787 (JCC, 32:262–66, 34:502). Under the provisions of "An Act for settling the Accounts between the United States and individual States" (1 STAT. 49 [5 Aug. 1789]), the president was empowered to fill vacancies in the board of commissioners, and on 7 Aug. 1789 he appointed John Kean to the position on the board left vacant by Abraham Baldwin's election to Congress (DE PAUW, 2:25–26). Both Irvine and Kean

Edward Savage's portraits of George and Martha Washington. (The Adams National Historic Site, National Park Service, U.S. Department of the Interior)

were appointed in Aug. 1790 as commissioners of accounts under "An Act to provide more effectually for the settlement of the Accounts between the United States and the individual States" (1 STAT. 178–79 [5 Aug. 1790]; DE PAUW, 2:92).

Christopher Gore (1758–1827), a 1776 graduate of Harvard, practiced law in Boston. He was a member of the Massachusetts Ratifying Convention in 1788 and served in the state legislature 1788–89. A leading Massachusetts

Federalist, he was deeply involved in support of Federalist policies in state politics. In Sept. 1789 GW appointed him United States attorney for the district of Massachusetts (EXECUTIVE JOURNAL, 1:29).

Friday 9th.   Exercised on Horseback in the forenoon.

Received the "Act for the encouragement of Arts from a Comee. of Congress."

The company who visited Mrs. Washington this afternoon was very numerous—both of Gentlemen & Ladies.

ACT: This statute, the first patent law, provided the administrative machinery for registering patents and granted inventors for any term not exceeding 14 years "the sole and exclusive right and liberty of making, constructing, using and vending to others to be used, the said invention or discovery" (1 STAT. 109–12 [10 April 1789]).

Saturday 10th.   Exercised in the Coach with Mrs. Washington and the Children. Walked in the afternoon around the Battery and through some of the principal Streets of the City.

In the Afternoon the Secretary of State submitted for my approbation Letters of credence for Mr. Short as Charges de affaires at the Court of Versailles, & his own Letter to Monsr. Montmorin taking leave of that Court both directed to that Minister—also to Mr. Short on the Subject of our Prisoners at Algiers. And at Night he submitted the Copy of a letter he had drafted to Mr. Carmichael respecting the Governor of the Island of Juan Fernandez who had been disgraced & recalled from his government of that Island for having permitted the ship Washington which had suffered in a storm to put into that Port to repair the damages she had sustained in it, & to recruit her wood & water. This Ship belonged to Barrel & Co. of Boston.

Although the documents submitted by Jefferson, all dated before 10 April 1790, were enclosed in a letter to GW dated 5 April, it is likely that the secretary of state held the drafts and submitted them to the president on this day (see JEFFERSON [1], 16:310n). Jefferson's two letters to Armand Marc, comte de Montmorin Saint-Herem, French minister for foreign affairs, 6 April, announcing his recall, are in JEFFERSON [1], 16:313–15. Jefferson may also have submitted for GW's approbation the draft of a letter from the president to Louis XVI, 6 April, notifying the court of Jefferson's recall (DNA: RG 59, Diplomatic and Consular Instructions). In his letter to William Short, 6 April (JEFFERSON [1], 16:315–17), Jefferson instructed him to continue to press for the relief of American prisoners at Algiers (see entry for 23 Mar. 1790).

Jefferson's letter to William Carmichael, 11 April 1790, is in JEFFERSON [1], 16:329–30. The letter concerned the *Columbia,* commanded by Capt. John Kendrick, and the *Lady Washington,* commanded by Capt. Robert Gray, both of which left Boston in 1787 on their way to the west coast of North America to open a fur trade with Russian settlements there. The *Lady Washington,* damaged in a storm in the vicinity of the Juan Fernandez Islands off the west coast of Chile, had been permitted by Gov. Don Blas Gonzalez to put into one of the islands' ports for repairs. "For this act of common hospitality," Jefferson informed Carmichael, "he was immediately deprived of his government unheard, by superior order, and remains still under disgrace."

Sunday 11th.   Went to Trinity Church in the forenoon and [wrote] several private letters in the afternoon.

April 1790

Monday 12th.   Exercised on Horse-back after which did business with the Secretaries of the Treasury and War Departments. The latter was directed to authorize the Judge of the Western district Harry Innis to permit the County Lieutenants of that District to employ 4 Scouts in each of the Frontier Counties for the purpose of discovering the movements of the Indians & giving the alarm in case they are about. The other Frontier Counties along the River Ohio East side above the Kentucke district was also authorized to keep out the same Number of Scouts.

The Secretary of State submitted the draught of a Report to me, which he was about to make to the House of Representatives in Congress consequent of a letter & other Papers which had been refered to him on the subject of Coinage—which report appeared to me to be sensible & proper.

Harry Innes (1753–1816) was at this time United States judge for the district of Kentucky, a post he held from 1789 to 1816. Innes was born in Caroline County, Va., and studied law there but moved to Bedford County, Va., where he began practice and held a number of local offices. In 1784 he was state attorney general for the western district and in 1785 moved to Kentucky, where he became involved in the so-called Spanish Conspiracy and in the struggle for Kentucky statehood. Knox wrote to Innes authorizing the scouts, 13 April 1790 (VSP, 5:133). REPORT: On 8 April 1790 the House of Representatives ordered Jefferson to report on a letter from John H. Mitchell of South Carolina to Thomas Tudor Tucker, 22 Mar. 1790, "reciting certain proposals of Matthew Boulton, of the Kingdom of Great Britain, for supplying the United States with copper coinage to any amount that government shall think fit to contract with him for" (DE PAUW, 3:360). Jefferson's "Report on Copper Coinage," 14 April 1790, advised that although Boulton's abilities appeared equal to his proposals, it was imperative that the coinage of the United States be managed at home rather than in a foreign country. For this reason "he is of opinion, the present proposals should be declined." The report was read and tabled in the House 15 April (DE PAUW, 3:368). Mitchell's letter and Jefferson's report are in JEFFERSON [1], 16:342–48.

Tuesday 13th.   Exercised on Horseback about 10 Oclock.

A good deal of Company at the Levee to day.

Received from the Joint Committee of Congress "An act furthr. to suspend pt. of an Act entitled, An Act to regulate the Collectn. of the Duties imposed by Law on the Tonnage of Ships &ca. &ca.

According to the journal of the House of Representatives the joint committee for enrolled bills brought the enrolled bill "An act further to suspend part of an act, entitled 'An act to regulate the collection of the duties imposed by law on the tonnage of ships or vessels, and on goods, wares and merchandizes imported into the United States,' and to amend the said act" to GW on Wednesday, 14 April, rather than Tuesday, 13 April (DE PAUW, 3:368).

Wednesday 14th.   Exercised in the Post Chaise with Mrs. Washington.

Thursday 15th.   Returned the above Act (presented to me on Tuesday) to the House of Representatives in Congress in which it originated with my approbation & signature.

The following Company dined here to day—viz—

The Vice President & Lady, the Chief Justice of the United States & Lady, Mr. Izard & Lady, Mr. Dalton and Lady, Bishop Provost & Lady, Judge Griffin & Lady Christina, Colo. Griffin & Lady, Colo. Smith & Lady, The Secretary of State, Mr. Langdon Mr. King, & Major Butler. Mrs. King was invited but was indisposed.

Bishop Samuel Provoost married in England in 1766 Maria Bousfield of County Cork, Ire., daughter of Thomas Bousfield, a member of the Irish House of Commons.

Friday 16th.   Had a long conference with the Secretary of State on the subject of Diplomatic appointments & on the proper places & characters for Consuls or Vice Consuls.

After which I exercised on Horseback.

The Visitors of Gentlemen and Ladies to Mrs. Washington this evening were very numerous.

CONFERENCE: See entries for 23 and 26 Mar. 1790.

Saturday 17th.   Exercised in the Coach with Mrs. Washington and the Children.

Sunday 18th.   At home all day—the weather being very stormy & bad.

Wrote private letters.

Monday 19th.   Prevented from beginning my tour upon long Island to day from the wet of yesterday and the unfavourableness of the Morning.

Conversed with the Secretary at War on the formation of the Troops proposed, by the amendments in the Senate to be Established.

The bill "for regulating the military establishment of the United States" was read in the Senate for the first time 26 Mar. 1790 and was sent to committee 30 Mar. The Senate committee reported 6 April and on 16 April it was sent back to committee. The amended bill passed the Senate 21 April (ANNALS OF CONGRESS, 1:995, 996, 998, 1001) .

Tuesday 20th.   About 8 Oclock (having previously sent over my Servants, Horses and Carriage I crossed to Brooklin and proceeded to Flat Bush—thence to Utrich—thence to Gravesend—thence through [   ] Jamaica where we lodged at a Tavern kept by one Warne—a pretty good and decent house. At the House of a Mr. Barre, at Utrich, we dined. The Man was obliging but little else to recommend it. He told me that their average Crop of Oats did not exceed 15 bushls. to the Acre but of Indian Corn they commonly made from 25 to 30 and often more bushels to the Acre but this was the effect of Dung from New York (about 10 Cart load to the Acre) —That of Wheat they sometimes got 30 bushels and often more of Rye.

The land after crossing the Hills between Brooklyn & flat Bush is perfectly level, and from the latter to Utrich, Gravesend and in short all that end of the Island is a rich black loam. Afterwards, between [   ] and the Jamaica Road it is more Sandy and appears to have less strength, but is still good & productive. The grain in general had suffered but little by the openess, and Rains of the Winter and the grass (clover &ca.) appeared to be coming on well. The Inclosures are small & under open Post & Rail fencing. The timber is chiefly Hiccory & Oak, mixed here and there

View of the City of New York taken from Long Island.

View of New York from Long Island; a nineteenth-century copy by Abram Hosier of a Saint-Mémin watercolor, c. 1794. (New-York Historical Society)

[63]

with locust & Sasafras trees and in places with a good deal of Cedar. The Road until I came within a mile or two of the Jamaica Road, calld the middle road kept within sight of the Sea but the weather was so dull & at times Rainy that we lost much of the pleasures of the ride.

From Brooklyn to Flat bush is called 5 miles—thence to Utrich 6—to Gravesend 2 and from thence to Jamaica 14—in all this day 27 Miles.

Before I left New York this Morning I signed Commissions appointing Mr. Carmichael Chargé des Affaires at the Court of Versailles, & Mr. Short Chargé des Affaires at the Court of Versailles which though not usually given to Diplomatic characters of their Grades was yet made necessary in the opinion of the Secretary of State by an Act of Congress.

ONE WARNE: probably William Warne, who is listed in the 1790 census as living in Jamaica (HEADS OF FAMILIES, N.Y., 150). MR. BARRE: The 1790 census for New Utrecht contains no entry for "Barre" but does list a William Barry, whose household consisted of eight whites and five slaves (HEADS OF FAMILIES, N.Y., 98).

Wednesday 21st.   The Morning being clear & pleasant we left Jamaica about Eight O'clock, & pursued the Road to South Hempstead passing along the South edge of the plain of that name—a plain said to be 14 miles in length by 3 or 4 in breadth witht. a Tree or a Shrub growing on it except fruit trees (which do not thrive well) at the few settlemts. thereon. The Soil of this plain is said to be thin & cold and of course not productive, even in Grass. We baited in South Hemstead (10 Miles from Jamaica) at the House of one Simmonds, formerly a Tavern, now of private entertainment for Money. From hence turning off to the right we fell into the South Rd. at the distance of about five miles where we came in view of the Sea & continued to be so the remaining part of the days ride, and as near it as the road could run for the small bays, Marshes and guts, into which the tide flows at all times rendering it impassible from the height of it by the Easterly Winds. We dined at one Ketchums wch. had also been a public House but now a private one receivg. pay for what it furnished. This House was about 14 Miles from South Hemstead & a very neat & decent one. After dinner we proceeded to a Squire Thompsons such a House as the last, that is, one that is not public but will receive pay for every thing it furnishes in the same manner as if it was.

The Road in which I passed to day, and the Country were more mixed with sand than yesterday and the Soil of inferior quality; Yet with dung wch. all the Corn ground receives the land yields on an average 30 bushels to the Acre often more. Of Wheat they do not grow much on acct. of the Fly but the Crops of Rye are good.

ONE KETCHUMS: A number of Ketchams were living in Huntington in 1790 (HEADS OF FAMILIES, N.Y., 163–65). Fitzpatrick identifies the house as "Zebulon Ketcham's Inn" (DIARIES, 4:117, n.2). SQUIRE THOMPSONS: probably Judge Isaac Thompson's Apple Tree Neck farm in Islip. Thompson (1743–1816) married Mary Gardiner (d. 1786) in 1772, and five years after her death he married Sarah Bradnor, who died in 1819 (THOMPSON, 1:451; WERNER, 4:106). At the time of GW's visit, Thompson's household consisted of five whites and four slaves (HEADS OF FAMILIES, N.Y., 165).

Thursday 22d.   About 8 Oclock we left Mr. Thompson's—halted a while at one Greens distant 11 Miles and dined Harts Tavern in Brookhaven town ship five miles farther. To this place we travelled on what is called the South road described yesterday but the Country through which it passed grew more and more Sandy and barren as we travelled Eastward, so as to become exceedingly poor indeed but a few miles further Eastward the lands took a different complexion we were informed. From Harts we struck across the Island for the No. side, passing the East end of the Brushey Plains and Koram 8 Miles—thence to Setakit 7 Mi. more to the House of a Captn. Roe which is tolerably dect. with obliging people in it. The first five Miles of the Road is too poor to admit Inhabitants or cultivation being a low scrubby Oak, not more than 2 feet high intermixed with small and ill thriven Pines. Within two miles of Koram there are farms but the land is of an indifferent quality much mixed with Sand. Koram contains but few houses. From thence to Setalket the Soil improves, especially as you approach the Sound; but is far from being of the first quality—still a good deal mixed with Sand. The road a cross from the So. to the No. Side is level, except a small part So. of Koram but the hills there are trifling.

HARTS TAVERN: probably run by Gilbert Hart, listed in the 1790 census for Brookhaven. Hart, whose household consisted of five whites, owned no slaves (HEADS OF FAMILIES, N.Y., 160).

Friday 23d.   About 8 Oclock we left Roes, and baited the Horses at Smiths Town, at a Widow Blidenbergs—a decent House 10 Miles from Setalkat—thence 15 Miles to Huntington where we dined and afterwards proceeded Seven Miles to Oyster-bay, to the House of a Mr. Young (private & very neat and decent) where we lodged. The house we dined at in Huntingdon was kept by a Widow Platt and was tolerably good. The whole of this days ride was over uneven ground and none of it of the first quality but intermixed in places with pebble-stone. After passing Smithstown & for near five Miles it was a mere bed of white Sand, unable to produce trees 25 feet high; but a change for the better took place between that & Huntington, which is a sml. village at the head of the Harbour of that name and continued to improve to Oyster-bay about which the Lands are good and in the Necks between these bays are said to be fine. It is here the Lloyds own a large & valuable tract, or Neck of Land from whence the British whilst they possessed New York drew large supplies of Wood and where, at present, it is said large flocks of Sheep are kept.

In the Long Island Sound between Oyster Bay and Huntington Bay, the peninsula known as Lloyd's Neck was divided among four brothers of the Lloyd family when the British attacked Long Island in Aug. 1776. During its occupation of the island, the British army despoiled the extensive stands of timber on the Lloyd farms. The 50,000-cord stand on the farms of Joseph Lloyd (1716–1780) and John Lloyd (1711–1795) was reduced to one quarter its original size (BARCK, 2:777–78). Henry Lloyd (1709–1795), who remained a loyal subject of the king, received £5,834 14s. 1d. for the loss of timber and other damages to his farm (BARCK, 2:828). The farm of James Lloyd (1728–1810) probably suffered similarly.

Saturday 24th.   Left Mr. Youngs before 6 Oclock, and passing Musqueto Cove, breakfasted at a Mr. Underduncks at the head of a little bay; where we were kindly received and well entertained. This Gentleman works a Grist & two Paper Mills, the last of which he seems to carry on with Spirit, and to profit—distc. from Oyster bay 12 Miles. From hence to Flushing where we dined is 12 more & from thence to Brooklyne through Newton (the way we travelled and which is a mile further than to pass through Jamaica) is 18 miles more. The land I passed over to day is gen-erally very good, but leveller and better as we approached New York. The soil in places is intermixed with pebble, and towards the Westend with other kind of stone which they apply to the pur-poses of fencing which is not to be seen on the South side of the Island nor towards the Eastern parts of it. From Flushing to New Town 8 Miles, & thence to Brooklyn, the Road is very fine, and the Country in a higher State of Cultivation & vegitation of Grass & grain forwarded than any place else I had seen—occasioned in a great degree by the Manure drawn from the City of New York. Before Sundown we had crossed the Ferry and was at home.

April 1790

Observations

This Island (as far as I went) from West to East seems to be equally divided between flat, & Hilly land—the former on the South next the Sea board & the latter on the No. next the Sound. The high land they say is best and most productive but the other is the pleasantest to work except in wet seasons when from the levelness of them they are sometimes (but not frequently having a considerable portion of Sand) incommoded by heavy & continual rains. From a comparitive view of their Crops they may be averaged as follow. Indian Corn 25 bushels—Wheat 15—Rye 12—Oats 15 bushels to the Acre. According to their accts. from Lands highly manured they sometimes get 50 of the first, 25 of the 2d. & 3d. and more of the latter. Their general mode of Cropping is—first Indian Corn upon a lay, manured in the hill, half a shovel full in each hole (some scatter the dung over the field equally) —2d. Oats & flax—3d. Wheat with what Manure they can spare from the Indian Corn land. With the wheat, or on it, towards close of the snows, they sow Clover from 4 to 6 lb; & a quart of Timothy seed. This lays from 3 to 6 years, according as the grass remains, or as the condition of the ground is, for so soon as they find it beginning to bind they plow. Their first plowing (with the Patent, tho' they call it the Dutch plough) is well executed at the depth of about 3 or at most 4 Inches—the cut being 9 or 10 Inches & the sod neatly & very evenly turned. With Oxen they plough mostly. They do no more than turn the ground in this manner for Indian Corn before it is planted; making the holes in which it is placed with hoes the rows being marked off by a stick. Two or three workings afterwards with the Harrows or Plough is all the cultivation it receives *generally*. Their fences, where there is no stone, are very indifferent; frequently of plashed trees of *any* & *every* kind which have grown by chance; but it exhibits an evidence that very good fences may be made in this manner either of white Oak or Dogwood which from this mode of treatment grows thickest, and most stubborn. This, however woud be no defence against Hogs.

MR. UNDERDUNCKS: Hendrick Onderdonck (Onderdonk, b. 1725) built New York's first paper mill at Hempstead (then South Hempstead) in 1768. Onderdonck may have had a number of partners in the venture, among them his son Andrew, a Henry Remsen, and possibly Hugh Gaine, editor of the *New York Gazette and Mercury*. At the time of GW's visit, Onderdonck's household consisted of eight whites and seven slaves (BUNKER, 316; BISHOP, 1:200; WEEKS, 37, 60; HEADS OF FAMILIES, N.Y., 152).

April 1790

Sunday 25th.   Went to Trinity Church, and wrote letters home after dinner.

Monday 26th.   Did business with the Secretaries of State, Treasury, and War, & appointed a quarter before three tomorrow to receive from the Senators of the State of Virga. an Address from the Legislature thereof.

The undated congratulatory address of the Virginia legislature is in DLC: GW. GW's reply, 27 April 1790, is in CSmH.

Tuesday 27th.   Had some conversation with Mr. Madison on the propriety of consulting the Senate on the places to which it would be necessary to send persons in the Diplomatic line, and Consuls; and with respect to the grade of the first. His opinion coincides with Mr. Jays and Mr. Jeffersons—to wit—that they have no Constitutional right to interfere with either, & that it might be impolitic to draw it into a precedent their powers extending no farther than to an approbation or disapprobation of the person nominated by the President all the rest being Executive and vested in the President by the Constitution.

At the time appointed, Messrs. Lee & Walker (the Senators from Virginia) attended, & presented the Address as mentioned yesterday & received an answer to it.

A good deal of respectable Company was at the Levee to day.

CONVERSATION WITH MR. MADISON: See entries for 23 and 26 Mar., 16 April 1790. Although James Madison and John Jay apparently did not present GW with written opinions, Jefferson's views on the appointment of the diplomatic establishment are expressed in his "Opinion on the Powers of the Senate Respecting Diplomatic Appointments," 24 April 1790 (DLC: Jefferson Papers). That GW also may have consulted John Adams on the question is indicated by the fact that a fair copy of Jefferson's opinion, in his own hand and endorsed by GW, is found among Adams's papers (MHi-A). It was GW's frequent habit to submit the written opinions of one cabinet member to other members for their comments. See also JEFFERSON [1], 16:378–82.

John Walker (1744–1809) was born at Castle Hill, Albemarle County, Va., the son of Dr. Thomas Walker (1715–1794) and his first wife, Mildred Thornton Meriwether Walker (d. 1778), who was a granddaughter of GW's aunt, Mildred Washington Gregory. In 1764 John Walker graduated from the College of William and Mary and became a planter at Belvoir in Albemarle County. During the Revolution he held the rank of lieutenant colonel and in Feb. 1777 was sent by the Virginia legislature to GW's headquarters as an observer, with orders to report to the legislature any events of interest from camp. The appointment proved to be a considerable embarrassment to GW who wrote Gov. Patrick Henry, 24 Feb. 1777, stating that he had appointed Walker an "Extra Aid de Camp" in order "that he may obtain the best information, and, at the same time, have his real design hid from the World; thereby avoiding the evils which might otherwise result from such Appointments, if adopted by other States. It will naturally occur to you, Sir, that there are some Secrets, on the keeping of which so, depends, often-times, the salvation of an Army. . . . If Mr. Walker's Commission, therefore from the Commonwealth of Virginia, should be known, it would, I am per-suaded, be followed by others of the like nature from other States, and be no better than so many marplots" (DLC:GW; General Orders, 19 Feb. 1790, DLC:GW). In 1780 Walker served in the Continental Congress. After the war he practiced law in Virginia and in Mar. 1790 was appointed United States senator to fill the vacancy left by the death of William Grayson.

Wednesday 28th.   Fixed with the Secretary of State on places & characters for the Consulate but as some of the latter were un-known to us both he was directed to make enquiry respecting them.

Sent the nominations of two Officers in the Customs of North Carolina, and one in the place of Mr. Jacob Wray of Hampton in Virginia—who has requested to resign his appointment to the Senate for their advice & consent thereon.

Received from the Secretary for the Department of War a re-port respecting the Sale of certain Lands by the State of Georgia; and the consequent disputes in which the United States may be involved with the Chicasaws & Choctaw Nations; part, if not the whole of whose Countries, are included within the limits of the said Sale. This report refers to the Act of the Legislature of Georgia, by which this sale is authorized and to the opinion of the Attorney General respecting the Constitutionality of the Proceeding—submitting at the same time certain opinions for the consideration of the Presidt.

Today's consultation with Jefferson on consular appointments was in prepa-ration for the list of nominations sent by GW to the Senate on 4 June 1790, when 14 names were submitted for confirmation (DE PAUW, 1:74–78). GW's letter to the Senate, 28 April 1790, nominated George Wray to succeed Jacob Wray as collector of the customs at Hampton, Va.; John McCullough as surveyor of Swansborough in the district of Wilmington, N.C.; and William Benson as surveyor for Winsor in the district of Edenton, N.C. (DLC:GW).

Knox's report concerned the sale in 1789 by the state of Georgia of over 15 million acres of land in western Georgia to three land companies, the South Carolina Yazoo Company, the Virginia Yazoo Company, and the Tennessee Yazoo Company at a projected cost to the companies of approxi-mately $200,000 ("An Act for disposing of certain vacant lands or territory within this State," 21 Dec. 1789, ASP, INDIAN AFF., 1:114). Some settlers had already moved into the area under the authority of "An Act for laying out a district of Land situated on the river Mississipi and within the Limits of this State to be called Bourbon," 7 Feb. 1785 (MS "Journal of the General As-sembly of the State of Georgia," 212, DLC: Microfilm Collection of Early

State Records). The land sold conflicted with still unsettled Indian claims in the area, involving the Creek, Chickasaw, Cherokee, and Choctaw, and with treaties negotiated by the United States with the tribes during the Confederation. Although neither Knox's nor Randolph's opinions have been found, it is likely that Knox's views were similar to those expressed in his report to GW, 22 Jan. 1791, that "although the right of Georgia to the preemption of said lands should be admitted in its full extent, yet, it is conceived, that, should the State, or any companies or persons, claiming under it, attempt to extinguish the Indian claims, unless authorized thereto by the United States, that the measure would be repugnant to the aforesaid treaties, to the constitution of the United States, and to the law regulating trade and intercourse with the Indian tribes" (ASP, INDIAN AFF., 1:112–13). In Mar. 1790 as a result of Indian depredations caused by increasing Georgian encroachment on Indian lands, the government sent three companies of federal troops to Georgia to keep the peace (Anthony Wayne to Knox, 10 April 1790, MHi: Knox Papers). Wayne observed that "while these troops are received with joy by part of the Citizens of Georgia, there are others who affect to believe that the troops are designed rather as a curb on Georgia, or to assist the laws of the Union, than to protect that State" ("Summary statement of the situation of the frontiers," 27 May 1790, DLC:GW). The federal government took as strong action as possible during the summer of 1790 to prevent the companies from implementing their claims. During the negotiations for the Treaty of New York in Aug. 1790, Creek chief Alexander McGillivray "protested strongly against the behavior of the new western companies, in the terms in which Georgia has formed them, and I have the word of the government that said companies will be broken up" (McGillivray to Carlos Howard, 11 Aug. 1790, CAUGHEY, 273–76). "An act to regulate trade and intercourse with the Indians" (1 STAT. 137–38 [22 July 1790]) stipulated that "no sale of land or lands made by any Indians, or any nation or tribe of Indians within the United States, shall be valid to any person or persons, or to any state, whether having the right of pre-emption to such lands or not, unless the same shall be made and duly executed at some public treaty, held under the authority of the United States." The signing of the Treaty of New York gave GW an opportunity to issue an additional warning with two proclamations, 14 and 26 Aug., enjoining United States citizens to abide by the treaties (DLC:GW). On 10 June 1790 the legislature of Georgia struck a further blow to the companies' plans by passing a resolution requiring that all payments to the Georgia treasury, except for taxes, be made in specie rather than paper or certificates of Georgia debt, a regulation which made it impossible for the companies to abide by the requirements of the Dec. 1789 act stipulating payments for the grants within two years (MS "Journal of the House of Representatives" [Georgia], DLC: Microfilm Collection of Early State Records). For the companies' protests, see ASP, PUBLIC LANDS, 1:165–79.

Thursday 29th.   Received from the joint Committee of Congress two Acts for my approbation & Signature—viz—one for "Regulating the Military Establishment of the United States" and the other "An Act for the Punishment of certain crimes against the United States."

Fixed with the Secretary of State on the present which (according to the custom of other Nations) should be made to Diplomatic characters when they return from that employment in this Country and this was a gold Medal, suspended to a gold Chain—in ordinary to be of the value of about 120 or 130 Guineas. Upon enquiry into the practice of other Countries, it was found, that France generally gave a gold Snuff-box set with diamonds; & of differt. costs; to the amount, *generally,* to a Minister Plenipotentiary of 500 Louisdores—That England usually gave to the same grade 300 guineas in *Specie*—And Holld. a Medal & Chain of the value of, in common, 150 or 180 Guineas the value of which to be encreas'd by an additional weight in the chain when they wished to mark a distinguished character. The Reason why a medal & Chain was fixed upon for the American present, is, that the die being once made the Medals could at any time be struck at very little cost, & the Chain made by our own artizans, which (while the first should be retained as a memento) might be converted into Cash.

The following Gentlemen dined here—viz—Of the Senate, Messrs. Strong, Doctr. Johnston, Mr. Patterson, Mr. Morris, Mr. Carroll, Mr. Lee, Mr. Walker, Govr. Johnston, & Mr. Gunn and of the House of Representatives, Mr. Sturges, Mr. Benson, Mr. Floyd, Mr. Scureman, Mr. Vining Mr. Smith Maryland, Mr. Bland, and Mr. Sumpter.

TWO ACTS: 1 STAT. 119–21 (30 April 1790) and 1 STAT. 112–19 (30 April 1790). PRESENT: On 20 April 1790 Louis Guillaume Otto had written to Jefferson suggesting that the United States, in accord with European diplomatic custom, might present former French minister to the United States Anne César, chevalier de La Luzerne, with some token, preferably valuable, in recognition of his services to the United States. Although he opposed such gifts, Jefferson wrote to William Temple Franklin, Benjamin Franklin's grandson and secretary, now in New York, inquiring what practice was followed in other countries and what was "the estimated value and the form" of the gift given Franklin on his departure from France. "Not foreseeing that I might ever have any thing to do with the decision of such a question, I did not inform myself of the usage even in the court with which I resided." Franklin replied, 27 April, that the usual value of the gift depended on the rank of the recipient and the esteem with which he was regarded. "These Presents vary as to their Nature, consisting either of Jewels, Plate, Tapestry, Porcelain, and sometimes Money" (JEFFERSON [1], 16:354–56, 363–66). On 30 April Jefferson instructed William Short at Paris to have the gold medal, which the administration had decided on as the gift for departing diplomats, made in France: "The medal must be of 30 lines diameter, with a loop on the edge to receive the chain. On one side must be the Arms of the United States, of which I send you a written description and several impressions in wax to render that more intelligible, round them as a Legend must be 'the United States of America.' The device of the other side we do not decide on. One suggestion has been a Columbia (a final female figure) delivering the emblems of peace and commerce to a Mercury, with the Legend 'Peace and Commerce' circumscribed, and the date of our Republic . . . subscribed as an Exergum. But having little confidence in our own ideas in an Art not familiar here, they are only suggested to you, to be altered, or altogether postponed to such better device as you may approve on consulting with those who are in the habit and study of Medals" (JEFFERSON [1], 16:395–96) . For a discussion of the final version of the medal, see JEFFERSON [1], 16:xli–xlii.

James Gunn (1753–1801) was born in Virginia but began the practice of law in Savannah, Ga. He served as a brigadier general in the Georgia militia during the Revolution and was elected to the Continental Congress in 1788 and 1789, although he did not attend. In 1789 he was elected to the United States Senate from Georgia.

Friday 30th.   Conversed with the Secretary of the Treasury, on the Report of the Secretary at War's propositions respecting the Conduct of the State of Georgia in selling to certain Compa[nies] large tracts of their Western territory & a proclamation which he conceived expedient to issue in consequence of it. But as he had doubts of the clearness of the ground on which it was proposed to build this proclamation and do the other acts which were also submitted in the report. I placed it in the hands of the Secretary of State to consider & give me his opinion thereon.

Returnd. the Bills which had been presented to me by the joint Committee of Congress on Thursday to the Houses in which they originated with my signature, though I did not conceive that the Military establishment of the one was adequate to the exigencies of the Government & the protection it was intended to afford.

The Visitors to Mrs. Washington this evening were not numerous.

PROPOSITIONS: See entry for 28 April 1790. BILLS: "An Act for regulating the Military Establishment of the United States" (1 STAT. 119–21 [30 April 1790]) provided for an army of 1,216 "non commissioned officers, privates and musicians" enlisted for a three-year period and formed into a regiment composed of three battalions of infantry and one battalion of artillery. GW and Knox had been particularly anxious that Congress should also pass a militia bill (see entries for 18 and 19 Dec. 1789 and 20 Jan. 1790) .

[May]

May 1st.   Exercised in the Coach with Mrs. Washington & the Children in the forenoon & on foot in the afternoon.

Mr. Alexr. White, representative from Virginia, communicated his apprehensions that a disposition prevailed among the Eastern & northern States (discoverable from many circumstances, as well as from some late expressions which had fallen from some of their members in the Ho.) to pay little attention to the Western Country because they were of opinion it would soon shake of its dependence on this; and in the meantime, would be burthensome to it. He gave some information also of the temper of the Western Settlers, of their dissatisfactions, and among other things that few of the Magestrates had taken the Oaths to the New Government not inclining in the present state of things and under their ideas of neglect to bind themselves to it by an Oath.

Sunday 2d.   Went to Trinity Church in the forenoon—writing letters on private business in the Afternoon—Among other letters one by my order to Genl. Moylan, to know if he wd. accept the Consulate at Lisbon, as it was not proposed to give Salaries therewith.

Monday 3d.   Exercised on horseback about 9 Oclock.

After my return, the Secretary of the Treasury called upon, and informed me that by some conversation he had had with Mr. King (of the Senate) it appeared that there was a probability the Senate would take up the Sales by the Legislature of Georgia, and the Affairs of the Indians which would be involved therein in a serious manner, and gave it as his opinion that if this was likely to be the case, it might be better for me to let the matter originate there, than with the Executive.

The Secretary of State furnished me with his opinion on these Subjects—see his Statement. The substance of it is, that the State of Georgia by having adopted the Constitution relinquished their right to treat with, or to regulate any matters with the Indians who were not subject thereto—consequently could not delegate a power they did not possess to others and that there was good & strong ground on which to contend this matter but, inasmuch as there was a party in the State opposed to the Sales before mentioned, but which might unite to defeat a Proclamation if one should be issued upon the Plan of the Secretary at War, he suggested the propriety of a representation to the State in the first instance for the purpose of undoing in a manner least hurtful to the feelings of it the impolitic act of the Legislature & in the meantime—at the meeting proposed to be held by the Indians in the Month of June ensuing to make these people perfectly sensible of the Sentiments and intentions of the general Government towards them.

May 1790

STATE OF GEORGIA: See entries for 28 and 30 April 1790. Jefferson's "Opinion on Certain Georgia Land Grants," 3 May 1790, is in JEFFERSON [1], 16:406–9.

Tuesday 4th.   Exercised in the forenoon on Horse back.
A respectable Company at the Levee to day.

Wednesday 5th.   Requested General Rufus Putnam—lately appointed a Judge in the Western Government and who was on the eve of his departure for that Country to give me the best discription he could obtain of the proximity of the Waters of the Ohio & Lake Erie—the nature of their Navigations—Portages—&ca.—Also of the occurrences in the Country—the population of it—Temper of the people &ca. &ca.

Rufus Putnam (1738–1824) was born in Sutton, Mass., and was largely self-educated. After serving in the French and Indian War, he engaged in farming and surveying. During the Revolution he served as a colonel of engineers and as commander of a Massachusetts regiment, ending the war as a brigadier general. In 1785 he was appointed surveyor of western lands by the Continental Congress and was active 1786–87 in the formation of the new Ohio Company, bringing the first party of settlers to Marietta in 1788. In Mar. 1790 GW appointed him a judge of the Northwest Territory (DE PAUW, 2:66).

Thursday 6th.   Exercised on horseback in the forenoon. The following, out of several others who were invited, but prevented

Brig. Gen. Rufus Putnam, by John Trumbull. (Yale University Art Gallery)

by sickness, dined here—viz.—Mr. Wingate, Mr. Maclay, Mr. Walker (of the Senate) and Messrs. Gilman, Aimes, Genl. Muhlenburg, Wynkoop, Page and Lady, Smith So. Carolina & Lady, and Mr. White & his Lady of the House of Representatives.

William Maclay noted in his diary that today he "went to dine with the President agreeably to invitation. He seemed in more good humor than I ever saw him, though he was so deaf that I believe he heard little of the conversation" (MACLAY, 251).

Friday 7th.   Exercised in the forenoon. Endeavoured through various Channels to ascertain what places required, and the characters fittest for Consuls at them.

As the House of Representatives had reduced the Sum, in a Bill to provide for the expences of characters in the diplomatic line, below what would enable the Executive to employ the number which the exigencies of Government might make it necessary I thought it proper to intimate to a member or two of the Senate the places that were in contemplation to send persons to in this Line—viz to France & England (when the latter manifested a disposition to treat us with more respect than She had done upon a former occasion) Ministers Plenipotentiary and to Spain, Portugal & Holland Chargé des Affaires and having an opportunity, mentioned the matter unofficially both to Mr. Carroll & Mr. Izard.

Much Company—Gentlemen & Ladies visited Mrs. Washington This Evening.

CONSULS: See entry for 28 April 1790. DIPLOMATIC LINE: See entries for 23 and 26 Mar., 16 and 27 April 1790. GW and Jefferson had agreed in their meeting of 26 Mar. that the sum required for the adequate support of a foreign diplomatic establishment might range between $36,000 and $50,000, and House Bill No. 35 had stipulated $40,000 for the support of American diplomats abroad. Opposition to so large an amount appropriated "to uses with the propriety of which no gentlemen seemed to be well acquainted" had been a major factor in the tabling of the bill (ANNALS OF CONGRESS, 1:1130). The amended bill No. 52 had apparently reduced the appropriation to $30,000. GW's efforts to raise the appropriation were successful. On 23 June, while the bill was still pending, William Maclay, whose views vividly express opposition opinion, noted: "The Intercourse bill, or that for appointing ambassadors, had been referred to a committee of conference so long ago that I had forgotten it, but the thing was neither dead nor sleeping. It was only dressing and friends-making. The report increased the salaries and added ten thousand dollars to the appropriations. I concluded they had secured friends enough to support it before they committed it to the House. This turned out to be the case. The whole appropriation was forty thousand dollars, and they were voted with an air of perfect indifference by the affirmants, although I consider the money as worse than thrown away, for I know not a single thing that we have for a minister to do at a single court in Europe. . . . Our business is to pay them what we owe, and the less political connection the better with any European power. It was well spoken against. I voted against every part of it" (MACLAY, 296).

Saturday 8th.   Exercised in the Coach with Mrs. Washington & the Children in the forenoon.

Received from Genl. Knox Secretary Genl. of the triennial Genl. Meeting of the Cincinnati held at Philadelphia the first Monday of this Month, the Copy of an Address from that body to me to which I was to return an answer on [   ] next.

The address of the triennial meeting of the Society of the Cincinnati, 4 May 1790, and GW's undated reply are in DLC:GW.

Sunday 9th.   Indisposed with a bad cold, and at home all day writing letters on private business.

GW's cold rapidly developed into pneumonia. Local physicians Dr. Samuel Bard, Dr. Charles McKnight, and Dr. John Charlton were summoned to the president's bedside, but in spite of their efforts GW grew steadily worse. On 12 May, William Jackson wrote to Clement Biddle in Philadelphia enclosing a letter to Dr. John Jones, a prominent Philadelphia physician, requesting him to attend the president in New York. "The Doctor's prudence will suggest the propriety of setting out as privately as possible; perhaps it may be well to assign a personal reason for visiting New York, or going into the

Maj. Gen. Henry Knox, by Gilbert Stuart. (Museum of Fine Arts, Boston)

Country" (WRITINGS, 31:41, n.73). By 15 May, however, the seriousness of GW's condition was widely known. "Called to see the President," William Maclay noted in his diary. "Every eye full of tears. His life despaired of. Dr. MacKnight told me he would trifle neither with his own character nor the public expectation; his danger was imminent, and every reason to expect that the event of his disorder would be unfortunate" (MACLAY, 258–59; see also JAY, 3:399). By the next day the outlook was more hopeful. On 16 May Jefferson wrote his daughter Martha Jefferson Randolph: "On Monday last the President was taken with a peripneumony, of threatening appearance. Yesterday (which was the 5th. day) he was thought by the physicians to be dying. However about 4. oclock in the evening a copious sweat came on, his expectoration, which had been thin and ichorous, began to assume a well digested form, his articulation became distinct, and in the course of two hours it was evident he had gone thro' a favorable crisis. He continues mending to-day, and from total despair we are now in good hopes of him" (JEFFERSON [1], 16:429).

Monday 10th.   A severe illness with which I was seized the 10th. of this Month and which left me in a convalescent state for several weeks after the violence of it had passed; & little inclination to do more than what duty to the public required at my hands occasioned the suspension of this Diary.

June 1790

Thursday 24th.   Exercised on horse back betwn. 5 & 7 Oclock P.M.

Enter[t]ained the following Gentlemen at Dinner—viz—Messrs. Gerry, Goodhue, Grout, Leonard Huntingdon, Benson, Boudinot, Cadwalader, Sinnickson, Heister, Scott, Contee, Stone, Brown and Moore of the House of Representatives.

Received from the Committee of Enrollment the Act for extending the Judiciary Law to the State of Rhode Island & Providence Planns.

ACT: According to the House of Representatives journal the joint committee for enrolled bills brought this bill to GW on 22 June 1790. On 23 June "A message was received from the President of the United States, by Mr. Lear his Secretary" in the House assenting to the bill (DE PAUW, 3:469, 473; see also 1 STAT. 128 [23 June 1790]).

Friday 25th.   Constant & heavy Rain all day, prevented Company from visiting Mrs. Washington this afternoon & all kinds of Exercise.

Saturday 26th.   Exercised in the Coach with Mrs. Washington & the Children in the forenoon & by walking in the Afternoon.

Sunday 27th.   Went to Trinity Church in the forenoon and employed myself in writing business in the afternoon.

Monday 28th.   Exercised between 5 & 7 Oclock in the Morning & drank Tea with Mrs. Clinton (the Governors Lady) in the Afternoon.

Gov. George Clinton's residence was at 10 Queen Street, near the end of Cedar Street. The house, for which Clinton paid £300 a year rent, had been confiscated from Loyalist Henry White and was "a two-story and attic house, five windows wide, with a sloping tiled roof, containing five dormer windows" (SMITH [4], 31; SPAULDING, 194). It was presumably this residence rather than the Clinton's farm on the Hudson outside the city which GW visited today. GW and Mrs. Washington had frequent social contacts with Clinton and his wife, Cornelia Tappan Clinton, during the Revolution and after the war a friendly correspondence had been maintained, Clinton sending GW trees and various plants for Mount Vernon. In spite of political differences between Clinton and GW after the new government was established, social relations between the two families remained warm. As a rule, partly because of Mrs. Clinton's ill health, the Clintons did little entertaining. Abigail Adams Smith found Mrs. Clinton "not a showy, but a kind, friendly woman" (ROOF, 197; SPAULDING, 192–94).

Tuesday 29th.   Exercised between 5 & 7 Oclock in the Morning on horse back.

A good deal of Company, amongst which several Strangers and some foreigners at the Levee to day.

On a consultation with the Secretary of State to day, it was thought advisable to direct him to provide two Medals one for the Marqs. de la Luzerne, formerly Minister Plenipo. from France to the U. States of America, & the other for Mr. Van Berkel late Minister from Holland; & To have the Dies with which they were to be struck in France, sent over here. The cost of these Medals would be about 30 Guineas; but the Chain for that designed for the Marqs. de la Luzerne (on Acct. of his attachment & Services to this Country) was directed to Cost about 200 Guineas—the other about 100 Guins.

MEDALS: See entry for 29 April 1790.

Wednesday 30th.   Recd. from the Committee of Enrollment the following Acts. viz. "An act providing the means of intercourse between the United States and foreign Nations" By which the President of the United States is authorised to draw from the Treasury 40,000 dollars annually, for the suppt. of such persons as he shall Commission to serve the U. States in foreign pts. and for the expence incident to the business in which they may be employed. Not *more* than 9,000 Dollars to be allowed to a Minister Plenipotentiary nor 4,500 to a Chargé des Affaires, except the out fit to each, which shall not exceed one years Salary; nor shall more than 1300 dollars be allowed to the Secretary of any Minister Plenipotentiary. The President is to acct. specifically for all such Expenditures as in his judgement may be made public and also for the amount of such Expenditures as he may think it advisable not to specify, and cause a regular statement thereof to be laid before Congress Annually. "An Act for the relief of Nathaniel Twining" And "An Act to satisfy the Claims of John McCord against the United States." These several Acts were presented to me about 10 Oclock A.M.

For background to "An Act providing the means of intercourse between the United States and foreign Nations," see entries for 23 and 26 Mar., 16 and 27 April, 7 May 1790.

"An Act for the relief of Nathaniel Twining" (6 STAT. 3 [1 July 1790]) remitted a penalty incurred by Twining's failure to abide by his contract to deliver the mail between Charleston, S.C., and Savannah in 1787. "An Act to satisfy the claims of John McCord against the United States" (6 STAT. 2–3 [1 July 1790]) granted McCord $809.71 for supplies furnished the Continental Army in Canada in 1776.

[July]

Thursday July 1st.   Exercised between 5 and 7 Oclock on Horseback.

Announced to the House of Representatives (where the Bills originated) that my signature had been given to the Acts above mentioned.

Having put into the hands of the Vice President of the U: States the communications of Mr. Gouvr. Morris, who had been empowerd to make informal enquiries how well disposed the British Ministry might be to enter into Commercial regulations with the United States, and to fulfil the Articles of Peace respecting our Western Posts, and the Slaves which had been carried from this Country, he expressed his approbation that this step had been taken; and added that the disinclination of the British Cabinet to comply with the two latter, & to evade the former, as evidently appears from the Corrispondence of Mr. Morris with the Duke of Leeds (the British Minister for Foreign Affairs) was of a piece with their conduct towds. him whilst Minister at that Court; & just what he expected; & that to have it ascertained was necessary. He thought as a rupture betwn. England & Spain was almost inevitable, that it would be our policy & interest to take part with the latter as he was very apprehensive that New Orleans was an object with the former; their possessing which would be very injurious to us; but he observed, at the sametime, that the situation of our affairs would not Justify the measure unless the People themselves (of the United States) should take the lead in the business.

Received about three Oclock, official information from Colo. Willet, that he was on the return from the Creek Nation (whither he had been sent with design to bring Colo. McGillivray, and some of the Chiefs of these people to the City of New York for the purpose of treating) that he, with the said McGillivray and many of the head Men, were advanced as far as Hopewell in So. Carolina on their way hither and that they should proceed by the way of Richmond with as much expedition as the nature of the case wd. admit.

It having been reported, upon information being recd. at St. Augustine of Colo. McGillivrays intention of coming to this place that advice thereof was immediately forwarded by the Commandant of that place to the Governor of the Havanna And a Mr. Howard Secretary of East Florida and an influencial character There under pretext of bad health and a Spanish Armed Brig of 20 Guns, ostensibly to bring 50,000 dollars for the purpose of buying Flour, arriving here immediately thereupon, affording strong ground to suspect that the Money & the character abovementioned were sent here for the purpose of Counteracting the Negotiations which was proposed to be held with Colo. McGillivray & the other Chiefs of the Creeks & this suspicion being corroborated by Mr. Howards visit to Philadelphia I directed the Secretary at War to advertise Colo. Willet thereof, that he might, if a meeting should take place at Philadelphia, or elsewhere on the Rd. observe their Conduct & penetrate, if possible, into the object of it. He was desired at the sametime to make suitable provision for lodging, & otherwise entertaining Colo. McGillivray & his party.

The following Gentn. & Ladies dined here to day. viz. The Secretary of State, Secretary of the Treasury and Secretary at War & their Ladies—Mr. Dalton & Mr. King & their Ladies Mr. Butler & his two daughters—Mr. Hawkins, Mr. Stanton & Mr. Foster & Mr. Izard. The Chief Justice & his Lady, Genl. Schuyler & Mrs. Izard were also invited but were otherwise engaged.

Chief Justice John Jay, by John
Trumbull. (Yale University Art
Gallery)

In the fall of 1789 GW had requested Gouverneur Morris to open unofficial
discussions with the British ministry on outstanding differences between the
United States and Great Britain (see entry for 7 Oct. 1789). Among the
letters that GW showed to Adams today was probably Morris to GW, 7 April
1790, describing in detail his polite but unsatisfactory interview with the
duke of Leeds, British minister for foreign affairs. "On Monday the twenty
ninth I waited upon him at Whitehall and after the usual Compliments, presented your Letter telling him that it would explain the Nature of my
Business. Having read it, he said with much Warmth and Gladness in his
Appearance 'I am very happy Mr. Morris to see this Letter and under the
Presidents own Hand. I assure you it is very much my Wish to cultivate a
friendly and commercial Intercourse between the two Countries *and more,*
and I can answer for the Rest of his Majesty's Servants that they are of the
same Opinion.' . . . I assured him of our sincere Disposition to be upon
good Terms and then proceeded to mention those Points in the Treaty of
Peace which remained to be performed: and first I observed that by the
Constitution of the United States which he had certainly read all Obstacles
to the Recovery of British debts are removed. . . . He said he was very happy
to receive this Information, that he had been of Opinion and had written
so to Mr Adams that the Articles ought to be performed in the Order in
Which they stood in the Treaty. . . . I took Occasion to observe that the
Southern States who had been much blamed in this Country for obstructing
the Recovery of british Debts, were not liable to all the Severity of Censure
which had been thrown upon them—that their Negroes having been taken
or seduced away, and the Payment for those Negroes having been stipulated
by Treaty they had formed a Reliance on such Payment for Discharge of
Debts contracted with british Merchants both previously and subsequently
to the War." Morris then brought up the main questions of British retention
of the frontier posts and payment for slaves that had been taken away by
the British army after the war. Leeds "became a little embarrassed" and could
not say how the question of the posts stood. "That as to the Affair of the

Negroes he had long wished to have it brought up and to have Something done, but Something or other had always interfered. He then changed the Conversation but I brought it back, and he changed it again. Hence it was apparent that he could go no farther than general Professions and Assurances." Leeds was equally noncommittal on the subject of an exchange of ministers between the two countries. "Wherefore as it was not worth while to discuss the Winds and the Weather I observed that as he might probably chuse to consider the matter a little and to read again the Treaty and compare it with the American Constitution. He said that he should and wished me to leave your Letter which he would have copies and return to me. . . . Thus Sir this Matter was began but nine Days have since lapsed and I have heard Nothing farther from the Duke of Leeds" (DLC:GW). Morris's correspondence with the duke of Leeds was enclosed.

A letter of 1 May from Morris to GW, also enclosing correspondence with Leeds, reported little progress in the negotiations. "It seems pretty clear that they wish to evade a commercial Treaty but not peremptorily to reject it, and therefore I have construed into Rejection his Graces abstruse Language. . . . I have some Reason to believe that the present Administration intend to keep the Posts, and withhold Payment for the Negroes" (DLC:GW).

The RUPTURE BETWN. ENGLAND & SPAIN involved a conflict between the two powers at Nootka Sound on the west coast of North America. When the British attempted in 1789 to establish a post in territory claimed but not effectively occupied by Spain, Spanish forces in the area resisted and captured several British ships. By mid-June reports reached the United States from London that the British were preparing for war and that a conflict appeared imminent (see John Rutledge, Jr., to Jefferson, 6 May 1790, JEFFERSON [1], 16:413–15).

For the background of Alexander McGillivray's trip to New York, see entry for 10 Mar. 1790. McGillivray, Marinus Willett, and their party apparently started north in mid-May, "McGillivray and several others on horseback, twenty-six chiefs and warriors in three wagons, and Willett riding in a sulky. All along the way the delegation was greeted with great interest and McGillivray was feted by the more prominent citizens. Particularly was this the case at Guildford Courthouse, North Carolina, at Richmond and Fredericksburg in Virginia, and at Philadelphia" (CAUGHEY, 43). Carlos Howard was an Irish officer who joined the Hibernia Regiment of the Spanish army in 1761. He had attained the rank of captain when in 1784 he was appointed provisional secretary of the captaincy-general of St. Augustine, serving in that post for the next 11 years (LOCKEY, 183–84, n.2). American suspicions about Howard's role were undoubtedly justified. He was sent to New York from St. Augustine ostensibly on sick leave but actually to keep an eye on the negotiations. John Leslie of the trading firm of Panton, Leslie & Co. wrote McGillivray from St. Augustine, 13 May 1790, concerning "our mutual friend Captain Carlos Howard, who by chance is about to make an excursion, which he has contemplated for some time past to the northern States in order to get for his health a change of climate and the benefits of the sea air." Leslie noted that the two men were sure to meet in New York and since Howard had "seen much of the world" his advice would be useful. "If you meet in New York, it will be in his power to introduce you to the Spanish minister in case you do not carry letters from the Governors. . . . Anyhow you will find him useful in other ways, for I am persuaded that he will be most happy to render you every possible service in any affair in which you conceive that he can contribute to further your views or facilitate your wishes, especially in connection with any communications that you may have to make to the Spanish governors or even to the court at Madrid" (CAUGHEY, 264). McGillivray and his party arrived in New York City on 20 July, and Howard made every effort to insinuate himself into the negotiations. "We are by no means satisfied with the conduct of the Spanish Officer, who arrived lately from the foreign possessions of that Crown," Hamilton stated. "We cannot prove it positively, but have every reason to think, that he has been using endeavours to check or even to frustrate our negotiations with the Creek Indians, and with this view that he has made them large presents in this city; this we consider as perfectly unwarrantable" (HAMILTON [2], 6:547). Howard himself, in his lively account of his activities in New York, stated that the United States government "appointed people to watch and follow my footsteps. . . . McGuillivray was convinced that my presence . . . contributed to the fact that the Americans did not insist on an unqualified recognition on the part of the Indians of the sovereignty of the United States as well as that a secret article concerning the settling of the question of Indian trade was deferred for two years" (Howard to Juan Nepomuceno de Quesada, governor of East Florida, 24 Sept. 1790, CAUGHEY, 281–84). The negotiations with the Creek continued in July and early August, and the Treaty of New York was signed on 7 Aug. 1790 (KAPPLER, 25–29).

Joseph Stanton, Jr. (1739–1807), newly elected senator from Rhode Island, had just arrived in New York. He served in the Rhode Island legislature 1768–74 and during the Revolution as a colonel of a Rhode Island regiment and brigadier general in the Rhode Island militia. In 1790 he was a member of the Rhode Island Ratifying Convention.

Theodore Foster (1752–1828), a native of Brookfield, Mass., graduated from Rhode Island College (Brown University) in 1770 and began the practice of law in Providence about 1771. He held several local positions, including judge of the court of admiralty in 1785. In June 1790 GW appointed him naval officer for Providence. At this time he had just been elected to represent Rhode Island in the United States Senate.

Friday 2d.   Exercised between 5 & 7 on horse back.

About one oclock, official accounts of the safety of Major Doughty (who was sent on important business to the Chiccasaw and Choctaw Nations of Indians) were received; together with the detail of his proceedings to the Country of the former, and the misfortune that attended him in ascending the River Tenessee to the intended place of meeting the Chicasaws, by the Treachery of a Banditti composed of Cherokees, Shawanese & Creek Indians who to the Number of 40 in 4 Canoes (Doughty's party consisting of no more than 15 Soldiers) under colour of a white flag, & professions of friendship rose, fired upon, & killed five & wounded Six more of his men; obliging him (when within Six miles of Ochappo the place of Rendezvous) to retreat down the Tennessee

& which he was able to effect by his gallant behaviour & good conduct; notwithstanding the superior force of the enemy & a pursuit of 4 hours and attempts to board the Barge in wch. he was. But being too weak to ascend the Ohio after he had entered it he was induced to follow the Currt. into the Missisippi & thence down the same to a Spanish post A [   ] de grass about [   ] Miles below the Mouth of the Ohio where he was treated with great kindness & Civility by Monsr. [   ] the Commandant. He contrived after this to see the Piemingo & other head Men of the Chicasaw Nation with whom he did the business he was sent on nearly as well as if he had got to Occhappo the place of his destination as will appear by his detail transmitted to the Secretary at War.

Received from the Committee of Enrollment two Acts—One "For giving effect to an Act entitled 'An Act providing for the enumeration of the Inhabitants of the United States' in respect to the State of Rhode Island & Providence Plantations"—The other "An Act to authorize the purchase of a tract of Land for the use of the United States."

Much company of both Sexes to visit Mrs. Washington this Evening.

John Doughty (1757–1826) served in the Revolution as aide-de-camp to Maj. Gen. Philip Schuyler and as a captain in the artillery. He was brevetted major 30 Sept. 1783. In 1789 he was appointed with the same rank to the artillery. He helped in the design and construction of Forts Harmar and Washington. He was sent by Knox in early 1790 to carry guarantees of American friendship to the Chickasaw (GW to Chiefs and Warriors of the Chickasaw, 30 Dec. 1790, DLC:GW). His report to Knox on his mission, 7 April 1790, is in MiU-C: Harmar Papers. Henry Knox's account of Doughty's misfortunes agrees substantially with that in GW's diary (see Knox's "Causes of the existing Hostilities between the United States, and certain Tribes of Indians North-West of the Ohio," 26 Jan. 1792, in CARTER [4], 2:364). The secretary of war had earlier mentioned the attack in his "Summary statement of the situation of the frontiers," 27 May 1790 (DLC: GW). The incident occurred on 22 Mar., and on 25 Mar. Doughty wrote to Maj. John P. Wyllys, describing the attack: "We fought them four hours, and then escaped in this distressed situation. I found it impossible to ascend the Ohio, or, after I reached the Mississippi, to ascend it. My wounded men were in so distressed a situation as to require immediate assistance. The only resource left me was to come to this place, where I have met with every civility" (ST. CLAIR PAPERS, 2:134). The commandant of Ansa á la grasa or Ainse à la graisse (New Madrid), to which Doughty and the surviving members of his party had fled, was Pedro Foucher (NASATIR, 285, n.1; THORNBROUGH, 231, n.2). Piomingo was a pro-American Chickasaw chief. OCCHAPPO: Occochappo (see entry for 26 Jan. 1790). ACTS: For the act providing for the census in Rhode Island, see 1 STAT. 129 (5 July 1790). The second act cited by GW authorized him to purchase for the federal government "the whole or such part of that tract of land situate in the state of New York, commonly called West Point, as shall be by him judged requisite for the purpose of such fortifications and garrisons as may be necessary for the defence of the same" (1 STAT. 129 [5 July 1790]).

Saturday 3d.   Exercised between 9 and 11 in the Coach with Mrs. Washington and the Children.

The policy of treating Colo. McGillivray, & the Chiefs of the Creek Nation who were coming with him, with attention as they passed through the States to this City induced me to desire the Secretary at War to write to the Governors of Virginia, Maryland & Pensylvania requesting that they might be provided at the expence with whatever might be deemed a proper respect that they might be kept in good humour.

Nominated, *Yesterday,* to the Senate, persons for the Judiciary of Rhode Island; and a person as Naval Officer in the District of Providence, in the place of Mr. Foster, who was sent by the State as one of their Senators—also Surveyors for the smaller Ports in the District & the District of New Port.

CHIEFS: See entry for 1 July 1790. Knox's circular letter to the governors was dated 3 July 1790. The letter sent to John Eager Howard of Maryland is in MdAA.

GW's appointments for Rhode Island included Henry Marchant (1741–1796), federal judge; William Channing (1751–1793), district attorney; William Peck (d. 1832), United States marshal; and Ebenezer Thompson to replace Theodore Foster (1752–1828) as naval officer of Providence. For the appointments to the Rhode Island customs service, see DE PAUW, 2:83.

Sunday 4th.   Went to Trinity Church in the forenoon.

This day being the Anniversary of the declaration of Independency the celebration of it was put of until to morrow.

Monday 5th.   The Members of Senate, House of Representatives, Public Officers, Foreign Characters &ca. The Members of the Cincinnati, Officers of the Militia, &ca., came with the compliments of the day to me. About One Oclk. a sensible Oration was delivered in St. Pauls Chapel by Mr. Brockholst Levingston on the occasion of the day—the tendency of which was, to shew the different situation we are now in, under an excellent government of our own choice, to what it would have been if we had not succeeded in our opposition to the attempts of Great Britain to enslave us; and how much we ought to cherish the blessings which are within our reach, & to cultivate the seeds of harmony & unanimity in all our public Councils. There were several other points touched upon in a sensible manner.

In the afternoon many Gentlemen & ladies visited Mrs. Washington.

I was informed this day by General Irvine (who recd. the acct. from Pittsburgh) that the Traitor Arnold was at Detroit & had viewed the Militia in the Neighbourhood of it twice. This had occasioned much Speculation in those parts—and with many other circumstances—though trifling in themselves led strongly to a conjecture that the British had some design on the Spanish settlements on the Mississipi and of course to surround these United States.

This oration was part of New York's Independence Day celebration. As part of the festivities in the early afternoon, local military units "escorted the Society of THE CINCINNATI to St. Pauls—where an elegant oration was delivered by BROCKHOLST LIVINGSTON, Esq., to a very numerous audience [including] The PRESIDENT and Vice-President of the United States Members of both Houses of Congress—a brilliant assembly of Ladies and of the most respectable citizens" (*Gaz. of the U.S.* [Philadelphia], 7 July 1790). GW may have dined this evening with the Society of the Cincinnati at Bardin's. Henry Brockholst Livingston (1757–1823) was the son of William Livingston, governor of New Jersey. A graduate of Princeton in 1774, he had accompanied his brother-in-law John Jay on the latter's mission to Spain in 1779 and served at various times during the Revolution in the Continental Army. In 1783 he was admitted to the New York bar and became prominent in New York legal circles. Under the new government he became an active Antifederalist.

After the Revolution, Benedict Arnold lived in England with his family until 1785. In that year, finding his inflated claims for compensation for his services to the British government during the Revolution were not successful, he sailed for the Loyalist settlement of St. John, New Brunswick, where he established a mercantile and shipping business (WALLACE [2], 288–92).

Tuesday 6th.   Exercised on Horse-back betwn. 5 & 7 Oclock in the Morning. At 9 Oclock I sat for Mr. Trumbull to finish my pictures in some of his historical pieces.

Anounced to the House of Representatives (where the Bills originated) my Assent to the Acts which were presented to me on Friday last—One of which Authorises the President to purchase the whole, or such part of that tract of Land situate in the State of New York commonly called West point as shall be by him judged requisite for the purpose of such fortifications & Garrisons as may be necessary for the defence of the same.

The Visitors were few to day on Acct. of the numbers that paid their Compliments yesterday.

HISTORICAL PIECES: John Trumbull was continuing the series of paintings depicting the events of the American Revolution that he had begun soon after the war. After considerable preparatory work in Europe, he returned to New York in 1789, "for the purpose of pursuing my work of the Revolution; all the world was assembled there, and I obtained many portraits for the Declaration of Independence, Surrender of Cornwallis, and also that of General Washington in the battles of Trenton and Princeton" (TRUMBULL [2], 88, 92, 164). See also entry for 14 Jan. 1790.

Wednesday 7th.   Exercised between 5 & 7 this Morning on Horse-back.

Thursday 8th.   Sat from 9 o'clock till after 10 for Mr. Jno. Trumbull, who was drawing a Portrait of me at full length which he intended to present to Mrs. Washington.
    About Noon the Secretaries of State, and of the Treasury called upon me—the last of whom reported a communication made to him by Majr. Beckwith Aid de Camp to Lord Dorchester—Governor of Canada wch. he reduced to writing, and is as follow.

"Memorandum of the substance of a communication made on Thursday the eighth of July 1790 to the Subscriber by Major Beckwith as by direction of Lord Dorchester"

"Major Beckwith began by Stating that Lord Dorchester had directed him to make his acknowledgmts. for the politeness which had been shewn in respect to the desire he had intimated to pass by N York in his way to England; adding that the prospect of a War between Great Britain & Spain would prevent or defer the execution of his intention in that particular."
    "He next proceeded to observe that Lord Dorchester had been informed of a negotiation commenced on the other side of the Water through the Agency of Mr. Morris; mentioning as the subscriber understood principally by way of proof of Lord Dorchesters knowledge of the transaction that Mr. Morris had not produced any regular Credentials, but merely a letter from the President directed to himself, that some delays had intervened partly on account of Mr. Morris's absence on a trip to Holland as was understood and that it was not improbable those delays & some other circumstances may have impressed Mr. Morris with an idea of backwardness on the part of the British Ministry."
    "That his Lordship however had directed him to say that an inference of this sort would not in his opinion be well founded as he had reason to believe that the Cabinet of Great Britain enter-

[87]

tained a disposition not only towards a friendly intercourse but towards an alliance with the United States.

"Major Beckwith then proceeded to speak of the particular cause of the expected rupture between Spain & Britain observing it was one in which all Commercial Nations must be supposed to favor the views of G. Britain. That it was therefore presumed, should a War take place, that the United States would find it to be their interest to take part with G. Britain rather than with Spain."

"Major Beckwith afterwards mentioned that Lord Dorchester had heard with great concern of some depredations committed by some Indians on our Western frontier. That he wished it to be believed that nothing of this kind had received the least countenance from him. That on the contrary he had taken every proper opportunity of inculcating upon the Indians a pacific disposition towards us; and that as soon as he had heard of the outrages lately committed he had sent a message to endeavor to prevent them. That his Lordship had understd. that the Indians alluded to were a banditti composed chiefly or in great part of Creeks or Cherokees, over whom he had no influence; intimating at the sametime that these tribes were supposed to be in connection with the Spaniards."

"He stated in the next place that his Lordship had been informed that a Captain Hart in our Service and a Mr. Wemble and indeed some persons in the Treaty at Fort Harmer had thrown out menaces with regard to the Posts on the Frontier & had otherwise held very intemperate language; which however his Lordship considered rather as effusions of individual feelings than as effects of any instruction from authority."

"Major Beckwith concluded with producing a letter signed Dorchester; which letter contained ideas similar to those he had expressed, though in more guarded terms and without any allusion to instructions from the British Cabinet. This letter it is recollected hints at the Non-execution of the treaty of peace on our part."

"On the subscriber remarking the circumstances that this letter seemed to speak only the Sentiments of his Lordship Major Beckwith replied that whatever reasons there might be for that course of proceeding in the present Stage of the business, it was to be presumed that his Lordship knew too well the consequence of such a step to have taken it without a previous knowledge of the intentions of the Cabinet."

The aspect of this business in the moment of its communication to me, appeared simply, and no other than this; We did not incline to give any satisfactory answer to Mr. Morris who was officially Commissioned to ascertain our intentions with respect to the evacuation of the Western Posts within the Territory of the United States and other matters into which he was empowered to enquire until by this unauthenticated mode we can discover whether you will enter into an Alliance with us and make Common cause against Spain. In that case we will enter into a Commercial Treaty with you & *promise perhaps* to fulfil what they already stand engaged to perform. However, I requested Mr. Jefferson & Colo. Hamilton, as I intend to do the Vice-President, Chief Justice & Secretary at War, to revolve this Matter in all its relations in their minds that they may be the better prepared to give me their opinions thereon in the course of 2 or three days.

The following Gentlemen dined here to day—viz—Messrs. Wingate Strong McClay, Lee, & Johnson (No. Carolina) of the Senate and Messrs. Gilman, Aimes Sturges, Schureman, Fitzsimmons, Wynkoop, Vining, Smith, Madison, Sevier, & Sumpter of the House of representatives.

PORTRAIT: See entry for 14 Jan. 1790.

George Beckwith (1753–1823), a member of a prominent Yorkshire, Eng., family, became an ensign in 1771 in the British army, achieving the rank of lieutenant in 1775, captain in 1777, and major in 1781. During the years of the American Revolution he saw extensive service in America and ended the war as aide-de-camp to Sir Guy Carleton (1724–1808). Carleton, who was raised to the peerage as the first Baron Dorchester in 1786, was made governor-in-chief of the Province of Quebec, also in 1786. When he went to Canada, Beckwith accompanied him. Between 1787 and 1790 Beckwith made four visits to the United States where he acted as an unofficial agent for Dorchester and the British ministry in acquiring information about the United States and where he carried on extensive conversations with such prominent Americans as Philip Schuyler, Alexander Hamilton, William Samuel Johnson, and John Trumbull (see JEFFERSON [1], 17:35–64).

The memorandum quoted by GW is in Hamilton's handwriting and is in DLC:GW. Canadian officials had already learned of the impending crisis between Britain and Spain over the seizure of British ships in Nootka Sound through a letter from William Wyndham, Lord Grenville, secretary of state for home affairs, to Lord Dorchester, 6 May 1790, marked "Secret." Grenville, who was concerned about the United States' position, particularly in regard to the frontier posts still held by the British, wrote Dorchester that in case war should break out, "I conceive that it would by no means be impossible to turn the tide of opinion and wishes of America in our favor in case of a Contest with Spain on the business now in question. . . . The object which we might hold out to them, particularly to the Kentucke and other Settlers at the back of the old colonies, of opening the Navigation of the Mississippi to them, is one at least as important as the possession of the Forts, and perhaps it would not be difficult to shew, that the former is much more easily attainable with the assistance of Great Britain against Spain, than the latter is by their joining Spain in offensive operations against this Country" (P.R.O., C.O. 42/67, f. 93–97). Two additional letters from Grenville of the same date reiterated his concern in regard to the United States (BRYMNER, 1890, 131–33). Grenville also forwarded to Dorchester Gouverneur Morris's correspondence with the duke of Leeds (see entry for 1 July 1790) with the comment that "this communication coming from Genl. Washington however vague and inexplicit it is, seems however to indicate some disposition on the part of the United States to cultivate a closer connection with this country than has hitherto subsisted since their separation from Great Britain."

Beckwith was the logical choice as an agent to present Britain's views unofficially and to sound out the administration on Grenville's, and although he had only returned to Canada from the United States in May 1790, he again set out for New York. Beckwith carried with him two sets of instructions, both dated 27 June 1790. The first instructions, which Beckwith showed to Hamilton, expressed Dorchester's hope that the difficulties between Spain and Britain would not "make any alteration in the good disposition of the United States to establish a firm friendship and Alliance with Great Britain to the Mutual advantage of both Countries; I am persuaded it can make none on the part of Great Britain, whose liberal treatment of the United States in point of Commerce sufficiently evinces her friendly disposition, notwithstanding the non execution of the Treaty on their part, which, and various misrepresentations I have always attributed to an unsettled state of their government, and of the minds of the multitude, influenced perhaps by a power not very cordial even to the United States" (P.R.O., C.O. 42/68, f. 225).

The second instructions, marked "Secret," which the secretary of the treasury did not see, instructed Beckwith to learn as much as possible about the attitudes of both the government and people in case of war but to be cautious about carrying out Grenville's suggestion regarding the navigation of the Mississippi as bait to westerners for a British connection: "You will be cautious in advancing anything specific on that head, but rather lead them to explain the different lines of policy, each party may have in view. . . . In general you may assert it as your own opinion, that in case of a War with Spain you see no reason why we should not assist in forwarding whatever their interests may require" (P.R.O., C.O. 42/68, f. 258–60).

The Indian depredations that Dorchester deplored may have been the attack on Maj. John Doughty's party (see entry for 2 July 1790) or the attacks along the Scioto River (see entry for 9 July 1790). Indian raids on all the frontiers had been widespread during the spring of 1790. CAPTAIN HART: Jonathan Heart (see entry for 9 July 1790). The Treaty of Fort Harmar had been negotiated 9 Jan. 1789 by Gov. Arthur St. Clair with the Wyandots (KAPPLER, 2:18–23).

William Maclay noted that this evening's entertainment "was a great dinner, in the usual style, without any remarkable occurrences. Mrs. Washington was the only woman present" (MACLAY, 310).

John Sevier (1745–1815) was elected United States senator from North Carolina in 1789. Sevier in Dec. 1773 moved from his native Virginia to the North Carolina frontier and settled on the Nolichucky River in an area which in 1796 became a part of the state of Tennessee. During the Revolution he led a force of frontiersmen at King's Mountain and in 1781 and 1782 led several expeditions against Indians who were raiding the frontier. In the 1780s he was governor of the short-lived State of Franklin and deeply involved in the Muscle Shoals speculation. From 1796 to 1801 and 1803 to 1809 he served as governor of Tennessee.

Friday 9th.   Exercised on Horse-back between 5 and 7 in the morning.

A letter from Genl. Harmer, enclosing copies of former letters; and Sundry other papers, were put into my hands by the Secretary at War. By these it appears that the frequent hostilities of some Vagabond Indians, who it was supposed had a mind to establish themselves on the Scioto for the purpose of Robbing the Boats, and murdering the Passengers in their dissent or assent of the Ohio, had induced an Expedition composed of 120 effective men of the Regular Troops under his (Harmers) command, and 202 Militia (mounted on Horses) under that of Genl. Scott of the District of Kentucky. This force rendezvoused at the Mouth of Lime-stone on the 20 of April; and intended by a detour to fall on the Scioto high up: five Miles above the Mouth of paint Creek (which runs through the finest land in the world, & Surveyed for the Officers of the Virginia line) it accordingly struck the Scioto on the 25th, 50 Miles from its mouth. But the Militia, according to custom, getting tired, & short of Provisions, became clamorous to get home; & many of them would have gone off but for the influence of Genl. Scott; however, the March was continued and on the 27th. the Troops arrived at the Mouth of the Scioto where crossing the Ohio the Militia seperated for their respective homes & the regular Troops proceeded up to their head Quarters at Fort Washington. In this expedition little was done; a small party of 4 Indians was discovered—killed & Scalped and at another place some Bever traps & Skins were taken at an Indian Camp. The detour made was about 128 miles & had the Militia crossed to the East side of the Scioto it is supposed several parties of Indians would have been fallen in with. The Scioto is 65 Miles below the Mouth of Licking.

Among the Enclosures with Genl. Harmers letter, were Captn. Harts report of the Navigations of Big beaver and the Cayahoga, and Country between; & of other waters: also Majr. Hamtrameks report of the distances &ca. from Post Vincennes on the Wabash to Detroit—Copies of which I desired to be furnished with.

Many Visitors (male & female) this Afternoon to Mrs. Washington.

Josiah Harmar (1753–1813), a native of Philadelphia, served as major, lieutenant colonel, and colonel of various Pennsylvania regiments during the Revolution and in Aug. 1784 became commander of the new United States

Army. From that time until his resignation in 1792, he served mainly on the Ohio frontier, repelling Indian attacks against the area's few settlements. In Sept. 1790 he was to engage in an unsuccessful campaign against the Shawnee in the area of the Miami villages on the Maumee River. The letter that GW mentions was probably Harmar's letter of 9 June 1790 to Henry Knox, although GW must have obtained additional details from other papers submitted by Knox (ASP, INDIAN AFF., 1:91–92). Lt. Col. James Wilkinson wrote Harmar 7 April 1790 that for "more than one month past a party of savages has occupied the Northwestern bank of the Ohio, a few miles above the mouth of the Scioto, from whence they make attacks upon every boat which passes, to the destruction of much property, the loss of many lives, and the great annoyance of all intercourse from the northward . . . their last attack was made against five boats, one of which they captured" (ASP, INDIAN AFF., 1:91). On 30 May, Ens. Asa Hartshorne of the 1st United States Regiment reported that he and a small party had been attacked near Limestone; "in the afternoon, myself with five men went up to the place where we were attacked; we found one man, one woman, and three children, killed and scalped. . . . There are eight missing; the whole killed and missing is thirteen souls; they took none of the property but one horse" (ASP, INDIAN AFF., 1:91). Both of these documents were enclosed in Harmar's letter to Knox. Limestone was a small post town in Kentucky on the south side of the Ohio River "and on the west side of the mouth of a small creek of its name" (MORSE [2]).

Charles Scott (c.1739–1813) was born in Goochland (later Powhatan) County, Va., and served under GW in Braddock's campaign during the French and Indian War. During the Revolution he was a lieutenant colonel in the 2d Virginia Regiment, colonel of the 5th Virginia Regiment, and in 1777 was commissioned brigadier general in the Continental Army. He was brevetted major general in 1783. In 1785 he moved to Kentucky and represented Woodford County in the Virginia Assembly 1789–90. In 1791 he led Kentucky troops in the St. Clair expedition. Concerning his role in the Scioto expedition, Harmar noted in his letter to Knox that "General Scott detached a small party of horsemen, who fell in with the savages, killed them, and brought four scalps into Limestone" (ASP, INDIAN AFF., 1:91).

Jonathan Heart (d. 1791) of Connecticut entered the Revolution in 1775 as a volunteer, became an ensign in 1776, a captain lieutenant in 1779, and a captain in 1780. He served as a brigade major until Nov. 1783 and in 1785 was appointed a captain in the United States Infantry Regiment. In Sept. 1789 he became a captain in the 1st United States Infantry Regiment and served with Harmar's command on the Ohio frontier. He was killed during Arthur St. Clair's battle with the western Indians 4 Nov. 1791.

John Hamtramck (c.1756–1803), a native of Quebec, served during the Revolution as a major in the New York line. In 1785 he became captain of a New York company serving under Harmar on the Ohio frontier. Joining the United States forces at Vincennes in 1787 he remained as one of the fort's officers for the next six years. His "report of the distances" from Vincennes to Detroit was enclosed in a letter to Harmar of 17 Mar. 1790, and is printed in THORNBROUGH, 225–27.

Saturday 10th. Having formed a Party, consisting of the Vice-President, his lady, Son & Miss Smith; the Secretaries of State,

Treasury & War, and the ladies of the two latter; with all the Gentlemen of my family, Mrs. Lear & the two Children we visited the old position of Fort Washington and afterwards dined on a dinner provided by Mr. Mariner at the House lately Colo. Roger Morris but confiscated and in the occupation of a common Farmer. I requested the Vice-President & the Secretary at War as I had also in the Morning the Chief Justice, to turn their attention to the Communications of Majr. Beckwith; as I might in the course of a few days, call for their opinions on the important matter of it.

MISS SMITH: probably Louisa Smith. See entry for 8 Oct. 1789. GENTLEMEN OF MY FAMILY: GW's secretaries, Tobias Lear, William Jackson, Bartholomew Dandridge, Jr., David Humphreys, and Robert Lewis. Dandridge (d. 1802) was the son of Mrs. Washington's brother Bartholomew Dandridge.

Mrs. Lear, Tobias Lear's wife, was Mary (Polly) Long Lear of Portsmouth, N.H. The Lears were married in April 1790 in Portsmouth, and upon their return to New York they were invited to make their home with the Washingtons. Mrs. Washington in particular apparently became very fond of young Mrs. Lear, who made herself useful to the presidential household in a number of ways. The living arrangements continued after the household moved to Philadelphia. Polly Lear died, at the age of 23, in Philadelphia, 28 July 1793 (DECATUR, 128–29). The two children were Mrs. Washington's grandchildren George Washington Parke Custis and Eleanor Parke Custis.

Fort Washington, in the vicinity of present W. 183d Street in Manhattan, had fallen to the British in Nov. 1776. Later Fort Knyphausen had been constructed by the British on the site of the American works. The Morris Mansion (Jumel Mansion), constructed by Lt. Col. Roger Morris in 1765, was confiscated at the end of the Revolution as Loyalist property and was advertised in Mar. 1790 for sale at public auction: "A Farm at the 11 mile stone on New York Island late the property of Col. Roger Morris—the mansion house in point of elegance and spaciousness is equal to any in this state, and from its elevated position not only enjoys the most salubrious air, but affords a prospect extensively diversified and beautiful. The farm contains about 140 acres, the greatest part of which is mowing ground, and extends across the Island from the East to the North river. On the premises are a large coach house and barn, with a garden containing a variety of the best fruits" (*Daily Adv.* [New York], 12 Mar. 1790, cited in STOKES, 5:1263). The house was to be sold on 3 May 1790.

Although there are no written communications from GW on the subject of Beckwith's communications (see entry for 8 July 1790) to Adams or Knox, on 9 July Hamilton wrote Jay that "certain Circumstances of a delicate nature have occurred, concerning which The President would wish to consult you." In view of the serious illness of Jay's father-in-law, Gov. William Livingston of New Jersey, "I cannot say the President directly asks it, lest you should be embarrassed; but he has expressed a strong wish for it" (HAMILTON [2], 6:488).

On 12 July Jefferson wrote to GW that he "had a conference yesterday with Mr. Madison on the subject recommended by the President. He has the honor of inclosing him some considerations thereon, in all of which he believes Mr. Madison concurs" (DNA: RG 59, Misc. Letters). For the enclosure, "Jefferson's Outline of Policy Contingent on War between England and Spain," see JEFFERSON [1], 17:109–10.

Sunday 11th.   At home all day dispatching some business relative to my own private concerns.

Monday 12th.   Exercised on Horse back between 5 & 6 in the Morning.

Sat for Mr. Trumbull from 9 until half after ten.

And about Noon had two Bills presented to me by the joint Committee of Congress–The one "An Act for Establishing the Temporary & permanent Seat of the Government of the United States"–The other "An Act further to provide for the payment of the Invalid Pensioners of the United States."

BILLS: 1 STAT. 130 (16 July 1790) and 1 STAT. 129 (16 July 1790). The Residence Bill, establishing a new federal district on the banks of the Potomac River for the permanent capital, had been under debate in Congress since 31 May, but the struggle over the location for the capital long preceded the bill's advent in Congress. GW's close personal involvement in the matter will be fully treated in the correspondence volumes. Under the terms of the Residence Act the president was authorized to appoint three commissioners who would "under the direction of the President" oversee the surveying and construction of the new city, a provision which guaranteed GW's continued close involvement with the Federal City for the rest of his administration. The act also provided that the capital would move from New York to Philadelphia by Dec. 1790 and remain there until Dec. 1800 when the new Federal City would presumably be finished.

Tuesday 13th.   Again sat for Mr. Trumbull from 9 until half past 10 Oclock.

A good deal of Company at the Levee to day.

Wednesday 14th.   Exercised on horseback from 5 until near 7 Oclock.

Had some further conversation to day with the Chief Justice and Secretary of the Treasury with respect to the business on which Majr. Beckwith was come on. The result–To treat his communications very civilly–to intimate, delicately, that they carried no marks, official or authentic; nor, in speaking of Alliance, did they convey any definite meaning by which the precise objects of the British Cabinet could be discovered. In a word, that the Secretary of the Treasury was to extract as much as he could from

Major Beckwith & to report it to me, without committing, by any assurances whatever, the Government of the U States, leaving it entirely free to pursue, unreproached, such a line of conduct in the dispute as her interest (& honour) shall dictate.

BUSINESS ON WHICH MAJR. BECKWITH WAS COME ON: See entries for 8 and 10 July 1790.

Southern Tour

March–July 1791

EDITORIAL NOTE. From the first days of his presidency, GW was determined "to visit every part of the United States" during his term of office if "health and other circumstances would admit of it" (GW to Edward Rutledge, 16 Jan. 1791, ScCMu). A month after GW returned from his New England tour, Gov. Charles Pinckney of South Carolina wrote him suggesting a tour of the southern states (14 Dec. 1789, DLC:GW), and GW replied 11 Jan. 1790 that nothing would give him more pleasure although his time was not his own (DNA: RG 59, Misc. Letters).

By the following summer rumors were circulating in the South that GW would come that fall, but when William Blount of North Carolina called on GW at Mount Vernon in September, he learned that the southern tour would start by spring. "You may shortly expect to hear of pompous Orders for equiping and training the Cavalry," Blount confidently wrote his brother in North Carolina; "and perhaps," he added, news of GW's tour "may induce the Overseers of Roads and Ferry-Keepers to mend *their Ways* and repair or build new Boats. If the very greatest Attention and Respect is not paid him he will be greatly disappointed and Mortified for to the North the Contention has been who should pay him the most" (William Blount to John Gray Blount, 20 Sept. 1790, BLOUNT, 2:117–20).

Congress adjourned 3 Mar. 1791. Bad roads delayed GW's departure from Philadelphia for a while, but the need to traverse the route before "the warm and sickly months" were upon the South prompted him to leave on 21 Mar. (GW to William Washington, 8 Jan. 1791, and GW to David Humphreys, 16 Mar. 1791, DLC:GW).

Before setting off GW prepared a careful itinerary describing the dates, places, and mileages for his proposed "line of march." His route south was to be an eastern one through Richmond and Petersburg, Va., New Bern and Wilmington, N.C., and Georgetown and Charleston, S.C., to Savannah, and his return by "an

The World of President Washington, 1789–1797

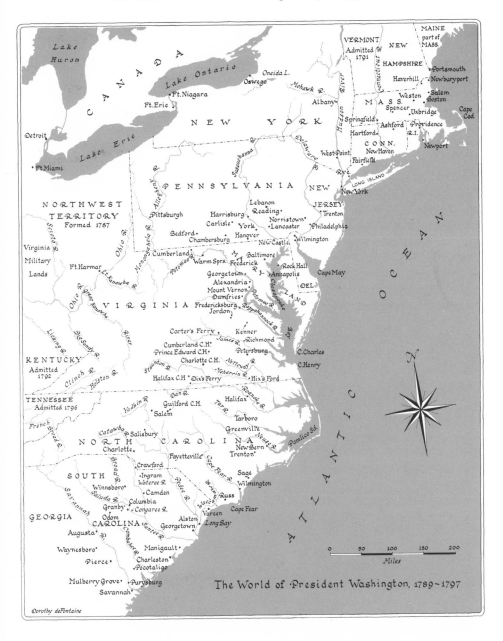

The World of President Washington, 1789–1797

Dorothy deFontaine

upper road" from Augusta through Columbia and Camden, S.C., Charlotte and Salem, N.C., and Fredericksburg. In all he was to be gone more than three months and would travel an estimated 1,816 miles ("Route & Stages of G. Washington in the yr. 1791," GW to Thomas Jefferson, Alexander Hamilton, and Henry Knox, 4 April 1791, and GW to Alexander Hamilton, 13 June 1791, DLC:GW).

As on the New England tour GW planned to lodge only at public houses and to refuse all offers to stay in private homes. "I am persuaded you will readily see the necessity of this resolution both as it respects myself and others," GW wrote his relative William Washington of South Carolina. "It leaves me unembarrassed by engagements, and by a uniform adherence to it I shall avoid giving umbrage to any by declining all invitations of residence" (8 Jan. 1791, DLC:GW). Nevertheless, lack of suitable ordinaries along several parts of his route was to oblige him to make exceptions to this rule on more than one occasion.

March 1791

Monday 21st.   Left Philadelphia about 11 O'clock to make a tour through the Southern States. Reached Chester about 3 oclock —dined & lodged at Mr. Wythes—Roads exceedingly deep, heavy & cut in places by the Carriages which used them.

In this tour I was accompanied by Majr. Jackson. My equipage & attendance consisted of a Chariet & four horses drove in hand— a light baggage Waggon & two horses—four Saddle horses besides a led one for myself—and five Servants including to wit my Valet de Chambre, two footmen, Coach man & Postilion.

MR. WYTHES: Mary Withy's inn (see entry for 13 May 1787). The words "Servants including" were struck out by GW in MS.

The coachman John Fagan, said to be "by birth a Hessian," had been hired the previous December (Robert Lewis to John Fagan, 28 Nov. 1790, DLC:GW; CUSTIS, 424). The postilion Giles proved to be "too much indisposed to ride the journey" by the time the party reached Mount Vernon (GW to Thomas Jefferson, 1 April 1791, DNA: RG 59, Misc. Letters).

Tuesday 22d.   At half past 6 Oclock we left Chester, & breakfasted at Wilmington. Finding the Roads very heavy and receiving unfavourable Accts. of those between this place and Baltimore I determined to cross the [Chesapeake] Bay by the way of Rockhall and crossing Christiana Creek [Christina River] proceeded through Newcastle & by the Red Lyon to the Buck tavern 13 Miles from Newcastle and 19 from Wilmington where we dined and lodged. At the Red Lyon we gave the horses a bite of Hay—during their eating of which I discovered that one of those wch. drew the Baggage Waggon was lame and appd. otherwise much indisposed. Had him bled and afterwards led to the Buck tavern.

This is a better house than the appearances indicate.

The Red Lion Tavern, located at the site of present-day Red Lion, Del., was opened sometime after the end of the War of Independence by a Huguenot woman named Elisse Roussier. The Buck Tavern where GW had dined 3 Sept. 1774, was, according to one patron, "indifferent for bed and table—good for horses" (W.P.A. [3], 461–62, 485).

Wednesday 23d.   Set off at 6 Oclock—breakfasted at Warwick— bated with hay 9 miles farther and dined and lodged at the House of one Worrells in Chester; from whence I sent an Express to Rock-hall to have Boats ready for me by 9 Oclock tomorrow Morning—after doing which Captn. Nicholson obligingly set out for that place to see that every thing should [be] prepared against my arrival.

The lame horse was brought on, and while on the Road appd. to move tolerably well, but as soon as he stopped, discovered a stiffness in all his limbs which indicated some painful disorder. I fear a Chest founder. My riding horse also appeared to be very unwell, his appetite havg. entirely failed him.

The Winter grain along the Road appeared promising and abundant.

The village of Warwick, Md., lies in southern Cecil County near the Maryland-Delaware line.

Thursday 24th.   Left Chester town about 6 Oclock. Before nine I arrivd at Rock-Hall where we breakfasted and immediately; after which we began to embark — The doing of which employed us (for want of contrivance) until near 3 Oclock and then one of my Servants (Paris) & two horses were left, notwithstanding two Boats in aid of The two Ferry Boats were procured. Unluckily, embarking on board of a borrowed Boat because She was the largest, I was in imminent danger, from the unskilfulness of the hands, and the dulness of her sailing, added to the darkness and storminess of the night. For two hours after we hoisted Sail the Wind was light and a head. The next hour was a stark calm after which the wind sprung up at So. Et. and encreased until it blew a gale — about which time, and after 8 Oclock P.M. we made the mouth of Severn River (leading up to Annapolis) but the ignorance of the People on board, with respect to the navigation of it run us aground first on Greenbury point from whence with much exertion and difficulty we got off; & then, having no knowledge of the Channel and the night being immensely dark with heavy and variable squals of wind — constant lightning & tremendous thunder — we soon grounded again on what is called Hornes point where, finding all efforts in vain, & not knowing where we were we remained, not knowing what might happen, 'till morning.

GW's vessel, according to the *Maryland Gazette,* "did not enter the river Severn until ten o'clock, in a dark tempestuous night. She struck on a bar, or point, within about a mile from the city; and although she made a signal of distress, it was impossible, before day-light, to go to her relief" (*Md. Gaz.* [Annapolis], 31 Mar. 1791). Greenbury Point marks the entrance to the Severn on the north. Horn Point is on the opposite side of the river, about a mile to the west (now part of the Annapolis suburb Eastport).

Friday 25th.   Having lain all night in my Great Coat & Boots, in a birth not long enough for me by the head, & much cramped; we found ourselves in the morning with in about one mile of

View of Annapolis in 1797, from an extra-illustrated copy of *Public Men of the Revolution* by William Sullivan, 1847. (Beinecke Rare Book and Manuscript Library, Yale University)

Annapolis & still fast aground. Whilst we were preparing our small Boat in order to land in it, a sailing Boat came of to our assistance in wch. with the Baggage I had on board I landed, & requested Mr. Man at whose Inn I intended lodging, to send off a Boat to take off two of my Horses & Chariot which I had left on board and with it my Coachman to see that it was properly done —but by mistake the latter not having notice of this order & attempting to get on board afterwards in a small Sailing Boat was overset and narrowly escaped drowning.

Was informed upon my arrival (when 15 Guns were fired) that all my other horses arrived safe, that embarked at the same time I did, about 8 Oclock last night.

Was waited upon by the Governor (who came off in a Boat as soon as he heard I was on my passage from Rock hall to meet us, but turned back when it grew dark and squally) as soon as I arrived at Mans tavern, & was engaged by him to dine with the Citizens of Annapolis this day at Manns tavern and at his House tomorrow—the first I accordingly did.

Before dinner I walked with him, and several other Gentlemen to the State house, (which seems to be much out of repair) —the College of St. John at which there are about 80 Students of every description—and then by the way of the Governors (to see Mrs. Howell) home.

GW was taken to a hostelry operated by George Mann (1753–1795), called Mann's Tavern or the City Hotel. A 1787 travel journal kept by an English visitor to Annapolis described these lodgings: "Mr. Mann keeps an excellent publick house 4 rooms on a floor, & one for company 66 by 21 feet—the second story Lodging Rooms, all wainscoted to the ceiling, might vie with any tavern in England" (VAUGHAN, 60–61). The large room was probably used for GW's dinner with some of the citizens of Annapolis.

The dinner at Mann's began at 3:00 P.M. "with a numerous company of inhabitants" in attendance and continued until 15 patriotic toasts had circulated around the table, each "announced by the discharge of cannon" (*Md. Gaz.* [Annapolis], 31 Mar. 1791). Like the presentation of laudatory addresses, the rituals of the public dinner would occur often in the coming weeks.

The governor of Maryland was John Eager Howard, and "Mrs. Howell," whom GW stopped to see at the governor's house before dinner, must have been the governor's wife Peggy Chew Howard (see entry for 23 May 1787).

St. John's College, where GW arrived about 10:00 A.M., was chartered by the Maryland General Assembly in 1784 but did not open its doors until Nov. 1789. From the school's faculty on the following day, GW received the first of the many formal congratulatory addresses that were to be pressed on him during his tour. "We the faculty of St John's College beg leave to express the sincere joy; which the honour of your presence in our infant seminary afforded us," wrote Principal John McDowell in this typical address. "In common with all those who superintend the education of youth, we must feel a lively gratitude to the defender of liberty, the guardian of his country's peace and consequently the great patron of literature. . . . Our earnest prayer is, that a kind providence may continually watch over you and preserve a life, long indeed already, if measured by deeds of worth and fulness of honour, but too short as yet for your Country" (26 Mar. 1791, DLC:GW). In reply GW expressed satisfaction with his visit to the college and hopes for its future progress. "You will do justice to the sentiments, which your kind regard towards myself inspires," he concluded, "by believing that I reciprocate the good wishes contained in your address, and I sincerely hope the excellence of your seminary will be manifested in the morals and science of the youth who are favored with your care" ([26 Mar. 1791], DLC: GW). Seven years later GW sent George Washington Parke Custis to St. John's to be one of those youths.

Saturday 26th.   Spent the forenoon in my room preparing papers &ca. against my arrival at George Town. Dined at the Governors and went to the Assembly in the Evening where I stayed till half past ten oclock.

In the Afternoon of this day Paris and my other two horses arrived from Rock-hall.

GW "again dined with a large company" at the governor's house, "and in the evening," reported the *Maryland Gazette*, "his presence enlivened a ball, at which was exhibited everything which this little city contained of beauty and elegance" (*Md. Gaz.* [Annapolis], 31 Mar. 1791).

Sunday 27th.   About 9 oclock this morning I left Annapolis under a discharge of Artillery, and being accompanied by the Governor a Mr. Kilty of the Council and Mr. Charles Stuart proceeded on my Journey for George Town. Bated at Queen Ann, 13 Miles distant and dined and lodged at Bladensburgh. Many of the Gentlemen of Annapolis (among [whom] was the Chanceller of the State) escorted me to the ferry over So. River.

John Kilty (1756–1811) of Annapolis, apparently a brother of Dr. William Kilty (see entry for 8 Aug. 1788), was a member of the Maryland council 1785–91 and 1792–93. During the first years of the War of Independence he served as a lieutenant in the Maryland line and later as a captain in the Continental dragoons. GW appointed him supervisor of the revenue for Maryland in 1795 (*Md. Hist. Mag.*, 6 [1911], 357; MD. ARCH., 71:64, 149, 227, 301, 72:58, 153, 235, 300).

The chancellor of Maryland was Alexander Contee Hanson (1749–1806) of Annapolis. In June 1776 he was appointed GW's assistant secretary at headquarters but resigned a few months later because of bad health. A justice of the Maryland General Court for many years, he was appointed chancellor in 1789 and served until his death.

Queen Anne, Md., was described by the English traveler Samuel Vaughan in 1787 as a "pleasant Village" with "12 houses" and a tobacco warehouse from which about 1,100 hogsheads of tobacco were shipped annually (VAUGHAN, 60). At Bladensburg, Md., according to a local tradition, GW lodged at the Indian Queen Tavern, now called the George Washington House (DIARIES, 4:152, n.5; MD. GUIDE, 262).

The South River ferry crossed to Londontown, Md. GW had used this ferry often on his way to and from Annapolis (HOWARD & SHRIVER, Map, No. 60; MD. GUIDE, 232–33).

Monday 28th.   Left Bladensburgh at half after Six, & breakfasted at George Town about 8; where, having appointed the Commissioners under the Residence Law to meet me, I found Mr. Johnson one of them (& who is chief Justice of the State) in waiting & soon after came in David Stuart & Danl. Carroll Esqrs. the other two.

A few miles out of Town I was met by the principal Citizen[s] of the place, & escorted in by them; and dined at Suters tavern (where I also lodged) at a public dinner given by the Mayor & Corporation—previous to which I examined the Surveys of Mr. Ellicot who had been sent on to lay out the district of ten miles square for the federal seat; and also the works of Majr. L'Enfant who had been engaged to examine, & make a draught of the grds.

in the vicinity of George town and Carrollsburg on the Eastern branch making arrangements for examining the ground myself tomorrow with the Commissioners.

The Residence law, which authorized the establishing of a new capital, also provided for the president to appoint three commissioners to supervise the land surveying, the layout of the Federal City in the district, and the construction of public buildings (see entry for 12 July 1790). The three commissioners, appointed by GW in 1791, were Thomas Johnson of Fredericktown, Md., Dr. David Stuart, of Hope Park in Fairfax County, and Daniel Carroll (1730–1796).

Andrew Ellicott (1754–1820) was appointed by GW to survey the district lines, which he began in the late winter of 1791. Pierre Charles L'Enfant (1754–1825), born and trained in engineering and artistic design in France, volunteered as an officer of engineers in the Revolution, entering the American army during the winter encampment at Valley Forge. During the next decade his artistic activity in America included a sketch of GW and several architectural designs in Philadelphia and New York City. In 1791 GW appointed L'Enfant to design a Federal City to be built within the district. Carrollsburg, still only a paper town in 1791, was laid out c.1770 on the neck between James Creek and the Anacostia River for Charles Carroll, father of Daniel Carroll of Duddington.

Tuesday 29th. In a thick mist, and under strong appearances of a settled rain (which however did not happen) I set out about 7 Oclock for the purpose abovementioned—but from the unfavorableness of the day, I derived no great satisfaction from the review.

Finding the interests of the Landholders about George town and those about Carrollsburgh much at varience and that their fears & jealousies of each were counteracting the public purposes & might prove injurious to its best interests whilst if properly managed they might be made to subserve it—I requested them to meet me at Six oclock this afternoon at my lodgings, which they accordingly did.

To this meeting I represented, that the contention in which they seemed engaged, did not in my opinion, comport either with the public interest or that of their own; that while each party was aiming to obtain the public buildings, they might, by placing the matter on a contracted scale, defeat the measure altogether; not only by procrastination but for want of the means necessary to effect the work; That neither the offer from George town, or Carrollsburgh, seperately, was adequate to the end of insuring the object—That both together did not comprehend more ground nor would afford greater means than was required for the federal City; and that, instead of contending which of the two should have it they had better, by combining there offers make a common cause of it and thereby secure it to the district. Other arguments were used to shew the danger which might result from delay and the good effects that might proceed from a Union.

Dined at Colo. Forrests to day with the Commissioners & others.

Although the Residence Bill did not specify the size of the capital, the Georgetown and Carrollsburg landholders assumed that the land to be set aside in the federal district for government buildings would consist of at most a few hundred acres. According to an early plan of Thomas Jefferson, the new town would require only about 100 acres (JEFFERSON [1], 17:460–61, 463). The landholders of Georgetown believed that 400 acres located somewhere between Rock and Goose creeks could accommodate the new capital (SCISCO, 128–29). In Jan. 1790 Daniel Carroll, one of the commissioners of the federal district and owner of land in the Carrollsburg area, proposed his 160-acre paper town as an alternative (SCISCO, 132; REPS, 254). At today's meeting, GW makes the first official public pronouncement on the size of the new capital; it would encompass the sites promoted by both the Georgetown and Carrollsburg interests, making the city a project far more ambitious than either group of landholders originally conceived.

Uriah Forrest (1756–1805), of Georgetown, Md., served as an officer in the Revolution and received wounds at Germantown and Brandywine. During the time he was a Federalist member of the United States House of Representatives (1793–94) he had a house built on Ordway Street near Wisconsin Avenue. In partnership with Benjamin Stoddert, Forrest owned nearly 1,000 acres of land north of Georgetown that fell within the newly surveyed federal district boundaries (BRYAN, 413).

Wednesday 30th.   The parties to whom I addressed myself yesterday evening, having taken the matter into consideration saw the propriety of my observations; and that whilst they were contending for the shadow they might loose the substance; and therefore mutually agreed, and entered into articles to surrender for public purposes, one half of the land they severally possessed with in bounds which were designated as necessary for the City to stand with some other stipulations which were inserted in the instrument which they respectively subscribed.

This business being thus happily finished & some directions given to the Commissioners, the Surveyor and Engineer with respect to the mode of laying out the district—Surveying the grounds for the City & forming them into lots—I left Georgetown —dined in Alexandria & reached Mount Vernon in the evening.

GW's directions for laying out the district were based upon his proclamation dated Georgetown, 30 Mar. 1791, establishing a district ten miles square beginning at Jones Point at the mouth of Hunting Creek on the south side of Alexandria. The survey was done by "the Surveyor" Andrew Ellicott, with the assistance of Benjamin Banneker (see REPS, 252). The "Engineer" was Pierre L'Enfant. For the agreement dated 30 Mar. 1791, see DNA: RG 42, Proceedings of the Commissioners.

Thursday 31st. From this time, until the 7th. of April, I remained at Mount Vernon—visiting my Plantations every day—and

Was obliged also, consequent of Colo. Henry Lees declining to accept the command of one of the Regiments of Levies and the request of the Secretary of War to appoint those Officers which had been left to Colo. Lee to do for a Battalion to be raised in Virginia East of the Alligany Mountains to delay my journey on this account—and after all, to commit the business as will appear by the letters & for the reasons there-mentioned to Colo. Darke's management.

From hence I also wrote letters to the Secretaries of State—Treasury and War in answer to those received from [them] on interesting subjects—desiring in case of important occurrances they would hold a consultation and if they were of such a nature as to make my return necessary to give me notice & I would return immediately. My rout was given to them & the time I should be at the particular places therein mentioned.

The regiment of which Henry Lee was offered command was one of two regiments of six-month levies that Congress had recently authorized to be raised as part of an expeditionary force that Maj. Gen. Arthur St. Clair was preparing to lead against hostile Indians in the Ohio Valley. Lee's refusal of the command, about which GW did not definitely learn until 31 Mar., was unwelcome news, for it meant delay in officering and recruiting of the regiment's three battalions, one to be raised in Pennsylvania, one in Maryland, and one in Virginia. To minimize the delay Secretary of War Henry Knox suggested in letters of 24 and 27 Mar. 1791 that the command be offered to either Col. Josias Carvill Hall or Col. Moses Rawlings, both of Maryland, and that GW in the meantime appoint the officers for the Virginia battalion (Knox to William Jackson, 24 Mar. 1791, and Knox to GW, 27 Mar. 1791, DLC:GW). Unprepared for Lee's refusal, GW hastily approved offering the command to Hall but was reluctant to take time out of his schedule to secure the Virginia officers (William Jackson to Henry Knox, 30 Mar. 1791, and GW to Henry Knox, 1 April 1791, DLC:GW). GW settled the matter by writing to Lt. Col. William Darke of Berkeley County on 4 April to ask him to appoint the officers for the Virginia battalion and to accept command of the regiment if Hall declined it (GW to Darke, 4 and 7 April 1791, DLC:GW). Hall did decline, and Darke accepted. In the defeat that St. Clair's force suffered at the hands of the Indians near the Wabash River 4 Nov. 1791, Darke was severely wounded and his son Capt. Joseph Darke mortally wounded (William Darke to GW, 9 Nov. 1791, DLC:GW).

The letters that GW wrote from Mount Vernon to Secretary of State Thomas Jefferson are dated 31 Mar. and 1 and 4 April 1791, to Secretary of the Treasury Alexander Hamilton 4 April 1791, and to Secretary of War Henry Knox 1, 4, and 7 April 1791 (DLC:GW). The instructions for "important occurrances" are in a letter of 4 April 1791 addressed jointly to the three cabinet members. Vice-President John Adams was not included in the consultations only because he was going to Boston (DLC:GW).

[April]

Thursday 7th. April.   Recommenced my journey with Horses apparently well refreshed and in good spirits.

In attempting to cross the ferry at Colchester with the four Horses hitched to the Chariot by the neglect of the person who stood before them, one of the leaders got overboard when the boat was in swimming water and 50 yards from the Shore—with much difficulty he escaped drowning before he could be disengaged. His struggling frightned the others in such a manner that one after another and in quick succession they all got over board harnessed & fastened as they were and with the utmost difficulty they were saved & the Carriage escaped been dragged after them as the whole of it happened in swimming water & at a distance from the shore. Providentially—indeed miraculously—by the exertions of people who went off in Boats & jumped into the River as soon as the Batteau was forced into wading water—no damage was sustained by the horses, Carriage or harness.

Proceeded to Dumfries where I dined—after which I visited & drank Tea with my Niece Mrs. Thos. Lee.

GW's niece at Dumfries was Mildred Washington Lee, daughter of John Augustine Washington. Her husband Thomas Lee (1758–1805), a son of Richard Henry Lee, was practicing law in the town at this time.

Friday 8th.   Set out about 6 oclock—breakfasted at Stafford Court House and dined and lodged at my Sister Lewis's in Fredericksburgh.

GW reached Fredericksburg "about 1 o'clock, P.M." The citizens of the town, "not being apprized of his approach, were disappointed in the opportunity of evincing their respect . . . by meeting him previous to his arrival" (*Phila. Gen. Adv.*, 22 April 1791).

Saturday 9th.   Dined at an entertained [entertainment] given by the Citizens of the town. Received and answered an address from the Corporation.

Was informed by Mr. Jno. Lewis, who had, not long since been in Richmond, that Mr. Patrick Henry had avowed his interest in the Yazoo company; and made him a tender of admission into it whh. he declined—but asking, if the Company did not expect the Settlement of the lands would be disagreeable to the Indians was answered by Mr. Henry that the Co. intended to apply to Congress for protection—which, if not granted they would have recourse to their own means to protect the settlement—That General Scott had a certain quantity of Land (I think 40,000 acres in the Company's grant, & was to have the command of the force which was to make the establishment—and moreover that General Muhlenberg had offered £1000 for a certain part of the grant—the quantity I do not recollect if it was mentioned to me.

"An elegant dinner was prepared at the Town-Hall . . . ; at 2 o'clock [GW] was waited on by some of the officers and principal inhabitants of the corporation, conducted to the place of entertainment, received by the Mayor, and introduced to those present" (*Phila. Gen. Adv.*, 22 April 1791). The address delivered by Mayor William Harvey and a copy of GW's response are in DLC:GW.

Patrick Henry was a leading member of the Virginia Yazoo Company (MEADE [3], 422–23; see entry for 28 April 1790).

Sunday 10th.   Left Fredericksburgh about 6 Oclock. Myself, Majr. Jackson and one Servant breakfasted at General Spotswoods. The rest of my Servants continued on to Todds Ordinary where they also breakfasted. Dined at the Bowling Green and lodged at Kenner's Tavern 14 Miles farther—in all 35 M.

GW left town "attended by a large company of Gentlemen, of whom he took leave a few miles distant" (*Phila. Gen. Adv.*, 22 April 1791). Dr. George Todd of Caroline County had died during the previous year, but his tavern at the site of present-day Villboro, Va., apparently remained open under his name. Kenner's "Red house" stood about nine miles south of John Hoomes's Bowling Green tavern and about two miles north of Burk's Bridge, where the main road to Richmond crossed the Mattaponi River (RICE, 2:176; COLLES, 189).

Monday 11th.   Took an early breakfast at Kinners—bated at one Rawlings's half way between that & Richmd.—and dined at the latter about 3 Oclock. On my arrival was Saluted by the Cannon of the place—waited on by the Governor and other Gentlemen—and saw the City alluminated at Night.

GW arrived in Richmond about 2:00 P.M. and during the evening "viewd the Capitol" (*Va. Gaz.* [Richmond], 13 April 1791; James Currie to Thomas Jefferson, 13 April 1791, DLC: Jefferson Papers). Beverley Randolph served as governor of Virginia 1788–91.

[108]

A view of Richmond from William Wirt's *Letters of the British Spy*, 1811. (Library of Congress)

Tuesday 12th.   In company with the Governor, The Directors of the James River Navigation Company—the Manager & many other Gentlemen. I viewed the Canal, Sluces, Locks & other Works between the City of Richmond & Westham. These together have brought the navigation to within a mile and half, or a Mile and ¾ of the proposed Bason; from which the Boats by means of Locks are to communicate with the tide water Navigation below. The Canal is of Sufficient depth every where but in places not brought to its proper width; it seems to be perfectly secure against Ice, Freshes & drift Wood. The locks at the head of these works are simple—altogether of hewn stone, except the gates & Cills and very easy & convenient to work. There are two of them, each calculated to raise & lower 6 feet. They cost, according to the Manager's, Mr. Harris acct. about £3,000 but I could see nothing in them to require such a sum to erect them. The sluces in the River, between these locks and the mouth of the Canal are well graduated and easy of assent. To complete the Canal from the point to which it is now opened, and the Locks at the foot of them Mr. Harris thinks will require 3 years. Received an Address from the Mayor, Aldermen & Common Council of the City of Richmond at Three oclock, & dined with the Governor at four Oclock.

In the course of my enquiries—chiefly from Colo. Carrington— I cannot discover that any discontents prevail among the people at large, at the proceedings of Congress. The conduct of the Assembly respecting the assumption he thinks is condemned by them as intemperate & unwise and he seems to have no doubt but that the Excise law—as it is called—may be executed without difficulty —nay more, that it will become popular in a little time. His duty as Marshall having carried him through all parts of the State lately, and of course given him the best means of ascertaining the temper & dispositions of its Inhabitants—he thinks them favorable towards the General Government & that they only require to have matters explained to them in order to obtain their full assent to the Measures adopted by it.

GW was president of the James River Company 1785–95, but in name only. Edmund Randolph, one of the original directors of the company, acted as president from 1785 to 1789, when another director, Dr. William Foushee, assumed those duties. Besides Foushee, the current directors were John Harvie and David Ross. James Harris continued as manager (see entries for 17 May 1785 and 11 Mar. 1786).

GW and his party began today's tour at Harris's home and ascended the canal "in 2 fine new Batteaus of David Ross, who had his Watermen dressed in red Coaties on the Occasion." The boats, according to Dr. James Currie of Richmond, "took . . . 7 Minutes & 4 seconds by a stop watch" to pass through the canal's two locks (Currie to Thomas Jefferson, 13 April 1791, DLC: Jefferson Papers). The address from the Richmond city officials and a copy of GW's answer are in DLC:GW. The mayor was George Nicholson (CHRISTIAN, 44).

Edward Carrington, having been appointed United States marshal for Virginia 26 Sept. 1789 and supervisor of the federal revenue for the state 4 Mar. 1791, was now undertaking to perform the duties of both offices (Carrington to Alexander Hamilton, 4 April 1791, HAMILTON [2], 8:240). ASSUMPTION: State debts incurred during the War of Independence were to be assumed by the federal government under terms of a plan established by "An Act making provision for the [payment of the] Debt of the United States" (1 STAT. 138–44 [4 Aug. 1790]). The Virginia General Assembly objected to this scheme on two principal grounds: that it would enlarge the powers of the federal government at the expense of state powers and that it would oblige Virginia, which had discharged much of its war debt, to pay part of the heavy debts that some northern states still had outstanding. Declaring the act warranted by "neither policy, justice, nor the constitution," the assembly petitioned Congress on 16 Dec. 1790 to revise the act generally and in particular to repeal the part relating to the assumption of state debts (ASP, FINANCE, 7:90–91). EXCISE LAW: "An Act repealing, after the last day of June next, the duties heretofore laid upon Distilled Spirits imported from abroad, and laying others in their stead; and also upon Spirits distilled within the United States, and for appropriating the same" (1 STAT. 199–214 [3 Mar. 1791]).

Wednesday 13th.   Fixed with Colo. Carrington (the supervisor of the district) the Surveys of Inspection for the District of this State & named the characters for them—an acct. of which was transmitted to the Secretary of the treasury.

Dined at a public entertainment given by the Corporation of Richmond.

The buildings in this place have encreased a good deal since I was here last but they are not of the best kind. The number of Souls in the City are [   ].

The Virginia revenue district was divided into six surveys, each of which was overseen by an inspector of the revenue under the general direction of the district supervisor. Nominations for the six Virginia inspectors were forwarded today to Secretary of the Treasury Alexander Hamilton by William Jackson (DLC:GW). Tobias Lear sent Hamilton commissions for the appointees on 1 June 1791 (Hamilton to Lear and Lear to Hamilton, 1 June 1791, and Lear to GW, 5 June 1791, DLC:GW).

The dinner given for GW by the citizens of Richmond was held at the fashionable Eagle Tavern on Main Street (James Currie to Thomas Jefferson, 13 April 1791, DLC: Jefferson Papers). The population of Richmond in 1790 was 3,761.

Thursday 14th.   Left Richmond after an early breakfast & passing through Manchester received a salute from cannon & an Escort of Horse under the command of Captn. David Meade Randolph as far as Osbornes where I was met by the Petersburgh horse & escorted to that place & partook of a Public dinner given by the Mayor & Corporation and went to an assembly in the evening for the occasion at which there were between 60 & 70 ladies.

Petersburgh which is said to contain near 3000 Souls is well situated for trade at present, but when the James River navigation is compleated and the cut from Elizabeth River to Pasquotanck effected it must decline & that very considerably. At present it receives at the Inspections nearly a third of the Tobacco exported from the whole State besides a considerable quantity of Wheat and flour—much of the former being Manufactured at the Mills near the Town. Chief of the buildings in this town are under the hill & unpleasantly situated but the heights around it are agreeable.

The Road from Richmond to this place passes through a poor Country principally covered with Pine except the interval lands on the [James] River which we left on our left.

The small town of Manchester, established in 1769, was "a sort of suburb to Richmond," lying on the south bank of the James River across from the city (CHASTELLUX, 2:427).

David Meade Randolph (1760–1830), who lived at Presque Isle on the James River near Bermuda Hundred, was a captain of dragoons during the War of Independence. In the fall of this year GW named him to succeed Edward Carrington as United States marshal for Virginia (HENDERSON, 59–62).

GW's welcome to Petersburg was apparently a tumultuous one. "So great was the desire of the people to see him," reported Edward Carrington, who accompanied GW to the town, "that by the time of his arrival, there were not less than several thousands after him" (Carrington to James Madison, 20 April 1791, DLC: Madison Papers). At the dinner, held at Robert Armistead's tavern on Sycamore Street, "a number of patriotic toasts were drank, attended by a discharge of cannon," and it was probably there that Mayor Joseph Westmore presented GW with yet another civic address (*Dunlap's American Daily Adv.* [Philadelphia], 29 April 1791). The text of Petersburg's address and of GW's brief reply are in DLC:GW. The evening assembly was at the Mason's Hall in Blandford, which had become part of Petersburg in 1784. The town fathers had decided against a general illumination for fear of fire among the many wooden buildings (SCOTT AND WYATT, 44–47, 133–35). Petersburg's population in 1790 was 2,828.

Plans to link the Elizabeth River, a branch of the James, with the Pasquotank River in northeastern North Carolina by digging a canal through the Dismal Swamp were approved by the Virginia General Assembly in 1787 and by the North Carolina General Assembly in 1790 (HENING, 12:479–94, 13:145–46; N.C. STATE REC., 25:83–93; BROWN [3], 31–39).

Friday 15th.   Having suffered very much by the dust yesterday and finding that parties of Horse, & a number of other Gentlemen were intendg. to attend me part of the way to day, I caused their enquiries respecting the time of my setting out, to be answered that, I should endeavor to do it before eight O'clock; but I did it a little after five, by which means I avoided the inconveniences abovementioned.

I came twelve miles to breakfast, at one Jesse Lees, a tavern newly set up upon a small scale, and 15 miles farther to dinner and where I lodged, at the House of one Oliver, which is a good one for horses, and where there are tolerable clean beds. For want of proper stages I could go no farther. The road along wch. I travelled to day is through a level piney Country, until I came to Nottaway, on which there seems to be some good land. The rest is very poor & seems scarce of Water.

Finding that the two horses wch. drew my baggage waggon were rather too light for the draught; and, (one of them especially) losing his flesh fast, I engaged two horses to be at this place this evening to carry it to the next stage 20 Miles off in the Morning, and sent them on led to be there ready for me.

The Nottoway River joins the Blackwater River at the North Carolina line to form the Chowan River, which empties into Albemarle Sound.

Saturday 16th.   Got into my Carriage a little after 5 Oclock, and travelled thro' a cloud of dust until I came within two or three miles of Hix' ford when it began to rain. Breakfasted at one Andrews' a small but decent House about a mile after passing the ford (or rather the bridge) over Meherrin river. Although raining moderately, but with appearances of breaking up, I continued my journey—induced to it by the crouds which were coming into a general Muster at the Court House of Greensville who would I presumed soon have made the Ho. I was in too noizy to be agreeable. I had not however rode two miles before it began to be stormy, & to rain violently which, with some intervals, it contind. to do the whole afternoon. The uncomfortableness of it, for Men & Horses, would have induced me to put up; but the only Inn short of Hallifax having no stables in wch. the horses could be comfortable, & no Rooms or beds which appeared tolerable, & every thing else having a dirty appearance, I was compelled to keep on to Hallifax; 27 miles from Andrews—48 from Olivers and 75 from Petersburgh. At this place (i.e., Hallifax) I arrived about Six Oclock, after crossing the Roanoke on the South bank of which it stands.

This River is crossed in flat Boats which take in a carriage & four horses at once. At this time, being low, the water was not rapid but at times it must be much so, as it frequently overflows its banks which appear to be at least 25 ft. perpendicular height.

The lands upon the River appear rich, & the low grounds of considerable width but those which lay between the different rivers—namely Appamattox—Nottaway—Meherrin—and Roanoke are all alike flat, poor & covered principally with pine timber.

It has already been observed that before the rain fell I was travelling in a continued cloud of dust but after it had rained sometime, the Scene was reversed, and my passage was through water; so level are the Roads.

From Petersburgh to Hallifax (in sight of the road) are but few good Houses, with small appearances of wealth. The lands are cultivated in Tobacco—Corn—Wheat & oats but Tobacco, & the raising of Porke for market, seems to be the principal dependence of the Inhabitants; especially towards the Roanoke. Cotten & flax are also raised but not extensively.

Hallifax is the first town I came to after passing the line between the two states, and is about 20 Miles from it. To this place Vessels by the aid of Oars & setting poles are brought for the produce which comes to this place and others along the River; and may be carried 8 or 10 Miles higher to the falls which are neither great nor of much extent; above these (which are called the great falls) there are others; but none but what may with a little improvement be passed. This town stands upon high ground; and it is the reason given for not placing it at the head of the navigation there being none but low grounds between it and the falls. It seems to be in a decline, & does not it is said contain a thousand souls.

Hicks's (Hix's) ford, now the site of Emporia, Va., was designated the seat of Greensville County when the county was formed in 1780, and seven years later a permanent courthouse was finished on the south side of the river (GAINES [1], 40). The bridge was described by an English traveler during or shortly before the Revolution as being "remarkably lofty, and built of timber" (SMYTH, 1:81). The Meherrin River is a branch of the Chowan.

Halifax was laid out in 1758 as the county seat of Halifax County and during the Revolution was a frequent meeting place for the North Carolina legislature. The falls of the Roanoke River are near present-day Roanoke Rapids, N.C. The river flows into the Albemarle Sound.

Sunday 17th.   Colo. Ashe Representative of the district in which this town stands, and several other Gentlemen called upon, and invited me to partake of a dinner which the Inhabitants were desirous of seeing me at & excepting it dined with them accordingly.

"The reception of the President at Halifax," wrote Samuel Johnston of Edenton to James Iredell on 23 May 1791, "was not such as we could wish tho in every other part of the Country he was treated with proper attention." There is a local tradition that the dinner for GW was held at the Eagle Tavern near the river (HENDERSON, 75–76). John Baptista Ashe (see entry for 1 April 1790) served in Congress 1789–93. He was later elected governor of North Carolina but died before his inauguration.

Monday 18th.   Set out by Six oclock—dined at a small house kept by one Slaughter 22 Miles from Hallifax and lodged at Tarborough 14 Miles further.

This place is less than Hallifax, but more lively and thriving; it is situated on Tar River which goes into Pamplico Sound and is crossed at the Town by means of a bridge a great height from the Water and notwithstanding the freshes rise sometimes nearly to the arch. Corn, Porke and some Tar are the exports from it. We were recd. at this place by as good a salute as could be given with one piece of artillery.

Slaughter's tavern was probably operated by James Slaughter (died c.1799) of Halifax County, who was listed in the 1790 census as head of a household of 12 whites and 20 slaves (HEADS OF FAMILIES, N.C., 64).

Tarboro, N.C., seat of Edgecombe County, was settled in 1732 and officially established in 1760. The town gave GW a somewhat feeble welcome, undoubtedly because the citizens learned only at eight o'clock the previous evening that GW might pass through Tarboro, and even then it was not clear when he would arrive, if at all (Thomas Blount to Samuel Simpson, 17 April 1791, BLOUNT, 2:168–69).

The Tar River becomes the Pamlico River lower down and flows into Pamlico Sound. Floods on the river had previously carried away several wooden bridges at Tarboro, despite their considerable height and width for the times (SMYTH, 1:101).

Tuesday 19th.   At 6 Oclock I left Tarborough accompanied by some of the most respectable people of the place for a few Miles. Dined at a trifling place called Greenville 25 Miles distant and lodged at one Allans 14 Miles further a very indifferent house without stabling which for the first time since I commenced my Journey were obliged to stand without a cover.

Greenville is on Tar River and the exports the same as from Tarborough with a greater proportion of Tar—for the lower down the greater number of Tar markers [makers] are there. This article is, contrary to all ideas one would entertain on the subject, rolled as Tobacco by an axis which goes through both heads. One horse draws two barrels in this manner.

Greenville, N.C., seat of Pitt County, was incorporated in 1771 as Martinsborough; its name was changed in 1786 to honor Nathanael Greene. Allen's tavern was run by Shadrach Allen (born c.1752) of Pitt County, one of the county's delegates to the state legislature 1788–89 and to the state convention of 1789 that ratified the United States Constitution. In 1790 he had 8 whites in his household and 15 slaves (HEADS OF FAMILIES, N.C., 148).

Wednesday 20th.   Left Allans before breakfast, & under a misapprehension went to a Colo. Allans, supposing it to be a public house; where we were very kindly & well entertained without knowing it was at his expence until it was too late to rectify the mistake. After breakfasting, & feeding our horses here, we proceeded on & crossing the River Nuse 11 miles further, arrived in Newbern to dinner.

At this ferry which is 10 miles from Newbern, we were met by a small party of Horse; the district Judge (Mr. Sitgreave) and many of the principal Inhabitts. of Newbern, who conducted us into town to exceeding good lodgings. It ought to have been mentioned that another small party of horse under one Simpson, met us at Greensville, and in spite of every endeavor which could comport with decent civility, to excuse myself from it, they would attend me to Newburn. Colo. Allan did the same.

This town is situated at the confluence of the rivers Nuse & Trent, and though low is pleasant. Vessels drawing more than 9 feet Water cannot get up loaded. It stands on a good deal of ground, but the buildings are sparce and altogether of Wood; some of which are large & look well. The number of Souls are about 2000. Its exports consist of Corn, Tobacco, Pork—but principally of Naval stores & lumber.

The home that GW mistook for a tavern was apparently that of John Allen of Craven County, who was one of Craven's representatives in the legislature 1788–94 and in the convention of 1789. He was probably the John Allen listed in the 1790 census as head of a household of 5 whites and 27 slaves and may have been a brother of Shadrach Allen (HEADS OF FAMILIES, N.C., 131–32; BLOUNT, 3:33, n.78; HENDERSON, 80). Allen's military title must have derived from state or local service (N.C. STATE REC., 22:954).

The citizens of New Bern, seat of Craven County and the "place . . . generally reckon'd to be the Capital of North Carolina" despite the fact that the legislature often met elsewhere, were better prepared for GW's coming than their neighbors to the north had been (ATTMORE, 45). Three military units were mustered to welcome him. His escort from West's ferry was the recently formed Craven County Light Horse commanded by a Captain Williams. At the edge of town the New Bern Volunteers, infantrymen commanded by Capt. Edward Pasteur, one of the state's assistant United States marshals, joined the procession, and at GW's lodgings—said to be the John Wright Stanly house at Middle and New streets—"he was saluted by a discharge of fifteen guns from Captain Stephen Tinker's Company of Artillery," followed by "fifteen vollies and a feu-de-joye from the Volunteers. In the evening the town was elegantly illuminated" (*Dunlap's American Daily Adv.* [Philadelphia], 13 May 1791; DILL, 227).

The ferry over the Neuse River, where GW crossed about 1:00 P.M., was West's ferry, also called at various times in its long history Graves's, Kemp's, Curtis's, and Street's ferry (POWELL [3], 479; ATTMORE, 14–15, 21; ASBURY, 1:534, 2:628).

The horsemen who crossed the Neuse with GW were members of the Pitt County Light Horse, commanded by Capt. Samuel Simpson, who served the county in the state legislature in 1792 and 1796–97 (WHEELER, 2:347). This troop was to have met GW in Tarboro, but so short was the notice given of his approach that the men apparently were unable to assemble until GW arrived in Greenville, almost halfway through their county (Thomas Blount to Samuel Simpson, 17 April 1791, BLOUNT, 2:168–69).

John Sitgreaves (1757–1802), a prominent New Bern lawyer and the town's representative in the state legislature 1786–89, was named United States attorney for the district of North Carolina by GW in June 1790 and was raised to judge of the district the following December. He was a militia officer during the War of Independence, seeing action at the disastrous Battle of Camden in 1780, and served in the Continental Congress 1784–85 (ASHE, 2:398–400).

The Trent River is a relatively short tributary of the Neuse River, which rises in central North Carolina and flows into Pamlico Sound near Ocracoke Inlet, where vessels entered from the Atlantic.

Thursday 21st.   Dined with the Citizens at a public dinner given by them; & went to a dancing assembly in the evening—both of which was at what they call the Pallace—formerly the government House & a good brick building but now hastening to ruins. The company at both was numerous—at the latter there were abt. 70 ladies.

This town by Water is about 70 miles from the Sea but in a direct line to the entrance of the river not over 35 and to the nearest Seaboard not more than 20, or 25. Upon the River Nuse, & 80 miles above Newbern, the Convention of the State that adopted the federal Constitution made choice of a Spot, or rather district within which to fix their Seat of Government; but it being lower than the back Members (of the Assembly) who hitherto have been most numerous inclined to have it they have found means to obstruct the measure but since the Cession of their Western territory it is supposed that the matter will be revived to good effect.

GW sat down to dinner with the citizens at 4:00 P.M.; he remained at the ball until 11:00 P.M. Earlier in the day he walked around New Bern and during the afternoon received an address from a committee of local freemasons representing St. John's Lodge No. 2. A general address from the town's inhabitants was also given to him apparently at West's ferry the previous day. (*Dunlap's American Daily Adv.* [Philadelphia], 13 May 1791; HENDERSON, 84–87; both addresses and copies of GW's replies are in DLC:GW).

The palace, built in 1767–70 at the urging of Gov. William Tryon (1729–1788), served as residence for North Carolina's governors until 1780 and as an occasional meeting place for the General Assembly until 1794 (DILL, 110–19, 206, 258). It was "almost in ruins" in 1784 when the German traveler Johann David Schoepf saw it. "The inhabitants of the town," he explained, "took away everything they could make use of, carpets, panels of glass, locks, iron utensils, and the like, until watchmen were finally installed to prevent the carrying-off of the house itself. The state would be glad to sell it, but there is nobody who thinks himself rich enough to live in a brick house" (SCHOEPF, 2:128–29). William Attmore of Philadelphia who visited the palace in 1787 reported that "the Town's people use one of the Halls for a Dancing Room & One of the other Rooms is used for a School Room. . . . The King of G. Britain's Arms, are still suffered to appear in a pediment at the front of the Building; which considering the independent spirit of the people averse to every vestige of Royalty appears Something strange" (ATTMORE, 16).

The question of a new capital had troubled North Carolina politics since 1777. Unable to decide the matter, the legislature referred it to the state's Ratifying Convention of 1788, which rejected the United States Constitution. On 2 Aug. 1788 the convention voted to fix the seat of government within ten miles of Isaac Hunter's tavern in Wake County near the falls of the Neuse, but to let the legislature determine the exact spot within that radius. In 1792 land was purchased and the city of Raleigh was laid out in Wake County; by the end of 1794 a small brick statehouse was erected there (N.C. STATE REC., 22:26–29, 33; LEFLER AND NEWSOME, 243–45).

Friday 22d.   Under an Escort of horse, and many of the principal Gentlemen of Newbern I recommenced my journey. Dined at a place called Trenton which is the head of the boat navigation of the River Trent wch. is crossed at this place on a bridge and lodged at one Shrine's 10 M farther—both indifferent Houses.

GW left New Bern "under a discharge of cannon." He was undoubtedly relieved that the light horse and citizens accompanied him only "a few miles out of town" (*Dunlap's American Daily Adv.* [Philadelphia], 13 May 1791). Some of the strains of traveling were now beginning to tell. "We have, all things considered, come on tolerably well," GW had written Tobias Lear the previous day, "yet, some of the horses, especially the two last bought, are not a little worsted by their journey; and the whole, if brought back, will not cut capers as they did at starting out" (WRITINGS, 31:284–85). At Trenton, N.C., seat of Jones County, GW is said to have dined at a tavern known as "the Old Shingle House" (W.P.A. [8], 286). There also he was greeted by more freemasons, the members of King Solomon's Lodge, who presented him with a short address (DLC:GW). No reply has been found.

Shine's tavern, which a contemporary informant described as "one of the best," was apparently run by John Shine of Jones County. He appears in the 1790 census as head of a household of nine whites and eight slaves ("memorandum of distances," 1791, N.C. STATE REC., 15:380; ASBURY, 2:722; HEADS OF FAMILIES, N.C., 144).

Saturday 23d.   Breakfasted at one Everets 12 Miles—bated at a Mr. Foys 12 Miles farther and lodged at one Sages 20 Miles beyd. it—all indifferent Houses.

John Everit of Duplin County may have been proprietor of the place where GW breakfasted (HEADS OF FAMILIES, N.C., 190). Foy's tavern, described by an informant as "but tolerable," was apparently operated by James Foy of Onslow County, a bachelor who owned 31 slaves ("memorandum of distances," 1791, N.C. STATE REC., 15:380; HEADS OF FAMILIES, N.C., 143). Robert Sage of Onslow County, whom a traveler in 1786 called "a fine jolly Englishman," had his tavern at Holly Shelter Bay about a mile south of present-day Holly Ridge (WRIGHT, 279; POWELL [3], 233).

Sunday 24th.   Breakfasted at an indifferent House about 13 miles from Sages and three Miles further met a party of Light Horse from Wilmington; and after them a Commee. & other Gentlemen of the Town; who came out to escort me into it, and at which I arrived under a federal salute at very good lodgings prepared for me, about two O'clock. At these I dined with the Commee. whose company I asked.

The whole road from Newbern to Wilmington (except in a few places of small extent) passes through the most barren country I ever beheld; especially in the parts nearest the latter; which is no other than a bed of white Sand. In places, however, before we came to these, if the ideas of poverty could be seperated from the Land, the appearances of it are agreeable, resembling a lawn well covered with evergreens and a good verdure below from a broom or course grass which having sprung since the burning of the woods had a neat & handsome look especially as there were parts entirely open and others with ponds of water which contributed not a little to the beauty of the Scene.

Wilmington is situated on Cape Fear River, about 30 Miles *by water* from its mouth, but much less by land. It has some good houses pretty compactly built—The whole undr. a hill; which is formed entirely of Sand. The number of Souls in it amount by the enumeration to about 1000, but it is agreed on all hands that the Census in this state has been very inaccurately & shamefully taken by the Marshall's deputies; who, instead of going to Peoples houses, & there, on the spot, ascertaining the Nos.; have advertised a meeting of them at certain places, by which means those who did not attend (and it seems many purposely avoided doing it, some from an apprehension of its being introductory of a tax, & others from religious scruples) have gone, with their families, unnumbered. In other instances, it is said these deputies have taken their information from the Captains of militia companies; not only as to the men on their Muster Rolls, but of the souls in their respective families; which at best, must in a variety of cases, be mere conjecture whilst all those who are not on their lists—Widows and their families &ca. pass unnoticed.

Wilmington, unfortunately for it, has a mud bank [   ] miles below, ovr. which not more than 10 feet water can be brought at common tides; yet it is said vessels of 250 Tonns have come up. The qty. of shipping, which load here annually, amounts to about 12,000 Tonns. The exports consist chiefly of Naval Stores and lumber—Some Tobacco, Corn, Rice & flax seed with Porke. It is at the head of the tide navigation: but inland navigation may be extended 115 miles farther to and above Fayettesville which is from Wilmington 90 miles by land, & 115 by Water as above. Fayettesville is a thriving place containing near [   ] Souls. 6,000 Hhds. of Tobacco, & 3000 Hhds. of Flax Seed have been recd. at it in the course of the year.

The New Hanover County tavern at which GW breakfasted was probably Jennett's. Its proprietor may have been Jesse Jennett (Jinnett) who appears in Currituck County in the 1790 census, but in New Hanover in that of 1800 ("memorandum of distances," 1791, N.C. STATE REC., 15:380; HEADS OF FAMILIES, N.C., 20; N.C. 1800 CENSUS, 118).

The Wilmington Troop of Horse, commanded by Capt. Henry Toomer, met GW about 12 miles from town, and the gentlemen of the town, all on horseback, greeted him about six miles farther down the road. Stepping out of his chariot, GW mounted one of his horses and rode the remaining distance to Wilmington, preceded by four dragoons with a trumpet and followed by the rest of his escort. His servants and baggage brought up the rear of the procession.

The federal salute which GW received on reaching the town was a "tripple" one—three rounds of fifteen shots each—fired by a battery of four guns under the command of Capt. John Huske. GW then, according to a newspaper account, was escorted to his lodgings "through an astonishing concorse of people of the town and country, whom, as well as the ladies that filled the windows and balconies of the houses, he saluted with his usual affability and condencension. Upon his alighting, the acclamations were loud and universal. The Ships in the harbour, all ornamented with their colours, added much to the beauty of the scene." GW's lodgings were at Mrs. Ann Quince's house on the east side of Front Street near the river. "Authenick information" of GW's approach had arrived at Wilmington only the previous day, and "the House which was at first intended by the inhabitants for his reception and accommodation not being ready," Mrs. Quince, widow of John Quince (died c.1776), "cheerfully made an offer to the town of her elegant House and furniture for that purpose, which was gratefully accepted." Mrs. Quince lodged elsewhere during GW's stay. The dinner with the seven members of the town's welcoming committee, said to have been at Dorsey's tavern also on Front Street, was short. Afterwards GW "took a walk round the town, attended by them and many other gentlemen" (*Columbian Centinel* [Boston], 11 June 1791; HENDERSON, 104–7, 115).

Wilmington, seat of New Hanover County, and Fayetteville, seat of Cumberland County, were both settled in the early 1730s. Wilmington was incorporated in 1739/40, and Fayetteville, first called Campbelltown, in 1762. The name was changed in 1786 to honor the marquis de Lafayette. Fayetteville's population in 1790 was 1,536 (HEADS OF FAMILIES, N.C., 9). Wilmington's exact population is not given in the 1790 census. Robert Hunter, Jr., a Scottish traveler who visited the town in 1786, reported: "The inhabitants, white and black, are estimated at 1,200—the proportion four blacks to a white" (WRIGHT, 286–87).

Monday 25th.   Dined with the Citizens of the place at a public dinner given by them. Went to a Ball in the evening, at which there were 62 ladies—illuminations, Bonfires &ca.

The town's welcoming committee today presented GW with an address of the inhabitants to which GW replied briefly as usual. The address and the text of GW's remarks are both in DLC:GW. The dinner is said to have been at Jocelin's (Joslin's) tavern, and the ball at the Assembly Hall on Front Street between Orange and Ann streets. A newspaper account of the ball reported that GW "appeared to be equally surprised and delighted, at the very large and brilliant assembly of ladies, whom admiration and respect for him had collected together" (*Columbian Centinel* [Boston], 11 June 1791; HENDERSON, 114–15).

Tuesday 26th.   Having sent my Carriage across the day before, I left Wilmington about 6 oclock accompanied by most of the Gentlemen of the Town, and breakfasting at Mr. Ben. Smiths lodged at one Russ' 25 Miles from Wilmington—an indifferent House.

GW crossed the Cape Fear River in a "Revenue-barge, manned by six American Captains of ships, in which the standard of the United States was displayed." As previously arranged, the gentlemen of the town attended him in "boats from the shipping in the harbour, under their national colours," while in the background could be heard "the firing of cannon, accompanied by the acclamations of the people, from the wharves and shipping" (*Columbian Centinel* [Boston], 11 June 1791).

Col. Benjamin Smith (c.1756–1826) of Brunswick County lived at Belvidere plantation about four miles west of Wilmington on the Brunswick River, an arm of the Cape Fear. Owner of 221 slaves in 1790, Smith was, despite a hotheaded tendency to duel, a prosperous and influential planter. He represented his county in the legislature for many years and from 1810 to 1811 was governor of North Carolina. During the early days of the War of Independence, he apparently served under GW in some capacity—as an aide it is often said—although he was not a commissioned officer in the Continental Army; his rank of colonel was a militia appointment made in 1789 (N.C. STATE REC., 22:358). In forwarding some letters to GW six days after this visit, Smith took the opportunity to profess his great attachment to him— "that Attachment with which I was inspired at New York & Long Island in 1776" (Smith to GW, 1 May 1791, DNA: RG 59, Misc. Letters; ASHE, 2:401–5; HEADS OF FAMILIES, N.C., 190).

From Belvidere GW was escorted for ten miles by the Wilmington troop and Col. Thomas Brown (1744–1811) of neighboring Bladen County, commander of the horse for the district of Wilmington (*Columbian Centinel* [Boston], 11 June 1791). Russ's tavern, run by Francis, John, or Thomas Russ of Brunswick County, was typical of the "very bad" public accommodations that GW had been warned to expect between Wilmington and his next major stop, Georgetown, S.C. ("memorandum of distances," 1791, N.C. STATE REC., 15:380; HEADS OF FAMILIES, N.C., 189).

At Russ's this evening Congressman William Barry Grove (1764–1818) of Fayetteville arrived with an address from "the Merchants, Traders, and Principal Inhabitants" of that town. Grove had expected to present it to GW at Belvidere, but reaching that place about an hour after GW's departure, he had been obliged to ride on to Russ's (*Columbian Centinel* [Boston], 11 June 1791). The address dated 15 April 1791 and a copy of GW's reply to it are in DLC:GW.

Wednesday 27th.   Breakfasted at Willm. Gause's a little out of the direct Road 14 Miles—crossed the boundary line between No. & South Carolina abt. half after 12 oclock which is 10 miles from Gauses. Dined at a private house (one Cochrans) about 2 miles farther and lodged at Mr. Vareens 14 Miles more and 2 Miles short of the long bay. To this house we were directed as a Tavern, but the proprietor of it either did not keep one, or would not acknowledge it. We therefore were en[ter]tained (& very kindly) without being able to make compensation.

William Gause (died c.1801) of Brunswick County also ran a "very indifferent" tavern ("memorandum of distances," N.C. STATE REC., 15:380). Listed as head of a household of 8 whites and 37 slaves in 1790, he later became a strong Methodist supporter and a good friend of Bishop Francis Asbury, who stopped at his place several times (HEADS OF FAMILIES, N.C., 189; ASBURY, 2:109, 185, 283, 324). James Cochran of All Saints Parish, Georgetown District, S.C., was living alone in 1790 according to the census (HEADS OF FAMILIES, S.C., 50).

Jeremiah Vareen, Sr., of All Saints Parish (now Horry County, S.C.), kept a public house for some years "near the Long Bay, and a little out of the road," but apparently quit the business before this time. His son, Jeremiah Vareen, Jr., was said to be now living in the house, which was described as "a wretched one" ("memorandum of distances," 1791, N.C. STATE REC., 15:381). Both Vareens still resided in this sparsely populated parish in 1800 (HEADS OF FAMILIES, S.C., 50; S.C. 1800 CENSUS, 543; SCHOEPF, 2:156).

The Long Bay is the part of the Atlantic Ocean that washes the curving Carolina coast between Cape Fear, N.C., and Georgetown, S. C., but on many eighteenth-century maps the name seems to apply specifically to the waters off the 16-mile stretch of sand called the Long Beach, now Myrtle Beach, S.C., and its vicinity (MOUZON, MAP).

Thursday 28th. Mr. Vareen piloted us across the Swash (which at high water is impassable, & at times, by the shifting of the Sands is dangerous) on to the long Beach of the Ocean; and it being at a proper time of the tide we passed along it with ease and celerity to the place of quitting it which is estimated 16 miles. Five Miles farther we got dinner & fed our horses at a Mr. Pauleys a private house, no public one being on the road; and being met on the Road, & kindly invited by a Docter flagg to his house, we lodged there; it being about 10 miles from Pauleys & 33 from Vareens.

Both the Long Beach and the swash, a narrow channel cutting inland from the ocean, had to be crossed at low tide ("memorandum of distances," 1791, N.C. STATE REC., 15:381; VERME, 52–53). On Henry Mouzon's 1775 map of the Carolinas the name "Lewis Swash" appears at the northernmost entrance to the beach, about two miles south of a house labeled "Varene." The beach itself is labeled "Eight Mile Swash," apparently indicating the fact that the road there was often washed over by the high tide. Johann David Schoepf, who traversed the Long Beach in 1784, noted, "Here for 16 miles the common highway runs very near the shore. Lonely and desolate as this part of the road is, without shade and with no dwellings in sight, it is by no means a tedious road. The number of shells washed up, sponges, corals, sea-grasses and weeds, medusae, and many other ocean-products which strew the beach, engage and excite the attention of the traveller at every step. . . . This beach-road consisted for the most part of shell-sand, coarse or fine. . . . So far as the otherwise loose sand is moistened by the play of the waves it forms an extremely smooth and firm surface, hardly showing hoof-marks" (SCHOEPF, 2:161–62).

George Pawley of All Saints Parish was in 1790 head of a household of 4 whites and 15 slaves (HEADS OF FAMILIES, S.C., 50).

Dr. Henry Collins Flagg (1742–1801), a physician, lived at Brookgreen plantation on the Waccamaw River in All Saints Parish. He came to South Carolina from Rhode Island before the War of Independence and during the war was chief surgeon of Nathanael Greene's southern army. In 1784 he married Rachel Moore Allston, widow of Capt. William Allston (1738–1781), who developed Brookgreen (ROGERS [2], 172–73, 256; LACHICOTTE, 24, 55).

Friday 29th.   We left Doctr. Flaggs about 6 oclo[ck] and arrived at Captn. Wm. Alstons' on the Waggamaw to Breakfast.

Captn. Alston is a Gentleman of large fortune and esteemed one of the neatest Rice planters in the state of So. Carolina and a proprietor of some of the most valuable grounds for the Culture of this article. His house which is large, new, and elegantly furnished stands on a sand hill, high for the Country, with his rice fields below; the contrast of which with the lands back of it, and the Sand & piney barrens through which we had passed is scarcely to be conceived.

At Captn. Alstons we were met by General Moultree, Colo. Washington & Mr. Rutledge (son of the present Chief Justice of So. Carolina) who had come out that far to escort me to town. We

Maj. Gen. William Moultrie, by John Trumbull. (Yale University Art Gallery)

dined and lodged at this Gentlemens and Boats being provided we [left] the next morning.

William Alston (1756–1839), a veteran of Francis Marion's partisan brigade, bought 1,206 acres on the Waccamaw River in 1785 and developed it into the prosperous plantation that he called Clifton. Below his two-story mansion, his marshy rice lands were cultivated by work gangs from his force of 300 slaves, the largest holding in All Saints Parish and one of the largest in the state (GROVES, 53; LACHICOTTE, 22–24; HEADS OF FAMILIES, S.C., 50).

William Moultrie (1730–1805), William Washington (1752–1810), and John Rutledge, Jr. (1766–1819), came to Clifton to escort GW not just to Georgetown but to their own city, Charleston. Moultrie, hero of the defense of Charleston harbor against a British fleet in June 1776, became a Continental major general before the end of the war and served as governor of South Carolina 1785–87 and 1792–94. GW's kinsman William Washington was also a war hero. Born in Virginia, he distinguished himself as an infantry captain in the Virginia line during the northern campaign of 1776. Switching to the cavalry, he rose to the rank of lieutenant colonel and in Dec. 1779 was ordered to take his dragoons to the Carolinas where he proved his personal bravery in a succession of skirmishes and battles. In 1782 he married a South Carolina heiress and settled in an elegant Charleston town house. Young Rutledge, recently returned from a long gentleman's tour of Europe, was representing his father John Rutledge, Sr. (1739–1800), who, having been elected chief justice in February of this year, was now obliged to attend the court's spring circuit (John Rutledge, Sr., to GW, 15 April 1791, DLC:GW; see entry for 3 May 1791). John Rutledge, Jr., later became a controversial Federalist politician, serving in the United States Congress 1797–1803 (COMETTI, 186–219).

Saturday 30th.   Crossed the Waggamaw to George town by descending the River three miles. At this place we were recd. under a Salute of Cannon, & by a Company of Infantry handsomely uniformed. I dined with the Citizens in public; and in the afternoon, was introduced to upwards of 50 ladies who had assembled (at a Tea party) on the occasion.

George Town seems to be in the shade of Charleston. It suffered during the war by the British, havg. had many of its Houses burnt. It is situated on a pininsula betwn. the River Waccamaw & Sampton *Creek* about 15 Miles from the Sea. A bar is to be passed, over which not more than 12 feet water can be brot. except at spring tides; which (tho' the Inhabitants are willing to entertain different ideas) must ever be a considerable let to its importance; especially if the cut between the Santee & Cowper Rivers should ever be accomplished.

The Inhabitants of this place (either unwilling or unable) could give no account of the number of Souls in it, but I should not compute them at more than 5 or 600–Its chief export Rice.

GW was rowed to Georgetown "by seven captains of vessels, dressed in round hats trimmed with gold lace, blue coats, white jackets, &c. in an elegant painted boat. On his arriving opposite the market he was saluted by the artillery, with fifteen guns, from the foot of Broad-street; and on his landing he was received by the light-infantry company with presented arms, who immediately after he passed, fired thirteen rounds" (*Md. Journal* [Baltimore], 17 May 1791). A committee of seven gentlemen escorted GW to his lodgings, said to be Benjamin Allston's house on Front Street, and at 2:00 P.M. they presented GW with an address from the inhabitants of Georgetown and its vicinity. Immediately afterwards he received another address from the Masonic brethren of Prince George's Lodge No. 16. Both addresses and copies of GW's replies are in DLC:GW.

At the public dinner, which began at 4:00 P.M., GW sat in a chair that "was beautifully ornamented with an arch composed of laurel in full bloom." A similarly decorated chair awaited him in the festooned assembly room where the tea party was held following the dinner, but GW "declined the formality of being placed in a manner unsocial." Instead of sitting in the chair after being introduced to the ladies, he "seated and entertained several of them" there "in succession." The dress of the ladies on this occasion was conspicuously patriotic. "There appeared," said a newspaper account, "sashes highly beautified with the arms of the United States, and many of the ladies wore head-dresses ornamented with bandeaus, upon which were written, in letters of gold, either 'Long life to the President,' or 'Welcome to the hero'" (*Md. Journal* [Baltimore], 31 May 1791). A ball apparently followed the tea party.

Georgetown, established 1735, lies at the head of Winyah Bay where the Waccamaw, Pee Dee, and Sampit rivers converge. A detachment of British soldiers occupied the town from July 1780 to May 1781, but the burning resulted from internecine warfare between Patriot and Loyalist partisans after the British departure: on 25 July 1781 Thomas Sumter sent some of his South Carolina State Troops to plunder the property of Loyalists in the Georgetown area, and a few days later a Loyalist privateer retaliated by attacking and burning the town (BASS [2], 202–3; Nathanael Greene to Continental Congress, 25 Aug. 1781, DNA: PCC, Item 155).

The Santee River, which enters the Atlantic a short distance south of Georgetown, is fed by several large branches extending far into the Carolina piedmont, but its usefulness as a trade route from that rapidly developing region was limited by lack of a good harbor at its mouth. As early as 1770 a proposal was made to build a canal linking the Santee, about 100 miles above its mouth, with the headwaters of the Cooper River, which flows into Charleston harbor, and in Mar. 1786 the South Carolina General Assembly chartered a company to build such a canal. Construction, however, did not begin until 1793, and work was not completed until 1800 (SAVAGE, 240–53; PORCHER).

May

Sunday—May first.   Left Georgetown about 6 Oclock, and crossing the Santee Creek [Sampit River] at the Town, and the Santee

River 12 miles from it, at Lynchs Island, we breakfasted and dined at Mrs. Horry's about 15 Miles from George town & lodged at the Plantation of Mr. Manigold about 19 miles farther.

GW was rowed across the Sampit River "in the same manner, and by the same Captains of vessels," as he had been rowed to Georgetown the previous day. The artillery again saluted him from the foot of Broad Street, and "on the opposite shore [he] was received by the light-infantry company" (*Md. Journal* [Baltimore], 31 May 1791). The Santee River divides near its mouth into two branches, the North Santee and South Santee, between which lies Lynch's Island, a marshy area patented to Thomas Lynch, Sr. (1675–1752), in the 1730s. A causeway about two miles long was built across the island 1738–41 to connect the public ferries on the two branches, and it was rebuilt in the 1770s (ROGERS [2], 23, 43–44, 201).

Harriott Pinckney Horry (1748–1830) of St. James Santee Parish, Charleston District, was the widow of Col. Daniel Horry (d. 1785), who commanded state troops at Sullivan's Island in 1776 and later led a regiment of state dragoons, but was heavily fined by the General Assembly in 1782 for swearing allegiance to the crown during the 1780–81 British occupation (MCCRADY, 145, 298, 305; *S.C. Hist. and Geneal. Mag.*, 19 [1918], 177, 34 [1933], 199, 39 [1939], 24–25). Mrs. Horry had written to GW 14 April 1791 inviting him to stop at Hampton, her large rice plantation on the south side of the South Santee (DNA: RG 59, Misc. Letters). According to one account, GW was greeted at the entrance to the house by Mrs. Horry, her mother and daughter, and several nieces, all "arrayed in sashes and bandeaux painted with the general's portrait and mottoes of welcome" (RAVENEL, 311–12). Mrs. Horry was listed in the 1790 census as holding 340 slaves in St. James Santee Parish and 40 in Charleston, where she apparently had another house (HEADS OF FAMILIES, S.C., 37, 40).

Joseph Manigault (1763–1843) of Charleston inherited about 12,000 acres on Awendaw (Auendaw, Owendow) Creek (now in Berkeley County, S.C.) from his grandfather Gabriel Manigault (1704–1781) when he came of age in 1784 (*S.C. Hist. and Geneal. Mag.*, 5 [1904], 220–21, 12 [1911], 115–17, 20 [1919], 205, 208). "This great tract of land," says one South Carolina historian, "was not a beautiful, well cultivated plantation . . . but was almost entirely pine forest and swamps, devoted principally to raising scrub cattle and razorback hogs. The house . . . was an unpretentious structure which was never occupied as a home by its owner. He lived in Charleston in one of the handsomest homes in the city, on Meeting Street" (SALLEY [2], 9).

Monday 2d.   Breakfasted at the Country Seat of Govr. Pinckney about 18 miles from our lodging place, & then came to the ferry at Haddrels point, 6 miles further, where I was met by the Recorder of the City, Genl. Pinckney & Edward Rutledge Esqr. in a 12 oared barge rowed by 12 American Captains of Ships, most elegantly dressed. There were a great number of other Boats with Gentlemen and ladies in them; and two Boats with Music; all of whom attended me across and on the passage were met by a number of others. As we approached the town a salute with Artillery commenced, and at the wharf I was met by the Governor, the Lt. Governor, the Intendt. of the City; The two Senators of the State, Wardens of the City—Cincinnati &ca. &ca. and conducted to the Exchange where they passed by in procession. From thence I was conducted in like manner to my lodgings—after which I dined at the Governors (in what I called a private way) with 15 or 18 Gentlemen.

It may as well in this as in any other place, be observed, that the country from Wilmington through which the road passes, is, except in very small spots, much the same as what has already been described; that is to say, sand & pine barrens—with very few inhabitants. We were indeed informed that at some distance from the Road on both sides the land was of a better quality, & thicker settled, but this could only be on the Rivers & larger waters—for a perfect sameness seems to run through all the rest of the Country. On these—especially the swamps and low lands on the rivers, the soil is very rich; and productive when reclaimed; but to do this is both laborious and expensive. The Rice planters have two modes of watering their fields—the first by the tide—the other by resurvoirs drawn from the adjacent lands. The former is best, because most certain. A crop without either is precarious, because a drought may not only injure, but destroy it. Two and an half and 3 barrels to the Acre is esteemed a good Crop and 8 or 10 Barrls. for each grown hand is very profitable; but some have 12 & 14, whilst 5 or 6 is reckoned the average production of a hand. A barrel contains about 600 weight, and the present price is about 10/6 & 11/. Sterg. pr. 100.

The lodgings provided for me in this place were very good, being the furnished house of a Gentleman at present in the Country; but occupied by a person placed there on purpose to accomodate me, & who was paid in the same manner as any other letter of lodgings would have been paid.

Gov. Charles Pinckney (see entry for 17 May 1787) had written to GW 26 April 1791 inviting him "to make a stage" at Snee Farm, a small tract that he owned in Christ Church Parish. "I must apologise," said Pinckney in his letter, "for asking you to call at a place so indifferently furnished, & where your fare will be entirely that of a farm. It is a place I seldom go to, or things perhaps would be in better order" (DLC:GW).

Haddrell's Point, near present-day Mount Pleasant, was the eastern terminus of the ferry that crossed Charleston harbor to the city (SALLEY [2], 11; NAMES IN S.C., 13:48–49). The recorder of Charleston was John Bee Holmes (1760–1827), a lawyer who held that position 1786–92 and 1811–19 (*S.C. Hist. and Geneal. Mag.*, 29 [1928], 239). Charles Cotesworth Pinckney, the governor's cousin, was brevetted a brigadier general in the Continental

Army near the end of the Revolution after having served most of the war as a colonel (see entry for 4 Nov. 1786; ZAHNISER, 50, 70, n.58). Edward Rutledge (1749–1800), a lawyer like Holmes and the two Pinckneys, served in the Continental Congress 1774–76, was an artillery officer in the South Carolina militia for much of the Revolution, and became governor of the state in 1798. On 24 May 1791, when GW was in Columbia, S.C., he wrote a letter addressed to Charles Cotesworth Pinckney and Edward Rutledge, offering either of them the seat on the United States Supreme Court that Rutledge's brother John had recently vacated to become chief justice of South Carolina. Both men declined because of distressed finances (GW to Pinckney and Rutledge, 24 May 1791, ScC; Pinckney and Rutledge to GW, 12 June 1791, DLC:GW; ZAHNISER, 111–13).

The 12 captains who rowed GW across the harbor, plus a thirteenth captain who acted as coxswain of the barge, "were uniformly and neatly dressed in light blue silk jackets, and round black hats decorated with blue ribbons on which were impressed the arms" of South Carolina. "During the passage vocal and instrumental music were performed on the water by the Amateur Society, assisted by a voluntary association of singers; and upwards of forty boats attended with anxious spectators, which formed a most beautiful appearance" (*Gaz. of the U.S.* [Philadelphia], 21 May 1791; SALLEY [2], 13; HENDERSON, 159, n.1). The opening stanza of the laudatory lyrics sung by the waterborne chorus—"young gentlemen of considerable vocal powers"— revealed the high pitch to which the patriotic fervor of Charleston's citizens had risen in anticipation of GW's arrival:

> He comes! he comes! the hero comes.
> Sound, sound your trumpets, beat your drums,
> From port to port let cannons roar,
> His welcome to our friendly shore

(HENDERSON, 156; *Dunlap's American Daily Adv.* [Philadelphia], 10 and 16 May 1791).

The cannon salute that GW heard as he approached the temporary steps erected for him at Prioleau's wharf were fired by the men of the Charleston battalion of artillery, who on his landing offered "to mount guard" for him during his stay, but GW "politely declined . . . saying that he considered himself perfectly safe in the affection and amicable attachment of the people." Mingled with the sound of the cannon were the ringing bells of St. Michael's Church and "reiterated shouts of joy" from "an uncommonly large concourse of citizens" (*Gaz. of the U.S.* [Philadelphia], 21 May 1791).

The officials who stood with Governor Pinckney at the wharf were: Lt. Gov. Isaac Holmes (1758–1812), Charleston intendant (mayor) Arnoldus Vanderhorst (1748–1815), Sen. Pierce Butler (see entry for 15 Nov. 1789), and Sen. Ralph Izard (see entry for 10 Oct. 1789). The 12 wardens of Charleston (city councilmen) are identified in SALLEY [2], 15. The local Cincinnati turned out in full uniform as did the militia officers of the city and the entire Charleston Company of Fusiliers, who were also present at the wharf (*Dunlap's American Daily Adv.* [Philadelphia], 16 May 1791; HENDERSON, 150–52).

The Exchange, an elegant customs house built 1767–71 by the commercially ambitious Charlestonians and used as their city hall until 1818, stood on the harbor at the east end of Broad Street. From its steps GW "received the honors of the procession, to whom he politely and gracefully bowed as they passed in review before him." Joining the high officials, Cincinnati, militia officers, and fusiliers in this procession were members of the city's various professions and handicrafts, each group marching in its allotted place (*Gaz. of the U.S.* [Philadelphia], 21 May 1791; *Dunlap's American Daily Adv.* [Philadelphia], 10 May 1791; HENDERSON, 149–51, n.1).

GW lodged on Church Street in the town house of Thomas Heyward, Jr. (1746–1809), who had retired in 1789 to his plantation in St. Luke's Parish, Beaufort District (see entry for 11 May 1791). The house, which was currently occupied by Mrs. Rebecca Jamieson, had been leased with its furnishings for a week by the city council at a cost of £60. The council also supplied a housekeeper, several servants, and "a proper stock of liquors, groceries, and provisions" (HENDERSON, 159–60, n.1; *Gaz. of the U.S.* [Philadelphia], 27 April 1791). Governor Pinckney's house was on Meeting Street near the harbor (SALLEY [2], 19–20).

Tuesday 3d. Breakfasted with Mrs. Rutledge (the Lady of the Chief justice of the State who was on the Circuits) and dined with the Citizens at a public dinr. given by them at the Exchange.

Was visited about 2 oclock, by a great number of the most respectable ladies of Charleston—the first honor of the kind I had ever experienced and it was as flattering as it was singular.

John Rutledge's wife was Elizabeth Grimké Rutledge (d. 1792). Their house stood on Broad Street between King and Legare. After the visit of the ladies, the events of the day followed a more familiar pattern. At 3:00 P.M. the city officials presented GW with a welcoming address, and half an hour later the merchants of Charleston "in a body" delivered another address. Both addresses and copies of GW's replies are in DLC:GW. At the public dinner, which began at 4:00 P.M., GW ate sitting beneath "a beautiful triumphal

Miniature of John Rutledge, by John Trumbull. (Yale University Art Gallery)

arch" and afterwards heard 15 toasts, accompanied by cannon shots. "It is almost unnecessary to add," observed the writer of the next day's newspaper account, "that the day and evening were spent with all that hilarity, harmony, and happy festivity, which was suited to the occasion" (*Md. Journal* [Baltimore], 24 May 1791). The city council had repaired the bells and employed bellmen for GW's visit (HENDERSON, 160, n.1).

Wednesday 4th. Dined with the Members of the Cincinnati, and in the evening went to a very elegant dancing Assembly at the Exchange—At which were 256 elegantly dressed & handsome ladies.

In the forenoon (indeed before breakfast to day) I visited and examined the lines of Attack & defence of the City and was satisfied that the defence was noble & honorable altho the measure was undertaken upon wrong principles and impolitic.

At the Cincinnati dinner, held in the "long-room" of Edward McCrady's tavern on East Bay Street, "a choir of singers entertained the company with several pieces of vocal music," and there were again patriotic toasts punctuated by the guns of the Charleston battalion of artillery. The evening ball, given by the city corporation, was attended by "a great number of gentlemen," but the "brilliant assemblage of ladies" was clearly the center of attention. "The ladies," said a newspaper account, "were all superbly dressed; and most of them wore ribbons with different inscriptions, expressive of their respect for the President, such as, 'long live the President,' &c. &c. Joy, satisfaction and gratitude illumined every countenance, and revelled in every heart; whilst the demonstrations of grateful respect shewn him seemed to give him the most heartfelt satisfaction, which visibly displayed itself in his countenance. The beautiful arch of lamps in front of the Exchange was illuminated; and over the entrance there was a superb transparency, in the centre *Deliciis Patriae,* and at the top G.W. The fusileer company was drawn up before the Exchange to maintain order, and exhibited a very pleasing appearance. In short, every circumstance of the evening's entertainment was truly picturesque of the most splendid elegance" (*Md. Journal* [Baltimore], 24 May 1791). A supper at 10:30 P.M. finished the evening's festivities (HENDERSON, 178).

Earlier in the day a delegation from the Grand Lodge of the State of South Carolina Ancient York Masons, headed by Mordecai Gist, called on GW and presented him with their address of welcome. The address dated 2 May 1791 is printed in *Md. Journal* (Baltimore), 24 May 1791, and *Dunlap's American Daily Adv.* (Philadelphia), 25 May 1791. GW's reply, which also appears in those newspapers, is in DLC:GW.

The lines of attack and defense that GW toured this morning were constructed across Charleston neck, north of the city, in the spring of 1780 when British forces commanded by Sir Henry Clinton laid seige to American forces in Charleston commanded by Maj. Gen. Benjamin Lincoln (BOATNER [1], 205–14; BOATNER [2], 462). At the time of the seige GW was much concerned about Lincoln's decision to commit all of his men to the defense of the city, leaving the rest of the South with little protection. "It is putting much to the hazard," GW wrote Baron von Steuben 2 April 1780; "I have the greatest reliance on General Lincoln's prudence; but I cannot forbear dreading the event" (DLC:GW). The key to the defense of Charleston, GW believed, was control of the harbor (GW to Benjamin Lincoln, 15 April 1780, DLC:GW; GW to John Laurens, 26 April 1780, PHi: Gratz Collection). Unfortunately, the deteriorating forts guarding the harbor were ineffective against Adm. Marriot Arbuthnot's ships, which crossed the bar in force 8 April 1780. On 12 May the American garrison surrendered. GW, nevertheless, supported Lincoln to the end. "This consolation . . . offers itself," GW wrote him 28 April 1780 when the fate of Charleston was sealed, "that the honour of our Arms is safe in your hands, & that if you must fall, you will not fall without a vigorous struggle" (MH). Lincoln later played a prominent role at Yorktown.

Thursday 5th.   Visited the Works of Fort Johnson on James's Island, and Fort Moultree on Sullivans Island; both of which are in ruins, and scarcely a trace of the latter left—the former quite fallen.

Dined with a very large Company at the Governors, & in the evening went to a Concert at the Exchange at wch. there were at least 400 lad[ie]s—the Number & appearances of wch. exceeded any thing of the kind I had ever seen.

GW visited the two forts in Charleston harbor by boat, accompanied by "several . . . gentlemen of great respectability," including William Moultrie whose courageous defense of the sand and palmetto-log fort on Sullivan's Island 28 June 1776 earned him his status as a hero. Originally called Fort Sullivan, the post was renamed in his honor after the battle, but both it and Fort Johnson on the other side of the harbor failed to stop the British in 1780 (*Md. Journal* [Baltimore], 24 May 1791; BOATNER [1], 197–205, 750).

Governor Pinckney's dinner, which began at 4:00 P.M., was attended by "the principal gentlemen of the civil, clerical and military professions." At the concert "an excellent band of music played in the orchestra, and were accompanied in the vocal strain by the choir of St. Philip's church." For this occasion the Exchange "was decorated with various ornaments—the pillars were ingeniously entwined with laurel, and the following devices inscribed in different parts of the Hall: *'With grateful praises of the hero's fame,' 'We'll teach our infants' tongues to lisp his name.'* " Several Latin mottoes were also displayed (*Gaz. of the U.S.* [Philadelphia], 21 May 1791).

Friday 6th.   Viewed the town on horse back by riding through most of the principal Streets.

Dined at Majr. Butlers, and went to a Ball in the evening at the Governors where there was a select company of ladies.

Saturday 7th.   Before break I visited the Orphan House at which there were one hund. & Seven boys & girls. This appears to be a charitable institution and under good management. I also viewed the City from the balcony of [   ] Church from whence the whole is seen in one view and to advantage. The Gardens & green trees which are interspersed adding much to the beauty of the prospect.

Charleston stands on a Pininsula between the Ashley & Cowper Rivers and contains about 1,600 dwelling houses and nearly 16,000 Souls of which about 8,000 are white. It lies low with unpaved Streets (except the footways) of Sand. There are a number of very good houses of Brick & wood, but most of the latter. The Inhabitants are wealthy—Gay—& hospitable; appear happy, & satisfied with the Genl. Governmt. A cut is much talked off between the Ashley & Santee Rivers but it would seem I think, as if the accomplishment of the measure was not very near. It would be a great thing for Charleston if it could be effected. The principal exports from this place is Rice, Indigo and Tobacco; of the last from 5 to 8,000 Hhds. have been exported, and of the first from 80 to 120,000 Barrels.

The Charleston Orphan House, established by city ordinance 18 Oct. 1790, was located in rented quarters on Ellery (now Market) Street until a permanent building for the institution was completed in Oct. 1794 (DUKE ENDOWMENT, 105–6; HENDERSON, 185). GW was greeted today at the orphan house by its six commissioners, who laid out their records for inspection. After receiving GW's approbation of their management, the commissioners escorted him to the breakfast room where the children and attendants waited "in their proper places" to meet him. "On taking leave of the children," said a newspaper account, "he very pathetically pronounced his benediction on them." The visit ended with "a genteel breakfast . . . in the Commissioners' room" (*Md. Journal* [Baltimore], 31 May 1791).

GW's panoramic view of Charleston was from the second balcony of St. Michael's steeple.

About 4:30 P.M. the merchants of Charleston gave an elaborate dinner for GW at the Exchange. "Upwards of 300" guests dined on "every delicacy that the country and season could afford" and sipped "wines excellent and in great variety." In the harbor the ship *America* of Charleston fired a federal salute when GW arrived at the Exchange and a salute of 13 guns following each of the 17 afterdinner toasts. At 8:00 P.M. "fire-works [were] displayed on board the ship, which was illuminated with lanterns; amidst them the letter V.W. (*Vivat Washington*) were strikingly conspicuous" (*Md. Journal* [Baltimore], 31 May 1791). Today the Charleston City Council passed a resolution asking GW to sit at his convenience for a portrait by John Trumbull to hang in the city hall in commemoration of his visit (resolution in DLC:GW). GW consented, and a portrait was finished by May 1792 (*Md. Journal* [Baltimore], 31 May 1791; GW to William Moultrie, 5 May 1792, DNA: RG 59, Misc. Letters; TRUMBULL [2], 170–71).

Sunday 8th. Went to Crouded Churches in the Morning & afternoon—to [   ] in the Morning & [   ] in the Afternoon.

Dined with General Moultree.

GW attended services at St. Philip's Church in the morning and at St. Michael's in the afternoon (*Md. Journal* [Baltimore], 31 May 1791; minutes of the St. Philip's vestry, 3 May 1791, DLC:GW).

Monday 9th. At Six oclock I recommenced my journey for Savanna; attended by a Corps of the Cincinnati, and most of the principal Gentlemen of the City as far as the bridge over Ashly river, where we breakfasted and proceeded to Colo. W. Washington's at Sandy-hill with a select party of particular friends—distant from Charleston 28 Miles.

To reach the Ashley River bridge GW and his escort traveled up Charleston neck, crossing the city boundary line, where they were met by Intendant Vanderhorst and the city wardens. Vanderhorst delivered a brief farewell address, to which GW replied with a few words of thanks. Then "the whole cavalcade, joined by the Intendant, moving on, they were saluted with a federal discharge from the field-pieces of the Charleston battalion of artillery, and a volley of musketry by the fusileer company, who were drawn up at some distance from the skirts of the city" (*Md. Journal* [Baltimore], 31 May 1791).

On the bridge, a wooden structure about three-fourths of a mile long with a draw in the middle, "a triumphal arch was constructed, adorned with flowers, laurel, &c." Breakfast was provided by John Freazer (Frazer, Fraser) of St. Andrew's Parish, who apparently kept a tavern near the south end of the bridge (*Md. Journal* [Baltimore], 31 May 1791; *S.C. Hist. and Geneal.*

Lt. Col. William Washington of South Carolina, by Charles Willson Peale. (Independence National Historical Park Collection)

Mag., 14 [1913], 203–6, 20 [1919], 83–84, 47 [1946], 211–13, 71 [1970–71], 172–73; HENDERSON, 201).

Sandy Hill plantation in St. Paul's Parish, Charleston District, was inherited by William Washington's wife, Jane Reiley Elliott Washington (c.1763–1830), from her father, Charles Elliott (1737–1781). In 1790 William Washington held 380 slaves in St. Paul's Parish (*S.C. Hist. and Geneal. Mag.,* 10 [1909], 245–46, 11 [1910], 60–61, 66; HEADS OF FAMILIES, S.C., 37; SALLEY [2], 22). The select party that accompanied GW to Sandy Hill consisted of Gov. Charles Pinckney, Sen. Pierce Butler, Sen. Ralph Izard, Gen. William Moultrie, and Gen. Charles Cotesworth Pinckney (*Md. Journal* [Baltimore], 31 May 1791).

Tuesday 10th. Took leave of all my friends and attendants at this place (except General Moultree & Majr. Butler—the last of whom intended to accompany me to Savanna, and the other to Purisburgh, at which I was to be met by Boats) & breakfasting at Judge Bees 12 Miles from Sandy Hill lodged at Mr. Obrian Smiths 18 or 20 further on.

Thomas Bee (1730–1812) was nominated judge of the United States district court for South Carolina by GW 11 June 1790 and was confirmed by the Senate three days later. A wealthy aristocratic lawyer, he had played a prominent political role in the Revolution in South Carolina, serving as a member of the council of safety 1775–76, a state judge 1776–78, speaker of the state House of Representatives 1777–79, lieutenant governor 1779–80, and a member of the Continental Congress 1780–82. In 1790 he held 165 slaves on his lands in St. Paul's Parish and 19 more in Charleston, where he had a town house (GADSDEN, 154; *S.C. Hist. and Geneal. Mag.,* 37 [1936], 87–88; HEADS OF FAMILIES, S.C., 37, 39).

O'Brian Smith (c.1756–1811) came to South Carolina from Ireland about 1784. He later served in the state legislature and from 1805 to 1807 was a member of the United States Congress. His plantation was in St. Bartholomew's Parish, Charleston District, where in 1790 he owned 146 slaves, and he also had a town house in Charleston, where he kept 8 slaves (HEADS OF FAMILIES, S.C., 34, 43).

Wednesday 11th. After an early breakfast at Mr. Smiths we road 20 Miles to a place called Pokitellico, where a dinner was provided by the Parishoners of Prince William for my reception; and an Address from them was presented and answered. After dinner we proceeded 16 Miles farther to Judge Haywards w[h]ere we lodged, &, as also at Mr. Smiths were kindly and hospitably entertained. My going to Colo. Washingtons is to be ascribed to motives of friendship & relationship; but to Mr. Smiths & Judge Haywards to those of necessity; their being no public houses on the Road and my distance to get to these private ones increased at least 10 or 12 miles between Charleston and Savanna.

Pocotaligo, an Indian settlement taken over by whites in the early years of the century, was on the Pocotaligo River, a branch of the Broad River (SALLEY [2], 23). The address of the people of Prince William's Parish and a copy of GW's very brief answer are in DLC:GW.

Thomas Heyward, Jr., in whose Charleston town house GW had lodged, lived at White Hall plantation on Hazzard Creek, another tributary of the Broad River. He also owned nearby Old House plantation and on his two plantations in 1790 had a total of 440 slaves. A lawyer educated at the Middle Temple in London, Heyward served in the Continental Congress 1776–78 and fought as a militia officer in 1780 at Charleston, where he was captured. He was elected a state circuit judge in 1779 and held that position until 1789, when he resigned to pursue his serious interest in agriculture at White Hall. In 1785 he helped to found and became first president of the Agricultural Society of South Carolina (SALLEY [2], 16–17, 24).

Thursday 12th.   By five oclock we set out from Judge Haywards and road to Purisburgh 22 Miles to breakfast.

At that place I was met by Messr. Jones, Colo. Habersham, Mr. Jno. Houston Genl. McIntosh and Mr. Clay, a Comee. from the City of Savanna to conduct me thither. Boats also were ordered there by them for my accomodation; among which a handsome 8 oared barge rowed by 8 American Captns. attended. In my way down the River I called upon Mrs. Green the Widow of the decreased [deceased] Genl. Green (at a place called Mulberry grove) & asked her how she did. At this place (12 Miles from Purisburgh) my horses and Carriages were landed, and had 12 Miles farther by Land to Savanna. The wind & tide being both agt. us, it was 6 oclock before we reached the City where we were recd. under every demonstration that could be given of joy & respect. We were Seven hours making the passage which is often performed in 4, tho the computed distance is 25 Miles. Illumns. at night.

I was conducted by the Mayor & Wardens to very good lodgings which had been provided for the occasion, and partook of a public dinner given by the Citizens at the Coffee room. At Purisbg. I parted w' Genl. Moultree.

Purrysburg, S.C., a village first settled by Swiss colonists in 1732, is on the Savannah River about 25 miles upstream from the city of Savannah (*S.C. Hist. and Geneal. Mag.,* 10 [1909], 187–219, 73 [1972–73], 187–88).

The five Savannah committeemen who greeted GW here had all been in the vanguard of the Revolution in Georgia. Noble Wimberley Jones (c.1724–1805), a physician, was speaker of the Commons House of the Georgia Assembly 1768–70, but because of his vigorous opposition to royal policies, his elections to that post in 1771 and 1772 were disallowed by the royal executive. Jones later played a leading role in the council of safety and the provincial congresses and served in the Continental Congress 1781–82.

Joseph Habersham (1751–1815), a merchant, was appointed major in a battalion of Georgia state troops in July 1775 and by 1778 was a lieutenant colonel in the Continental service. In 1795 GW appointed him United States postmaster general, a position he held until 1801. John Houstoun (1744–1796), a lawyer, was another prominent member of the council of safety and the provincial congresses. Elected to the Continental Congress in 1775, he attended only a few weeks, but was more active in political affairs at home, serving as governor of Georgia 1778–79 and 1784–85. Lachlan McIntosh (1725–1806), remembered as the man who killed Georgia signer of the Declaration of Independence Button Gwinnett in a duel in 1777 in which he himself was wounded, was well known to GW for his military services during the Revolution. Appointed a colonel by the state in Jan. 1776, he became a Continental brigadier general later that year. He was at Valley Forge and in May 1778 was given command of the Western Department. Conflicts with subordinates obliged GW to relieve him the next year, and McIntosh returned south where he fought at the seiges of Savannah and Charleston. Joseph Clay (1741–1804), a merchant and rice planter, was also a leader in the council of safety and the provincial congresses. He was appointed paymaster general for the Continental Army in the South in 1777 and later served as state treasurer. GW also was met at Purrysburg by Anthony Wayne (1745–1796), who, although a native Pennsylvanian, had been living since 1785 in Chatham County, Ga., on a 1,134-acre Savannah River plantation known as Richmond and Kew, which the state of Georgia had confiscated from its Loyalist owner and had presented to Wayne as a reward for his military services in the South (GRANGER, 114–21).

Mulberry Grove, home of Catherine Littlefield Greene (see entry for 1 Oct. 1789), lay near Richmond and Kew and, like Wayne's plantation, was a confiscated Loyalist estate, which Georgia had used to reward Nathanael Greene for his wartime services. Greene settled on this 2,171-acre plantation in 1785 and began to restore its deteriorated rice fields, but made little progress before his death in June 1786, leaving his wife and children in financial difficulties (GRANGER, 71–74).

Savannah officials expected GW and his escort to spend the night at Mulberry Grove. "Indeed," wrote Mayor Thomas Gibbons to Wayne on 11 May, "it seems necessary that the President should be delayed there, because from the uncertainty of his arrival, no satisfactory provision will be made on that day. To land [at Savannah] in the Evening, will be unfavorable to the wishes of the Ladies, Citizens &c who wish to see the procession." If GW was to come on to the city today, Wayne was instructed "to effect a Landing at Mulberry Grove, if only for an hour," and send a warning to the city from there (MiU-C: Wayne Papers).

GW's late arrival this afternoon, however, did little if anything to dampen the festivity of Savannah's welcome. Rowed by the eight captains with a ninth as coxswain, all "dressed in light blue silk jackets, black satin breeches, white silk stockings, and round hats with black ribbons having the words 'Long live the President,' in letters of gold," GW was met "within ten miles of the city . . . by a number of gentlemen in several boats, and as the President passed by them a band of music played the celebrated song, 'He comes, the Hero comes,' accompanied with several voices. On his approach to the city the concourse on the Bluff, and the crowds which had pressed into the vessels', evinced the general joy which had been inspired by the visit of this most beloved of men. . . . Upon arriving at the upper part of the harbor he was saluted from the wharves and by the shipping," and at the public wharf where he landed, he was received by Sen. James Gunn (see entry for 29 April 1790) and Congressman James Jackson (see entry for 21 Jan. 1790), who introduced him to Mayor Thomas Gibbons (1757–1826) and the aldermen of the city (*Dunlap's American Daily Adv.* [Philadelphia], 31 May 1791). Gibbons, a wealthy lawyer and plantation owner and a passive Loyalist during the Revolution, served several terms as mayor of Savannah between 1791 and 1801, when he was appointed a federal judge.

After a salute of 26 shots by the Chatham County Artillery Company, GW was escorted to his lodgings in St. James's Square by a long procession which included, besides the city officials, the welcoming committee, the artillery company, the local light-infantry company, officers of the militia, members of the Cincinnati, and "citizens two and two." Dinner was to have been a small private affair either at GW's lodgings or Mayor Gibbons's house. Instead, it turned out to be a rather formal public affair at Brown's Coffeehouse, attended by numerous judges, clergymen, legislators, Cincinnati, militia field officers, and other distinguished citizens. After dinner there were 16 toasts punctuated as usual by artillery fire (*Dunlap's American Daily Adv.* [Philadelphia], 31 May 1791; Thomas Gibbons to Anthony Wayne, 11 May 1791, MiU-C: Wayne Papers).

The general illumination of the city this evening was elaborately done. One alderman's house displayed "no less than three hundred lights, arranged in a beautiful symmetry, with fifteen lights contained in the form of a W in front" (LEE & AGNEW, 70), and in the river the ship *Thomas Wilson* "with a great number of lanterns . . . made a fine appearance" (*Dunlap's American Daily Adv.* [Philadelphia], 31 May 1791).

Friday 13th.   Dined with the Members of the Cincinnati at a public dinner given at the same place and in the evening went to a dancing Assembly at which there was about 100 well dressed & handsome Ladies.

At the Cincinnati dinner more toasts "were drank under federal salutes from the artillery company," and it was probably there that Anthony Wayne, as president of the Georgia Cincinnati, presented its undated address of welcome to GW (*Dunlap's American Daily Adv.* [Philadelphia], 31 May 1791). During his stay in Savannah, GW received more than the usual number of such addresses. Besides the address of the Georgia Cincinnati, there was an undated one from the citizens of Savannah and its vicinity; one of 12 May 1791 from the Congregational Church and Society of Midway, Ga., a town about 30 miles southwest of Savannah; one of 13 May 1791 from the mayor and aldermen of Savannah; one of 14 May 1791 from the freemasons of Georgia; and another of 14 May 1791 from John Earnst Bergman, minister of the German Congregation of Ebenezer, Ga., a town about 30 miles northwest of Savannah. GW replied to each address, except apparently the one from Bergman, which, unlike the others, was in Latin. All of these addresses and copies of the answers are in DLC:GW; a draft of the Savannah citizens' address and GW's signed reply to them are owned by Mr. Sol Feinstone, Washington Crossing, Pa.; GW's signed reply to the Georgia freemasons is at DMS.

The evening ball was held in the Long Room of the Filature, a large building on Reynolds Square erected in the 1750s and used for silk manufacturing until about 1770 when it became a public assembly hall. GW arrived at the ball at 8:30 P.M., "and was personally introduced," according to a newspaper account, "to 96 ladies, who were elegantly dressed, some of whom displayed infinite taste in the emblems and devices on their sashes and head dresses, out of respect to the happy occasion. The room, which had been lately handsomely fitted up, and was well lighted, afforded the President an excellent opportunity of viewing the fair sex of our city and vicinity, and the ladies the gratification of paying their respects to our Federal Chief. After a few minuets were moved, and one country dance led down, the President and his suite retired about 11 o'clock. At 12 o'clock the supper room was opened, and the ladies partook of a repast, after which dances continued until 3 o'clock" *Dunlap's American Daily Adv.* [Philadelphia], 31 May 1791).

Saturday 14th.   A little after 6 Oclock, in Company with Genl. McIntosh Genl. Wayne the Mayor and many others (principal Gentlemen of the City) I visited the City, and the attack & defence of it in the year 1779, under the combined forces of France and the United States, commanded by the Count de Estaing & Genl. Lincoln. To form an opinion of the attack at this distance of time, and the change which has taken place in the appearance of the ground by the cutting away of the woods, &ca., is hardly to be done with justice to the subject; especially as there is remaining scarcely any of the defences.

Dined to day with a number of the Citizens (not less than 200) in an elegant Bower erected for the occasion on the Bank of the River below the Town. In the evening there was a tolerable good display of fireworks.

Savannah, which fell to the British 29 Dec. 1778, was attacked 9 Oct. 1779 by an American force under Benjamin Lincoln and a French force under Charles Hector, comte d'Estaing (1729–1794), but the poorly coordinated assault ended in disaster. Lachlan McIntosh, who had commanded the American reserves on 9 Oct. 1779, today gave GW and the accompanying gentlemen "an account of every thing interesting" relating to the attack (*Dunlap's American Daily Adv.* [Philadelphia], 31 May 1791; BOATNER [1], 980–88; BOATNER [2], 89–91).

The bower where GW dined this afternoon was described in a newspaper account as "a beautiful arbor, supported by three rows of pillars, entirely covered with laurel and bay leaves, so as to exhibit uniform green columns. The pillars were higher than the arbor, and ornamented above it by festoons, and connected below by arches covered in the same manner. The place on which it stood was judiciously chosen, presenting at once a view of the city and the shipping in the harbor, with an extensive prospect of the river and rice lands both above and below the town." GW, as usual, was the focus of all attention, and there were many toasts and much firing of artillery in his honor after dinner. A concert, following the fireworks display, concluded the day's activities *(Dunlap's American Daily Adv.* [Philadelphia], 31 May 1791).

Sunday 15th.   After morning Service, and receiving a number of visits from the most respectable ladies of the place (as was the case yesterday) I set out for Savanna [Augusta], Escorted beyd. the limits of the City by most of the Gentlemen in it and dining at Mulberry grove—the Seat of Mrs. Green—lodged at one Spencers —distant 15 Miles.

Savanna stands upon what may be called high ground for this Country. It is extremely Sandy wch. makes the walking very disagreeable; & the houses uncomfortable in warm & windy weather as they are filled with dust whensoever these happen. The town on 3 sides is surrounded with cultivated Rice fields which have a rich and luxurient appearance. On the 4th. or back side it is a fine sand. The harbour is said to be very good, & often filled with square rigged vessels but there is a bar below over which not more than 12 Water can be brot. except at Spg. tides. The tide does not flow above 12 or 14 miles above the City though the River is swelled by it more than dble. that distance. Rice & Tobacco (the last of wch. is greatly encreasing) are the principal Exports. Lumber & Indigo are also Expord. but the latter is on the decline, and it is supposed by Hemp & Cotton. Ship timber—viz—live Oak & Cedar, is (and may be more so) valuable in the expt.

Maj. Gen. Nathanael Greene, by Charles Willson Peale. (Independence National Historical Park Collection)

The morning service was at Christ Church on Johnson Square. GW was escorted out of Savannah not only by a large number of the city's gentlemen but also by a detachment of Augusta, Ga., dragoons commanded by Maj. Ambrose Gordon (1751–1804), a Revolutionary War cavalryman formerly of Virginia. On the outskirts of the city GW halted briefly at Spring Hill, site of a British redoubt where much fighting had occurred during the 1779 Allied attack on Savannah. Today at this place James Jackson, as commander of the militia in the eastern district of Georgia, stood at the head of the local artillery and light-infantry companies, and GW received a parting salute: "39 discharges from the field pieces, and 13 vollies of platoons" (*Dunlap's American Daily Adv.* [Philadelphia], 31 May 1791).

Before GW left Savannah today, he "politely expressed his sense of the attention shewn him by the corporation & every denomination of people during his stay" (*Dunlap's American Daily Adv.* [Philadelphia], 31 May 1791). That attention, however, was burdensome as well as flattering. Writing to Tobias Lear in the midst of his Savannah visit, GW observed that at Charleston "the continual hurry into which I was thrown by entertainments —visits—and ceremonies of one kind or another, scarcely allowed me a moment that I could call my own—nor is the case much otherwise here." Outside the two cities "the abominably Sandy & heavy" low-country roads were the principal inconvenience. "My horses (especially the two I bought just before I left Philadelphia, & my old white horse) are much worn down," GW wrote Lear from Savannah, "and I have yet 150 or 200 miles of heavy sand to pass before I fairly get into the upper, & firmer roads" (GW to Lear, 13 May 1791, MeHi).

Monday 16th. Breakfasted at Russells–15 Miles from Spencers. Dined at Garnets 19 further & lodged at Pierces 8 miles more in all, 42 Miles to day.

GW probably dined today with Thomas Garnett (1750–1793) of Effingham County, Ga. Born in Essex County, Va., Garnett married Rachel Willson at Ebenezer Jerusalem Church in Effingham County 8 Jan. 1772 and was commissioned a first lieutenant in the local militia 25 June 1776. Joshua Pearce (Pierce), Jr. (d. 1810), of Effingham County was GW's host for the night. Although his father was a Loyalist during the Revolution, Pearce and two of his brothers fought with the Patriots (MC CALL, 1:72, 139–40, 3:86, 183, 185; CANDLER [1], 1:145, 3:174, 178).

Tuesday 17th. Breakfasted at Skinners 17 Miles–dined at Lamberts 13–and lodged at Waynesborough (wch. was coming 6 miles out of our way) 14 in all 43 Miles. Waynesborough is a small place, but the Seat of the Court of Burkes County–6 or 8 dwelling houses is all it contains; an attempt is making (without much apparent effect) to establish an Accademy at it as is the case also in all the Counties.

Waynesboro, Ga., named in honor of Anthony Wayne, was established by an act of the General Assembly in July 1783. The same act, in obedience to a stipulation made in Georgia's 1777 constitution that schools should "be erected in each county and supported at the general expense of the State," provided for an academy for Burke County at Waynesboro, an academy for Richmond County at Augusta, and a "free school" for Wilkes County at newly created Washington, Ga. (CANDLER [2], 19:248–56, pt.2; KILPATRICK, 4; COULTER, 11–12).

Wednesday 18th.   Breakfasted at Fulchers, 15 Miles from Waynesborough; and within 4 Miles of Augusta met the Govr. (Telfair), Judge Walton, the Attorney Genl., & most of the principal Gentlemen of the place; by whom I was escorted into Town, & recd. under a discharge of Artillery. The distance I came to day was about 32 miles. Dined with a large company at the Governors, & drank Tea there with many well dressed Ladies.

The Road from Savanna to Augusta is, for the most part, through Pine barrans; but more uneven than I had been accustomed to since leavg. Petersburgh in Virginia, especially after riding about 30 Miles from the City of that name; here & there indeed, a piece of Oak land is passed on this road, but of small extent & by no means of the first quality.

On coming in sight of the welcoming party from Augusta, Georgia's temporary capital 1785–95, GW got out of his chariot, mounted a horse, and rode forward to meet Gov. Edward Telfair. After Telfair "congratulated the President on his near approach to the residence of government," Major Gordon and the Augusta horsemen who had accompanied GW from Savannah joined the distinguished citizens of the town to form the procession that escorted GW to his lodgings on Broad Street. The cannon salute that greeted him was fired by Capt. Howell's artillery (HENDERSON, 234–38; JONES AND DUTCHER, 141).

Edward Telfair (c.1735–1807), a wealthy merchant and early Revolutionary War leader, served Georgia in the Continental Congress frequently between 1778 and 1782 and was governor of the state 1786–87 and 1789–93. For today's 4:00 P.M. dinner at his residence, the Grove, Telfair invited "several federal and state Officers," and as so often before, there were "a number of memorable and patriotic toasts." The ladies came to the governor's house this evening for a ball given by his wife, Sally Gibbons Telfair, but GW only "attended for a short time," apparently just long enough to meet the ladies over tea (*Dunlap's American Daily Adv.* [Philadelphia], 16 June 1791).

George Walton (1741–1804), judge of the superior court of Georgia, was, like Telfair, an early supporter of the Patriot cause in Georgia. He attended many sessions of the Continental Congress between 1776 and 1781, was wounded and captured at the seige of Savannah where he fought as a militia colonel, and served as governor of the state 1779–80 and 1789.

Thursday 19th.   Received & answered an Address from the Citizens of Augusta; dined with a large Company of them at their

Court Ho.; and went to an Assembly in the evening at the Accadamy; at which there were between 60 & 70 well dressed ladies.

The address of the Augusta citizens and a copy of GW's reply are in DLC:GW.

About 3:00 P.M. GW reviewed the Augusta Light Horse, and at 4:30 P.M. he attended the public subscription dinner at the Richmond County courthouse, where again "a variety of the most patriotic toasts and sentiments were drank" (*Dunlap's American Daily Adv.* [Philadelphia], 16 June 1791; HENDERSON, 241–42).

This evening's ball was held "in the large room" of the Richmond Academy on Bay Street. According to the *Augusta Chronicle,* the ball was attended by "the largest number of Ladies ever collected at this place" (BELL AND CRABBE, 29).

Friday 20th.　Viewed the ruins, or rather small remns. of the Works which had been erected by the British during the War and taken by the Americans—also the falls, which are about 2 Miles above the Town; and the Town itself.

These falls (as they are called) are nothing more than rapids. They are passable in their present state by boats with Skilful hands, but may at a very small expence be improved, by removing a few rocks only to straighten the passage. Above them there is good boat navigation for many Miles; by which the produce may be, & in some measure is, transported. At this place, i.e., the falls, the good lands begin; & encrease in quality to the westward & No. ward. All below them, except the Interval lands on the River and Rice Swamps wch. extend from them, the whole Country is a Pine barren. The town of Augusta is well laid out with wide & spacious Streets. It stands on a large area of a perfect plain but is not yet thickly built, tho' surprizingly so for the time; for in 1783 there were not more than half a dozen dwelling houses; now there are not less than [   ] containing about [   ] Souls of which about [   ] are blacks. It bids fair to be a large Town being at the head of the *present* navigation, & a fine Country back of it for support, which is settling very fast by Tobacco planters. The culture of which article is encreasing very fast, and bids fair to be the principle export from the State; from this part of it, it certainly will be so.

Augusta, though it covers more ground than Savanna, does not contain as many Inhabitts. the latter having by the late census between 14 & 1500 hundred Whites and about 800 blacks.

Dined at a private dinner with Govr. Telfair to day; and gave him dispatches for the Spanish Govr. of East Florida, respecting the Countenance given by that Governt. to the fugitive Slaves of the Union—wch. dispatches were to be forwarded to Mr. Sea-grove, Collector of St. Mary's, who was requested to be the bearer of them, and instructed to make arrangements for the prevention of these evils and, if possible, for the restoration of the property—especially of those Slaves wch. had gone off since the orders of the Spanish Court to discountenance this practice of recg. them.

Forts Grierson and Cornwallis were erected at Augusta after Loyalist forces occupied the town in June 1780. Both works fell in the spring of 1781 when beseiged by Patriot militia aided by the Continental troops of Henry Lee's Legion (BOATNER [1], 49–51; BOATNER [2], 75–77).

Under the terms of an act passed by the Georgia General Assembly 13 Feb. 1786, the falls of the Savannah River were to have been cleared for naviga-tion and a lock built at the lower end. This improvement scheme collapsed when the land tax that was to finance the work was repealed the following year (JONES AND DUTCHER, 446; CANDLER [2], 19:534–40, pt.2).

Augusta in 1791 was reported to have 250 houses and 1,100 people within its boundaries (JONES AND DUTCHER, 137).

The private dinner with Governor Telfair may have been the occasion for presenting a congratulatory address to GW that Telfair signed today at the statehouse. Telfair's address and a copy of GW's reply are in DLC:GW.

The fugitive slave problem, which GW discussed at length with Telfair during his stay in Augusta, had troubled Georgia planters for years, but particularly since 1783 when Spain regained the Floridas from Great Britain. Under an old Spanish policy any American slave who crossed the St. Marys River into East Florida was granted freedom, and it was only after many protests from the Georgians that authorities in Spain consented to a change. By a letter of 28 Aug. 1790 from Juan Nepomuceno de Quesada, newly appointed governor of East Florida, the American Secretary of State Thomas Jefferson learned that the Spanish monarch had given orders "not to permit, under any pretext, that persons sold in slavery in the United states introduce themselves, as free, into the province of East Florida" (Quesada to Jefferson, 28 Aug. 1790, and Jefferson to José Ignacio de Viar, 27 Oct. 1790, JEFFERSON [1], 17:341n, 638–39).

The new policy, however, did not satisfy Georgia's planters, for it applied only to the future and no mention was made of returning slaves lost since 1783 (Edward Telfair to Thomas Jefferson, 12 Jan. 1790, JEFFERSON [1], 18:491–92). Jefferson was reluctant to push the matter further, considering it a relatively trivial affair that might jeopardize the more important goal of inducing Spain to open the Mississippi River to American traffic, but the final decision was left to GW and Telfair. Jefferson promised the Georgia governor in a letter of 26 Mar. 1791 that when GW reached Augusta "you will have an opportunity of explaining to him the extent of the losses complained of, and how far they could probably be recovered, even were the dispositions of your [Spanish] neighbors favourable to the recovery, and what those disposi-tions may actually be" (JEFFERSON [1], 19:429–33, 519).

Although GW acquiesced in Telfair's arguments, the instructions he wrote today for James Seagrove, collector for the port of St. Marys, Ga., show that he shared much of Jefferson's cautious attitude toward the matter. Seagrove's "first care" was to insure that the Spanish king's new orders to stop sheltering

American slaves were fully enforced by Governor Quesada; his second, to seek the return of any slaves who had fled to Florida since the announcement of the new orders; and his third, to recover the slaves lost since 1783. "This last instruction," GW warned, "will require peculiar delicacy, and must be entered on with caution and circumspection, or not to be taken up at all" (GW to Seagrove, 20 May 1791, DLC:GW).

Seagrove, a Savannah merchant whom GW had named to his rather unremunerative post in Aug. 1789, adhered to GW's injunction. While conferring with Quesada at St. Augustine in early August, he apparently brought up only the first two "cares" and succeeded in making detailed arrangements for returning future fugitives to their masters and in convincing Quesada to issue an order to penalize East Florida inhabitants who harbored runaways. Seagrove, however, failed in the request that he made for immediate restoration of slaves who had entered East Florida since the date of the king's orders. Not "even a single Slave," Quesada replied, had come into his province between the date of the royal orders and their promulgation in East Florida. Even if slaves had fled into Florida, however, his instructions would not allow them to be returned (Seagrove to Quesada, 2 and 7 Aug. 1791, and Quesada to Seagrove, 6 Aug. 1791, all enclosed in Thomas Jefferson to Edward Telfair, 15 Dec. 1791, DLC: Jefferson Papers). Seagrove's skill in carrying out this mission was apparently a factor in his being appointed federal agent to the Creeks in September of this year (SMITH [7], 42–43).

GW's tour of the town today included a stop at the Richmond Academy, where "he honored the examination of the students with his presence, and was pleased to express himself handsomely of their performances" (BELL AND CRABBE, 29; CORDLE, 79–80; HENDERSON, 243–47).

Saturday 21st.   Left Augusta about 6 oclock, and takg. leave of the Governor & principal Gentlemen of the place at the bridge over Savanna river where they had assembled for this purpose, I proceeded in Company with Colos. Hampton & Taylor, & Mr. Lithgow a Committee from Columbia (who had come on to meet & conduct me to that place) & a Mr. Jameson from the Village of Granby on my rout.

Dined at a house about 20 Miles from Augusta and lodged at one Oden about 20 miles farther.

GW crossed the Savannah River bridge into South Carolina "under the salute of Major Gordon's horse and Captain Howell's artillery" (BELL AND CRABBE, 29).

The members of the Columbia committee were Wade Hampton (c.1751–1835), the recently elected sheriff of Camden District; Thomas Taylor (1743–1833), one of the original commissioners of Columbia; and Robert Lithgow (Lythgoe), a newly appointed town commissioner. Hampton and Taylor both distinguished themselves as militia colonels under Thomas Sumter during the latter part of the War of Independence. Earlier in the war Hampton was a junior officer in the South Carolina line, serving until the state fell to the British in 1780. He then took an oath of loyalty to the crown, an oath that he soon broke to join Sumter's partisans. An aggressive land speculator, he became one of the wealthiest planters in the state, served in the United States Congress 1795–97 and 1803–5, and participated as a major general in the War of 1812. Taylor, who with a brother provided the land on which Columbia was laid out in 1786, was a member of the state's first provincial congresses 1775–76, served in the militia in 1779, and joined Sumter as a captain in Aug. 1780. After the war he served frequently in the legislature, and although an opponent of the federal constitution in 1788, he raised an influential voice against nullification in 1830 (TAYLOR, 204–11). Robert Lithgow, apparently a Columbia merchant, was a judge of the Richland County court as well as a town commissioner (GREEN [2], 176).

Granby's representative may be Archibald Jamison, who appears in the 1790 census as a resident of the north part of Orangeburg District, which included Granby; Dr. Van de Vastine Jamison, who is also listed in the northern part of the district, lived near Orangeburg well to the east of Granby (HEADS OF FAMILIES, S.C., 94, 98; NAMES IN S.C., 13 [1966], 52–55).

The house at which GW dined was the Piney Woods House, a log tavern near present-day Trenton, S.C. The house belonged to Capt. Van Swearingen of Edgefield County, a veteran of the Revolution. Swearingen's daughter Frances Swearingen apparently inherited the tavern about this time and ran it with her husband Ezekiel McClendon (NAMES IN S.C., 11 [1964], 44). ODEN: The census of 1790 lists four families of Odens, three of Odums, and one of Odem in Edgefield County (HEADS OF FAMILIES, S.C., 62–63, 65–66). The house is said to have been near present-day Ridge Spring (SALLEY [2], 25).

Sunday 22d.   Rode about 21 Miles to breakfast, and passing through the village of Granby just below the first falls in the Congaree (which was passed in a flat bottomed boat at a rope ferry) I lodged at Columbia, the newly adopted Seat of the Government of South Carolina about 3 miles from it, on the No. side of the river, and 27 from my breakfasting stage.

The whole Road from Augusta to Columbia is a pine barren of the worst sort, being hilly as well as poor. This circumstance added to the distance, length of the Stages, want of water and heat of the day, foundered one of my horses very badly.

Beyond Granby 4 miles, I was met by sevl. Gentlemen of that place & Wynnsborough; and on the banks of the River on the No. Side by a number of others, who escorted me to Columbia.

Breakfast may have been at Lee's Stage Tavern near present-day Batesburg and Leesville (SALLEY [2] 25).

Granby, called Congarees before the Revolution, began in 1718 as an Indian trading post and was at this time the seat of Lexington County. Eclipsed by its newer neighbor, Columbia, the village later disappeared (GREEN [2], 15–22).

GW crossed the Congaree River, a major branch of the Santee, at Friday's ferry, which was started in 1754 by Martin Fridig (Friday) and was purchased in 1785 by Wade Hampton and one of his brothers. On 10 Feb. 1791 the General Assembly authorized the Hamptons to build a toll bridge at the ferry, a project that was to have been completed before GW's arrival, and provided that the president of the United States should cross without paying the toll. Work was begun promptly, but a flood destroyed the bridge as it neared completion (GREEN [2], 113–21).

It was "about sun set" when GW reached the ferry. Nevertheless, "the banks of the river at that place were lined with the neighbouring inhabitants, who anxiously waited for the President's arrival." The gentlemen from Granby and from Winnsboro, a town about 28 miles north of Columbia, met GW before he reached Granby and escorted him without stopping through the village to the ferry. The Winnsboro group was headed by Brig. Gen. Richard Winn (1750–1818), the revolutionary soldier for whom the town was named when it was incorporated in 1785 (*Dunlap's American Dailey Adv.* [Philadelphia], 24 June 1791).

As GW approached the statehouse in Columbia, a body of light horse commanded by a Captain Kershaw "formed on the left, near the edge of the woods, and saluted him with much respect; he was then conducted to a house commodiously prepared for his reception, where a few gentlemen, and the officers of the troops were introduced" (*Dunlap's American Daily Adv.* [Philadelphia], 24 June 1791).

Columbia was ordered laid out as the new state capital by the General Assembly in 1786, and the executive offices were moved there in late 1789. The General Assembly first met in the new statehouse 4 Jan. 1790 (GREEN [2], 146–55).

Monday 23d. Dined at a public dinner in the State house with a number of Gentlemen & Ladies of the Town of Columbia, & Country round about to the amt. of more than 150, of which 50 or 60 were of the latter.

At noon today GW rceived "the gentlemen of Columbia, Granby, Winnsboro', Camden, Statesburgh, Bellville and Orangeburgh, and their vicinity (who were present at Columbia). . . . At four o'clock he was conducted to the room of the representatives in the state-house, where were assembled sixty-seven ladies, who upon his entering the room, arose and made an elegant appearance, to whom he was individually introduced. The ladies were then led by the gentlemen (there being present 153) to the Senate room, where they set down together in a well conceived arrangment: to a farmer's dinner, where plenty abounded." GW left the statehouse after several toasts were given, but returned at 8:00 P.M. for a ball that lasted until 11:00 P.M. (*Dunlap's Daily American Adv.* [Philadelphia], 24 June 1791).

Tuesday 24th. The condition of my foundered horse obliged me to remain at this place, contrary to my intention, this day also.

Columbia is laid out upon a large scale; but, in my opinion, had better been placed on the River below the falls. It is now an uncleared wood, with very few houses in it, and those all wooden ones. The State House (which is also of wood) is a large & commodious building, but unfinished. The Town is on dry, but cannot be called high ground, and though surrounded by Piney & Sandy land, is, itself, good. The State house is near two miles from the River, at the confluence of the broad River & Saluda. From Granby the River is navigable for Craft which will, when the River is a little swelled, carry 3000 bushels of Grain—when at its usual height less, and always some. The River from hence to the Wateree below which it takes the name of the Santee is very crooked; it being, according to the computed distance near 400 miles—Columbia from Charleston is 130 miles.

GW dined today "in private with a few gentlemen" (*Dunlap's American Daily Adv.* [Philadelphia], 24 June 1791). The Broad and Saluda rivers meet at Columbia to form the Congaree, which is joined by the Wateree River lower down to form the Santee.

Wednesday 25th.   Set out at 4 'Oclock for Cambden (the foundered horse being led slowly on). Breakfasted at an indifferent house 22 miles from the town (the first we came to) and reached Cambden about two oclock, 14 miles further where an address was recd. & answered. Dined late with a number of Gentlemen & Ladies at a public dinner. The Road from Columbia to Cambden, excepting a mile or two at each place, goes over the most miserable pine barren I ever saw, being quite a white sand, & very hilly. On the Wateree with in a mile & half of which the town stands the lands are very good—the culture Corn Tobacco & Indigo. Vessels carrying 50 or 60 Hhds. of Tobo. come up to the Ferry at this place at which there is a Tobacco Warehouse.

An address from the citizens of Columbia, Granby, and vicinity, bearing today's date, was presented to GW before he left town by Alexander Gillon (1741–1794), a wealthy merchant and early revolutionary leader who had been embroiled in much controversy as a commodore in the South Carolina navy during the war. Gillon was one of the original commissioners of Columbia, a member of the General Assembly 1783–91, and a member of the United States Congress 1793–94. The address and a copy of GW's reply are in DLC:GW.
   The welcoming address from the citizens of Camden and vicinity apparently was presented to GW by the town's intendant and patriarch, Col. Joseph Kershaw (c.1723–1791), a militia veteran of the Revolution. The address and a copy of GW's reply are in DLC:GW.
   GW, according to local tradition, lodged in Camden at the house of Adam Fowler Brisbane (1754–1797), a Lancaster County justice, and the public dinner was probably at the house of Col. John Chesnut (1743–1813), a veteran of the South Carolina line and prominent indigo planter, who discussed agriculture at some length with GW during his stay in town. A month later GW sent Chesnut a drill plow from Mount Vernon to try in sowing indigo seed (GW to Chesnut, 26 June 1791, anonymous donor). At the dinner GW "was introduced to the ladies individually. The ladies rose after the 2d or 3d toast, and the President sat till near twelve o'clock" (*Md. Journal* [Baltimore], 17 June 1791). In all there were 17 toasts, including 2 given after

GW retired for the night (KIRKLAND AND KENNEDY, 307–12, 351–52; REYNOLDS AND FAUNT, 186, 196–97, 251).

Thursday 26th.   After viewing the british works about Cambden I set out for Charlotte. On my way—two miles from Town—I examined the ground on wch. Genl. Green & Lord Rawden had their Action. The ground had but just been taken by the former —was well chosen—but he not well established in it before he was attacked; which by capturing a Videt was, in some measure by surprize. Six miles further on I came to the ground where Genl. Gates & Lord Cornwallis had their Engagement wch. terminated so unfavourably for the former. As this was a night Meeting of both Armies on their March, & altogether unexpected each formed on the ground they met without any advantage in it on either side it being level & open. Had Genl. Gates been ½ a mile further advanced, an impenitrable Swamp would have prevented the attack which was made on him by the British Army, and afforded him time to have formed his own plans; but having no information of Lord Cornwallis's designs, and perhaps not being apprised of this advantage it was not siezed by him.

Cambden is a small place with appearances of some new buildings. It was much injured by the British whilst in their possession.

After halting at one Suttons 14 M. from Cambden I lodged at James Ingrams 12 Miles farther.

Camden became an important outpost for the British army when it occupied South Carolina after the fall of Charleston in May 1780, and much fighting occurred in the vicinity during the ensuing 12 months. About 2:30 A.M. on 16 Aug. 1780 a British force under Lord Cornwallis and an American one under Maj. Gen. Horatio Gates, both advancing to attack the other at daylight, met by accident in the pine woods north of Camden. Cornwallis, although hampered by swamps on either flank and Saunders Creek less than a mile to his rear, deployed his troops, and at dawn British regulars attacked and routed the Virginia militia at the east end of Gates's position. The battle rapidly became a full-blown disaster for the Americans despite a courageous stand by Maryland Continentals under Johann Kalb (1721–1780), the Bavarian-born French army officer known as Baron de Kalb in America. Kalb, mortally wounded in the fighting, was buried at Camden. On the way out of town today, GW paused "a few minutes" at his grave (*Md. Journal* [Baltimore], 17 June 1791; BOATNER [1], 159–70, 570–71; BOATNER [2], 456–58).

The fortifications that GW viewed in Camden were built by the British after the battle of 16 Aug. 1780. Incorporated into the defenses were Joseph Kershaw's stockaded house, the local jail, and the town's powder magazine (BOATNER [2], 458–60).

The battle between Nathanael Greene and Francis, Lord Rawdon, the young acting commander of British forces in South Carolina and Georgia, occurred 25 April 1781 at Hobkirk's Hill, a sandy ridge where Greene camped with his army to await reinforcements and supplies after finding Camden's defenses too strong for the force that he had on hand. Rawdon in a daring move assembled all available troops in Camden and made a surprise attack on the American camp about 10:00 A.M. on 25 April. Although several Continental units broke, the 5th Virginia Regiment held, enabling Greene to make a short orderly retreat. Rawdon, having failed to destroy the American army, abandoned Camden on 10 May. The British, Greene informed GW 14 May 1781, "left . . . with great precipitation after burning the greater part of their baggage and Stores and even the private property belonging to the Inhabitants. They also burnt the Gaol, mills and several other buildings, and left the Town little better than a heap of rubbish" (MiU-C: Greene Papers; BOATNER [1], 503–8; BOATNER [2], 458–59).

William Loughton Smith of Charleston found Camden when he stopped there on 9 May 1791 to be "a pretty town of about seventy houses and some very good buildings," but at the site of Gates's defeat, he noted, "the marks of balls against the trees" were still visible (SMITH [6], 75).

Jasper Sutton of Lancaster County, stepfather of John Chesnut, settled near Granny's Quarter Creek about 1757. In 1790, according to the census, he held 17 slaves. James Ingram of Lancaster County lived near Hanging Rock, a geological landmark south of present-day Heath Springs. The 1790 census credits him with 3 slaves (SALLEY [2], 27–28; HEADS OF FAMILIES, S.C., 23, 25; KIRKLAND AND KENNEDY, 366; BOATNER [2], 478).

Friday 27th. Left Ingrams about 4 Oclock, and breakfasting at one Barrs 18 miles distant lodged at a Majr. Crawfords 8 Miles farther. About 2 miles from this place I came to the Corner where the No. Carolina line comes to the Rd. from whence the Road is the boundary for 12 Miles more. At Majr. Crawfords I was met by some of the Chiefs of the Cutawba Nation who seemed to be under apprehension that some attempts were making or would be made to deprive them of part of the 40,000 Acres wch. was secured to them by Treaty and wch. is bounded by this Road.

Nathan Barr of Lancaster County kept a tavern a short distance north of the present-day town of Lancaster. During the Revolution he served in the militia as a lieutenant. The head of a household of 11 whites in 1790, he held no slaves (SALLEY [2], 28; HEADS OF FAMILIES, S.C., 24). Robert Crawford (1728–1801) of Lancaster County, a militia officer during the War of Independence, lived on the north side of Waxhaw Creek. His household in 1790 consisted of 11 whites and 15 slaves (SALLEY [2], 28–30; *S.C. Hist. & Geneal. Mag.*, 50 [1949], 57; HEADS OF FAMILIES, S.C., 23).

The Catawba Indians were granted by the Treaty of Augusta in 1763 a tract of land 15 miles square in this part of South Carolina, a total of 144,000 acres embracing the sites of present-day Fort Mill and Rock Hill, S.C. Much of the tract the Catawba leased to white settlers for long terms, but as the settlers grew steadily in number, the Catawbas began to worry about the security of their land. In 1782 Catawba representatives appealed to the Continental Congress to protect their tract from forcible intrusion or alienation "even with their own consent." Congress, deeming the problem to be a South Carolina one, referred it to the state's legislature, which in 1786 took steps to safeguard the Catawbas' rights (BROWN [4], 250–51, 279–94). GW apparently did not interfere in this matter although the Catawba continued to press their case with him. Writing to Secretary of War James McHenry from Mount Vernon 18 July 1796, GW complained that "I have already, been incommoded, at this place, by a visit of several days, from a party of a dozen Cuttawbas; & should wish while I am in this retreat, to avoid a repetition of such guests" (NhD).

The road on the boundary line between the two Carolinas followed that line for eight miles. It did not form part of the Catawba boundary line but did pass through the eastern corner of the tract before entering North Carolina (SALLEY [2], 28–29).

Saturday 28th. Sett off from Crawfords by 4 Oclock and breakfasting at one Harrisons 18 Miles from it & got into Charlotte, 13 miles further, before 3 oclock. Dined with Genl. Polk and a small party invited by him, at a Table prepared for the purpose.

It was not, until I had got near Barrs that I had quit the Piney & Sandy lands—nor until I had got to Crawfords before the Lands took quite a different complexion. Here they began to assume a very rich look.

Charlotte is a very trifling place, though the Court of Mecklenburg is held in it. There is a School (called a College) in it at which, at times there has been 50 or 60 boys.

GW apparently breakfasted with Isaiah Harrison of Mecklenburg County, N.C., who lived between McAlpine and Sixmile creeks a short distance southeast of present-day Pineville, N.C. In 1790 he was head of a household of seven whites and two slaves (RAY, 365, 367, 369, 380–81; HENDERSON, 287, n.2).

Thomas Polk (c.1732–1794) of Mecklenburg County became a justice of the county when it was formed in 1762 and a commissioner and treasurer of Charlotte when it was established six years later. A colonel in the North Carolina line during the War of Independence, he was at Brandywine and Valley Forge but resigned in June 1778 after failing to obtain a desired promotion (Polk to GW, 26 June 1778, DNA: RG 93, Ms. File No. 14498). He was appointed Continental commissary of purchases for the southern army in 1780, and in Feb. 1781 Nathanael Greene designated him brigadier general of militia for the Salisbury, N.C., district. The General Assembly, however, consented to give him only the title of colonel commandant of the district, an action that prompted him to resign in May. Polk lived on a plantation on Sugar Creek near present-day Pineville and in 1790 owned 47 slaves (RAY, 358, 369, 380–81, 414).

Charlotte, reported William Loughton Smith who visited there three weeks before GW did, "does not deserve the name of a town, it consists only of a wretched Court House, and a few dwellings falling to decay. There is a good tavern kept by Mason, where, however, I paid the dearest bill on the road" (SMITH [6], 74). There was a school at Charlotte chartered as Queen's College by the colonial assembly in 1771, and although the charter was subsequently disallowed by the crown, it remained open and was chartered by the state assembly in 1777 as Liberty Hall Academy. By 1780, however, this academy was in "an entire state of decay," and four years later it was moved to Salisbury, N.C. (LEFLER AND NEWSOME, 135).

Sunday 29th. Left Charlotte about 7 Oclock, dined at a Colo. Smiths 15 Miles off, and lodged at a Majr. Fifers 7 Miles farther.

Martin Phifer, Jr. (1756–1837), of Mecklenburg County lived at Red Hill plantation on Irish Buffalo Creek, now in Cabarrus County, a short distance west of present-day Concord. Appointed captain of a company of North Carolina light horse by the General Assembly in April 1776, he was in Continental service from Mar. 1777 to April 1780. His household, according to the 1790 census, consisted of 7 whites and 16 slaves (HENDERSON, 294, n.3; HEITMAN [1], 327; HEADS OF FAMILIES, N.C., 161).

Monday 30th. At 4 Oclock I was out from Major Fifers; and in about 10 Miles at the line which divides ·Mecklenburgh from Rowan Counties, I met a party of horse belonging to the latter, who came from Salisbury to escort me on. (It ought to have been mentioned also that upon my entering the State of No. Carolina, I was met by a Party of the Mecklenburgh horse–but these being Near their homes I dismissed them). I was also met 5 Miles from Salisbury by the Mayor of the Corporation, Judge McKoy, & many others; Mr. Steel, Representative for the district, was so polite as to come all the way to Charlotte to meet me. We arrived at Salisbury about 8 Oclock, to breakfast, 20 miles from Captn. Fifers. The lands between Charlotte & Salisbury are very fine, of a reddish cast and well timbered, with but very little under wood. Between these two places are the first meadows I have seen on the Road since I left Virga.; & here also, we appear to be getting into a Wheat Country.

This day I foundered another of my horses.

Dined at a public dinner givn. by the Citizens of Salisbury; & in the afternoon drank Tea at the same place with about 20 ladies, who had been assembled for the occasion.

Salisbury is but a small place altho' it is the County town, and the district Court is held in it; nor does it appear to be much on the encrease. There is about three hundred Souls in it and tradesmen of different kinds.

The Rowan County Troop of Horse was commanded by Capt. Montfort Stokes (1762–1842), a revolutionary veteran who later became a United States senator and governor of North Carolina. The mayor of Salisbury, Spruce Macay (McCay, McCoy, McKay, McKoy), was appointed a judge for the frontier counties of Washington and Sullivan in 1782 and in Dec. 1790 became a judge of the state superior court, a position that he retained until his death in 1808 (N.C. STATE REC., 16:175, 21:854). John Steele (1764–1815) of Salisbury served in the United States Congress 1789–93 and was appointed comptroller of the United States Treasury by GW in 1796. All three men were prosperous planters and slaveholders. In 1790 Stokes had 15 slaves, Macay 19, and Steele 16 (HEADS OF FAMILIES, N.C., 176).

As GW entered Salisbury today, he "was saluted by about forty boys in uniform, who had chosen officers, and arranged themselves for that purpose," and on arriving at his lodgings, he received a salute from the local artillery company. Breakfast is said to have been at Capt. Edward Yarborough's tavern on Main Street, and the public dinner and the tea at Joseph Hughes's Hotel (HENDERSON, 298–99, 302, 305–6; RUMPLE, 178–81). The dinner concluded with the customary patriotic toasts accompanied by the firing of cannon (*State Gaz. of N.C.* [Edenton], 10 June 1791; HENDERSON, 303–4). An address from the inhabitants of Salisbury was presented to GW apparently during the morning. It and a copy of GW's reply are in DLC:GW.

GW's impressions of Salisbury are confirmed by William Loughton Smith's remarks about the town in his journal. Salisbury, observed Smith who stopped there 6 May 1791, "consists of about forty or fifty straggling houses in an open pretty plain; it looks like a poor place and has but little business. The Court House is not half finished: the town contains about 300 inhabitants among them a great number of children" (SMITH [6], 74).

Tuesday 31st. Left Salisbury about 4 Oclock; at 5 Miles crossed the Yadkin, the principal stream of the Pedee, and breakfasted on the No. Bank (while my Carriages & horses were crossing) at a Mr. Youngs; fed my horses 10 miles farther, at one Reeds; and about 3 oclock (after another halt) arrived at Salem; one of the Moraviann towns 20 miles farther—In all 35 from Salisbury.

The Road between Salisbury & Salem passes over very little good land, and much that is different; being a good deal mixed with Pine, but not Sand.

Salem is a small but neat Village; & like all the rest of the Moravian settlements, is governed by an excellent police—having within itself all kinds of artizans. The number of Souls does not exceed 200.

From Salisbury GW was escorted by the Rowan County Troop of Horse to Long's ferry on the Yadkin River, where he crossed (*State Gaz. of N.C.* [Edenton], 10 June 1791). The Yadkin and the smaller Uwharrie River join in Montgomery County, N.C., to form the Pee Dee River. Young and Reed lived in the part of Rowan County that later became Davidson County. There are several listings for each name in the 1790 Rowan County census (HEADS OF FAMILIES, N.C., 169, 172–76; RUMPLE, 118–22).

On the road to Salem GW was met by three Moravian ministers who had ridden out to greet him, Frederic William Marshall, John David Koehler, and Christian Ludwig Banzien. As the party approached the town, "several tunes were played" by some of the community's renowned musicians, "partly by trumpets and French horns, partly by the trombones." At the Salem Tavern on Main Street, where GW lodged, he stepped out of his chariot and, according to the town's official diary, "greeted those who stood around in a friendly manner, showing his good will especially to the children who were there. Then he talked on various matters with several Brethren who accompanied him to the room that had been prepared for him. At first he said that he was leaving in the morning, but when he heard that the Governor of this State had expressed a wish to wait on him the next day he decided to rest here over one day. He sent word to our musicians that he would like some music during his evening meal, and it was furnished to him" (Salem Diary, 1791, FRIES, 5:2324).

Salem, now part of Winston-Salem, was founded by Moravian settlers in 1776 near two other North Carolina towns previously established by them, Bethabara and Bethania.

[June]

Wednesday June 1st.   Having received information that Governor Martin was on his way to meet me; and would be at Salem this evening, I resolved to await his arrival at this place instead of halting a day at Guilford as I had intended.

Spent the forenoon in visiting the Shops of the different Trades Men—The houses of accomodation for the single men & Sisters of the Fraternity & their place of worship. Invited Six of their principal people to dine with me—and in the evening went to hear them Sing, & perform on a variety of instruments Church music.

In the Afternoon Governor Martin as was expected (with his Secretary) arrived.

Alexander Martin (1740–1807), governor of North Carolina 1782–85 and 1789–92, was a bachelor who lived at Danbury plantation on the Dan River in Rockingham County about 40 miles northeast of Salem. During the War of Independence he served as a colonel in the North Carolina line but resigned in Nov. 1777 after being tried for and acquitted of cowardice at the Battle of Germantown. Guilford Court House was 27 miles east of Salem.

During the morning tour of Salem, GW was especially impressed by the waterworks, a system of pipes that brought water from nearby streams to every house in the town. At 2:00 P.M., a time set by GW, Rev. Frederic William Marshall read and presented him an address from the United Brethren of Wachovia, the official name of the North Carolina Moravians. GW "in the same manner gave his answer, couched in favorable terms" (Salem Diary, FRIES, 5:2324–25; SMITH [6], 73). The Moravian address dated 31 May 1791 is in DLC:GW; GW's answer is in NcWsM, and a copy in DLC:GW.

Governor Martin accompanied GW to the "singstunde [song service] in the evening, the singing being interspersed with instrumental selections, and they expressed their pleasure in it. In the evening the wind instruments were heard again, playing sweetly near the tavern." Music was also furnished for the dinner with the six Brethren (Salem Diary, 1791, FRIES, 5:2325).

Many people from the neighborhood and the other Moravian congregations came to Salem to see GW during his stay in town, and according to the Salem diary, "the President gladly gave them opportunity to gratify their wish" (Salem Diary, FRIES, 5:2325).

Thursday 2d. In company with the Govr. I set out by 4 Oclock for Guilford. Breakfasted at one Dobsons at the distance of eleven Miles from Salem [1] and dined at Guilford 16 Miles farther, where there was a considerable gathering of people who had receivd notice of my intention to be [2] there to day & came to satisfy their curiosity.

On my way I examined the ground on which the Action between Generals Green and Lord Cornwallis commenced and after dinner rode over that where their lines were formed [3] and the scene closed in the retreat of the American forces [4]—The first line of which [5] was advantageously drawn up, and had the Troops done their duty properly, the British must have been sorely galded in their advance, if not defeated.

The Lands between Salem and Guilford are, in places, very fine; but upon the whole can [6] not be called [7] more than midling —some being very [8] bad.

On my approach to this place (Guilford) I was met by a party of light horse which I prevailed on the Governor to dismiss, and to countermand his orders for others to attend me through the State.

William Dobson of Stokes County ran a popular tavern at the site of present-day Kernersville, N.C., where he had settled about 1770. William Loughton Smith, who stopped at Dobson's tavern on the morning of 5 May 1791, reported that he "got a very good breakfast" there. Dobson, he added, "has a very decent house; his wife, who sat down to breakfast with me, is a huge fat woman of about eighty, whom he calls 'Honey' " (SMITH [6], 72).

Guilford Court House, established in 1774 as the seat of Guilford County, was designated 11 years later as site of the town of Martinville, but the small community that developed around the courthouse disappeared after 1809 when the county court moved to nearby Greensboro (ARNETT, 18).

The battle at Guilford Court House occurred 15 Mar. 1781. Having evaded Cornwallis's regulars for three weeks, Nathanael Greene took a stand with his army on the road south of the courthouse and invited attack on the favorable terrain there. When the British advanced, the North Carolina militia in the center of the American front line fired one volley and fled in disorder, but the Continentals on the flanks and in the second line fought well, inflicting heavy casualties on the British until Greene ordered a withdrawal later in the day. Two days after the battle, Cornwallis, having won the field but at the cost of 532 dead and wounded out of a force of about 1,900 men, was obliged to begin retreating toward the coast (BOATNER [1], 460–71; BOATNER [2], 350–54).

"Although the honors of the field did not fall to your lot," GW wrote

Greene 18 April 1781, "I am convinced you deserved them. The chances of War are various and the best concerted measures, and the most flattering prospects may, & often do deceive us, especially while we are in the power of Militia" (owned by Mr. Sol Feinstone, Washington Crossing, Pa.).

In the manuscript of the diary for 2 June–4 July GW made many changes and corrections, inserting words between lines and crossing out parts of the text, apparently intending to recopy the diary. The changes consist primarily of corrections in grammar and syntax. Although a few of the changes were obviously made as GW was writing the entry, the majority of the revisions appear to have been made at a later time, probably after his return from his southern tour. GW's changes have been incorporated into the present text and the original wording of the corrected passages is indicated in numbered notes.

1. "from Salem" inserted above line.
2. "to be" substituted for "of being."
3. "up" deleted.
4. "in the retreat of the American forces" inserted above line.
5. "which" substituted for "the American Troops."
6. "can" inserted above line.
7. "be called" added above line.
8. "being very" inserted above line.

Friday 3d.   Took my leave of the Governr. whose intention was to have atten[d]ed me to the line, but for my request that he would not; and about 4 Oclock proceeded on my journey. Breakfasted at troublesome Iron works (called 15, but which[1] is at least) 17 Miles from Guilford partly in Rain and from my information or for[2] want of it was obliged to travel 12 miles further than I intended to day—to one Gatewoods within two Miles of Dix' ferry over the Dan, at least 30 Miles from the Iron works.

The Lands over which I passed this day were of various qualities and as I approached the Dan, were a good deal covered[3] with pine.

In conversing with the Governor on the State of Politics in No. Carolina I learnt with pleasure that opposition to the Genl. Government, & the discontents of the people were subsiding fast and that he should, so soon as he received the Laws which he had written to the Secretary of State for, issue his proclamation requiring all Officers & members of the Governmt. to take the Oaths prescribed by Law. He seems to condemn the Speculators in Lands and the purchases from the State of Georgia, & thinks as every sensible & disinterested man must that schemes of that sort must involve the Country in trouble—perhaps in blood.

The Troublesome Iron Works, built by William Patrick in 1770, were on Troublesome Creek in southern Rockingham County, about a mile and a half north of present-day Monroeton (POWELL [3], 500; BOATNER [2], 371–72).

William Loughton Smith toured the works on 4 May 1791 and found that "the buildings, large reservoir of water, creek, and the people at work, with the noise of the machinery of the mills and the rapid currents which work them, have a pleasing and singular appearance just as you ascend the hill which overlooks them, after traveling a number of miles through the woods" (SMITH [6], 72). GW apparently lodged with Dudley Gatewood, of Caswell County, who in 1790 had been appointed one of the trustees responsible for extending the navigation of the Roanoke River above the falls (HEADS OF FAMILIES, N.C., 79; N.C. STATE REC., 25:107).

Dix's ferry, located near the site of present-day Danville, Va., was established in 1766 to run from the land of John Dix (died c.1784) on the north side of the Dan River across to Lewis Green's land. By 1777 John Dix owned the land on both banks, and by 1791 the ferry had passed to Col. William Dix of Pittsylvania County, who also kept a tavern nearby (HENING, 8:193, 9:334–35; SMITH [6], 71). The Dan River is a main branch of the Roanoke.

1. "which" inserted above line.
2. "for" inserted above line.
3. "covered" substituted for "grown."

Saturday 4th.   Left Mr. Gatewoods about half after Six oclock and between his house & the Ferry passed the line which divides the States of Virginia and No. Carolina—dining at one Wisoms 16 Miles from the Ferry, lodged at Hallifax old Town. The Road from Dix' ferry to Wisom's, passes over very hilly (& for the most part) indifferent land, being a good deal mixed with pine though it is said here that [1] pine when mixed with Oak, & more especially with [2] hiccory is not indicative of a poor [3] Soil. From Wisom's to Hallifax old Town the Soil is good, & of a reddish cast.

Having this day passed the line of No. Carolina, and of course finished my tour thro' the three Southernmost States a general [4] description of them may be comprised in the [5] few following [6] words.

From the Sea board to [7] the falls of all the Rivers which water this extensive region,[8] the lands, except the Swamps, on the Rivers, and the lesser streams which empty into them; & the interval lands higher up the Rivers [9] is, with but few exceptions, neither more nor less [10] than a continued pine barren [11] very thinly inhabited. The part next the Sea board, for many miles, is a dead level & badly watered. That above it is [12] hilly & not much better watd. but [13] if possible, less valuable on account of its hilliness and because they are [14] more inconvenient to Market supposing them [15] as capable as the lands below [16] of producing [17] Beef Porke Tar, pitch & Turpentine. The Lands above the falls of the several [18] Rivers from information, and as far as [19] my own observation has extended, is of a very superior kind from these [20] being of a greasy red, with large oaks, intermixed with hiccory Chestnut

&ca. producing,[21] Corn Tobo., Wheat, Hemp & other articles in great abundance & are generally [22] thickly inhabited comparitively speaking with those below.

In the lower Country (next the Seaboard) in the States of So. Carolina & Georgia, Rice, as far up as the low Swamps extend is almost the sole article that is raised for market; Some of the planters of which, grow [23] as much Corn as, with the Sweet Potatoes, support their people; The middle Country—that is—between the Rice lands and the falls of the Rivers & a little above them, is cultivated chiefly in Corn & Indigo and the upper Country in Tobacco, Corn, Hemp & in some [24] degree the smaller grains.

It is nearly the same in No. Carolina, with this difference however [25] that, as not much rice is planted there, especially in the Northern parts of the State, Corn, some Indigo, with naval Stores & Porke, are substituted in its place, but as Indo. is on the decline Hemp, Cotton &ca. are comg. in its place.[26]

The Inland navigations of the Rivers of these three States, may be improved (according to the ideas I have formed of the matter) [27] to a very extensive degree—to great & useful purpose and at a very moderate expence compared with the vast utility of the measure; [28] inasmuch as the falls in all of [29] them are trifling and their lengths great; (quite to the Mountns.) [30] penetrating the Country in all directions by their lateral branches [31] and in their present State except at the falls wch. as has been observd before are trifling except that of the Pedee [32] navigable for vessels carrying sevl. Hhds. of Tobo. or other Articles in proportion.

The prices at which the Rice lands in the lower parts of the ⟨st.⟩ [33] are held is very great—those of them wch. have been [34] improved, comd.[35] from 20£ to 30£ Sterlg. £50 has been given for some and from £10 to 15 is the price of it [36] in its rude state. The Pine barrens adjoining these sell from one to two dollars pr. Acre [37] according to Circumstances. The interval Lands on the River below the falls, & above the Rice Swamps also command a good price but not equal to the abe. & the pine barrens less than those below.[38] The lands of the upper Country sell from 4 to 6 or 7 dollars according to the quality and Circumstances thereof.

In the upper part of No. Cara. Wheat is pretty much grown, & the Farmers seem disposed to try Hemp but the Land Carriage is a considerable drawback having between 2 & 300 Miles to carry the produce either to Chs. Town, Petersburgh or Wilmington wch. are their three great Marts though of late Fayettesville receives a gd. deal of the bulky Articles & they are [39] water borne from thence to Wilmington.

Excepting the Towns, (and some Gentlemens Seats along the Road from Charleston to Savanna) [40] there is not, within view of the whole road I travelled [41] from Petersburgh to this place, a single house which has anythg. of an elegant appearance. They are altogether of Wood & chiefly of logs—some [42] indd. have brick chimneys but generally the chimnies [43] are of Split sticks filled with dirt between them.

The accomadations on the whole Road (except in the Towns,[44] and even there, as I was informed [45] for I had no opportunity of Judging, lodgings having been provided for me in them [46] at my own expence) we found extremely indifferent—the houses being small and badly provided either for man or horse; though extra exertions when it was known I was coming,[47] wch. was generally the case, were made to receive me. It is not easy to say on which road—the one I went or the one I came—the entertainment is most indifferent—but with truth it may be added,[48] that both are bad, and to be accounted for from the kind of travellers which use them; which with a few exceptions only on the uppr. Rd.[49] are no other than [50] Waggoners & families removing; who, generally, take their provisions along with them. The people however appear to have abundant means to live well the grounds where they are settled yielding grain in abundance and the natural herbage a multitude of meat with little or no labr. to provide food for the support of their Stock—especially in Georgia where it is said the Cattle live through the winter without any support from the owners of them.

The manners of the people, as far as my observations, and means of information extended, were orderly and Civil. And they appeared to be happy, contented and satisfied with the genl.[51] governmt. under which they were placed. Where the case was otherwise, it was not difficult to trace the cause to some demago[g]ue, or speculating character. In Georgia the dissatisfied part of them at the late treaty with the Ck. Indians were evidently Land Jobbers, who, Maugre every principle of Justice to the Indians [52] & policy to their Country would, for their own immediate emolument, strip the Indns. of all their territory if they could obtain the least countenance to the measure. But it is to be hoped the good sense of the State will set its face against such diabolical attempts: And it is also to be wished and by many it was said it might be expected—that the Sales by that State to what are called the Yazoo Companies would fall through.

The discontents which it was supposed the last Revenue Act

(commonly known by the Excise Law) would create subside as fast as the law is explained and little was said of the Banking Act.

GW apparently dined today with Francis Wisdom (died c.1794) of Pittsylvania County (HEADS OF FAMILIES, VA., 42, 99; SMITH [6], 71).

Halifax Old Town, established as Peytonsburg in 1759, lay south of Elkhorn Creek in eastern Pittsylvania County (GAINES [4], 6). "Halifax Old Town," remarked William Loughton Smith who breakfasted there 3 May 1791, "has no other pretension to the name than by containing two or three old houses, inhabited by some wretched old women" (SMITH [6], 71). GW, nevertheless, found a tavern in which to lodge this night (Richard N. Venable Diary, ViHi). The town no longer exists. LATE TREATY WITH THE CK. INDIANS: See entry for 1 July 1790. YAZOO COMPANIES: See entry for 28 April 1790. LAST REVENUE ACT: "An Act repealing, after the last day of June next, the duties heretofore laid upon Distilled Spirits imported from abroad, and laying others in their stead; and also upon Spirits distilled within the United States, and for appropriating the same" (1 STAT. 199–214 [3 Mar. 1791]). BANKING ACT: "An Act to incorporate the subscribers to the Bank of the United States" (1 STAT. 191–96 [25 Feb. 1791]).

1. "here that" added above line.
2. "with" inserted above line.
3. "a poor" substituted for "the poverty of the."
4. "general" inserted above line.
5. "the" substituted for "a."
6. "following" inserted above line.
7. "the Sea board to" added above line.
8. "this extensive region" substituted for "these three States, quite to the sea board."
9. "than the Rice swamps extend" deleted.
10. "neither more nor less" substituted for "no other."
11. "with" deleted.
12. "That above it is" substituted for "The residue is more."
13. "& not much better watd. but" substituted for "and."
14. "less valuable on account of its hilliness and because they are" substituted for an illegible line; the rest of the substitution reads "because they are hilly & broken &."
15. "supposing them" substituted for "if they are."
16. "as the lands below" inserted above line.
17. "any Thing but" deleted.
18. "several" inserted above line.
19. "as far as" added above line.
20. "superior kind from these" substituted for "different kind."
21. "yielding" inserted above line, however, GW did not cross out "producing."
22. "generally" inserted above line.
23. "grow" substituted for "raise."
24. "some" substituted for "a."
25. "however" inserted above line.
26. "but as Indo. is on the decline Hemp, Cotton &ca. are comg. in its place" added at the end of sentence.

27. "of the matter" inserted above line.
28. "the measure" substituted for "them."
29. "in all of" substituted for "of."
30. "quite to the Mountns." added in parentheses above line.
31. "by their lateral branches" inserted above line.
32. "wch. as has been observd. before are trifling except that of the Pedee" inserted above line for an entry GW made illegible by marking through it.
33. "in the lower parts of the St." inserted above line.
34. "those of them wch. have been" substituted for "that wch. is."
35. "comd." substituted for "is."
36. "is the price of it" inserted above line.
37. "pr. Acre" inserted above line.
38. "& the pine barrens less than those below" inserted above line.
39. "they are" substituted for "is."
40. Parentheses added before "and" and after "Savanna."
41. "I travelled" inserted above line.
42. "some" substituted for "many."
43. "the chimnies" substituted for "they."
44. "in the Towns" substituted for "as before."
45. "was informed" substituted for "am told."
46. "in them" added above line.
47. "when it was known I was coming" substituted for "where I was expected."
48. GW inserted "affirmed" above line but did not mark through "added."
49. "on the uppr. Rd." inserted above line.
50. "no other than" inserted above line.
51. "genl." added above line.
52. "to the Indians" inserted above line.

Sunday 5th. Left the old Town about 4 Oclock A.M.; & breakfasting at one Pridies (after crossing Banister River 1½ Miles) abt. 11 Miles from it, came to Staunton River about 12; where meeting Colo. Isaac Coles (formerly a member of Congress for this district &) who pressing me to it, I went to his house about one mile off to dine and to halt a day, for the refreshment of myself and horses; leaving my Servants and them at one of the usually indifferent Taverns at the Ferry that they might give[1] no trouble, or be inconvenient to a private family.

The Banister River, a branch of the Dan River, was apparently crossed at a bridge near present-day Meadville, Va. (SMITH [6], 71). The Staunton River is the main branch of the Roanoke. "Pridie's," where William Loughton Smith spent the night of 2 May 1791, was in his opinion "a sorry tavern; I had for company an idiot, the landlord's brother, who was himself but one remove from it, and I was waited on by an ugly broken backed old negro woman. My fare was indifferent, and . . . I was kept awake a great part of the night by bugs and fleas, and the united groaning and grunting of hogs under the window" (SMITH [6], 71). The landlord may be Richard Preddy (Priddy), of Halifax County, who appears in the census lists of 1782 and

1785, or Robert Priddy for whom an inventory was recorded in the Halifax County court in 1795 (HEADS OF FAMILIES, VA., 23, 87; TORRENCE, 345).

Isaac Coles of Halifax County (see entry for 26 Dec. 1789) probably met GW at Coles Ferry about ten miles southeast of present-day Brookneal, Va. Coles, observed William Loughton Smith in May, "is a man of genteel fortune, and has a pretty considerable plantation here, with other estates" (SMITH [6], 70).

1. "give" substituted for "be."

Monday 6th. Finding my Horses fared badly at the ferry for want of Grass, & Colo. Coles kindly pressing me to bring them to his Pasture, they were accordingly brought there to take the run of it till night. Dined at this Gentlemans to day also.

The Road from Hallifax old Ct. Ho. or town to Staunton River passes for the most part over thin land a good deal mixed with Pine.

Tuesday 7th. Left Colo. Coles by day break, and breakfasted at Charlotte Ct. Ho. 15 Miles[1] where I was detained sometime to get Shoes put on such horses as had lost them. Proceeded afterwards to Prince Edward Court House 20 Miles further.

The Lands from Coles ferry on[2] Staunton to Charlotte Ct. Ho. are in genl. good; & pretty thickly settled. They are[3] cultivated chiefly in Tobo. wheat & Corn, with Oats & flax. The Houses (tho' none elegt.) are in genl. decent, & bespeak[4] good livers; being for the most part weatherboarded & Shingled, with brick Chimnies—but from Charlotte Ct. Ho.[5] to Prince Edward Ct. Ho. the lands are of an inferior quality with few[6] inhabitants[7] in sight of the Road.[8] It is said they are thick settled off it, the Roads by keeping the Ridges pass on the most indifferent ground.

Richard N. Venable (1763–1838), a Peytonsburg lawyer who was at Charlotte Court House on 6 June 1791, noted in his diary the "great Anxiety in the people to see Genl. Washington. Strange is the impulse which is felt by almost every breast, to see the face of a Great good man & one of whom we have heard much spoken" (Richard N. Venable Diary, ViHi). Established in 1765, Charlotte Court House remains the seat of Charlotte County (GAINES [2], 7).

Prince Edward Court House, established 1754, was at the site of present-day Worsham, about six miles south of Farmville, the present county seat (GAINES [3], 41). Venable was at Prince Edward Court House today and reported that the way where GW was expected to pass was crowded with people "anxious to see the Saviour of their Country & object of their love" (Richard N. Venable Diary, ViHi).

1. "15 Miles" inserted above line.
2. "Coles ferry on" inserted above line.
3. "They are" substituted for "&."

4. "bespeak" substituted for "indicative of."
5. "Ct. Ho." added above line.
6. "or no" deleted.
7. "with" deleted.
8. "Tho" deleted.

Wednesday 8th.   Left Prince Edward Ct. Ho. as soon as it was well light, & breakfasted at one Treadways 13 Miles off.[1] Dined at Cumberland Ct. Ho. 14 Miles further and lodged at Moores Tavern within 2 miles from [2] Carters ferry over James River.

The road from Prince Edward Court Ho. to Treadways was very thickly settled, although the land appeared thin, and the growth in a great degree pine, & from Treadways to Cumberland Ct. Ho. they were equally well settled on better land, less mixed, and in places not mixed at all,[3] with pine. The buildings appear to be better.

Cumberland Court House (now Cumberland, Va.) was established as the seat of Cumberland County in 1777. GW probably dined at the Effingham Tavern, a popular establishment opposite the courthouse (GAINES [5], 39–41; W.P.A. [4], 490).

Carter's ferry became the site of Cartersville in Oct. 1790, when the Virginia General Assembly authorized trustees to lay out the town on 27 acres of land that John Woodson (d. 1793) owned at the south landing. Established in 1744, the ferry was originally designated to run between "the land of Ashford Hughes, on the north side of James river," and "the land of Robert Carter" (apparently the deceased Robert "King" Carter) on the opposite shore, but by 1763 the land on both banks, including the ferry, belonged to the Hughes family, the family into which John Woodson married (HENING, 5:250, 6:16, 13:155, 171; WMQ, 1st ser., 11 [1902–3], 52–53).

1. "off" inserted above line.
2. "from" substituted for "of."
3. "in" deleted.

Thursday 9th.   Set off very early from Moores but the proper ferry boat being hauled up, we were a tedious while crossing in one of the Boats used in the navigation of the River; being obliged to carry one carriage at a time, without horses [1] & crossways the Boat on planks. Breakfasted at a Widow pains 17 [2] Miles on the No. side of the River, and lodged at a Mrs. Jordans a private house where we were kindly entertained and to which we were driven by necessity having Rode not less than 25 miles from our breakfasting stage through very bad Roads in a very sultry day witht. any refreshments [3] & by missing the right road had got to it.

From the River to the Widow Pains, & thence to Andersons bridge over the North Anna Branch of Pamunky, the Lands are not good, nor thickly settled on the Road but are a good deal mixd. w. Pine; [4] nor does the Soil & growth promise much (except in places) from thence for several miles further; but afterwards, throughout the County of Louisa, which is entered after passing the Bridge, the River over which it is made dividing it from Goochland they are much better & continued so with little exception quite to Mrs. Jordons.

GW apparently breakfasted with Jane (Jean) Smith Chichester Payne of White Hall, Goochland County, widow of Col. John Payne (1713–1784), whom she married in 1757 (*Va. Mag.*, 6 [1898–99], 315–16, 427–38, 31 [1923], 174). GW's lodgings were at Jerdone Castle, home of Sarah Macon Jerdone of Louisa County, whose husband Francis Jerdone (1720–1771) had been a prominent merchant (*Va. Mag.*, 62 [1954], 208; WMQ, 1st ser., 6 [1897–98], 37–38).

GW was mistaken about Anderson's bridge. It was on the South Anna River near the mouth of Deep Creek and lay entirely in Louisa County, being about a mile northeast of the Goochland County line. The South Anna roughly parallels the boundary between Louisa and Goochland but forms no part of it. The North Anna River, which GW crossed the next day, forms Louisa's northern border with Orange and Spotsylvania counties. Both the South and North Anna are branches of the Pamunkey River.

1. "without horses" added above line.
2. "17" substituted for "15."
3. "witht. any refreshments" inserted above line.
4. "but are a good deal mixd. w. Pine" inserted above line.

Friday 10th.   Left Mrs. Jordans early, & breakfasting at one Johnstons 7 Miles off reached Fredericksburgh after another (short) halt about 3 Oclock & dined and lodged at my Sister Lewis's.

The Lands from Mrs. Jordans to Johnsons, and from thence for several miles further are good but not rich afterwards (as you approach nearer to Rappahannock River) they appear to be of a thinner quality & more inclined to black Jacks.

GW reported to Tobias Lear that he arrived at Fredericksburg "in good health, but with horses much worn down" (GW to Lear, 12 June 1791, CSmH). BLACK JACKS: *Quercus marilandica,* blackjack oak, is adapted to barren and sterile soils.

Saturday 11th.   After a dinner with several Gentlemen whom my Sister had envited to dine with me I crossed the Rappahannock & proceeded to Stafford Ct. House where I lodged.

Sunday 12th.   About Sun rise we were off – breakfasted at Dumfries and arrived at Mt. Vn. to D.

From[1] Monday 13th. until Monday the 27th. (being the day I had appointed to meet the Commissioners under the residence Act, at George town) I remained at home; and spent my time in daily rides to my severl. farms and in receiving[2] many visits.

    1. "From" inserted at the beginning of the line.
    2. "in receiving" substituted for "during it had."

Monday 27th.   Left Mount Vernon for George town before Six Oclock; and according to appointment met the Commissioners at that place by 9—then[1] calling together[2] the Proprietors of the Lands on which the federal City was proposed[3] to be built who had agreed to cede them on certain conditions at the last meeting I had[4] with them at this place but from some misconception with respect to the extension of their grants had refused to make conveyances and recapitulating the principles upon which my comns. to them at the former meeting were made and giving some explanations of the present State of matters & the consequences of delay in this business they readily waved their objections & agd. to convey to the utmost ex[t]ent of what was required.

After their meetings with GW in late March 1791 five of the landholders protested the large size of the proposed Federal City. GW called this meeting today to warn the owners, some of whom were speculators, that there might not be a capital there at all if they did not abide by their agreement (see entry for 30 Mar. 1791).

    1. "at that place by 9—then" substituted for "and."
    2. "together" inserted above line.
    3. "proposed" substituted for "intended."
    4. "I had" added above line.

Tuesday 28th.   Whilst the Commissioners were engaged in preparing the Deeds to be signed by the subscribers[1] this afternoon, I went out with Majrs. L'Enfant and Ellicot to take a more perfect view of the ground, in order to decide finally on the spots on which to place the public buildings and to direct how[2] a line which was to leave out a Spring (commonly known by the name of the Cool Spring) belonging to Majr. Stoddart should be run.

THE SPOTS: GW accepted L'Enfant's suggestions for placing the Capitol "on the west end of Jenkins heights which Stand as a pedestal waiting for a monument," while the president's house, "situated on that ridge which attracted your attention . . . will see *10* or *12* Miles down the potowmak," thus "adding to the sumptousness of a palace the convenience of a house and the agreableness of a country seat" (L'Enfant to GW, 22 June 1791, DLC: L'Enfant Papers).

    1. "to be signed by the subscribers" added in place of "for signing."
    2. "how" inserted above line.

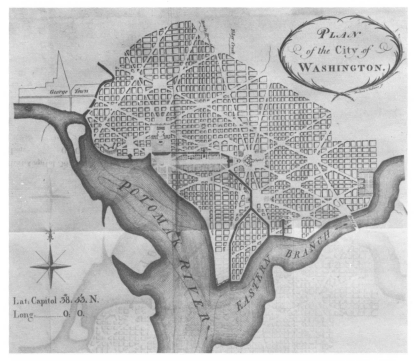

Original plan for the city of Washington (1800) from Kenneth W. Leish's *White House,* New York, 1972. (Boston Athenaeum)

Wednesday 29th.   The Deeds which remained unexecuted yesterday were signed to day and the Dowers of their respective wives [1] acknowledged according to Law.

This being [2] accomplished, I called the Several subscribers together and made known to them the Spots on which I meant to place the buildings for the P. & Executive departments of the Government and for the Legislature of Do. A Plan [3] was also laid before them of the City in order to convey to them general ideas of the City—but they were told that some deviations from it [4] would take place—particularly in the diagonal Streets or avenues, which would not be so numerous; and in the removal of the Presidents house more westerly for the advantage of higher ground. They were also told that a Town house, or exchange wd. be placed on some convenient ground between the spots designed for the public buildgs. before mentioned. And it was with much pleasure that a general approbation of the measure seemed to pervade the whole.

On 22 June 1791 L'Enfant sent GW "the plan here anexed, for the Intended federal city," regretting that "due to the shortness of time . . . together with the hurry with which I had it drawn" it was neither complete nor entirely accurate (DLC: L'Enfant Papers).

1. "of their respective wives" substituted for "of the several different."
2. "done" deleted.
3. "Plan" inserted for "Map."
4. "from it" inserted above line.

Thursday 30th.   The business which brot. me to George town being finished & the Comrs. instructed with respect to the mode of carrying the plan into effect—I set off this morning a little after 4 oclock in the prosecution of my journey towards Philadelphia; and being desirous of seeing the nature of the Country North of Georgetown, and along the upper road, I resolved to pass through Frederick town [1] in Maryland & York & Lancaster in Pennsylvania & accordingly.

Breakfasted at a small village called Willamsburgh in which stands the Ct. House of Montgomerie County 14 M. from George Town. Dined at one Peters's tavern 20 [2] miles further and arrived at Frederick town about Sun down—the whole [3] distance 43 miles.

The road by wch. I passed [4] is rather hilly, but the lands are good, and well timbered. From Monocasy to F. T. 4 Miles they are very rich & fine.[5] The Country is thicker [6] settled and the farm Houses of a better kind [7] than I expected to find. This is [8] well calculated for small grain of wch. a good deal is now [9] on the grd. but thin—owing as the farmers think [10] to the extreme drought of the Spring [11] though more, it appeared to me, to the frosts & want of Snow to cover their fds. during the Winter.

Williamsburg (now Rockville), Md., was established in 1784 but had been the site of the Montgomery County courthouse since 1777. Peter's tavern was on Bennett Run near present-day Urbanna, Md. Its proprietor may have been Enoch or Richard Peter of Frederick County, Md. (HOWARD & SHRIVER, MAP; HEADS OF FAMILIES, MD., 68, 72).

GW arrived in Frederick at 7:25 P.M. "So sudden and unexpected was the visit of this amiable and illustrious character," declared a newspaper account, "as to leave it entirely out of the power of the citizens to make the necessary preparations for his reception. On notice being given of his arrival, the bells of the Lutheran and Calvinist churches were rung—fifteen rounds from Cannon-Hill were discharged—and a band of music serenaded him in the evening. He was politely invited to spend the succeeding day in town; but answered (as an apology for not accepting the invitation), that public business obliged him to hasten to Philadelphia" (*The Mail, or Claypoole's Daily Adv.* [Philadelphia], 9 July 1791, BAKER [2], 224–25). GW is said to have lodged at Brother's tavern (DIARIES, 4:201, n.3); Henry Brother was a tavernkeeper in Frederick in the 1790s (SCHARF [3], 1:486–87).

1. "town" added above line.
2. "20" substituted for "9."
3. "the whole" inserted above line.
4. "by wch. I passed" added above line.
5. This sentence inserted above line.
6. "is thicker" substituted for "better."
7. "and the farm Houses of a better kind" added above line.
8. "This is" substituted for "it, being."
9. "is now" substituted for "was."
10. "think" substituted for "thought."
11. "of the Spring" inserted for "but."

[July]

Friday July 1st.   Received an Address from the Inhabitants of Frederick town and about 7 Oclock left it. Dined at one Cookerlys 13 Miles off & lodged at Tawny town only 12 Miles farther—being detained at the first stage by rain and to answer the address wch. had been presented to me [1] in the Morning. Tawny town is but a small place with only the Street through wch. the road passes, built on. The buildings are principally of wood. Between Cookerly's & this place we crossed the little & great Pipe Cks.—branches of Monocasy.[2] The latter (about half way betwn. them) [3] is a considerable stream and from its appearance capable of Navigation. The lands over wch. we travelled this day are remarkably fine—but, as was observed yesterday the fields were [4] thinly covered with grain—owing, as I conceive, to the cause already mentioned. The farm houses are good mostly of Stone [5] and the settlers compact with good Barns & meadows appertaining to them.

The address of the Frederick inhabitants and a copy of GW's answer are in DLC:GW. Cookerly's tavern, located at the site of present-day New Midway, Md., may have been operated by Jacob or John Cookerly of Frederick County, Md. (HOWARD & SHRIVER, MAP; HEADS OF FAMILIES, MD., 59, 61). Taneytown, Md., was founded about 1740.
1. "to me" added above line.
2. "branches of Monocasy" inserted above line.
3. "betwn. them" and parentheses inserted above line.
4. "the fields were" added above line.
5. "mostly of Stone" inserted above line.

Saturday 2d.   Set out a little after 4 Oclock and in [1] abt. 6 Miles crossed the line wch. divides the States of Maryland & Pennsylvania— [2] the Trees on wch.[3] are so grown up [4] tht. I could not perceive the opening [5] though I kept a lookout for it. 9 Miles from Tawny town, Littles town is past, they are of similar appe.

but the latter is [6] more insignificant than the former. Seven Miles farther we came to Hanover (commonly called McAlisters town) a very pretty village with a number of good brick Houses & Mechanics [7] in it. At this place, in a good Inn, we breakfasted and in 18 Miles more reached York Town [8] where we dined and lodged.

The Country from Tawny Town to York town [9] is exceedingly pleasant thickly inhabited [10] and well improvd. The dwelling Houses, Barns & meadows being good. After dinner in company with Colo. Hartley & other Gentlemen I walked through the principal Streets of the Town and drank Tea at Col. Hartleys. The Ct. Ho. was illuminated.

Littlestown, Pa., was founded in 1765 by the German settler Peter Klein; Hanover, Pa., was founded about 1763 by Col. Richard McAllister (d. 1795), a Scotch-Irish innkeeper who served in the Continental Army during the War of Independence.

GW arrived at York about 2:00 P.M. and lodged at Baltzer Spangler's tavern on Market Street. He was greeted by the ringing of bells and a salute from the Independent Light Infantry Company commanded by Capt. George Hay. "In the evening," reported one citizen, "there was a general illumination, and in the court house in each pane was set a light" (JORDAN, 46–48).

1. "with" deleted.
2. "but" deleted.
3. "on wch." inserted above line.
4. "up" inserted above line.
5. "the opening" substituted for "it."
6. "they are of similar appe. but the latter is" inserted above line.
7. "& Mechanics" added above line.
8. "Town" added at end of line.
9. "town" inserted above line.
10. "thickly inhabited" inserted above line.

Sunday 3d.   Received, and answered an address from the Inhabitants of York town—& there being no Episcopal Minister *present* [1] in the place, I went to hear morning Service performed [2] in the Dutch reformed Church—which, being in that language [3] not a word of which I understood I was in no danger of becoming [4] a proselyte to its religion [5] by the eloquence of the Preacher.

After Service, accompanied by Colo. Hartley & half a dozen other Gentlemen, I set off for Lancaster. Dined at Wrights Ferry where I was met by Genl. Hand [6] & many of the principal characters of Lancaster [7] & escorted to the town by them, arriving [8] abt. 6 oclock.

The Country from York to Lancaster is [9] very fine, thick settled, and well cultivated. About the ferry they are extremely [10] rich.

The river Susquehannah at this place is more than a mile wide and some pretty views on the banks of[11] it.

The address from the citizens of York and a copy of GW's reply are in DLC: GW. The church service was at the German Reformed Church on Market Street that burned six years later (JORDAN, 47).

Wright's ferry, established by the Quaker settler John Wright after his arrival in 1726, crossed the Susquehanna River to Columbia, Pa., the town laid off by his grandson Samuel Wright in 1788. This area was one of several proposed in 1789 as the site of the new national capital (ESPENSHADE, 42, 210–11).

Edward Hand (1744–1802), physician, politician, and former major general in the Continental service, was appointed an inspector of revenue earlier this year by GW (Hand to GW, 18 April 1791, DNA: RG 59, Misc. Letters).

The time of GW's arrival in Lancaster, according to one of the town's residents, was 6:30 P.M. "The colors," she reported, "were fixed in the cupola of the Court House, and all the Bells rung at his entrance" (LANDIS [2], 222).

1. *"present"* inserted above line.
2. "performed" added above line.
3. "that language" substituted for "Dutch ⟨illegible⟩."
4. "becoming" substituted for "being ad."
5. "religion" added above line.
6. "Genl. Hand" inserted above line.
7. "Lancaster" substituted for "that place."
8. "arriving" substituted for "whence I arrived."
9. "in general" deleted.
10. "extremely" inserted above line for "very."
11. "the banks of" added above line.

Monday 4th.   This being the Anniversary of American Independence and being kindly requested to do it, I agreed to halt here this day and partake of the entertainment which was preparing for the celebration of it. In the fore noon I walked about[1] the town. At half passed 2 oclock I received, and answered an address from the Corporation and[2] the complimts. of the Clergy of different denominations. Dined between 3 & 4 Oclock. Drank Tea with Mrs. Hand about

"This morning before day the cannon was fired, the drums beat and fifes played" (LANDIS [2], 222). The address from the inhabitants of Lancaster is in DLC:GW, and GW's answer is in PHi: William Smith Papers. A copy of the reply can also be found in DLC:GW. The dinner was held in the Lancaster County courthouse. The tea given by Catharine Ewing Hand (d. 1805) was apparently attended by a number of the town's ladies (LANDIS [2], 222).

With this entry GW's account of his southern tour ends. He returned to Philadelphia on 6 July 1791, his approach being announced as it had been so often during the past weeks "by the firing of cannon, and the ringing of bells" (*Dunlap's American Daily Adv.* [Philadelphia], 7 July 1791).

1. "about" substituted for "down."
2. "received" deleted.

Whiskey Insurrection

September–October 1794

EDITORIAL NOTE. GW's brief journal for 30 Sept.–20 Oct. 1794 records his journey from Philadelphia to western Pennsylvania with the militia raised to suppress the so-called Whiskey Insurrection that erupted in the fall of 1794 in the Pennsylvania counties of Westmoreland, Fayette, Washington, and Allegheny. The Excise Act, passed by Congress 3 Mar. 1791, had imposed substantial duties on domestically distilled spirits and provided an elaborate system for efficient collection.[1] Under the law the United States was divided into fourteen districts or surveys, each under a supervisor of the revenue. Inspectors were to be appointed for each district to serve under the supervisor and an elaborate system of penalties and forfeitures was devised to deal with infractions of the law. Considered as a necessary revenue measure by the Federalists, the legislation did not have an easy passage through Congress. Such antiadministration congressmen as Josiah Parker maintained that the excise would "convulse the Government; it will let loose a swarm of harpies, who, under the denomination of revenue officers, will range through the country, prying into every man's house and affairs, and like a Macedonian phalanx bear down all before them." In Sen. William Maclay's view the measure was "the most execrable system that ever was framed against the liberty of a people. . . . War and bloodshed are the most likely consequence of all this."[2]

Public opposition to the collection of the excise was evident before 1794. Popular enough with affluent easterners, the laws

[1] "An Act repealing, after the last day of June next, the duties heretofore laid upon Distilled Spirits imported from abroad, and laying others in their stead; and also upon Spirits distilled within the United States, and for appropriating the same" (1 STAT. 199–214 [3 Mar. 1791]). Two additional acts, passed in 1792 and 1794, supplemented the original Excise Act: "An Act concerning the Duties on Spirits distilled within the United States" (1 STAT. 267–71 [8 May 1792]); and "An Act making further provision for securing and collecting the Duties on foreign and domestic distilled Spirits, Stills, Wines and Teas" (1 STAT. 378–81 [5 June 1794]).

[2] ANNALS OF CONGRESS, 2:1891–92; MACLAY, 375–76, 377.

evoked only sullen compliance in western counties of the southern and middle states where small distilleries abounded and there were large numbers of individually operated stills. Already disenchanted with the course of events under the new government—the drain of specie to the east, an Indian policy considered ineffectual by frontier areas, the operation of the militia laws, failure to open the Mississippi to western trade—westerners made the excise law the focus for dissatisfaction.

Sporadic outbreaks of opposition in 1792 prompted GW to issue a proclamation, 15 Sept. 1792, condemning activities that tended "to obstruct the operation of the laws of the United States for raising a revenue upon spirits distilled within the same."[3]

Over the next two years opposition continued to grow, with much of the agitation centered in the four western counties of Pennsylvania—Washington, Westmoreland, Fayette, and Allegheny—constituting the state's federal Survey No. 4. Beginning peacefully enough with petitions and memorials requesting repeal, in July 1794 the situation suddenly erupted into violence. The immediate cause of the outbreak was the attempt by federal revenue officers to serve processes issued by the United States District Court at Philadelphia against distillers who had not registered the previous year. One of the provisions of the excise law which westerners found most obnoxious was the requirement that such cases be tried in a district court, usually held at a considerable distance from the residence of the accused. Although legislation was pending to remedy the situation, United States Marshal David Lenox was sent to western Pennsylvania to serve the processes under the original law. He presented the documents without incident in Fayette, Cumberland, and Bedford counties, but in Westmoreland on 15 July 1794 while he was accompanied on his rounds by Col. John Neville, inspector of the revenue for Survey No. 4, he met armed opposition. Quickly serving as many of his processes as possible, he retreated to Pittsburgh. Somewhat later in the day, Neville's house on Bower Hill was attacked by

[3] The proclamation appeared in the *National Gazette*, 29 Sept. 1792. For opposition to the excise before the summer of 1794, see Hamilton to GW, 5 Aug. 1794, DLC: Hamilton Papers; FINDLEY; BALDWIN [3], 76–104; HAMILTON [2], 12:305–10, 311–13, 330–33, 336–42, 344–47. On 24 Feb. 1794 GW issued another proclamation offering a reward for the apprehension of members of a band of armed men who had attacked the collector for Westmoreland and Fayette counties (*Pittsburgh Gaz.*, 22 Mar. 1794).

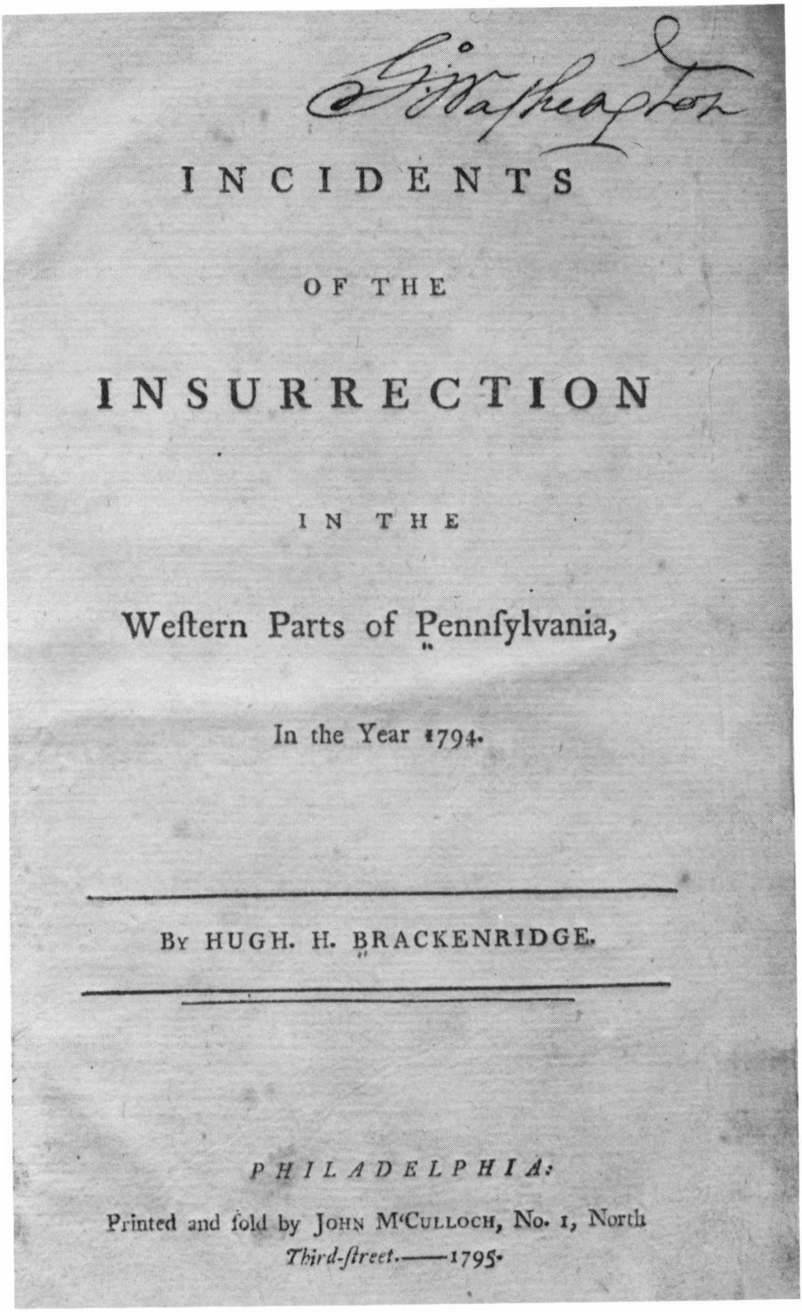

INCIDENTS

OF THE

INSURRECTION

IN THE

Weſtern Parts of Pennſylvania,

In the Year 1794.

By HUGH. H. BRACKENRIDGE.

PHILADELPHIA:

Printed and ſold by John M'Culloch, No. 1, North
Third-ſtreet.——1795.

Title page of Hugh H. Brackenridge's account of the Whiskey Insurrection, from Washington's library. (Boston Athenaeum) a group of armed men and Neville appealed for state militia to put down the rioters. On 17 July the house was again attacked and this time burned.[4]

Word of the violence quickly reached Philadelphia, and on 2 Aug. GW and members of the cabinet met with Gov. Thomas Mifflin and state officials Jared Ingersoll, attorney general, Thomas McKean, chief justice, and Alexander Dallas, secretary of the commonwealth, to consider whether the situation warranted calling out the Pennsylvania militia—a step the state officials plainly opposed.[5] According to an account by Secretary of State Edmund Randolph, the cabinet advised GW to present information on the violence in Westmoreland to one of the associate justices of the Supreme Court or to the district judge of Pennsylvania. "This step was urged by the necessity of understanding without delay all the means, vested in the President for suppressing the progress of the mischief. A caution, however, was prescribed to the attorney-general, who submitted the documents to the judge; not to express to him the most distant wish in the President, that the certificate should be granted." GW decided the documents should be presented to Associate Justice James Wilson. Hamilton advised that if Wilson issued the required certificate, "it will follow that a competent force of Militia should be called forth and employed to suppress the insurrection and support the Civil Authority." A "competent force" appeared to Hamilton to be 12,000 militia. Since Mifflin had stated in the 2 Aug. conference that Pennsylvania's militia forces would be inadequate, Hamilton advised that New Jersey, Maryland, and Virginia also be requested to furnish troops. Associate Justice James Wilson issued the required certificate on 4 Aug. stating that the evidence laid before him indicated that "in the counties of Washington and Alleghany in Pennsylvania, Laws of the United States are opposed, and the Execution thereof obstructed by Combinations too powerful to be suppressed by the ordinary

---

[4] For the attacks on Bower Hill, see BALDWIN [3], 110–28; Hamilton to GW, 5 Aug. 1794, DLC: Hamilton Papers; FINDLEY, 84–91.

[5] PA. ARCH., 2d ser., 4:122–24. Probably the best account of the progress of the insurrection to the beginning of August is Hamilton's lengthy and detailed description of events in his letter to GW of 5 Aug. 1794, DLC: Hamilton Papers. The letter was printed in *Dunlap and Claypoole's American Daily Advertiser* [Philadelphia], 21 Aug. 1794.

Course of judicial Proceedings, or by the Powers vested in the Marshal of that District."[6]

On 7 Aug. GW issued a proclamation recapitulating the events in Pennsylvania's western counties and, citing as his authority the 2 May 1792 Militia Act, stated his determination "under the circumstances of the case, to take measures for calling forth the Militia . . . and I have accordingly determined to do so, feeling the deepest regret for the occasion, but withal, the most solemn conviction, that the essential interests of the Union demand it." All persons "being insurgents, as aforesaid," were commanded "on or before the first day of September next, to disperse and retire peaceably to their respective abodes."[7] Gov. Thomas Mifflin issued a similar proclamation on the same day, promising full support of the state government, and Henry Knox sent a circular letter, also dated 7 Aug., to the governors of Pennsylvania, New Jersey, Maryland, and Virginia, requesting those states to supply a total of 12,950 militia.[8]

In a final effort to restore order, GW appointed three federal commissioners to meet with the insurgents—Atty. Gen. William Bradford, Federalist Sen. James Ross of Washington County, and Jasper Yeates, associate justice of the Pennsylvania Supreme Court.[9] On 21–23 Aug. the commissioners met at Pittsburgh with a committee of conference representing the western Pennsylvania

[6] Randolph to GW, 5 Aug. 1794, and Hamilton to GW, 2 Aug. 1794, DLC:GW; Wilson to GW, 4 Aug. 1794, DNA: RG 46, President's Messages. Wilson was consulted in compliance with Section 2 of "An Act to provide for calling forth the Militia to execute the laws of the Union, suppress insurrections, and repel invasions" (1 STAT. 264–65 [2 May 1792]). This section provided "that whenever the laws of the United States shall be opposed, or the execution thereof·obstructed, in any state, by combinations too powerful to be suppressed by the ordinary course of judicial proceedings, or by the powers vested in the marshals by this act, the same being notified to the President of the United States, by an associate justice or the district judge, it shall be lawful for the President of the United States to call forth the militia of such state to suppress such combinations, and to cause the laws to be duly executed." See also Randolph to GW, 5 Aug. 1794, DLC:GW.

[7] PA. ARCH., 2d ser., 4:105–8.

[8] PA. ARCH., 2d ser., 4:104–5, 108–10.

[9] Copies of Edmund Randolph's instructions to the commissioners, 8 Aug. 1794, are in DLC: Pa. Miscellany, Whiskey Rebellion. See also ASP, MISC., 1:86–87; PA. ARCH., 2d ser., 4:116–18. A similar state commission, appointed by Mifflin, consisted of Thomas McKean and William Irvine.

counties, followed by a second meeting 1–2 Sept., and received some assurances that the committee would work toward restoring order. It was soon evident that the committee of conference's conciliatory attitude was not shared by their constituents. During September the commissioners' reports to Philadelphia grew more pessimistic.[10] Incidents of violence increased, and it appeared that resistance was spreading to western Virginia and Maryland and even eastward in Pennsylvania.[11] On 24 Sept. after their return to Philadelphia the three federal commissioners submitted a detailed report on conditions in western Pennsylvania, reaching the ominous conclusion that "there is no probability that the acts for raising a revenue on distilled spirits and stills can at present be enforced by the usual course of civil authority, and that some more competent force is necessary to cause the laws to be duly executed. . . . This opinion . . . is confirmed by that which is entertained by many intelligent and influential persons, officers of justice and others resident in the western counties, who have lately informed one of the commissioners that whatever assurances might be given, it was, in their judgment, absolutely necessary

[10] PA. ARCH., 2d ser., 4:155–64, 168–77, 179, 180–82, 198–201. See also BRACKENRIDGE [2], 100–107. The committee of conference was appointed by a meeting of delegates from Westmoreland, Fayette, Allegheny, Washington, and part of Bedford counties, Pa., and Ohio County, Va., on 14 Aug. at a meeting at Parkinson's Ferry (Williamsport) on the Monongahela River. The committee consisted of 15 members, including such prominent western Pennsylvania leaders as David Bradford, Albert Gallatin, and Hugh Henry Brackenridge.

[11] During August and September reports of local meetings, musters of local irregular troops, and addresses against the excise multiplied. Liberty poles, the favorite revolutionary device of the insurgents, appeared in western Pennsylvania townships. For accounts of the sporadic outbreaks of violence in Maryland and Virginia during these months, see the *Gazette of the United States* [Philadelphia], 3 Sept. 1794; GALLATIN, 13; VSP, 7:29, 267; *Va. Gaz.* [Richmond], 15, 29 Sept. 1794. On 23 July leading radicals held an inflammatory meeting at Mingo Creek Presbyterian Church (BALDWIN [3], 129–37; FINDLEY, 91–93). On 26 July the Pittsburgh-Philadelphia post was held up near Greensburg and letters from Pittsburgh residents condemning the insurrection were seized and retaliation carried out against the writers. At the end of July a muster was held on Braddock's Field, 8 miles from Pittsburgh, at which 5,000 or 6,000 opponents of the excise gathered to listen to inflammatory speeches and engage in target practice (BALDWIN [3], 141–55; FINDLEY, 98–101). For an account of events from the Federalist point of view, see Hamilton to GW, 5 Aug. 1794, DLC: Hamilton Papers.

that the civil authority should be aided by a military force in order to secure a due execution of the laws." [12]

In the view of the administration, further conciliatory measures would be useless. On 25 Sept. GW issued a proclamation stating that since he had hoped that "the combinations against the Constitution and the Laws of the United States, in certain of the Western counties of Pennsylvania would yield to time and reflection, I thought it sufficient, in the first instance, rather to take measures for calling for the militia, than immediately to embody them; but the moment is now come, when the overtures of forgiveness, with no other condition, than a submission to Law, have been only partially accepted—when every form of conciliation not inconsistent with the being of Government, has been adopted without effect . . . when, therefore, Government is set at defiance, the contest being whether a small portion of the United States shall dictate to the whole union, and at the expence of those, who desire peace, indulge a desperate ambition; Now therefore I, George Washington, President of the United States, in obedience to that high and irresistible duty, consigned to me by the Constitution, 'to take care that the laws be faithfully executed;' deploring that the American name should be sullied by the outrages of citizens on their own Government; . . . but resolved . . . to reduce the refractory to a due subordination to the law; Do Hereby declare and make known, that with a satisfaction, which can be equalled only by the merits of the Militia summoned into service from the States of New-Jersey, Pennsylvania, Maryland, and Virginia, I have received intelligence of their patriotic alacrity, in obeying the call of the present, tho' painful, yet commanding necessity; that a force, which, according to every reasonable expectation, is adequate to the exigency, is already in motion to the scene of disaffection; . . . And I do, moreover, exhort all individuals, officers, and bodies of men, to contemplate with abhorrence the measures leading directly or indirectly to those crimes, which produce this resort to military coercion. . . . And lastly, I again warn all persons, whomsoever and wheresoever, not to abet, aid, or comfort the Insurgents aforesaid, as they will answer the contrary at their peril." [13]

[12] PA. ARCH., 2d ser., 4:293–302.
[13] *Gaz. of the U.S.* [Philadelphia], 25 Sept. 1794.

GW decided to accompany the troops at least as far as Carlisle and to decide later whether to continue further on the march.[14]

[14] GW to William A. Washington, 28 Sept. 1794, PPRF. In response to GW's proclamation of 7 Aug., the governors of Pennsylvania, Maryland, Virginia, and New Jersey had already issued proclamations calling out the militia of their respective states; Thomas Mifflin's proclamation is dated 7 Aug.; Thomas S. Lee's, 14 Aug.; Henry Lee's, 16 Aug.; Richard Howell's, 16 Sept. (PA. ARCH., 2d ser., 4:114, 131–33, 136–37, 258–60; *Pa. Gaz.* [Philadelphia], 24 Sept. 1794) .

September

Tuesday 30th.   Having determined from the Report of the Commissioners, who were appointed to meet the Insurgents in the Western Counties in the State of Pennsylvania, and from other circumstances—to repair to the places appointed for the Rendezvous, of the Militia of New Jersey Pennsylvania Maryland & Virginia; I left the City of Philadelphia about half past ten oclock this forenoon accompanied by Colo. Hamilton (Secretary of the Treasury) & my private Secretary. Dined at Norris Town and lodged at a place called the Trap—the first 17, and the latter 25 Miles from Philadelphia.

At Norris Town we passed a detachment of Militia who were preparing to march for the rendezvous at Carlisle—and at the Trap, late in the evening, we were overtaken by Major Stagg principal Clerk in the Department of War with letters from Genl. Wayne & the Western Army containing official & pleasing accounts of his engagement with the Indians near the British Post

Bartholomew Dandridge, Jr., Washington's secretary, by John Trumbull. (American National Bank and Trust Company of Chattanooga, Tennessee)

at the Rapids of the Miami of the Lake and of his having destroyed all the Indian Settlements on that River in the vicinity of the said Post quite up to the grand Glaize—the quantity not less than 5000 acres—and the Stores &ca. of Colo. McGee the British Agent of Indian Affairs a mile or two from the Garrison.

PRIVATE SECRETARY: Bartholomew Dandridge, Jr., Mrs. Washington's nephew, had succeeded Tobias Lear as GW's secretary in mid-1793.

The Trappe was the name given to a small German settlement and to the area surrounding it. It was on the Germantown Road about nine miles from Pottsgrove.

John Stagg (1758–1803), of New York, had served during the Revolution in Malcolm's Additional Continental Regiment, in Spencer's Additional Continental Regiment, and as brigade major of Conway's Brigade. He was now chief clerk in the War Department. The message he brought GW was a letter of 28 Aug. 1794 from Maj. Gen. Anthony Wayne to Secretary of War Henry Knox describing his decisive victory over some 2,000 Indians at Fallen Timbers near the Maumee Rapids on 20 Aug. After their defeat the Indians, with Wayne's army in close pursuit, had fled to Fort Miami, a small British garrison at the rapids of the Maumee. Although to the Indians' consternation Maj. William Campbell, the fort's commanding officer, did not open the gates to Britain's Indian allies, he and Wayne engaged in an acrimonious exchange of letters concerning Wayne's approach to the fort, copies of which were submitted with Wayne's letter of 28 Aug. Wayne's dispatch had been received in Philadelphia 30 Sept., and in view of its importance Edmund Randolph immediately sent Stagg to carry news of the victory to GW (Randolph to GW, 30 Sept. 1794, "½ past 1 o'Clock," DLC:GW). MCGEE: Alexander McKee (see entry for 20 Oct. 1770) was now British deputy agent for Indian affairs in the area of Detroit. McKee was with the Indians during their retreat from Wayne's victorious army.

October

1st. Left the Trap early, and breakfasting at Potts grove 11 Miles we reach Reading to Dinner 19 Miles farther where we found several detachmts. of Infantry & Cavalry preparing for their March to Carlisle.

Pottsgrove (Pottstown), on the northeast bank of the Schuylkill River, at this time contained about 90 dwellings, "several . . . neat and commodious," and a Quaker meetinghouse (SCOTT [2]). Quartermaster John Hugg Clunn found it "a fine Village, some elegant buildings and the Streets broad" (CLUNN, 47). During the Revolution, GW had his headquarters at Pottsgrove 21–26 Sept. 1777.

2d. An accident happening to one of my horses occasiond. my setting out, later than was intended. I got off in time, however, to make a halt (to bait my horses) at Womeldorfs 14 miles and to view the Canal from Myers town towards Lebanon—and the Locks between the two places; which (four adjoining each other, in the dissent from the Summit ground along the Tulpihockin; built of Brick;) appeared admirably constructed. Reached Lebanon at Night 28 miles.

Womelsdorf (Middletown) in Berks County, Pa., was a "flourishing town . . . containing about 40 dwellings, and a German Luthern and Calvinist church, united" (scott [2]). Clunn counted "about 50 Houses mostly built of log. The Church was built by the Lutheran's & Presbyterian's for their joint use" (clunn, 48).

Myerstown, Dauphin County, Pa., was about 77 miles from Philadelphia on the north side of Tulpehocken Creek, a few miles below the canal. The canal was part of a construction project of the Schuylkill and Susquehanna Navigation Company and connected Quitipihilla Creek and Tulpehocken Creek (*Pa. Mag.,* 71 [1947], 48, n.25). Quartermaster John Hugg Clunn of the New Jersey militia, visiting the area on 8 Oct. 1794, found Myerstown to be "a Village built of Log. Rode on by the Canal. The Lock is remarkably curious. An Irishman . . . very humbly pulld of his Hatt and asked if I knew the Custom when Gent. came to see the Works. I saw plainly it was 2/ out of my pocket & without further ceremony gave it him—took another look thought it worth 4/" (clunn, 48). Another New Jersey officer noted that the "canal is already dug ten miles, in which are five locks, to embrace thirty feet; that they are executed in a masterly manner—that in the distance already done there is a great number of elegant arched bridges over the canal, wherever it goes across the road. There are now employed 600 hands at it, and every prospect of succeeding in this part of the bold enterprise" (ford [6], 81). Lebanon, in Dauphin County, at this time consisted of 2 churches and about 40 houses, mostly built of log (clunn, 48).

3d. Breakfasted at Humels T. 14 M. and dined and lodged at Harrisburgh on the Banks of the Susquehanna 23 miles from Lebanon.

At Harrisburgh we found the first Regiment of New Jersey (about 560 strong) commd. by Colo. Turner drawn out to receive me. Passed along the line, to my Quarters—and after dinner walked through and round the Town which is considerable for its age (of about 8 or 9 years). The Susquehanna at this place abounds in the Rockfish of 12 or 15 Inches in length & a fish which they call Salmon.

Hummelstown, Dauphin County, ten miles east of Harrisburg, had around 90 buildings and a German Lutheran church (scott [2]).

Harrisburg at this time "is regularly laid out, and contains upwards of 300 houses; several of these are neat, commodious dwellings; some of brick, and others of stone; a handsome brick court houses, a stone jail, & a German church" (SCOTT [2]).

TURNER: The 1st New Jersey Regiment was under the command of Lt. Col. Francis Davenport (GOULD, 181). Apparently no Colonel Turner accompanied the New Jersey troops. GW may have meant to write "Forman." Lt. Col. Jonathan Forman was in command of the 3d New Jersey Regiment, infantry, and New Jersey militia (CLUNN, 58, n.80). Captain Gould notes this day that he, Colonel Forman, and another militia officer "accepted an invitation from the President to take a glass of wine with him (GOULD, 178).

After his arrival in Harrisburg, a group of the town's citizens presented GW with an address supporting the government. GW replied before his departure early on 4 Oct. (DLC:GW; *Gaz. of the U.S.*, 16 Oct. 1794).

4th.   Forded the Susquehanna; nearly a mile wide, including the Island—at the lower end of wch. the road crosses it.

On the Cumberland Side I found a detachment of the Phila-delphia light horse ready to receive, and escort me to Carlisle 17 miles; where I arrived at about 11 Oclock. Two miles short of it, I met the Governors of Pennsylvania & New Jersey with all the Cavalry that had rendezvouzed at that place drawn up—passed them—and the Infantry of Pennsylvania before I alighted at my quarters.

Traveling the same route in 1783–84, Johann David Schoepf observed that the Susquehanna at Harrisburg was "three quarters of a mile wide, but in the summer months so shallow that only canoes can cross; horses and wagons ford over. In the middle are a few small islands, called Harris's and also Turkey Islands" (SCHOEPF, 1:212). Captain Gould noted today that the troops "suffered much with the cold in crossing [the Susquehanna], it being a very cold morning. The President, General Washington, forded the river in a coach—drove it himself, &c." (GOULD, 179).

The detachment of the Philadelphia Light Horse had left Carlisle at 3:00 A.M. and met GW just after he crossed the river (*Dunlap's American Daily Adv.* [Philadelphia], 17 Oct. 1794).

At Carlisle, GW found a town "regularly laid out, consisting of several parallel streets, crossed by others at right angles. It contains upwards of 400 dwellings, chiefly of stone and brick. The public buildings are, a college, a jail, a handsome brick court-house, which stands in the centre of the town; and four houses for public worship" (SCOTT [2]). During the Revolution, Carlisle Barracks had been an ordnance depot and in 1791 had been designated as a general rendezvous for federal troops and supplies. It is estimated that during the insurrection between 10,000 and 15,000 troops encamped on the common (TOUSEY, 164–65).

There was "the greatest vieing between the New Jersey and Pennsylvania horse," Captain Ford of the New Jersey troops noted, as to "who should be first on the ground to receive the President. At ten o'clock, the signal for mounting came, and away went the horse" (FORD [6], 85). At 12 o'clock it was announced that the president was approaching. "Immediately the 3 troops from Philadelphia, Gurney's and Macpherson's battalions, and the artillery paraded. The horse marched down the road about two miles, followed by the Jersey cavalry in great numbers. We were drawn up on the right of the road, when our beloved Washington approached on horseback in a traveling dress, attended by his Secretary, &c. As he passed our troop, he pulled off his hat, and in the most respectful manner bowed to the officers and men; and in this manner passed the line. . . . As soon as the President passed, his escort followed, we joined the train, and entered the town whose inhabitants seemed anxious to see this very great and good man; crowds were assembled in the streets, but their admiration was silent. In this manner the President passed to the front of the camp, where the troops were assembled in front of the tents; the line of artillery, horse and infantry, appeared in the most perfect order; the greatest silence was observed" ("Notes on the March from September 30, until October 29, 1794," PA. ARCH., 2d ser., 4:361).

While at Carlisle, GW and his party occupied two houses belonging to Ephraim Blaine (1741–1804), former commissary general in the Continental Army. Blaine and his family not only provided lodging but also meals and hostelry service for the president and his staff (FREEMAN, 7:202, n.212).

Governor of New Jersey Richard Howell (1754–1802) was born in Newark, Del., but moved with his family to Cumberland County, N.J. He studied law there and was admitted to the bar. In 1775 he joined the 2d New Jersey Regiment as a captain, served as brigade major with Stark's Brigade in 1776, and again with the 2d New Jersey Regiment until his resignation in 1779. He became an active Federalist and was elected governor of New Jersey in 1793, serving until 1801. Something of a poet, Howell is credited with having composed the stanzas in honor of GW for the president's reception at Assanpink Bridge on his way to New York in April 1789 (see also AGNEW, 221–30).

5th. – Sunday.   Went to the Presbiterian Meeting and heard Doctr. Davidson Preach a political Sermon, recommendatory of order & good government; and the excellence of that of the United States.

The First Presbyterian Church of Carlisle was on the northeast corner of the town's center square. In 1785 Dr. Robert Davidson (d. 1812) had been called to the church's pulpit (NEVIN, 238). Dr. Davidson was an outspoken critic of the rebellion. In a sermon of 28 Sept. 1794 he had railed against the "sinners" who had taken up arms against their government. "But if they will *resist,* and involve themselves in the *guilt* of rebellion, they deserve not to be pitied nor spared" (BALDWIN [3], 226).

6th. to the 12th.   Employed in Organizing the several detachments, which had come in from different Counties of this State, in a very disjointed & loose manner; or rather I ought to have said in urging & assisting Genl. Mifflin to do it; as I no otherwise took the command of the Troops than to press them forward, and to provide them with necessaries for their March, as well, & as far, as our means would admit.[1]

To effect these purposes, I appointed General Hand Adjutant General on the 7th.[2]

On the 9th. William Findley and David Redick—deputed by the Committee of Safety (as it is designated) which met on the 2d. of this month at Parkinson Ferry arrived in Camp with the Resolutions of the said Committee; and to give information of the State of things in the four Western Counties of Pennsylvania to wit—Washington Fayette Westd. & Alligany in order to see if it would prevent the March of the Army into them.[3]

At 10 oclock I had a meeting with these persons in presence of Govr. Howell (of New Jersey) the Secretary of the Treasury, Colo. Hamilton, & Mr. Dandridge: Govr. Mifflin was invited to be present, but excused himself on acct. of business.

I told the Deputies that by one of the Resolutions it would appear that they were empowered to give information of the disposition & of the existing state of matters in the four Counties above men[tioned]; that I was ready to hear & would listen patiently, and with candour to what they had to say.

Mr. Findley began. He confined his information to such parts of the four Counties as he was best acquainted with; referring to Mr. Reddick for a recital of what fell within his knowledge, in the other parts of these Counties.

The substance of Mr. Findleys communications were as follows

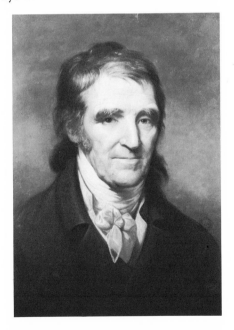

Rembrandt Peale's portrait of Congressman William Findley of Pennsylvania. (Independence National Historical Park Collection)

—viz.—That the People in the parts where he was best acquainted, had seen there folly; and he believed were disposed to submit to the Laws; that he thought, but could not undertake to be responsible, for the re-establishment of the public Offices for the Collection of the Taxes on distilled spirits, & Stills—intimating however, that it might be best *for the present,* & until the peoples minds were a little more tranquilized, to hold the Office of Inspection at Pitsburgh under the protection—or at least under the influence of the Garrison; That he thought the Distillers would either enter their stills or would put them down; That the Civil authority was beginning to recover its tone; & enumerated some instances of it; That the ignorance, & general want of information among the people far exceeded any thing he had any conception of; That it was not merely the excise law their opposition was aimed at, but to all law, & Government; and to the Officers of Government; and that the situation in which he had been, & the life he had led for sometime, was such, that rather than go through it again, he would prefer quitting this scene altogether.

Mr. Redicks information was similar to the above; except as to the three last recitals—on wch. I do not recollect that he expressed any sentiment further than that the situation of those who were not in the opposition to government whilst the frenzy was at its height, were obliged to sleep with their Arms by their bed Sides every night; not knowing but that before Morning they might have occasion to use them in defence of their persons, or their properties.

He added, that for a long time after the riots commenced, and until lately, the distrust of one another was such, that even friends were affraid to communicate their sentiments to each other; That by whispers this was brought about; and growing bolder as they became more communicative they found their strength, and that there was a general disposition not only to acquiesce under, but to support the Laws—and he gave some instances also of Magistrates enforcing them.

He said the People of those Counties believed that the opposition to the Excise law—or at least that their dereliction to it, in every other part of the U. States was similar to their own, and that no Troops could be got to March against them for the purpose of coercion; that every acct. until very lately, of Troops marching against them was disbelieved; & supposed to be the fabricated tales of governmental men; That now they had got alarmed; That many were disposing of their property at an under rate, in order to leave the Country, and added (I think) that they wd. go to Detroit. That no person of any consequence, except one, but what had availed themselves of the proffered amnesty; That those who were still in the opposition, and obnoxious to the laws, were Men of little or no property, & cared but little where they resided; That he did not believe there was the least intention in them to oppose the Army; & that there was not three rounds of ammunition for them in all the Western Country. He (& I think Mr. Findley also) was apprehensive that the resentments of the Army might be productive of treatment to some of these people that might be attended with disagreeable consequences; & on that account seemed to deprecate the March of it: declaring however, that it was their wish, if the people did not give proofs of un-equivocal submission, that it might not stop short of its object.

After hearing what both had to say, I briefly told them—That it had been the earnest wish of governmt. to bring the people of those counties to a sense of their duty, by mild, & lenient means; That for the purpose of representing to their sober reflection the fatal consequences of such conduct Commissioners had been sent amongst them that they might be warned, in time, of what must follow, if they persevered in their opposition to the laws; but that coercion wou'd not be resorted to except in the dernier resort: but, that the season of the year made it indispensible that prepara-tion for it should keep pace with the propositions that had been made; That it was unnecessary for me to enumerate the trans-actions of those people (as they related to the proceedings of government) forasmuch as they knew them as well as I did; That the measure which they were not witness to the adoption of was not less painful than expensive—Was inconvenient, & dis-tressing—in every point of view; but as I considered the support of the Laws as an object of the first magnitude, and the greatest part of the expense had already been incurred, that nothing Short of the most unequivocal *proofs* of absolute Submission should retard the March of the army into the Western counties, in order to convince them that the government could, & would enforce obedience to the laws—not suffering them to be insulted with impunity. Being asked again what proofs would be required, I answered, they knew as well as I did, what was due to justice & example. They understood my meaning—and asked if they might have another interview. I appointed five oclock in the After noon for it. At this second Meeting there was little more than a repeti-[ti]on of what had passed in the forenoon; and it being again mentioned that all the *principal* characters, except one, in the Western counties who had been in the opposition, had submitted to the propositions—I was induced, seeing them in the Street the next day, to ask Mr. Redick who that one was?—telling him at the same time I required no disclosure that he did not feel himself entirely free to make. He requested a little time to think of it, and asked for another meeting—which was appointed at 5 oclock that afternoon—which took place accordingly when he said David Bradford[4] was the person he had alluded to in his former conversations.

He requested to know if a Meeting of the people, by their deputies, would be permitted by the Army at any given point, on their March into that Country (with fresh evidence of the sincerity of their disposition to acquiesce in whatever might be required). I replied I saw no objection to it, provided they came unarmed; but to be cautious that not a gun was fired, as there could be no answering for consequences in this case. I assured them that every possible care should be taken to keep the Troops from offering them any insult or damage and that those who always had been subordinate to the Laws, & such as had availed themselves of the amnesty, should not be injured in their persons or property; and that the treatment of the rest would depend upon their own conduct. That the Army, unless opposed, did not mean to act as executioners, or bring offenders to a Military Tribunal; but merely to aid the civil Magistrates, with whom offences would lye. Thus endd. the matter.

On the 10th. the light & legionary Corps under the immediate Command of Majr. McPherson[5]—The Jersey Regiment & Guirney's[6] from Philadelphia commenced their March under the Orders of Governor Howell; and the day following the whole body of Cavalry (except the three Troops of Phila. Horse commanded by Captn. Dunlap,[7] as part of the legion above mentioned) under Genl. White[8]—a new formed Corp of Independant uniform Companies under [   ] & several other Corps under the Command of Govr. Mifflin Marched—all for the rendezvous at Bedford.

The Rank of the principal officers of the Army being first settled by me, as follow.

First—Govr. Lee of Virginia to be commander in chief if I do not go out myself.

Second—Govr. Mifflen.

Third—Govr. Howell.

Fourth—Majr. General Danl. Morgan,[9] or Majr. Genl. Irvine,[10] according to the dates of their ⟨Militia⟩ Commissions.

The Brigadiers in like manner, according to seniority.[11]

1. On 6 Oct. GW wrote Secretary of State Edmund Randolph: "As I reached this place Saturday only, & have no very precise information from the Insurgent counties I cannot decide definitely at this moment whether I shall proceed into them with the Troops, or return in time for the meeting of Congress. As soon as I can ascertain the true state of the Troops & other matters at this place I intend to proceed to Williamsport, & probably from thence to Fort Cumberland and Bedford; at one or other of which my ulterior resolution must be taken and in either case communications must be prepared for the meeting of Congress" (NIC). By 9 Oct. he had decided to go on with the army at least as far as Bedford and ordered Bartholomew Dandridge to request that Henry Knox send on "sundry Articles such as tents, &ca. &ca." Knox was to forward only such articles "as you conceive will be *absolutely necessary* for the President's accommodation. . . . As the President will be going, if he proceeds, into the Country of Whiskey he proposes to make use of that liquor for his drink, and presuming that beef and bread will be furnished by the contractors he requires no supply of these Articles from you" (Dandridge to Knox, 9 Oct. 1794, List of Supplies, 11 Oct. 1794, and GW to Daniel Morgan, 8 Oct. 1794, DLC:GW).

On 6 Oct. the citizens of Carlisle presented an address to GW, supporting the laws of the United States. The address and GW's reply are in DLC:GW. See also *Gaz. of the U.S.* [Philadelphia], 18 Oct. 1794.

2. After an outstanding military career during the Revolution, Edward Hand (see entry for 3 July 1791) resumed the practice of medicine. In GW's view he was "a sensible and judicious man . . . and was esteemed a pretty good Officer. But, if I collect rightly, not a very active one" (WRITINGS, 31: 510).

On 8 Oct. there was a general review of the New Jersey horse "at a sight of which the President was pleased to express his great satisfaction" (FORD [6], 85).

3. On 2 Oct. a meeting was held at Parkinson's Ferry, composed largely of the same individuals as the 14 Aug. meeting. Its members agreed to a series of conciliatory resolutions in an effort to prevent the army from marching into the insurgent counties and sent two emissaries to present the resolutions to GW at Carlisle (GALLATIN, 22–23). For the resolutions and a description of the Parkinson's Ferry meeting, see BRACKENRIDGE [1], 253–54.

William Findley (1750–1821), one of the meeting's representatives, was born in Ireland, immigrated to the United States, and settled in Westmoreland County, Pa., soon after the Revolution. He served in the Pennsylvania legislature, in the 1790 state constitutional convention, and in 1791 was elected to the United States House of Representatives where he became a vigorous opponent of administration policies (PA. ARCH., 2d ser., 4:41n). His colleague, David Redick (d. 1805), also a native of Ireland, had settled in Washington County, Pa., where he began the practice of law in 1782. He was a member of the Pennsylvania Supreme Executive Council 1786, vice-president of the state 1788–89, and prothonotary of Washington County in 1794 (PA. ARCH., 2d ser., 4:39n).

Findley and Redick approached Carlisle with some apprehension, having heard on their way "alarming accounts of the army, rendezvoused at that place, being very ungovernable and exceedingly inflamed against the people of the western country indiscriminately"; they were even strongly advised by nearby residents not to venture into the town. After their arrival in the town, "having early in the morning waited on the President to deliver the papers, and obtained an appointment for an interview, we withdrew in a short time. This was to have been expected; it was about seven o'clock; but before ten the report was current through both the town and the army, that the President had driven us out in six minutes, and was not to see us again; and notwithstanding the President's established character for discretion and politeness, and the frequent interviews to which we were admitted, this ridiculous story was believed by many in the army" (FINDLEY, 140–42). When they met GW to deliver the resolutions, he was alone and received them well. After a short conversation he informed them he had some pressing duties and after breakfast "was going to see a division of the army march" but would see them at ten. For Findley's account of the succeeding meeting, much more detailed than GW's, see FINDLEY, 169–89. As the second meeting drew to a close, the representatives expressed a wish that GW would remain with the army if it continued on its western march. "He replied on this occasion, that if when at Bedford he discovered that his presence would be necessary, and he was not under the necessity of returning to Philadelphia, he possibly would stay with the army, if it advanced into the western country.

"I do not pretend that we were treated with attention, from any peculiar attachment to us, whether that was so or not is a matter of no importance in this case. The attention however that he paid to us was the result of sound discretion. He was anxious to prevent bloodshed, and at the same time to enforce due submission to the laws, with as little trouble as possible. . . . The President was very sensible of the inflammatory and ungovernable disposition that had discovered itself in the army before he arrived at Carlisle, and he had not only laboured incessantly to remove that spirit and prevent its effects, but he was solicitous also to remove our fears. As often as we suggested apprehensions of danger from that quarter, he consoled us with assurances of good discipline and subordination to the laws being enforced, and of the disorderly corps being dispersed among such as were more orderly, or if that would not do, that they should be discharged with infamy. Orders were actually given to this effect, and at least in some instances punctually executed" (FINDLEY, 187–88).

For a description of various incidents involving the behavior of the soldiers toward the civilian population, see BRACKENRIDGE [2], pt.2, 30–33; FORD [6], 84; FINDLEY, 143–44.

Findley was correct in believing that other, and contradictory, versions of the meeting were circulating. Capt. David Ford of the New Jersey militia noted that the "committee consisted of the damned scoundrel Finley, who most certainly was the first founder of the opposition to law in the four western counties, and of a Mr. Reddick. . . . The President received them; coldly told them he was determined . . . to march the army to the seat of rebellion, and told them, if they met with the least resistance, he would not answer for the consequences. This stern reply seemed to discompose the old villan, and to please every federalist" (FORD [6], 86).

4. David Bradford, one of the most popular and vocal of the insurgent leaders, was a native of Maryland but moved to Washington County, Pa., in 1773 or 1774 and was admitted to the Pennsylvania bar in 1783. He was elected to the Pennsylvania General Assembly in 1792. Bradford, who was specifically exempted from the amnesty extended to the other insurgents

after order was restored, eventually fled to Louisiana (PA. ARCH., 2d ser., 4: 333–34; MULKEARN AND PUGH, 322).

5. William MacPherson (1756–1813), a native of Philadelphia, was a graduate of Princeton. He had served as an officer in the British army before the Revolution but joined the Continental Army in 1779. In Sept. 1789 GW appointed him surveyor for the port of Philadelphia; in 1792, Philadelphia port inspector; and in 1793, Philadelphia naval officer (EXECUTIVE JOURNAL, 1:25, 104, 143, 144). During the Whiskey Insurrection he was in command of a battalion of Philadelphia volunteers called "MacPherson's Blues" (PA. ARCH., 2d ser., 4:317).

6. Francis Gurney (1738–1815), a native of Bucks County, Pa., served in the French and Indian War, and as a colonel with Pennsylvania troops during the Revolution. After the war he became a merchant in Philadelphia and for a time was warden of the post of Philadelphia, a Philadelphia alderman, and a member of the city council (*Pa. Mag.*, 47 [1923], 175–76). In 1794 he was in command of the 1st Regiment of the Philadelphia Brigade with the rank of colonel. Apparently Gurney had considerable difficulty maintaining discipline among his troops, for GW wrote Hamilton, 26 Oct., on his way back to Philadelphia, that "I heard great complaints of Gurney's Corps (& some of the Artillery) along the road to Strasburgh. . . . In some places, I was told they did not leave a plate, a spoon, a glass or a knife; and this owing, in a great measure I was informed, to their being left without Officers. At *most* if not *all* the encampments, I found the fences in a manner burnt up. I pray you to mention this to Govr. Mifflin" (DLC: Hamilton Papers).

7. John Dunlap (1744–1812), born in County Tyrone, Ire., came to the United States as a child and was apprenticed to his uncle, William Dunlap, a prominent Philadelphia printer. In 1771 he became printer of the *Pennsylvania Packet* and in 1784 joined with David C. Claypoole to publish the paper as a daily. Dunlap & Claypoole were printers to the Continental Congress during the Confederation and in 1794 were publishing the *Daily Advertiser* in Philadelphia. Dunlap had served in the 1st Troop of Philadelphia Light Horse during the Revolution and was captain of the troop during the insurrection (PA. ARCH., 2d ser., 4:324; THOMAS, 386–87, 393–94).

8. In 1793 Anthony Walton White moved from New York to New Brunswick, N.J., and in 1794 was commissioned brigadier general of cavalry in the campaign against the whiskey insurgents (*Pa. Mag.*, 47 [1923], 172–73). See also entry for 1 Jan. 1787.

9. After the Revolution, Daniel Morgan had returned to his estate Saratoga in Frederick County (see entry for 3 Sept. 1784). Now 58 and plagued by ill health, he came out of retirement to serve with the Virginia militia in the 1794 campaign. After the insurrection was repressed, he remained in command of some 1,500 troops which remained in western Pennsylvania to keep order during the winter of 1794–95.

10. William Irvine, who held the rank of major general in the Pennsylvania militia, was in command of a brigade composed of troops from Cumberland and Franklin counties (TOUSEY, 165).

11. On 10 Oct. "the Philadelphia horse, McPherson's blues and a number of other corps were formed into a legion, to be put under the command of Gen. [Frederick] Frelinghuysen, to lead the van of the army. This corps

began their march and was reviewed with a critical eye, by the President. They were followed by the train of artillery, and were to have been followed by the Jersey horse, but by some mistake or other the wagons for transporting our baggage were not provided. This default was severely censured by the President" (FORD [6], 86).

12th. Octr.   Having settled these Matters, seen the Troops off, as before mentioned; given them their rout & days Marching; and left Majr. Genl. Irvine to organise the remainder of the Pennsylvania detachments as they might come in, & to March them & the Jersey Troops on when refreshed, I set out from Carlisle about 7 Oclock this Morning—dined at Shippensburgh 21 miles further & lodged at Chambersburgh 11 M. farther where I was joined by the Adjt. Genl. Hand.

Chambersburg, in Franklin County, about 150 miles west of Philadelphia, consisted of "one long street, on which are erected about 200 dwellings, two Presbyterian churches, a stone jail, and handsome brick court-house, a paper and a merchant mill" (SCOTT [2]). According to local tradition, GW may have lodged tonight with Dr. Robert Johnson, a surgeon in the Pennsylvania line during the Revolution (EGLE [2], 1st-2d ser., 1:225).

13th.   Breakfasted at Greencastle 10 Miles, & lodged at Williamsport, 14 Miles further.
    Having now passed thro' the States of Pennsylvania & Maryland, Williamsport being on the Banks of the Potomac, at the Mouth of Conogocheaque; I shall summarily notice the kind of land, & State of improvements, along the Road I have come.
    From the City of Philadelphia, or rather from Norris Town to Reading the road passes over a reddish, & slaty, or shelly kind of land, through a very open and hilly Country, tolerably well cultivated by the farmers. The farm houses are good, and their Barns above mediocrity—The former chiefly of Stone. The whole Road indeed from Philadelphia to Reading goes over Hilly & broken grounds—but very pleasant notwithstanding.
    From Reading to Lebanon, along what is called the Valley, the Country is extremely fine—The lands rich—The Agriculture good—as the buildings also are, especially their Barns, which are large & fine; and for the most part of Stone. This settlement is chiefly of Dutch, and upon the Tulpahocken.
    From Lebanon to Harrisburgh, along the same Vale, the Lands are also good; but not in so high a state of cultivation as between Reading & Lebanon.
    From Harrisburgh to Carlisle the lands are exceedingly fine,

but not under such cultivation & improvement as one might have expected.

From Carlisle along the left Road, which I pursued, to be out of the March of the Army, and to avoid the inconvenience of passing the Waggons belonging to it; the Lands are but indifferent until we came within a few miles of Shippensburgh — The first part of a thin and dry Soil, succeeded by piney flats (not far from the South Mountain). For a few miles before we arrived at Shippensbg. the Lands were good, but uncultivated. The improvements along this road were mean; the farms scattered; the houses but indifferent; and the husbandry apparently bad. Along the Road which the Troops Marched, both the land & the Improvements I was told are much better. The Roads came together again at the East end of the Town.

From Shippensburgh to Chambersburgh, the Road passes over pretty good land; better, (but not well) cultivated than that betwn. Carlisle & Shippensburgh.

From Chambersburgh to Williamsport the Lands are fine, and the Houses and improvements amended, considerably.

Greencastle was 11 miles southwest of Chambersburg, in Franklin County, and consisted of about 80 houses and 2 churches (SCOTT [2]).

From Shippensburg to Bedford the army was able to make use of a well-kept state road, generally following the route of Forbes Road, constructed during the French and Indian War (CLUNN, 50, n.38).

14th.   About Seven oclock, or half after it, we left Williamsport; and travelling upon the Maryland side of the River, we breakfasted at one [   ] 13 miles on our way — & crossing the Potomac a mile or two below Hancock Town lodged at the Warm Springs; or Bath; 16 miles from our breakfasting stage — and 29 from Williamsport.

Johann David Schoepf described his trip through this region as a journey "through fertile valleys and over a few barren hills, consisting wholly of limestone soil and growing almost nothing but white-oaks. I came to Hancocktown on the Potowmack; a small place begun shortly before the war and numbering only a dozen houses. It belongs to Maryland which province here runs very narrow, for but a mile and a half from the town I crossed the boundary-line" (SCHOEPF, 1:308).

15th.   Left Bath by seven oclock; & crossing the Cacapohon Mountain, & the Potomack River by a very rough road, we breakfasted at one Goldens — distant about 7 Miles — Bated our horses at a very indifferent place abt. 13 Miles further on — and lodged at the Old Town 33 or 34 Miles. This distance from the extreme badness of the Road, more than half of it being very hilly, & great part of it Stoney, was a severe days Journey for the Carriage horses; they performed it however, well.

16th.   After an early breakfast we set out for Cumberland — and about 11 Oclock arrived there.

Three miles from the Town I was met by a party of Horse under the command of Major Lewis (my Nephew) and by Brigr. Genl. Smith of the Maryland line, who Escorted me to the Camp; where, finding all the Troops under Arms, I passed along the line of the Army; & was conducted to a house the residence of Major Lynn of the Maryland line (an old Continental Officer) where I was well lodged, & civily entertained.

Cumberland, Md., was the rendezvous for the militia from Maryland and Virginia; the Pennsylvania and New Jersey militia were to rendezvous at Bedford, Pa.

George Lewis (see entry for 3 April 1785) was now a captain in command of the Fredericksburg Troop of Volunteers. He was promoted to major on 17 Oct. The troops under Lewis's command had left Fredericksburg on 22 Sept. (WELLFORD, 2, 8; SORLEY, 154).

Samuel Smith (1752–1839), Baltimore merchant, was born in Pennsylvania but in 1759 moved with his family to Baltimore. During the Revolution, Smith served with Maryland regiments from 1776 to 1779, resigning in 1779 with the rank of lieutenant colonel. From 1790 to 1792 he served in the Maryland House of Delegates. In 1793 he was elected as a Democrat to the Third Congress and served until 1803 when he was elected to the Senate. At this time he was a major general in the Maryland militia (CASSELL, 58–59).

David Lynn (d. 1835) served in various Maryland regiments from 1776 to 1783.

Dr. Robert Wellford of Fredericksburg, who was with the Virginia troops, noted in his diary GW's arrival at Cumberland: "Between eleven & twelve o'clock this day arrived the President of the United States escorted into the town & to Head Quarters near the Fort by three troops of light dragoons, every man of whom cheerfully left ye encampment to pay the President a compliment, every regiment was drawn up in excellent order to receive him, & as he passed the line of Infantry he deliberately bowed to every officer individually. The Artillery at the same time announced his arrival" (WELLFORD, 7).

17th. & 18th.   Remained at Cumberland, in order to acquire a true knowledge of the strength — condition — &ca. of the Troops; and to see how they were provided, and when they could be got in readiness to proceed.

I found upwards of 3200 Men (Officers included) in this Encampment; Understood that about 500 more were at a little

Village on the Virginia side, 11 Miles distant, called Frankfort, under the command of Majr. Genl. Morgan; that 700 more had arrived at that place the evening of the 18th. undr. Brigr. Mathews and 500 more were expected in the course of a few days under Colo. Page and That the whole were well supplied with Provns., Forage & Straw.

Having requested that every thing might be speedily arranged for a forward movement, and a light Corps to be organized for the advance under the command of Major Genl. Morgan, I resolved to proceed to Bedford next Morng.

At this place a deputation was received from the County of Fayette consisting of a Colo. Mason [   ] Terrence and [   ] Clinton who came to give assurances that deposits for the Army might safely be made in that County, and any person sent from it for this purpose would be safe in doing it.

They were desired to get there wheat ground up, and their Oats threshed out, to be in readiness to be drawn to any place, or places that might be required after the Army had crossed the Mountains.

From Colo. Mason (who has been a uniform friend to Government) and from a variety of concurrant accounts, it appears evident that the people in the Western Counties of this State have got very much alarmed at the approach of the Army; but though Submission is professed, their principles remain the same; and that nothing but coercion, & example will reclaim & bring them to a due & unequivocal submission to the Laws.

On 17 Oct., Dr. Wellford of the Fredericksburg troops reported that he "was this day invited to dine with the President, and with a number of Officers, dined under Genl. Lee's Marque, and was treated very affably by the President, who was pleased to express his approbation of my conduct" (WELLFORD, 8). TERRENCE: probably Joseph Torrence of Franklin Township, Fayette County, Pa. Clinton may have been Charles Clinton of Union Township, Fayette County.

19th.   In company with Genl. Lee, who I requested to attend me, that all the arrangements necessary for the Army's crossing the Mountns. in two columns might be made; Their routs, & days Marches fixed, that the whole might move in Unison—and accompanied by the Adjutant General and my own family we set out, abt. eight oclock, for Bedford, and making one halt at the distance of 12 Miles, reached it a little after 4 oclock in the afternoon being met a little out of the Encampment by Govr. Mifflin—Govr. Howell—& several other Officers of distinction.

Quarters were provided for me at the House of a Mr. Espy.

Prothonotary of the County of Bedford—to which I was carried & lodged very comfortably.

The Road from Cumberld. to this place is, in places, stoney but in other respects not bad. It passes through a Valley the whole way; and was opened by Troops under my command in the Autumn of 1758. The whole Valley consists of good farming land, & part of it—next Cumberland—is tolerably well improved in its culture but not much so in Houses.

On 19 Oct., Dr. Wellford noted in his diary that "this morning the President of the United States set out for Bedford on his return to the right wing of the Army, & from there to the seat of Government. . . . The Cavalry this morning escorted the President about five miles from (camp), when he requested the Troops to return, & taking leave spoke to Major George Lewis as follows: 'George, You are the eldest of five nephews that I have in this Army, let your conduct be an example to them, and do not turn your back until you are ordered.' Major Lewis made a suitable reply, but from this address of the President it was conjectured that the Troops would not be entirely disbanded at the end of the three months' service.

"Mem: The President's five nephews are Major George Lewis, Commandant of the Cavalry. Major Laurence Lewis, Aid de Camp to Major Genl. Morgan. Mr. Howell Lewis, in Capt. Mercer's troop, and Mr. Saml. Washington (son of Col. Ch's Washington), and Mr. Laurence Washington (son of Col. Saml. Washington), both of whom are light horsemen in the troop lately commanded by Capt. Lewis" (WELLFORD, 8–9). At this time Bedford, some 110 miles west of Philadelphia, contained 41 log and 9 stone dwellings, a brick market house, a stone jail, a courthouse, and a brick building for keeping the records of the county (SCOTT [2]). "The President's reception at Bedford on his return to the seat of Government was affectionate and interesting," Dr. Wellford continued. "When it was announced that He was approaching, the troops & the artillery paraded, the Cavalry marched down the road two miles, & drew up on the right of the road. As General Washington passed he pulled off his hat, &, in the most respectful manner, bowed to the officers & men, and in this manner passed the line, who were affected by the sight of their Chief, for whom each individual seemed to show the affectionate regard that would have been to an honoured Parent. As soon as the President passed, his escort followed the Troops, joined the train, & entered the town, whose inhabitants seemed anxious to see this very great and good Man. Crowds were assembled in the streets, but their admiration was silent. In this manner the President passed in front of the Camp, where the troops were assembled in front of the Tents. the line of Artillery Horse & Infantry appeared in the most perfect order, the greatest silence was observed. Genl. Washington approached the right uncovered, passed along the line bowing in the most respectful & affectionate manner to the officers—he appeared pleased" (WELLFORD, 9–10).

David Espy was one of Bedford's first settlers. His house was "a two-story stone structure with three windows across the front and a high hipped roof giving almost a full floor in the attic." The house had been used by Arthur St. Clair when he was prothonotary of Bedford County (MULKEARN AND PUGH, 130, 139). ROAD: For GW's route to join Gen. John Forbes for the march on Fort Duquesne in 1758, see FREEMAN, 2:324–33.

20th.　　Called the Quarter Master General, Adjutant General, Contractor, & others of the Staff departmt. before me, & the Commander in chief, at 9 Oclock this morning, in order to fix on the Routs of the two Columns & their Stages; and to know what the situation of matters were in their respective departments—and when they wd. be able to put the Army in motion. Also to obtain a correct return of the strength—and to press the commanding Officers of Corps to prepare with all the Celerity in their power for a forward movement.

Upon comparing accts., it was found that the army could be put in motion 23d.—and it was so ordered, by the Routs which will be mentioned hereafter.

Matters being thus arranged I wrote a farewell address to the Army through the Commander in Chief—Govr. Lee—to be published in orders—and having prepared his Instructions and made every arrangement that occurred, as necessary I prepared for my return to Philadelphia in order to meet Congress, and to attend to the Civil duties of my Office.

I should have mentioned before that I found (on my arrival at Bedford) the judge, and Attorney for the district of Pennsylvania attending, as they had been required to do, the Army.

I found also, which appeared to me to be an unlucky measure —that the former had issued his warrants against, and a party of light horse had actually siez'd, one Harman Husband & one Filson as Insurgents or abetters of the Insurrection. I call it unlucky because my intention was to have suspended all proceedings of a Civil Nature until the Army had united its columns in the Center of the Insurgent Counties & then to have ciezed at one & the same all the leaders and principals of the Insurrection and because it is to be feared that the proceeding above mentioned will have given the alarm and those who are most obnoxious to punishment will flee from the Country.

STAFF DEPARTMT.: It is uncertain in some instances to which officers GW was referring. Henry Miller was quartermaster for the militia army as a whole; Clement Biddle was quartermaster for Pennsylvania. Edward Hand was adjutant general. The contractor was probably Elie Williams who was in Bedford at this time. Ephraim Blaine of Carlisle was responsible for wagons, horses, forage, and fuel. George Gale, supervisor of the revenue for Maryland, was responsible for supplying the Maryland militia; Joel Gibbs was contractor for the artillery (RISCH, 110; HAMILTON [2], 17:150–52).

GW's farewell to the army was contained in his letter of this day to Henry Lee expressing "the very high sense I entertain of the enlightened and patriotic zeal for the constitution and the laws which has led them chearfully to quit their families and homes and the comforts of private life to undertake and thus far to perform a long and fatiguing march and to encounter the hardships and privations of a Military life." He warned every officer and soldier, however, that he had come to western Pennsylvania to support the laws and "that it would be peculiarly unbecoming in him to be in any way the infractor of them. . . . The dispensation of . . . justice belongs to the civil Magistrate and let it ever be our pride and our glory to leave the sacred deposit there unviolated" (DLC:GW). Lee included the letter in his General Orders of 21 Oct. 1794 (PA. ARCH., 2d ser., 4:350–53).

GW's instructions were submitted through Alexander Hamilton in a letter from Hamilton to Lee, 20 Oct. 1794: "I have it in special instruction from the President of the United States . . . to convey to you on his behalf, the following instructions for the general direction of your conduct in the command of the Militia army." The instructions directed Lee to march the army in two columns in the direction of Parkinson's Ferry and suggested that upon the army's arrival in the insurgents' area a proclamation should be issued exhorting all citizens to abide by the laws. Armed insurgents should be turned over to the civil authority and the rest sent home. When the insurrection was suppressed the army was to withdraw "detaching such a force as you deem adequate; to be stationed within the disaffected Country. . . . You are to exert yourself by all possible means to preserve discipline among the troops, particularly a scrupulous regard to the rights of persons and property and a respect for the authority of the civil magistrate; taking especial care to inculcate and cause to be observed this principal, that the duties of the army are confined to the attacking and subduing of armed opponents of the laws, and to the supporting and aiding of the civil officers in the execution of their functions" (HAMILTON [2], 17:331–36).

JUDGE, AND ATTORNEY FOR THE DISTRICT OF PENNSYLVANIA: Richard Peters (1744–1828), judge of the United States district court of Pennsylvania and a native of Philadelphia, served as secretary of the Board of War 1776–81 and as a member of the Continental Congress 1782–83. William Rawle (1759–1836) of Philadelphia studied law in London at the Middle Temple. After his return to the United States in 1783 he practiced law in Philadelphia. GW appointed him United States attorney for the district of Pennsylvania in 1791. Peters and Rawle accompanied the army on its march west from Bedford.

Herman Husbands (1724–1795) was living at Coffee Springs Farm in Somerset County, Pa., in 1794. Born probably in Cecil County, Md., he moved to North Carolina around 1755. About 1759 he returned to Maryland but moved back to North Carolina in 1761. He soon became a spokesman for frontier rights and was a leader of the Regulators in North Carolina in the backwoods attack on Gov. William Tryon's taxation policies. He was forced to flee to Pennsylvania in 1771. Settling in Somerset County, he served in the Pennsylvania legislature 1777, 1778, and 1790, where he was particularly interested in the development of the iron industry in Pennsylvania (MUL-KEARN AND PUGH, 290). Johann David Schoepf encountered this frontier eccentric. "barefoot and dressed in dirty clothes," on his journey west in 1783–84. After his flight from North Carolina, Schoepf observed, Husbands "betook himself hither into the mountains, where under a changed name and wearing strange clothing, he contrived to avoid further persecution. . . . Instead of matters of state he concerns himself now with prophecies of which several have appeared in Goddard's Maryland Calendar under the name of Hutrim Hutrim, or the Philosopher of the Alleghany. In one of these he had calculated the time of his death, but has already lived some years beyond the term" (SCHOEPF, 1:292–97). When the revolt against the excise erupted, Husbands not surprisingly assumed a leading role.

Robert Philson was a storekeeper in Berlin, Bedford County, Pa. Husbands, Philson, and two other prisoners taken at approximately the same time were sent to Philadelphia for trial, and GW wrote Hamilton 31 Oct. that they "were safely lodged in this City on Wednesday afternoon" (DLC: Hamilton Papers).

On his return to Philadelphia, GW apparently followed a route from Bedford to Chambersburg, from Chambersburg to York, and then to Lancaster, from which place he proceeded to Philadelphia. On Tuesday evening 21 Oct. he wrote Hamilton from "Hartley's" (DLC:GW). This was William Hartley's stone house, some four miles east of Bedford (MULKEARN AND PUGH, 141). By 26 Oct. he had reached Wright's ferry on the Susquehanna. From there he wrote Hamilton that "thus far I have proceeded without accident to man, horse or Carriage, altho' the latter has had wherewith to try its goodness; especially in ascending the North Mountain from Skinners by a wrong road. . . . I rode yesterday afternoon thro' the rain from York Town to this place, and got twice in the height of it hung, (and delayed by that means) on the rocks in the middle of the Susquehanna, but I did not feel half as much for my own situation as I did on acct. of the Troops on the Mountains, and of the effect the rain might have on the Roads through the glades" (DLC: Hamilton Papers). On 31 Oct. he wrote Hamilton from Philadelphia that "by pushing through the rain (which fell more or less on Saturday, Sunday and Monday) I arrived in this City before noon on Tuesday [28 Oct.]; without encountering any thing so unpleasant than the badness of the ways, after the rains had softened the earth and made them susceptible of deep impression of the Wheels" (DLC: Hamilton Papers).

After GW's departure from Bedford, the army, unruly and poorly disciplined, continued on the march to the Pittsburgh area and to Washington County, reaching the disaffected counties early in November, and by 17 Nov. Hamilton, who had accompanied the army, wrote GW that "the list of prisoners has been very considerably increased, probably to the amount of 150. . . . Subsequent intelligence shews that there is no regular assemblage of the fugitives where it is supposed—there are only small vagrant parties in that quarter affording no point of Attack. Every thing is urging on for the return of the troops" (DLC:GW). On 19 Nov., Hamilton wrote that "the army is generally in motion homeward" (DLC:GW). A regiment of infantry, with nine months' enlistment, was raised by Lee to maintain order in the counties involved in the insurrection (Hamilton to GW, 8 Nov. 1794, NjP: De Coppet Collection). The insurgents' trials dragged on through much of 1795 and most of the accused were acquitted for lack of evidence, GW issuing a proclamation 10 July pardoning most of those who were not sentenced or under indictment (PHi: Wallace Papers).

In his Sixth Annual Address to Congress, 19 Nov. 1794, GW recapitulated the course the government had taken to suppress the insurrection and gave his own views as to its cause: "During the session of the year 1790, it was expedient to exercise the legislature power, granted by the constitution of the United States, 'to lay and collect excises.' In a majority of the States, scarcely an objection was heard to this mode of taxation. In some indeed, alarms were at first conceived; until they were banished by reason and patriotism. In the four western counties of Pennsylvania, a prejudice, fostered and embittered by the artifice of men who labored for an ascendency over the will of others by the guidance of their passions, produced symptoms of riot and violence. It is well known, that Congress did not hesitate to examine the complaints which were presented; and to relieve them, as far as justice dictated, or general convenience would permit, But the impression, which this moderation made on the discontented, did not correspond, with what it deserved. The arts of delusion were no longer confined to the efforts of designing individuals. The very forbearance to press prosecutions was misinterpreted into a fear of urging the execution of the laws; and associations of men began to denounce threats against the officers employed. From a belief, that, by a more formal concert, their operation might be defeated; certain self-created societies assumed the tone of condemnation. Hence, while the greater part of Pennsylvania itself were conforming themselves to the acts of excise; a few counties were resolved to frustrate them. It was now perceived, that every expectation from the tenderness which had been hitherto pursued, was unavailing, and that further delay could only create an opinion of impotency or irresolution in the government. Legal process was, therefore, delivered to the Marshal, against rioters and delinquent distillers" (*Gaz. of the U.S.* [Philadelphia], 19 Nov. 1794).

Mostly Weather

April–December 1795

EDITORIAL NOTE. In Feb. 1795 GW resumed making notations on the calendar pages of his almanacs and continued to do so until the end of 1798. In some cases the notations are clear. For example, in Jan. 1797, he temporarily kept some daily temperature readings on that month's calendar, and during 1795 and 1796 he occasionally recorded stops on his journeys between Mount Vernon and Philadelphia, apparently after the fact. On the April 1795 calendar the notation "Bla" in the margin next to the 17th corresponds with his regular diary entry for that date: "Arrived at Bladensburgh." Other travel notes appear in the "Remarkable Days, &c." columns, such as in July 1795 when "Wilmington" is written to the right of the 15th and "Spurriers" to the right of the 18th, days on which he lodged at those places according to his fuller entries on another page. And in October of that same year, the entire record for his trip home from Philadelphia is kept under "Remarkable Days, &c." The fact remains, however, that the meaning of many of GW's calendar notations for these years, as in previous ones, are obscure, for they consist of letters, circles, dashes, x's, and personal names that have no clear connection with the rest of his diary. The names may be names of slaves, and the letters and abstract marks may relate to the administration of his household or plantation, for some of them are connected with names of Mount Vernon farms—Home House, Dogue Run, and Union Farm—on the July 1795 calendar. See illustration on 1:328 in the present edition of GW's diaries.

[April]

Tuesday 14th.   Left Phila. for Mt. V.
Reached Wilmington.

15.   Do.   Roger's Susqa.

ROGERS'S SUSQA: John Rodgers (see 7 May 1775) had died in 1791 and his wife, Elizabeth Reynolds Rodgers (c.1743–c.1816), was continuing to run her husband's old stone ferry house at Perryville, Md., on the east bank of the Susquehanna River.

16.   Baltimore.

17.   Bladensburgh.

18.   George Town.

19.   Mount Vernon & remained there until the 26th.

26.   Came to George Town.

27.   In the federal City.

28.   Arrived at Bladensburgh.

29.   Baltimore.

30.   Rogers's–Susquehanna.

[May]

May–1st.   Came to Wilmington.

2.   Arrived at Philadelphia.

15.   Thunder, lightning & rain–cool.

16.   Wind Northerly in the Morng.

17–18.   Cool & cloudy, with the Wind easterly. Same till the 21st.

21.   Wind at So. Wt. Warm & very heavy rain.

22.   Cloudy all day—Wind So.

23.   Raining moderatly till Noon—W[in]d S. W.

24.   Clear with the Wind Westerly—rather cool.

25.   Clear, & rather cool. Wd. East[er]ly.

26. ⎫
    ⎬ Wind Southerly & Warm.
27. ⎭

28.   Do.   Do.   Do. cloudy.

29.   Do.   Do.   Rain.

30.   Raining in the Night—do. about Noon—and at Night.

31.   Wind Westerly & clear.

[June]

1st.   Wind hard at No. Wt. & cold—all day.

2.   Do. at So. Wt.—fresh—& heavy showers—Aftern[oon].

3.   Clear & pleasant Wind Easterly.

4.   Clear wind Westerly.

5.   Do. fine air—Wind at So. W.

6.   Do. Wind at Do. & fresh. Warm.

7.   Do.   Do. Easterly.   Do.

8.   Do.   Do.   Do.   do.

9.   Do. Wind fresh at S. W. all day.

10.   Do. Do.   Do.   Do. Rainy night.

11. Wind at N. Et. Raining all day.

12. Do.   do.   Raing. more or less.

13. Do.   do.   Cloudy & cool till aft[ernoon].

14. Clear forenoon but cloudy afterwd.

15. Cold & disagreeable Wind N. E.

16. Wind at So. Wt. Showers & variable.

17. Do.   at No. Et. Cloudy forenoon clear aft.

18. Wind at So. Wt. Clear & growing warm.

19. Do.   Do.   Clear & very warm.

20. Do.   Do.   Clear forenoon – rain afterwd.

21. Do.   Do.   Very warm Morng. & day.

22. Do. So. Wt. – warm.

23. Do.   Do.   Warm with showers.

24. Do.   Do.   Showers – heavy – rain all N[ight].

25. Do.   Do.   Rain in the morng. & afternn.

26. Do. No. Wt. Clear & cooler all day.

27. Do. Westerly – clear & getting warmr.

28. Do. Westerly. Clear & pleast.

29. Do. So. Wt.   Clear & warm.

30. Do.   Do.   Cloudy forenoon. Rain after.

[July]

1. Wind at So. Et. Raing. more or less all day.

2. Do. at East—cloudy more or less.

3. Do. do. Clear & growing warm.

4. Do. do.—heavy morng. but clear afterwds.

5. Do. do. in the morning West in the aftern.

6. Do. So. Wt. & fresh—Warm also.

7. Cool morning—fresh No. Wind all day.

8. Southerly & warm—but little Wind.

9. Much as yesterday.

10. Very sultry, with little or no Wind.

11. Wind at No. Et. & fresh but very wa[rm].

12. Do. Easterly—very warm—clear.

13. Do. So. Wt. Sultry.

14. Do. Northerly & fresh—cooler.

15. Do. Easterly. Cloudy all day.

16. Do. Do. but clear & warmer.

17. Southerly & growing warmer.

18. Do. & very warm.

19. Do. Do. Do.

20. Do. Do. Do.

21. Do. Still warmer.

22. Do. Very warm.

23. Do. Appearance of Rain.

24. No. Wt. but very warm, Rain.

25. No. Wt. but warm.

26. West—warm—then East.

27. Easterley—a great deal of Rain.

28. Wind at No. West—clear—pleast.

29. Wd. variable. Showers abt.

30. Do. variable much rain.

31. Do. Showery. Do. Do. in the Night.

July

15th.   Left Philaa. with Mrs. Washington & my family for Mt. Vernon. Dined at Chester & lodged at Wilmigton.

LEFT PHILAA.: "President Washington about eight o'clock this morning set out for Mount Vernon in a two-horse phaeton for one person, his family in a coach and four horses, and two servants on horseback leading his saddle horse" (HILTZHEIMER, 215).

16.   Breakfasted at Christa.—dined at Elkton & lodgd at Susquehanna. One of my horses overcome with heat.

CHRISTA.: GW probably breakfasted at the village of Christiana Bridge (now called Christiana), Del., on the road from Wilmington to Charlestown, Md., rather than at Christina (Christiana) ferry, which crosses the Delaware River at Wilmington.
    On this journey GW probably stopped at Havre de Grace on the west bank of the Susquehanna River. The tavern, formerly run by John Rodgers, was at this time under the management of John H. Barney, a brother of the naval hero Capt. Joshua Barney.

17.   Breakfasted before I set out. Dined at Hartford & lodged at Websters. Brot. on the sick horse led.

HARTFORD: Harford Town, Md., now called Bush. The town was the county seat of Harford County from 1744 to 1782. WEBSTERS: probably the tavern at the head of Bird River that earlier was called Skerrett's and also Cheyns's.

18.   Breakfasted in Baltim[or]e—dined & lodged at Spurriers where my sick horse died.

SPURRIERS: This is probably the same tavern that GW on 21 Sept. 1787 had called "the Widow Balls (formerly Spurriers)." Either Spurrier had again taken over as proprietor or the tavern was still known by his name.

19.   Breakfasted at Vanhorn—dined at Bladensburgh & lodged in Geo. Town.

VANHORN: Gabriel P. Van Horne ran a post-stage line from Philadelphia to Alexandria and operated several taverns on the road, including this one in Prince George's County, 14 miles from Spurriers and 9 from Bladensburg. The location was known as Vans Ville at the time. Van Horne had been captain of a company of militia in Harford County, Md., during the Revolution, and GW refers to him after the Revolution as Colonel Van Horne. Van Horne also rented his carriages and horses for private trips; GW solicited his services in transporting Mrs. Washington and her party to New York in May 1789 (SCHARF [5], 1:311–12; BRUMBAUGH [2], 2:366; GW to Elizabeth Powel, 26 Mar. 1797, ViMtV; Van Horne to GW, 13 June 1789 and 22 Aug. 1795, and Van Horne to George Augustine Washington, 12 May 1789, DLC: GW).

20.   After doing business with the Comrs. of the fedl. City I proceeded on my journey & got home to dinner.

The commissioners of the Federal City at this time were Gustavus Scott, William Thornton, and Alexander White. There had been endless disputes arising from the planning and development of the city. This meeting with the commissioners, however, dealt with an especially serious matter. Robert Morris and John Nicholson, who had bought hundreds of lots in the city for speculation and development, had failed to make their scheduled payments on the land. GW promised to try to get Morris and Nicholson to live up to their contract (FREEMAN, 7:266–67). He wrote Edmund Randolph two days later: "I should be glad if you would call upon Messrs. Morris & Nicholson . . . and in earnest & strong terms represent to them, the serious consequences which must inevitably result to the public buildings in the federal City, if the deficiency, or part thereof, due on their contract, is not paid. Besides arresting the work in the present critical state, & compelling the discharge of some valuable workmen, who may never be recovered; it would throw such a cloud over the public & private concerns of the City, & would be susceptible of such magnified & unfavorable interpretations, as to give it a vital wound. . . . If to pay the whole deficiency is not, at present, within the means of Messrs. Morris & Nicholson, a part thereof, & to keep pace with the current demand, might possibly enable the Commissioners to proceed without much embarrassment in the *principal* work. Between forty & fifty thousand dollars, I am informed, is now due on the Contract" (22 July 1795, DLC:GW).

[August]

1.   Wind at No. Wt.—flying clouds, warm.

2. Do. Easterly—violent Rain & wind aftn.

3. Do. No. Wt. Much rain fell last night.

4. Sml. Westerly breeze—quite clear.

5. Do.   Do.   Do. Clear.

6. Clear, still & warm.

7. Wind Southerly & very warm.

8. Same as yesterday with R[ain] af[ternoon].

9. Still very warm with clouds.

10. Very warm rain afternoon.

11. Cloudy & showery more or less.

12. Wind Easterly cloudy & someti[mes] R[ain].

13. Do.   Do.   Do. Rain in the Night.

14. Do.   Do.   Do. Cooler.

15. Do. No. Easterly—cool & clear.

16. Do.   Do.   Clear & pleast.

17. Do. Southerly Rain in the Afn.

18. Do.   Do.   Growing much warmr.

19. Do.   Do.   Very warm.

20. Do.   Do.   Do. Rain in the Eveng.

21. Do. No. Et. Cool & raing. more or less.

22. Do.   Do.   Do. Thick mist all day.

23. Do.   Do.   Cleared abt. noon & grew W[arm].

24.   Do.   Do.   with sunshine & showers.

25.   Do. Southerly & growing warm.

26.   Do.   Do.   Clear & rather warm.

27.   Do.   Do.   Clear & warm.

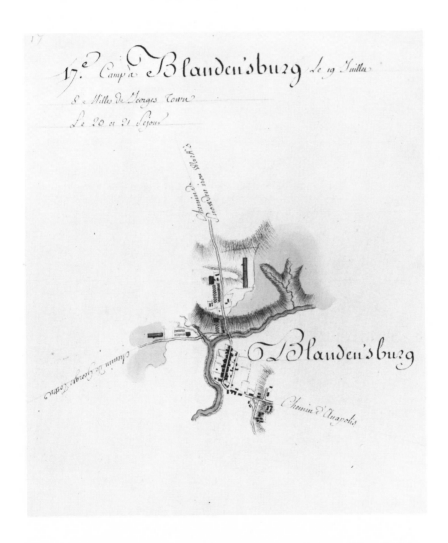

Plan of Bladensburg, Md., drawn during the Revolution. (Map Division, Library of Congress)

28. Cloudy forenoon clear afterwds.

29. Thick morning clear & hot afterwd.

30. Fresh So. Westerly wind – warm & clear.

31. Wind same. Showery all day & a good deal of rain in the night.

For August

6th.   Left home on my return to Philadelphia. Met the Potok. Co. at Geo. Town & lodged there.

GW had expected to leave for Philadelphia on 3 Aug., stopping in Georgetown for the meeting of the Potomac Company on that date. However, several weeks of rainy weather culminated in a bad storm and heavy rains on 2 and 3 Aug. which swelled the streams and washed out roads and bridges. GW then planned to attend the rescheduled meeting of the Potomac Company on 6 Aug. and leave on 8 Aug. for Philadelphia. However, the first post to get through from Philadelphia to Alexandria after the storm arrived on 5 Aug. and brought news that made him change his plans. He wrote hurriedly to David Stuart the same day: "By the Mail which came into Alexandria this day, I have received letters, advising me of the recall of Mr. Hammond; & some other matters which have induced me to determine to proceed from Georgetown to Phila." (PPRF). Among the "other matters" referred to was a reference in Secretary of War Timothy Pickering's letter which arrived on that day. Pickering wrote: "On the subject of the [Jay] treaty I confess I feel extreme solicitude; and for a *special reason* which can be communicated to you only in person I entreat therefore that you will return with all convenient speed to the seat of Government. In the mean time, for the reason above referred to, I pray you to decide on no important political measure in whatever form it may be presented to you" (31 July 1795, DLC:GW). Pickering was undoubtedly referring to the intercepted dispatch from the French envoy Fauchet that seemed to incriminate Secretary of State Edmund Randolph in a bribery plot.

GW lodged at Suter's tavern in Georgetown, which, since John Suter's death in 1794, had been run by his son John Suter, Jr. (ECKER, 28–29; GW's Cash Memorandum, 29 Sept. 1794–17 Aug. 1797, RPJCB). GW had maintained his interest in the Potomac Company during the presidential years but had been unable to attend the meetings. This general meeting was an important one, and Tobias Lear, now a director of the company, had urged GW to attend, or, if he could not, to send his proxy. At the meeting it was decided to open the books for 100 additional shares in the company, 60 to be subscribed by the state of Maryland and the remaining 40 by individuals. The locks and works at Little Falls were reported to be completed, with all impediments in the river between there and Great Falls removed. A decision was reached to start collecting tolls above Great Falls (BACON-FOSTER, 90; Lear to GW, 3 Aug. 1795, DLC:GW).

7.   Breakfasted at Bladensburgh—din. at Vanhornes & lodged at Spurriers.

The roads in Maryland were still in very bad condition after the recent torrential rains. The journey from Bladensburg, where GW breakfasted, to Van Horne's, where he dined, was only nine miles. It was probably on this stretch of road that the horses became mired and GW had to pay £1 7s. 6d. to have them extricated (GW's Cash Memorandum, 29 Sept. 1794–17 Aug. 1797, RPJCB).

8.   Breakfasted at Baltimore and dined and lodged at Websters.

9.   Breakfasted at Hartford dined at Susquehanna and lodged at Charles town.

On this day GW probably stopped at John H. Barney's tavern on the west bank of the Susquehanna River. On 17 Aug., GW's cash memorandum notes "By a Bank bill of five dollars, sent Mr. Barney of Havre de grace, out of wch. to rec[eiv]e the ferriage I forgot to pay when I crossed on my last journey from Virga. the bal[anc]e to be returned to me—or paid when I call there again. Note, this Bill was returned in a letter from Mr. Barney informing me that I had paid the ferriage" (29 Sept. 1794–17 Aug. 1797, RPJCB).

10.   Breakfasted at Elkton—Dined at Newcastle and lodged at Wilmington.

11.   Breakfasted at Chester and dined in Phila.

For September

1st.   Wind westerly—some rain—A good deal fell in the Night. Cool.

2.   Wind Northerly cloudy & springling till Noon.

3.   Do. No. W. Fine, clear & pleast. all day.

4.   Do.   Do. Much such a day as yester.

5.   Do.   Do. Cloudy in the morng., clear.

6.   No. Et. Showery and Cool.

7.   Do. Do. Do.   Do. Much rain in N.

8.   So. Wt. with mists in the forenoon.

9.   Do. Clear & very warm.

10.   Same as yesterday.

11.   Do.   Do.

12.   Wind at No. Et. Cool & cloudy.

13.   Do. at So. Wt. with Showers. Warmr.

14.   Do. Clear & very warm.

15.   Do. Do.   Do. Do.

16.   Do. Do.   Do. Do.

17.   Do. Do.   Do. Do.

18.   Do. Do.   With rain at Night.

19.   Do. No. Wt. & cold.

20.   Do. Do.   Do.

21.   Do. Do.   Do.

22.   Do. Do.   Do. Frost slight.

23.   Do. Do.   Do. Do. Do.

24.   Do. Southerly warmer.

25.   Do.   Do. and warm.

26.   Do. No. Et. & lowering. Equinoctial gale all night.

27.   Raing. till noon, with high wind from No. Et. & So. Et.

28. Clear & warm—wind Wester[ly].

29. Wind at No. Wt. & cool.

30. Do. in same place but warmer.

September

8th. Left Phila. for Mt. Vernon. Dined at Chester & lodged at Wilmington.

9. Breakfasted at Christiana dined at Elkton & lodged at Charles town.

10. Breakfasted at Susquehanna (Mrs. Rogers's) dined at Hartford & lo[d]ged at Websters.

11. Breakfasted at Baltimore. Dined & lodged at Spurriers.

12. Breakfasted at Van Horns. Dined at Bladensburgh & lodged at George Town.

13. Breakfasted in George Town and reached Mt. Vernon to dinner.

25. Went to Alexandria. Dined with Mr. & Mrs. Lear.

Tobias Lear's first wife, Mary Long Lear, had died in 1793, and Lear in early August 1795 married Fanny Bassett Washington (*Columbian Mirror* [Alexandria], 6 Aug. 1795), widow of GW's nephew George Augustine Washington, who had also died in 1793.

26. Returned home to dinner.

[October]

1. Little or no wind & very pleasant.

2. Wind Easterly—clear & pleasant.

3. Do. Southerly & warm.

4. Do. Do. Do.

5. Do. Easterly good deal of Rai[n].

6. Do. N. Wt. clear cooler.

7. Do. Do. and still cool.

8. Do. Do. and cold.

9. Do. Easterly.

10. Do. Lowering & a little R.

11. Wd. at So. Wt. Light Showers.

12. Do. Do. Clear & growg. warm.

13. Calm clear & very warm.

14. Lowering—not much wind.

15. Rain & very high Wd. So. Wt. & N. W.

16. Clear & Cool—Wind at No. Wt.

17. Rain in the Morng. Clear afterwds.

18. Clear Wind pretty fresh. No. W. & S. W.

19. Do. & pleasant.

20. Lowering.

21. Rain in the night. Wd. at East.

22. Misty morning.

23. Clear.

24. Variable—sometimes cloudy.

25. Clear & pleast. Wd. Westerly.

26. Same as yesterday.

27. Do. Do. Do.

28. Do. Do. Do.

29. Do. Do. Do.

30. Do. Do. Do. Warmer.

31. Very thick fog—rain afterwds. & fresh Westerly wind.

[October]

12. Set out for Phila.

Entries for 12–20 Oct. appear on the printed almanac page.

13. Stayed at Geo. Town.

14. Lodged at Spurriers.

16. Lodged at Websters.

17. Do. at Hartford.

18. Do. at Elkton.

19. Do. at Wilmington.

20. Arrived at Phil.

[November]

1. Cool & variable—Wind Easterly.

2. Clear till evening then cloudy.

3. Very threatning forenoon & variable.

4.   Clear & pleasant. Wind Westerly.

The whole Month of November has been remarkable pleasant. The ground has never been froze—but few white frosts, and No Snow.

The words "turned away" appear on the printed almanac page under 18 Nov.

[December]

1.   Mild & pleast. Wind Southerly.

7.   A good deal of rain fell last night with the wind at East.

12.   Rain, with the Wind at East.

13.   Misting and Raining a little through the day.

20.   Snow, about 2 Inches deep.

24.   Raining.

A Few Entries
1796

[January]

1. Remarkably mild and pleasant—perfectly clear.
Received the National Colours from Mr. Adet the Minister Plenipo. to day.
Much company visited.

Pierre Auguste Adet, French minister plenipotentiary, had arrived in the United States on 13 June 1795 to replace Fauchet. He brought with him a French flag, a gift of the French Committee of Public Safety, and an accompanying speech of warm friendship for the United States. His awareness of the anti-French bias in the American government, however, caused him to delay presenting the flag. In Dec. 1795 he finally notified GW that he desired to make the presentation, and GW chose New Year's Day for the ceremony. GW answered the French address in a friendly manner, but he included the statement that the French flag would be placed in the archives. Adet took violent exception to this. An American flag presented earlier by James Monroe to the French National Convention was on prominent display in the French chamber, and Adet had expected the French flag to be accorded a conspicuous place in the halls of Congress. The Federalists, however, felt that Adet's presentation was a flagrant attempt to sway American feeling during the discussion of the Jay Treaty (DECONDE, 424, 435–36).

2. Equally fine with yesterday. Saw the Stem of the Frigate raised.

On 27 Mar. 1794 Congress passed "An Act to provide a Naval Armament," providing for the construction of six frigates, to be built in various shipyards around the country. This measure was designed to protect American shipping from marauding Algerines (1 STAT. 350–51 [27 Mar. 1790]). The frigate mentioned here was being built at Southwark, near Philadelphia. It was the *United States*, 44 guns, and was to be commanded by Commodore John Barry. After the treaty with the Dey of Algiers in 1795, three of the frigates, including the *United States*, were ordered to be completed immediately, and work on the other three was to be put off for an indefinite period (ASP, NAVAL AFF., 1:6, 18, 25). The visit to the shipyard with GW that George Washington Parke Custis later recalled was probably this one: "I well remember visiting with Washington the *United States* Frigate at Southwark, when her Keel was laid, & stem & starnpost only up. The Chief expressed his admiration at the great size of the Vessell that was to be. Commodore Barry was present, & Mr. [Joshua] Humphreys [naval constructor] explained to the President, several of his cabinet, and other persons who were present, the great principle which he had originated & was now by consent of the authorities putting into successful practice, all of which met with Washington's approbation, & he expressed himself on the return in his coach, much gratified with all he had seen & heard in this, his *First visit to an American Navy Yard"* (HUMPHREYS, 391) .

3.   Rain in the night–foggy till Noon–then clear. Wind S.W.

4.   Remarkably mild–clear & pleasant. Wind So. Wt.

5.   Very white frost–Southerly Wind & lowering sun.

6.   Rain in the Night and violent Storm–variable wind & a little Snow.

7.   Clear forenoon–lowering afternoon. Wind No. Wt.

8.   Clear but cool. Wind at N.W.

9.   Clear & cold. Wind at Do. lowering towards night.

10.   Lowering all the forenoon–about 2 oclock begun to Snow. Wind at So. Wt.

11.   Snowing very moderately till Noon with the Wind at No. Et. Then Rain–wch. carrd. all off.

12.   Clear with the Wind at West and moderate.

13.   Clear in the forenoon, lowering afterwards. Wind at No. Et.

14.   Raining all day moderately & Steadily. Wind at No. Et. but warm.

15.   Cloudy most part of the day. Wind Westerly.

16.   Similar to yesterday in all respects.

17.   Snowing more or less all day with the wind at No. Et.

18.   Cloudy, & now and then Snowing. Wind Westerly.

19.   Clear in the forenoon, cloudy afterwards with great appearances of Snow.

20.   Some Snow fell in the night and at intervals & with a mixture of rain through the day. Wind Easterly.

21.   Clear with the Wind Westerly.

22d.   Clear—wind westerly. Mercury in the morning at 16 degrees.

23.   Perfectly calm, clear and pleasant. Mercury 18 in the morning.

24.   Clear in the forenoon—a little lowering afterwards. Wind at So. West. Mercury at 30 & falling.

25.   Lowering all day with appearances of Rain. W[in]d No. Et.

26.   Thick weather, but mild & thawing. Wind at So. Wt.

27.   Rain fell in the night. Fine Snow all the forenoon. Wind Easterly.

28.   Light Snow in the morning. Clear afterwards & mild. Wind So. Wt.

29.   Clear & turned much colder. Mercury at 18. Wind at No. Wt.

30.   Quite clear—mercury at 8 degrees. Wd. at No. Wt. but not strong.

31.   Very cold. Mercury at 4 degrees—very clear with little wind but a piercing Air.

[February]

Feb. 1.   Clear all day. Wind westerly in the forenoon & So. Wt. after wards.

2.   A sprinkle of Snow in the morning—cloudy afterwards with appearances of Rain. Wind So. W.

3.   A slight Snow fell in the Night. Clear day. Mild in the fore-noon–Cooler afterwards. Wind at N.W.

4.   Clear and rather cold. Not much wind & that N.W.

5.   Very clear & pleasant with but little Wind from the No. Et.

6.   A Slight Snow, not an Inch deep fell last night, clear without wind.

7.   Clear all day with but little wind from the Eastward.

8.   Cloudy all day. Wind Westwardly–moderate.

9.   Clear with the Wind at No. Wt. and rather cold–but fine notwithstanding for the Season.

10.   About 7 Oclock it began to Snow and kept steadily at it until 11, then changd. to rain & contd. all the day afterwards. Wind Easterly.

11.   Raining in the Morning. Clear afterwards and as mild as April. Wind at So. Wt.

12.   Wind from No. Wt. & cool, but fine notwithstanding.

13.   Clear & pleasant with but little wind and that from the Southward.

14.   Warm in the forenoon with the Wind Southerly. Cooler afterwards–Wind getting r[oun]d to the No. Wt.

15.   Cool, & clear all day, but not unpleasantly cold, Wind continuing at No. Wt. but not hard nor disagreeable.

16.   A little variable with the wind westerly.

17.   Clear, & remarkably fine with the Wind Southerly.

18th.   Wind at No. Et. and raing. all day. In the Night Snow abt. one inch thick fell.

19.   Clear with the wind at West & rather cool.

20.   Clear & cool – Wind westerly.

21.   Clear in the forepart of the day but lowering afterwards. Wind So. Wt.

22.   Snow abt. 2 Inches deep fell in the Night – forenoon cloudy; afternoon clear. Wind westerly.

23.   Wind at No. Wt. pretty fresh & cold.

24.   Cold & towards evening lowering & likely for Snow. Wind at No. Wt.

25.   Thick foggy morning with appearances of Wet, but none fell. Wd. at West.

26.   Much such a day as yesterday – but Wind more Southerly.

27.   Very thick morning again, but clear afternoon. Wind Southerly.

28.   Very clear and remarkably fine & pleasant.

29th.   A good deal of Rain fell in the Night. Fine Rain all day with the Wind at East.

[March]

1.   Thick heavy morning with the Wind at North. The afternoon not much better.

2.   Same kind of day, & Wind as yesterday – with spitting of Snow.

3.   A little Snow fell in the Night – heavy and thick all day. Wind abt. North.

4.   Again a little Snow fell in the Night – but not eno' to cover the ground.

5.   Heavy morning with clouds all day. Wind at North, a little Easterly.

6.   Thick morning but very pleasant afternoon with but little wind.

7.   Cloudy morning but clear afternoon. Wind West—shifting more Northerly & Easterly, & clouding towards Night.

8.   Snow 4 Inches deep fell in the Night & continued Spitting until 10 or 11 Oclock—then cleared & grew cold. Wind at No. Wt.

9.   Cold & clear. Wind No. Wt. & Westerly.

10.   Cold & cloudy in the forenn. but clear & mild afterwds. Wind getting to the So. Wt.

11.   Clear & pleasant all day. Wind getting more Westerly.

12.   Clear and warmer than yesterday—Wind more South.

13.   Forenoon clear & still. Afternoon very windy from the So. West.

14.   Lowering ⟨   ⟩ likely to rain with the Wind in the same place. Cloudy more or less all day.

15.   Tuesday clear and warm. Wind still Southerly and pretty brisk.

16.   A good deal of Rain fell last night and this morning. About 7 P.M. it cleared & blew violent from abt. No. Wt. all day & Night.

17.   Clear with the Wind from the same point.

18.   Dull & heavy forenoon with light falls of Snow from the No. Et. Clear afternoon.

19.   Clear & cold all day with the Wind fresh from No. W.

20.   Clear morning. Wind Westerly—pleasant all day.

21.   Morning lowering—but clear afterwards. Wind So. Et. growing warm.

22.   Heavy morning but clear afterwards and warm. Wind still at So. Et.

23.   Clear and warm Wind fresh from So. Wt.

24.   Cloudy morning & cooler. Wind at No. Wt. and clear afternoon.

25.   Wind in the Same place. Clear & cool all day.

26.   Wind Easterly—but clear & very pleasant notwithstanding.

PLEASANT: MS reads "pleasand."

27th.   Clear all day. The Wind at East & pleasant tho' a little cool.

28.   Thick, foggy morning with moderate rain about Noon, with the Wind at East. About 3 Oclock it cleared & was pleast. but afterwds. grew cloudy & cold.

29.   Very pleasant all day with the Wind westerly but variable.

30.   Clear in the forenoon with the wind mostly at west—cloudy afternoon.

31.   Clear and warm but little Wind & that Easterly.

[April]

1st.   Thick morning but clear afterwards & warm—very little wind & that No. Et.

2.   Hazy & smoaky—very little wind & that westerly. In the night a little rain.

3.   Clear with the Wind No. Easterly—somewhat cooler.

4.   Same wind & weather as yesterday.

5.   Clear and still cooler. The Wind, tho' not fresh, at No. W.

6.   Clear & rather cool—Wind being at No. Et. in the Morning. Warmer in the Afternoon wind being at So. W.

7.   Cool in the morning, but warmer afterwards wind getting to South West.

8.   Warm with appearances of Rain. Wind at So. W.

9.   Thick morning, but clear afterwards with a brisk So. Westerly wind—ground very dry. Smoaky.

10.   Again very thick and Smoaky in the morning. Wind Easterly & fresh last night—afterwards Northerly.

11.   Wind at No. Wt. and cold all day.

12.   Thick morning, but clear afterwards, rather cool wind Easterly in the morning & westerly afterwards.

At the top of the diary page for 1–15 April is the notation in GW's hand-writing: "Mr. Washington Craik joined as private Secrety. 12th. April 1796." George Washington Craik, Dr. James Craik's youngest son, held the position for about a year.

13.   Just such a day as yesterday & Wind the same.

14.   Wind at East in the Morning and very thick light Rain about Noon.

15.   Very thick morning—with but little wind. Clear Noon and rain in the Afternoon.

16.   Wind at No. Et. and from Nine until 11 a close and constant rain—clear afterwards.

17.   Wind at East & clear all day—a little cool.

18.   Clear & serene with very little wind.

19.   Clear forenoon—with the wind pretty fresh from the So. Wt.

20.   Clear all day with little Wind—that from So. W.

21.   Clear with the wind at No. Et. but warm & pleast. notwithstanding.

April 1796

Portraits of George and Martha Washington, by James Sharples, c. 1796. (Mount Vernon Ladies' Association of the Union)

22. Clear morning with the wind at East, wch. shifted in the afternoon to So. Wt. & grew warm.

23. Clear morning with the Wind fresh from No. Et. wch. continued so through the day & weather cooler.

24. Thick heavy morning with drops of Rain, Wind at So. W. In the afternoon there was pretty good Shower—Cool.

25. Cloudy morning but clear afterwards & cool all day. Wind at No. Et.

26. Cloudy morning & evening clear mid day. Cool all day with the Wind at No. Et.

27. Wind at No. Et. About 8 Oclock in the morning it began a fine Rain and continued till Noon. Towds. Night there was a very fine rain for an hour or two.

28. Clear and pleasant with the Wind Westerly.

29. Wind at No. Wt.—fresh—cold & disagreeable all day.

30. Wind and weather the same as yesterday.

[May]

1. Clear and cool all day. Wind at No. Wt.

2. Much such as yesterday: both in wind & weathr.

3. Wind at So. Wt. and warmer.

4. Clear morning. Wind variable from So. Et. to South.

5. Wind at So. Et. and fresh with Clouds in the forenoon, & mostly thro the day.

6. About 6 oclock it began a moderate rain, with the wind from East and continued raining moderately but steadily until 7 oclock in the evening.

7. Wind in the same quarter with a little rain in the forenoon. Clear afterwds.

8. Wind still at East with Clouds & sprinkling rain.

9. Cloudy with appearances of Rain—some of which fell in the night. Wind Easterly.

10. Cloudy with the Wind Westerly.

11. Weather variable, with small Showers. Wind abt. So. Wt. & growing warm.

12. For the most part clear but at times threatning rain. Wind Westerly.

13. Wind Westerly—shifting to So. W. & getting warm. Clear & very pleasant.

14. Wind at So. Et. and lowering more or less all day.

15. Wind in the same quarter, with clouds, & sometimes Sprinkling of Rain; in the afternoon a pretty heavy Shower with Sharp thunder.

16.   Wind Westerly & So. West.

17.   Cloudy more or less all day with light drippings now & then of Rain. Wind at S. Et.

18.   Wind at East. A thick Mist till 7 Oclock—then a steady rain till ten. Variable afterwards with a Shower abt. 6 oclock & Wind —N.W.

19.   Wind at East in the forenoon with constant rain from 6 till 12 Oclock. Wind westerly afterwds.

20.   Wind Southerly & weather. Rain in the afternoon.

21.   Clear with little or no Wind—until the afternn.

22.   Clear with hard wind from So. Wt. & South.

23.   Brisk Wind from South all day with great appearances of Rain.

24.   Wind Northerly and cool and for the most part of the day clear.

25.   Wind at No. Et., & fresh with constant rain until 4 O'clock— thick & mistg. afterwds.

26.   Wind in the same place with constant rain till abt. 4 oclock when it ceased & began at Night.

27th.   Thick morning, with some drops of Rain. Wind Easterly. About 9 Oclock the Wind Shifted to So. Wt. cleared & grew warm.

28.   Wind at So. Wt. in the Morning—varying to West and No. Wt. with changeable weather & a Shower.

29.   Clear forenoon—lowering afternoon with Wind at So. Wt.

30.   Rain in the Night—wch. continued steadily till Noon when it cleared. Wind still at So. West.

31.   Variable—with rain at times and wind at So. West.

[June]

1. Clear, with the Wind varying, but chiefly Westwardly.

2. Clear all day with the wind at So. West & Warm.

3. Clear & warm with but little wind and that Southerly.

4. Warm with but very little Wind. In the afternoon there was appearances of Rain but none fell.

5. Clear morning & showery afternoon—with variable wind from So. W. to N. Et.

6. Raining a little in the forenoon—clear afterwards. Wind Easterly.

7. Wind Easterly—very heavy morning and raining more or less all day with the Wind at East.

8. Heavy morning with the Wind at East, variable afterwards & Wind South.

9. Tolerably clear all day with the wind at So. & Warm but rain in the Night.

10. Wind at East in the Morning with Rain. In the Evening and Night a great deal fell.

11. Wind at East with a little Rain. Very warm.

12. Cloudy all day with great appearances of Rain. Wind Easterly in the Morning and Westerly afterwards.

13. Cloudy for the most part of the day—but no Rain.

GW left Philadelphia for Mount Vernon on 13 June and remained there until 17 Aug.

14. Clear Morning—but Rainy afternoon. Wind vary[ing].

15. Cloudy but no Rain and tolerably cool.

16.   Thick heavy Morning & heavy Showers of Rain in the afternoon.

17.   Clear all day and very warm—especially in the afternoon.

18.   Clear & very warm all day with sprinkling Rain in the Afternoon.

19.   Very warm with very little wind.

20.   Slight rain in the Morning but fair before and after noon.

21.   Clear and warm all day and but little wind.

Philadelphia and Mount Vernon
1797

January

1. Clear—Wind Westerly. Went to church. [23]

The information in brackets (indicating morning temperatures for the days in January) appears as marginal notes on one diary page and one almanac page.

2. Cloudy forenoon—wind westerly. Much company to complement the Season. [18]

New Year's Day having fallen on Sunday this year, the New Year's celebration was postponed until today.

3. Snowing from 10 oclock until 4—Wind westerly. Went to see Davenports Duck Manufy. [18]

Pages from Washington's diary for 1797. (Mount Vernon Ladies' Association of the Union)

After the Revolution there was a continuing demand in the United States for canvas, or duck, for sails. James Davenport (d. 1797) installed in 1794 at the old Globe Mills on the Germantown Road water-powered machinery of his own invention for "spinning and weaving flax, hemp and tow" (NEEDLES, 298). His patent, procured in 1794 for "weaving and beating sail duck," was the first one issued in the United States for any kind of textile machine (21st Cong., 2d sess., House Doc., No. 50, p. 140; BAGNALL, 222). The work was done by a few boys, one of whom could in a 10- to 12-hour day weave 15–20 yards of sailcloth or spin 292,000 feet of flax or hempen thread. According to a later newspaper advertisement, GW, accompanied by several members of Congress and others, was visiting the manufactory by invitation. After the death of James Davenport later in the year the machinery was sold and the business broken up (BISHOP, 2:71–72).

4. Wind Southwesterly, and cold moderating; a large Company of Gentlemen & ladies dined with me. [10]

5. Clear—Wind still So. Westerly and more moderate tho' cold. A large Compy. of Gentn. dined. [12]

6. Clear & moderate—Wind still at So. Wt. Road out between 10 & 12 Oclock. A good deal of company in the evening. [22]

7. Wind at No. West and cold with clouds. Road to German Town with Mrs. Washington to see Mr. Stuarts paintings. [14]

Gilbert Stuart (1755–1828) had recently returned to America after a long stay in England and Ireland, first as a student and then as a successful painter of portraits. He painted three portraits of GW from life between 1794 and 1796. From each of these life-portraits he made numerous copies to answer the great demand from both Americans and foreigners for likenesses of the first president. In the summer of 1796 Stuart had moved his studio from Philadelphia to a stone barn in Germantown.

8. Clear & Cold—wind at No. Wt. Went to a charity Sermon in Christ Church. Alarmed by a cry of fire while there. [6]

9. Clear & very cold—wind in the same place. Went to the Theatre, for the first time this Season. The Child of Nature & The Lock & Key were performed. [2]

WENT: GW has inadvertently written "Wind" in the MS. The New Theatre on Chestnut Street above Sixth Street had opened in 1794, and was said to be the finest theater in America at this time. It was copied after the theater at Bath, Eng., and seated 2,000 people. A stock company had been formed by Hugh Reinagle and Thomas Wignall, and they spent money lavishly to procure costumes and scenery and to obtain a supply of good actors, many from England (SCHARF [1], 2:970–71). *The Child of Nature* was a comedy in four

Self-portrait by Gilbert Stuart, painted in London 1786–88. (Metropolitan Museum of Art, Fletcher Fund, 1926)

acts, and *The Lock and Key,* a comic opera in two acts. The latter had been a resounding success in London, where it had played at Covent Garden Theatre for about 130 nights (*Gaz. of the U.S.* [Philadelphia], 5 and 9 Jan. 1797). The performance this evening was by request, and a local newspaper proclaimed that "the PRESIDENT OF THE UNITED STATES, and Family, will honor the Theatre with their company" (*Claypoole's Adv.* [Philadelphia], 9 Jan. 1797; *Gaz. of the U.S.* [Philadelphia], 9 Jan. 1797).

10.   Clear. Wind Westerly—or rather Southerly & moderating. [o]

11.   Wind at No. Et. Sprinkling of Snow in the Morning and raining soberly afterwds. [24]

12.   Clear & pleasant all day. Wind at So. Wt. All the Diplomatic Corp (except France) dined with me. [34]

The absence of the French minister, Pierre Auguste Adet, from GW's dinner party was undoubtedly a reflection of the strained relations existing between France and the United States at this time.

13.   Wind still Southerly. Exercised on horseback, on the River Delaware Crossing to Cowpers Tavern & recrossing below. [24]

COWPERS TAVERN: probably the ferry house erected by Samuel Cooper (1744–1812) in 1770 at Cooper's Point in what is now Camden, N.J. Samuel's son William was running the ferry by this time. There were actually several ferries within a short distance of each other, all owned by the Cooper family and all crossing the Delaware to Philadelphia (*N.J. Documents,* 542). December 1796 had produced unusually cold weather, and the Delaware River at Philadelphia was completely frozen over for several weeks. Jacob Hiltzheimer recorded on 8 Jan. that "from Race Street wharf I walked on the ice to Cooper's Ferry and back; saw thousands of people horses and sleighs, and booths on the ice" (HILTZHEIMER, 237).

14.   Wind Southerly. Morng. very heavy, with rain from Noon. Company dined with 5 Gent[leme]n. [32]

15.   Wind at So. Wt. mild & pleasant. [36]

16.   Wind Westerly with Sunshine & Clouds alternately thro' the day. [34]

17.   Clear with the wind at No. Wt. [36]

18.   Snowing until abt. 11 Oclock then clear & pleast. wind at So. Wt. [27]

19.   Wind Westerly, & clear & cold. [21]

20.   Wind at No. Wt. Colder than yesterday—clear until evening then cloudy.

21.   Three or 4 Inches of Snow fell last Night. Cloudy all day Wind at No. Et. Large compy. dined here. [26]

22.   Several Inches of Snow fell last Night. Variable weather with the wind at No. Et. [26]

23.   Wind at So. Wt. & thawing. Small compy. dined here. [21]

24.   Wind in the same quarter & thawing fast. Went to the Pantheon in the evening. [26]

WENT TO THE PANTHEON: The following advertisement appeared in a Philadelphia newspaper on 23 Jan.: "Pantheon, AND RICKETTS'S AMPHITHEATRE. MR. RICKETTS takes the liberty of announcing to his friends and the public, that to-morrow evening there will be a variety of performances, at the Pantheon BY DESIRE OF THE PRESIDENT OF THE UNITED STATES" (*Gaz. of the U.S.* [Philadelphia], 23 Jan. 1797). Ricketts's Amphitheatre, or Circus, was devoted principally to equestrian performances and slack and tightrope walking. John Bill Ricketts, a Scotsman, had come to Philadelphia in 1792 and had shortly afterwards built his large, circular amphitheater at the corner of Chestnut and Sixth streets. Ricketts and his son were the two main equestrians, performing dangerous feats of riding and acrobatics on horseback. The amphitheater burned in 1799, and Ricketts, bankrupt, returned to England (SCHARF [1], 2:952–53).

25.   Wind more westerly—clearer & somewhat cooler. Lar. company dined here. [24]

26.   Wind Northerly—then So. Westerly. Clear. Large Compa. dined. [24]

27.   Wind Southerly—thawing fast. [30]

28.   Do.   Do.   Do. Rain last Night [42]

29.   But little wind, dull and variable weather; misting. [34]

30.   Clear, & somewhat cooler than yesterday &ca. [28]

31.   Snowing in the Morning & raining the remainder of the day or rather misting. Wind at No. Et. [22]

February

1.   Wind No. Easterly in the Morning—So. Westerly afterwards and raining more or less all day. Mercury at 34 in the morning.

2.   A good deal of rain fell last [night]. Cloudy Morning but clear & very pleasant afterwards. Wind westerly. Mercury 42.

3.   Much such a day as yesterday but rather cooler. Wind same place. Mer. 30.

4.   Wind at So. West—weather pleasant. Mercury at 32 in the morning.

5.   Clear & pleasant with the Wind Westerly. Mery. 28. Morn.

6.   Fine Rain most part of the day. Wind So. Wt. Mer: 48. Went to the Play of Columbus in the evening.

Columbus; or a World Discovered, a historical play, was presented at the New Theatre at six o'clock this evening "BY PARTICULAR DESIRE." Also on the bill was a farce called *Barnaby Brittle; or a Wife at Her Wit's End.* The production of *Columbus* was an unusually ambitious one. The theater had been closed for several days before the first performance on 30 Jan., "on account of the extensive preparations" necessary for the new scenery, machinery, and decorations. Included in the production were a representation of a storm, an earthquake, a volcano eruption, and "A PROCESSION OF INDIANS and the first Landing of COLUMBUS" (*Gaz. of the U.S.* [Philadelphia], 23 Jan. and 6 Feb. 1797).

7.   Clear & cool. Wind at No. Wt. Mercury 34 in the Morn.

Benjamin Latrobe's watercolor of a view from the lawn at Mount Vernon, 1796. (The Papers of Benjamin Henry Latrobe, Maryland Historical Society)

8.   Clear & pleasant but Cool. Wind westerly. Mercury at 26.

9.   Cloudy all day. Wind Southerly. Mercury 34.

10.   Morning Rainy & stormy afterwards—Wind at So. Wt. Mercury at 50 in the Morn.

11.   Clear after the morning & Wind Westerly Mer: 35.

12.   Clear & pleasant. Wind Westerly—Mercury at 35.

13.   Cloudy morning, and fine rain all day afterwards. Wind Easterly—Mery. 38.

14.   Fine Rain—Wind in the same quarter. Mercury 38.

15.   Cloudy forenoon with flakes of Snow—clear afterwards. Wind Westerly. Mercury 34. Large Compy.

16.   Clear & pleasant. Wind Westerly. Mercury at 28. Large company dined here.

17.   Wind still westerly. Cloudy forenoon & rainy afternoon & Night. Mercury at 38. A very crouded drawing Room.

A VERY CROUDED DRAWING ROOM: That the drawing room, or levee, was particularly crowded on this day was undoubtedly the result of a rumor that this was to be Mrs. Washington's last levee before the Washingtons retired to Mount Vernon. John Adams was to be inaugurated as the new president on 4 Mar., and GW's last weeks in office were marked by a hectic round of visits and addresses from various groups including congressmen, merchants, the Pennsylvania governor and legislature, the Society of the Cincinnati, and army officers. There were also elaborate dinners and entertainments given in his honor. The Washingtons themselves on 3 Mar. gave a farewell dinner followed by Mrs. Washington's last drawing room. On 4 Mar. at noon GW attended the inauguration of the new president.

18.   Heavy morning & variable all day—Wind West. Mercury at 30. One third of the Pennsylvania Ho. of Representatives dined here.

Jacob Hiltzheimer, one of the members of the Pennsylvania legislature, listed in his diary Speaker George Latimer and 20 other members as present. "Our Speaker sat between the President and his lady, and I on the left of the President" (HILTZHEIMER, 240).

19.   Clear, Wind Westerly in the Morning but cloudy afterwards. Mer: 30. Went to church.

20.   Cloudy with a little rain in the forenoon—variable afterwards. Wind So. West. Mercury 39. Another third of the Penna. Reps. dined here.

21.   Wind westerly & remarkably pleasant in the forenoon—but lowering afterwards. Mery. at 30.

22.   Rain in the Night cloudy forenoon with the Wind at East—afterwards at S. W. clear & very fine. Went in the evening to an elegant entertainmt. given on my birth night. Mery. 38.

The "elegant entertainment" took place at Ricketts's Amphitheatre and was followed by dinner and a ball "which for Splendour, Taste and Elegance, was, perhaps, never excelled by any similar Entertainment in the United States." This entertainment was the culmination of a whole day of celebration which had begun by the ringing of bells and the firing of cannon (*Claypoole's Adv.* [Philadelphia], 23 Feb. 1797). See the description of the events of the day in MCREE, 2:493.

23.   Clear & pleasant forenoon. Wind brisk at So. Wt. lowerg. aftds. W. at So. Et. Mer. 36. The last third of the Pennsa. Assembly dined with me.

24.   Rain fell last Night & a little this Morng. Cloudy until afternoon Wind Westerly. Mery. 50.

25.   Wind pretty fresh from the No. W. and cool with lowering clouds towards evening—Mercury 32.

26.   Clear & cold all day Wind at No. Wt. & Mercury 19. All the Military & Naval Officer[s] dined with me yesterd. Mercury at 19 degs.

27.   Wind at So. Et. & lowering but no fall, Mer: 36. Went to the theatre in the Evening.

Playing at the New Theatre were a comedy, *The Way to Get Married;* a farce, *Animal Magnetism;* and "a new Pantomime Ballet Dance . . . called Dermot & Kathleen," composed by Mrs. Byrne, a member of the theater company (*Gaz. of the U.S.* [Philadelphia], 27 Feb. 1797; SCHARF [1], 2:971).

28.   Wind variable and grt. appearances all day of Snow. Mer. 35. Went to Mrs. Grattons concer[t] in the Evening.

"Mrs. Grattan Respectfully informs the Ladies and Gentlemen of the City, that the 5th ladies' concert will be on TUESDAY, the 28th day of February, at the Assembly-Room." The concert was to begin at 6:30, and "at half past eight, the music will attend for the ball." The program, part instrumental and part vocal, consisted of selections by Haydn, Handel, and others. Mrs. Grattan was among the vocalists. This may be the same Mrs. Grattan who opened a linen and muslin warehouse on North Sixth Street (*Gaz. of the U.S.* [Philadelphia], 28 Feb. 1797).

March

1.   Mercury at 24. Wind Westerly and cold all day.

2.   Wind as yesterday; cloudy, cold & Raw all day. Towards night it began to Snow. Mercury at 26.

3.   Mercury at 34. Morning very lowering & threatning but clear & pleasant afterwards. Wind fresh from the So. Wt.

4.   Much such a day as yesterday in all respects. Mercury at 41.

5.   Not unlike the two preceding days. M. at 50.

6.   The wind Shifted to the No. Wt. and turned Cold M: 24.

7.   A hard No. Wt. [wind] all day. Hard frost this morning & but little [sun] all day—snowing at times. Mer. at 24.

8.   Very thick morning with sprinkling rain clear afterwards with a brisk So. Westerly wind. Mer. 52.

9.   Wind changed to No. Wt. blew very hard & turned very cold. Mer. at 28. Left Phila. on my return to Mt. Vernon—dined at Chester & lodged at Wilmington.

Accompanying GW and Mrs. Washington on the trip home to Mount Vernon were Nelly Custis and the marquis de Lafayette's son, George Washington Motier Lafayette (1779–1849), accompanied by his tutor, Felix Frestal. George Washington Parke Custis was in school in Princeton, and Tobias Lear and Bartholomew Dandridge, Jr., had been left in Philadelphia to supervise the packing and moving of the Washingtons' belongings and the cleaning of the presidential house. Lear was to follow them to Mount Vernon, but Dandridge would leave shortly for The Hague where he was to be secretary to the United States minister, William Vans Murray. Young Lafayette had fled France with his tutor in 1795, three years after his father's arrest and imprisonment. The young man's arrival in America had been an embarrassment to GW. As much as he wished to have this only son of his close friend come to live in his family, he wanted to do nothing to offend the French government or the French partisans in this country. He therefore arranged for the boy and Frestal to live in New York under his family name, Motier. Finally, in April 1796, in spite of warnings by some members of the government, GW invited young Lafayette and Frestal to Philadelphia for a visit with his family. The visit lengthened into a permanent residency (GOTTSCHALK, xxi–xxiii; FREEMAN, 7:304, 323, 359–60, 388–99, 403–12). DINED AT CHESTER: "At Chester, Mr. Anderson keeps such a house *now,* as Mrs. Withy did *formerly;* and that is encomium enough. At Wilmington, twelve miles further, Mr. O Flin's (sign of the Ship) is a quiet Inn, with good Beds, and a tolerable good Table" (GW to Elizabeth Willing Powel, 26 Mar. 1797, ViMtV).

10. Dined & lodged at Elkton. Tolerably pleasant all day.

"At Elkton . . . Hollingsworth's is a quiet orderly Tavern, with good beds, and well in other respects" (GW to Elizabeth Willing Powel, 18 Mar. 1797, ViMtV). "We encountered no adventures of any kind, & saw nothing uncommon, except the light Horse of Delaware, & Maryland, who insisted upon attending us through their states" (Eleanor Parke Custis to Elizabeth Bordley, 18 Mar. 1797, ViMtV).

11. Snowing from day light until 10 Oclock – in the Afternoon a little rain. Breakfasted at Susquehanna – dined & lodged at Hartford.

"At the Ferry, on both sides, are good Taverns: Mrs. Rogers' on the East, & Mr. Barney's on the West. From thence to Hartford (commonly called Bushtown) twelve miles from the ferry, a good house *used* to be kept but . . . it was to be sold the Wednesday after we passed it" (GW to Elizabeth Willing Powel, 26 Mar. 1797, ViMtV). GW stopped at both Mrs. Rodgers's and Barney's on this day (GW's Cash Memorandum, 29 Sept. 1794–17 Aug. 1797, RPJCB).

12. Lowering, but tolerably pleasant. Breakfasted at Websters. Dined & lodged in Baltimore. Met & escorted into town by a great concourse of people.

WEBSTERS: "Thirteen miles from thence [Harford] a pretty good Inn is kept by one Webster. From that to Baltimore is 14 Miles" (GW to Elizabeth Willing Powel, 26 Mar. 1797, ViMtV).

GW's entrance into Baltimore was described in a contemporary account: "At a distance from the city he was met by a crowd of citizens, on horse and foot, who thronged the road to greet him; and by a detachment from capt. Hollingsworth's troop, who escorted him in thro' as great a concourse of people as Baltimore ever witnessed. On alighting at the Fountain Inn, the general was saluted with reiterated and thundering huzzas from the spectators" (*Gaz. of the U.S.* [Philadelphia], 16 Mar. 1797). Mayor James Cal-

A primitive view of Mount Vernon, painted in 1797. (Mount Vernon Ladies'
Association of the Union)

houn read an address from the council of Baltimore which GW answered
(FREEMAN, 7:446). The Fountain Inn, where GW lodged, had been sold
by Daniel Grant in 1795, and the present owner was a Scot, James Bryden
(ANDREWS, 60–63).

13.   Breakfasted at Spurriers & dined & lodged in Bladensburgh.
Morning lowered but clear afterwards.

Spurrier's was "much resorted, not because it is well kept but because there
is no other; the lodging is bad—the eating tolerable . . . better for lodging
than eating. At Bladensburgh nine miles beyond a good house is kept by one
Ross (sign of the Indian Queen)" (GW to Elizabeth Willing Powel, 26 Mar.
1797, ViMtV).

14.   Dined at Mr. Laws & lodged at Mr. Thos. Peters. Day warm.

MR. LAWS: Thomas Law (1759–1834), son of Edmund Law, bishop of Carlisle, was in India from 1773 to 1791 in the service of the East India Company, where he held several important administrative positions and acquired
a sizable fortune. Apparently sometime during his stay in India, Law was
married, for when ill health forced his return to England, he brought his
three Indian sons with him. In 1794 Law and his children came to America.
He met James Greenleaf in New York and purchased from him a large
section of lots in the new Federal City. Law came to the Federal City on
23 Feb. 1795 to inspect his newly acquired property, located south of the
Capitol between the Potomac River and the Eastern Branch (Anacostia

River). In 1796 he married young Eliza Parke Custis, Martha Washington's eldest grandchild. Law built numerous houses in the city for speculation and for his own use, but at this time he was probably living at the northeast corner of Sixth and N streets, S.W., near Greenleaf Point (DOWNING [3], 27). The Englishman Thomas Twining, who visited the Laws in 1796, wrote of his difficulty in finding the isolated house several miles from the Capitol: "His house, built by himself, was only a few yards from the steep bank of the Potomac, and commanded a fine view across that river, here half a mile wide. In the rear of the house Mr. Law was building a street, consisting of much smaller houses than his own. . . . The position at least was favorable, being on a point of land between the Potomac and a tributary stream called 'the eastern branch,' thus offering a double waterfront" (TWINING, 104). Thomas Law, aside from his land activities in the capital, was a strong advocate of the need for a national currency and wrote numerous addresses and pamphlets promoting it. Law lost much of his fortune in his land speculations and spent his later years in relative poverty. Always eccentric, he became more so with age, and his marriage to Eliza Parke Custis ended in a much publicized separation and divorce.

MR. THOS. PETERS: Thomas Peter was the son of Robert Peter, a prominent merchant and first mayor of Georgetown. In Jan. 1795 Thomas Peter married Martha Washington's granddaughter Martha Parke Custis. The couple lived in Washington in a house located near Rock Creek on the south side of K Street between 26th and 27th.

15.   Recd. the Compliments of the Citizens of George Town as I had done the day before of those of the City of Washington. Stopped in Alexa. & got to Mt. V. to dinner.

CITY OF WASHINGTON: The *Washington Gazette* on this day reported that "Yesterday George Washington (God bless him) passed through the city on his way to Mount Vernon. When he reached the Capitol the company of Artillery, under the command of Captain [James] Hoban, welcomed him by a discharge of cannon. After dining in the City, he was escorted to George Town by several of our most respectable Citizens. As he passed the President's house, a salute of 16 guns was fired by the said company and followed by repeated huzzas, dictated by hearts sensibly alive to his merits" (DIARIES, 4:255, n.1). Nelly Custis wrote a friend that "The gentlemen of George Town also attended us to the River, & four of them rowed us over in a barge" (Eleanor Parke Custis to Elizabeth Bordley, 18 Mar. 1797, ViMtV). ALEXA.: "Yesterday General Washington accompanied by his Lady, the son of the Marquis de la Fayette, &c. passed through town on their way home. The General's desire to reach Mount-Vernon that evening prevented the citizens of Alexandria from offering those public marks of their gratitude and esteem, which they were now more than ever solicitous of manifesting for their illustrious neighbour. . . . We are informed that Gen. Washington has accepted of an invitation to a public dinner, to be given in this town on Thursday" (*Columbian Mirror* [Alexandria], 16 Mar. 1797). MT. V.: They arrived at Mount Vernon at 4:00 P.M. (Eleanor Parke Custis to Elizabeth Bordley, 18 Mar. 1797, ViMtV). Of the journey from Philadelphia and the conditions prevailing at Mount Vernon when he arrived, GW wrote: "We got home without accident, & found the Roads drier, & better than I ever

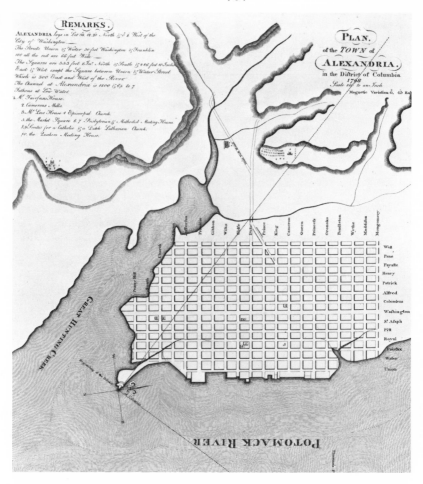

Plan of the town of Alexandria, 1798, engraved by T. Clarke. (Map Division, Library of Congress)

travelled them at that Season of the year. The attentions we met with on our journey were very flattering, and to some whose minds are differently formed from mine would have been highly relished, but I avoided in every instance where I had any previous knowledge of the intention, and c[oul]d by the earnest entreaties prevail, all parade, or escorts. . . . I find myself in the situation, nearly, of a new beginner; for although I have no houses to build (except one, which I must erect for the accommodation & security of my Military, Civil & private Papers . . .) yet I have not one or scarcely anything else about me that does not require considerable repairs. In a word I am already surrounded by Joiners, Masons, Painters & ca." (GW to James McHenry, 3 April 1797, NN: Washington Collection).

16.   At home all day alone. Wind at East & very cloudy all day.

17. Wind in the same place with rain from 10 oclock until 12 – clear afterwards.

18. Clear – with the Wind fresh from So. Wt. in the forenoon and at No. Wt. in the afternoon.

19. Wind at No. Wt. and fresh after the morning continuing so all day & cold.

20. Cool in the morning with the wind still at No. W. but very moderate afternoon.

21. Wind Southerly and fresh all day – clear.

22. Wind still Southerly and fresh with appearances of Rain. In the Afternoon wind came out brisk at N. W.

23. Cool in the morning but clear & very pleasant afterwards with but little Wd.

24. Wind at So. Et. with Rain more or less all day.

25. Wind for the most part Southerly – and clear.

26. Wind varying from No. Et. to So. Et. and blowing very fresh.

27. A little rain fell last Night. Wind Southerly in the Morning & violently all day afterwards & night from No. Wt.
   Omitted to enter the Acct. of the Weather & Occurrences the remainder of this month.

April

Omitted keeping any Acct. of the Weather and Occurrences in this Month.

May — 1797

1. Went to Alexandria to settle some matters at the Bank. Day warm – wind at So. Wt.

MATTERS AT THE BANK: "To Cash recd. from the Bank of Alexa. dividend on 10 Sh:—100 Dollrs." (GW's Cash Memorandum, 29 Sept. 1794–17 Aug. 1797, RPJCB).

2.   Blew violently hard all day from the No. Wt. & grew very Cold.

3.   A frost in the morning—Weather variable & cold. Wind So. Wt. & fresh.

4.   Warm, with very little Wd. and that So. Wt.

5.   Warm in the forenoon with the wind at So. Wt. Rain in the Afternoon. Went to Alexa. on business. Retd. in the afternoon.

ON BUSINESS: GW had "Dinner &ca." at Gadsby's tavern today (GW's Cash Memorandum, 29 Sept. 1794–17 Aug. 1797, RPJCB).

6.   Warm with the Wind at So. Et.—but not hot.

7.   Wind, after the morning very fresh from the N. W. & turning very cold.

8.   Wind No., a little Easterly and Cool with a shower of Rain abt. 1 Oclock & squally.

9.   Disagreeably cool—tho' the Wind was shifting to the South-ward.

10.   Very pleasant—warm & clear.

11.   Brisk So. Westerly Wind & warm.

12.   Wind in the same quarter but not so much of it but very warm.

13.   Wind No. Westerly and much cooler with appearances of Rain.

14.   Wind at No. Et. & rather Cool—indeed quite so.

15.   Very pleasant, & but little wind—that however was from the No. Et.

16. Wind No. Easterly, & then to the westward of No. but not much of it. Appearances of Rain but none fell.

17. Wind Easterly all day and pretty fresh & cool.

18. Very cloudy all day with the Wind at So. Et. Showers with thunder & lightening in the afternoon.

19. Wind at No. Et. & cloudy all day with moderate Rain from ½ after 10 until near two.

20. Wind from the So. Et. with appearances of Rain but none fell—very warm.

21. Wind more Southerly with great appearances of Rain but none fell here.

22d. Morning rather cooler but warm afterwards with but little wind.

23. Wind Easterly & rather Cool.

24. Wind Southerly and warm with appearances of Rain but none fell.

25. Very brisk Southerly wind & still great appearances of Rain but none fell here.

26. Wind at No. W. & fresh in the morning, but less of it & at So. Wt. in the Afternn. Cool till evening.

27. Wind at So. Wt. Clear and warm all day. In the evening Sultry.

28. Wind in the forepart of the day very high, from the No. W. and cold.

29. Clear & rather Cool with but little Wind.

30. Cloudy & much like rain all day with the Wind at No. Et. In the afternoon & night a little rain fell.

31. Wind at No. Wt. and cool.

June

1.   Wind at No. Et. in the morning and at So. Wt. in the afternoon but not much of it—Cool.

2.   Wind at So. Wt. with great appearances of rain but very little fell—rather cool.

3.   Wind in the same quarter tho' not much of it. Warm.

4.   Very warm with the Wind at So. Wt.; much appearances of Rain, but very little fell.

5.   Cool again with the Wind fresh from No. Wt.

6.   Wind at So. Wt. and warm.

7.   Ditto—   Do.   Do.

8.   Wind at No. Et. in the Morning—but Southerly afterwards and warm.

9.   Very warm with the wind at So. Wt. and great appearances of Rain but none fell here.

10.   Very warm with a Southerly wind and great appearances of rain but none fell here.

NONE: MS reads "not."

11.   Wind at No. Wt. All day but neither hard nor cold.

12.   Wind Southwesterly—clear & warm.

13.   Very Warm with a brisk Southerly wind—a slight Shower of Rain. Mercury 83.

14.   Very Warm with the [wind] Southerly. Mercury 84. Weather extremely dry.

15.   Same Wind, & heat as yesterday.

16.   Wind in the same quarter Mer. at 87. Clear.

17.   Mercury at 90—day Sultry with the wind Southerly—a scud of Rain for a minute or two.

18.   A refreshing Rain fell in the Night and a tolerable good shower about 3 Oclock this day. Wind variable. Mercury at 83 only.

19.   Cool in the morning with the wind at No. Wt. Mercury 69 only.

20.   Wind Southerly but cool Mercury 71. Two showers in the Afternoon.

21.   Wind at No. Et. but variable. Mercury 74. Cloudy in the afternoon with appearances of Rain but none fell.

22.   Wind Southerly & growing warmer. Cloudy & likely for rain all day. Began Wheat harvest at Union & Dogue R. Farms.

GW wrote a friend on 26 June, "Until last week, I had no suspicion that the Hessian fly was among my Wheat, but upon examination I found there were many. They have come too late, *this year,* however, to do me much damage; but . . . I view them as the harbingers of those who will visit me

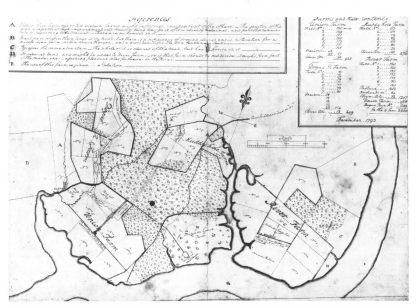

Washington's map of the farms comprising his Mount Vernon estate, 1793. (The Henry E. Huntington Library)

next year." He added, however, "Where this calamity has not visited the Wheat, the grain is remarkably fine, and the quantity not to be complained of" (GW to Richard Peters, PHi: Peters Manuscripts).

23.   Cloudy morning with light showers, & wind Southerly until Noon then clear with the wind from No. W. M. 77.

24.   Wind Westerly, but very little of it. Mery. 73.

25.   Clear & tolerable pleasant with the Wind Westerly. Mer. 77.

26.   Wind southerly & clear. Mer. 78.

27.   Wind Easterly with some appearances of Rain but none fell. Mer. 79.

28.   Wind Southerly and Warm. Mer. 78.

29.   Clear & Warm—Wind So. Mer. 79.

30.   Clear & warm—Wind Southerly. Mercury 80.

July

1.   Warm with variable Wind—sometimes East & sometimes West of So. M. 80.

2.   Wind Southerly with a slight Shower 2 Oclock. Mer. 88 before the Rain.

3.   Clear in the forenoon with a slight shower for a few minutes about 2 Oclock; afternoon Wind Southerly Mer. 81.

4.   Wind Westerly all day with appearances of Rain but none fell. Mercury at 81.

5.   Cool in the morning with the Wind at No. Wt.—calm afterwards. Mery. 79.

6.   Clear until the Afternoon with but little wind then hazy clouds with the Wind at So. Et. Mer. 80.

Silhouette of George Washington. (Independence National Historical Park Collection)

Silhouette of Martha Washington drawn in 1796 by her granddaughter, Nelly Custis. (Mount Vernon Ladies' Association of the Union)

7. Heavy morning with Rain more or less from 7 in the Morning until 2 Oclock in the afternoon but very moderate. Wind So. Easterly—Mer. 74.

8. Clear after the morning & warm. Wind Southerly Mer. 82.

9. Wind pretty fresh from No. Wt. all day. Weather clear and Mercury at 82.

10. Clear with the Wind Southerly. Mery. at 84.

11. Wind at No. Wt. all day a little rain having fallen in the Night but not on my Farms. M. 81.

12. Little or no wind. Mercury at 83.

13. Calm and clear all day—Mery. at 85.

14. Very little wind and clear—Mery. 91.

15.   Last Night extremely warm—clear & calm—Mer. 88.

16.   Very warm with the Wind at So. Mer. 90. Fine Rain in the Afternoon—suff[icien]t to wet the g[round].

17.   Appearances of Rain most part of the day but none fell— pleasant. Went up to the Fedl. City.

18.   Warm with appearances of Rain in the Afternoon—but none fell. In the City all day.

19.   Went by the bridge at the little falls to the Gt. Falls & re- turned home in the Afternoon.

BRIDGE AT THE LITTLE FALLS: Pierre Charles L'Enfant's original plan for the Federal City called for a bridge over the Potomac River at Little Falls and one over the Eastern Branch (Anacostia River). In 1791 the Georgetown Bridge Company was chartered and subscriptions taken. On 1 July 1795 the company's books were opened for 400 shares at $200 per share. Timothy Palmer was to undertake the erection of the bridge at Little Falls. The bridge, which opened for use on 3 July 1797, was a "wooden roofed-in struc- ture" with high stone and iron abutments (BRYAN, 1:243, 491–92; *National Intelligencer* [Washington], 16 Mar. 1808; *Columbian Mirror* [Alexandria], 12 Aug. 1797).

20.   Clear & warm. Mercury at 83.

21.   Much such a day as yesterday—M. 83.

22.   Warm morning & cloudy with very fine Showers from 11 Oclock in the Morning until near 3 oclock wetting the grd. thor- oughly. Mery. 80.

23.   Cloudy forenoon but clear afterwards—but little Wind. Mer. 81.

24.   Clear & warm—Wind Southerly. A little rain in the Night. M. 85.

25.   Great appea[ra]nces of Rain in the morning clear & warm afterwards—Mer. 83.

26.   Clear all day with but little wind and that So. Mer. 84.

27.   Wind Southerly & warm. A fine rain about 3 Oclock for an hour. Mercury 81.

28.   Mercury at 82. Clear forenoon but Showers in the Afternoon.

29.   Clear all day—Wind Easterly. Mer. 79.

30.   Mercy. 79—A Slight Shower abt. 2 Oclock rather cool afterwds.

31.   Mercury at 76. Wind Easterly—and frequent Showers of Rain in the Afternoon.

August

1.   Wind Southerly—heavy shower in the afternoon & much rain fell in the Night. Mer. 78. Mr. Bolling & Mr. L. Washington of King George came here.

Robert Bolling (born c.1759) of Centre Hill, Petersburg, was the son of Robert Bolling (1730–1775) and Mary Tabb Bolling of Bollingbrook. He married in 1796 his third wife, Sally Washington, daughter of Lawrence Washington of Chotank. Bolling had served in the Virginia militia during the Revolution (DAVIDSON, 154–56; *Va. Mag.*, 4 [1897], 330–31). L. WASHINGTON OF KING GEORGE: probably Bolling's brother-in-law, Lawrence Washington, Jr. (see entry for 27 July 1785).

2.   Wind Easterly. Showers in the Morng. & Afternoon. Mer. 77. B. & W. went away.

3.   Raining more or less from 10 Oclock—M. 77.

4.   Wind at So. Et. & Easterly—appearances of Rain but none fell. Warm Mer. 85. Mrs. Peake & Miss Evelin dined here.

MISS EVELIN: GW undoubtedly means Fanny Edelen (see entries for 28 Dec. 1771 and 7 Nov. 1785). Mrs. Peake is probably Humphrey Peake's widow, Mary Stonestreet Peake.

5.   Warm & sultry in the forepart of the day with great appearances afterwards & a slight Shower in the evening—Mer. 85. Doctr. Stuart & daughter Nancy came here.

Dr. David Stuart (see entry for 3 Jan. 1785) was appointed by GW as one of the three original commissioners for the Federal City but resigned that office in Sept. 1794. The settlement of a long-standing dispute with Robert Alexander (see entry for 27 Mar. 1788) over the nearby Abingdon property (see entry for 12 Mar. 1785) had necessitated the Stuart family's removal from there about 1792. They were at this time living at Hope Park, a 2,000-acre estate about 10 miles west of Abingdon in a more isolated area of Fairfax County. Stuart's daughter Ann Calvert (Nancy) Stuart was about 14 years old at this time.

6.   Showery in the morning & cloudy most part of the day. Mer. 76. Wind at No. Et.

7.   Appearances of Rain until 10 Oclock & a sprinkle at Night. Mer. 76. Dr. Stuart & daughter returned home. I went to the annual Meeting of the Potk. Co. at George town. Dined at the Union tavern & lodged at Mr. Thos. Peter's.

POTK. CO.: Work on building locks and clearing the Potomac River and its tributaries for navigation had been under way for more than a decade. When money was plentiful, the work progressed rapidly, with the employment of many Irish and German indentured servants and hired laborers; but from 1788 until the present year, funds for the work on the river gradually became harder to procure. Efforts were largely bent on obtaining enough money to complete the locks at Great Falls, the only part of the Potomac River at which a portage was still necessary. There were repeated calls on shareholders for additional contributions; the legislatures of Maryland and Virginia were petitioned at various times for the sale of more shares to be added to the capital stock; attempts were made to force delinquent subscribers to pay their quotas. Despite all efforts to raise money, funds were at this time entirely exhausted. At the 1797 annual meeting in Georgetown the shareholders of the Potomac Company found it necessary to agree to sell the indentures of the servants and discharge the company's laborers. Among the attempts to raise more money was an order to the directors to sell or mortgage all shares belonging to the company; to open the books for 30 additional shares at £130 each; to petition the Virginia and Maryland legislatures for permission to collect tolls at Great Falls; and "to mortgage the tolls for the amount of $16,000, all monies to be applied to the works at Great Falls" (BACON-FOSTER, 95). For further information on the activities of the Potomac Company during the period 1788 to 1797, see BACON-FOSTER, 82–100 and 169–71.

The Union Tavern, built in 1796 by the subscription of a number of Georgetown citizens, was a three-story brick structure located at the corner of Washington (30th) and Bridge (M) streets. It boasted an elegant assembly, or ball, room which was a favorite accommodation for birthday balls and other social assemblies (BRYAN, 1:280; EBERLEIN & HUBBARD, 10–12).

8.   Returned home to dinner. Drizling at times until one Oclock —clear afterwds. Mer. 75. Wind No. W. in the Aftern.

9.   No rain, but appearances of it in the afternoon. Wind Northerly—Mer. 73.

10.   Clear & cool all day with the wind varying from No. Wt. to No. Et. Mery. at 70. Miss Fanny Henley came.

Frances (Fanny) Henley (b. 1779) was the eldest child of Martha Washington's sister Elizabeth and her second husband, Leonard Henley, of James City County. Fanny later became the third wife of Tobias Lear.

11.   Morning & evening cloudy but no rain—Wind shifting from No. Et. to So. Wt.—Mer. 73.

12.   Fair until evening, when it began to rain moderately. Wind at So. West & Mer. 79. Genl. Lee, Lady & daughter came.

GENL. LEE: Henry (Light Horse Harry) Lee's first wife, Matilda, died in 1790 and in 1793 Lee married Anne Hill Carter (1773–1829), daughter of Charles Carter of Shirley and his second wife, Anne Butler Moore Carter. The daughter who accompanied the Lees was Lucy Grymes Lee (1786–1860), a child of Lee's first marriage.

13.   Wind rather variable with Showers in the afternoon. Mer. 79. General ⟨L.⟩ & ca. went away & Mr. Bourne and Mr. Lear came.

Anne Hill Carter Lee, second wife of "Light Horse Harry" Lee. (Washington and Lee University, Washington-Custis-Lee Collection)

MER.: GW has inadvertently written "Mer." twice in the MS. Mr. Bourne may be Sylvanus Bourne, who was vice-consul in Amsterdam about 1794 and in June 1797 was appointed consul general to the Batavian Republic. A notice in the Alexandria newspaper on 7 Nov. stated that he and his wife "sailed from Chester on Sunday last, in the ship Phoenix, for Amsterdam" (*Columbian Mirror* [Alexandria], 7 Nov. 1797).

Tobias Lear, whose second wife, Fanny Bassett Washington Lear, had died in late Mar. 1796, seems to have been living in Washington City. Lear, now a merchant in the Federal City, was also president of the Potomac Company and was on his way to the Great Falls on company business (Lear to GW, 16 Aug. 1797, DLC:GW). Lear wrote GW a few weeks later that he was resolved to take up residence in the fall at Walnut Tree Farm, a section of Clifton's Neck which GW had given to Fanny and George Augustine Washington in 1787 (see entry for 10 Feb. 1787). There he would take up farming and direct the studies of his "Charming boys"—Fanny Lear's two orphan sons, George Fayette Washington (1790–1867) and Charles Augustine Washington (b. 1791), and his own child, Benjamin Lincoln Lear (c.1791–1832), the son of his first wife, Mary Long Lear. He had hoped to rent GW's adjacent River Farm for the coming year, but the season was too far advanced and GW had already made other arrangements to farm the land himself (Lear to GW, 8 Sept. 1797, DLC:GW; GW to Lear, 11 Sept. 1797, NN: Washington Papers).

14. Wind at No. Wt. & Cool all day. Mer. 70. Mr. Bourne & Mr. Lear went away & Mr. Ferdd. Fairfax came.

Ferdinando Fairfax (see entry for 31 May 1769) inherited from his uncle George William Fairfax in 1787 all his property, including the Belvoir estate in Fairfax County and tracts of land in Berkeley (later in Jefferson) County. Ferdinando's home, Shannon Hill, on the Shenandoah River was about halfway between Key's ferry and Snickers' ferry. During this visit to Mount Vernon, Fairfax discussed with GW the possibility of hiring one of GW's jackasses to stand at Shannon Hill for the season and of GW's purchasing or hiring a cook to replace one who had recently run away (Ferdinando Fairfax to GW, 22 Aug. 1797 and 2 Mar. 1798, DLC:GW).

15. Clear & Cool—wind at No. W. Mer. 71. Mr. Fairfax went away.

16. Clear wind varying from No. W. to S. W. Mer. 73.

17. Wind inclining to the Westward—Mer. 73. Weather clear. Went with the family to Alexa. Dined with Mr. Potts. Doctr. Stuart came home with us in the evening.

Mr. Potts is John Potts, Jr., formerly of Pottsgrove (Pottstown), Pa. (see entry for 11 Sept. 1785).

18. Wind Southerly—Clear—Mer. at 79. Doctr. Stuart went away.

Edward Savage's portrait of the Washington family, painted in 1796. (National Gallery of Art, Gift of Henry Prather Fletcher)

19.   Wind Southerly all day. Mer. at 82. Some app[earanc]e of Rain.

20.   But little wind & that variable. Weather clear. Mer. 79.

21.   Clear with little or no wind. Mer. at 80.

22.   Clear & warm. Wind small & variable. Mer. 79.

23.   Very little wind rather inclining to the Westward. Mer. 80. Mr. Richd. Randolph & Mr. Carter Beverly came to dinner & Captn. Blackburn & lady in the Afternoon. Clouds but no R.

Richard Randolph, Jr. (c.1758–1799), of Curles in Henrico County was married to Maria Beverley Randolph (1764–1824), daughter of Robert Beverley (1740–1800) and Maria Carter Beverley (1745–1817) of Blandfield. Randolph's brother-in-law, Carter Beverley (1774–1844), was a justice of Culpeper County. CAPTN. BLACKBURN & LADY: Richard Scott Blackburn (died c.1804–5), the eldest son of Thomas and Christian Scott Blackburn of Rippon Lodge near Dumfries, had been appointed to a captaincy in the United

States Army in 1794. Earlier, in 1790–91, he served one term in the Virginia House of Delegates. Blackburn was married first to Judith Ball and then, sometime after Oct. 1796, to Ann Blause (c.1760–c.1804).

24. The latter Gentn. & lady went away after breakfast & the former after dinner. Calm. Mer. at 80.

25. Very warm with but little Wind in the forenoon—Mer. at 82. Mr. Wilson & Mrs. Ramsay—Mr. & Mrs. Potts & two daughters dined here.

Mr. Wilson is William Wilson, merchant, of Alexandria (see entry for 17 April 1785). Mrs. Ramsay is Mrs. Elizabeth Ramsay, mother of Eliza Ramsay Potts and widow of Patrick Ramsay, a Scottish merchant of Blandford, Prince George County. At the beginning of the Revolution, Patrick Ramsay returned with his family to Glasgow, where he died. His widow and children came back to America in the 1780s and settled in Alexandria (SLAUGHTER [3], 211). William Wilson may have been married to one of Mrs. Ramsay's daughters (deed of Elizabeth Ramsay to John Potts, Jr., and William Wilson, Fairfax County Deeds, Book T-1, 7–11, Vi Microfilm; WMQ, 1st ser., 14 [1905–6], 211–13). John Potts, Jr., and his wife, Eliza Ramsay Potts (see entry for 18 Nov. 1787), had at least three daughters: Sophia W., Anna, and W. D. Potts (SLAUGHTER [3], 211).

26. Mrs. Washington dined here and in the afternoon Genl. & Mrs. Spotswood—Captn. Spotswood Miss Spotswood & Miss Thornton came. But little wind & great appearances of Rain. Mer. 81.

Mrs. Washington is undoubtedly Lund Washington's widow, Elizabeth Foote Washington, of nearby Hayfield.

Alexander Spotswood of New Post and Nottingham, both in Spotsylvania County, and his wife, Elizabeth Washington Spotswood, were accompanied by two of their children and a niece; Capt. John Augustine Spotswood, a son, was captain of a schooner probably involved in the West Indies trade (see entry for 30 April 1785; John A. Spotswood's statement of his property, 1798, DLC:GW). Miss Spotswood was probably the eldest daughter, Mary; Miss Thornton was one of the four daughters of Mrs. Spotswood's sister Jane Washington Thornton (born c.1752) and her husband, Col. John Thornton, son of Col. Francis Thornton (d. 1784) of Society Hill.

27. Clear, with the wind at No. W. all day. Mer. at 78.

28. Clear—Mercury at 80. Wind Southerly.

29. Clear—Wind Southerly. M. at 80. Mr. Bushd. Washington Mr. Fieldg. Lewis & Wife and Miss Dade dined here & went away afterwards.

Bushrod Washington had moved his law practice from Alexandria to Richmond in 1790. Fielding Lewis, Jr., was married to Nancy Alexander, daughter of Gerard and Mary Dent Alexander of Fairfax County. The Miss Dade who accompanies the Lewises is undoubtedly one of Mrs. Lewis's relatives; there were numerous marriages between the Alexander and Dade families over several generations.

30.   Clear, with the Wind, tho little of it Southerly. Mercury 80. Ludwell Lee Esqr. & Lady & Miss Armistead dined here.

Richard Henry Lee's eldest son, Ludwell Lee (1760–1836), served in the Virginia House of Delegates 1787–90 and was now speaker of the Virginia Senate. His first wife, Flora Lee, had died, and he was married again on 30 May 1797 to Elizabeth (Betsey) Armistead, daughter of Bowles and Mary Fontaine Armistead. The Miss Armistead who appears with the Lees is undoubtedly one of the bride's sisters.

31.   Appearances of rain in the Morning—clear & warm afterwards. Mer. at 84. Genl. Spotswoods family & ours dined with Mr. Ludwell Lee. And Mr. Nichs. Fitzhugh & his wife came here to dinner & Mr. Lawe. Lewis in the evening.

DINED WITH MR. LUDWELL LEE: at Shuter's (Shooter's) Hill, Lee's home just outside Alexandria. Nicholas Fitzhugh (1764–1814), one of 14 children of Henry Fitzhugh (1723–1783) of Bedford and Sarah Battaile Fitzhugh (1731–1783), lived at Ravensworth in Fairfax County. He served in the House of Delegates 1790–91 and 1800–3, and then was appointed judge of the United States circuit court for the district of Washington. He married in 1788 Sarah Ashton, daughter of Burdett Ashton and his wife, Ann Washington Ashton, GW's niece.

Lawrence Lewis, son of GW's sister Betty, had been invited by GW to reside at Mount Vernon to help with the entertainment of the many guests. GW informed Lewis, however, that he would "expect no Services from you for which pecuniary compensation will be made. I have already as many on wages as are sufficient to carry on my business and more indeed than I can find means to pay, conveniently. As both your Aunt and I are in the decline of life, and regular in our habits, especially in our hours of rising & going to bed; I require some person (fit & proper) to ease me of the trouble of entertaining company; particularly of Nights, as it is my inclination to retire (and unless prevented by very particular company, always do retire) either to bed, or to my study, soon after candle light. In taking these duties (which hospitality obliges one to bestow on company) off my hands, it would render me a very acceptable service, and for a little time *only,* to come, an hour in the day, now and then, devoted to the recording of some Papers which time would not allow me to complete before I left Philadelphia, would also be acceptable" (4 Aug. 1797, ViMtV).

September

1.   Clear & extremely warm being calm—Mer. at 90.

2.   Calm in the forenoon & very warm—Mer. being at 91. In the afternoon a little rain fell here for a few minutes & apparently a good deal elsewhere.

3.   A sprinkle of rain for a few minutes—Wind at No. Wt. Mer. at 79. Mr. & Mrs. Fitzhugh went away after breakfast & Mr. Lear came to dinner.

4.   Wind at No. Wt. & clear—Mer. 77. Genl. Spotswood & family went away after breakfast.

5.   Clear—Mercury at 79.

6.   Clear—Do.   —72.

7.   Do.—Do. 70. Dined, with all the family, at Mr. Willm. Wilsons & returnd in the Even.

8.   Clear—Wind varying from No. Et. to So. Et. Mercury at 68.

9.   Very great appearances of Rain in the Morning with some mist—but not to lay the dust. Mer. at 68. Wind at No. Et. all day.

10.   Clear & Cool Wind at No. Et. Mer. 68. Mr. Jno. Bassett— wife & 3 Childn. came here to Dinnr.

Martha Washington's nephew John Bassett and his wife, Elizabeth Carter Browne Bassett, had at least four children at this time.

11.   Wind at No. Et. & Cool. Mer. 70—Colo. Sam Griffin and Lady came to dinner.

12.   Wind at So. Et. Mer. 70. Appearances of Rain in the Eveng. but none fell. Col. Otway Byrd, Doctr. Barraud came to Dinr. & Mr. Saml. Washington in the Afternoon.

Francis Otway Byrd (1756–1800), son of William Byrd III (1729–1777) and his first wife, Elizabeth Hill Carter Byrd, resigned his post in the British navy at the beginning of the Revolution to take the position of aide to Maj. Gen. Charles Lee. He later was appointed a lieutenant colonel of dragoons. After the Revolution, Byrd was sheriff and clerk of the court of Charles City County. On 24 Nov. 1797 he was appointed collector of the port of Norfolk (EXECUTIVE JOURNAL, 1:251).

Dr. Philip Barraud (1757–1830), son of Daniel Cary and Catherine Curle Barraud, practiced medicine in Williamsburg. He was on the board of visitors at the College of William and Mary and on the court, or board, of directors of the asylum in Williamsburg. In 1799 he moved to Norfolk where he practiced for 30 years (BLANTON, 343–44; VSP, 9:13).

Samuel Washington (c.1765–1832), the younger son of GW's brother Charles and Mildred Thornton Washington, lived in or near Charles Town, Berkeley County. Samuel, who had become responsible for his ailing father's debts and had suffered two disastrous years in which he lost his crops, wrote GW on 7 July requesting a loan. GW was short of money himself but agreed to let his nephew have $1,000 in order to prevent him from having to sell his land; at the same time he gave him a stern lecture on the evils of borrowing (Samuel Washington to GW, 7 July, 1797, owned by Mr. Sol Feinstone, Washington Crossing, Pa.; Samuel Washington to GW, 29 July 1797, ViMtV; GW to Samuel Washington, 12 July 1797, DLC:GW). On 19 Sept. Samuel gave GW a promissory note for the money (ViMtV).

13.   Some appearances of Rain in the evening but none fell. Wind southerly. Mer. 72. All the company went after breakfast.

14.   Wind at So. Wt. Mer. at 74, a Shower for abt. 6 Minutes in the afternoon.

15.   Great appearances of R. with light drippings in the forenoon–Mer. 78. In the Afternoon abt. 6 Oclock it began a sober rain & cond. till 11 Ock.

16.   Clear, with the Wind at No. W. but neither hard, nor cold. Mer. at 68. Mr. Lear came to dinner.

17.   Clear & calm. Mercury at 72. Mr. Lear went away after breakfast.

18.   Raining in the forenoon and afternoon–Mer. at 69. Wind Southerly.

19.   Clear all day and Wind fresh from No. Wt. Mer. 66. Mr. Geo. Lee of Loudoun dined here.

George Lee (c.1768–1805) was a son of Thomas Ludwell Lee (1730–1778).

20.   Clear with little or no wind. A slight white frost. M. 64.

21.   Clear & very pleasant–slight white frost. Wind Easterly. Mer. 68.

22.   Cloudy all day, with the Wind at No. Et. Mer. 67.

23.   Just such a day as yesterday. Mer. at 64. Wind at No. E.

24.   The same. Wind in the same quarter with a little sprinkling of Rain. Mer. at 62. Went to Church in Alexa.

25.   Wind at No. West and clear. Mer. at 72. Went to Alexandria on business.

26.   Clear in the forenoon lowering afterwards & turning cold. Wind brisk from the No. Wt. The Attorney Genl. Lee & Lady & Mrs. Edmund Lee dined here.

Charles Lee was appointed attorney general of the United States in 1795. He served in this post until 1801, then returned to his law practice. His last years were spent at his Fauquier County home near Warrenton. Lee was married in 1789 to Anne Lee (1770–1804), daughter of Richard Henry Lee, and later to Margaret Scott Peyton (1783–1843), a widow. MRS. EDMUND LEE: In MS this reads Mrs. Edmund Leed. Mrs. Lee was Sarah (Sally) Lee (1775–1837), daughter of Richard Henry Lee and his second wife, Anne Gaskins Pinckard Lee. She had married her cousin Edmund Jennings Lee in 1796.

27.   Cold No. Wt. Wind in the Morning—more moderate afterwards. Mer. at 62. Mr. H. Peake & a Romh. Priest—Mr. Caffray dind here.

Mr. H. Peake is Henry (Harry) Peake, son of Humphrey and Mary Stonestreet Peake. MR. CAFFRAY: Anthony Caffrey (McCaffrey), a Catholic priest who came from Ireland in 1792, was the founder and first pastor of St. Patrick's Church in Washington. In 1794 he bought the lots on which the church was built. Caffrey deeded the land to Bishop Carroll in 1804 and returned to Ireland the next year (O'BRIEN, 143; DOWNING [2], 44–45).

28.   A small white frost; clear, Calm & very pleasant. Mer. at 65. Mr. Edmd. Lee Mr. Scudder—Doctr. English & brother dined here.

Edmund Jennings Lee (1772–1843) was the fifth son of Henry Lee of Leesylvania. He and his wife had settled in Alexandria where he practiced law. Mr. Scudder may be a son or brother of Nathaniel Scudder (1733–1781) of Monmouth County, N.J., who had been a member of the Continental Congress and a colonel of New Jersey militia. Dr. English is probably Dr. James English of Upper Freehold Township, Monmouth County, N.J.

29.   A very thick & heavy fog with appearances [of rain] but none fell. But little wind & that at No. Wt. Mer. 65. Col. Gilpin & Mr. Hartshorne dined here.

30. Cloudy all day with the wind at No. Et. Mer. at 65. Mr. Carter of Shirley & Mr. Fitzhugh of Chatham came to Dinner.

MR. CARTER OF SHIRLEY: Charles Carter (1732–1806) of Shirley in Charles City County. MR. FITZHUGH OF CHATHAM: William Fitzhugh (1741–1809) of Chatham. The Fitzhughs planned to move to Alexandria, and the Fitzhugh home, Chatham, in Stafford County, was put on the market in 1796 (MOORE [1], 203). Martha Washington wrote her friend Elizabeth Powel in July that the Fitzhughs "expect to be living in alexandria in october, but not fixed their before november" (14 July 1797, ViMtV). In fact they did not take up residence in Alexandria until early in December (Martha Washington to Elizabeth Powel, 18 Dec. 1797, ViMtV).

October 1797

1. Began raining in the Night and contind. to do so, more or less, until Noon—when the Wind got to the Westward & cleard— Mer. 63.

2. Clear, warm & pleasant. Mer. at 66. Mr. Carter & Mr. Fitzhugh went away & Mr. Washington & Mr. Foot came to dinr. & returned afterwards.

Mr. Washington undoubtedly is Lawrence Washington (1740–1799) of nearby Belmont, brother of GW's cousin and wartime manager, Lund Washington (see entries for 10 Mar. and 27 July 1785). MR. FOOT: probably William Hayward Foote, usually called Hayward Foote. He was the son of Richard Foote (d. 1779) and Margaret Foote and was the nephew of both Catherine Foote Washington, Lawrence's wife, and Elizabeth Foote Washington, the widow of Lund Washington. Elizabeth Washington called Hayward Foote her "adopted son"; he evidently lived with her and helped her manage the farm after Lund's death (Fairfax County Wills, Book K-1, Vi Microfilm; Lund Washington's Account Book, MdAN).

3. Clear & very warm. Wind Southerly—Mer. at 68. Doctr. Stuart came hear to Dinner. Washington Custis came home.

George Washington Parke Custis was home after an unsuccessful year at the College of New Jersey at Princeton. His academic career was distinctly checkered and caused GW much concern. During the early years of the presidency, GW had sent the boy to a small private school in New York run by Patrick Murdoc (HAMILTON [2], 7:25–26n). When the seat of government was moved to Philadelphia he enrolled young Custis at the "College, Academy and Charitable School" associated with the University of Pennsylvania. Even at this early date there was dissatisfaction with his progress (DECATUR, 102, 169–70, 219–20). In 1796 young Custis matriculated at Princeton and, armed with much good advice from his grandfather, seemed for a time to be doing well. GW's letters to him during the fall and early winter are full of admonitions to exert himself in his studies and avoid bad habits; Custis's replies give repeated assurances of his good intentions and progress (see CUSTIS, 73–83). Soon after Custis's return to Princeton from his spring vacation, however, GW received a letter from the president of the college, Samuel Stanhope Smith (1750–1819), which, GW wrote Smith, "filled my mind (as you naturally supposed it would) with extreme disquietude. From his infancy I have discovered an almost unconquerable disposition to indolence in everything that did not tend to his amusements; and have exhorted him in the most parental and friendly manner often, to devote his time to more useful pursuits" (GW to Smith, 24 May 1797, CUSTIS, 83–84). Custis himself a few days later wrote GW a letter full of apologies and promises for improved conduct, and GW replied that he would "not only heartily forgive, but will forget also, and bury in oblivion all that has passed" (Custis to GW, 29 May 1797, and GW to Custis, 4 June 1797, CUSTIS, 84–87). However, despite much good advice from GW and frequent assurances of good conduct from Custis during the next few months, Washington Custis's homecoming on 3 Oct. marked the end of his schooling at Princeton. On 9 Oct., GW wrote Smith, acknowledging several recent letters regarding Custis's deportment. GW expressed regret at "the conduct and behaviour of Young Custis" and made arrangements to pay his grandson's outstanding accounts at Princeton (DLC:GW).

4. A Shower of Rain in the Morning & the wind very high from No. Wt. afterwards—Mer. at 65. Mr. B. Bassett & Mrs. Dunbar & Mr. McCarty came to dinner. The latter returned afterwards.

Mrs. Dunbar may be Elizabeth Thornton Dunbar, wife of Robert Dunbar, a Scots merchant of Falmouth. She was a sister of Charles Washington's wife, Mildred Thornton Washington. Mr. McCarty is Daniel McCarty, Jr. (1759–1801), son of GW's former neighbor Daniel McCarty of Mount Air. The younger McCarty had served in the Revolution as a lieutenant in Grayson's Additional Continental Regiment. He was now living at his grandfather Dennis McCarty's old home, Cedar Grove, and was married to Sarah Eilbeck Mason McCarty, daughter of Col. George Mason of Gunston Hall. McCarty was interested in moving west and tried to negotiate with GW for an exchange of his Loudoun County Sugar Lands for GW's Kanawha lands, but he decided that he would prefer to have property in the Louisiana area. For the correspondence regarding the negotiations, see Daniel McCarty, Jr., to GW, 2 and 6 Nov. 1797 and 19 Sept. 1798, DLC:GW; GW to McCarty, 30 Oct. 1797, ViMtV; GW to McCarty, 3 and 13 Nov. 1797, NN: Washington Papers.

5. Clear & very pleasant with but little Wind—Mer. at 62. Mr. Basset & Mrs. Dunbar wt. away after breakfast.

6. Warm & pleasant. Wind So. Mer. 65.

7. Calm, clear & warm in the forenoon with appearances of Rain afterwds. Mer. 66. Mr. La Colombe & a Doctr. Flood came here

to Dinner. The last returned. Mr. T. Peter & Mrs. Peter came in the Afternoon.

Louis Saint Ange Morel, chevalier de La Colombe (1755–c.1800), had come with Lafayette to America in 1777 as an aide-de-camp. He was later made a captain of the King's Dragoons and retired as a major in 1783. He also served in the French army in France, becoming colonel of an infantry regiment in 1791 and aide to the commander-in-chief, Lafayette, in 1792. He was arrested and imprisoned, but in 1794 escaped and came to the United States. Except for a brief return to France he lived in the United States the rest of his life (CONTENSON, 197). George Washington Lafayette, during the early part of his exile in the United States, probably stayed in La Colombe's home (George Cabot to GW, 16 Sept. 1795, DLC:GW). Dr. Flood may be William Pinckard Flood, son of Dr. William Flood and nephew of Dr. Nicholas Flood of Richmond County. William Pinckard Flood was married in 1793 to Ann Peyton (Nancy) Washington and probably resided in King George County.

8.   Clear, brisk Southerly Wind. Mer. 65. Mrs. Stuart & two of her daughters came to dinner as did Mr. Lear. Mr. La Tombe went awy.

MR. LA TOMBE: GW means Louis Saint Ange Morel, chevalier de La Colombe, who came on the previous day. He has confused the name with that of Philippe André Joseph de Létombe, the current French minister plenipotentiary to the United States.

9.   Wind brisk from the No. Wt. & turning cold–Mer. 64. Mr. Lear & Mr. Peter went awy.

10.   The Wind continuing at No. Wt. it brew colder–Mer. at 58.

11.   Wind at No. Wt. & fresh after the Morning. Mer. at 56– Mrs. Stuart & Daughters & Mrs. Peters went after breakfast.

12.   Cold & frosty Morning, Mer. 54. Mr. G. W. La Fayette & Mr. Frestal left this for Geo. Town to take the stage for New York to embark for France. I accompanied them to the Fedl. City.

Young George Washington Motier Lafayette had received reports from correspondents in Hamburg that his father, together with his mother and sisters who had voluntarily joined him in prison, had been released from Olmütz and were on their way to Paris. GW was unable to persuade him to wait until the reports were confirmed. He and his tutor, Felix Frestal, sailed from New York for Havre de Grace on 25 Oct. on the brig *Clio*. Definite word of the release of the Lafayette family reached GW several weeks later (GW to chevalier de La Colombe, 3 Dec. 1797, DLC:GW; Eleanor Parke Custis to Elizabeth Bordley, 23 Nov. 1797, ViMtV). There followed two years of exile for the Lafayette family in Hamburg, Holstein, and Holland (GOTTSCHALK, xxiii).

George Washington Motier Lafayette, by a member of the Sharples family. (Mount Vernon Ladies' Association of the Union, Robert E. Lee IV and Mrs. A. Smith Bowman Collection)

13.   I returned home to dinner. Captn. Huie dined here & went away afterwards. Mer. at 5< >. Wind Southerly.

Captain Huie may be Capt. James Huie of the Dumfries firm of Smith, Huie, Alexander & Co. (DIARIES, 4:261, n.3).

14.   Great appearances of Rain—but none fell. Wind Southerly —Mer. 54. Mr. McDonald & Mr. Rich Brith. Com. came to dinner. Christopher set out for Lebanon.

MR. MCDONALD & MR. RICH: Thomas Macdonald and Henry Pye Rich, British commissioners under Article VI of the Jay Treaty. Article VI provided that the United States make full compensation for losses owed to British merchants and others "in all such Cases where full Compensation for such losses and damages cannot, for whatever reason be actually obtained had and received by the said Creditors in the ordinary course of Justice" (BEMIS [2], 460). Five commissioners were to be appointed; two British, two American, and the fifth by "unanimous voice of the other Four" (BEMIS [2], 461). The four commissioners met at Philadelphia and, after much disagreement, were forced to appoint the fifth member by lot. This choice fell upon an Englishman, and since the principles subsequently laid down by the commission majority proved unacceptable to the Americans, the commission disbanded. A compromise was finally reached in 1802 by which the United States agreed to pay the British government a lump sum of £600,000 sterling in three annual installments (BEMIS [2], 438–39).

In August Thomas Macdonald wrote from Philadelphia informing GW that he was forwarding him a volume of reports sent by the British Board of Agriculture and entrusted to his care by Sir John Sinclair. He informed GW of the proceedings of the commission, stating his belief that an honorable agreement could be reached. He expressed the hope that he and his colleague Rich would be able to pay their respects to GW at Mount Vernon (19 Aug. 1797, DLC:GW). GW replied on 29 Aug. thanking him for the reports and assuring Macdonald that he and Rich would be welcome at Mount Vernon (DLC:GW). CHRISTOPHER: GW's body servant, Christopher (sometimes called Christopher Sheels), was "on Monday last . . . Bit by a Small Dog belonging to a Lady in my house, then as was supposed a little diseased. And Yesternight died (I do think) in a State of madness. As soon as the Boy . . . was Bit application was made to a medical Gentleman in Alexandria who has cut out so far as He could, the place Bit, applyed Ointment to keep it open, And put the Boy under a Course of Mercury" (GW to William Henry Stoy, 14 Oct. 1797, WRITINGS, 37:581). GW, upon hearing of the miraculous cures performed in such cases by Dr. William Henry Stoy (1726–1801) of Lebanon, Pa., sent Christopher to him for further treatment. Stoy wrote GW on 19 Oct. that the servant was in no further danger since he had taken his medicine (DLC:GW). Stoy's remedy consisted of "one ounce of the herb, red chickweed, four ounces of theriac and one quart of beer, all well digested, the dose being a wine glassful" (KELLY [2], 1177). Christopher survived Dr. Stoy's treatment and lived to attend GW during his final illness and death.

15. Clear & pleasant calm in the morning—wind at No. Wt. afterwds. Mer. at 58. Mr. Potts & Mr. Keith dined here & returned.

James Keith became a director of the Potomac Company in 1793 (see entry for 15 Aug. 1786).

16. Clear & moderate with but little Wind—Mer. 55. Mr. Macdonald & Mr. Rich went away after breakfast. Mrs. Nichols & Mr. Nichols & wife & Doctr. Stuart came to Din. The 3 first returnd after it.

Mr. Nichols and his wife are probably James Bruce and Mary Nichols of Fairfax County. Nichols may be the J. B. Nickolls who advertised in the Alexandria newspaper in 1797 as a broker "for the purchase of real and personal Estate, (negroes excepted) and procuring money on loan, &c." (*Columbian Mirror* [Alexandria], 8 June 1797). The Nichols family lived on land adjoining Thomson Mason's Hollin Hall farm (SPROUSE [2], 53).

17. Clear and pleasant. Doctr. Stuart went away after breakfast. Mr. Law & Cap: Turner came in the Aftern. Mer.—58.

CAP: TURNER: probably Thomas Turner, a son of Col. Thomas Turner (d. 1797) of Westmoreland County.

18. Clear & pleasant—Wind West. Mer. 61. Mr. Law & Cap. Turner went away after breakfast & Mr. Geo. Calvert came to Dinnr.

Don Carlos Martinez de Yrujo y Tacon, attributed to one of the Sharples family. (Independence National Historical Park Collection)

19.   Calm & very pleasant—M. 58.

20.   Cloudy morning with the wind at No. Et. Abt. Noon it began to Rain & contd. to do so more or less all day. Mer. at 56.

21.   Wind still at No. Et. & misting all day. Mer. at 56. Mr. Calvert went away after breakfast.

22.   Clear all day. Wind at No. Wt. M. 57. Mr. Potts & wife & Mr. Smith & wife & Mr. Lear dined here.

Mr. Smith may be Augustine Jaquelin Smith (1774–1830), son of Augustine Smith (1739–1774). Augustine Jaquelin Smith represented Fairfax County in the Virginia legislature 1796–98 and 1821–22. In 1796 he was married to Susannah Taylor, the daughter of Jesse Taylor, Sr., of Alexandria.

23.   Very clear & pleasant—M. 56. Went with the family to dine with Mr. Potts in Alexandria.

24.   Constant Rain from 8 in the Morning until 4 in the aftern. with the Wind at No. Et. then No. W. Mer. 42. Spanish Minister & Mr. Barry came to dinner.

SPANISH MINISTER: Don Carlos Martinez de Yrujo y Tacon .(1763–1834) had come to America as Spanish minister in 1797, succeeding Don José de

Jáudenes. In a previous visit, in 1796, Yrujo had spent two days at Mount Vernon at GW's invitation, and GW described him at that time as "a young man, very free and easy in his manners; professes to be well disposed towards the United States; and as far as a judgment can be formed on so short an acquaintance, appears to be well informed" (GW to Timothy Pickering, 4 July 1796, MHi: Pickering Papers). In 1798 Yrujo married Sally McKean, daughter of the chief justice of the Pennsylvania Supreme Court.

Mr. Barry was James Barry, an Irishman and a partner of Thomas Law in the East India trade. Barry had earlier acted as Spanish agent and Portuguese consul for the states of Maryland and Virginia. He was a heavy investor in lands in the new Federal City (O'BRIEN, 141–43). Barry had attempted to aid Yrujo in obtaining from the commissioners of the District of Columbia a site in the Federal City to put up housing for the Spanish representative, and GW had written the commissioners urging them to accommodate Yrujo. He thought such a move might persuade other countries to follow suit and thus stimulate the growth of the city (GW to Commissioners, 18 Sept. 1796, DLC:GW).

25. Wind moderately from So. Wt.–clear. Mer. at 52. The above gentlemn. went away after breakfast & Mrs. Craik & two sons & Mr. & Mrs. Harrison came to dinner.

Mrs. Mariamne Ewell Craik, wife of Dr. James Craik, had three sons living at this time—James, Jr., William, and George Washington Craik; Adam Craik seems to have died earlier. Mr. and Mrs. Harrison were Mrs. Craik's son-in-law and daughter, Richard and Ann (Nancy) Craik Harrison, who were married in 1791 (see entry for 14 Oct. 1773).

27. Clear & pleasant–Wind Southerly–Mer. 56. Mrs. Crk. &ca. went away before dinner.

28. Lowering in the Morning, but clear & pleasant afterwards. Wind Southerly. Mer. at 60.

29. Clear & pleasant tho' cool Wind getting to the No. Wt. Mer. at 55. Doctr. Stuart came to dinner.

30. Wind brisk from No. Wt. & cold. Mer. at 54. Doctr. Stuart went away after breakfast. Mr. Cottineau & Lady, Mr. Rosseau & Lady, the Visct. D'Orleans, & Mr. De Colbert came to Dinner & returned to Alexa. afterwards. A Mr. Stockton from N. Jerseys came in the afternoon.

MR. COTTINEAU & LADY: Denis Nicholas Cottineau de Kerloguen (c.1745–1808) was a Breton officer who had served with the Continental navy during the Revolution. He had commanded the United States frigate *Pallas,* serving under John Paul Jones's command during the fight between the *Bonhomme Richard* and *Serapis,* and had himself fought and captured the *Countess of*

Scarborough in the same battle. After the Revolution, Cottineau returned to his plantations in Saint Domingue but was forced to flee because of the insurrection there. He settled in Philadelphia and for a time became a shareholder and settler at the French Royalist colony of Azilum on the Susquehanna River. Later, he moved to Savannah. Although Cottineau was not qualified for membership in the Society of the Cincinnati, he had been made an honorary member of the Pennsylvania Society in 1795. Cottineau was married to Luce Moquet, a sister of the marquis de Montalet (HUME, 412; MOREAU DE SAINT-MÉRY, 3:1470; Cottineau to GW, 7 Sept. 1788, HUME, 335–37; chevalier d'Annemours to GW, 15 Feb. 1789, HUME, 340–42). MR. ROSSEAU & LADY: Fitzpatrick says this is Jean Rosseau, a volunteer on the *Bonhomme Richard* (DIARIES, 4:263). VISCT. D'ORLEANS: GW may mean Louis Philippe, duc d'Orleans (1773–1850) or one of his brothers, Antoine Philippe d'Orleans, duc de Montpensier (1775–1807), or Louis Charles d'Orleans, comte de Beaujolais (1779–1808). The three Princes of the Blood were in exile in America and had visited GW at Mount Vernon for four days in April 1797, before starting on a three-month tour through the wilderness of Tennessee, Kentucky, western Virginia, and Pennsylvania. GW had at that time given them letters of introduction and a map of the roads they were to follow on their journey. The duc d'Orleans in 1830 became King Louis Philippe of France (see LOUIS-PHILIPPE [1], xxi–xxxiii, and LOUIS-PHILIPPE [2]). MR. DE COLBERT: This is probably Édouard Charles Victurnin, chevalier Colbert de Maulevrier (1758–1820). Colbert later became comte de Colbert de Maulevrier. He entered the French navy in 1774 and served in America during the Revolution. At the beginning of the French Revolution he commanded a French vessel, but he lost his command and was eventually forced to flee France. He spent a part of his exile in America, returning to France in 1814 at the restoration of the Bourbons (BIOG. UNIVERSELLE, 8:562).

31.   Wind still at No. Wt. but moderate. Mer. at 55. Mr. Stockton went away after breakfast and Mr. Ford & Lady & a Mr. Richards came to dinner & proceeded on their Journey to So. Cara. afterwards.

Mr. Ford may be Timothy Ford (1762–1830), formerly of New Jersey. He served briefly in GW's bodyguard during the Revolution and later studied law under Robert Morris. In 1785 he moved to Charleston, S.C., where he was a member of the legislature and a trustee of the College of Charleston. He was married first in 1793 to Sarah Amelia DeSaussure and later to Mary Magdalen Prioleau. MR. RICHARDS: GW may mean a member of the prominent Richardson family of South Carolina.

November 1797

1.   Calm, clear & extremely pleasant. Mer. at 60.

2.   Calm, clear & pleasant as yesterday—Mer. at 60. Mr. Thomson Mason & Lady and Mrs. Nichols dined here.

Thomson Mason (1759–1820), son of Col. George Mason of Gunston Hall, lived at Hollin Hall, just north of GW's River Farm. The house had been built on land given Thomson by his father. He was a justice of Fairfax County and later served as a state senator (1801–4) and a delegate (1808–9) from Fairfax to the Virginia General Assembly. Mason married in 1784 Sarah McCarty Chichester, daughter of GW's neighbor Richard Chichester.

3.   Calm, Clear & pleasant—Mer. at [   ].

4.   Cloudy Morning, drisling afterwards until Night when it rained closely. Mer. 70.

5.   Clear in the forenoon & raing. afterwards until Sun down by showers—when the Wind came out strong & cold at No. Wt. & the Mer. fell from 72 to 52 degrees.

6.   Variable in wind & weather Mer. Cold. 42. Wind in the afternoon at No. Wt.

7.   Cold Morning—ground froze Wind at No. Wt. Morng. Southerly afterwards. Cold 41 deg[ree]s.

8.   More moderate—wind still at No. Wt. clear. Mer. 48.

9.   Calm, clear & remarkably pleasant. Mer. 52.

10.   Wind at No. Et. & great appearances of a fall of weather but it held up. Mer. at 46. Dr. Keith & a Mrs. Forest came to dinner & stayed all night.

DR. KEITH: GW may mean James Keith. He calls the man "Mr. Keith" when he leaves Mount Vernon on the next day.

11.   A thick heavy fog all day but no rain till night, when it began to rain very fast. Mer. at 50. Mr. Keith &ca. went away & Mrs. Ratcliff & Son came to Dinner.

MRS. RATCLIFF: may be either Louisiana (Lucian) Bowling Ratcliffe, wife of Richard Ratcliffe (c.1750–1825), or her daughter-in-law, the wife of Richard's son John Ratcliffe (b. 1766). Richard Ratcliffe was a justice and coroner of Fairfax County, served as a commissioner of the tax, and was deputy sheriff for Fairfax. John Ratcliffe was a merchant in Alexandria.

12.   Raining all the forenoon with a strong So. Et. Wind. Clear afterwards—Mer. 55.

13.   Clear, calm & remarkably fine & pleasant—Mer. 55 a 65. The British Envoy Mr. Liston & his Lady—Mr. Marchant & his lady & her Son Mr. Brown and Mr. Athill Speaker of the Assembly of Antigua came to Dinner as did a Doctr. Pinckard. The last went afterwards.

Robert Liston (1743–1836) served as British minister and ambassador at several important posts before being appointed in 1796 as envoy extraordinary and minister plenipotentiary to the United States. He served in this capacity until 1802. In Feb. 1796, just before coming to this country, he married Henrietta Merchant, "daughter of the late Nathaniel M. esq. of Antigua" (*Gentleman's Mag.*, 66 [1796], 254). Nelly Custis characterized Mrs. Liston as having "kind & friendly manners" and seemed fond of her, but she refused an invitation to spend part of the winter with the Listons in Philadelphia because of her reluctance to leave Mount Vernon and especially her grandmother (Eleanor Parke Custis to Elizabeth Bordley, 23 Nov. 1797, ViMtV). MR. MARCHANT: undoubtedly a relative of Mrs. Liston's. According to Nelly Custis, Mrs. Merchant was "a sweet beautiful engaging Woman, her husband very pleasing & entertaining. I am really sorry that his health is so very precarious. . . . Mr. Brown is a very genteel young man, I am sorry he has left Philadelphia, as I am sure the Belles will feel his loss— he was in my opinion one of the most elegant & pleasing young men last Winter" (Eleanor Parke Custis to Elizabeth Bordley, 23 Nov. 1797, ViMtV). Mr. Athill may be John Athill (DIARIES, 4:263). Nelly Custis thought him "a sensible agreeable man." The Listons were to accompany the Merchant family and Mr. Athill by water as far as Norfolk, from whence the Merchants, Brown, and Athill were to embark for Antigua (Eleanor Parke Custis to Elizabeth Bordley, 23 Nov. 1797, ViMtV).

14.   Remarkable fine morning but lowering & windy from No. W. in the afternoon. Mer. 58 & 42. Mrs. Ramsay, Mr. & Mrs. Potts Mr. Wilson, Mr. Harrison & Da[ughter] & son dined here. In the afternoon Majr. Pinckney & Lady arrived.

Maj. Thomas Pinckney (1750–1828), of South Carolina, was the son of Charles and Eliza Lucas Pinckney and brother of Charles Cotesworth Pinckney. Reared and educated in England, Pinckney attended the Inner Temple and was admitted to the bar in 1774. He returned to America and served in the Continental Army, receiving a promotion to major of the 1st South Carolina Regiment in 1778. From 1792 to 1796 he served as minister to Great Britain and from 1794 to 1795 was in Spain as special commissioner and envoy to settle the outstanding differences between the United States and Spain. In 1796 Pinckney was the Federalist candidate for vice-president. At the present time he was a member of the House of Representatives from South Carolina. Pinckney's first wife, Elizabeth Motte Pinckney, had died while he was in England, and on 19 Oct. 1797 he had married her sister, Frances Motte Middleton, widow of John Middleton. The Pinckneys were undoubtedly on their way to Philadelphia for the new session of Congress.

15.   Cold & windy with a little Snow just to whiten the grd. in the morning—clear afterwards. Mer.—38 & 48.

16.   Very hard frost—Wind at No. wt. & clear. Mer. at [   ]. All the Compy. above mentd. went away & Mr. B. Bassett came to dinner & a Mr. Augs. Woodward came in the Evening.

Augustus Woodward, of Greenbrier Court House, stopped at Mount Vernon on his way to Philadelphia with a "draft" from George Alderson, sheriff of Kanawha County, for taxes due for the years 1791–96 on four tracts of GW's land lying on the Kanawha River in Kanawha County (Alderson's draft to GW, Aug. 1797, NjMoNP). Since his knowledge of the county's tax laws was sketchy, GW declined to pay until he could make further inquiry. Woodward informed him that the necessary information could be obtained from the treasury or auditor's office in Richmond, and GW requested his nephew Bushrod Washington, then living in Richmond, to investigate (GW to Bushrod Washington, 18 Dec. 1797, DLC:GW). On 9 Jan. 1798 Bushrod informed his uncle that Sheriff Alderson was substantially correct, but that some of these lands and two lots in Berkeley County had also been returned for nonpayment of 1788 taxes and 1795 taxes, respectively, "with a view under a late Law, of subjecting them to forfeiture and future appropriation by any other person, or to be sold by the public." This, he urged GW, was the more urgent matter, and payment should be made at the treasury or the auditor's office promptly. The taxes due for the last six years should be paid directly to the "Sheriff or Collector of the County where the Lands lie" (ViMtV). Woodward stopped at Mount Vernon on 14–15 Jan. 1798 on his way home from Philadelphia and received the full amount of the taxes requested by the sheriff of Kanawha County. GW sent the amount due at the auditor's office promptly to Bushrod Washington for payment (GW to Bushrod Washington, 19 Jan. 1798, DLC:GW). See also GW to Bushrod Washington, 30 Jan. and 7 Feb. 1798, DLC:GW; Bushrod Washington to GW, 9 Feb. 1798, ViMtV; schedule of GW's western lands, Jan. 1798, DLC:GW.

17.   Snowing very fast from So. Et. until 9 Oclock when it ceased —grd. covered abt. 2 Inchs. Mer. 44. 36.

18.   Very pleasant, & clear after the morning. Wind moderate Mer. 48 & 42. Mr. Woodford went.

MR. WOODFORD: GW means Augustus Woodward, who came on 16 Nov.

19.   Clear & very pleasant—Wd. Southerly. Mer. 50 & 44—Mr. White came.

Mr. White is Alexander White, commissioner of the Federal City (see entry for 31 Dec. 1789).

20.   Wind shifting to No. Easterly, it grew cold & threatned Snow. Mer. from 32 to 42. Mr. White went away & I went to Alexandria & returned.

21.   A little Snow in the morning with a very heavy sleet all day.

Mer. from 36 to 48. A Mr. Lister introduced by Mr. Robt. Morris came here dined & returned.

Robert Morris wrote GW that Daniel Lister was "an English young Gentn." on a tour of the United States and "could not return contentedly without seeing the Saviour of this country, Thus you see that your well earned Fame subjects your time & attention to be taxed by Strangers" (6 Nov. 1797, DLC:GW).

22. Misting, & at times raining all day. The sleet was so heavy as to break down all the Willow Trees. Mer. 48 & 34.

23. Such a day as yesterday but more rain. Mer. as above. Mr. Bassett & Fanny Henly went away.

Mr. Bassett is probably Burwell Bassett, Jr. He wrote GW from Richmond three days later indicating that he had recently talked to GW about a cook and housekeeper for Mount Vernon (DLC:GW). FANNY HENLY: Nelly Custis wrote a friend, "My cousin left me this morning for her Home. I regret the loss of her society much, as she was great company for me, she is an affectionate amiable girl" (Eleanor Parke Custis to Elizabeth Bordley, 23 Nov. 1797, ViMtV).

24. Clear & cold. Wd. at No. Wt. Mer. as above—A Mr. Welch from Greenbrier dined here.

James Welch of Rockingham County, now living in Greenbrier County, arrived at Mount Vernon armed with a cautious letter of introduction from Daniel Morgan. He had no money but had a grandiose scheme for leasing GW's 23,000 acres of land on the Kanawha River and dividing it into small farms for sublease. On 29 Nov., Welch submitted a definite proposition for leasing the land with an option to buy. GW wrote Dr. James Craik in Alexandria to try to find out more about him before carrying negotiations any further (COOK, 71–73; PRUSSING, 119, 464–65).

25. Moderate with the Wind Southerly—Mer. 41 a 49. Mr. Russel came here abt. 9 Oclock A.M.

MR. RUSSEL: probably William Russell (1740–1818), a merchant and reformer of Birmingham, Eng., who engaged in an export trade from Birmingham and Sheffield to Russia, Spain, and the United States. In 1795 he came to the United States to clear up matters dealing with his American trade and to check on a family estate in Maryland. He stayed for five years. On 8 Sept. 1798 Russell wrote GW from Middletown, Conn., thanking him for the hospitality shown him at Mount Vernon and promising to send the ram and the recently completed chaff machine he had promised as soon as appropriate shipping could be had (DLC:GW). Owing to various delays, the sheep and the chaff machine did not arrive until May 1799. Russell also sent GW a gift of a new type of hoe and a new implement called a ground borer, designed for digging fence post holes but which could be put to military use making chevaux-de-frise (GW to Russell, 28 Sept. 1798, 6 Jan. and 26 May 1799, and Russell to GW, 11 May 1799, DLC:GW; Russell to GW, 20 Dec. 1798, ViMtV) .

26.   Wind fresh from No. West all day & clear. Mr. Russel went away after breakfast. Mr. Lear came to dinner & Mr. & Mrs. Law at Night.

27.   Wind in the same place & cold. Mer. [   ] No acct. taken.

28.   Wind still at No. Wt. & cold. Mer. neglected again.

29.   Wind in the same quarter & equally cold and spewing frost. Mer. 22 a 32.

30.   Wind & weather as yesterday—Mer. 24 a 34.

[December]

1.   More moderate—wind still at No. Wt. Mer. 29 & standing there.

2.   Wind at So. Wt.—raining and misting all day. Mer. from 32 to 33. Doctr. Fendall came in the afternoon.

3.   Wind hard and cold all day from No. Wt. Mer.—From 28 to 18.

4.   Excessively Cold wind in the same quarter—Mer. 10 to 18. All the creeks & great part of the River froze.

5.   Wind shifted Southerly but still very cold. Mery. as above.

6.   Mer. 18–32. River all most closed. Mrs. Forbes our House keeper arrived here this day. Wd. South.

The steady stream of visitors to Mount Vernon put quite a strain on Mrs. Washington. There was no steward or housekeeper at Mount Vernon, and to make matters worse, their slave cook, Hercules, had run away sometime in the early fall. GW wrote several friends requesting them to help him find either a housekeeper or a steward and a cook, either slave or for hire. He also inserted an advertisement in the newspaper for a housekeeper "competent to all the duties of that office in a large family—for such, one hundred and fifty dollars per annum will be allowed. OR In place of a HOUSE-KEEPER, a HOUSEHOLD STEWARD, well acquainted with the duties of a Butler, and skilled in the art of cookery (the manual part of which would not be required of him) would be employed at the above, or greater wages, if his qualifications entitled him to them" (*Columbian Mirror* [Alexandria], 12 Aug. 1797). The choice fell upon Mrs. Eleanor Forbes, a 50-year-old English widow who had served as housekeeper for Robert Brooke during his term as governor of Virginia. Mrs. Forbes was, according to Brooke, "active & Spirited in the execution of her business—sober & honest—well acquainted with Cookery & . . . capable of ordering & setting out a table . . . her appearance is decent & respectable & such is her general deportment" (Bushrod Washington to GW, 8 Nov. 1797, ViMtV). Mrs. Forbes was due to come to Mount Vernon immediately but was unable to come until December (GW to Bushrod Washington, 22 Nov. 1797, DLC:GW; Bushrod Washington to GW, 8 and 26 Nov. 1797, ViMtV). She proved satisfactory and remained at Mount Vernon until after GW's death.

7. Wind Southerly but still cold. Mer. from 26 to 32. Doctr. Fendall went away, & Docr. Stuart came.

Dr. Benjamin Fendall of Cedar Hill in Charles County, Md., was a dentist. He probably came to see Mrs. Washington, who was to have some new teeth made. GW wrote Dr. Fendall several months later, "Mrs. Washington has been long in expectation of receiving what you took away unfinished, and was to have completed and sent to her; and prays that it may be done with out further delay, as she is in want of them, & must apply elsewhere if not done" (6 Mar. 1798, DLC:GW). Over a year later Fendall wrote GW that he had been able to finish Mrs. Washington's teeth and was sending them by a servant. Whether these are the same ones GW had inquired about is not known. Fendall wrote, "They are—as nearly as I can now recollect, like the old ones—as there are so many ways, to make, & shape Teeth—'twoud be almost impossible, to make 'em, exactly alike—after some time, without having the old ones present. The Model, I took, has, also, by accident, sustain'd some injury. I am extremely sorry, indeed, yr. Lady has been obliged to wait so long owing to my long absence from home and my Illness after I had arriv'd at Cedar-Hill" (10 Aug. 1799, DLC:GW).

8. Lowering, but moderate—Wind Southerly. Mer. 32.

9. Wind cold again from the No. Wt. Mer. 24 a [   ]. Mr. Law & family & Doc. Stuart went away after breakfast & Mr. Welch came to Dinner & returned afterwards.

James Welch had come to Mount Vernon to deliver his final proposal for the Kanawha lands. There had been correspondence back and forth since his original proposal on 29 Nov., and GW had received some rather disquieting reports about Welch. However, Welch's offer of his 99,995-acre tract on Elk River in Randolph County (now W.Va.) to be held in trust by GW as security for payment induced GW to agree to Welch's latest proposal. He wrote James Keith the next day to draw up the necessary papers. Welch was to have a 30-year-lease on GW's four tracts of land on the

Kanawha River "to commence on the 1st. day of January next (1798) at the Rent of $5,000 for the first year . . . for $8,000 the next year, and from thence untill the expiration of the 30 yrs. for $11,143 annually, and for 99 years *thereafter* on an annual Rent of $22,286" (GW to Keith, 10 Dec. 1797, DLC:GW). If he so desired, Welch was to have the right to purchase the land in fee simple in four yearly installments beginning in 1804. The land was to be divided into tenements of 50 to 300 acres, with the usual specifications regarding improving the land (PRUSSING, 119–20, 466–71).

10.   Wind variable—Mer. 26 a [   ]. Mr. Burwell came to dinner.

Mr. Burwell is probably either Lewis Burwell, Jr., son of Col. Lewis Burwell (1716–1784) of Kingsmill, or Lewis Burwell (1764–1834) of Richmond, son of Lewis Burwell (1737–1779) of Fairfield, Gloucester County.

11.   Calm & pleasant—Wind Southerly—Mer. 28 a 34. Mr. Burwell went away after breakfast & a son of Colo. D. Henley came to dinner.

Col. David Henley was at this time War Department agent to the Southwest Territory. He and his wife Sarah Hesilrige Henley (d. 1786) had two sons, Arthur Hesilrige Henley (b. 1782) and David Henley (b. 1784). For information on the Henley family, see WYMAN, 1:493–94.

12.   Lowering Morning, but fine afternoon, Mer. 32 a 42. Mr. Henley went up to Alex. Revd. Mr. Fairfax dined he⟨re⟩.

Late in 1789 Bryan Fairfax had been ordained a minister in the Episcopal church, and on 15 Mar. 1790 he was inducted as rector of Fairfax Parish. He served as rector for only two years, retiring on 16 July 1792. In 1790 he moved his residence from Towlston Grange to Mount Eagle, a home he built on 329 acres he had purchased near Alexandria. There is some evidence that GW may have named Fairfax's new residence (KILMER, 39–42).

13.   Soft & moderate—Wind Southerly. Mer. 42. a 46. Mr. Lear dined here & Mr. Lawe. Lewis returned.

14.   Just such a day as the preceeding one. Mer. 46 a 52.

15.   Little or no Wind in the forenoon brisk So. Easterly & constant Rain afternoon. Mer. 38 a 50.

16.   Wind at No. Wt. but not very hard or cold. Mer. 26 a 40.

17.   Moderate with very little wind Mer. from 30 to 34. Gen. Huntingdon came to dinner.

GEN. HUNTINGDON: Maj. Gen. Jedediah Huntington (see entry for 18 Oct. 1789, n.3) had recently built a home in New London, Conn., which he called Mount Vernon (CROFUT, 2:729).

18.   Wind shifted to No. Wt. in the Night & grew cold. Mer. from 18 to 32. Went up to Alex. & finished my business w. Mr. Welch.

GW and James Welch signed the papers drawn up by James Keith for the Kanawha lands (PRUSSING, 471). See entry for 24 Nov. 1797.

19.   Wind got to the Southward again but was very cold not with standing. Mer. 26 to 34. Genl. Huntingdon went away after breakfast.

20.   Wind Southerly in the Morng. with appearances of Snow No. Wt. in the afternn. & Cold Mer. 28 a 38. Doctr. Stuart came to Dinn.

21.   Very cold—Wind at No. W. Mer. 9 a 28. Doctr. Stuart went away after breakfast.

22.   Very cold Wind fresh at No. Wt. Mer. 8 a [   ].

23.   Wind in the same quarter but not so hard. Mer. 10 a 26.

24.   Calm but still cold. Mer. 8 a 28.

25.   Appearance for Snow in the Morning but clear afterwards & moderate—Mer. 24 a 32. Mr. W. Dandridge came.

William Dandridge was a son of Martha Washington's brother Bartholomew Dandridge (1737–1785) and Mary Burbidge Dandridge (d. 1809). Young Dandridge had purchased garden seeds for GW at Georgetown (GW's Cash Memorandum, 1 Sept. 1797–20 Feb. 1799, RPJCB).

26.   Cloudy morning, & rainy afternoon—wind at So. Et. as it was yesterday. Mer. 32 a 36. Mr. Dandridge went away.

27.   Clear—wind having got to No. Wt. again. Mer. 20 to 25. Mr. Lear & Mr. W. Dandridge came to dinner.

28.   Clear with but little Wind. Mer. from 15 to 34. Mr. Lear went away after breakfast. Began to fill my Ice house.

29.   Clear with very little wind. Mer. from 20 to 41.

30. Just such a day as yesterday—Mer. 20 to 40. Mrs. Washington came here and Mr. Wm. Dandridge to do business for me in the way of writing.

William Dandridge probably did not stay long at Mount Vernon. The only mentions of him in the accounts after this date are an entry for $25 on 3 Feb. 1798, "By Cash *given* to Mr. Wm. Dandridge," and a similar entry on 11 April (GW's Cash Memorandum, 1 Sept. 1797–20 Feb. 1799, RPJCB). GW probably did not approve of the young man's requests for such sizable sums of money in so short a time after his employment.

31. Clear & pleasant all day with but little Wind. Mer. at 30 or thereabouts.

GW has written this last entry for 1797 on a page inadvertently headed "January."

Mount Vernon and Guests
1798

Remarks in January

1.   Much rain fell last night & a thick fog, with a Southerly Wind continued all the forenoon, clear afterwards. Mer. abt. 32.

2.   Clear with the Wind (tho' not much of it) at No. Wt. Mer. abt. 30. A Mr. Elliot came to dinnr. and stayed all Night.

MR. ELLIOT: Barnard Elliott, Jr. (c.1777–1806), only son of Lt. Col. Barnard Elliott (d. 1778), a former member of the King's Council in South Carolina and an officer of the South Carolina Regiment of Artillery in the Revolution. Young Elliott was at Mount Vernon to solicit GW's aid in securing a claim against the government for land for his father's service in the war. GW wrote a letter to Secretary of War James McHenry on this day asking him to aid the young man if possible in pressing his petition. A claim for seven years' half pay was finally approved in 1810 (GW to McHenry, 2 Jan. 1798, DLC:GW; *S.C. Hist. & Geneal. Mag.*, 17 [1916], 150–51, 50 [1949], 70, 63 [1962–63], 128).

3.   Mrs. L. Washington & Mr. Elliot went away after breakfast, & Mrs. Washington, myself &ca. went to Alexandria & dined with Mr. Fitzhugh. Morning clear but lowering afterwards. Mer. about 28. Wind No. Easterly.

4.   Wind at No. Et. and constant Rain all day, with a Sleet; Mer. at 30 in the morning, & continued thereat all day.

5.   Little or no wind all day. In the evening it sprung up at No. Wt. Mer. from 30 to 36. A Mr. Fisk who came here on Wednesday evening went away this morning. Last night there fell about three Inches of Snow. Thawing all day.

6.   Wind pretty brisk from No. Wt. Mer. from 33 to 40 and thawing.

7.   Morning calm & clear. Mer. at 28; in the evening it lowered with the wind at No. Et. Mer. at 34.

8.   Wind at So. Et. in the Morning and lowering. Mer. at 28. Abt. Noon it began to rain & contd. to do so all afternn. Mer. 30 at

Night. A Mr. Marshall Music Master came here—Tuned Nelly Custis's Harpsicord & returned after din⟨ner⟩.

9.　Very foggy with little or no Wind in the morning. Mer. at 32 —at the highest 42 and at Night 30 the Wind having got to No. Wt. abt. Noon.

10.　Clear fine morning—Mer. at 29. At Noon it lowered very much & towards night Spits of Snow fell. At night the Mer. was at 30 & its greatest height 34.

11.　Clear, with the wind fresh all the forenoon from No. Wt. Mer. at 25 in the Morng.—36 at its greatest height & 27 at Night. Mr. Lear dined here & returned.

12.　Clear, & wind Southerly. Mer. at 24 in the morning—42 greatest height and 32 at Night.

13.　Clear & no wind in the morning. Mer. at 28—greatest height 48—in the evening at 43. Calm & pleasant all day.

14.　A little lowering all day with but little wind and that Southerly. Mer. at 36 in the Morning 46 at Night & 48 when highest. Mr. Lewis Burwell came to dinner & Mr. Woodward in the evening.

Burwell requested a letter of introduction for a trip to inspect land in the Genesee country of western New York State (GW to Charles Williamson, 19 Jan. 1798, WRITINGS, 37:581).

15.　Southerly Wind—Soft morng. thin clouds. Mer. at 46 at Sunrise—50 at Noon & 50 at Night. Slow rain from 12 oclock with the wind Southerly. Mr. Burwell & Mr. Woodward went away & I went to Alexandria to a meeting of the Stockholders of that Bank to an Election of Directors.

GW on this day, "By Cash (in a check on the Bank of Alexa.) paid George Alderson Sheriff of Kanhawa Cty., his draught in favour of Augustus Woodward, taxes on four tracts of Land lying on the Kanhawa River for the years 1791. 2. 3. 4. 5 & 1796 pr. the said Woodwards receipt—£101.10. 3¾" (GW's Cash Memorandum, 1 Sept. 1797–20 Feb. 1799, RPJCB). See entry for 16 Nov. 1797.

GW attended a meeting to elect nine directors of the Bank of Alexandria for one-year terms under the charter granted by the Commonwealth of Virginia in 1792 (*Columbian Mirror* [Alexandria], 4 Jan. 1798; HOWE, 1–9).

16.   Clear morning & brisk Southerly Wind. Mer. at 43 in the morning–53 at its highest and 51 at Night. Day clear throughout & very pleasant.

17.   Clear & pleasant wind Southerly. Mer. 30 in the Morng.–56 at the height and 48 at Night. Abt. noon the Wind came out at No. Wt. but died away. Very clear & pleast.

18.   Lowering, with the wind pretty fresh from the Northward in the morning. Mer. then 38–32 at Night & 38 at its highest. Cold, raw & cloudy all day.

19.   More lowering & likely to snow than yesterday. Wind still Northerly–And Mer. at 26 in the morning–the same at Night & only raised two degrees in the course of the day. Afternoon threatned Snow much.

20.   Still likely for Snow–A small sprinkle, but not enough to cover the ground in the Morning. About 10 Oclock it cleared & became remarkably pleasant wind Southerly. Mer. at 26 in the Morning–40 at highest & 32 at Night. Mr. G. W. Craik came here to dinner.

21.   Morng. clear & wind at No. Wt.–Mer. at 30. Clear all day. Mer. at 40 & fallen to 39 at night.

22.   Very cloudy & heavy. Wind Southerly. Mer. 32 in the Morn. –40 at Noon & 42 at Night. About two oclock it began to rain & continued to do so about 2 hours when it ceased but remained cloudy.

23.   Snow, just sufft. to cover the ground, fell in the Night. Wind at No. Wt. in the Morning & Mer. at 30–at Noon 25 & at night 20. Wind fresh all day. Mr. Howell Lewis came to Dinner.

Howell Lewis (1771–1822), of Culpeper County, was the youngest child of Fielding and Betty Washington Lewis. In 1793 he served GW as an interim manager of Mount Vernon until GW found and hired William Pearce.

24.   Wind at No. Wt. in the morning–at noon 28 and at Night 22. Clear all day & afterno[o]n the wind was Southerly. Mr. Jno. Hopkins & Mr. Hodgden came to dinner.

MR. JNO. HOPKINS: probably John Hopkins (c.1757–1827), commissioner of continental loans for the state of Virginia (1780–c.1794) and a merchant and banker of Richmond. In 1806, after moving to Alexandria, Hopkins married Cornelia Lee (1780–1815), a daughter of William Lee of Greenspring.

25.   Wind Southerly all day & much like Snow in the forenoon —clear afterwards. Mer. 26–32 & 32. Mess. Hopkins & Hodgden went away after Breakfast.

26.   Mer. at 30 in the morning. Wind Southerly & raining until Noon, when it ceased but continued cloudy with the Wind in the same place. Mer. rising to 37 by Night.

27.   Raining with the wind at No. Et. Mer. at 32 in the morning —33 at Noon & 28 at Night. About 4 O'clock the Wind came out at No. Wt. & the Rain changed to Snow.

28.   Snow about an Inch deep. Clear & wind at No. Wt. & Mer. at 20 in the Morning—33 at its highest & 20 at Night. Mr. Craik & Mr. Howell Lewis went away after breakfast.

29.   Cold, raw & likely for Snow in the Morning. Mer. at 20 & wind at No. Et. Clear Afternoon with but little wind. Mer. 31 at highest & 27 at Night.

30.   Lowering—in the Morning, Wind still at No. Et. Mer. 24. Afternoon calm, clear & pleasant. Mer. at 42 at its height & 37 at Night.

31.   Clear with the Wind at No. Wt. and Mer. at 31 in the Morning—lowering towards night. Mer. 45 when highest and 35 at Night.

February— 1798

1.   Clear wind about So. Wt. & Mer. 28 in the Morning. Pretty brisk from No. Wt, about Noon & calm towards night & clear all day. Mer. 40 at Night & 45 when highest. A Mr. Lad & a Mr. Gibbes from Rhode Island dined here & returned to Alexandria.

John G. Ladd was a merchant in Alexandria. Of Mr. Gibbes from Rhode Island, Nelly Custis later remarked: "I do not know what subjects he discusses with *gentlemen* . . . as I have seen too little of him, to fathom his *scull,* yet his conversation to Ladies is composed of . . . *Hearts, darts, hopes, fears, heart achs,* & all the etcetera superfluous of the *tender passion"* (Eleanor Parke Custis to Elizabeth Bordley, 20 Mar. 1798, ViMtV).

2.   Clear, moderate & pleasant all day with but little wind & that Westerly. Mer. 32 in the Morning—56 at highest & 52 at Night.

3.   Wind brisk from No. Wt. & Mer. 42 in the Morning—clear and but little of it afterwards. Mer. 44 at highest & 38 at Night. A Mr. Adamson from Hamburgh & Doctr. Stuart came to Dinner.

William Adamson wrote GW a letter on 5 Feb. 1798 thanking him for "the polite & kind reception" that he had received at Mount Vernon (DLC:GW).

Dr. David Stuart was at Mount Vernon to discuss with GW what was to be done with Washington Custis. After young Custis's return from Princeton in October (see 3 Oct. 1797), GW made out a schedule of study with the intention of having the boy pursue his education at Mount Vernon (7 Jan. 1798, DLC:GW). The results, as may have been expected, were not satisfactory. GW wrote to Stuart on 22 Jan. to see if he and Custis's mother could find out what the boy wanted to do (MH: Autograph File). Stuart replied on 26 Jan. that Custis himself "found his habits of indolence and inattention so unconquerable, that he did not expect to derive any benefit from the plans pursued in [a college]." Stuart promised GW that he would be at Mount Vernon soon to talk over the situation (DLC:GW). He came again on 18 Feb.

4.   Wind Southerly, & weather lowering. Mer. at 31 in the morning. 44 at Noon, & at Night. Afternoon clear. Mr. Adamson went away after breakfast & Mr. Craik & Mr. Marshall came to dinner —the latter returned after it.

5.   Wind violent at No. Wt. in the morning & Mer. at 40—46 at highest & 37 at Night. Clear all day & wind ceasing towards Night. Doctr. Stuart went away after breakfast.

6.   Clear, with a brisk Southerly Wind. Mer. at 29 in the morning—46 at highest & 41 at Night.

7.   Wind Southerly in the Morning but shifted before 10 oclock & turned very cold. Mer. 31 in the Morng. Went to a meetg. of the Potomak Co. in George Town. Dined at Colo. Fitzgeralds & lodged at Mr. T. Peters.

This was a special meeting of the Potomac Company shareholders, called to try to shore up the crumbling financial condition of the company (see entry for 7 Aug. 1797). The president (Tobias Lear) and directors (James Keith, John Mason, and John Templeman) were authorized "to borrow not more than 100 shares from the proprietors to mortgage for loan, said stock

February 1798

Thomas Peter in an early nine-teenth-century portrait, by William Williams (Mr. Armistead Peter III)

to be returned on or before August, 1800." A report was read which told of unsuccessful attempts to procure further aid from the Virginia and Maryland legislatures. However, the two legislatures had passed a law allowing the company to collect additional tolls, and the time for completion of the work had been again extended until 1802. Although the president and directors had obtained "on their notes, for the use of the Potomac Company, from the Bank of Columbia, $4500, and from the Bank of Alexandria $1500," in order to carry on the work at Great Falls, the financial condition of the company became increasingly precarious (BACON-FOSTER, 95–97).

8.   Visited the Public buildgs. in the Morng. Met the Compy. at the Union Tavern & dined there—lodged as before. Weather very cold. Wind Northerly.

Visitors to the Capitol and the president's residence in Feb. 1798 found the buildings well along. At the Capitol the superintendent reported "the free-stone work on the outside is raised as high as the top of the Corinthian capitals all round the building. . . . The brickwork is also raised as high as the roof, and the naked flooring of the building is almost entirely laid." At the "President's House" the stone work was almost finished, the chimneys were up to the roof, which was finished except for the laying of the slate, and the doors "of the two principal stories" were all framed, "and some of them are panelled" (*Columbian Mirror* [Alexandria], 27 Feb. 1798).

9.   Returned home to Dinner—hard freezing the three last

Nights. Weather still cold. Wind No. Easterly. Mer. at night 20. Found Mr. Geo. Calvert here.

10.   Clear morning with but little W. Mer. at 18. Pleasant all day. Mer. 28 at Night. Mr. Calvert left this after breakfast. Wind freshened from the Southward.

In MS "left" is written "let."

11.   Clear—Mer. at 30, & wind Southerly in the Morning. 47 at highest & 40 at Night. Towards Night the Wind shifted to the No. Et. & the weather became lowering.

12.   Clear—Mer. at 35 and Wind at No. Wt. in the Morning— little or none afterwards—& at Night lowering. Went with the family to a Ball in Alexa. given by the Citzen[s] of it & its vicinity in commemoration of the Anniversary of my birth day.

Feb. 11 was GW's birthday according to the Julian (Old Style) calendar, but in 1752 the corrections of the Gregorian (New Style) calendar were adopted by England, Ireland, and the colonies, and GW's birthday became 22 Feb. The citizens of Alexandria chose to celebrate GW's birthday on the Old Style date, but it fell on a Sunday in 1798, and consequently the ball was held on Monday, 12 Feb. (see entry for 11 Mar. 1747/48 for a discussion of the transition from the Julian to Gregorian calendar). Nelly Custis accompanied GW's party to the ball, where she found her old music "master for singing" from Philadelphia who "performed with the band . . . and his clarinet sounds as sweetly as ever." She also found "the room . . . crouded, there were twenty five or thirty couples in the first two setts . . . we danced until two o'clock" (Eleanor Parke Custis to Elizabeth Bordley, 20 Mar. 1798, ViMtV).

13.   A sprinkle of Snow fell in the Night. Wind at No. Et. Raw & threatning a fall of Weather all day. Returned home to dinner. Mer. 30 at Night.

14.   About an inch deep of Snow fell last Night. Weather cloudy & cold. Wind at No. & Mer. 25 in the morning—Clear afterwds. Mer. 33 at Night. Mr. Alexr. Spotswood & Wife & Mr. Fieldg. Lewis & Mr. Lear came to dinner. The latter returned afterwards.

15.   Clear morning—wind still at N. W. & Mer. at 24—the evening—32 & at highest 36. Afternoon clear & evening lowering. Mr. Fieldg. Lewis went away after dinner.

16.   Cloudy, & Wind No. Westerly & Mer. at 30 in the Morning. No. Easterly afterwards. Mer. 28 at Night & 32 at highest. Cloudy most part of the day. Mr. & Mrs. Spotswood left us after breakfast.

17.   Mer. at 24—Wind at No. cold & fresh in the morning & all day. Mer. 30 at Night & 36 at highest—clear.

18.   Quite clear & little wind, Mer. 21 in the morning—Wind at No. Et. afterwards. Mer. 24 at Night & 34 at highest. Doctr. Stuart came in the evening.

19.   Mer. at 22 in the morning. Wind at No. Et. & extremely cloudy. About 4 O'Clock it began to Hail. At Night Mer. was at 21 & at highest 24. Doctr. Stuart went away after Breakt.

20.   An extremely heavy Sleet—with little or no wind. Mer. at 28. A mixture of Hail & rain had fallen in the Night. Abt. noon the Wind came out, but not hard at No. W. Cloudy all day. Mer. 32 at Night—as high as it had been in the day.

21.   Mer. at 32 in the Morning & very cloudy—the wind at No. Et.—where it remained all day. In the evening it began a steady rain. Mer. stood at 32 all day.

22.   About an inch of Snow fell last Night—Mer. 32—morning clear. Wind So. Westerly till 10 Oclock—then No. Wt. & fresh. Mer. 42 at Night & 50 at highest.

23.   Heavy morning—no wind. Mer. 32 very cloudy all day—wind at So. Et. & in the aftern. fine Rain. Mer. 36 at Night & not more all day.

24.   Very foggy Morng. & Mer. at 36. Cloudy all day without Wind. Mer. at 40 at Night & at highest.

25.   Rain fell last Night. Morning cloudy & heavy—Wind Easterly & Mer. at 36. No. Wt. in the afternn. Mer. 44 at higt. & 40, Night.

26.   Morning calm & heavy—clear afterwards. Wind at No. Wt. in the Morning & Mer. 36. Clear the remainder of the day & a little cool. Mer. 40 at Night & 43 at highest.

27.   Morning clear. Wind at No. Wt. but not fresh—grd. a little froze & Mer. at 30. Clear & pleasant all day. Mer. 40 at Night & 44 at higt.

28.   Clear morning & very white fr. No wind—Mer. at 30. About 10 Oclock the wind came out at No. Et. clouded up immediately & at 12 began to snow & contd. to do so until night, by which the grd. was covered about 4 Inches. Mer. contd. at 30 all day.

March — 1798

1.   Wind at East—Morning heavy. M. at 30. About 9 or 10 Oclock began a slow foggy rain which continued through the day. Mer. remained at 30.

2.   A very thick fog & very little Wind. Mer. at 31 in the morning. In the afternoon the weather cleared & towds. Night the Wind came out fresh at No. W. Snow all gone. Mer. 33 at Night 40 at high.

3.   Cloudy with appearances of Snow. Wind at No. a little Easterly. Mer. 29 & ground frozen in the morning. Abt. noon it cleared, & the wind shifted to the Southward. Mer. 30 at Night & 34 at highest. Mr. G. W. Craik dined here & returned.

4.   Morning clear & calm—White frost—Mer. 26 grd. frozen. Clear & pleasant all day with the Wind at So. Mer. 41 at night & 43 at highest. Doctr. Stuart came to dinner.

5.   Calm morng. with Indications of a change in the weather. Mer. at 30. Doctr. Stuart left this, to accompany Washington Custis to St. Johns College at Annapolis. Messrs. Bowne & Lawrence from New York & young Hartshone dined here & retd. Mer. 40 at N. 46.

After much thought GW had finally decided to enroll Washington Custis in St. John's College, a small nondenominational school opened in 1789 in Annapolis. Custis's uncle George Calvert had recommended the college. GW thought the boy might like it better than a school farther from home and also he felt "there is *less* of that class of people which are baneful to youth, in that City, than in any other" (GW to David Stuart, 26 Feb. 1798, NN: Washington Papers). GW sent by Dr. Stuart's hand a letter to John McDowell, president of the college, in which he warned McDowell of Custis's indolence. He added, however, that he knew of no vice in the boy. "From drinking and gaming he is perfectly free and if he has a propensity to any other impropriety, it is hidden from me. He is generous, and regardful of truth" (5 Mar. 1798, NN: Washington Collection). YOUNG HARTSHONE: may be William Hartshorne, Jr. (SPROUSE [2], 2:50).

6. Morning clear—Wind No. Easterly M. 32. Afternoon wind South Easterly. Mer. 38 at Night & 46 at highest. Doctr. Craik dined here & went away afterwards.

7. A very white frost—heavy fog. No wind & Mer. at 32 in the morning. Clear & at So. Et. afterwards though but little of it. Mer. at 46 at Night and 50 at highest.

8. Cloudy, with the wind at No. Et. but not much of it & Mer. at 40 in the Morng. Clear afterwards & wind Southerly. Mer. 50 at Night & 60 at the highest. Colo. Heth—Colo. Fitzgerald & Mr. Patten dined here. The two last left it after dinner.

Col. William Heth (see entry for 22 Feb. 1788), of Virginia, was one of the officers GW preferred for the army formed in 1798 in response to the threat of war with France.

9. Morning—Sun rose red—thin gauz Clouds—Wind No. Et. Mer. 38. Clear afterwards & wind at So. Wt. Mer. 50 at Night 52 at height. Colo. Heath went away after breakfast.

10. Morning—clear & smoaky—Wind at South & Mer. at 50. Clear all day & wind in same quarter. Mer. 62 at Night & 66 at highest. Ludwell & Geo. Lee Esqrs. & Mr. Robt. Beverly dined here & returned & Mr. & Mrs. Peter & Nelly Custis came after dinner.

Ludwell Lee was a first cousin of George Lee of Loudoun, who appears at Mount Vernon also on this day. ROBT. BEVERLY: may be either the father or the brother of George Lee's wife, Evelyn Byrd Beverley Lee. The elder Robert Beverley (1740–1800) lived at Blandfield in Essex County; his son Robert Beverley (1769–1823) inherited the estate upon the death of his father.

11. Morning—thin clouds—brisk South wind Mer. at 57. In the afternoon Rain with thunder & lightening—Mer. at 55 & 63 at highest. Colo. Ball & Doctr. Stuart came to Dinner.

Col. Burgess Ball moved from his Spotsylvania estate in 1791 and was at this time living at Springwood in Loudoun County.

12.   Morning—High No. Wt. Wind—Mer. at 33. Clear all day. Mer. 42 at Night & 44 at highest. Calm evening. Colo. Ball & Dr. Stuart went after Bt.

13.   Morning—Cloudy, & but little Wind—Mer. at 40. Clear afterwds. with the wind at No. Wt. but not hard. Mer. 40 at Night & 46 at hig. Mr. Peter went away after breakt.

14.   Morning—Clear & pleasant—Wind Southerly—Mer. 38. Wind increased from same quarter—and in the evening lowered. Mer. rose to & stood at 56.

15.   Morning cloudy with but little Wind. Mer. at 46. Abt. Noon the Wind came out strong at No. Wt. & sprinkled Rain— after wch. it cleared & became calm. Mer. at 40 at Night & 46 at its height.

16.   Morning—clear, Wind at No. Wt. Mer. 38. Clear all day & wind pretty fresh. Mer. 41 at Night & 46 at the height.

17.   Morning cloudy—Wind at East & Mer. at 35. Clear afterwards with but little wind and that Easterly. Mer. 44 at Night & 49 at highest. Mr. Snow of Massachusetts dined here & returned to Alexa.

Mr. Snow is probably Gideon Snow, who settled in Boston, Mass. (see entry for 17 Sept. 1786).

18.   Morning—thick—Wind at No. East—Mer. at 38. Clear about Noon cloudy & much like rain afterwards wind still at No. Et. Mer. 39 at Night & 43 at highest. Mr. Steer Senr. & Junr. Miss Steer & Mrs. Vanhaver dined here & returned to Alexa. afterwards. Mr. Peter came in the afternoon.

Henri Joseph Stier (1743–1821), member of the States General of the Province of Antwerp, Belgium, fled the wars of the French Revolution in 1794 and brought his family to America, settling in Annapolis, Md. With him at Mount Vernon today were his son, Jean Charles Stier, his daughter Rosalie Eugenia Stier, and another daughter, Isabel, wife of Jean Michel Van Havre, who appears in the diaries 20 June 1799.

19.   Morning—Raining slow—Wind at No. Et. Mer. at 37. Cloudy until late in the afternoon without rain, when it cleared; Mer. at 42 at Night, & no higher all day. Horns of the New Moon up. Dined with Mrs. Washington &ca. at Mr. Thomson Mason's.

20. Morning—Soft & cloudy without Wind—Mer. at 42. Raining at times from about noon with the Wind at No. Et. Mer. contd. at 42 all day. Mr. Lawe. Washington of Chotanck & Mr. Lawe. Washington of Belmont came to Dinner. Albin Rawlins came to live with me as Clerk.

GW, upon "finding it impracticable to use the exercise on horse back which my health business and inclination requires, and at the same time to keep my acots., and perform all the writing, which my late Public Occupations have been the means of involving me in, I resolved to employ a clerk," preferably "a single man . . . on very moderate wages . . . [to] be content to eat with, and live in the same manner the Housekeeper does, having a room to himself to write in, and another to lodge in, over the same" (GW to William Augustine Washington, 27 Feb. 1798, DLC:GW; GW to Albin Rawlins, 31 Jan. 1798, DLC:GW; WRITINGS, 36:150–51, 171–74). The clerk's "principle employment" would be "to copy and record letters and other Papers, to keep Books (if required) and an account of articles received from and delivered to the Farms . . . to go . . . to such places as my business may require, to receive grain, and attend to the measurement of it, and other things when it is necessary to send a trustworthy person to see it done" (GW to Albin Rawlins, 12 Feb. 1798, DLC:GW; WRITINGS, 36:164–66). After some dickering GW hired Albin Rawlins, of Hanover County, for $150 per year (see Rawlins to GW, 26 Jan. and 7 Feb. 1798, DLC:GW).

21. Morning—hard rain with thunder & lightening—wind at East & Mer. at 41. Showery until 3 Oclock when the wind came out violently at No. W. & cleared. Mer. 40 at Night & 46 at its height. Mr. L. Washington Belmont went away.

BELMONT: GW wrote "Vermt.," apparently a slip of the pen.

22. Morning—Clear—Wind at No. Wt. Mer. at 35. Clear all day & wind hard until evening at same point. Mer. 40 at Night & 48 high.

23. Morning—Clear & calm—Mer. 33. Lowering afterwards with a brisk So. Easterly Wind. Mer. 46 at Night & no higher all day. Mr. L. Washington of Chotanck & Mr. Peter went away after breakfast.

24. Morning—Storming with Rain & Wind at So. Et. Mer. 48. Abt. Noon the Rain ceased, & the wind shifted to the West of South. Mer. 50 at Night and 51 at highest.

25. Morning—clear & Wind So. Wt. Mer. 42. Squally afternoon, Wind shifting to No. Wt. Mer. 42 at Night & 48 at high. Mr.

Nichols & wife & Mr. Lear & family dined here. Mr. Peter returnd.

MR. LEAR & FAMILY: Besides his son Benjamin Lincoln Lear and stepsons George Fayette Washington and Charles Augustine Washington, the Lear family may have included Lear's mother, Mary Lear, who had come to care for the boys after Fanny Lear's death. Lear's stepdaughter, Anna Maria Washington (1788–1814), had gone to live with her uncle Burwell Bassett, Jr., at Eltham.

26. Morning–Clear–Wind at No. Wt. & Mer. 40. Afternoon wind shifted to So. W. & lowered. Mer. 50 at Night 51 hight.

27. Morning–Clear & pleasant with but little Wind from So. Wt. Mer. 46. Wind more westerly afterwards clear & still very pleasant and warm. Mer. at 53 at Night & 56 at highest. Mr. Charles Carroll Jun. & Mr. Willm. Lee came to dinner.

Charles Carroll, Jr. (b. 1775), of Homewood, was the son of Charles Carroll of Carrollton. His attentions to Nelly Custis at an Alexandria ball the previous spring set off rumors of romance that were discounted by Nelly, who, although finding Carroll "a pleasing young man," was left with the impression that he "unfortunately has been told too often of his merit and accomplishments, and it has given him more affectation than is by any means agreeable" (Eleanor Parke Custis to Elizabeth Bordley, 30 May 1797, ViMtV). With this visit by Carroll the romantic rumors resumed, and to Nelly's brother, George Washington Parke Custis, GW wrote: "Young Mr. C[   ] came . . . to dinner, and left us next morning after breakfast. If his object was such as you say has been reported, it was not declared here; and therefore, the less is said upon the subject, particularly by your sister's friends, the more prudent it will be until the subject develops itself more" (15 April 1798, CUSTIS, 102).

WILLM. LEE: probably William Lee (1775–1845), of Frederick County, Md., third son of Thomas Sim Lee and Mary Digges Lee.

28. Morning clear & calm–Mer. 42–So. East afterwards. 53 at Night & 56 at highest. Mr. Carroll & Mr. Lee went away after breakfast & the family here went to dine with Mr. Nichols.

29. Morning–heavy without wind. Mer. 50. Clear afternoon & Calm. Mer. 53, greatest 54.

30. Morning tolerably clear Wind abt. South Mer. 49. Clear & warm all day, wind in the same place. Mer. 64 at Night & 67 at highest. Doctr. Flood dined here.

31. Morning—Hazy & a little cloudy. Wind pretty fresh from South. Mer. 58. Clear afterwards—Wd. same place. Mer. 65 at Night 68 at highest. A Mr. Fevot—a French Gentleman recomd. by Count de Rochambeau dined here & a Mr. Freeman Member in Congress from N. Hamps. came in the afternoon & returned.

Paul Ferdinand Fevot (b. 1756) was born in Lausanne, Switzerland, the son of Jean Samuel Fevot. Lausanne was at this time ruled by the Canton of Berne, and Fevot was "Lawyer at the Soverign Council of Berne." He was, however, in ill favor with the French whose influence was strong in his country at this time and had come to the United States with a cautious, unsigned letter of introduction from Rochambeau, whose own position in France was extremely precarious. Fevot wrote GW a long, rambling letter a few days after this visit expressing disillusionment in general with people and conditions in America, and particularly dissatisfaction with GW's reception and entertainment at Mount Vernon. "I was not surprised in beholding your reserved Countenance at first meeting, but I entertained a chearfull hope that it would clear up when I should have made myself better Known. I respectfully presented to You my note of recomandation, & Your Excellency told me You did not read French; upon which I took the Liberty to Express my hope that You Knew the hand writing; & Your answer was You *rather* thought it was! If I am still acquainted with the English language this expression is to carry with it if not a thourough doubt of an allegation at least a strong shade of it injurious in this instance to any honest man, and very ungenerous, very cruel indeed to a Stranger of a genteel appearance & behaviour; 1200 leagues distant from his native Country, who having exposed himself to run 400 more at a grievous expence for him, relying on a recomandation, does not get by it the least token of interest or protection but not even a Kind word!" He continued, "If to obtain in life a high Situation, if the worship of the Multitude is to be captivated by divesting oneself of humanity & generosity there is much more comfort in my [lowly] position than I thought." Fevot added, however, that he found Mrs. Washington a civil and polite lady. GW was nonplussed by Fevot's letter and replied on 15 April: "Not perceiving what has been your object in addressing such sentiments as your letter of the 4th inst. contained—and not being conscious of having merited the reprehension you have judged it expedient to inflict on me, I shall not give you the trouble of reading an answer in detail. I can not forbear observing however that as it is not usual with me, to treat any Gentleman with incivility or even with indifference (especially under my own Roof) I am unable to recollect any part of my behaviour which could give rise to such misconception of my motives" (Fevot to GW, 16 Oct. 1797 and 4 April 1798, and GW to Fevot, 15 April 1798, DLC:GW; Fevot's certificate from the magistrate of Lausanne, 14 April 1797, MHi-A: Adams Family Papers).

Jonathan Freeman (1745–1808) lived in Hanover, N.H., where he farmed and served as treasurer of Dartmouth College for over 40 years. After holding a number of local and state offices he was twice elected as a Federalist to the United States House of Representatives, serving from 1797 to 1801.

April — 1798

1.   Morning—Smoaky & a little cloudy with the wind fresh from the Southward. Mer. 60—at night 66 & not higher all day. Mr. Law, a Mr. Taylor Lieutt. Walton of the Navy & young Mr. Barry came to dinner & Chs. Alexander junr. came at Night.

Young Mr. Barry is probably James David Barry, nephew and adopted son of James Barry. Charles Alexander, Jr. (d. 1812), was the oldest son of Charles Alexander (1737–1806) of Preston.

2.   Morning—very heavy—Wind at No. Et. Mer. 56. Raining more or less from 10 oclk. Wind more Northerly. Mer 40 at Night. Mr. Law & the Gentlemen who came with [him] left this about noon.

3.   Morning—Raining—Wind fresh from No. Et. Mer. 39. Raining all day—wind in the same quarter. Mer. 38 at Night 42 highest.

4.   Morning very thick and misting. Wind high from No. Et. Mer. 38. Misting & sometimes raining through the day. Wind in the same quarter. Mer. 39 at Night & 42 at highest. Mr. Alexander went away after breakfast.

5.   Morning—Heavy & misting, Wind at No. Et. Mer. 42—The same through the day. Mer. 46 at Night & no higher.

6.   Morning—Sun rose clear, but cloudy notwithstanding. Wind at No. Et. & Mer. at 46. Clear afterwards Wind still Easterly but moderate; Mer. 54 at Night—58 at highest.

7.   Morning thick & misting. Wind easterly Mer. 48. Clear at Noon & cloudy afterwards. Mer. 50 at night & 58 at highest.

8.   Morning—Began to rain about 6 Oclock—Wind at No. Et. & Mer. at 48. Ceased before 8 oclock & became a fine clear day with the wind moderately from No. Wt. Mer. 58 at Night & 63 at highest. Cap. John Spotswood & Mr. Lear came to dinner—the last went away after it.

9.   Morning—clear, calm & extremely pleasant. Mer. 46. Clear all day—wind first at No. Et. then Southerly. Mer. 53 at Night, &

56 at highest. Mr. Peter went away after breakfast—leaving Mrs. Peter behind him.

10.   Morning—Calm & clear Mer. 47. The wind springing up from the Eastward it lowered in the Afternoon & began to rain at Night. M. 52 at Night and 53 at highest.

11.   Morning—Very cloudy havg. rained through the Night. Wind at So. Et. & Mer. at 52.

12.   Morning—Clear—Wind Southerly & Mer. 45. Wind variable and weather apparently unsettled. Mer. 47 at Night 52 at highest. Mr. Peter ret[urned].

13.   Morning heavy & lowering. Wind Southerly & Mer. at 44—variable appearances of weather thro the day. Mer. 48 at Night & 50 at highest. Genl. Lee came to dinner & Colo. Heath & son in the afternn.

Col. William Heth had two sons, William M. Heth and Henry Gray Heth (d. 1816).

14.   Morning—Clear & but little Wd. & that at No. W. Mer. 46. Wind varying from No. W. to So. W. & then back again with squalls without Rain. Mer. 45 at Night & not higher than 46. Genl. Lee & Colo. Heath went away after breakfast & Dr. Stuart came to D.

TO D.: probably means "to dinner" or "to dine."

15.   Morning clear & cool, but no frost. Wind abt. West & Mer. 38. Clear & Cold all day wind getting to and blowing cold from the No. Wt. Mer. at 40 all day. Mrs. Fitzhugh & her daughters & son came in the afternoon.

Mrs. Anne Randoph Fitzhugh, wife of William Fitzhugh of Chatham, had one son, William Henry Fitzhugh (1790–1830), who later lived at Ravensworth, the vast Fitzhugh estate in Fairfax County. Her two daughters were Anne Fitzhugh (b. 1784), who later married Dr. Craik's eldest son, William Craik, and Mary Lee (Molly) Fitzhugh (1788–1835), who was to marry Martha Washington's grandson, George Washington Parke Custis.

16.   Morning Calm & clear Mer. at 40. Afterwards Wind at No. Wt. & variable & weather also, Cold and disagreeable. Mer. at Night 32. 40 at highest. Doctr. Stuart went away. I went to Alexa. to an Election of Delegates for the Cty. of Fairfax—voted for

William Henry Fitzhugh, only son of William Fitzhugh of Chatham; portrait attributed to Cephas Thompson. (Washington and Lee University, Washington-Custis-Lee Collection)

Messrs. West & Jno. Herbert—returned to Dinner. Mr. Fitzhugh came in the Afternoon.

Roger West (d. 1801), son of John West, Jr., and John Carlyle Herbert (1777–1846), elder son of William Herbert of Alexandria, were elected.

17.   Morning—Wind at No. Wt. & disagreeably cold—Mer. at 28. Clear and cold all day. A very severe frost—ground hard frozen. Ice sufficient to bear. Fruit supposed to be all Killed—leaves of trees bit &ca. Mer. 36 at night 37 highest.

18.   Morning—Clear & more moderate—Wind still at No. Wt. Mer. at 32. Clear all day & but little wind after morng. Mer. 50 at Night & no higher all day. Peaches not killed, & hoped other fruit not hurt. Points of the New Moon upwards. Mr. Fitzhugh & family left this after breakfast. Began to plant Corn at Union farm.

19.   Morning—clear & calm & continued so through the day. Mer. 40 in the Morning—53 at Night & 54 at highest.

20.   Morning—lowering—wind Southerly & Mer. at 54. Variable weather all day. Mer. 62 at Night, & 64 at highest. Mr. Peter went

away after breakfast and Mr. Townshend Dade & Mr. Nichs. Fitzhugh came to Din.

Nicholas Fitzhugh's sister Susannah Fitzhugh Dade (1757–1808) was married
to Col. Townshend Dade of King George County.

21.   Rained the greater part of last Night. Wind still Southerly
& fresh. Mer. 58 in the morning 62 at Night & 64 at highest. A very
heavy shower of Rain & high wind abt. 2 Oclock. Mr. Dade & Mr.
Fitzh. went after breakf.

22.   Morning–calm & clear–Mer. 55. Clear all day with the
wind at No. Wt. but not hard or cold. Mer. 62 at Night & 65 at
height. Doctr. Craik came on a Visit to Eleanor Peter.

Martha Eliza Eleanor Peter (1796–1800) was the eldest child of Thomas and
Martha Parke Custis Peter.

23.   Morning lowering & calm–Mer. 52. Clear afternoon–wind
at No. Wt. Mer. 66 & at its highest. Mr. Peter returned–sent for.

24.   Clear with but little wind, from No. W. Mer. 51 morning.
Calm mid day & wind at So. Et. at Night. Mer. 56 then & 62 at
highest. Doctr. Craik came in the afternoon to visit Mr. Peter's
Children.

Thomas Peter and Martha Parke Custis Peter had two children at this time;
the younger was named Columbia Washington Peter (1797–1820).

25.   Morning–Lowering–Wind at S. E. Mer. at 52. Clouds
heavier towds. Night. Mer. 52 at Night–60 at highest. Doctr. went
away after breakf.

26.   Morning very heavy–Wind at S. E. Mer. 53. Clear afterwards & turning very Warm. Mer. at 67 at Night & not higher all
day. The Revd. Mr. Fairfax and Doctr. Craik (to visit Mr. Peter's
children) came to dinner. The first returned afterwards.

27.   Morning, & the day throughout clear. Wind at So. Et. Mer.
56 in the M. & 68 at Night & no higher all day. Doctr. Craik went
away after breakfast & Mr. & Mrs. Law and a Mr. Ghan, a Swedish
Gentleman came to dinner.

MR. GHAN: Henry Gahn (d. 1834), a young Swede from Stockholm, was
established in New York where he carried on "a very lucrative commerce"

with Spain. He later served as a commercial agent for Sweden (NIEMCEWICZ, 17, 299, n.49).

28.   Morning clear—wind Southerly. Mer. 64. Some appearances of Rain in the afternoon but none fell. Mer. 66 at Night 68 at high.

29.   Morning—clear, wind still Southerly—Mer. 61. Calm all day with appearances abt. 2 Oclock of Rain but none fell. Mer. 70 at Night & 73 at height. Mr. Ghan wt. away after breakfast.

30.   Morning—Clear, wind Southerly Mer. at 62—70 at Night & 74 at highest. Mr. Law & Mr. Peter went away after breakfast— and Doctr. & Mrs. Craik & Son—Mr. & Mrs. Harrison—and Mrs. Jenifer & a Miss Barnes came to dinner & returned afterwards.

Mrs. Jenifer is probably Dr. and Mrs. Craik's daughter Sarah, wife of Dr. Daniel Jenifer. Miss Barnes is probably a member of the Barnes family of Charles County, Md. The 1790 census included several heads of households by that name (HEADS OF FAMILIES, MD., 47–48).

May 1798

1.   Morning—clear—wind at South & Mer. at 63. Clear & warm all day—wind in the same place. Mer. 71 at Night—75 at highest.

2.   A light sprinkling of Rain & cloudy in the morning—Mer. 66. Clear afterwards & very warm. Mer. 71 at Night & 75 at highest. Mr. Law returned to dinr.

3.   Morning—clear—wind Southerly Mer. 60 very little wind & appearances of Rain in the afternoon. Mer. 74 at Night & not higher.

4.   Morning—Clear & wind Southerly Mer. at 66. Appearances of Rain abt. Noon but none fell. Mer. 81 at Night & 82 at highest. Mr. and Mrs. Law went away after breakfast & Nelly Custis went up to Hope Park.

5.   Clear Morning & little Wind—Mer. 70. Between 2 & 4 Oclock fine showers at intervals. Mer. 70 at Night & 81.

6.   Morning—perfectly clear with a light breeze from the West- ward—Mer. 62. High wind from No. West afterwards—Mer. 67

A Sharples portrait of Nelly Custis, circa 1796. (Mount Vernon Ladies' Association of the Union, Collection of the heirs of Stephen Decatur, Jr.)

thro' the day. A Mr. Tayler & a Mr. Crips—introduced by Mr. Potts dined here as did Mr. T. Peter & Mr. Lear. All except Mr. Peter went away after dinner.

7.   Morng. Cloudy with a little drippg. of Rain. Mer. at 60. Clear Afternoon. Mer. 64 at Night.

8.   Morning perfectly clear & pleasant—Calm—Mer. at 64. Lowering afternoon. Mr. Peter, Mrs. Peter & their Children left this and the Revd. Mr. Lewis from Connecticut came in the Afternoon.

REVD. MR. LEWIS: probably Zechariah Lewis (1773–1840), son of Rev. Isaac Lewis of Greenwich, Conn. Young Lewis had graduated from Yale in 1794 and studied theology under Dr. Ashbell Green in Philadelphia. During this time he had also acted as a tutor to George Washington Parke Custis. In 1796 Lewis was licensed to preach at Fairfield West Association, and later in the year became a tutor at Yale College, a position he held until his health failed in the summer of 1799. He then became editor of the *New York Spectator* and the *Commercial Advertiser* but retained his theological interests, becoming involved in various religious societies (SPRAGUE, 1:662–68; Zechariah Lewis to GW, 17 June 1797, CtY).

9.   Morning clear with but little Wind. Mer. at 58. Wind afterwards fresh indeed hard from the Westward until Night when it ceased. Mer. at 64 at Night. Mr. Lewis went away after breakfast. I went to the Proclamn. Sermon in Alexandria.

SERMON: On 23 Mar. 1798 Pres. John Adams issued a proclamation recommending that "as the United States of America are at present placed in a hazardous and afflictive situation, by the unfriendly disposition, conduct, and demands of a foreign power [France] . . . the 9th of May next, be observed throughout the United States, as a day of solemn humiliation, fasting and prayer" (ADAMS [2], 9:169).

10.   Morning—clear & calm—Mer. at 52. Lowering all the afternoon with the Wind Southerly, but no Rain fell.

11.   Morning—clear & but little wind—Mer. at 54. Great appearances of Rain abt. 2 Oclock with the Wind at No. Et. but none well. Eveng. Clear Mer. at 56 & no higher.

12.   Morning—clear & cool—Wind Northerly & Mer. at 44. Clear & Cold all day—a White frost this Morning. Mer. 56 at Night.

13.   Morning—clear & cool—Wind No. Easterly—Mer. at 50. Lowering towards evening. Mer. 56 at N. not much higher all day. Mr. White & Doctr. Craik dined here. The latter went away after dinr.

14.   Morning—Clear & cool, Calm—Mer. at 49. Some appearances of Rain abt. noon but they went off. Wind No. Et. & Mer. at 60 at Night. Mr. White left this after breakfast.

15.   Morning–clear, with but little Wind & that No. Easterly Mer. 52–same through the day. Mer. 64 at Night.

16.   Morning perfectly clear–Wind northerly & Mer. at 58. Wind fresh after morning & cool all day. Mer. 60 at Night.

17.   Morning–Clear & calm–Mer. 52. Very lowering & likely for Rain afterwards with the Wind at So. Wt. Mer. 66 at Night.

18.   Clear Morning–no rain fell–clear all day. Mer. 60 in the Morning & 66 at Night. Horns, or points of the Moon upwards.

19.   Morning–Clear, Wind Southerly and Mer. at 55. About 8 Oclock in the forenoon Mrs. Washington & Myself sat out on a visit to Hope Park & the Federal City. Got to the former to Dinner and remained there until Morning when we proceeded to the City. Dined at Mr. Thos. Peter's & remained there until Wednesday, and then went to Mr. Laws & remained there until friday when we sat out on our return home & called at Mount Eagle to take our leave of the Revd. Mr. Fairfax who was on the point of Embarking for England.

The weather during this time was as follow–20th. a brisk Southerly wind & Cool. 21. Appearances of Rain & very warm. 22. Warm & still greater shew for Rain but none fell. 23. Wind still Southerly–Clouds gathering from all quarters and in the Afternoon a very fine Rain. 24. Warm–Southerly Wind & moderate Rain in the Afternoon.

Another guest of Thomas Law was Julian Ursyn Niemcewicz (1758–1841) who visited Mount Vernon on 2 June. Niemcewicz was a Polish literary and political figure who came to America in 1797 as the companion of Tadeusz Kościuszko, leader of the Polish insurrection against Russia. Upon their release from a Russian prison the two Poles had come to America where Kościuszko had earlier gained fame as a colonel of engineers in the Revolution. GW and Mrs. Washington came to the Law home on 23 May for a two-day stay while Niemcewicz was still there. "The whole time he [GW] was courteous, polite, even attentive; he talked very little, now and then on agriculture, on natural history, on all that one would wish, except politics, on which he maintains an absolute silence and reserve." During this visit GW renewed his interest in billiards. "He plays with a mace and although it is 25 years since he has played, his attention and skill made up for the lack of practice" (NIEMCEWICZ, 86–87). A billiard mace is a cue with a knob on the end.

REVD. MR. FAIRFAX: GW wrote the earl of Buchan that "ill health and advice of Physicians have induced him [Bryan Fairfax] to try the effect of Sea Air, & his inclinations have led him to give a voyage to England the preference" (15 May 1798, DLC:GW).

25.   Very brisk So. Westerly wind with misting showers at Intervals from about Noon. Rain in the afternoon. Mrs. Peaks fam. dined here.

26.   Clear all day, with the Wind at No. Wt. Mer. at 60 in the Morning & 62 at Night.

27.   Clear Morning & Calm—Mer. at 54. Wind brisk from the Eastward abt. 8 Oclock & appearances of Rain in the Evening. Mer. at 60 at Night. Mr. Lear dined here.

28.   Morning—Misty & sometimes raining—Mer. at 59, & growing Warm with the wind Easterly. Mer. 65 at Night.

29.   Morning warm & cloudy—Mer. 60, & wind No. Easterly at which pt. & Easterly it contind. all day with appearances of Rain but none fell. Went up to Alexa. on business & returned home to dinner.

30.   Morning—a thick Mist with the wind at No. Et.—Mer. 62. A good deal of Rain afterwards, before One oclock and a very heavy shower mixed with hail about 5 oclk. Colo. Morris, Lady & 4 children came here after dinner.

Colonel Morris is probably Lewis Morris (d. 1829), who had visited Mount Vernon with his brother Jacob Morris on 6 Nov. 1786. Morris had settled in South Carolina after the Revolution, and was an original member of the South Carolina Society of the Cincinnati. Morris, with his wife and children, was probably on his way to or from the Morris family home in New York.

31.   Cloudy more or less through the day but no rain fell here. Wind Southerly. Mer. 64 at Nigt. Colo. Morris & family left this after breakfast—and Mr. Herbert & Son—the Revd. Mr. Addison a Mr. Rogers of Baltimore—Mr. Delius of Bremen & a Mr. Pekmoller of Hamburgh dined here & returned afterwards.

Mr. William Herbert became president of the Bank of Alexandria in 1798. His two sons were John Carlyle Herbert (1777–1846) and William Herbert. Rev. Mr. Addison was Rev. Walter Dulany Addison (b. 1769), eldest son of Thomas Addison (d. 1775), of Oxon Hill and Rebecca Dulany Addison. In 1792 Walter married Elizabeth Dulany Hesselius, daughter of the artist John Hesselius (1728–1778), of Bellefield, Prince George's County, Md.

   Mr. Delius may be Arnold Delius, who was appointed by GW in May 1794 as United States consul to Bremen, Germany (EXECUTIVE JOURNAL, 1:157, 158). MR. PEKMOLLER: For the mid-nineteenth-century memoir of "a German gentleman" who visited Mount Vernon in May 1798, see CUSTIS, 460n.

June — 1798

1.   Morning—clear & pleasant—Wind Southerly, & Mer. at 62. Cloudy more or less all day. Mer. 70 at Night. Mr. Hartshorne & Mr. Lear dined here.

2.   Morning clear & warm—With but little wind. Mer. 62—at Night 70. Mr. Law & a Polish Gentleman, the Companion of General Kosciaski came here to dinner, as did Miss Lee of Greenspring with Nelly Custis who returnd to day.

A POLISH GENTLEMAN: See entry for 19 May 1798. Neimcewicz made a full report of his Mount Vernon visit in his journal, including a detailed description of the Mansion House, farms, gardens, and something about the daily lives of the Washingtons. He immediately became infatuated with Nelly Custis: "This was one of those celestial figures that nature produces only rarely, that the inspiration of painters has sometimes divined and that one cannot see without ecstacy . . . she plays the harpsichord, sings, and draws better than any woman in America or even in Europe" (NIEMCEWICZ, 97).
   Although GW refers to Portia Lee (1777–1840) as being of Greenspring, the home of her recently deceased father, William Lee, she was at this time living with her cousin Richard Bland Lee at Sully, his home in the neighborhood of Hope Park where Nelly Custis had been visiting.

3.   Morning—Calm & Warm Mer. 65. Warm all day with very little wind & that Southerly. Mer. 76 at Night, & in the Night Thunder Lightning & Rain. Mrs. Law came down to dinner & Mr. & Mrs. McClanahan dined here, & returned afterwds.

Niemcewicz said that GW wrote letters all day. In the evening there was no music or games; it was Sunday and everyone retired at 9:00 P.M. On the following day Thomas Law took the guest to see the distillery. "If this distillery produces poison for men, it offers in return the most delicate and the most succulent feed for pigs. They keep 150 of the Guinea type, short feet, hollow backs and so excessively bulky that they can hardly drag their big bellies on the ground" (NIEMCEWICZ, 100).

4.   Morning heavy—wind southerly—Mer. 64. In the afternoon Easterly & a great deal of Rain. Mer. 70 at Night.

5.   Morning, Mer. 65—but little wind & that Southerly. Appearances of Rain in the afternoon but none fell.

6.   Morning—Mer. at 65. Calm & thin clouds; thunder abt. 10 Oclock & Showers at a distance. In the Afternoon Rain for near an hour. Mer. 64 at Night. Mr. Law went away this morning & Dr. Stuart Mrs. Stuart & three daughters came to breakfast & dinner.

Tadeusz Kościuszko, by Julian Rys. (Independence National Historical Park Collection)

According to Niemcewicz, the Stuarts arrived in a coach and four with two postilions and two men on horseback (NIEMCEWICZ, 103). The Stuarts' three daughters were Ann (b. 1784), Sarah, and Arianne (b. 1789).

7.   Morning clear—Wind westerly Mer. 60. Appearances of Rain in the afternoon but none fell. Mer. 70 at Night. Wind West[erl]y.

8.   Morning—Clear & calm. Mer. 65. Clear most of the day & towards evening appearances of Rain but none fell.

9. Morning—clear calm & Warm. Mer. 66. Much the same through the day. Mer. 74 at Night.

10. Morning—Wind pretty fresh from No. Et. but clear—Mer. 70. Very lowering in the Evening—Mer. 66. Doctr. Stuart returned, & Mr. Lear dined here.

11. Morning very heavy & misting. Wind at No. Et. No rain had fallen. Mer. 64. Fine Rain from 8 Oclock through the day. Mer. 64 at Night. Mr. Tracy came in the evening.

Thomas Tracy was a local music master whose students included Nelly Custis (GW's Cash Memorandum, 1 Sept. 1797–20 Feb. 1799: entry for 20 Dec. 1798, RPJCB).

12. Morning Misty. Mid day clear & afternoon moderate Rain. Wind Easterly all day. Mer. 64 in the Morning & 70 at Night. Mr. Law returned in the Evening.

13. Morning, Mer. 68 & clear. Clouds but no rain all day. Mer. 72 at Night. Mr. Fitzhugh, Lady & daughter—Mrs. Beverley Randolph, with her daughter & Son in Law Randolph & his Sister dined here.

Beverley Randolph married Martha Cocke of Williamsburg; their daughter Lucy Randolph married William Randolph (born c.1769) of Chitower, son of Thomas Randolph of Tuckahoe, Goochland County, and his first wife, Anne Cary Randolph. William Randolph's sister is probably one of his two youngest sisters, Harriet Randolph (b. 1783) or Virginia Randolph (b. 1786).

Returning from a fishing trip, Niemcewicz found a "notable and unexpected company from Alexandria." He said the table in the great hall was set out with porcelain service for 20. "The General, in high spirits, was gracious and full of attention to everybody." Of the young Randolphs, he wrote, "I do not know whether both their ages would add up to 38, and already they are the parents of three children" (NIEMCEWICZ, 106–7). In the evening Nelly Custis played the harpsichord and sang for Niemcewicz, who was leaving the following morning.

14. Morning Clear—Mer. 64. Wind at East—So. Westerly afterwards. At N. Mer. 76. Mrs. Stuart & her family & Mr. Law Mrs. Law and Mr. Niemcewitz (the Polish Gentn.) went away after breakfast.

"The next day, after having risen before dawn, I walked, now for the last time, about the green groves of Mo[u]nt Vernon. . . . Then at six in the morning . . . I took my leave of the honorable Washington, his worthy wife and the beautiful, good and kind Miss Custis" (NIEMCEWICZ, 107–8).

15.   Morning—clear, calm & warm. Mer. at 70—80 at Noon & 78 at Night. Calm all day. Mrs. Lund Washington dined here.

16.   Morning—Calm, clear & Warm. Mer. at 72. Clear all day & calm till the afternoon then a brisk Easterly Wind. Mer. 80 at N. & 72 at N.

17.   Morning—Wind fresh from No. Et. and cloudy Mer. at 66. Clear afterwards. Mer. 66 at Night. Mr. [   ] sent by Mr. Pearce to attend my Cradlers in harvest arrived.

On 6 May 1798 GW wrote to his ex-manager, William Pearce, who was now living in the wheat belt of the Eastern Shore in Kent County, Maryland: "In cradling my Wheat the coming Harvest I wish to catch it in the hand, in the manner practised on the Eastern Shore and other places; but as none of my People have been in the habit of cutting in this way, they might need an Instructor. Would it be in your power to engage a person who understands this business *perfectly,* as fixing the Cradles, to be here by the 25th. June, to be paid by the day while here and for coming & returning, and his reasonable travelling expences?" (NBLiHi). Pearce's reply of 16 June 1798 introduces "Mr. John Costalaw . . . the person who I have Sent to you to make and Fix Cradels for you, and to Instruct your people In Cradeling wheat In the manner practised here" (DLC:GW).

18.   Morning—lowering, wind Easterly & Mer. at 62. Afternoon slow Rain—Mer. 70.

19.   Morning Wind still at East & Mer. at 70. Slow rain on & off all the forenoon—then clear—afterwds. cloudy & misting—Mer. [   ].

20.   Morning—heavy, a good deal of Rain fell in the Night. Wind at East Mer. 70. Variable through the day. Mer. 76 at Night—80 at highest.

21.   Morning—Mer. 72—but little wind and that Southerly. Tolerably clear all day & wind fresher from South. Mer. 78 at Noon & Night. Mr. Lear & Mr. Tracy dined here—the first returned afterwards.

22.   Morning clear—wind Southerly—Mer. at 72. Clear & warm all day—fresh breeze from So. Mer. 83 at height & 80 at Night. Mr. Tracy went away [after] dinner.

23.   Morning very lowering with the Wind at So. Wt. & light sprinkling of Rain. Mer. 74—at Night 80.

24.   Morning Clear, Wind So. Wt. Mer. 76. About 3 oclock a very heavy rain for 15 or 20 Minutes and more, but moderate at Night. Mer. at 82 Noon & 74 Night.

25.   Morning very heavy & cloudy with the wind at So. Wt. and Mer. 72. Cloudy all day & sprinkling now and then. Mer. 78 at Noon & 73 at N.

26.   Morning Cloudy, & contd. so all day with the wind at So. Mer. 70 in the Morng. 75 at Noon and 72 at Night. Mr. Law & two French Gentn.—viz. Mr. La Guin & Mr. Clarmont.

Anna Maria Brodeau Thornton wrote in her diary on 24 June 1798 that "Mr. La Guin & Mr. Flamand two French Gentlemen from New York came" (DLC: William Thornton Papers). Nelly Custis recorded that they were "old friends" of Thomas Law's (Eleanor Parke Custis to Elizabeth Bordley, 1 July 1798, ViMtV). MR. LA GUIN: probably the Frenchman Louis Le Guen, who came to the United States in 1794, went into trade in New York City and Philadelphia, and invested in land in eastern Pennsylvania.

27.   Morng. Cloudy—Wind No. Westerly Mer. 67. Clear afterwards & calm. Mer. 75 at Noon & 74 at Night.

28th.   Morning—clear, Wind at So. Mer. 70. Cloudy & likely for Rain all the afternoon but none fell. Mer. 75 at Noon & 74 at Night. Col. Simm dined here.

29.   Morning cloudy, & raining moderately between 7 & 9 Oclock. Clear afterwards & warm Wind Westerly. Mer. 74 in the Morng. 80 at Noon & 76 at Night.

30.   Morning & day clear & calm. Mer. 76 in the Morning, 80 at Noon & 78 at Night.

July — 1798

1.   Morning—Clear & wind Southerly Mer. 74. Day clear & very warm. Mer. 86 at Noon & 84 at Night. Mr. Fitzhugh of Chatham & Doctr. Welford dined here—as did Dr. Fld.

Dr. Robert Wellford (1753–1823), originally of Hertfordshire, Eng., came to America as a surgeon with the British army under Gen. William Howe in 1776. While stationed in Philadelphia, Wellford distinguished himself for his treatment of sick and wounded American prisoners, and in 1781, after resigning his commission, he established a practice in Fredericksburg. In 1794 GW chose him as surgeon general of the army called out to put down the Whiskey Rebellion, and in June 1799 GW, recommending him for the provisional army, wrote: "Doctor Wellford ranks high in his profession, and his Character as a friend to the Government and as a man of integrity, is, I believe, unimpeachable" (GW to James McHenry, 6 June 1799, DLC:GW; BLANTON, 356–57). DR. FLD.: GW probably means William Pinckard Flood. He may, however, be referring to either Richard Feild (1767–1829) or his brother Alexander Feild, both of whom received medical degrees from the University of Edinburgh.

2.   Clear with very little wind & that southerly in the Morng. Mer. 79 at Noon 88 & at Night 86—clear.

3.   Clear morning & but little wind—Mer. at 80–90 at Noon & 82 at N. Abt. 7 Oclock a Cloud arose wch. produced a good shower of Rain & pretty severe Thunder. Mrs. Fairfax, her Sister, daughter & widow Price Mrs. [   ] Mr. Ferdd. Fairfax & Lady, and Mr. Jno. Herbert & his two Sisters dined here & returned.

MRS. FAIRFAX: After the death of his first wife, Elizabeth Cary Fairfax, Bryan Fairfax married Jane (Jenny) Dennison (sometimes Donaldson), who died in 1805, and who bore him a daughter, Anne, who appears here with her today. Mrs. Fairfax's sister is probably the Miss Dennison who appears with her elsewhere in the diaries.

WIDOW PRICE: probably Mrs. Mary Price, widow of David Price (d. 1785). In 1797 she was renting land in Fairfax County from Nicholas Fitzhugh, and in 1799 she was involved in a suit in Fairfax County court for nonpayment of tobacco (will of David Price, Fairfax Wills, Book E-1, 62–63, Vi Microfilm; SPROUSE [2], 2:54, 63).

Ferdinando Fairfax's "Lady," whom he married in 1796, was Elizabeth Blair Cary Fairfax (b. 1765), daughter of Col. Wilson Miles Cary (1734–1817) of Rich Neck, Ceely's, and Carysbrook and his wife Sarah Blair Cary.

These two sisters of John Carlyle Herbert were possibly the two oldest, Margaret and Sarah.

4.   Morning clear—breeze from the No. but light—Mer. 78. 80 at Night. Went up to the Celebration of the anniversary of Independance and dined in the Spring Gardens near Alexa. with a large Compa. of the Civil & Military of Fairfax County.

THE CELEBRATION: "The auspicious morning was ushered in by a discharge of sixteen guns . . . GEN. WASHINGTON was escorted into town by a detachment from the troop of Dragoons. He was dressed in full uniform, and appeared in good health and spirits. At 10 o'clock . . . uniform companies paraded . . . the different corps were reviewed in King street by General Washington, and Col. Little, who expressed the highest satisfaction at their appearance and manoeuvering; after which they proceeded to the Episcopal Church, where a suitable discourse was delivered by the Rev. Dr. Davis.

"A dinner was prepared at Spring Gardens by Mr. John Stavely; which, considering the number of citizens and military that partook of it (between 4 and 500) was conducted with the greatest propriety and decorum. Ludwell Lee, esq. presided at the head of the table—the foot was honored by Col. Charles Little . . . the troops went through a number of military evolutions during the day, with all of which the General was particularly pleased, and bestowed many encomiums on their martial appearance" (*Claypoole's American Daily Adv.* [Philadelphia], 19 July 1798) .

Spring Gardens, a modest building surrounded by gardens set in the fields south of Alexandria, was a popular setting for large gatherings (see MOORE [1], 197–98; POWELL [1], 134–35) .

5.   Morning lowering, with heavy rain about 3 Oclock for near half an hour. Mer. 74 in the M. & 73 at Night.

6.   Morning Clear—Mer. 70 Wind Northerly. Pleasant & clear all day. Doctors Thornton & Dalson—Mr. Ludwell Lee, Lady & Miss Armistead, & Mr. David Randolph & a Son of Colo. R. Kidder Mead came here to Dinner. The two last proceeded to Alexa. afterwards.

William Thornton (1759–1828), born in the Virgin Islands, raised in England, and educated in medicine in Scotland, came to America in 1787 and became a United States citizen the following year. Among his many

Dr. William Thornton, by Robert Field. (National Collection of Fine Arts, Smithsonian Institution)

talents was architectural design, and in 1789 he won an award for his design for the Library Company of Philadelphia building. In 1793 his design, preferred by both GW and Jefferson, was accepted for the United States Capitol and, although later modified, was the basis for that building. In 1794 GW appointed Thornton a commissioner for the District of Columbia, where he soon settled. From 1802 until his death he was director of the United States patent office. Most of Thornton's subsequent architectural work, primarily residential, grew out of his associations with GW and his connections, particularly GW's double town house (1798–99), John Tayloe's Octagon House (1798–1800), Woodlawn (c.1805) for Lawrence and Eleanor Parke Custis Lewis, and Tudor Place (c.1805–15) for Thomas and Martha Parke Custis Peter. DOCTORS THORNTON & DALSON: Anna Maria Brodeau Thornton records in her diary that on this day her husband Dr. William Thornton and Dr. Dawson went to Mount Vernon. She had identified Dr. Dawson when he came to visit their home at the beginning of February as "of Tortola" in the British Virgin Islands (DLC: William Thornton Papers).

After the death of his first wife, none of whose children survived infancy, Richard Kidder Meade married, in 1780, Mary Grymes Randolph, widow of William Randolph of Chatsworth. Among their eight children were three sons who survived infancy: Richard Kidder Meade (1784–1833), William Meade (1789–1862), later the third bishop of the Protestant Episcopal Church in Virginia, and David Meade (1793–1837).

7.   Morng. Clear & but little Wind. Mer. at 68 in the Morng.– clear all day. Mr. R. Bland Lee & Mr. Hodgden came here to dinner & Mr. Ludwell Lee & Lady went away after Din.

MR. HODGDEN: GW probably means William Hodgson.

8.   Morning clear with the Wind brisk from the Southward. Abt. 3 oclock a heavy Shower of Rain for half an hour. Mer. at 70 in the Morng. 75 at Night. Mr. Lee & Miss Portia Lee Mr. Hodgden, & Doctr. Stuart who came in the afternoon of yesterday went away after breakfast & Mr. & Mrs. Potts, Miss Fitzhugh Mrs. Conway Miss Brown Mr. Wm. Wilson Mr. Wm. Ramsay & Mr. Lear came to Dinner & returned.

Portia Lee and William Hodgson were married 2 May 1799.

Dr. William Ramsay had died c.1795 (Arlington County Complete Records, Book A, 169–70, Vi Microfilm). The William Ramsay who appears today at Mount Vernon is probably the son of Patrick and Elizabeth Ramsay and the brother of Eliza Ramsay Potts, who is also a Mount Vernon guest. William and his twin brother Andrew Ramsay were merchants in Alexandria (SLAUGHTER [3], 211; *Columbian Mirror* [Alexandria], 21 Oct. 1797 and 15 Feb. 1799).

9.   Clear morning wind at No. West Mer. 66–72 at Night–clear all day.

10.   Clear morning—Wind, tho' little still No. Westerly, Mer. 64—Southerly afterwards & at Night 74. Doctr. Craik, Wife & Son—a Mr. Craig of Alexa. & Mr. Hunter of Baltimore—Mr. Jno. Herbert—Mr. de Bourg Presid. of the College at George Town another of the Professors & two of the Studts. Viz.—a Son of Mr. Laws & a Neph. of Barrys dined here & all retd.

Mr. Craig is probably Samuel Craig, who in 1799 was the treasurer for the Alexandria Library (*Columbian Mirror* [Alexandria], 10 Jan. 1799).
    Louis Guillaume Valentin DuBourg (1766–1833) was born in Santo Domingo and raised and educated a Roman Catholic priest in France. In 1794 he migrated to the United States and two years later was appointed president of Georgetown College (later Georgetown University), the first Roman Catholic college in the United States, founded in 1789 (see DALEY).

11.   Morning lowering—Wind fresh from the So. Mer. 72. Rain in the afternoon. Mer. 74 at Night. Mr. Fitzhugh & his oldest daughter dined here. He went away afterwards & Mr. McHenry —Secy. of war came in the evening.

James McHenry, the secretary of war, brought GW's commission as "Lieutenant General and Commander in Chief" of the provisional army then being raised in expectation of a war with France. GW's commission, dated 4 July 1798, is in DLC:GW. GW accepted the commission with the proviso that he would not enter active service until the army was in the field, which never occurred. The army was disbanded in 1800.

12.   Morng. Clear & Calm—Mer. at 69. Clear through the day. M. 72 at [   ]. The following Compy. dined here Colos. Fitzgerald & Simms Mr. Herbert & Son—Doctr. Craik & Son—Mr. L. Lee Col. Ramsay—Cap. Young & Lt. Jones Mr. Potts Wm. Wilson Mr. Porter Doctr. Cook Mr. Riddle Mr. Lear—Mr. Tracey—& six Ladies & 4 Gentn. from Mr. Rozers.

CAP. YOUNG: Capt. Robert Young (1768–1824) of the Alexandria Dragoons. By 1800 Young and Philip Richard Fendall were "merchants & partners" in the Alexandria firm of Robert Young & Co. This probably is the same man who was a general of militia in the War of 1812 (*Columbian Mirror* [Alexandria], 12 June 1798; SPROUSE [2], 2:65; POWELL [1], 363).
    Lieutenant Jones is probably Walter Jones (c.1773–1861), an attorney in Alexandria and Washington City, who studied law with Bushrod Washington and later married a daughter of United States Atty. Gen. Charles Lee (BROCKETT, 169). DOCTR. COOK: possibly Dr. Stephen Cooke who emigrated from Bermuda to Alexandria after 1788 and later settled in the Leesburg neighborhood at his farm called The Forest.
    Mr. Riddle was probably the merchant Joseph Riddle whom GW credited on 20 July 1798 for rent received for a house owned by GW in Alexandria (GW's Cash Memorandum, 1 Sept. 1797–20 Feb. 1799, RPJCB).

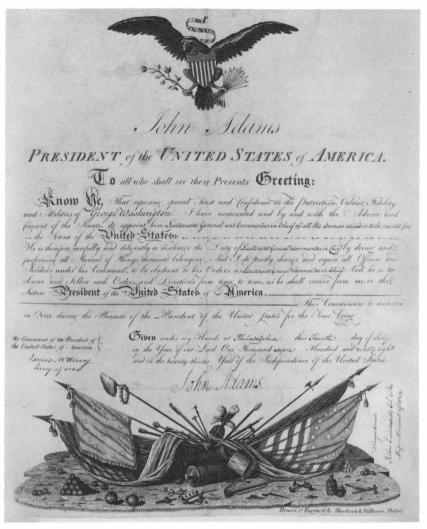

Washington's commission as commander-in-chief of the army, 4 July 1798. (Library of Congress)

13.   Lowering in the Morng. No Wind Mer. 70. Clear afternoon Mer. 66.

14.   Clear Morng. Mer. 62 but little Wd. 68 at Night—wind westerly. The Secy. of War left this after dinner.

15.   Morning clear but little wind Mer. 68. Clear & cool all day with the [wind] So. Easterly Mer. 70 at Night. Mr. Law dined here & returned afterwds.

16.   Raining or Misting all day—with but little w. & that Southerly. Mer. 68 all day.

17.   Hea[v]y Morng. & even.—clear midday. Mer. 70. Mr. & Mrs. Fitzhugh & their Younger daughter & son & Mr. Lear came to dinner. The last retd. after.

18.   Rain with thunder in the morng. Mer. at 70. Clear afterwards and Wind Northerly. Mer. 72 at N. Mr. Fitzhugh & all his family went away after dinner.

19.   Morning—clear—Wind North. Mer. 60. Clear all day. Wind blowing fresh from No. Wt. Mer. 66 at Night. Miss Digges & her niece Miss Carroll dined here.

MISS DIGGES: Ann Digges (died c.1804) of Warburton was a sister of Elizabeth Digges Carroll (1743–1845), whose daughter Ann is probably the "niece Miss Carroll" accompanying Ann Digges today.

20.   Morning—clear & Cool—Wind brisk from No. W. Mer. 60 in Morning 68 at Night. Went up to Alexa. with Mrs. W. & Miss Cus. dined at Doctr. Craiks retd. in the Aftn.

21.   Morning & throughout the day clear with very little Wind. Mer. 63 in the Morning & 74 at Night.

22.   Morning quite clear—Wind Southerly—Mer. at 68. Clear all day—Mer. 76 at Night. Mr. Mrs. Dalton & their two daughters came here to dinner.

Tristram and Ruth Hooper Dalton had six daughters, three of whom lived to maturity.

23. Morng. clear—Wind Southerly Mer. 70. Remained so all day. Mer. 76 at N. Mr. Lear came in the M[ornin]g—stayed all day.

24. Morng.—clear & still—Mer. 72. Clear thro' the day with a southerly Wind. Mer. 80 at Night. Doctr. Stuart & Mr. Geo. Graham dined here. The last went away afterwards.

Graham is probably George Graham (c.1772–1830), who grew up at Gunston Hall with the children of George Mason. He was a son of Richard Graham, merchant of Dumfries, and his wife, Jane Brent Graham. Young Graham had come to live at Gunston Hall in 1780 when his aunt, Sarah Brent, became the second wife of George Mason. After graduation from Columbia College, Graham studied law and practiced in Dumfries. He married Elizabeth Mary Ann Barnes Hooe Mason, the widow of his friend George Mason (1753–1796) of Lexington.

25. Morng. Clear—Wind Southerly Mer. 74. In the Afternoon Rain below us—but none fell here. Mer. 78 at Night. This family & Mr. Daltons dind with Mr. Le[a]r.

Tristram Dalton was a business partner of Tobias Lear (Fairfax County Deeds, Book B-2, 39–42, Vi Microfilm).

26. Mer. at 76 in the Morning very little wind. Rain pretty smartly abt. 3 Oclock for 5 or 6 Minutes. Mer. 80 at Night. Mr. Herbert wife 2 daughters son & Mr. & Mrs. Whiting dined here— as did the Count Inznard & Mr. Merchant—all went awy.

William Herbert and his wife Sarah, eldest daughter of John Carlyle, had two sons and five daughters. Sarah's sister, Anne Carlyle (1761–1778), married Henry (Harry) Whiting (1748–1786), son of Francis (Frank) Whiting. She died during the delivery of their only child, Carlyle Fairfax Whiting (1778–1831), later of Morven, who appears here with his bride, Sarah Little Whiting (1776–1835), daughter of Col. Charles and Mary Manley Little.

COUNT INZNARD: This may be Joseph M. Yznardy (Iznardi), Jr., American consul at Cadiz, or his father Josef Yznardy, a merchant of Cadiz who was acting consul during his son's absences from the city.

27. Morng. clear & calm—Mer. 77. Clear all day & but little W. Mer. 87 at [   ].

28. Clear Morng. but rain in the Afternoon at a distance from us. Mer. 80 in the M. 90 at noon & 86 at Night.

29. Mer. 80 in the Morng. 90 at N. & 86 at Night. Clear all day Wind Southerly. Doctr. Craik dind he[re].

30.   Morning lowering—wind brisk from South & Mer. at 79. Clouds gathered & Rain fell in difft. quarters before Noon. Abt. 3 oclock we had a fine shower for half an hour with a little more at Night. Mer. 72 at N.

31.   Morng. clear—afternoon appearance of Rain but none fell. Mer. 68 in the Morng. 76 at Night. Very little wind. Mrs. L. Washington—Mr. Foot & a Majr. Parker dined here & returned.

MAJR. PARKER: probably Maj. Alexander Parker (died c.1820), who had served as an officer in the 2d Virginia Regiment throughout the Revolution. He was the son of Richard Parker (1729–1813) and Elizabeth Beale Parker of Westmoreland County. In 1790 Parker was appointed a major in the United States Army (EXECUTIVE JOURNAL, 1:45–47).

August 1798

1.   Clear Morning & day—Mer. 72 in the Morning & 80 at Night.

2.   Morning clear & calm—Mer. at 74. Clear all day—Wind Southerly. M. 80 at Night. Mr. Lear dined here & Mrs. Washington of Bushfield & her G. daughter Ann Washn. came in the Afternn.

Ann Aylett Washington (1783–1804), daughter of Jane Washington (1759–1791) and William Augustine Washington (d. 1810), was the granddaughter of Jane's mother, Hannah Bushrod Washington of Bushfield, widow of GW's brother John Augustine Washington (1736–1787).

3.   Morning cloudy, & Showers of rain about in the afternoon, but none here. Mer. 74 in the morning 80 at N.

4.   Morning—Clear & but little wind & that So. Easterly. Mer. at 76. Appearances of Rain all the forenoon. In the Afternoon heavy clouds and rain all around us but none fell here. Mer. 77 at Night.

5.   Morning clear—Wind at So. Mer. 74. Clouds around us in the Afternoon & rain—but none here. Mer. 79 at N. Washn. Custis came home fm. College.

Washington Custis had been at St. John's College just over four months when GW received a letter from him asking whether he should pack only for the coming vacation or to come home to stay (21 July 1798, CUSTIS, 109). GW was astonished and outraged and wrote young Custis that "it would seem as if *nothing* I could say to you made more than a *momentary* impression" (24 July 1798, CUSTIS, 110). It was by this time evident, however, that sending the boy back to school would serve no useful purpose. After some correspondence with David Stuart on the subject (GW to Stuart, 13 Aug. 1798, PHi: Dreer Collection; Stuart to GW, 22 Aug. 1798, DLC:GW), GW decided to keep Custis at home and have him tutored by Tobias Lear, who at this time was acting as GW's military secretary (GW to Stuart, 10 Sept. 1798, WRITINGS, 36:435; for correspondence regarding Custis's college career see CUSTIS, 73–116). GW's final attempt to solve the problem of what to do with Washington Custis was made in December of this year: he had the young man appointed a cornet in a troop of horse (GW to David Stuart, 30 Dec. 1798, ViMtV; CUSTIS, 51).

6. Morning heavy with great appearances of Rain but none fell. Mer. at 74 in the morng. & 80 at N. Went to Alexa. to a meeting of the Poto. Co. Mr. Bur: Bassett came home with me.

In May 1798 the president and directors of the Potomac Company had been authorized by the shareholders "to mortgage as many shares as could be obtained and to borrow as much stock as could be had" to the amount of $10,000. At the August annual meeting the president announced that loans had been made by Daniel Carroll of Duddington "of $2,500 of six per cent. stock of the United States, and by General Washington of $3,498 of the same" and an additional amount might be had of Carroll. Although over $2,000 had been collected in tolls in the last year, the superintendent and overseer were discharged and horses and wagons sold because lack of money had brought the work on the project to a virtual standstill (BACON-FOSTER, 97–98).

7. Morning–clear & calm Mer. 76. Clear all day. Mer. 85 at Noon & 80 at Night. Mr. Lear & the boys dined here & with Mr. Basset went afterwards.

8. Morng. clear, but the Sun rose red. Calm & Mer. at 74 in the Morning 88 at Noon & 84 at N.

9. Morning clear & calm M. 78. Clear all day. Mer. 90 at Noon & 84 at Night. Clear & calm all day. Doctr. Stuart came to dinner.

10. Morning–clear & calm Mer. 78. Pretty fresh from the Southward afterwards. Mer. 90 at highest 86 at Night. Mr. & Mrs. Thornton & Jno. Herbert & G. W. Craik came to dinner. The two last returned.

11. Morng. perfectly clear & calm. Mer. at 78–at Noon 90–and at Night. Fine Showers appeared all around us–but none fell here. Genl. & Mrs. & Miss Spotswood & two younger daughters came in the Afternoon.

Gen. Alexander Spotswood and Elizabeth Washington Spotswood had five daughters; the four younger ones were Elizabeth, Anne, Henrietta, and Martha.

12.   Morning clear—Wind Westerly Mer. 73. 78 at Night.

13.   Morng. cloudy & so it contd. thro the day. In the afternoon a shower for a few Minutes. Mer. [   ] in the morning & 76 at Night.

14.   Morning cloudy—raing. a few Minutes about 8 Oclock. The same about one. Showery from about 4 until after dark. M. [   ] in the Morng. and 73 at Night. Mr. Booker came in the afternn.

William Booker erected a threshing machine of his own design for GW at the Union Farm in July 1797. The machine's performance had been disappointing, and Booker was back at Mount Vernon to make repairs (GW to Booker, 15 April 1798, DLC:GW; GW's Cash Memorandum, 29 Sept. 1794–17 Aug. 1797: entry for 6 July 1797, RPJCB; GW's Cash Memorandum, 1 Sept. 1797–20 Feb. 1799: entry for 18 Aug. 1798, RPJCB).

15.   Morning—Cloudy, wind southerly Mer. [   ]. A slight shower in the evening. Mer. 78 at Night. Mr. & Mrs. Ludwell [Lee] & Miss Armistead & Mr. Fielding Lewis dined here & returnd.

16.   Morning Cloudy—Wind Southerly Mer. 78. Clouds & showers about in the afternoon—but none fell here. Mer. 80 at Night.

17.   Morning clear & calm M. 77. At Noon 88 & at Night 78. Clouds all round & rain in places but none fell here. Wind variable. Mr. Tracy came in the Morng. & Mr. Harper at Night.

18.   Morng. clear—Mer. at 76—Noon 88 and at Night 84. Clear all day. Mr. Tracy went away after dinner & Mr. Booker in the Morng.

19.   Morning clear & Calm Mer. 80 at noon 89 and at Night 79. Showers around us in the Afternoon but none fell here. Colo. Simms & lady, & Mr. Herbert & Son dined here.

Charles Simms's wife, Nancy Douglass Simms, was the daughter of William Douglass of New Jersey.

20.   A heavy fog. Mer. at 76 Morn. 82 at Night. Thunder in the forenoon & rain around us but none fell here. Mr. Harper went away after Breakfast.

No acct. kept of the Weather &ca. from hence to the end of the Month—on acct. of my sickness which commenced with a fever on the 19th. & lasted until the 24th. which left me debilitated.

On the 28th. there was a very refreshing Rain but not sufft. to go to the Roots of Indian Corn which was suffering very much for want of it.

MY SICKNESS: GW suffered a severe fever for about a week, for which he received quinine treatments, but lost about 20 pounds. On 14 Sept. he was still "recovering my flesh fast—nearly a pound, & half a day" (GW to Alexander Spotswood, 14 Sept. 1798, owned by Mr. Sol Feinstone, Washington Crossing, Pa., on deposit at PPAmP; see FREEMAN, 7:527).

September 1798

1.   Morning—A little lowering with appearances of rain in the Afternoon but not fell here. Mer. 68 in the Morn. & [   ] at N.

2.   Morning—Clear—Mer. 68. Clear all day—wind fresh at East. Mer. 72 at Night. Mr. White came to dinner.

3.   Morning Calm & lowering—Mer. 65. Lowering all day with a little misting rain in the afternoon. Mer. 70 at N. In the Morning to breakfast came Genl. Marshall & Mr. Bushrod Washington and to dinner the Atty. Genl. Chas. Lee Mr. Herbert Mr. Keith & Doc. Craik. The last went away.

John Marshall, after serving as one of the three American peace commissioners to France in 1797 had recently returned home to Virginia. GW had invited Marshall to Mount Vernon to urge him to run for Congress as a Federalist for the district around Richmond.

4.   Morng. Cloudy—Mer. at 69. Clear afterwards. Mer. 80 in the Aftern. & 74 at Night. In the Afternoon Mr. & Mrs. Parks of Fredericksbg. came here.

Mr. and Mrs. Parks were Andrew Parks, a merchant in Fredericksburg, and his wife, Harriot Washington Parks (1776–1822), youngest child of GW's brother Samuel Washington and his fourth wife Anne Steptoe Allerton Washington. When the topic of their marriage arose in 1796, GW, acting in place of Harriot's deceased father, assured Parks that if he were "a gentleman of respectable connexions; and of good dispositions," and able to support her decently, he would assent to the marriage, declaring: "my wish is to see my niece happy" (GW to Parks, 7 April 1796, DLC:GW; Betty Washington Lewis to GW, 27 Mar. 1796, ViMtV). GW sent his niece "a great deal of good advice which," Harriot replied, "I am extremely obliged to you for." The wedding took place in July 1796 (Harriot Washington Parks to GW, 17 July 1796, DLC:GW).

5. Morning clear & Cool—Afternoon clouds, & a light shower. Mer. at [   ] in the Morning 62 at Night. Genl. Marshall & Mr. B. Washington went to a dinner in Alexa. given to the former by the Citizen's there & returned.

DINNER IN ALEXA.: "Every preparation and arrangement for the day was elegant and patriotic. The dinner was served in the best style, and the good humor and conviviality of the company, which was numerous and respectable, gave a zest to the wines, which were of the best quality. The Toasts . . . were accompanied by a number of patriotic songs, and discharges from the train of Artillery, together with repeated huzzas and plaudits from the Citizens both within and without doors." The first of the 19 toasts was to "The United States, free, Sovereign and Independent forever"; the fourth to "Lieut. General George Washington"; the thirteenth, "God speed the plough"; the eighteenth to Marshall, and the last to the other honored guest, United States Atty. Gen. Charles Lee, of Alexandria (*Columbian Mirror* [Alexandria], 6 Sept. 1798).

6. Morning Clear—Mer. 65—at Night 66. Clear all day. Mr. Marshall & Mr. B. Washington went away before breakfast. Mr. Wm. Craik came to Breakfast & returned afterwards and Mr. Jno. Herbert & Mr. Robt. Burwell came to dinner. The latter returned after it. The former stayed all Night.

7. Morning—thunder & Rain for about an hour—Mer. 58—at Night 59. Clear afternoon. Mr. Herbert went away after dinner.

8. Morning clear Mer. at 58—70 at Noon and 66 at Night. Mr. & Mrs. Parks left this after breakfast.

9. Morning clear—Mer. at 59. Wind though but little of it Westerly—clear all day. Mer. 70 at Night.

10. Omitted to take any Acct. but the weather was clear & warm.

11. Morning a little cloudy, but clear afterwards. Mer. at 65—at Night 74—but little wind & that Southerly.

12.   Morning lowering & calm—M. 68. Wind brisk from the Eastward—Mer. 70 at Night.

13.   Morning Clear except a fog and but little wind through the day. Mer. 68 in the Morning 70 at Night. Mrs. Fairfax and daughter—Miss Dennison and a Mrs. Tebbles dined here.

14.   Morning clear—wind Southerly—Mer. 64—78 at Noon & 72 at Night. Clear all day.

15.   Morning & throughout the day clear—Mer. 68 in the warm mid day & 76 at Night So. & then Easterly. Mr. White came to dinner.

16.   Morning clear—Wind Southerly—Mer. 71. Doctr. Stuart & Doctr. Craik came to dinner. Day warm.

17.   Mer. at 75 in the Morning 85 at hight & 80 at Night. Day clear—wind Southerly. Mr. White & the Doctors went away this Morning.

18.   Morning cloudy—Wind Southerly & Mer. at 75. After 2 Oclock there were showers with intervals till Night, when it had the appearance of a settled rain. Mer. 75 at N.

19.   Morning cloudy—wind South—Mer. [   ] and at Night 80. Doctr. Craik came in the Morning to visit Mr. L. Lewis & stayed all day & Night.

20.   Morning clear—wind Southerly—Mer. at 75. Went up to the Federal City. Dined & lodgd at Mr. Thos. Peters.

21.   Great appearances to Rain & some fell about 8 Oclock A.M. —clear afterwds. Examined in company with the Comrs. some of the Lots in the vicinity of the Capital & fixed upon No. 16 in [square] 634 to build on. Dined & lodged at Mr. Laws.

Lot 16, square 634 was on the west side of North Capitol Street between B and C streets, about the middle of the block. GW was to pay $535.71 for it in three annual installments, the first of which was paid in 1798. The construction of a double town house on the lot, which GW hoped would "promote the necessary improvements in the City," was begun that fall (GW to the Commissioners of the District of Columbia, 27 Oct. 1798, DLC:GW; DIARIES, 4:284).

22. Came home with Mr. T. Peter wife & 2 Children to Dinner. Mer. at 70 at Night and evening cool.

23. Morning clear—Wind Easterly & Mer. at 63. Lowering in the evening Mer. at 72. Mr. & Mrs. Nichols & his brother & Mrs. Swanwick dined here.

Mrs. Swanwick is undoubtedly the widow of John Swanwick who had died the previous month. Swanwick was James B. Nichols's brother-in-law (John Swanwick to GW, 22 April 1789, DLC:GW).

24. Morning clear—Wind Southerly Mer. at 64. No. West afterwards.

25. Morning Mer. 60. Wind hard at No. W. all day. Mr. Geo. Steptoe Washington who came to dinner yesterday returned to day & Mr. Peter set off for New Kent. Mer. 64 at Noon and 58 at Night.

George Steptoe Washington was now living at Harewood with his wife, Lucy Payne Washington, sister of Dolley Madison.

George Steptoe Washington and his wife, Lucy Payne Washington, painted by C. P. Polk. (Dr. and Mrs. John A. Washington)

26.   Morning–Clear–Wind at No. Wt. but little of it. Mer. at 48. Wind shifted to the Southward & blew fresh. Mer. 62 at N. Mr. Tracey came here to dinner.

27.   Morning cloudy–wind fresh from So. Wt. with a scud or two of Rain in the afternoon. Mr. Jno. Herbert came to dinner and a Major Simons of Charleston in the afternn.

MAJOR SIMONS: Simons may be Maj. William Simons who was commissioned a captain in the 5th Infantry in 1799 but declined the appointment (WRIT-INGS, 36:468n). The rank of major was probably from service in the militia. Simons brought a letter of introduction to GW from William Washington of South Carolina. GW returned an answer by Simons in which he urged Washington to accept a commission in the army during the diplomatic crisis with France and also asked him to recommend officers for the regimental ranks from South Carolina, Georgia, and North Carolina. "It has been said . . . that the twelve Regiments, under the Act for augmenting the force of the United States, will be proportioned among them; whereof Virginia, the two Carolinas, Georgia, Tennessee & Kentucky, will be called upon for four; & perhaps the additional Troops of Cavalry. If this plan should be adopted, I presume each of these states will be called upon for a certain part. I do not mean the *authority* of the State will be required to furnish them—but that, so many Men will be recruited in each, & furnish Officers in proportion thereto" (GW to William Washington, 27 Sept. 1798, DLC:GW).

28.   Morning clear & cold–wind fresh from No. Wt. Mer. at 51. Wind high all day. Majr. Simons went away in the Morning & Mr. Herbert & Mr. Tracey in the Afternoon.

29.   Morning & whole day clear and very cold. Mer. at Night 48.

30.   Morning clear & calm–Mer. at 44. Clear all day. Went to church in Alexa. Mer. 59 at N.

October—1798

1.   Morning clear, Wind Southerly and Mer. at 50. Wind in the same place all day & clear. Mer. 60 at N.

2.   Morning clear–wind at So. Et. Mer. at 55. Clear & warm all day.

3.   Day clear & warm. Wind Southerly. Mer. 65 at Night.

4.   Very thick fog in the Morng. Clear & warm afterwards–wind Southerly. Mer. 68 at Noon & 66 at Night. Mr. Jno. Herbert &

Mr. G. W. Craik dined here & returnd & Cap. Jno. Spotswood came in the evening.

5.   Clear all day. Mer. 60 in the Morning. Doctr. Thornton – Mr. Law and a Mr. Baldo a Spanish Gentleman from the Havanna came to Dinner.

6.   Morning clear – Very little Wind Mer. at 60. Clear all day. Mer. 65 at Night. Mr. Bushrod Washington & Captn. Blackburn came to dinner & Mr. Thos. Peter returned in the afternoon from New Kent.

Bushrod Washington had, just a week earlier, been appointed by John Adams to the Supreme Court of the United States to fill the vacancy left by the death of James Wilson. The appointment was confirmed in December, and he served on the bench until his death 31 years later.

7.   Morning Mer. 58. Wind brisk & thro' the whole day at No. Wt. with clouds & appearances of Rain. M. 64 at Night. Mr. B. Washington & Captn. Blackburn went away after Breakft.

8.   Morning cloudy – wind at No. W. M. 58 and fresh all day.

9.   Morning a little cloudy Wind still at No. Wt. Mer. at 55. 9th.

10. and eleventh absent – in the Federal City – Weather warm & dry the whole time. Mr. Welch & Mr. Tracy came in the afternoon.

James Welch's visit was for the purpose of persuading GW to accept some of Welch's other lands in place of a portion of the Elk Creek tract as security for his payment on GW's Kanawha lands. Welch thought he had a buyer for some of the Elk Creek lands, and he needed the money to make his first payment of $5,000 due 31 Dec. for the Kanawha lands. GW was agreeable to the exchange provided the lands were of equal value (PRUSSING, 471–72). See entries for 24 Nov. and 18 Dec. 1797.

12.   Morning lowering Wind Southerly – Mer. 62. Brisk from East afterwards & very cloudy. Mer. 64 at Night. Mr. Welch & Mr. Tracy went away in the Forenoon & Mr. Wm. Craik came to dinner.

13.   Morning – Misty, but not sufficiently so to lay the dust – cloudy all day. Genl. Lee, Captn. Presley Thornton & Mr. T. Peters came to dinner. Wd. Easter[ly].

14.   Morning very heavy & likely for rain. Wind at East – Mer. 56. Very cloudy all day but no Rain – Mer. at 56. Genl. Lee &

Captn. Thornton went away after breakfast & Mr. Booker came at Night.

15.   Very Cloudy & likely to Rain in the Morning but clear afterwards—Wind getting to No. Wt.

16.   Clear & pleasant all day & very little wind. Mer. 51 in the Morning & 66 at Night. The Attorney Genl. of the United States Lee and Lady & Mr. Wm. Craik dined here & retd.

17.   Morning clear & calm M. at 56—very warm midday. Mr. Law—a Mr. David Barry and a Mr. Shedden came to dinner & staid the Night.

David Barry may be James Barry's nephew James David Barry.
    MR. SHEDDEN: Robert Shedden (1741–1826), a native of Scotland, immigrated to America at the age of 18, settling in Portsmouth, Va. In 1767 he married Agatha Wells Goodrich, daughter of John Goodrich who was, like Shedden, loyal to the British. Shedden's illegal trade with British merchants brought about his arrest and the seizure of his property in 1776. Upon release he fled first to Bermuda, then to New York, and finally to London when the British evacuated in 1783. There he raised four sons and prospered at the head of a successful commercial house. Shedden's affairs in Virginia were still unresolved as late as 1789. He or one of his sons may have returned to America to settle old debts and establish new commercial ties, not an uncommon practice among displaced merchants.

18.   Morning clear & calm Mer. 56 day very warm. Mr. Law & his Company went away after breakfast.

19.   Morning very lowering. Mists afterwards and rain at Night. Mer. 55 in the Morning. Wd. No. E.

20.   Raining by Intervals in the forenoon Wind at No. Et. & Mer. 54—afternoon clear. Mer. 54 at Night.

21.   Morning Cloudy—Wind still at No. E. Mer. at 52. Clear all day—warm & smokey. Mer. 63 at Night.

22.   Morning clear Mer. 52. Calm. Wind afterwards Southerly & in the afternoon appearances of Rain. Mer. 66 at Night.

23.   Morning very cloudy with appearances of Rain—Wind Southerly—And Mer. 62. No. W. afterwards blowing hard & turning cold.

24.   Morning clear & calm M: 42. Light wind afterwards from No. W. Mrs. Washington—Mrs. Peake and Doctor Stuart dined here. The two first went away afterwards. M. 56 at Night.

25.   Morning clear & calm—Mer. at 58. Calm & clear all day—towards night Southerly Wind. Doctr. Stuart & Mr. Booker went away after breakfast. M. 65 at N.

26.   Morning clear & calm—Mer. 54. Very clear & pleasant all day. Mr. & Mrs. Law, with Govr. Crawford (late of Burmuda) & Lady came to dinner.

James Craufurd was governor of Bermuda from 1794 to 1796, after which he left Bermuda for New York, where he met and married Alice Swift Livingston (1751–1816), widow of Robert Cambridge Livingston.

27.   Morning Cloudy—Wind North East & cold. Mer. at 39 in the Morning & 40 at Night. From about 8 oclock slow Rain by Intervals.

28.   Morning clear & pleasant & continued so all day. Mer. 39 in the Morng. & 40 at Night. The Atty. Genl. U.S. Mr. Jno. Hopkins & Mr. Chs. F. Mercer dined here & returned.

Charles Fenton Mercer (1778–1858), younger son of James Mercer (1736–1793), graduated from Princeton in 1797 and eventually settled at Aldie in Loudoun County. Mercer, who had a distinguished political career, later became the first president of the Chesapeake and Ohio Canal Company after it succeeded the Potomac Company in the 1820s.

29.   Morning a little cloudy M. 32. Wind No. Wt. and afterwards blew hard & cold from thence. Mr. & Mrs. Law—Mr. & Mrs. Peter and Govr. Crauford & lady all went after breakfast.

30.   Morning clear & Cold Mer. 27. Wind Southerly & fresh all day afterwards. At Night M. 37.

31.   Clear—wind shifting in the Night to the No. Wt. & blowing hard—Mer. at 30. Clear and blowing fresh all day. Doctr. Craik visited Patients at Union farm & dined here.

November 1798

1.   Morning—Wind Easterly & lowering Mer. at 30. About 8 Oclock it began to snow but soon changed to rain & contd. a slow rain all day. Mer. 30 at Night.

2.   Morng. Clear, calm & pleast. Mer. 34. Wind afterwards North Easterly. Mr. Law Mr. Hasler of Demarara & Lady came to dinner.

3.   Morning very heavy—Wind in the same place and M. 35.

4.   Clear—but cool. Mr. Fitzhugh Mr. David Randolph & Mr. Alexr. White came to dinner, & the two first went away afterwards. Mr. Hasler & Lady went away after breakfast & Mrs. Law came at Night.

5.   Mr. White went away before breakfast. I set out on a journey to Phila. about 9 Oclock with Mr. Lear my Secretary—was met at the Turnpike by a party of horse & escorted to the Ferry at George Town where I was recd. with Military honors. Lodged at Mr. T. Peters.

GW was going to Philadelphia to make plans for the provisional army then being raised in case of an invasion by the French. The "military honors" began as he entered Alexandria where, at about 11 o'clock, "his Excellency Lieutenant-General GEORGE WASHINGTON, accompanied by his Secretary Colonel LEAR . . . was met at West End and escorted into town by Colonel Fitzgerald's and Captain Young's troops of cavalry, and the company of Alexandria blues. . . . When the General alighted at Gadsby's tavern, the blues fired a continental salute of 16 rounds. The troops of horse escorted the General to the ferry at George Town where . . . five gentlemen of George Town, in uniform, received him into a yawl and passed the river while the infantry and artillery on the Maryland side, by several discharges, honoured their illustrious chief. The George Town troop of horse and the other military companies then escorted him into the city of Washington and after firing a number of rounds, they and the whole assemblage of spectators retired" (*Claypoole's American Daily Adv.* [Philadelphia], 10 Nov. 1798).

6.   Breakfasted at Bladensburgh—dined & lodged at Spurriers. Escorted by horse.

7.   Breakfasted at Baltimore—dined at Websters, & lodged at Hartford. Met at Spurriers by the Baltimore horse & escorted in and out by the same. Viewed a Brigade of Militia at Balte.

"This morning arrived in town, the Chief who unites all hearts. He left Spurrier's pretty early, and lighted at Bryden's about 8 o'clock, escorted in by captains Hollingsworth's and Bentalou's troops, who went out last evening for that purpose. About 10 [o'clock], the 5th and 17th regiments (as many as from the shortness of the notice could get ready,) had the gratification of being reviewed by him, in Market street, much to the satisfaction of a large concourse of spectators, who thronged around him . . . the City Company . . . made open ranks for him to pass through as he came out to review the troops" (*Claypoole's American Daily Adv.* [Philadelphia], 10 Nov. 1798).

8.   Breakfasted at Susquehanna escorted by the Hartford horse. Dined at Elkton and lodged at Christiana bridge.

HARTFORD HORSE: A cavalry unit from Harford County, Md.

9.   Breakfasted in Wilmington & dined & lodged at Chester— waitg. at the latter the return of an Exps. At this place was met by sevl. Troops of Phila. horse.

10.   With this Escort I arrived in the City about 9 Oclock & was recd. by Genl. McPhersons Blues & was escorted to my lodgings in 8th. Street (Mrs. Whites) by them & the Horse.

"November 12. Lieutenant General WASHINGTON, Commander in Chief of the Armies of the United States, arrived here on Saturday morning last, escorted by the different troops of horse—and, notwithstanding the short notice which had been given the Blues, almost the whole of that corps, with an alacrity which does them honor, were drawn up on the commons, to receive their beloved General. On his arrival, the cavalry and infantry were drawn up, and the General . . . passed in review down their front . . . the procession then moved from the commons, the General accompanied by his secretary Mr. Lear, in the centre of the cavalry. On his arrival at his lodgings in Eighth-street, he was saluted by the acclamations of the citizens who had collected once more to behold their Chief. The General was dressed in his uniform" (*Claypoole's American Daily Adv.* [Philadelphia], 12 Nov. 1798). MCPHERSONS BLUES: William MacPherson's battalion, largely Federalist in its composition, had been reorganized and enlarged in June 1798 to include units of cavalry, infantry, and artillery. LODGINGS IN 8TH. STREET: Mrs. Rosannah White, a widow, kept a boardinghouse at 9 North Eighth Street.

11, 12, & 13.   Dined at my Lodgings receiving many Visits. Weather clear & pleasant.

14.   Dined at Majr. Jacksons.

15.   Dined at Mr. Tench Francis's. Rain at Night.

16.   Dined at the Secrety. of the Treay.

Oliver Wolcott, Jr., of Connecticut, was appointed by GW in 1795 to succeed Alexander Hamilton as secretary of the treasury. He served through most of John Adam's presidency, finally resigning late in 1800.

17.   Do. at Mr. Willings.

18.   Do. at my lodgings. Weather cloudy & heavy.

19.   Do. at Doctr. Whites—Bishop. Raining.

Oliver Wolcott, Jr., secretary of the treasury, painted by Gilbert Stuart. (Yale University Art Gallery, Gift of George Gibbs, M.A. 1808)

20.   Dined at the Secretary of Wars. Violent Snow Storm from No. Et.

21.   Dined at Majr. Reeds—Senator's.

Jacob Read (1752–1816) was a Federalist United States senator from South Carolina for one term (1795–1801).

22.   Dined at Mr. Binghams.

23.   Ditto at Mr. Saml. Meridiths. Treasurer.

24.   Ditto at the Secretary of States.

Timothy Pickering, a leading Massachusetts Federalist, was appointed by GW as secretary of state in 1795. Reappointed by Pres. John Adams in 1797, he continued in that office until dismissed by Adams in May 1800.

25.   Ditto at my Lodgings.

26.   Dined at the Presidents of the U. States.

27.   Dined in a family with Mr. Morris.

John Adams, by William Winstanley. (The Adams National Historic Site, National Park Service, U.S. Department of the Interior)

Walnut Street Prison in Philadelphia.
(Library of Congress)

Robert Morris was at this time confined to the Prune Street Prison, the section of the Walnut Street Prison used for debtors. Morris had overextended himself in land speculation so that with the financial problems caused by the war in Europe he could not meet taxes on his lands or interest on loans. He was to remain in prison until 1801, when he obtained his release under the federal bankruptcy law.

28.   Dined with Judge Peters.

29.   Do. with the British Minister.

30.   Do. with the Govr. of the State. Govr. Mifflin.

December

1.   Dined with Mr. Rawle.

2.   Ditto with Bingham. From hence until my leaving the City on the

13.   I dined at my lodgings.

14.   After dinner set out on my journey home. Reached Chester.

15.   Breakfasted at Wilmington bated at Christiana and dined and lodged at Elkton.

16.   Set out after a very early breakfast; and was detained at Susquehanna from 10 Oclock until the next morning, partly by Ice and Winds but principally by the Lowness of the tides occasioned by the No. Westerly Winds.

17.   Breakfasted at Barneys—bated at Hartford. Dined at Websters and lodged at Baltimore.

18.   Breakfasted at Spurriers—dined at Rhodes's—and lodged at Mr. Laws in the Federal City.

RHODES'S: Rhodes tavern was a three-story building about six miles north of Bladensburg near the present town of Beltsville (W.P.A. [2], 311).

19.   Stopped at Doctr. Thorntons and Mr. Peter's & dined at home. Snow having fallen about 3 Inches deep in the Night.

20.   Appearances of more Snow but none fell. Wind at No. W.

21.   Clear & pleasant, with but little wind—that at No. Wt.

22.   Snowing the whole day, without much wind, Snow 8 or 10 Inches deep.

23.   Clear—wind at No. West. Mercury at 20 in the Morning.

24th.   Clear all day with the Wind fresh from No. Wt. & Snow driving. Mer. 25. Doctr. Craik came to D. & Judge Cushing & lady in the afternoon—as did a Mr. Dinsmoor Agent in the Cherokee Country on his way to Philadelphia—with a Mr. [   ].

Silas Dinsmoor (Dinsmore), son of John and Martha McKeen Dinsmoor of Londonderry, N.H., graduated from Dartmouth College in 1791. In 1794 he received an appointment as lieutenant in the United States Army Corps of Engineers and Artillery but resigned after only a few weeks (NOYES, 421; EXECUTIVE JOURNAL, 1:159–60; CARTER [4], 4:362n). Late in 1794 Dinsmoor was sent as an agent to reside among the Cherokee Nation to keep the peace. In 1805 he was one of the United States commissioners who signed treaties with the Chickasaws and Choctaws (ASP, INDIAN AFFAIRS, 531–32, 639–40, 697, 749).

25.   Perfectly clear, Calm & pleasant in the Morning—Mer. at 18. Genl. Pinckney, Lady & daughter came to dinner—and Captain Jno. Spotswood in the afternoon.

GENL. PINCKNEY, LADY & DAUGHTER: Charles Cotesworth Pinckney in July had been appointed a major general in the army, ranking just below GW and Alexander Hamilton. The daughter accompanying Pinckney and his wife was Eliza, the youngest of Pinckney's three daughters.

26. Clear & not much wind. Mer. at 14 in the Morng.

27. Clear morning, but spitting of Snow in the Evening little however fell. Mer. at 25 in the Morning. The following Gentlemen dined here the 27th. viz. Messrs. Wm. Fitzhugh—Wm. Herbert Potts—Wilson—Doctr. Craik & son Geo: Washington Craik, Heath & Doctr. Greenhow of Richmond.

Mr. Heath is possibly John Heath (d. 1810), son of Capt. John Heath (d. 1783) of Northumberland County. The younger Heath was a member of the Virginia General Assembly in 1782 and 1784–85 and first president of Phi Beta Kappa after its founding at the College of William and Mary in 1776. He was living in Richmond about this time. In 1803 he married Sarah Ewell, niece of Mrs. James Craik.

Dr. Greenhow is young James Greenhow who had graduated from the University of Edinburgh the previous year.

28. Clear morning but a little lowering afterwards. Mer. at 29 in the Morng. & thawing afterwards. Genl. Pinckney—Lady & daughter left this after breakfast.

29. Rain in the Night—a thick fog, & thawing in the morning— Mer. at 34. In the afternoon wind high from the No. Wt.

30. In the morning wind very high from the same point. Mer. at 30— in the eveng. at 35. Calm & pleasant afternoon.

31. Calm & pleasant—thawing. Mer. higher than yesterday.

Benjamin Latrobe's 1796 watercolor of the Mount Vernon piazza, depicting members of the Washington family. (Mount Vernon Ladies' Association of the Union)

The Final Year
1799

[January 1799]

Jany. 1. Raining Slowly until the Afternoon when it cleared. Wind southerly. Mer. 38. Ih.

Diary entries for 1–21 Jan. 1799 are from a diary page at PHi: Gratz Collection. The first part of this section of the diary has a number of cryptic abbreviations in GW's handwriting, some of which appear to have been added at a later date. See editorial note to the 1795 diary.

2. Clear. Wind at No. Wt. but moderate. Mer. at 30 – W – little Kx.

3. Cold. A little Snow fell. Mer. 28.

4. Very cold. Wind at No. and Mer. 24. – V – x

5. Extreme cold. Mer. at 10. Wind at No. Wt. and in the Night a considerable fall of Snow.

6. Clear but very cold. Wind still at No. Wt. & Mer. at 9.

7. Clear. Mer. at 8. Wind at No. Wt.

8. Clear in the forenoon but lowering afterwards. Raining in the Night but Not much. Mer. at 16. – Gr. – Wind Southerly.

9. Cloudy Morning but clear afterwards. Wind Southerly. Mer. at 30.

10. Lowering. Wind Southerly. Mer. 32. Left home for the City of Washington W – x. Dined at Mr. T. Peters.

11. Very heavy fog but little wind and that Southerly. Clear after the fog went off & very warm. Quite a Spring day – Petr. A – dined at Doctr. Thorntons.

12. Heavy fog. Nearly calm. Clear after morning & warm Sun. Returned home to dinner. Snow all gone.

13th.   Mer. 42. Wind at No. Et. and misting in the forenoon & raining afterwards—and faster at Night.

14.   Heavy Morning but No Rain & but little wind. Mer. at 38. Foggy & thick through the day.

15.   Perfectly clear & calm in the Morning. Mer. at 36. Wind afterwards fresh but not hard at N. W.

16.   Clear. Mer. 38. Wind at No. W. in the Morning but moderate calm and exceedingly pleasant afterwards.

17.   Clear & calm in the Morning & a white frost. Mer. 30 in the Morning & 40 at Night. Clear all day with very little wind—that Easterly.

18.   Heavy morning (a fog). Little or no Wind & that Southeasterly. Afternoon clear. Mer. 36.

19.   Morning misting—afterwards Slow rain at Intervals. Wind what there was of it in the same quarter. Nelly Custis accompanied by Doctr. & Mrs. Stuart and their three daughters came to Dinner. Mer. 36.

20.   Morning dull. Mer. at 35. Wind but little, & that Southerly. Clear afterwards.

21.   Morning clear. Mer. at 32. Wind hard & cold from the No. Wt. till Noon, when it moderated. Went up to Court, and to an Election of Bank Directors in Alexandria—was chosen Guardian by Miss Eleanor Parke Custis & gave in my Suffrage for Directors. Dined at Mr. Fitzhughs.

On 23 Jan., GW wrote Lawrence Lewis of his errand to Alexandria, "whither I went to become the guardian of Nelly, thereby to authorize a license for your nuptials on the 22d of next month" (CUSTIS, 45).

22.   Clear morning. Mer. at 30. Wind from the Southward. Lowering afternoon & likely for rain. Turning Warm.

The entries for 22 Jan.–9 Feb. 1799 are from a diary page at PHi: Dreer Collection.

23.   Lowering. Mer. at 40. Wind (tho' but very little of it) Southerly. Lowering through the day. Mr. Bushrod Washington came to dinner.

24.　Mer. at 33. A sprinkling of Snow fell in the night—succeeded by R which continued steadily thro' the day, though not hard.

25.　Mer. at 28; with a very heavy Sleet. Thick heavy day throughout. Sleet continuing. No wind but an air from the No. Et. Doctr. Stuart & family & Mr. Bushd. Washn. went away after breakfast.

26.　Mer. at 30. Sleet increased & weather very thick & foggy all day.

27.　Mer. at 36 in the Morning. Cloudy all day with the Wind at No. Wt. & turning cold.

28.　Morning clear. Mer. at 26 and wind at No. Wt. where it remained all day but not hard tho' cold. Mer. 26 at Night.

29.　Mer. at 23 in the Morning wch. was lowering with the wind what there was of it at No. Wt.

30.　Mer. at 29. Morning clear. Wind southerly and a remarkable large hoarfrost. Remained at So. all day & fresh. Mer. 44 at Night.

31.　Clear Morning. Mer. at 33 and wind at No. Wt. Afterwards calm & remarkably pleasant.

[February]

February 1.　Mer. at [　　]. Brisk southerly Wind all day & towards Noon lowering with appearances of rain. Mer. 44 at Night.

2.　Mer. at 42 in the Morning. Wind Southerly & raining. 37 at Night and raining also. From ten oclock in the forenoon until near 5 in the afternoon it ceased raining but was thick & foggy.

3.　Wind shifting to No. Wt. in the Night. It cleared—blew hard & turned cold. Mer. at 27 in the Morning. Wind Moderated in the day wch. was clear throughout.

4.　Lowering in the Morning. Wind at the same place. Mer. 24. Calm clear & pleasant afterwards.

5.   Wind at No. Et. Mer. at 28—and commenced Snowing about 7 OClock, left off about Noon—grd. slightly covered.

6.   Clear. Wind at No. Wt. Mer. 22. Calm & moderate in the Afternoon.

7.   Clear & pleasant all day. Mer. at 20 in the Morning but little Wind and that Easterly. Doctr. Thorn. & Majr. Turner came to dinner.

Major Turner is probably Dr. William Thornton's good friend George Turner. Turner, originally from South Carolina, had served as a lieutenant and captain in the 1st South Carolina Regiment during the Revolution and in 1778 became an aide to Maj. Gen. Robert Howe, with the rank of major. In 1789 Turner was appointed judge of the western territory but resigned the office in 1798.

8.   Wind Easterly. Morning heavy & Mer. at 28. Dripping rain now & then through the day. Wind shifting to the southward & fresh. Mr. Thos. Digges dined here & returned. Mr. Tracy came to dinner.

Thomas Atwood Digges (1742–1821) was the sole surviving son of William Digges of Warburton. Thomas and his brother George (d. 1792) had been in school in England when the Revolution broke out, and although George soon returned home to Maryland, Thomas remained in England. There he followed a controversial and frequently discreditable career. During the Revolution he undoubtedly worked to alleviate the sufferings of American prisoners of war in Britain, but he also seems to have pocketed a large portion of the money sent him for this purpose and was accused of being both a double agent and a thief (wmq, 3d ser., 22 (1965), 486–92; *Pa. Mag.*, 77 (1953), 381–438). Thomas Digges arrived back in America in 1799 and took up residence at Warburton.

9.   A heavy storm of Wind from the So[uth]ward & rain in the night—also in the Morning but clear afterwards. Wind getting to the Westward. Mer. at 54 in the Morning & 50 at Night. Thornton & Turner went away abt. Noon.

10.   Wind shifted in the Night to N.W., blew fresh & turned cold. Mer. at 30 in the morning & 34 at Night. Clear all day.

11.   A little lowering—W. in the Morning—Wind Southerly and Mer. at 27. Went up to Alexandria to the celebration of my birth day. Many Manœuvres were performed by the Uniform Corps and an elegant Ball & Supper at Night.

Participating in the maneuvers were the Alexandria Silver Grays, the "Volunteer Troop of Light Dragoons," and the Alexandria Dragoons (*Columbian Mirror* [Alexandria], 9 Feb. 1799). The ball was held at Gadsby's tavern, which was located on Royal Street at the corner of Cameron. John Wise in 1792 had built a large three-story building adjoining the old City Tavern which Wise boasted as having "twenty commodious, well-furnished rooms in it" (*Va. Gaz. and Alexandria Adv.,* 14 Mar. 1793). In 1794 Wise leased both this new building and the old City Tavern to John Gadsby, an Englishman. Gadsby combined the two buildings into one tavern which for many years provided some of the best accommodations in the country.

12. Wind Westerly & day clear and pleasant. Returnd home. Mr. N. Fitzhugh & brother & Mr. Hen. Wash. came to dinnr.

N. FITZHUGH: Nicholas Fitzhugh had ten brothers. HEN. WASH.: probably Henry Washington (1765–1812), son of Lawrence Washington (b. 1749) and Susannah Washington, both of whom were distant cousins of GW. He may be the same Henry Washington who had earlier been sheriff of Prince William County.

13. Morning clear—wind Southerly. Mer. 34. Wind very fresh all day. Mer. 46 at Night.

14. Mer. 33—morning clear and Wind at South and very pleasant forepart of the day—Lowering afterwards.

15. Wind shifted to the No. Wt. in the Night. Blew hard and turn cold. Mer. 30 in the Morning & 26 at Night.

16. Hard frost—clear and calm—Pleasant after the Morning. Mer. at 18 in the Morning and 26 at Night. Mr. & Mrs. Peters came to dinner.

17. Morning Snowing with little or no wind. Snow abt. 4 Inches deep. Mer. at 24. Before Noon it cleared & became a fine day with very little Wind. Mer. 30 at Night.

18. Morning clear and calm. Mer. at 30. Wind fresh, but not hard, from No. Wt. afterwards. Mrs. Stuart and her 3 daughters came here in the afternoon. Mer. at 24 at Night.

19. Mer. at 30 in the Morning and at Night. Very Cloudy in the forenoon and spitting Snow from 8 Oclock until Noon—clear afterwards.

Nelly Custis in her wedding gown, painted by James Sharples. (Woodlawn Plantation, Mount Vernon, Va.; a property of the National Trust for Historic Preservation)

20.   Morning very thick & Misting; Wind Easterly. Mer. at 30 Morng. & Evening with Rain at Intervals through the day. Doctr. Baynham dined here.

21.   Mer. at 30 in the Morning—very little wind & that Easterly. Heavy & misting all day. Mer. 30 at Night. Mr. Chs. Carter wife & daughter came to dinner & Mr. Robt. Lewis in the Afternoon.

The Carters' daughter was Maria Ball Carter (1784–1823).

22.   Morning Raining—Mer. at 30. Wind a little more to the Northward. Afterwards very strong from the No. Wt. and turning clear & cold.

The Revd. Mr. Davis & Mr. Geo. Calvert came to dinner & Miss Custis was married abt. Candle light to Mr. Lawe Lewis.

REVD. MR. DAVIS: Thomas Davis, Episcopalian clergyman of Charles City County, was an usher at the College of William and Mary 1768; was ordained in London 1773; and served as rector of Elizabeth City Parish in Norfolk County 1773–76, St. Stephen's Parish, Northumberland County 1779–92, Fairfax Parish, Fairfax County 1792–1806, Elizabeth City Parish 1806–8, and Hungar's Parish, Northumberland County 1808. During the Revolution, Davis served as chaplain to several Virginia regiments. Davis later this year presided at GW's funeral.

23.   Morning clear & very cold. Mer. at 12 & wind at No. Wt. which afterwards shifted to the Southward but still continued cold. Mr. Davis retd. after dinner.

24.   Mer. at 18 in the Morning and Wind Southerly—but it soon shifted to the No. Wt. & blew fresh. Weather clear and very cold.

25th.   Clear & very cold in the Morning, and through the day. Mer. at 12 in the Morning and 22 at Night. Wind at No. Wt. River nearly closed with Ice. Mr. L: Lee, Mrs. Lee & Miss French —Mr. Herbert, Mr. Jno. Herbert & Miss Herbert—Doctr. Craik & Mr. G. W. Craik—Miss Fitzhugh Miss Moly Fitzhugh & Miss Chew & Colo. Fitzgerald dined here & returned.

Mrs. Lee was Ludwell Lee's second wife, Elizabeth Armistead Lee, whom he married in 1797. MISS FRENCH: GW may be following the custom of referring to elderly widows as "Miss," in which case his visitor might be Penelope Manley French, aged widow of Daniel French (d. 1771) of Rose Hill, Fairfax County.

   Miss Chew is perhaps Harriet Chew, of Philadelphia, who married Charles Carroll, Jr., of Homewood in July 1800.

26.   Morning cold & cloudy with the Wind at No. Et. & Mer. at 22 Morng. & Eveng. Abt. 3 Oclock it began to snow, & continued steadily to do so. Mrs. Potts—Mrs. Fendall—Mr. Andw. Ramsay & Wife—Mr. Wm. Ramsay—Mr. Edmd. Lee & Sister Lucy—and Mr. Hodgden dined here & returned—and Mr. Bushrod Washington came in the afternoon.

Mrs. Fendall was Philip R. Fendall's third wife, Mary Lee Fendall (born c.1775), a sister to Edmund, Charles, and Light Horse Harry Lee.

   Andrew Ramsay was married in 1795 to Catherine Graham (d. 1844), daughter of Richard Graham (d. 1796) and Jane Brent Graham of Dumfries.

   Lucy Lee (b. 1774), a daughter of Henry Lee of Leesylvania, was Mrs. Fendall's sister.

27.   The Snow which fell in the afternn. was about 4 Inches deep this morng. Morning heavy & but little wind. Mer. 22 and at Night 26. Mr. Thomson Mason & Wife and Mr. Nicholls & Wife dined here & returned.

28.   Clear—wind at No. Wt. but not hard. Mer. at 28 in the Morning and 32 at Night. Evening lowering & calm.

March

1.   Snowing fast. Mer. at 30. More or less snow through the day with the wind though but little of it at No. Et. Snow 6 In. deep.

2.   Morning very heavy & likely for more Snow. Mer. at 25 and Wind at No. Et. Mer. 26 at Night.

3.   Morning moderate with little or no wind & Mer. at 26. Towds. Sundown it came out at No. W. & turned cold. Mer. 28 at Night. Mrs. Stuart & her 3 daughters (Stuarts) and Mr. & Mrs. Peters went away after breakfast.

4.   Clear, hard frost. Mer. at 24 and wind at No. Wt. at which it continued all day and very cold. Mr. & Mrs. Carter went away after Breakfast.

5.   Wind still at No. Wt. and Mer. at 8 in the Morning & 17 at Night. River almost closed with Ice. Clear all day. Mr. Lawe. Lewis & Wife went up to the Fedl. City.

6.   Clear with a light breeze from the South. Mer. at 15 in the Morng. River closed—except in holes—32 at Night & Lowering. Mr. & Mrs. Law went away to day.

Maj. Thomas Pinckney, by John Trumbull.
(Yale University Art Gallery)

7. Morning—Mer. at 31, & a little cloudy with a light breeze from No. Wt. Clear & pleasant afterwards. Mer. 35 at N.

8. But little wind & that No. Westerly. Morng. clear & Mer. at 28. Southerly in the afternoon—clear all day & Mer. 40 at Night. Mr. Mrs. & Miss Carter returned this afternoon.

9. Morning clear but lowering, and, at times raining through the day. Major Pinckney came in the Evening. Mer. 40 and wind Southerly.

Thomas Pinckney was returning home to South Carolina from a session of the United States Congress in Philadelphia. He was interested in experimental farming, and during this visit one of the topics of discussion was GW's jackasses, two of which were for sale (GW to Charles Cotesworth Pinckney, 31 Mar. 1799, DLC:GW).

10. Mer. at 40 in the Morning. Wind and Weather very variable after 12 oclock with squalls & Rain by intervals. Mr. Carter & family and Major Pinckney left this after breakfast and young Mr. Barry—with a Spanish officer—a Mr. O'Higgens came to dinner & returned afterwards.

Mr. O'Higgins may be Capt. Thomas O'Higgins of the Spanish navy (DIARIES, 4:300n).

11. Mer. at 32 in the Morning and Wind at No. Wt. Afterwards So. Et. & very lowering. Mer. 34 at Night.

12. In the Night the wind shifted to No. Wt. again, and blew very hard & continued to do so through the day turning very cold. Mer. 22 in the morning & 18 at Night when it grew calm.

13. Mer. at 17 in the Morning and 20 at Night. Snowing all day —sometimes fast, at other times slow with very little wind.

14. Mer. at 15 in the Morning & quite Calm. Wind at So. Et. afterwards & lowering. Mer. at 30 at Night.

15. Mer. at 30 Morning & Evening. Wind (though not much of it) Easterly. Raining more or less all day.

16. A very thick Fog, with the wind Southerly. Mer. at 30 in the Morning & 40 at Night. At Night it shifted to No. West. Snow all gone. A Mr. Boyd & his Brother from Boston dind here.

17.   Wind about North & mer. at 30 in the morning & lowering. At Night No. Wt. clear & Mer. at 24.

18th.   Mer. at 22 in the Morning. Wind hard all day at No. Wt. and clear. Mer. at 24 at Night.

19.   Calm in the Morning, & somewhat lowering afterwards, Wind Southerly & Mer. at 34 at Night.

20.   Raining & drizling all day with the Wind at South. Mer. at 32 in the morning and 40 at Night.

21.   Mer. at 50 in the Morning and at Night—higher at Noon. Raining by intervals all day with the Wind at South.

22.   Morning Cloudy, with but little wind (that No. Westerly). Mer. at 42 in the Morning and 44 at Night.

23.   Mer. at 35 in the Morning and 34 at Night. Wind at No. Wt. all day and cool. Mr. & Mrs. Lawe. Lewis returned from the Federal City.

24.   Mer. at 32. Wind westerly—clear and pleasant. Mr. Robt. Stith came to dinner & stayed all N.

25.   Calm & clear in the Morning. Wind Southerly & lowering in the afternoon. Mer. at [   ] in the Morning & 52 at Night. Doctr. Craik & Mr. Foot dined here & returned in the afternoon.

26.   A very light breeze from the Eastward in the morning. Clear & Mer. at 42. Very lowering towards evening. Mer. 52 at Night. Mr. Stith went away after breakfast.

27.   Storming from N. a little Easterly. Mer. at 46 in the Morning. Raining more or less all day. Towds. Night the wind came out Violently at No. Wt. & began to clear. Mer. at 44.

28.   Morning clear, Mer. at 32 in the Morning—ground a little froze. Wind high all day at No. Wt. until sundown. Mer. 34 at Night.

29.   Mer. at 32 in the Morning & the Wind Southerly & Lowering. Clear afterwards. Wind towds. Night shifting to West. Mer. 50 at [   ]. Mr. Burwell Bassett came in the Evening.

30. Mer. at 45 in the Morning. Wind Southerly. Weather hazy & Smokey but otherwise pleasant. Mer. 56 at Night.

31. Clear Morning except being very smoky. Mer. at 48 and Wind Southerly. 62 at Night. Mr. Bassett went away after breakfast.

April

1. Clear (except being smoky). Mer. at 46. Wind Northerly—afterwds. Easterly and towards Night lowering.

2. Very thick mist—afterwards Raining with the Wind at East & Mer. at 48 in the Morning. In the afternoon the wind shifted to No. Wt. Blew fresh & turned cold.

3. Extreme cold (but forgot to see what the Mercury was). Wind very high from the No. Wt. and continued so all day. Went up to four mile run to run round my land there. Got on the grd. about 10 Oclock and in Company with Captn. Terret and Mr. Luke commenced the Survey on 4 mile run & ran agreeably to the Notes taken. In the evening went to Alexa. & lodged myself at Mr. Fitzhughs.

MY LAND THERE: This plot of about 1,200 acres on Four Mile Run, bought by GW in 1775, lay about four miles north of Alexandria on the road to Leesburg. It had been losing timber to trespassers for years, and GW particularly suspected the owners of adjoining lands, among whom were Capt. William Henry Terrett, Jr. (d. 1826), and John Luke (see entry for 27 Jan. 1775; STETSON [1], 57–59, 72–73, 78–79). Terrett was the son of William Henry and Margaret Pearson Terrett. Luke was the son of the John Luke who bought this 330-acre tract in 1773 from Mrs. Susanna Pearson Alexander, daughter of the original patentee, Simon Pearson (STETSON [1], 78–79).

4. The No. Wt. [wind] contd. through the Night & all this day & cold. Recommenced the Survey at the upper end where we left off in Company with Colo. Little—Captn. Terret and Mr. Willm. Adams & contd. it agreeably to the Notes until we came to 4 Mile run again which employed us until dark. Returnd. to Alexa. and again lodged at Mr. Fitzhughs.

Col. Charles Little and William Adams both owned land adjoining GW's land being surveyed this day. William Adams (1723–1809), son of Gabriel Adams, Sr. (d. 1750), and Priscilla Pearson Adams, had served as a colonel of militia, vestryman of Truro Parish, justice of the peace, and sheriff of

Fairfax County. His home, Church Hill, adjoined GW's land on the south-west. Adams was an early Methodist convert, and his home was headquarters for Bishop Francis Asbury when he was traveling in the area (STEADMAN [2], 223–24).

5. Returned home to Breakfast. But little wind in the forenoon & quite calm in the afternoon—cool notwithstanding. Mer. 42 at Night.

6. Mer. at 38 in the Morning. Very cloudy & wind at No. Et. Clear afterwards with but little wind. Mer. 46 at Night. Mr. White the Fedl. Commr. came to dinner and Colo. Ball after dinner.

7. Clear & calm in the Morning. Mer. at 41. Wind moderately from the No. Wt. the remainder of the day. Mer. 52 at Night.

8. Hazy & smokey with a light breeze from the Southward in the Morning & Mer. at 46. Wind fresh from the same point after-wards. Mer. 62 at Night. Colo. Ball & Mr. White went away after breakfast.

9. In the morning Mer. at 56. Wind very fresh from South & very likely for Rain. Shifted abt. 9 Oclock & blew violently at No. W. turned cold. Mer. 32 at Night. Mrs. Washington of H: came.

MRS. WASHINGTON OF H: Elizabeth Foote Washington of Hayfield.

10th. A hard frost—morning clear and Cold. Wind at No. Wt. & Mer. at 28.

11. Mer. at 32 in the morning and 49 at Night. Wind Southerly and towards evening the Weather was a little lowering. Mr. Foot dined here & with Mrs. Washington returned home in the after-noon.

12. Morng. Calm & Heavy. Mer. 45. Wd. afterwards, first Southerly & then Easterly but not fresh. Weather clear. Mer. 54 at Night. Doctr. Wade came this Aftn. Spread Plaster of Paris this Morning on the circle & sides before the door & on the Lawn to the Cross Path betwn. the Garden gates & on the Clover by the Stable.

Dr. Robert H. Wade had been to Mount Vernon three times during March and April to attend sick slaves (Wade's account with GW, 13 Mar.–12 April 1799, PU: Early American Letters).

Mount Airy in Richmond County, the home of John Tayloe.
(Virginia Historical Society)

13.   A little rain fell last night. Wind at No. Wt. & Mer. 45 in the Morning—contd. at No. Wt. all day—but not hard. Mer. 50 at Night.

14.   Clear Morning; Mer. at 30, Wind at No. Wt. but light. Calm afterwards & lowering; Mer. 58 at Night.

15.   Clear & Calm morning. Mer. at 43. Clear & calm all day. Mer. 62 at Night.

16.   Calm & clear in the Morning. Brisk Southerly wind afterwards. Mer. 48 in the Morning & 62 at Night.

17.   Lowering morning—brisk Southerly wind. Mer. at 58 in the morning and 66 at Night. Jno. Tayloe Esqr. & Mr. Jno. Herbert came here to dinner.

John Tayloe (1771–1828) was one of the most notable owners of racehorses in Virginia at the turn of the century. He divided his time between his family home, Mount Airy, in Richmond County and his town house—the Octagon House—built for him in the Federal City.

18th.   Calm & pleasant—a refreshing Rain fell in the night. Mer. at 60 in the morning & 66 at Night. About 9 Oclock the wind sprung up from No. Wt. but did not blow fresh nor cold. In the afternoon it shifted to So. Wt. Mr. Tayloe & Mr. Jno. Herbert went away after breakfast.

19.   Mer. 54 in the morning. Wind Northerly & cool, & beginning to lower. Clear afterwards wind encreasing. Mer. 46 at Night & blowing.

20.   Mer. at 32. Wind still fresh from No. Wt. & having blown (it is believed) throu the Night. It is hoped the fruit has escaped, altho' there Ice had formed. Mrs. Washington of Hayfield—Genl. O'Donald, Mr. Barry, Mr. Oliver Mr. Thompson & a Doctr. [   ] dined here & returned. Mer. 47 at N.

GENL. O'DONALD: probably John O'Donnell (died c.1805), eldest son of John O'Donnell (1715–1780) of County Clare in Ireland. O'Donnell ran away from home as a young man and became bookkeeper to the captain of an East Indiaman. He later amassed a fortune while in the employment of the East India Company but was robbed of most of it on his way back to Europe. O'Donnell became master and owner of a merchant ship trading between Bombay and Baltimore and brought the first direct importation of goods from Canton to Baltimore in 1785. He settled in Baltimore probably about 1780 and became colonel of the 27th Regiment of militia and a member of the Maryland legislature. His estate, Canton, was near Baltimore (BURKE [1], 533; WILLIAMS [4], 135n; GW to O'Donnell, 4 Sept. 1797, NN: Washington Papers).
    Mr. Oliver is probably either John Oliver or Robert Oliver (c.1757–1834), both of whom were merchants in Baltimore.

21.   Morning clear & calm. Mer. at 42. But little wind all day & that No. Westerly. Mer. 54 at Night. A B. Heppesley Coxe Esqr. recomd. by Mr. Bingham came here to dinnr.

B. HEPPESLEY COXE: probably John Francis Buller Hippisley Coxe of Stone Easton, Somerset, Eng. He was the son of James Buller of Devon and his wife, Mary Hippisley Coxe Buller, of Somerset. In 1793 Young Buller by royal license had assumed the surnames of Hippisley Coxe (BURKE [2], 3:459).

22.   Morng. clear & Wind Easterly. Mer. at 44 in the Morning & 49 at Night. Mr. Coxe went awy. after breakfast & Mr. Vanstapherst came to dinner & Doctr. Craik to see Mr. Lear afterwards.

MR. VANSTAPHERST: probably a connection of the Amsterdam banking firm of Nicholaas and Jacob Van Staphorst. The Van Staphorst brothers, in connection with the Amsterdam firm of Jan and Wilhem Willink and a third partner, Nicholas Hubbard, had acted as the bankers of the United States in

April 1799

Amsterdam during the Confederation and early federal period. MR. LEAR: On 18 Mar. Dr. William Thornton wrote GW from the Federal City: "Col. Lear complained of one of his Legs very much. I examined & found it in a very bad state, but promised if he would stay with me for a week to attempt to render him some Service" (DLC: William Thornton Papers). On 24 April Thornton wrote GW: "we lament exceedingly the relapse of our Friend Colonel Lear and wish he could have staid a little longer with us; but I must own he is in some respects not a very patient Patient" (DLC:GW).

23d.   Morning very heavy & cloudy with the wind at East & the Mer. at 46. About 6 oclock in the afternoon a fine rain began & continued for an hour. Mer. 54 at Night. Doctr. Craik went away before breakfast & a Majr. Jones—a british Officer came to dinner & Mr. George Peter at Night.

George Peter (1779–1861), youngest brother of Thomas Peter of Georgetown, had come to Mount Vernon soliciting a commission in the provisional army. GW wrote him a recommendation, describing "the young Gentleman . . . [as] likely, well grown, and of good behaviour," and added, "all of the family of them are warm Federalists" (GW to James McHenry, 1 Feb. 1799 and 24 April 1799, DLC:GW). After participating in western exploration in the early years of the nineteenth century, Peter returned to Maryland, settling in Georgetown and Montgomery County, where he represented his district in Congress as a Democrat (ECKER, 150–51).

24.   Mer. at 52. Morning clear no Wind—afterwards at No. Wt. & high. Mer. 46 at Night. Gentlemen who came yesterday went away after breakfast and I went up to Alexa. to an Election of a Representative from the District to Congress & from the County to the State Legisla[tur]e.

FROM THE DISTRICT: GW voted for Henry (Light Horse Harry) Lee, who won election to the United States House of Representatives for the Sixth Congress, which was the only term he served. Three weeks after the first session opened, on 26 Dec. 1799, Lee spoke for the whole Congress on the death of GW and reminded his fellow Americans that while GW was "First in war—first in peace—and first in the hearts of his countrymen, he was second to none in the humble and endearing scenes of private life" (ANNALS OF CONGRESS, 10:1310). FROM THE COUNTY: Richard Bland Lee and Thomas Swann were elected to the Virginia House of Delegates from Fairfax County.

25.   Mer. at 50 in the morng. & 58 at Night. Calm Morning & evening & a light Southerly wind abt. Midday. Doctr. Stuart came to dinner.

26.   Mer. at 50 in the Morning and Wind at No. Et. which afterwds. shifted to So. Et. Mer. 58 at Night. Doctr. Stuart went away after breakfast and Mr. & Mrs. Law. Lewis came from Hope Park in the afternoon.

May 1799

27.   Mer. at 57 in the Morning. Rain last Night—wind at So. Et. and from abt. 8 oclock in the Morning continual Rain until Night —with thunder & lightning after dark. Mer. 62 at Night.

28.   Morning clear—with a light breeze from the Southward. Mer. at 60 & at night 68. About 9 Oclock the Wd. came from the No. Wt. & blew pretty fresh but not cold. Doctr. Craik & a Mr. Halsted dined here & returned.

29.   A little cloudy & Wind about North in the Morning. Mer. 62. Clear afterwards. Went up to run round my land on 4 Mile run. Lodged at Colo. Littles.

Although GW mentions no one else as being present this day, he had met all of the major owners of the lands adjoining his Four Mile Run land at the election in Alexandria (24 April). At that meeting, GW later wrote, "all the parties . . . engaged to meet me at the beginning Corner . . . by nine o'clock" on this morning to "ascertain all the Corners and . . . re-mark any of the lines" around GW's 1200-acre plot (GW to Ludwell Lee, 26 April 1799, DLC:GW; and see entry for 3 April 1799).

30.   Engaged in the same business as yesterday & returned home in the afternoon. Morning clear & fine. Wind Easterly—afterwards fresh from the Southward. Clouded up and between 2 & 3 began to rain. Conti[nue]d to do so steadily until I went to bed. Mer. then at 50.

May 1799

1.   Morning Cloudy & very heavy. Wind Easterly & Mer. at 50. After dark a heavy squall of Wind & Rain from the No. Wt. Mer. 52 at Night.

2.   Clear & calm in the Morning. Mer. at 52. Brisk So. westerly wind afterwards—still clear. Mer. 58 at Night.

3d.   Wind fresh from No. Et. & very Cloudy. Mer. at 50 in the morning. About 9 Oclock it began to rain & contd. to do so until near 2 Oclk. when it ceased & became a clear afternoon. Mer. 43 at night.

4.   Morning clear & pleasant, but cool. Mer. at 40. Wind, what there was of it—North westerly. Mer. 46 at night. Messrs. Wm. & Washington and a Mr. Jeffries dined here & returned.

MESSRS. WM. & WASHINGTON: GW probably meant William and George Washington Craik.

5th.   Morning calm & pleasant. Mer. 46. Wind afterwards at No. Wt. but not hard or cold. At night Mer. 54.

6.   Morning clear, Wind brisk from the Southward. Mer. at 50. At Night it lowered. Mer. 62. Mr. & Mrs. Lewis set out on their journey.

Nelly and Lawrence Lewis left Mount Vernon on a prolonged round of visits to the homes of various members of Lawrence's family. They were away from Mount Vernon most of the time until late October or early November (Eleanor Parke Custis Lewis to Elizabeth Bordley, 14 Nov. 1799, ViMtV).

7.   Morning clear—wind still Southerly & Mer. at 56. About 9 Oclk. it shifted to No. Wt. & blew hard—but did not turn suddenly cold. Mer. 59 at Night.

8.   Clear, but cool—wind still at No. Wt. and Mer. at 46. Calm in the Evening and Mer. at 54.

9.   No clouds, but smokey; Wind (tho' not much of it) at No. Wt. Mer. at 56 and at Night 60. Genl. Lee Messrs. Rd. B. Lee & Wm. Ludwell Lee—Mr. Fitzhugh Mr. Page Mr. T. Turner dined here & returned in the Evening.

Mr. Page is probably William Byrd Page (1772–1818), brother-in-law of Henry and Richard Bland Lee. Page, eldest son of Mann and Mary Mason Seldon Page (1754–1787) of Fairfield, Clarke County, was married c.1793 to Anne Lee, daughter of Henry Lee of Leesylvania.

Mr. Turner is probably Capt. Thomas Turner, "highly spoken of as a horse Officer, and a very respectable character," who wished a calvary commission in the provisional army (GW to James McHenry, 23 April 1799, WRITINGS, 37:192; GW to James McHenry, 6 June 1799, DLC:GW; Bushrod Washington to GW, 10 April 1799, ViMtV).

10th.   Morning lowering & Mer. at 60. Clear afterwards with a brisk Wind from So. Wt. which in the Evening veered to No. Mer. 72 at Night. Mr. Thos. Digges & Mr. Jas. Welch dined here & retd.

The due date for Welch's first payment on the Kanawha lands (31 Dec. 1798) had gone by without GW receiving any word from Welch. GW wrote several times requesting the money due him. He not only needed the money, but as he finally wrote Welch on 7 April 1799, "I have heard too much of your character lately, not to expect tale after tale, and relation after relation, of your numerous disappointments, by way of excuses for the noncompliance of your agreement with me . . . however you may have succeeded in imposing upon and deceiving others, you shall not practice the like game with me, with impunity" (DLC:GW). Welch protested his good intentions and promised to come to Mount Vernon in May. Welch was still unable at this time to come up with the money, and although GW gave him a further extension until November, he never received a penny from Welch for the lands. After GW's death, his executors seem to have canceled the contract and permitted Welch to keep his Elk River lands (PRUSSING, 120–21, 472–75). See entries for 24 Nov. and 18 Dec. 1797 and 10 Oct. 1798.

11. Morning clear – wind at No. Wt. & Mer. at 60 – at Night 56. Doctr. Stuart came to dinner & a Mr. Small afterwards. Both stayed all Night.

MR. SMALL: GW is somewhat confused on the man's name (see entry for 12 May 1799). He probably means Peyton Short (1761–1825), son of William and Elizabeth Skipwith Short of Spring Garden, Surry County, and brother of William Short, former chargé d'affaires to France and minister to The Hague and to Spain. Peyton Short, who attended the College of William and Mary where he was a member of the Phi Beta Kappa Society, moved to Kentucky in 1790 and from 1792 to 1796 represented Fayette County in the Kentucky Senate. GW carried on a correspondence with Short for a year regarding his Kentucky lands on Rough Creek. GW was concerned about the status of his taxes on the land, and was also interested in buying some adjoining property that might be for sale. GW wrote Short on 31 July 1799 that he would avail himself of Short's "obliging offer (when last in Virginia) to serve me in Kentucky, by requesting the favour of you to have the Deed, herewith sent admitted to Record in the County of Kentucky" (WRITINGS, 37:321; GW to Short, 16 July 1798, and Short to GW, 22 July 1798, DLC: GW; Short to GW, 1 Nov. 1798, NbO; TYLER [3], 261–62; TYLER [1], 237–39).

12. Morning clear & cool. Mer. at 48 and wind at No. W. Doctr. Stuart went away after Breakfast & Mr. Short after dinner. Mr. White came to dinner.

13. Clear & calm all day. Mer. at 47 in the Morning and 60 at Night. Mr. White went away before breakfast.

14. Morning clear & very smoaky. Mer. at 52 and but little wind – that Southerly. Mery. 62 at Night. Majr. Wm. Harrison came here to dinner.

William B. Harrison, of Loudoun County, owned land adjoining Mount Vernon. GW, who believed Harrison's tenants were stealing timber and livestock from Mount Vernon, wished to lease or buy Harrison's land to rid himself of those particular neighbors. On 10 April 1799 GW wrote to Harrison: "if you will come & take a bed at my house, I have a Clerk (living with me) who Surveys very well & shall do it for you without cost, the next day" (DLC:GW).

15.   Clear & warm. Mer. at 60, and Wind brisk from the Southward especially towards Night when it lowered. Mr. Thomson Mason came here to breakfast and attended Majr. Harrison & me on the Survey of the latters land & both dined here, as did a Mr. Season. Mer. 72 at Night.

Thomson Mason owned land adjoining Harrison's, which lay near GW's mill on Dogue Run.

MR. SEASON: John Searson (b. 1750), of Ireland, New York City, and Philadelphia, sometime merchant, teacher, and poet, wrote GW on 17 April 1799 of his intention "of waiting on your Excellency, so as to Obtain an Adequate Idea of mount Vernon" (DLC:GW). Searson, "wishing to compose a poem on that beautiful seat," planned the visit "to enable me to make an exact poetical description of it" (SEARSON, iv, v). The book of poems he published later in 1799 included several inspired by this visit. In the title poem, "Mount Vernon, a Poem," a 372-line paean to nature, Searson described some aspects of his visit: he was "invited to dine," after which he visited the gardens, the greenhouse, and the fish landings, and took a view from the cupola (SEARSON, 10, 22).

16.   Mer. at 65 in the morning. Wind fresh from the Southward, but variable—great appearances of Rain & some sprinkles. Went up to Alexandria to the Purse Race, & returned in the Evening. Mr. Law & Doctr. Thornton here. Mer. at 70 at N.

PURSE RACE: At 3:00 P.M. there was to be run "a Purse of Fifty-five pounds, the best two in three, 4 mile heats, free for any horse, mare or gelding" (*Columbian Mirror* [Alexandria], 11 May 1799).

17th.   Morning a little clouded but calm. Mer. 66 in the morning & 60 at Night. Great appearances of Rain all the latter part of the day (and distant thunder) at Night.

18.   Some rain fell last night & two or three hours of Slow rain this forenoon. Wind abt. North—clear afternoon. Mer. at 56 in the Morning & 55 at Night. A Mr. Boies & Lady from Boston dined here & returned to Alexa.

19.   Morning clear & calm. Mer. 50—but little wind afterwards and that So. Easterly. Mer. 60 at Night. Mrs. Peak Miss Eaglin & a Mr. Brent dined here and went away afterwards—as did Mr. Law & Doct. Thornton.

20.   Morning clear & wind abt. So. Et. Mer. at 56 in the Morning & 58 at N. A Mr. Hancock from Boston & a Mr. Smith from Portsmouth dined here.

21. Morning cloudy with appearances of Rain. Mer. at 52 & wind at South. Clear afternoon & Mer. 63 at Night. Mr. Fitzhugh & two daughters—Mr. Mrs. & Miss Turner Messrs. W. & Washington Craik & Mr. Jno. Herbert dined here. The last & Mr. Turners family stayed the night.

22d. Morning a little cloudy. Wind at South & Mer. at 58—78 at Night. Mr. Mrs. & Miss Turner and Mr. Herbert went away after breakfast.

23. Morning a little lowering. Mer. at 70 & wind at So. Very warm all day—about Noon a moderate shower. Mr. Thos. Adams, third son to the President & Mr. Joshua Johnson, Lady & son came to dinr.

Thomas Boylston Adams (1772–1832) was the third son of Pres. John Adams. Joshua Johnson (b. 1742), a brother of Gov. Thomas Johnson of Maryland, served as an American agent in France during the American Revolution and was later appointed by GW as the first American consul at London. Joshua and his wife, Catherine Nuth Johnson, had one son, Thomas Baker Johnson. The families were related by the marriage of a daughter, Louisa Catherine Johnson (1775–1852), to John Quincy Adams, eldest son of President Adams.

24. A good deal of Rain fell last Night; day warm, & Wind Southerly. Mer. 78 abt. Noon & 70 at Night. Rain in the afternoon by Showers. Colo. Ball came to breakfast, and went away after dinner. Mr. T: Peter & Mrs. Peter & young Powell came to dinner.

Young Powell may be William H. Powell (d. 1802), who asked GW for a recommendation for an officer's commission in the provisional army (GW to James McHenry, 30 June 1799, DLC:GW).

25. Morning clear, wind Southerly & Mer. at 67. In the afternoon a light Shower & Mer. at 68. All the company except Mr. & Mrs. Peter went away after breakfast.

26. Clear with the Wind at No. Wt. but not cold. Mer. at 64 in the Morng. and 66 at Night. Mr. & Mrs. Peter went away after breakfast. Mr. & Mrs. Nichols came to dinner & Majr. Geo. Lewis & Doctr. Welford came in the afternoon.

27. Morning perfectly clear. Wind rather fresh at No. Et. but died away. Mer. at 59 in the morning & 66 at night. Captn. Presley Thornton & Lady came to dinner—as did Mr. Lear.

June 1799

Elizabeth Thornton, daughter of Francis and Sarah Fitzhugh Thornton of Society Hill, King George County, married her cousin Presley (Presly) Thornton of Northumberland County about 1783 (wmq, 1st ser., 5 [1896–97], 58).

28. Morning Calm & Mer. at 60–at night 68–clear thro' the day. All the strangers went away after breakfast.

29. Morning perfectly clear–wind brisk from the Southward & contd. so all day. Mer. 60 in the Morning & 72 at Night.

30. Morning clear–Wind Southerly and Mer. at 64. Great appearances of Rain all the forenoon & a fine shower (of an hour) in the afternoon. Mer. 64 at Night.

31. More rain last night. Morning clear–wind at No. Wt. & Mer. at 60–blowing hard all day. Went up to the Fedl. City–dined & lodged with Mr. Peter.

June

1. Wind still fresh from No. Wt. & cold for the Season–sd. to be a frost. Dined & lodged at Mr. Laws.

2. Growing warmer, & cloudy–likely for Rain, but none fell. Returned home to dinner–takg. Church at Alexa. in my way. Found Doctr. Stuart here.

3. Mer. at 60 in the Morning and 64 at Night. Wind Easterly–great appearances of Rain without any falling. Doctr. Stuart went away after Breakfast.

4. Wind still Easterly with clouds. Mer. at 62 in the morning & 67 at N. Clear afternoon.

5. Wind So. Easterly–Mer. 62. Morning lowering as the Evening also was. Mer. 66 at Night. A Mr. Chs. Newbald from New Jersey dined here & went away afterwds.

CHARLES NEWBALD: GW paid Charles Newbold $12.00 on 27 Nov. 1799 for a plow (GW's Cash Memorandum, RPJCB). Newbold had received on 26 June 1797 the first patent for a plow issued in the United States (21st Cong., 2d sess., House Doc., No. 50, p. 46).

6. Morning cloudy—wind Southerly and Mer. at 64 & at Night 66. Towards night the wind got more to the Eastward & the clouds had more the appearance of Rain.

7. Morning calm & very heavy—Mer. at 66. Very likely for rain all day—with thunder about Noon & showers to the So. ward & Eastward of us. Mer. 68 at Night.

8. Morning still heavy & cloudy. Mer. at 65 and wind at So. Et. but variable. Sprinkling at times through the day—but no rain to wet the grd. Mer. at 62 at Night.

9. Clear through the day. Wind fresh and cool from No. Wt. Mer. 58 in the morning & 63 at Night. Mr. Alexr. White came to dinner.

10. Morning calm & clear. Mer. at 60. Southerly wind afterwards. Mer. 73 at Night. Mr. Page & Mr. Seldon dined here, & went away afterwds.

Mr. Seldon is probably a relative of William Byrd Page. Page's mother, a member of the Seldon family, married Wilson Cary Seldon after the death of her first husband.

11. Morning clear & calm. Evening a little cloudy with the wind Southerly. Mer. 62 in the morning & 76 at Night. Bishop Carroll, Mr. Digges & his Sister Carroll—Mr. Pye & Doctr. Craik all dined here.

Bishop John Carroll (1735–1815), son of Daniel Carroll (1696–1750/51) of Upper Marlboro, was born in Upper Marlboro, Md., studied for the priesthood at the Jesuit College at Liège, and returned to Maryland in 1774. While sympathetic to the American revolutionaries his only major activity in the Revolution was in accompanying the American mission to Canada in 1776. After the Revolution, Carroll became the first Roman Catholic bishop in the United States. HIS SISTER CARROLL: Although GW may have meant Bishop Carroll's unmarried sister Elizabeth Carroll, he probably meant Thomas Digges's sister Elizabeth Digges Carroll (1743–1845), widow of Bishop Carroll's nephew Daniel Carroll, Jr., of Rock Creek (d. 1790).
  Mr. Pye is probably one of the members of the Pye family of Charles County, Md. A Mr. Charles Pye had been entrusted by Thomas Atwood Digges with a box of seeds sent GW by a London seedsman during the previous year (Digges to GW, 10 April 1798, DLC:GW).

12. Clear & calm all the forenoon—a light So. Westerly breeze in the afternoon. Mer. at 70 in the Morning & 80 at Night.

June 1799

13.   Clear, with very little wind in the Morning. Mer. at 74 brisk Southerly wind afterwards. Mer. 82 at Nig. Mrs. & Miss Fairfax & Miss Denison dined here.

14.   Morning–calm, but the wind soon came out at No. Wt. & blew very hard all day–appearances of Rain in the forenoon but clear afternoon. Mer. at 80 in the Morning & 72 at Night.

15.   Mer. 66 in the Morning–clear with the wind at No. Wt. and fresh in the forenoon. Captn. Geo. S. Washington & Mr. Robt. Lewis came in the afternoon.

George S. Washington had received a commission in the provisional army in Jan. 1799. He was married in 1793 to Lucy Payne, sister of Dolley Madison. Later he moved to South Carolina and died in Augusta, Ga.

16.   Morning clear & calm. Mer. at 62–calm all day. Mer. 74 at Night. Doctr. & Mrs. Stuart & their 3 daughters came here to dinner.

17.   Morning Mer. at 69–Wind Southerly & perfectly clear– calm afterwards & Mer. 83 at Night. Captn. Washington & Mr. Lewis went away early this morning & Dr. Stuart aft. B[reakfast].

18.   Morning calm & clear. Mer. at 74. So. Wt. wind afterwards. Mer. 91 at Noon & 84 at Night. Mrs. Washington came to dinner.

19.   Morning clear, calm & very Warm. Mer. at 79 in the Morning 92 abt. 2 oclock and 82 at Night. About 5 oclock in the afternoon a moderate shower for 10 minutes. Mrs. & Miss Fairfax, & Mr. Donaldson and Mr. Foote came to Dinner & went away afterwards–as did Mrs. Washington.

Mr. Donaldson may be a relative of Mrs. Jane Dennison (Donaldson) Fairfax.

20.   Morning cloudy–Mer. at 76 and Wind So. Easterly and fresh all day towards night appearances of Rain. Mer. at 71 only. The following company dined here–Chief Justice of the U.S. Ellsworth Mr. & Mrs. Steer Senr.–Mr. & Mrs. Steer Junr. Mr. Van Havre–Mr. & Mrs. Ludwell Lee–Mrs. Corbin Washington Mr. & Mrs. Hodgson & Miss Cora. Lee Mr. & Mrs. Geo. Calvert and a Captn. Hamilton & Lady from the Bahama Islands.

GW's dinner guests today included: Oliver Ellsworth, whom GW appointed in 1796 to the United States Supreme Court as chief justice of the United

States; Henri Joseph Stier and his wife, Marie Louise Peeters Stier; their son Jean Charles Stier and his wife, Marie Van Havre Stier; Marie's brother Jean Michel Van Havre, an emigré from Belgium; Ludwell Lee and his second wife, Elizabeth Armistead Lee; William Hodgson and his bride, Portia Lee Hodgson; Portia's younger sister Cornelia; and George Calvert and his bride of nine days, Rosalie Eugenia Stier (1778–1821), daughter of Henri and Marie Stier (see HOYT [2]). MRS. CORBIN WASHINGTON: Hannah Lee (1766–c.1801), second daughter of Richard Henry Lee, married Corbin Washington in 1787.

21.   Cloudy morning & wind at South. Mer. 70 appearances of Rain all day, but none fell. Mer. 80 at Night.

22.   Morning clear—brisk Southerly wind. Mer. at 72. Very much like Rain in the Afternoon but none fell. Mer. at 86 at its highest & 82 at Night. Doctr. Stuarts family & Mr. & Mrs. Calvert went away after breakfast.

23.   Morning clear—Wind Southerly & Mer. at 76. Distant thunder & appearances of Rain in the afternoon but none fell. Mer. at 90 (highest) and 84 at night.

24.   Calm & very warm. Mer. at 80 in the morning—92 at highest & 86 at Night. Thunder in the So. Wt. quarter but no rain.

25.   Calm & very warm. Mer. at 80 in the morning—93 at highest & 88 at Night.

26.   Morning clear—wind fresh from the So. W. Mer. at 82. Fresh from the same quarter all day, with a good deal of rain to the Eastward but a sprinkle only fell here. Mer. 91 at highest & 79 at Night.

27.   Brisk Southerly wind in the morning & cloudy. Mer. at 74 & the same at Night. Great appearances of Rain in the afternoon and showers around us but none fell here.

28.   A little breeze from the Southward in the morning & Mer. at 72 84 at highest & 76 at Night. Great appearances of Rain & considerable quantities fell No. & East of us—but none here.

29.   Morning lowering—Wind Southerly and Mer. at 74. A great deal of rain appeared to fall all around us, but none here. Mer. 75 at Night.

ESSAYS AND NOTES

ON

HUSBANDRY

AND

RURAL AFFAIRS.

By J. B. BORDLEY.

Still let me COUNTRY CULTURE fcan:
My FARM's my Home: " My Brother, MAN :
" And GOD is every where."

PHILADELPHIA:

PRINTED BY BUDD AND BARTRAM,

FOR THOMAS DOBSON, AT THE STONE HOUSE,
No 41, SOUTH SECOND STREET.

1799.
[*Copy-Right Secured according to Law.*]

Washington owned this copy of John Beale Bordley's popular book on husbandry. (Mount Vernon Ladies' Association of the Union)

30.   Morning cloudy—Wind Southerly & Mer. at 72—84 at highest & 80 at night.

July 1799

1.   Morning clear—wind fresh from the So. Wt. and Mer. at 76 —89 at highest and 76 at Night. A fine shower for about 15 minutes abt. 5 oclock & light rain afterwards until bed time 9 oclock. Doctr. Tazewell & Mr. Burwell Bullett came to dinner.

Dr. William Tazewell wrote GW six weeks later to request that he be put in charge of a proposed marine hospital in Norfolk. His qualifications included a five-year attendance at hospitals in Edinburgh, London, and Paris (Tazewell to GW, 14 Aug. 1799, DLC:GW). Tazewell practiced medicine in Williamsburg during the War of 1812 and later practiced in Richmond. MR. BURWELL BULLETT: Benjamin Bullitt (d. 1766), of Fauquier County, had nine sons, one of whom was named Burwell.

2.   Mer. at 74 in the Morning and 79 at Night. Clouds & appearances of rain, but none fell. Doctr. Tazewell & Mr. Bullett went away in the Morning & a Captn. Moore from East Indies & a Mr. Teal from Phila. came to dinner & returned to Alexa. in the afternoon.

3.   Mer. at 74 in the Morning and 76 at Night. Wind brisk from the So. Et. Doctr. Stuart, & a Parson Lattum from Pennsylvania dined here & left it in the afternoon.

PARSON LATTUM: probably Rev. James Latta (1732–1801), Presbyterian minister of Chestnut Level, Lancaster County, Pa., or one of his sons. James Latta was born in Ireland of Scotch-Irish parents who emigrated to America and settled near Elkton, Md. Latta's two elder sons, Francis Alison Latta (c.1767–1834) and William Latta (c.1768–1847), were both ordained ministers at this time and had churches in Pennsylvania (SPRAGUE, 3:199–208).

4.   Morning heavy. Mer. at 74 and Wind So. Et. Clouds in every qr. & sprinklings of Rain. Mer. 80 at Night. Went up to Alexa. and dined with a number of the Citizens there in celebration of the anniversary of the declaration of American Independe. at Kemps Tavern.

KEMPS TAVERN: Peter Kemp ran the Globe Tavern at the northeast corner of Cameron and Fairfax streets. The tavern had had several earlier proprietors, including George H. Leigh, John Abert, and Henry Lyles. John Wise, who built the newer of the two buildings now comprising Gadsby's tavern.

had also been the proprietor at one time (POWELL [1], 129, 133; *Alexandria Journal,* 19 April 1787; *Columbian Mirror* [Alexandria], 15 Oct. 1799; BROCKETT, 54, 76).

5.   Morning clear—wind fresh from the Southward. Mer. 74— at highest 88—and at Night 84. Appearances of Rain with distant thunder & lightning in the No.

6.   Morning very heavy with great appearances of Rain—but little Wind & Mer. at 80—87 at highest & 84 at Night. Doctors Tazewell & Thornton came in the evening.

7.   Morning Cloudy—Wind altho' but little of it, No. W. Mer. 76—83 at highest and 78 at Night. Mr. Willm. Booker came in the evening.

On 3 Mar. 1799 GW wrote the agricultural mechanic William Booker that "a Mill grinding from 15 to 20 bushls. a day, with two horses, would nearly, if not entirely, answer all my purposes; with the occasional aid of the Water Mills which in the driest Seasons, grinds a little" (NN: Washington Papers). Booker was at Mount Vernon to build GW a horse-powered grist mill (GW's Cash Memorandum, 20 Feb.—3 Dec. 1799: entry for 12 July, RPJCB).

8.   Morning clear with very little wind. Mer. at 71—84 afterwards at highest, & 78 at Night. Wind Southerly & weather clear.

9.   Clear, with a very light air from the N.W. Mer. at 70 in the evening & Morning both. Much appearances of rain—but a sprinkling only fell. Doctors Thornton & Tazewell went away before breakfast.

10.   Morning perfectly clear with very little wind. Mer. at 66— clear all day. Mer. 74 at Night. Mr. and Mrs. Law and a Mr. Dunn came here to dinner.

11.   Morning clear, with a light breeze from the No. Et. Mer. at 68 & at Night 75—breeze fresher from the same quarter.

12.   Fresh Southerly wind in the morning; clear; Mer. at 68. After noon a little lowering. Mer. 82 at Night. Doctr. Tazewell & Mr. G. W. Craik came here in the afternoon. Mr. Booker went away.

13.   Morning a little cloudy—wind from the So. Wt. and Mer. at 76—85 at highest & 80 at Night. Great appearances of Rain towds. Evening—but they went off.

14.   Morning a little Cloudy—Wind Southerly & Mer. at 77. Great appearances of Rain but none fell. Mer. 79 at Night. The Atty. Genl. Lee & Mr. W. Craik dined here. Doctr. Tazewell went away after dinner.

15th.   Morning clear—Wind at No. Wt. and Mer. at 80—at highest 88 & at Night 83. Wind fresh after the Morning from the above point.

16.   Morning calm. Mer. at 74. Wind brisk from the No. W. till the afternoon when it grew calm again. Mer. 78 at Night. Mr. Dunn left this after breakfast.

17.   Morning clear—Wind at No. Wt. & Mer. at 72 and at night 78. Colonels Powell & Simms and Mr. Herbert and Judge Washington Captn. Blackburn & Mr. H. Turner dined here. The three first went away in the afternoon.

Capt. Richard Scott Blackburn was interested in an appointment in the provisional army (GW to Bushrod Washington, 31 Dec. 1798, DLC:GW). MR. H. TURNER: probably Henry Smith Turner (1770–1834), of Smith's Mount, Westmoreland County, who married (1796) Capt. Richard Scott Blackburn's sister Catherine Blackburn. They later settled at Wheatland in Jefferson County.

18.   Cloudy, with drippings now and then till about 4 oclock, when it commenced a constant slow rain with the Wind at So. Et. & contd. until I went to bed at 9 oclock. Mer. 71 at Night. Captn. Blackburn went away after breakfast.

19.   A good deal of rain fell in the Night and the ground made sufficiently wet. Morning heavy with the wind at No. Et. and Mer. at 72. Misting, & sometimes pretty smart rain [at] Noon. Mer. 70 at Night. Judge Washington & Mr. H. Turner left this after dinner.

20.   Morning a little cloudy—Wind at No. Et. & Mer. at 66—at Night 74. Appearances of Rain. Mr. Law went away after breakfast.

21.   Morning cloudy—Wind at No. Et. and Mer. at 70. After One Oclk. several fine showers. Mer. 72 at Night.

22.   Morning clear—Wind still at No. Et. & Mer. at 68. Serene all day. Mer. 74 at Night. Mr. Law returned this afternoon.

23.   Morning clear with but little Wind all day. Mer. 68 in the Morning—80 at highest & 76 at Night. Mr. Needham Washington came in the afternoon.

Needham (Nedham) Langhorne Washington (d. 1833), eldest son of Lawrence Washington (b. 1728) of Chotank and Elizabeth Dade Washington, inherited his father's plantation in the Chotank neighborhood of King George County.

24.   Morning perfectly clear. Mer. at 68 and a light breeze from the Eastward. Calm afterwards. Mer. 82 at highest & 77 at Night.

25.   Very little wind and very warm—but being unwell, no acct. was taken of the Mer. Visited by Doctr. Craik.

26.   Mer. at 74 in the Morning—85 at highest & 84 at Night. Doctr. Craik went away after breakft.

27.   Morning calm. Mer. at 76. Calm all day. Mer. 88 at highest & 85 at Night.

28.   Wind Southerly, with appearances of rain all the forenoon but none fell. Mer. 79 in the morng. & 80 at Night.

29.   Morng., Mer. at 74—But little wind, and that Southerly. Weather clear thro' the day. Mer. 87 at highest & 83 at Night.

30.   Morning perfectly clear and calm. Mer. at 78—at highest & 85 at Night—a breeze from So. Wt. latter part of the day. A Major Riddle (a British Officer) Colo. Fitzgerald, & Mr. James Patton —and Mr. B. Bassett came to Dinner. The first three went away afterwds.

James Patton (Patten) took an oath of citizenship and was licensed as a merchant in Alexandria in 1791 (SPROUSE [2], 2:29).

31.   Clear, & wind lightly from the Southward. Mer. at 76—at its height 90 and at Night.

August

1.   Morning clear—wind Southerly, & Mer. at 74—hot about midday & 72 at Night. A moderate & fine Rain began about 4 oclock & contd. more or less until 6.

2. Rain in the Night, & Clouds very heavy abt. sunrise. Mer. at 74—at its highest 76 and at Night 75. Captn. Blue of the Amn. Army who came here yesterday to dinner returned to day after breakft.

Capt. William K. Blue (d. 1802), of Virginia, had been appointed cornet of light dragoons in 1793 and lieutenant in July 1794 and was honorably discharged on 1 Nov. 1796. On 12 July 1799 he was appointed captain of the 7th Infantry and was again honorably discharged 15 June 1800. He was killed in a duel in 1802 (HEITMAN [3], 1:226).

3. Morning cloudy, but clear afterwards. Mer. at 72 in the Morning—80 at Noon & 77 at Night.

4. Morning a little cloudy and very little wind. Mer. at 70 Noon, and afternoon, wind Easterly with heavy Clouds in the North, South & East, and light sprinkling rain here. Mer. 70 at Night. Doctr. Stuart & his brother Richard & Mr. Foot dined here & returned afterwards.

5. Clear & Warm. Went up to George Town, to a general Meeting of the Potomac Company—dined at the Union Tavern & lodged at Mr. Law's.

In July 1799 a letter had been sent to each shareholder in the Potomac Company, outlining the financial plight of the company and soliciting assistance. The president (James Keith) reported that tolls were down from the previous year and work had been at a standstill for the past two seasons. However, a new machine for hoisting cargo over the Great Falls had been installed, replacing an earlier one, and there was still hope that the state of Maryland would lend further assistance. This was the last meeting GW was to attend. The Potomac Company survived until 1828, when it was incorporated into the Chesapeake and Ohio Canal Company.

6. Clear & warm. Returned home to dinner—found Genl. Wm. Washington of So. Carolina & Son here. Wind Southerly.

William Washington was one of GW's particular choices for the officering of the provisional army. He was appointed brigadier general of the United States Army on 19 July 1798 and retired on 15 June 1800. William Washington had an only son, William Washington (1785–1830).

7. Mer. at 72 in the Morning, and 80 at Night. Wind Southerly. The following Gentlemen dined here—viz. Colo. Fitzgerald— Doctr. Craik & Son—Mr. Wm. Craik—Mr. Herbert & Son Jno. C. Herbert—Colo. Ramsay—Mr. Potts—Mr. Edmd. Lee—Mr. Keith— Lieut. Kean of the Marines—and Mr. Chas. Fenton Mercer.

Edmund Jennings Lee.
(The Society of the Lees of Virginia)

LIEUT. KEAN: probably Newton Keene (b. 1768), son of Capt. Newton Keene and Sarah Edwards Keene of Northumberland County (WMQ, 1st ser., 18 [1909–10], 131–32). Keene was appointed second lieutenant in the Marine Corps on 22 Dec. 1798 and was promoted to first lieutenant 1 Nov. 1800. He resigned his commission 1 Nov. 1805 (CALLAHAN [3], 689).

8.   Morning calm & clear. Mer. at 77–88 at highest & 80 at Night. About 4 o'clock their was a moderate rain for about 10 minutes— but the grd. was not wet by it. Genel. Washington & son went away after breakfast & Doctr. & Mrs. Jenifer came to dinner.

9.   Mer. at 73 in the Morning & a light breeze from No. Wt.— 82 at Night. Clear & warm all day. Doctr. & Mrs. Jenifer went away after breakfast—as did Mrs. Law.—Mr. Law havg. left it on Monday last.

10.   Morning perfectly clear. Wind from So. Wt. and Mer. at 75 —at highest 87—and at Night 74. In the afternoon heavy clouds & fine rains all around us but none fell here.

11.   Morning clear—wind Southerly—and Mer. at 73; 83 at high-est—& 80 at Night—clear all day—& wind pretty fresh.

August 1799

12.   Morning quite clear—wind westerly—and Mer. 70 at sunrising—82 at highest & 80 at Night. Clouds & some rain to the Southward—but none fell here.

13.   Morning perfectly clear and quite calm. Mer. at 73—82 at Night & close—thunder, lightning & rain in the West & No. Wt. but none fell here.

14.   Morning clear & calm. Mer. at 71 and at night 83. Wind Southerly & Fresh after the Morning—with clouds to the West.

15.   Morning Calm & clear. Mer. at 80. Wind Southerly afterwards & Mer. at 85—and 82 at Night. Mr. Thos. Digges dined here.

16.   Mer. at 71 in the Morning—No wind & clear—82 at highest and 78 at N. Young Mr. McCarty dined here.

YOUNG MR. MCCARTY: probably Daniel McCarty (d. 1811), son of Daniel McCarty (1759–1801) of Cedar Grove (SPROUSE [4], 15–20).

17.   A Slow, & moderate rain for an hour or more fell About Middle of last night—but not sufft. to wet the grd. more than an Inch or two. This morning a little cloudy. Mer. at 70—& 68 at Night. Clouds at day & wind fresh from No. West & cool.

18.   Morning—Mer. at 64—and 69 at Night. Wind No. & No. East and cool great appearances of Rain but none fell here.

19.   Morning Cloudy Wind at No. Et. & Mer. at 65—at highest 75 and at Night 69. Wind brisk at No. Et. all day.

20.   Mer. at 69 in the morning. About ½ after 5, it began a fine, rain, with the wind at No. Et. & continued to do so until near 11 oclock when it ceased, but recommenced about ½ after 3 & contd. raining slow & fine until 9 oclock when I went to bed. Mer. 65 at Night.

The rain this day must have been welcome to GW, who wrote to Robert Lewis 17 Aug. that the drought had caused his oat crop to fail and now endangered his corn crop. He added that "my Meadows, at this time, are as bare as the pavements" (ViMtV).

21.   Heavy morning, with the Wind at No. Et. & Mer. at 64—at highest 66 & at Night 65. The same slow & fine rain fell with

Intervals after 12 oclock & early in the morning. Ground now fully wet.

22d.   The sun rose clear, but very cloudy notwithstanding. Very little wind from the No. Et. Mer. at 64—afterwards & Clear. Mer. 72 at highest & 70 at Night.

23.   Morning quite calm & tolerably clear. Mer. at 68–80 at highest & 66 at Night. Wind Southerly & clear after the Morning. Mr. & Mrs. Law came here to Dinner.

24.   Morning clear—a light breeze from the Southward and Mer. at 70. Clear all day & warm. Mer. 80 at Night. Mr. White came to dinner—as did 4 Gentlemen from Phila. viz.—young Mr. Meridith (son of the Treasurer) Mr. Clifton, a Mr. Walter & _____. The 4 last returned after dinner.

YOUNG MR. MERIDITH: a son of Samuel Meredith, treasurer of the United States, and his wife, Margaret Cadwalader Meredith.

25.   A shower of rain in the Night with lightning & distant thunder. Morng. calm & clear. Mer. 76. Wind Southerly afterwards and Mer. 80 at Night.

26.   Morning calm & clear. Mer. at 76—at highest 86 and at night 75. A fine shower of Rain in the afternoon. Wind Southerly in the forenoon & northerly after the Rain.

27.   Morning clear & pleasant & Wind at No. Wt. Mer. 75—at highest 72. Pleasant all day. Wind westerly until the afternoon then Calm.

28.   Morning perfectly clear and Calm. Mer. at 66–76 at highest & 70 at Night. Clear all day with but little wind.

29.   Morning very lowering with a brisk Southerly wind, Mer. 70 & at Night 76. A good deal of rain fell to the No., & No. Wt. of us, with thunder & light[ning]. A few drops fell here—but not more than enough to lay the dust.

30.   Morning cloudy—Wind Northerly and Mer. at 70–82 at highest & 78 at Night.

31.   Morning clear. Mer. at 76. Calm—82 at highest & 78 at Night. Messrs. Willm. & George Craik dined here & returned.

September

1.   A brisk Southerly wind in the Morning—clear & Mer. at 70 and at night 83. Cloud, thunder, lightning & Rain to the Northward of us but none fell here. Doctr. Craik dined here—sent for to Mrs. Washington who was sick.

2.   Morning very likely for Rain being very cloudy with a brisk Southerly wind. Rain all around us but only [a] sprinkle here. Mer. 76 in the Morning 84 at highest and 83 at Night.

3.   Morning Cloudy—about noon a very black cloud to the West & No. Wt. and a good deal of rain in appearance but little or none fell here. Mer. 79 in the Morning—84 at highest & 77 at Night. Mrs. Washn. & her grd. Dr. of Bushfd. & B: Washn. & wife & Dr. Stuart came here.

4.   A moderate shower of rain in the night with a good deal of lightning & distant thunder. Morning very heavy—a breeze from the No. Et. and Mer. at 72. About 4 Oclock it began a moderate settled rain, which continued until I went to bed. Mer. then at 67.

5.   Morning very heavy & Mer. 66—the same through the day. About 5 oclock it began to rain & contd. until bed time. Wind tho' very little of it, at No. Et. Doctr. Stuart went away after breakfast.

6.   Much rain fell in the Night, without wind, thunder or lightning—making the ground wetter than it has been since March. Mer. 65 in the Morning—68 at highest and at Night 68. Cloudy & heavy with a light breeze from the No. Et. At Night began a drizling rain. Mr. B. W. & wife went after breakfast. Doctr. Craik who was sent for in the Night to Mrs. Washington came early this Morning.

DOCTR. CRAIK WHO WAS SENT FOR IN THE NIGHT: GW wrote Thomas Peter on 7 Sept. that "Mrs. Washington has been exceedingly unwell for more than eight days. Yesterday she was so ill as to keep her bed all day, and to occasion my sending for Doctr. Craik the night before, at Midnight. She is now better, and taking the Bark; but low, weak and fatigued—under his direction. Her's has been a kind of Ague & fever—the latter never, entirely, intermitting until now. I sent for the Doctor to her on Sunday last, but she could not, until he came the second time—yesterday morning—be prevailed upon to take anything to arrest them." After sealing the letter, GW added a postscript saying that the fever had returned "with uneasy & restless symptoms." He requested that Mrs. Eliza Law also be informed (ViMtV). Mrs. Washington's illness persisted for several weeks and not until late October did GW write that she was "tolerably well" (GW to William Augustine Washington, 22 Sept. 1799, ViMtV; FREEMAN, 7:602–6).

7.   Much rain fell last night. Very heavy morning with very little Wind. At times after noon the sun appeared. Mer. at 65 in the morning—76 at highest & 72 at Night. Mr. & Mrs. Peter and Genl. Washington came in the afternoon.

William Washington brought GW a "model of an improvement made on Gun Carriages" from Edward Rutledge of South Carolina. GW wrote Rutledge that he saw many advantages in the improvement and thought something of the sort should be adopted (8 Sept. 1799, ViMtV).

8.   Morning very heavy & wind at No. Et. & Mer. 68 in the Morning & 70 at Night. Cloudy all day. Some rain fell last night and a slight sprinkling this afternn. Genl. Washington went away after breakfast & Mr. & Mrs. Law came to dinner.

9.   Morning heavy & at times raining. About noon the Sun came out warm and the weather appeared to be clearing but in the afternoon it rained again as it did last night. Mer. 70 in the morning & 73 at night. Wind still Easterly.

10.   Morning heavy again—but abt. Noon the weather broke away warm, and had the appearance of being fair. Wind still Easterly. Mer. 70 in the Morning 75 at highest & 72 at Night. Mrs. Washington & her granddaughter went away after breakfast. Doctr. Stuart came to dinner, & Doctr. Craik (sent for) came in the afternoon.

11.   An extremely heavy fog—no wind—and Mer. at 68 in the morning—79 at Highest & 75 at Night. Clear with a southerly wind after the Fog. Doctors Craik & Stuart, & Mr. Peter went away after breakfast.

12.   Morning clear—wind brisk from the Southward and Mer. at 72–84 at highest & 80 at N. Clear all day. Cap: Truxton came to dinner.

Thomas Truxton (1755–1822) was owner and master of several privateers during the Revolution and later was a merchant trading with the Orient. In 1794 he was appointed captain in the United States Navy. In Feb. 1799 Truxton, commanding the frigate *Constellation,* met and captured the French frigate *L'Insurgent* in a battle in the West Indies; he returned to America to find himself acclaimed a hero. At the end of June, Truxton sailed his vessel to New York for refitting, recruiting, and provisioning. On 1 Aug. he resigned his commission in a dispute over rank but reconsidered and sailed for the West Indies on 24 Dec. 1799. Truxton was at Mount Vernon by GW's invitation (FERGUSON, 176–87).

13.   Morning clear—wind Southerly. Mer. at 76—at highest 84 and at Night 76. Wind Southerly & clear till afternoon. Then cloudy & about 6 Oclock Rain, with a good deal of Lightening & thunder, but none severe. Mr. & Mrs. Law went away after breakfast & Doctor Thornton came to dinner.

14.   Morning clear—Mer. at 72. Wind Westerly through the day & clear.

15.   Day omitted through mistake.

16.   Morning clear—no wind. Mer. at 64 at highest 76—and at Night 73. Clear & but little wind all day.

17.   Morning clear—but little wd. & that No. Westerly. Mer. 66—calm all day. Mer. 80 at highest & 74 at Night. Doctr. Thornton went away after breakfast & Mr. Thos. Peter & his brother Lieutt. Peter came to Dinner.

LIEUTT. PETER: George Peter had been appointed a second lieutenant in the 9th Infantry on 12 July 1799 (HEITMAN [3], 1:786).

18.   Morning very heavy—Wind Easterly and Mer. at 70. Towds. Night the appearance of a Storm increased. Mr. George Peter went away after breakft.

19.   Raining in the Morning early and by 8 oclock storming with a heavy fall of rain. Mer. at 70—wind at So. Et. Afterwards shifted to the No. Wt. and cleared. Mer. 70 at highest and 64 at Night.

20.   Morning cloudy—Wind at No. W. and Mer. at 60—at Night 66 & clear. Mr. Ludwell Lee, and Messrs. Stanton & Parker from the Eastern shore of Virginia and a Mr. Hilton dined here & went away afterwards.

STANTON & PARKER: probably John Stratton and Thomas Parker. Stratton, of Elkington, near Eastville in Northampton County, was in the salt business on the Eastern Shore in the 1790s, while Parker (d. 1819) was an Eastern

Shore merchant based at Pungoteague, in Accomack County (WHITELAW, 1:147, 174, 698).

GW received word this evening of the death of his last remaining brother, Charles Washington.

21.   Morning cloudy—Wind Northerly—and Mer. at 63. Variable all day. Mer. 66 at Night. Mr. Alex. White came to dinner.

22.   Morning a little cloudy. Wind at No. Et. & Mer. at 62. Wind shifted to No. Wt. Mer. 62 at Night.

23.   Morning clear—wind No. Wt. & continued so all day. Mer. at 60 in the morning—and 58 at night. Mr. White went away after breakfast.

24.   Morning clear & calm. Mer. at 50. A small white frost—clear all day with but little wind. Mer. 63 at highest & 58 at Night. Mr. Thos. Peter went away after break[fas]t.

25.   Clear & calm. Mer. at 52 in the Morning—but little wind all day. Mer. 66 at highest and 63 at N. Mrs. & Miss Fairfax & Miss Dennison dined here & returned & Doctr. Stuart came in the Evening.

26.   Clear & calm in the Morning. Mer. at 63—at highest 70 and at Night 64. But little wind all day.

27.   Clear, with the wind Northerly; Mer. at 62 in the morning—70 at highest & 66 at Night. Governor Davie on his way to the Northward to Embark as Envoy to France called, dined & proceeded on. Mr. T. Peter came.

William Richardson Davie (1756–1820), a distinguished veteran of the southern campaigns in the American Revolution and a strong Federalist, was elected governor of North Carolina in 1798. He recently had been commissioned by President Adams to join Oliver Ellsworth and William Vans Murray in a mission to France to settle the two countries' differences (SMITH [5], 2:994–1003, 1010–16).

28.   Clear & calm. Mer. at 60 in the morning—70 at the highest & 66 at night. Clear & calm all day.

29.   Morning cloudy—Wind at So. W. & Mer. at 62. Wind changed to No. Wt. & blew pretty fresh. Mer. 65 at night. Doctr. Craik came to dinner on a visit to Mrs. Wash. & stayed all night.

30.   Morning clear wind Northerly and Mer. at 50—at highest 66 and at night 60. Clear all day wind in the same place. Doctr. Craik went away after Break.

October

1.   Morning a little lowering. Mer. at 55 and air from the No. West. Clear afterwards. Mer. 65 at high. Mrs. Fairfax sister & daughter and Mrs. Herbert & Mrs. Nelson—Mr. Jno. Herbert & two of Mrs. Washington of Fairfields Sons dined here. Mrs. Fairfax &ca. went away after dinner—the others remained.

Mrs. Herbert was Sarah (Mrs. William) Herbert, mother of the John Carlyle Herbert mentioned here.

Mrs. Nelson is Catharine (Catherine) Washington Nelson (1769–1845), daughter of Warner Washington and his second wife, Hannah Fairfax Washington. In 1789 Catharine married Dr. John Nelson, son of Roger Nelson of Frederick, Md. Mrs. Hannah Washington of Fairfield had two sons, Fairfax and Whiting Washington.

2.   Morning again lowering. Mer. at 58 and Light breeze from No. Et.—afterwards quite calm. Mer. 72 at Night and highest. After dinner Mrs. Herbert Mrs. Nelson &ca. went away.

3.   Morning lowering & calm. Mer. at 66—at highest it was 73 and at Night 72. It continued lowering & calm all day.

4.   Morning again, heavy & lowering. Mer. 68—quite calm through the day. Mer. 75 at highest & 73 at Night. Mrs. Peak dined here and in the Afternoon Colo. Jno. Waker & Mr. Hugh Nelson came here.

COLO. JNO. WAKER: John Walker.

Hugh Nelson (1768–1836), son of Gov. Thomas Nelson (1738–1789), graduated from the College of William and Mary in 1780, served in the Virginia General Assembly and later (1811–23) in the United States House of Representatives, and was United States minister to Spain 1823–24. In April 1799 he married John Walker's granddaughter Eliza Kinloch (1781–1834) and, after Walker's death in 1809, resided at the Walker home, Belvoir, in Albemarle County (BRYDON, 155–60).

5.   Morning heavy—Wind Southerly. Mer. at 68. Between 7 & 8 it began to Rain & continued to do so moderately until the afternoon when it cleared.

This pair of engraved pastoral landscapes originally hung at Mount Vernon. (George Washington Masonic National Memorial Association)

6. Morning clear. Wind abt. No. Wt. & Mer. at 60. Clear all day & the Wind pretty fresh. Mer. 62 at highest & 57 at Night.

7. Morning a little cloudy—but little wind from the northward. Mer. 52—and at Night 62 the Wd. having shifted to the Southward and the weather turning cloudy with appearances of Rain. Mr. Peter went to Geo: Town this Morng.

8th. Morning—Raining fast with the wind at So. Et. & Mer. at 60. A good deal of Rain fell in the Night. At 8 oclock it ceased

raining but continued cloudy more or less all day. Mer. 65 at Night.

9.   Morning cloudy—wind from the No. Et. and Mer. 59. Clouds & sunshine alternately through the day, at night very lowering & Mer. at 62. Colo. Walker & Mr. Nelson set out for the City of Washington after breakfast.

10.   Much rain fell last night. Morning very cloudy with the Wind moderate from No. W. & Mer. 64. About 10 oclock it began

to Rain & contd. to do so without intermission until night. Mer. then 60. Mr. T. Peter returned tonight.

11. Morning clear wind (tho little of it) at No. Wt. & Mer. at 52. Clear all wind in the same place. Mer. 52 at Night.

12. Morning clear Wind at No. Wt. and Mer. at 48–a white frost, not heavy. Towards evening a little lowering & wind (tho very little of it No. Easterly). Mer. 57 at Night. Mr. Mrs. Peter & family went away after breakfast & Mr. Lawe. Lewis and his wife came to dinner.

13. A little rain fell in the Night. Morning foggy or misting. Wind at No. Et. & Mer. at 57. Appearances, at different times, through the day, of rain but none fell. Mer. 62 at Night. Mr. Lear returned from Berkley.

Diary entries for 13–23 Oct. 1799 are from a diary page at PHi: Dreer Collection.

14. Morning–steady Rain (& much fell in the Night) with the Wind at So. Et. & Mer. at 60. After noon the wind shifted to So. Wt. but contind. Raining. Mer. 62 at Night.

15. Morning clear–Wind No. Westerly. Mer. 60. Clear all day & very pleasant. Mer. 60 at Night. A Mr. Bourdieu of the House of Bourdieu, Chollet & Bordieu of London (accompanied by a Mr. Gardner) –Mr. Gill & Mr. B. Bassett dined here. The three first went away afterwards.

Mr. Bourdieu is either James Bourdieu or his son James, both partners in the important London firm of Bourdieu, Chollet & Bourdieu. The Bourdieus were a settled Huguenot family, probably seventeenth-century immigrants to England. The third partner, Samuel Chollet, was a Swiss, a former clerk in the business who had become a partner c.1769. Bourdieu, Chollet & Bourdieu remained in business at the same address in London from the 1740s to the 1840s. Their main interest was in trade with France, but their widespread concerns reached to many other areas, including North America and the West Indies. In the 1760s the company had been London agent for the French East India Company and from c.1771 until at least 1791 was agent of the French government in making large purchases of wheat and flour in North America to supplement scarce French supplies. During the 1770s and 1780s the company engaged in a protracted struggle with other important British firms for the contract to supply tobacco to France. The importance of the Bourdieu firm began to diminish after 1800 (PRICE [2], 2:687–88, 739–40, 798–800, 1066).

John Gill, whom GW termed "late of Alexandria," came to Mount Vernon to discuss his rental payments for GW's land on Difficult Run (GW to Charles Little, 20 Nov. 1799, DLC:GW).

16. Morning clear & calm. Mer. 52. A brisk So. westerly Wind afterwds. Mer. 62 at Noon & 63 at Night—appearances of Rain.

17. Clear—wind at No. Wt. & Mer. 46 in the Morning. Clear all day & wind in the same place. Mer. 43 at night.

18. Morning clear with a little breeze from No. Wt. A large Frost & Mer. at 40. Clear all day with but little Wind. Mer. 43 at Night.

19. Morning quite clear with a small breeze from the So. Et. Mer. at 43. A great circle round the Sun about Noon which contd. for hours & towards Night it began to lower much. Mer. 55 at Night.

20. Morning very heavy. Wind Southerly & Mer. at 54. A Struggle all day between the Sun & the Clouds—but no rain fell. Mer. 62 at Night. Doctr. Stuart wife & three daughters and young Danl. McCarty came to dinner & stayed all Night.

21. Morning clear—wind Southerly. Mer. at 60. The forepart of the day variable. The latter part clear warm & pleasant. Mer. at 64.

22. Clear, with the Wind at No. Wt. and Mer. at 58. In the Morning fresh Wind all day from the same quarter. Mer. 50 at Night. Mr. Liston (British Minister) & lady came to dinner—as did young Mr. McCarty.

23. Morning clear & calm. Mer. at 42. Clear all day wind coming out from the No. West but not fresh. Mer. 49 at Night. Mr. Herbert—Mr. & Mrs. Patton—Mr. [   ] Mr. Gilmar came to dinner. The last stayed all Night.

MR. & MRS. PATTON: probably James Patton (Patten) and his wife, Ann Patton, who was sometimes listed on official records as Mary Ann (SPROUSE [2], 2:87). Mrs. Patton was probably a daughter of Mrs. Ann Clifton Slaughter. MR. GILMAR: probably either the Baltimore merchant Robert Gilmor (1748–1822) or his son Robert Gilmor, Jr. (1773–1848). During the Revolution, when the ports of Charleston, Norfolk, Philadelphia, and New York were blockaded or captured, trade from Baltimore remained relatively unhindered and the prospering city attracted the older Gilmor from Maryland's Eastern Shore. In 1782 the young Baltimore merchant entered a partnership with the wealthy and powerful William Bingham (see entry for 21 May 1787). As a result of the death of one of the other partners, the firm was reorganized under the name of Robert Gilmor & Co. two years later (*Pa. Mag.*, 61 [1937], 396–97). Gilmor's ensuing success led a member of the famous Baring family to remark in 1799 that the older Gilmor was "by far the best merchant in the United States" and "the family looks likely to last" (ALBERTS, 415). That same year the business did become a family concern when Gilmor's sons, including Robert Gilmor, Jr., became partners in the firm and its name changed to Robert Gilmor & Sons. The younger Gilmor became famous for his philanthropy and support of the arts in Baltimore, but he also used his wealth to put together a valuable autograph collection. This hobby may be the reason why Jared Sparks sent Gilmor the page from GW's diary containing the above entry (obituary in the *Baltimore American*, 2 Dec. 1848, quoted in *Md. Hist. Mag.*, 17 [1922], 231; *Pa. Mag.*, 14 [1880], 182; see also illus., I:xliii.

24. Morning clear—Wind at No. Et. and Mer. 39. Calm afterwards. Mer. 46 at Night. Mrs. Swanwick dined here. Mrs. Stuart & family went up to Alex.

25. Morning a little lowering—brisk wind from South and Mer. at 46. At Night it was 59. Mr. & Mrs. Liston and Mr. Gilmar left this after breakfast and Mr. Lawe. Washington Junior came here at night.

26. Morning very heavy with drippings now & then of Rain. Wind Southerly & Mer. at 58. Clear afterwards—wind in the same place & Mer. 61 at Night. Doctr. Stuart & family, and young McCarty returned here to Dinner.

27. Morning heavy, with the Wind at No. Et., and Mer. at 54. Same weather & wind thro' the day. Mer. 52 at Night. Doctr. Stuart & family and Mr. Lawe. Washington & young McCarty all went away after breakfast.

28. Morning very cloudy with the wind at No. Wt. & Mer. at 52. Clear afterwards and Mer. at 53. A Mr. Ridout an English Gentleman and his Lady dined here as did Mr. G. W. Craik. Mr. Lear set out for Harpers Ferry to make some arrangement with Colo. Parker respecting Cantoning the Troops.

Col. Thomas Parker (d. 1820) was in charge of establishing the winter quarters for three of the new United States Army regiments, which were to be located in the neighborhood of Harpers Ferry (GW to Gov. Benjamin Ogle, 28 Oct. 1799, DLC:GW).

29.   Morning perfectly clear and Calm. Mer. at 44. Extremely pleasant all day. Mer. 52 at Night. Colo. Griffen Mr. Law and a Mr. Valangin (an Engh. Gentleman introduced by Mr. Barthw. Dandridge). The latter went away afterwards.

Charles W. Valangin, the son of Dr. de Valangin of London, came to the United States with the intention of making it his permanent residence. He planned to travel throughout the states before deciding where to buy a farm. A man "of liberal Education," Valangin had "made Law & Physic his more particular Studies" and was especially interested in agriculture. Dandridge had written him a letter of introduction to GW because he knew of GW's desire "to encourage improvement of our husbandry by the introduction of farmers of good character" and felt Valangin's information on modern English farming methods would make him a welcome visitor to Mount Vernon. Dandridge wrote that Valangin brought with him samples of many varieties of English seed which Dandridge "advised him in the first instance to entrust to yr. care & which he will do with pleasure" (Bartholomew Dandridge, Jr., to GW, 1 July 1799, DLC:GW).

30.   Morning again clear & calm, Mer. at 43. Calm all day, and Mer. 50 at Night.

31.   Clear morning—wind at So. Et. & Mer. at 48. Afterwards the wind got to So. Wt. & blew pretty fresh. Mer. 56 at Night. Colo. Griffen & Mr. Law went away after breakfast and Mr. William Craik came here in the Afternn.

November

1.   Morning clear. A little breeze from the northward. Mer. at 55. Clear all day, & calm in the Afternoon. Mr. Craik went away after Breakfast. Mer. 49 at Night.

2.   Morning clear. Mer. at 45. Wind at So. Wt. Afternoon a little hazy with indications of Rain. Mr. Jno. Fairfax (formerly an overseer of mine) came here before dinner and stayed all Night.

John Fairfax resigned from GW's employ in Dec. 1790 and settled in Monongalia County, where he became a justice of the peace in 1794 and later represented that county in the Virginia House of Delegates (1809–10, 1814–15). His first wife, Mary Byrne, of Virginia, bore him two sons, and his second wife, Anne Lloyd Franklin, of Charles County, Md., bore him two more, one of whom was named George Washington Fairfax.

3.   Morning Cloudy. Wind at No. Et. & Mer. at 42. Clear Evening. Mer. at 42. Mr. Valangin came to dinner.

4th.   Morning clear—Wind (though but little of it) No. Wt. and Mer. 34. A very large & white frost—remarkably clear & fine all day and nearly calm. Mer. 50 at Night. A Mr. Teakle from Accomack County dined here & returned as did Doctr. Craik. Mr. Lear returned from Berkeley.

MR. TEAKLE: There were several families named Teackle in Accomack County. This is probably either John Teackle of Kegotank or John Teackle of Craddock.

5th.   Morning and the whole day calm—clear & pleasant. Set out on a trip to Difficult-run to view some Land I had there & some belonging to Mr. Jno. Gill who had offered it to me in discharge of Rent which he was owing me. Dined at Mr. Nicholas Fitzhughs and lodged at Mr. Corbin Washingtons.

DIFFICULT-RUN: On his 15 Oct. visit John Gill offered to sign over some of his own land on Difficult Run to pay back rents he owed to GW (GW to Gill, 19 Oct. 1799, NN: Washington Papers; GW to Charles Little, 20 Nov. 1799, DLC:GW).

Corbin Washington had lived for many years at Walnut Farm, originally a part of the Bushfield farm in Westmoreland County, but by October 1799 was living at a home called Selby in Fairfax County (WAYLAND [1], 125).

6.   Set out from thence after 8 Oclk. being detained by sprinkling Rain, & much appearance of it until that hour. Reached Wiley's Tavern near Difficult Bridge to Breakfast and then proceeded to Survey my own Land. The day clearing & the weather becoming pleasant.

WILEY'S TAVERN: James Wiley was licensed by Fairfax County to keep a tavern from as early as 1790 until at least the second decade of the nineteenth century. For many years his tavern was located on the south side of the bridge over Difficult Run. This tavern may be the "Shepherd's Tavern" referred to by GW in 1784 (SPROUSE [2], 2:35; HARRISON [1], 570; see entry for 1 Sept. 1784, n.1). MY OWN LAND: See entry for 1 Sept. 1784, n.1.

7.   Weather remarkably fine. Finished Surveying my own Tract & the Land belonging to Gill—returning, as the Night before to Wileys Tavern.

John Gill's land lay on both sides of Difficult Run near the bridge. For this surveying GW brought along a surveyor and several local residents to help find old boundary markers (GW to John Gill, 12 Nov. 1799, DLC:GW).

8.   Morning very heavy and about 9 oclock it commenced Raining which it continued to do steadily through the day—notwithstanding which I proceed to ascertain by actual measurement the

qualities. This being finished betwn. 12 & 1 oclock I returned to Wiley's Tavern & stayed there the remainder of the day.

THE QUALITIES: GW was unimpressed by Gill's land. The 85 acres Gill specifically was offering GW were "not only extremely hilly & broken, but much worn and gullied. The (uninhabited) house thereon, is tumbling down, the Fence around the field is in ruins; and . . . no part of the land within less than 80 rod of mine" (GW to John Gill, 12 Nov. 1799, DLC: GW). GW made a counterproposal but died before any agreement was reached.

9. Morning & whole day clear warm & pleasant. Set out a little after 8 Oclock. Viewed my building in the Fedl. City. Dined at Mr. Laws & lodged at Mr. Thos. Peter's.

10. Still remarkably fine, clear & pleasant; Wind Southerly; Returned home about Noon. Mr. Law, Mr. Barry Mr. White & Doctr. Thornton came to Dinner & stayed all Night. Mer. 55 at Night.

11. Morning a little lowering & wind Southerly. Mer. 55 at Night. The Gentlemen above mentioned went away after breakft.

12. It rained a little in the Night & this Morning. Mer. at 50 — But the Wind getting to No. Wt. it turned cold but did not clear (although it ceased raining about 10 Oclock), until afternoon. Mer. 42 at Night.

13. Morning clear — Wind at No. W. and Mer. 36. Clear all day & Wind fresh, but not cold. Mer. 42 at N.

14. Morning foggy — or rather Smoaky. Wind (tho' but little of it) Southerly and Mer. at 40. About 9 it came out at No. Wt. & blew pretty fresh. Mr. Valangen came to dinner & stayed all night.

15. Morning very smoaky — but little wind and Mer. at 39. Calm all day. Rode to visit Mr. now Lord Fairfax who was just got home from a Trip to England. Retd. to dinner.

While in England, Bryan Fairfax applied for certification as eighth Baron Fairfax of Cameron, succeeding his deceased cousin Robert Fairfax (d. 1793), seventh Baron Fairfax of Cameron. In May 1800 his claim was accepted by the House of Lords.

16. Clear & calm all day. Mer. at 42 in the morning & 52 at Night. Doctr. Craik came here in the afternoon on a visit to sick people.

17.   A very heavy & thick fog—morning calm, & Mer. at 41. About 2 oclock the Sun came out and the afternoon was pleasant. Went to Church in Alexandria & dined with Mr. Fitzhugh. On my return fd. young Mr. McCarty here on his way back from the Federal City. Young McCarty came to Dinr.

18.   Morning clear with the Wind very fresh from the Southward and Mer. at 48. Cloudy afterwards, with Rain from No. Wt. abt. 3 or 4 oclock. Mer. 58 at highest and 50 at Night.

19.   Morning clear & wind fresh & cold from No. Wt. Mer. at 40 —at highest 46 and at Night 33.

20.   Morning clear & cold. Wind at No. Wt. and Ice. Mer. at 27. Calm in the afternoon & Mer. 34 at Night. Mr. McCarty went away after breakfast and Mrs. Summers—Midwife for Mrs. Lewis came here abt. 3 Oclk.

21.   Morning perfectly clear & calm. A remarkably white hoar frost and Mer. at 30—but little wind all day. Mer. 41 at Night. Mrs. Stuart and the two eldest Miss Stuarts came here to dinner.

22.   Morning a little lowering & raw, with appearances of Snow. Mer. at 41 and Wind Southerly. Clear afternoon & calm. Colo. Carrington & Lady came in the afternn.

Lt. Col. Edward Carrington was married to Elizabeth Jaquelin Ambler Brent (1765–1842), daughter of Jaquelin Ambler (1742–1798) and Mary Burwell Ambler. She was the widow of William Brent, Jr. (c.1755–1786), son of William Brent (1733–1782) of Richland, Stafford County.

23.   Early morning, had much the appearance of Snow; Wind Southerly and Mer. at 40. Clear & mild afterwards. Mer. 54 at Night. Colo. Carrington & Lady went away after Breakfast. Doctr. Craik came to dinner & Doctr. Stuart at Night.

24.   Morning calm & clear. Mer. at 41. Fresh Southerly wind afterwards with great appearances of Rain. Mer. 58 at Night.

25.   A little rain had fallen in the night. Morning cloudy. Wind brisk from the Southward and Mer. at 52. After 10 oclock the Clouds dispelled, and it became a clear & pleasant day. Mer. 50 at Night. Doctr. Craik & Doctr. Stuart both went away after Breakfast.

26.   Morning clear. Mer. at 31—wind at No. Wt. Cold & fresh all day. Mer. 30 at Night.

27.   Morning clear—Wind Southerly and Mer. at 30. Wind, and appearances of Clouds afterwards, variable. Mer. 34 at Night. Doctr. Craik who was sent for to Mrs. Lewis (& who was delivered of a daughter abt. [   ] oclock in the forenoon) came to Breakfast & stayed [to] dinner. Mr. Dublois dined here, and both went away afterwards.

Eleanor Parke (Nelly) Custis Lewis's daughter was named Frances Parke Lewis (d. 1875). DUBLOIS: probably Lewis Deblois.

28.   Morning Cloudy—Wind Southerly and Mer. at 32. About 2 oclock it began to rain & continued to do so all the afternoon. Mer. 33 at Night. Colo. & Mrs. Carrington came to Dinner.

29.   Morning until about 9 Oclock Snowing—but not to lay on the grd. Mer. at 33 and wind at No. Wt. but neither hard nor cold. Afterwards it increased & turned colder. Young D. McCarty came to dinner and Mr. Howell Lewis & wife after dinner.

Howell Lewis's wife was Ellen Hackley Pollard Lewis (1776–1859).

30.   Morning cloudy—but no appearance of Rain. Wind So. W. but soon Shifted to No. Wt. Mer. at 24 in the morning & 31 at Night. Colo. & Mrs. Carrington went away after B[reakfas]t.

December

1.   Morning clear & but little Wd.—that Southerly. Mer. 26. Lowering towards evening. Mer. 36. Mr. Foot dined here.

2.   Rained in the Night. Morning heavy. Wind Southerly and Mer. at 36. Afternoon calm, & less clouded. Mer. 38. Lord Fairfax, Lady, Daughter & Miss Dennison dined here.

3.   Morning extremely foggy. Mer. at 38 and wind what there was of it Southerly. Abt. 2 oclock the fog dispelled and it became extremely pleasant. Mrs. Stuart & daughters went away after breakfast.

4.   Morning clear—wind at No. Wt. and Mer. at 36. From 10 oclock until 2 very like for Snow. It then cleared & became mild & pleasant. Mer. 38 at N.

5.   Morning raining and it continued to do so moderately through the day with the Wind at So. Et. Mer. 38 in the Morning & 36 at Night.

6.   Morning heavy, with appearances of clearing now & then, but about 2 oclock it set in to raining. Mer. 34 in the morning & 37 at Night.

7.   Rainy morning, with the Wind at No. Et. & Mer. at 37. Afternoon clear & pleasant wind westerly. Mer. 41 at Night. Dined at Lord Fairfax's.

8th.   Morning perfectly clear, calm and pleasant; but about 9 oclock the wind came from the No. Wt. and blew fresh. Mer. 38 in the morning and 40 at Night.

9.   Morning clear & pleasant, with a light Wind from No. W. Mer. at 33. Pleasant all day—afternoon Calm. Mer. 39 at Night. Mr. Howell Lewis & wife set off on their return home after breakfast and Mr. Lawe. Lewis and Washington Custis on a journy. to N. Kent.

10.   Morning clear & calm. Mer. at 31. Afternoon lowering. Mer. at 42 and wind brisk from the Southward. A very large hoar frost this morng.

11.   But little wind and Raining. Mer. 44 in the Morning and 38 at Night. About 9 oclock the Wind shifted to No. Wt. & it ceased raining but contd. Cloudy. Lord Fairfax, his Son Thos. and daughter—Mrs. Warner Washington & son Whiting—and Mr. Jno. Herbert dined here & returned after dinner.

12.   Morning Cloudy—Wind at No. Et. & Mer. 33. A large circle round the Moon last Night. About 1 oclock it began to snow—soon after to Hail and then turned to a settled cold Rain. Mer. 28 at Night.

13.   Morning Snowing & abt. 3 Inches deep. Wind at No. Et. & Mer. at 30. Contg. Snowing till 1 Oclock and abt. 4 it became

Doctors James Craik and Elisha Cullen Dick. (Richmond Academy of Medicine)

perfectly clear. Wind in the same place but not hard. Mer. 28 at Night.

On 12 Dec. in the midst of the day's severe weather GW rode out to supervise winter activities at the various farms, becoming wet and chilled in the course of his ride. On the 13th, in spite of a developing cold and sore throat, late in the day he went out on the front lawn to mark some trees for cutting. During the night he awoke with an inflammation of the throat but dissuaded Mrs. Washington from waking any members of the household until morning. Through the day of 14 Dec. he received various treatments commonly in use for such an illness, and he was attended by doctors James Craik, Gustavus Richard Brown, and Elisha Cullen Dick. On the evening of 14 Dec. GW died in his bed at Mount Vernon (see FREEMAN, 7:618–25).

Chamber clock originally owned by GW's physician, Dr. Elisha Cullen Dick
(Alexandria-Washington Lodge No. 22, A.F. & A.M., Alexandria, Va.)

Undated Diary Fragment

March

2d. Planted 3 French Walnuts & 8 English Walnuts in new Garden. Note the French Walnuts next the Schoolhouse & 8 steps asundr.

This undated fragment from PHi: Gratz Collection is from one of the early diaries, possibly 1763.

7. Sowed 50 pints of Clover Seed & 20 pints of Timothy at the Mill.

17. Began to Sow at Muddy hole and on

20. Finished—Sowing 59 Bushels—Oats. Note John Alton had sowed 14½ Bushls. Do.

29. Grafted sevl. kinds of Fruits as pr. Memm. at the Latter part of this Book.

30. Began to Sow Lucern below Garden.

31. Finished Sowing of Ditto after Collo. Landon Carters direction's contained in a Letter to Collo. P— T—.

Col. Landon Carter (1710–1778) of Sabine Hall in Richmond County was the son of Robert "King" Carter and his second wife, Elizabeth Landon Willis Carter. Landon Carter held many county and parish offices, including that of county lieutenant. From 1752 to 1768 he served as one of the most active and influential members of the House of Burgesses, becoming one of the chief defenders of its rights and actions in a steady flow of pamphlets and essays. Carter strongly supported the prosecution of the war against the French during the French and Indian War and just as strongly opposed later British efforts to encroach on the rights of the colonists. COLLO. P— T—: GW is almost certainly referring to Presley Thornton (1721–1769) of Northumberland House in Northumberland County. Presley Thornton, a son of Col. Anthony Thornton and Winifred Presley Thornton, served in the House of Burgesses 1748–60 and on the council 1760–69.

[March]

13.   Put up 3 lambs to fatten.

16.   Sowed Tobacco Seed at Doeg Run. Also sowed Clover, Timothy & Lucerne by Garden gate—1st. Row Clover, next Timothy, & then Lucerne.
   Sowed Tobacco Seed at Muddy hole. Note out of a Peck of Timothy Seed in the Chaff was got 5 pints of Clean Se⟨ed.⟩

17.   Sowed Tobo. Seed at all Quarters.

Repository Symbols
and Abbreviations

Bibliography

Index

Repository Symbols and Abbreviations

CSmH	Henry E. Huntington Library, San Marino, Calif.
CtY	Yale University, New Haven
DLC	Library of Congress
DLC:GW	George Washington Papers, Library of Congress
DMS	[Masons] Supreme Council, Ancient and Accepted Scottish Rite, Washington, D.C.
DNA	National Archives
MdAA	Maryland Hall of Records, Annapolis
MdAN	U.S. Naval Academy, Annapolis, Md.
MdBAr	Archdiocese of Baltimore
MeHi	Maine Historical Society, Portland
MH	Harvard University, Cambridge
MHi	Massachusetts Historical Society, Boston
MHi-A	Adams Papers, Massachusetts Historical Society, Boston
MIU-C	Clements Library, University of Michigan, Ann Arbor
NBLiHi	Long Island Historical Society, Brooklyn, N.Y.
NbO	Omaha Public Library, Nebraska
NIC	Cornell University, Ithaca, N.Y.
NcWsM	Moravian Archives, Winston-Salem, N.C.
NhD	Dartmouth College, Hanover, N.H.
NjMoNP	Morristown National Historical Park, Morristown, N.J.
NjP	Princeton University
NN	New York Public Library
PHi	Historical Society of Pennsylvania, Philadelphia
PPAmP	American Philosophical Society, Philadelphia
PPRF	Rosenbach Foundation, Philadelphia
P.R.O.	Public Record Office, London
PU	University of Pennsylvania, Philadelphia
RPJCB	John Carter Brown Library, Brown University, Providence
ScCM	Medical College of the State of South Carolina, Charleston
ViHi	Virginia Historical Society, Richmond
ViMtV	Mount Vernon Ladies' Association of the Union
ViU	University of Virginia, Charlottesville

Bibliography

ABERNETHY

Thomas Perkins Abernethy. *Western Lands and the American Revolution.* 1937. Reprint, New York: Russell & Russell, 1959.

ADAMS [2]

Charles Francis Adams, ed. *The Works of John Adams, Second President of the United States: With a Life of the Author, Notes, and Illustrations.* 10 vols. Boston: Little, Brown, and Co., 1850–56.

AGNEW

Daniel Agnew. "A Biographical Sketch of Governor Richard Howell, of New Jersey." *Pennsylvania Magazine of History and Biography,* 22 (1898), 221–30.

ALBERTS

Robert C. Alberts. *The Golden Voyage: The Life and Times of William Bingham, 1752–1804.* Boston: Houghton Mifflin Co., 1969.

ANDREWS

Matthew Page Andrews. *The Fountain Inn Diary.* New York: Richard R. Smith, 1948.

ANNALS OF CONGRESS

Joseph Gales, ed. *The Annals of Congress: The Debates and Proceedings in the Congress of the United States.* 42 vols. Washington, D.C.: Gales and Seaton, 1834–56.

ARNETT

Ethel Stephens Arnett. *Greensboro, North Carolina: The County Seat of Guilford.* Chapel Hill: University of North Carolina Press, 1955.

ASBURY

Elmer T. Clark, J. Manning Potts, and Jacob S. Payton, eds. *The Journal and Letters of Francis Asbury.* 3 vols. London: Epworth Press, and Nashville, Tenn.: Abingdon Press, 1958.

ASHE

Samuel A'Court Ashe, ed. *Biographical History of North Carolina from Colonial*

Times to the Present. 8 vols. Greensboro, N.C.: C. L. Van Noppen, 1905–17.

ASP   Walter Lowrie et al., eds. *American State Papers, Documents, Legislative, and Executive, of the Congress of the United States*. 38 vols. Washington, D.C.: Gales and Seaton, 1832–61.

ATTMORE   William Attmore. *Journal of a Tour to North Carolina by William Attmore, 1787*. Ed. Lida Tunstall Rodman. James Sprunt Historical Publications, vol. 17, no. 2. Chapel Hill: University of North Carolina, 1922.

BACON-FOSTER   Corra Bacon-Foster. *Early Chapters in the Development of the Patomac Route to the West*. Washington, D.C.: Columbia Historical Society, 1912.

BAGNALL   William R. Bagnall. *The Textile Industries of the United States*. Cambridge, Mass.: Riverside Press, 1893.

BAKER [2]   William Spohn Baker. *Washington after the Revolution*. Philadelphia: J. B. Lippincott Co., 1898.

BALDWIN [3]   Leland D. Baldwin. *Whiskey Rebels*. 1939. Reprint, Pittsburgh: University of Pittsburgh Press, 1968.

BALLAGH   James Curtis Ballagh, ed. *The Letters of Richard Henry Lee*. 2 vols. New York: Macmillan Co., 1911–14.

BARCK   Dorothy Barck, ed. *Papers of the Lloyd Family of the Manor of Queens Village, Lloyd's Neck, Long Island, New York, 1654–1826*. 2 vols. New York: New-York Historical Society, 1927.

BASS [2]   Robert D. Bass. *Gamecock: The Life and Campaigns of General Thomas Sumter*. New York: Holt, Rinehart and Winston, 1961.

BELL AND CRABBE   Earl L. Bell and Kenneth C. Crabbe. *The Augusta Chronicle, Indomitable Voice of Dixie, 1785–1960*. Athens: University of Georgia Press, 1960.

BEMIS [2]   Samuel Flagg Bemis. *The Diplomacy of the American Revolution*. 1935. Reprint,

Bloomington and London: Indiana University Press, 1967.

BIOG. UNIVERSELLE — *Biographie universelle ancienne et moderne* . . . . 45 vols. Paris: A. Thoisnier Desplaces, 1843–65.

BISHOP — J. Leander Bishop. *A History of American Manufactures from 1608 to 1860.* 3 vols. 1868. Reprint, New York: Augustus M. Kelley, 1966.

BLANTON — Wyndham B. Blanton. *Medicine in Virginia in the Eighteenth Century.* Richmond: Garrett & Massie, 1931.

BLOUNT — Alice Barnwell Keith and William H. Masterson, eds. *The John Gray Blount Papers.* 3 vols. Raleigh, N.C.: State Department of Archives and History, 1952–65.

BOATNER [1] — Mark Mayo Boatner III. *Encyclopedia of the American Revolution.* New York: David McKay Co., 1966.

BOATNER [2] — Mark Mayo Boatner III. *Landmarks of the American Revolution.* Harrisburg, Pa.: Stackpole Books, 1973.

BRACKENRIDGE [1] — Henry Marie Brackenridge. *History of the Whiskey Insurrection in Western Pennsylvania, Commonly Called the Whiskey Insurrection, 1794.* Pittsburgh: W. S. Haven, 1859.

BRACKENRIDGE [2] — Hugh H. Brackenridge. *Incidents of the Insurrection in the Western Parts of Pennsylvania in the Year 1794.* Philadelphia: John McCulloch, 1795.

BROCKETT — Franklin London Brockett. *The Lodge of Washington: A History of the Alexandria Washington Lodge, No. 22, A.F. and A.M. of Alexandria, Va.* Alexandria: George E. French, 1876.

BROWN [4] — Douglas Summers Brown. *The Catawba Indians, the People of the River.* Columbia: University of South Carolina Press, 1966.

BRUMBAUGH [2] — Gaius Marcus Brumbaugh. *Maryland Records: Colonial, Revolutionary, County, and Church from Original Sources.* 2 vols. 1915. Reprint, Lancaster, Pa.: Genealogical Publishing Co., Baltimore, 1975.

BRYAN

Wilhelmus Bogart Bryan. *A History of the National Capital, from Its Foundation through the Period of the Adoption of the Organic Act.* New York: Macmillan Co., 1914.

BRYDON

Anne Page Brydon. "A Small Diary of 1845: Anne Kinloch Meriwether and Her South Carolina Kin." *Magazine of Albemarle County History,* 33–34 (1975–76), 141–62.

BRYMNER

Douglas Brymner, ed. *Report on Canadian Archives, 1890.* Ottawa, Can.:

BUNKER

Mary Powell Bunker, comp. *Long Island Genealogies.* 1895. Reprint, Baltimore: Genealogical Publishing Co., 1976.

BURKE [1]

Sir Bernard Burke. *Burke's Genealogical and Heraldic History of the Landed Gentry of Ireland.* Ed. L. G. Pine. 4th ed. London: Burke's Peerage Ltd., 1958.

BURKE [2]

Peter Townend, ed. *Burke's Genealogical and Heraldic History of the Landed Gentry.* 3 vols. London: Burke's Peerage Limited, 1965–72.

CALLAHAN [3]

Edward William Callahan, ed. *List of Officers of the Navy of the United States and the Marine Corps from 1775 to 1890.* New York: L. R. Hamersly & Co., 1901.

CANDLER [1]

Allen D. Candler, comp. *The Revolutionary Records of the State of Georgia.* 3 vols. Atlanta: Franklin-Turner Co., 1908.

CANDLER [2]

Allen D. Candler, comp. *The Colonial Records of the State of Georgia.* 26 vols. Atlanta: Franklin Printing and Publishing Co., Franklin-Turner Co., and C. P. Byrd, State Printer, 1904–19.

CARTER [4]

Clarence E. Carter and John Porter Bloom, eds. *The Territorial Papers of the United States.* 27 vols. Washington, D.C.: Government Printing Office, 1934–69.

CASSELL

Frank A. Cassell. *Merchant Congressman in the Young Republic: Samuel Smith of Maryland, 1752–1839.* Madison: University of Wisconsin Press, 1971.

Bibliography

CAUGHEY   John Walton Caughey. *McGillivray of the Creeks*. Norman: University of Oklahoma Press, 1938.

CHASTELLUX   François Jean de Beauvoir, Marquis de Chastellux. *Travels in North America in the Years 1780, 1781, and 1782*. 2 vols. Ed. Howard C. Rice, Jr. Chapel Hill: University of North Carolina Press, 1963.

CHRISTIAN   W. Asbury Christian. *Richmond: Her Past and Present*. Richmond: L. H. Jenkins, 1912.

CLARK [5]   Allen C. Clark. "Captain James Barry." *Records of the Columbia Historical Society*, 42–43 (1940–41), 1–16.

CLUNN   John Hugg Clunn. "March on Pittsburgh, 1794." Ed. Nicholas Wainwright. *Pennsylvania Magazine of History and Biography*, 71 (1947), 44–67.

COLLES   Christopher Colles. *A Survey of the Roads of the United States of America, 1789*. Ed. Walter W. Ristow. Cambridge: Harvard University Press, 1961.

COMETTI   Elizabeth Cometti. "John Rutledge, Jr., Federalist." *Journal of Southern History*, 13 (1947), 186–219.

CONTENSON   Ludovic de Contenson. *La Société des Cincinnati de France et La Guerre d'Amerique, 1778–1783*. Paris: Editions Auguste Picard, 1934.

COOK   Roy Bird Cook. *Washington's Western Lands*. Strasburg, Va.: Shenandoah Publishing House, 1930.

CORDLE   Charles G. Cordle. "The Academy of Richmond County." *Southern Association Quarterly*, 3 (1939), 78–84.

COULTER   E. Merton Coulter. "The Ante-Bellum Academy Movement in Georgia." *Georgia Historical Quarterly*, 5 (1921), 11–42.

CROFUT   Florence S. Marcy Crofut. *Guide to the History and the Historic Sites of Connecticut*. 2 vols. New Haven: Yale University Press, 1937.

Bibliography

CUSTIS

George Washington Parke Custis. *Recollections and Private Memoirs of Washington.* New York: Derby & Jackson, 1860.

DALEY

John M. Daley. *Georgetown University: Origin and Early Years.* Washington, D.C.: Georgetown University Press, 1957.

DAVIDSON

Nora F. M. Davidson. "Revolutionary Services of Robert Bolling, of Petersburg." *Virginia Magazine of History and Biography,* 12 (1904–5), 154–56.

DECATUR

Stephen Decatur, Jr. *Private Affairs of George Washington, from the Records and Accounts of Tobias Lear, Esquire, His Secretary.* Boston: Houghton Mifflin Co., 1933.

DECONDE [2]

Alexander DeConde. *Entangling Alliance: Politics & Diplomacy under George Washington.* Durham, N.C.: Duke University Press, 1958.

DE PAUW

Linda Grant De Pauw, ed. *Documentary History of the First Federal Congress of the United States of America.* Baltimore: Johns Hopkins University Press, 1972—.

DIARIES

John C. Fitzpatrick, ed. *The Diaries of George Washington, 1748–1799.* 4 vols. Boston and New York: Houghton Mifflin Co., 1925.

DILL

Alonzo Thomas Dill. *Governor Tryon and His Palace.* Chapel Hill: University of North Carolina Press, 1955.

DOWNING [2]

Margaret Brent Downing. "The Development of the Catholic Church in the District of Columbia from Colonial Times until the Present." *Records of the Columbia Historical Society,* 15 (1912), 25–53.

DOWNING [3]

Margaret Brent Downing. "Literary Landmarks: Being a Brief Account of Celebrated Authors Who Have Lived in Washington, the Location of Their Homes, and What They Have Written." *Records of the Columbia Historical Society,* 19 (1916), 22–60.

DUER

William Alexander Duer. *Reminiscences of an Old Yorker.* New York: W. L. Andrews, 1867.

Bibliography

DUKE ENDOWMENT

The Duke Endowment: Sixth Annual Report of the Orphan Section, 1930. Charlotte, N.C.: The Duke Endowment, 1931.

DUMBAULD [2]

Edward Dumbauld. *The Bill of Rights.* Norman: University of Oklahoma Press, 1957.

EBERLEIN & HUBBARD

Harold Donaldson Eberlein and Cortlandt Van Dyke Hubbard. *Historic Houses of George-Town & Washington City.* Richmond: Dietz Press, 1958.

ECKER

Grace Dunlop Ecker. *A Portrait of Old George Town.* 2d ed. Richmond: Dietz Press, 1951.

EGLE [2]

William H. Egle, ed. *Notes and Queries, Historical, Biographical, and Genealogical, Relating Chiefly to Interior Pennsylvania.* Reprint. 2 vols. 1st-2d ser., 1894–95.

EISEN

Gustavus A. Eisen. *Portraits of Washington.* 3 vols. New York: Robert Hamilton & Associates, 1932.

ESPENSHADE

A. Howry Espenshade. *Pennsylvania Place Names.* State College: Pennsylvania State College, 1925.

EVANS [3]

Paul Demund Evans. *The Holland Land Company.* Buffalo: Buffalo Historical Society, 1924.

EXECUTIVE JOURNAL, 1

Journal of the Executive Proceedings of the Senate of the United States of America. Vol. 1. Washington, D.C.: Duff Green, 1828.

FERGUSON

Eugene S. Ferguson. *Truxton of the* Constellation. Baltimore: Johns Hopkins Press, 1956.

FINDLEY

William Findley. *History of the Insurrection, in the Four Western Counties of Pennsylvania, in the Year M.DCC.XCIV, with a Recital of the Circumstances Specially Connected Therewith, and an Historical Review of the Previous Situations of the Country.* Philadelphia: Samuel Harrison Smith, 1796.

FORD [6]

David Ford. "Journal of an Expedition Made in the Autumn of 1794 . . . into Western Pennsylvania." *New Jersey His-*

torical Society Proceedings, 8 (1859), 76–88.

FREEMAN   Douglas Southall Freeman. *George Washington*. 7 vols. New York: Charles Scribner's Sons, 1949–57.

FRIES   Adelaide L. Fries et al., eds. *Records of the Moravians in North Carolina*. 11 vols. Raleigh, N.C.: Edwards & Broughton Printing Co., 1922–69.

GADSDEN   Christopher Gadsden. *The Writings of Christopher Gadsden, 1746–1805*. Ed. Richard Walsh. Columbia: University of South Carolina Press, 1966.

GAINES [1]   William H. Gaines, Jr. "Courthouses of Brunswick and Greensville Counties." *Virginia Cavalcade*, 19 (Winter 1970), 36–41.

GAINES [2]   William H. Gaines, Jr. "Courthouses of Bedford and Charlotte Counties." *Virginia Cavalcade*, 21 (Summer 1971), 5–13.

GAINES [3]   William H. Gaines, Jr. "Courthouses of Prince Edward and Nottoway Counties." *Virginia Cavalcade*, 20 (Autumn 1970), 40–46.

GAINES [4]   William H. Gaines, Jr. "Courthouses of Halifax and Pittsylvania Counties." *Virginia Cavalcade*, 20 (Spring 1971), 5–11.

GAINES [5]   William H. Gaines, Jr. "Courthouses of Cumberland and Powhatan Counties." *Virginia Cavalcade*, 20 (Winter 1968), 38–41.

GALLATIN   Albert Gallatin. *The Speech of Albert Gallatin, a Representative from the County of Fayette, in the House of Representatives of the General Assembly of Pennsylvania*. . . . Philadelphia: William W. Woodward, 1795.

GOTTSCHALK   Louis Gottschalk, ed. *The Letters of Lafayette to Washington, 1777–1799*. New York: privately printed, 1944.

GOULD   William Gould. "Journal by William Gould during an Expedition into Pennsylvania in 1794." *New Jersey Historical Society Proceedings*, 3 (1848–49), 173–91.

GRANGER   Mary Granger, ed. *Savannah River Plantations*. Savannah: Georgia Historical Society, 1947.

GREEN [2]

Edwin L. Green. *A History of Richland County*. Columbia, S.C.: R. L. Bryan Co., 1932.

GROVES

Joseph A. Groves. *The Alstons and Allstons of North and South Carolina, Compiled from English, Colonial and Family Records with Personal Reminiscences; Also Notes of Some Allied Families.* 1901. Reprint, Easley, S.C.: Southern Historical Press, 1976.

HAMILTON [2]

Harold C. Syrett et al., eds. *The Papers of Alexander Hamilton.* New York: Columbia University Press, 1961—.

HARRISON [1]

Fairfax Harrison. *Landmarks of Old Prince William.* Reprint. Berryville, Va.: Chesapeake Book Co., 1964.

HEADS OF FAMILIES, MD.

Heads of Families at the First Census of the United States Taken in the Year 1790: Maryland. 1907. Reprint, Baltimore: Genealogical Publishing Co., 1965.

HEADS OF FAMILIES, N.C.

Heads of Families at the First Census of the United States Taken in the Year 1790: North Carolina. Washington, D.C.: Government Printing Office, 1908.

HEADS OF FAMILIES, N.Y.

Heads of Families at the First Census of the United States Taken in the Year 1790: New York. Reprint. Baltimore: Genealogical Publishing Co., 1966.

HEADS OF FAMILIES, S.C.

Heads of Families at the First Census of the United States Taken in the Year 1790: South Carolina. Washington, D.C.: Government Printing Office, 1908.

HEADS OF FAMILIES, VA.

Heads of Families at the First Census of the United States Taken in the Year 1790: Virginia. 1908. Reprint, Baltimore: Genealogical Publishing Co., 1970.

HEITMAN [1]

Francis Bernard Heitman. *Historical Register of Officers of the Continental Army.* Washington, D.C.: F. B. Heitman, 1893.

HEITMAN [3]

Francis Bernard Heitman. *Historical Register of the United States Army.* 2 vols. Washington, D.C.: Government Printing Office, 1903.

HENDERSON

Archibald Henderson. *Washington's Southern Tour, 1791.* Boston and New York: Houghton Mifflin Co., 1923.

HENING

William Waller Hening, ed. *The Statutes at Large: Being a Collection of All the Laws of Virginia from the First Session of the Legislature, in the Year 1619.* 13 vols. New York, Philadelphia, Richmond: various publishers, 1819–23.

HILTZHEIMER

Jacob Cox Parsons, ed. *Extracts from the Diary of Jacob Hiltzheimer of Philadelphia, 1765–1798.* Philadelphia: Press of William F. Bell & Co., 1893.

HOLMES [2]

Jack D. L. Holmes. *Gayoso: The Life of a Spanish Governor in the Mississippi Valley, 1789–1799.* Baton Rouge: Louisiana State University Press for the Louisiana Historical Society, 1965.

HOUSE JOURNAL, 1

Journal of the House of Representatives of the United States. Vol. 1. Washington, D.C.: Gales and Seaton, 1826.

HOWARD & SHRIVER

J. Spence Howard and J. Alexis Shriver. "Routes Traveled by George Washington in Maryland" (Map). N.p.: Maryland Commission for the Celebration of the Two Hundredth Anniversary of the Birth of George Washington, c.1932.

HOWE

Charles E. Howe. "The Financial Institutions of Washington City in Its Early Days." *Records of the Columbia Historical Society,* 8 (1905), 1–42.

HOYT [2]

William D. Hoyt, Jr., ed. "The Calvert-Stier Correspondence." *Maryland Historical Magazine,* 38 (1943), 123–140.

HUME

Edgar Erskine Hume, ed. *General Washington's Correspondence concerning the Society of the Cincinnati.* Baltimore: Johns Hopkins Press, 1941.

HUMPHREYS

Henry H. Humphreys. "Who Built the First United States Navy?" *Pennsylvania Magazine of History and Biography,* 40 (1916), 385–411.

JANVIER

Thomas A. Janvier. *In Old New York.* New York: Harper & Brothers, 1894.

JAY

Henry P. Johnston. *The Correspondence and Public Papers of John Jay.* 4 vols. New York: G. P. Putnam's Sons, 1890–93.

Bibliography

JCC · Worthington Chauncey Ford et al., eds. *Journals of the Continental Congress, 1774–1789*. 34 vols. Washington, D.C.: Government Printing Office, 1904–37.

JEFFERSON [1] · Julian P. Boyd, ed. *The Papers of Thomas Jefferson*. Princeton, N.J.: Princeton University Press, 1950—.

JONES [3] · Rufus M. Jones. *The Quakers in the American Colonies*. London: Macmillan and Co., 1911.

JONES AND DUTCHER · Charles C. Jones, Jr., and Salem Dutcher. *Memorial History of Augusta, Georgia*. 1890. Reprint, Spartanburg, S.C.: Reprint Co., 1966.

JORDON · John C. Jordon. "York in Its Relation to the Revolution." *Historical Society of York County Proceedings and Collections*, 1 (1903), 27–53.

KAPPLER · Charles J. Kappler. *Indian Affairs: Laws and Treaties*. Vol. 2, 2d ed. Washington, D.C.: Government Printing Office, 1904.

KELLY [2] · Howard A. Kelly and Walter L. Burrage. *Dictionary of American Medical Biography*. New York and London: D. Appleton and Co., 1928.

KILMER · Kenton Kilmer and Donald Sweig. *The Fairfax Family in Fairfax County: A Brief History*. Fairfax, Va.: Fairfax County Office of Comprehensive Planning, 1975.

KILPATRICK · William H. Kilpatrick. "The Beginnings of the Public School System in Georgia." *Georgia Historical Quarterly*, 5 (1921), 3–19.

KIRKLAND AND KENNEDY · Thomas J. Kirkland and Robert M. Kennedy. *Historic Camden: Colonial and Revolutionary*. Columbia, S.C.: The State Co., 1905.

LACHICOTTE · Alberta Morel Lachicotte. *Georgetown Rice Plantations*. Columbia, S.C.: State Printing Co., 1955.

LANDIS [2] · Charles I. Landis. "Jasper Yeates and His Times." *Pennsylvania Magazine of History and Biography*, 46 (1922), 199–231.

LEE & AGNEW · F. D. Lee and J. L. Agnew. *Historical Rec-*

ord of the City of Savannah. Savannah: J. H. Estill, 1869.

LEFLER AND NEWSOME   Hugh Talmage Lefler and Albert Ray Newsome. *North Carolina.* Chapel Hill: University of North Carolina Press, 1954.

LOCKEY   Joseph Byrne Lockey. *East Florida, 1783–85, a File of Documents Assembled.* . . . Berkeley: University of California Press, 1949.

LOUIS-PHILIPPE [1]   *Louis-Philippe, Memoirs, 1773–1793.* Trans. John Hardman. New York and London: Harcourt Brace Jovanovich, 1977.

LOUIS-PHILIPPE [2]   Suzanne D'Huart, ed. *Louis-Philippe, Journal de Mon Voyage d'Amérique.* Paris: Flammarion, 1976.

LOWDERMILK   Will H. Lowdermilk. *History of Cumberland Maryland.* 1878. Reprint, Baltimore: Regional Publishing Co., 1971.

LYLE   Maria Cook Nourse Lyle. "James Nourse of Virginia." *Virginia Magazine of History and Biography,* 8 (1900–1901), 199–202.

MCCALL   Ettie Tidwell McCall, comp. *Roster of Revolutionary Soldiers in Georgia and Other States.* 3 vols. 1941. Reprint, Baltimore: Genealogical Publishing Co., 1968–69.

MACLAY   Charles A. Beard, ed. *The Journal of William Maclay: United States Senator from Pennsylvania, 1789–1791.* 1927. Reprint, New York: Frederick Ungar Publishing Co., 1965.

MCCRADY   Edward McCrady. *The History of South Carolina in the Revolution, 1775–1780.* New York: Macmillan Co., 1901.

MCREE   Griffith J. McRee. *Life and Correspondence of James Iredell.* 2 vols. New York: D. Appleton and Co., 1857–58.

MAY   Dwight L. Smith. *The Western Journals of John May.* Cincinnati: Historical and Philosophical Society of Ohio, 1961.

MD. ARCH.   *Archives of Maryland.* Baltimore: Maryland Historical Society, 1883—.

MD. GUIDE   Edward C. Papenfuse et al., eds. *Maryland:*

Bibliography

A New Guide to the Old Line State. Baltimore: Johns Hopkins Press, 1976.

MEADE [3]   Robert Douthat Meade. *Patrick Henry, Practical Revolutionary*. Philadelphia and New York: J. B. Lippincott Co., 1969.

MIFFLIN   Warner Mifflin. *Defence of Warner Mifflin against Aspersions Cast on Him on Account of His Endeavors to Promote Righteousness, Mercy, and Peace among Mankind*. . . . Philadelphia: Samuel Sansom, Jr., 1796.

MITCHELL   Stewart Mitchell, ed. *New Letters of Abigail Adams, 1788–1801*. New York: Houghton Mifflin Co., 1947.

MOORE [1]   Gay Montague Moore. *Seaport in Virginia: George Washington's Alexandria*. Reprint. Charlottesville: University Press of Virginia, 1972.

MOORE [3]   John Bassett Moore. *History and Digest of the International Arbitrations to Which the United States Has Been a Party*. 6 vols. Washington, D.C.: Government Printing Office, 1898.

MOREAU DE SAINT-MÉRY   Moreau de Saint-Méry, Médéric Louis Élie. *Description topographique, physique, civile, politique, et historique de la partie française de l'Isle Saint-Dominque*. 3 vols. Paris: Société de l'Histoire des Colonies Françaises et Librairie Larose, 1958.

MORSE [2]   Jedidiah Morse. *The American Gazetteer*. Boston: S. Hall and Thomas & Andrews, 1797.

MOUZON   Henry Mouzon. "An Accurate Map of North and South Carolina . . . ." London: printed for Robert Sayer and J. Bennett, Map and Print-sellers, 1775.

MULKEARN AND PUGH   Lois Mulkearn and Edwin V. Pugh. *A Traveler's Guide to Historic Western Pennsylvania*. Pittsburgh: University of Pittsburgh Press, 1954.

NASATIR   Abraham P. Nasatir. *Spanish War Vessels on the Mississippi*. New Haven and London: Yale University Press, 1968.

NEEDLES   Samuel H. Needles. "The Governor's Mill,

and the Globe Mills, Philadelphia." *Pennsylvania Magazine of History and Biography*, 8 (1884), 279–99.

NEVIN — Alfred Nevin. *Churches of the Valley*. Philadelphia: Joseph M. Wilson, 1852.

N.C. 1800 CENSUS — Ronald Vern Jackson, Gary Ronald Teeples, and David Schaefermeyer, eds. *North Carolina 1800 Census Index*. Bountiful, Utah: Accelerated Indexing Systems, 1974.

N.C. STATE REC. — Walter Clark, ed. *The State Records of North Carolina*. 16 vols. Winston, N.C.: M. J. & J. C. Stewart, and Goldsboro, N.C.: Nash Brothers, Book and Job Printers, 1895–1906.

NOYES — Harriette Eliza Noyes, comp. *A Memorial History of Hampstead, New Hampshire*. Boston: George B. Reed, 1903.

O'BRIEN — Michael J. O'Brien. *George Washington's Associations with the Irish*. New York: P. J. Kenedy & Sons, 1937.

PALMER — John McAuley Palmer. *General Von Steuben*. New Haven: Yale University Press, 1937.

PA. ARCH. — Samuel Hazard et al., eds. *Pennsylvania Archives*. 9 ser., 138 vols. Philadelphia and Harrisburg: various publishers, 1852–1949.

PORCHER — Frederick A. Porcher. *The History of the Santee Canal*. 1875. Reprint, Moncks Corner, S.C.: South Carolina Public Service Authority, 1950.

POUND — Merritt B. Pound. *Benjamin Hawkins—Indian Agent*. Athens: University of Georgia Press, 1951.

POWELL [1] — Mary G. Powell. *The History of Old Alexandria, Virginia, from July 13, 1749, to May 24, 1861*. Richmond: William Byrd Press, 1928.

POWELL [3] — William S. Powell. *The North Carolina Gazetteer*. Chapel Hill: University of North Carolina, 1968.

PRICE [2] — Jacob M. Price. *France and the Chesapeake: A History of the French Tobacco Monopoly, 1674–1791, and of Its Relationship to the British and American Tobacco*

Trades. 2 vols. Ann Arbor: University of Michigan Press, 1973.

PRUSSING   Eugene E. Prussing. *The Estate of George Washington, Deceased.* Boston: Little, Brown, and Co., 1927.

RAMSEY   J. G. M. Ramsey. *The Annals of Tennessee to the End of the Eighteenth Century.* 1853. Reprint, Kingsport, Tenn.: Kingsport Press, 1926.

RAVENEL   Harriott Horry Ravenel. *Eliza Pinckney.* New York: Charles Scribner's Sons, 1909.

RAY   Worth S. Ray. *The Mecklenburg Signers and Their Neighbors.* Austin, Tex.: published by the author, 1946.

REARDON   John J. Reardon. *Edmund Randolph: A Biography.* New York: Macmillan Co., 1974.

REDD   John Redd. "Reminiscences of Western Virginia, 1770–1790." *Virginia Magazine of History and Biography,* 7 (1899–1900), 1–16, 113–28.

REPS   John W. Reps. *Tidewater Towns: City Planning in Colonial Virginia and Maryland.* Williamsburg, Va.: Colonial Williamsburg Foundation, 1972.

REYNOLDS AND FAUNT   Emily Bellinger Reynolds and Joan Reynolds Faunt. *Biographical Directory of the Senate of the State of South Carolina, 1776–1964.* Columbia: South Carolina Archives Department, 1964.

RICE   Howard C. Rice, Jr., and Anne S. K. Brown, eds. *The American Campaigns of Rochambeau's Army, 1780, 1781, 1782, 1783.* 2 vols. Princeton, N.J., and Providence: Princeton University Press and Brown University Press, 1972.

RISCH   Erna Risch. *Quartermaster Support of the Army: A History of the Corps, 1775–1939.* Washington, D.C.: Government Printing Office, 1962.

ROGERS [2]   George C. Rogers, Jr. *The History of Georgetown County, South Carolina.* Columbia: University of South Carolina Press, 1970.

[401]

ROOF

Katherine Metcalf Roof. *Colonel William Smith and Lady*. Boston: Houghton Mifflin Co., 1929.

RUMPLE

Jethro Rumple. *A History of Rowan County, North Carolina, Containing Sketches of Prominent Families and Distinguished Men, with an Appendix.* 1881. Reprint, Salisbury, N.C.: Elizabeth Maxwell Steele Chapter, Daughters of the American Revolution, [1929].

SALLEY [2]

Alexander Samuel Salley. *President Washington's Tour through South Carolina in 1791.* Bulletins of the Historical Commission of South Carolina, No. 12. Columbia, S.C.: printed for the Commission by the State Company, 1932.

SAVAGE

Henry Savage, Jr. *River of the Carolinas: The Santee.* 1956. Reprint, Chapel Hill: University of North Carolina Press, 1968.

S.C. 1800 CENSUS

Gary Ronald Teeples, Ronald Vern Jackson, and Richard Moore, eds. *South Carolina 1800 Census.* 2d ed. Provo, Utah: Accelerated Indexing Systems, 1975.

SCHARF [1]

J. Thomas Scharf and Thompson Westcott. *History of Philadelphia, 1609–1884.* 3 vols. Philadelphia: L. H. Everts & Co., 1884.

SCHARF [3]

John Thomas Scharf. *History of Western Maryland.* 2 vols. Philadelphia: Louis H. Everts, 1882.

SCHARF [5]

John Thomas Scharf. *History of Baltimore City and County.* 1881. Reprint, Baltimore: Regional Publishing Co., 1971.

SCHOEPF

Johann David Schoepf. *Travels in the Confederation.* Ed. and trans. Alfred J. Morrison. 2 vols. Philadelphia: William J. Campbell, 1911.

SCISCO

Louis Dow Scisco. "A Site for the 'Federal City.'" *Records of the Columbia Historical Society,* 57–59 (1961), 123–47.

SCOTT [2]

Joseph Scott. *The United States Gazetteer: Containing an Authentic Description of the Several States. Their Situation, Extent, Boundaries, Soil, Produce, Climate, Population, Trade, and Manufactures, Together*

Bibliography

with the Extent, Boundaries and Population of Their Respective Counties, Also, an Exact Account of the Cities, Towns, Harbours, Rivers, Bays, Lakes, Mountains. Philadelphia: Lund R. Bailey, 1795.

SCOTT AND WYATT James G. Scott and Edward A. Wyatt. *Petersburg's Story, a History*. Petersburg, Va.: Titmus Optical Co., 1960.

SEARSON John Searson. *Mount Vernon, a Poem.* Philadelphia: published for the author, [1799].

SLAUGHTER [3] Philip Slaughter. *A History of Bristol Parish, Va.* Richmond: J. W. Randolph & English, 1879.

SMITH [4] Thomas E. V. Smith. *The City of New York in the Year of Washington's Inauguration, 1789.* Intro. Joseph Veach Noble. Rev. ed. Riverside, Conn.: Chatham Press, 1972.

SMITH [5] Page Smith. *John Adams.* 2 vols. New York: Doubleday & Co., 1962.

SMITH [6] Albert Matthews. *Journal of William Loughton Smith, 1790–1791.* Cambridge, Mass.: University Press, 1917.

SMITH [7] Daniel M. Smith. "James Seagrove and the Mission to Tuckaubatchee, 1793." *Georgia Historical Quarterly,* 44 (1960), 41–55.

SMYTH John Ferdinand Dalziel Smyth. *A Tour in the United States of America: Containing an Account of the Present Situation of That Country; the Population, Agriculture, Commerce, Customs, and Manners of the Inhabitants . . . .* 2 vols. London: printed for G. Robinson, J. Robson, and J. Stewell, 1784.

SORLEY Merrow Egerton Sorley. *Lewis of Warner Hall: The History of a Family.* Columbia, Mo.: E. W. Stephens Co., 1937.

SPAULDING E. Wilder Spaulding. *His Excellency George Clinton.* New York: Macmillan Co., 1938.

SPRAGUE William B. Sprague. *Annals of the American Pulpit or Commemorative Notices of Distinguished American Clergymen of*

[403]

Various Denominations. 9 vols. New York: Robert Carter & Brothers, 1859.

SPROUSE [2]   Edith Moore Sprouse, ed. *A Surname and Subject Index of the Minute and Order Books of the County Court, Fairfax County, Virginia, 1783–1802.* Fairfax, Va.: Fairfax County Historical Commission, 1976.

SPROUSE [4]   Edith Moore Sprouse. *Mount Air, Fairfax County, Virginia.* Fairfax, Va.: Fairfax County Division of Planning, 1970.

1 STAT.   Richard Peters, ed. *The Public Statutes at Large of the United States of America.* Vol. 1. Boston: Charles C. Little and James Brown, 1845.

6 STAT.   Richard Peters, ed. *The Public Statutes at Large of the United States of America.* Vol. 6. Boston: Charles C. Little and James Brown, 1846.

ST. CLAIR PAPERS   William Henry Smith, ed. *The St. Clair Papers: The Life and Public Services of Arthur St. Clair, Soldier of the Revolutionary War; President of the Continental Congress, and Governor of the North-Western Territory with His Correspondence and Other Papers.* 2 vols. Cincinnati: Robert Clarke & Co., 1882.

STETSON [1]   Charles W. Stetson. *Four Mile Run Land Grants.* Washington, D.C.: Mimeoform Press, 1935.

STOKES   I. N. Phelps Stokes. *The Iconography of Manhattan Island.* 6 vols. New York: Robert H. Dodd, 1895–1928.

TAYLOR   B. F. Taylor. "Col. Thomas Taylor." *South Carolina Historical and Genealogical Magazine,* 27 (1926), 204–11.

THOMAS   Isaiah Thomas. *The History of Printing in America.* 1810. Reprint, New York: Weathervane Books, 1970.

THOMPSON   Benjamin F. Thompson. *History of Long Island from Its Discovery and Settlement to the Present Time.* 2 vols. 2d ed. rev. New York: Gould, Banks, & Co., 1843.

THORNBROUGH   Gayle Thornbrough, ed. *Outpost on the*

Bibliography

Wabash, 1787–1791. Indianapolis: Indiana Historical Society, 1957.

TORRENCE
Clayton Torrence, comp. *Virginia Wills and Administrations, 1632–1800: An Index of Wills Recorded in Local Courts of Virginia, 1632–1800, and of Administrations on Estates Shown by Inventories of the Estates of Intestates Recorded in Will (and Other) Books of Local Courts, 1632–1800.* 1930. Reprint, Baltimore: Genealogical Publishing Co., 1972.

TOUSEY
Thomas G. Tousey. *Military History of Carlisle and Carlisle Barracks.* Richmond: Dietz Press, 1939.

TRUMBULL [2]
Theodore Sizer, ed. *The Autobiography of Colonel John Trumbull, Patriot-Artist, 1756–1843.* 1953. Reprint, New York: Da Capo Press, 1970.

TWINING
Thomas Twining. *Travels in America 100 Years Ago.* New York and London: Harper & Brothers, 1893.

TYLER [1]
Lyon G. Tyler. "Original Records of the Phi Beta Kappa Society." *William and Mary Quarterly,* 1st ser., 4 (1895–96), 213–59.

TYLER [3]
Lyon G. Tyler. "William Short." *William and Mary Quarterly,* 1st ser., 4 (1895–96), 261–63.

VAN NESS
Allen C. Clark. "General John Peter Van Ness, a Mayor of the City of Washington, His Wife, Marcia, and Her Father, David Burnes." *Records of the Columbia Historical Society,* 22 (1919), 125–204.

VAUGHAN
Samuel Vaughan. "Minutes Made by S. V. from Stage to Stage on a Tour to Fort Pitt or Pittsburgh in Company with Mr. Michl. Morgan Obrian, from Thence by S. V. Only through Virginia, Maryland, & Pensylvania (18 June to 4 Sept. 1787)." Manuscript diary in the collection of the descendants of Samuel Vaughan.

VERME
Francesco dal Verme. *Seeing America and Its Great Men: The Journal and Letters of Count Francesco dal Verme, 1783–1784.* Ed. and trans. Elizabeth Cometti. Char-

[405]

lottesville: University Press of Virginia, 1969.

VSP William P. Palmer et al., eds. *Calendar of Virginia State Papers and Other Manuscripts.* 11 vols. Richmond: various publishers, 1875–93.

WALLACE [2] Willard M. Wallace. *Traitorous Hero: The Life and Fortunes of Benedict Arnold.* New York: Harper & Brothers, 1954.

WATLINGTON Patricia Watlington. *The Partisan Spirit, Kentucky Politics, 1779–1792.* New York: Atheneum for the Institute of Early American History and Culture at Williamsburg, Va., 1972.

WAYLAND [1] John Walter Wayland. *The Washingtons and Their Homes.* 1944. Reprint, Berryville: Virginia Book Co., 1973.

WEEKS Lyman Horace Weeks. *A History of Paper Manufacturing in the United States, 1690–1916.* New York: Lockwood Trade Journal Co., 1916.

WELLFORD Robert Wellford. "A Diary Kept by Dr. Robert Wellford, of Fredericksburg, Virginia, during the March of the Virginia Troops to Fort Pitt (Pittsburg) to Suppress the Whiskey Insurrection in 1794." *William and Mary Quarterly,* 1st ser., 11 (1902–3), 1–19.

WERNER Benjamin F. Thompson. *History of Long Island from Its Discovery and Settlement to the Present Time.* 4 vols. 3d ed. rev. by Charles J. Werner. New York: Robert H. Dodd, 1918.

WHEELER John H. Wheeler. *Historical Sketches of North Carolina from 1584 to 1851 . . . .* 2 vols in one. Philadelphia: Lippincott, Grambo and Co., 1851.

WHITELAW Ralph T. Whitelaw. *Virginia's Eastern Shore: A History of Northampton and Accomack Counties.* 2 vols. 1951. Reprint, Gloucester, Mass.: Peter Smith, 1968.

WILLIAMS [3] Samuel Cole Williams. *Dawn of Tennessee Valley and Tennessee History.* Johnson City, Tenn.: Watauga Press, 1937.

WILLIAMS [4]

Calendar of the General Otho Holland Williams Papers in the Maryland Historical Society. Baltimore: Maryland Historic Project, 1940.

WMQ

The William and Mary Quarterly: A Magazine of Early American History. Williamsburg, Va.: published by the Institute of Early American History and Culture.

W.P.A. [2]

W. P. A. Writers' Project. *Maryland: A Guide to the Old Line State.* New York: Oxford University Press, 1940.

W.P.A. [3]

W.P.A. Writers' Project. *Delaware: A Guide to the First State.* American Guide Series. New York: Viking Press, 1938.

W.P.A. [4]

W. P. A. Writers' Project. *Virginia: A Guide to the Old Dominion.* New York: Oxford University Press, 1940.

W.P.A. [8]

W.P.A. Writers' Project. *North Carolina: A Guide to the Old North State.* Chapel Hill: University of North Carolina Press, 1939.

WRIGHT

Louis B. Wright and Marion Tinling, eds. *Quebec to Carolina in 1785–1786.* San Marino, Calif.: Huntington Library, 1943.

WRITINGS

John C. Fitzpatrick, ed. *The Writings of George Washington from the Original Manuscript Sources, 1745–1799.* 39 vols. Washington, D.C.: Government Printing Office, 1931–44.

WYMAN

Thomas Bellows Wyman. *The Genealogies and Estates of Charlestown, in the County of Middlesex and Commonwealth of Massachusetts, 1629–1818.* 2 vols. Boston: David Clapp and Son, 1879.

ZAHNISER

Marvin R. Zahniser. *Charles Cotesworth Pinckney, Founding Father.* Chapel Hill: University of North Carolina Press, 1967.

Index to Vols. I-VI

This is a comprehensive cumulative index for the six volumes of

The Diaries of George Washington.

Index

Index

Agriculture *(cont.)*

weather on, 4:316, 340, 5:58, 64, 196, 203, 250, 259, 266, 269; experiments with, 4: 330, 5:150, 207, 253; weeding, 4:348, 5:348, 352, 357, 369-71, 376, 381-82; yield of, 5:49, 58, 62, 64, 209, 215, 225-26, 255, 259, 261, 266, 269, 410; inventorying seeds of, 5:92, 96; fallowing, 5: 196; plowing, 5:357, 377-79, 387-88

potatoes, 5:133, 179, 218, 272, 338, 344, 379, 415, 426, 430, 433; id., 2:14; experiments with, 4:202, 204, 207, 254, 350, 434; preparing ground for, 4:310-12, 314, 5:4, 8, 94, 104, 126, 151, 187, 206-7, 253, 306-7, 330-33, 337-38, 341-42, 345, 348-49; fertilizing, 4:312, 320, 5:62, 202, 207, 323; effects of weather on, 4:319, 340, 5:131, 196, 250, 431, 434; weeding, 4: 348, 5:347-48, 363, 379-85, 387-89; plowing, 5:6, 342, 365, 376-77, 379-82, 390, 430; yield of, 5:57, 62, 66, 89-90, 202, 204, 207, 212-16, 226, 228, 251, 253-54, 256-57, 259, 406-7, 412, 415, 429-30, 432

potatoes, harvesting of, 5:219; at Muddy Hole, 5:57, 203-4, 207, 211-15, 217, 219-20, 251, 253, 256-59; at Dogue Run, 5:59, 212-15, 258-59, 385, 388, 404-8, 410-11, 415-16, 419, 426-28; at the Neck (River Farm), 5:61, 64-65, 210-11, 255-56, 403-4, 407, 410-13, 415, 420, 431; at Union Farm (Ferry, French's, United plantations), 5:211-13, 215, 218, 256-59, 416, 419, 425-26, 429, 430-34

potatoes, planting of: at Union Farm (Ferry, French's, United plantations), 4:332,

353, 5:66, 333, 337, 339, 341, 349, 350-51, 353, 354-55; at the Neck (River Farm), 4: 333, 337, 341-42; at Muddy Hole, 4:348, 5:310-11; at Dogue Run, 5:133, 331-32, 337, 341, 350, 352, 354

pumpkins: id., 4:317; planting, 4:321, 329, 5:151, 187, 314, 316, 319, 321-23, 331, 333; condition of, 4:329; inventorying seed of, 5:92; effects of weather on, 5:196, 250; preparing ground for, 5:319; weeding, 5:341-43, 365-66, 382; plowing, 5:364; harvesting, 5:406, 413

ribgrass (plantain, ribwort), 4: 311, 313, 316, 327; 5:208, 219, 254; id., 4:301

root of scarcity (mangel-wurzel), 5:298, 309, 323, 328, 333-34, 402, 413-14; id., 5:298

"row grass," 5:306, 307, 310

rutabaga ("turnip rooted cabbages"), 5:285, 430; id., 5: 285

rye, 5:112, 123, 128; fertilizing, 1: 256; condition of, 1:263, 4: 341, 344, 355, 5:118, 134, 147, 343-45, 349; effects of weather on, 1:295, 4:343, 5:5; id., 1:305; diseased, 4: 355, 5:345-46; yield of, 5:11-14, 64, 76, 79, 397; preparing ground for, 5:32, 35, 37, 42, 45, 51, 62, 78, 403; infested with insects, 5:51

rye, harvesting of, 1:311, 5:4, 9-10; at Muddy Hole, 1:311, 5:8, 11, 13-14, 40, 79-80, 111, 355-56, 360, 376, 388, 394-95, 427-28, 428; at Dogue Run, 1:311, 5:43, 64, 143, 354-56, 358, 374-76, 381, 397, 419; at Union Farm (Ferry, French's, United plantations), 4:355, 5:36, 62, 64, 188, 247, 338, 349, 351, 353-56, 375, 397, 416, 418-19; at the Neck (River Farm),

[415]

Index

Alexander, Frances Brown. *See* Brown, Frances

Alexander, G. (Fairfax County landowner), 2:219; 3:147

Alexander, George Dent, 2:96, 115, 159, 181, 182, 219, 223; 3:74, 75, 204, 308

Alexander, Gerard, 1:279, 299; 2:41, 126; 3:102, 161; 4:254; 6:255

Alexander, John (d. 1677), 1:279

Alexander, John (1711-1764), 1:279

Alexander, John (1735-1775), 2:44

Alexander, Lucy Thornton, 2:44

Alexander, Mariamne Stoddert, 2: 188, 189, 255

Alexander, Mary, 2:175

Alexander, Mary Ann, 3:102

Alexander, Mary Dent, 1:299; 2:126; 3:102; 6:255

Alexander, Morgan, 2:38, 39; 3:292, 293, 295

Alexander, Philip (son of John the immigrant), 1:279

Alexander, Philip (b. 1742), 4:253, 254, 255

Alexander, Philip (1704-1753), 2:44; 4:254

Alexander, Philip (d. 1790), 2:41, 44, 110, 166, 219, 223; 3:160, 161, 308; 4:253, 254, 255

Alexander, Robert (son of John the immigrant), 1:279

Alexander, Robert (d. 1793), 2:32, 33, 43, 96, 139, 219, 3:152, 4:101, 241, 5:103; breeding horses, 1: 279, 299, 300; id., 1:279, 299, 2:41; fox hunting with GW, 2: 30, 31, 37, 40, 44, 99, 121, 181, 207, 214, 219, 223, 3:160, 162; at Mount Vernon, 2:31, 37, 52, 77, 83, 96, 99, 108, 110, 115, 121, 136, 139, 159, 181, 187, 189, 207, 214, 223, 255, 3:21, 113, 162, 204, 225, 308; GW visits, 2:40, 41, 4:273; rides with GW, 2:77; surveying, 2:188; land transactions, 2:188, 189, 190, 245, 255, 256; legal transactions, 5:290, 291, 409, 414, 420, 6:249, 250

Alexander, Sarah Snickers, 3:292

Alexander, Susanna Pearson, 6:340

Alexander, William. *See* Stirling, William Alexander, earl of

Alexander's Island (Holmes Island), 3:160, 161

Alexander's ordinary. *See* Snickers's ordinary

Alexandria, 2:95, 103, 183, 213, 3:101, 4:113, 210, 232; GW at, 1:130, 174, 176, 216, 228, 231, 235, 238, 239, 254-55, 268, 281, 2:38, 46, 52, 67, 68, 69, 77, 78, 93, 94-95, 99, 109, 113, 115, 120, 128, 132, 141-42, 143, 154, 157, 159, 160, 167, 168, 180, 181, 182, 186, 188, 209, 213, 214-15, 221, 228, 254, 256, 263, 264, 271, 329, 3:2, 3, 14-15, 20, 33, 46, 47, 51, 53-54, 70, 74, 78, 81, 84, 103, 107, 108, 114, 119, 124-25, 131-32, 137, 138, 147, 149, 154, 155, 161, 170, 186, 187, 194, 197, 198, 199, 203, 204, 220, 227, 240, 245, 257, 260-61, 262, 264, 290, 291, 296, 297, 302, 303, 304, 309, 310, 321, 322, 323, 325, 327, 4:77, 88, 89, 93, 107, 113, 123, 124, 140, 141, 146, 157-58, 165, 170, 183, 191, 198, 210, 211, 221, 235, 241, 251, 311, 312, 347, 5:22, 29, 43, 49-50, 52, 65, 70, 89, 135, 187, 190, 210-11, 213, 216, 247, 248, 256, 257, 259, 260, 284, 286, 290, 301, 306, 351, 361, 373, 381, 409, 410, 419, 420, 426, 431, 435, 440, 444, 6:105, 211, 239, 241-42, 252, 258, 264, 269, 274, 276, 277, 282, 291-92, 296, 298, 309, 312, 318, 331, 333, 340, 344, 348, 350, 355, 376

Alexandria Academy, 4:93, 236, 241, 251, 330

Alexandria Inn and Coffee House (New Tavern, Lyles's tavern), 4:198; 5:17

Algerian captives, 6:51, 52

Alice (Lame; slave), 4:145, 277

Alison (Allison), Francis, 3:285

Alkers (Alker), Thomas, 5:480

Allan, Mr. (at Warm Springs), 2: 177, 180

Allan, Mr. (of Philadelphia), 3:281

Brooke, Richard, 2:221

Brooke, Robert, 6:272

Brooke, Sarah Mason, 4:150

Brooke, Thomas, 4:150

Brooke, Walter, 4:150, 297; 5:125, 384

Brookfield, Mass., 5:471, 472

Brookgreen (S.C.), 6:123

Brooks, James, 4:49

Brooks, John, 5:472, 473

Brother, Henry, 6:166

Brother Bucks. *See* Croghan, George

Brothers (sloop), 6:40

Brothers's tavern, 6:166

Brown (at Warm Springs), 2:175

Brown (clerk to William Hartshorne), 5:407

Brown (son of Mrs. Merchant), 6:268

Brown, Miss (Mount Vernon visitor), 6:306

Brown, Mr. (Mount Vernon visitor), 3:133, 136, 147

Brown, Mrs. (of Philadelphia), 5:510

Brown (Browne), Anne, 5:448, 449, 505; 6:2

Brown, Catherine Scott, 3:71, 74, 75, 108, 197, 210, 227, 228, 245, 322; 5:364

Brown, Frances, 2:69; 3:108, 219, 220; 5:449

Brown, Gustavus (1689-1762), 4:106

Brown, Gustavus Richard, 5:214; 6:379

Brown, Hope Power, 5:80

Brown, Jacob, 5:466, 467

Brown, James (Indian trader), 1:135

Brown, James (father of John Brown of Providence), 5:80

Brown, James (son of John Brown of Providence), 5:80, 81

Brown, John (1757-1837; of Ky.), 6:15, 17, 57, 77

Brown, John (of Providence), 4:78; 5:80

Brown, Margaret Graham, 5:214

Brown, Richard, 2:69

Brown, Sarah, 5:80

Brown, Thomas, 6:121

Brown, William (composer and organist), 5:163, 169

Brown, William (doctor), 3:197, 219, 5:449; id., 3:108; at Mount Vernon, 3:108, 133, 147, 219, 220, 227, 228, 244, 245, 4:108, 244, 254, 284, 5:364; accompanies GW, 3:147; GW visits, 3:260; treats ill servants, 4:85, 145, 203, 276, 286; and Alexandria Academy, 4:236

Browne (sister of Elizabeth Carter Browne Bassett), 5:362, 372

Browne (Brown), Bennett, 3:154, 203, 238

Browne (Brown), Judith Carter, 5:362, 449; 6:4

Browne (Brown), Judith Walker Carter, 4:155; 5:449; 6:4

Browne (Brown), Mary Burnet, 5:362

Browne, Mary French, 5:449

Browne, William, 5:449

Browne (Brown), William Burnet, 4:155; 5:449; 6:4

Brown's Coffeehouse, 6:137

Brown's Island. *See* Long Island

Brownsville, Pa. *See* Red Stone Old Fort

Bruce (shipmaster), 2:256

Bruce, James, 2:256

Bruce, Normand, 3:305; 4:11, 12, 13, 14

Brummitt (sons of William Brummitt), 3:122

Brummitt, William, 3:122

Brunswick, duke of, 3:362

Brunswick, N.J. *See* New Brunswick, N.J.

Brunswick River, 6:121

Bruton Parish Church (illus., 2:60), 1:274; 3:252

Bryan, John, 4:53

Bryan, Thomas, 4:53

Bryden, James, 6:238, 322

Buchan, David Stuart Erskine, eleventh earl of, 6:297

Buchanan, Mr. (Mount Vernon visitor), 2:140, 141

Buchanan, James, 3:320

Buchanan, Lloyd, 5:32

Buckland, William, 1:237; 3:206

Buck Marsh Run, 1:9; 2:173; 3:293

Custis, Martha Parke ("Patsy"; daughter of Martha Washington; illus., 1:212, 3:109), 1:xix, 272, 3: 60, 101; death of, 1:xvii, 3:188; id., 1:xxii, 211; GW manages affairs for, 1:xxiv, 304, 2:126, 128, 202, 209, 247, 253, 272, 3:21, 101; health of, 1:329, 2:39, 45, 47, 54, 68, 76, 108, 120, 123, 128, 141, 168, 177, 195, 197, 201, 257, 3:1, 2, 7, 9, 71, 114; placed in care of Lund Washington, 2:27; education of, 2:37, 40, 50, 182, 229, 253; accompanies Washington family, 2:46, 52, 54, 87, 94, 119, 141, 154, 157, 158, 168, 177, 179, 186, 190, 193, 195, 196, 197, 199, 200, 208, 256, 261, 3:2, 3, 21, 31, 45, 52, 70, 83, 103, 107, 118, 119, 123, 125, 128, 129, 138, 142, 173; rides to harvest field, 2:77, 165, 254; clothing, 2:199, 200, 213, 3:94, 120; gift from GW, 2:262; portrait of, 3:109; burial of, 3: 188

Custis, Martha Parke ("Patsy"; daughter of John Parke Custis; illus., 4:130), 5:307, 6:306; id., 4:72; at Mount Vernon, 4:72, 144, 145, 158, 159, 194, 262, 268, 5:5, 6, 43, 44, 50, 51, 57, 63, 84, 122, 123, 130, 188, 217, 234, 247, 263, 269, 274, 277, 289, 292, 293, 306, 330, 361, 420, 6:261, 285, 291, 296, 317, 321, 334, 337, 349, 364, 370; portrait of, 4:130; illness, 5:269; marriage of, 6:239; children, 6:293

Custis estate, 1:214-15, 272, 273-74, 303-4; 2:44, 50, 59, 61, 141, 151, 196, 245, 247, 274; 3:60, 142, 213, 215; 4:103, 294; 5:290, 291, 409, 420

Cut Creek (Fish Creek), 2:299, 301

Cutler, Manasseh, 5:159

Cuyahoga River, 4:59, 69

Cymon and Sylvia (opera), 5:502

Cypress Swamp, 1:321

Dade, Miss (Mount Vernon visitor), 6:254, 255

Dade, Elizabeth Alexander, 2:99

Dade, Francis, 2:128

Dade, Jane Stuart, 5:50

Dade, Parthenia Alexander Massey, 2:99; 4:241

Dade, Susannah Fitzhugh, 6:293

Dade, Townshend (son of Townshend Dade, d. 1781), 2:99

Dade, Townshend (b. 1743), 3:153; 5:50

Dade, Townshend (d. 1781), 2:99, 100; 3:152, 153; 4:241

Dade, Townshend (of King George County), 6:293

Daily, Richard, 5:425

Daingerfield, Hannah, 3:26, 213; 5: 320, 326, 331

Daingerfield, Mary Willis, 2:262; 4: 112

Daingerfield, Sarah Taliaferro, 2:195, 262

Daingerfield, William, 2:262

Daingerfield, William (d. 1783; of Belvidera), 1:297; 2:195, 262

Daingerfield, William (d. 1781; of Coventry), 1:297; 2:262; 4:112

Daingerfield, William (d. 1769; of Greenfield), 1:297

Daingerfield, Mrs. William, 2:262

Dalby, Mary Rose, 4:165

Dalby, Philip, 4:76, 165, 236, 306, 307

Dallas, Alexander, 6:173

Dalley, Gifford, 6:53, 54

Dalton (daughters of Tristram Dalton), 5:456; 6:309

Dalton, Elizabeth ("Betty," "Betcy"), 2:115, 175, 177, 213, 263

Dalton, Jenny, 3:227

Dalton, John, 1:217, 2:115, 175, 177, 3:152, 153, 227; id., 1:218, 2:120; partnership with John Carlyle, 1:269, 2:38; horse breeding, 1: 281, 282; at Mount Vernon, 2:68, 116, 3:269, 270, 292, 325; GW visits, 2:116, 120, 214; and association committee, 2:256; and petitions to the House of Burgesses, 3:250

Dalton, Mrs. John, 2:175

Dalton, Ruth Hooper, 5:456, 457, 501, 502, 504; 6:62, 80, 309

Dalton, Tristram, 5:132, 456, 457, 477, 486, 487, 495, 502, 504; 6:23, 40, 62, 80, 309, 310

Danbury (on the Dan River, N.C.), 6:153

Dance, John, 5:28

Dandridge, Anna Maria. *See* Bassett, Anna Maria Dandridge

Dandridge, Bartholomew, Jr. (illus., 6:178), 1:274; 2:60; 3:27, 215, 255; 4:127, 266; 5:101, 291, 362; 6:93, 178, 179, 183, 236, 373

Dandridge, Bartholomew, Sr., 6:93, 274

Dandridge, Elizabeth ("Betcy"), 2: 108, 109, 127, 143

Dandridge, Frances Jones, 1:272; 2:246; 3:100; 4:127

Dandridge, John, 4:266, 267

Dandridge, John (1700-1756), 1:272; 5:340

Dandridge, John (b. 1756), 4:266

Dandridge, John (d. 1799), 4:266, 333; 5:101, 104, 105

Dandridge, Martha Washington ("Patcy"), 5:362

Dandridge, Mary Burbidge, 3:215, 255; 5:101; 6:274

Dandridge, Nathaniel West, 4:266

Dandridge, William (Martha Washington's brother), 3:27

Dandridge, William (Martha Washington's uncle), 4:266

Dandridge, William (son of Bartholomew Dandridge, Sr.), 6:274, 275

Dan River, 6:155, 156

Dansie, Thomas, 1:274; 2:101

Dansie's ferry, 1:274; 2:101

Daphne, the (room in Raleigh Tavern), 2:148

Darby, Samuel, 3:380

Darcus (slave), 1:230

Darke, Joseph, 6:106

Darke, William, 5:69, 152; 6:106

Darnall, Henry (d. 1711), 2:75

Darnall, Henry (great-grandson of Henry Darnall, d. 1711), 2:75

Darnall, Mary, 2:75

Darrell, Ann. *See* Smith, Ann Darrell

Darrell, Augustus, 2:45, 254

Darrell, Sampson, 1:239, 241, 242, 245, 255, 268, 298; 2:45, 86, 142; 3:125, 131, 149; 5:236

Darrell, Sarah McCarty Johnston, 2:45

Darrell's Hill, 5:236

Dartmouth, William Legge, second earl of, 3:284

Daugherty, James, 4:18, 19

Dauphin (ship), 6:52

Davenport, Francis, 6:181

Davenport, James, 6:228, 229

Davenport, Joseph, 5:228

Davenport, P., Miss, 2:199, 200

David Ross & Co., 2:264; 3:3, 16, 19

Davidson, Robert, 6:182

Davie, William Richardson, 6:366

Davies, Elizabeth Perry, 2:61

Davies, Price, 2:61, 195; 3:27

Davis (midshipman), 2:253

Davis, Thomas (clergyman), 6:304, 335, 336

Davis (Davies), Thomas (of Fredericksburg), 3:323

Davis, Tom (slave, Home House), 4:190, 191, 335; 5:4, 331, 341, 356

Davison, John, 1:133, 135, 147, 148, 192

Davis Run. *See* Putnam's Run

Davy (slave; owned by Abraham Barnes), 1:269

Davy (carpenter; slave), 2:36; 3:122

Davy (cooper; slave, mill), 5:4, 355, 356

Davy (overseer; slave), 2:164, 165; 3:122; 4:185, 249, 252, 301, 308, 344; 5:3, 86, 135, 141, 143, 233, 307, 322, 377

Dawson (doctor; of the Virgin Islands), 6:305, 306

Dawson, Mr. (Mount Vernon visitor), 4:82

Dawson, Elizabeth Churchill Bassett: id., 2:58; GW visits, 2:58, 106, 152, 153, 194, 196, 197, 238, 239, 3:25, 41, 67, 68, 95, 96, 97, 142, 143, 211, 213, 216, 219, 251, 252, 255, 256, 268; GW's family visits, 2:195, 197

Dawson, George, 4:82

Digges, Ignatius (illus., 2:86), 1:246, 260, 281; 2:84, 85, 86; 3:54, 129, 154, 178, 197; 4:141, 170, 179

Digges, Jane ("Jenny"). *See* Fitzgerald, Jane ("Jenny") Digges

Digges, Joseph, 3:75, 76, 154, 174, 175, 260

Digges, Mary (daughter of William Digges of Warburton), 3:148

Digges, Mary Carroll (illus., 2:86), 2:84

Digges, Susannah, 3:148

Digges, Theresa ("Tracy"). *See* Foster (Forster), Theresa ("Tracy") Digges

Digges, Thomas Atwood, 6:333, 346, 351, 361

Digges, William (of Warburton), 1: 260, 2:75, 84, 3:308, 6:333; id., 1:236; at Mount Vernon, 1:236, 258, 2:53, 160, 3:125, 148, 154, 188, 193, 245, 260, 263, 271; and William Clifton's land, 1:237, 246, 258, 260; and agriculture, 1:238, 239, 317, 328, 2:50; breeds horses, 1:299, 302; and family, 2:53, 3:56, 75, 125, 148, 154, 155, 167, 174, 203; GW visits, 2:158, 3:54, 75, 76, 125, 129, 149, 167, 194, 197, 200, 203, 244, 245, 309

Digges, William (son of Edward Digges), 1:236

Digges, William (d. 1698), 2:84

Dinsmoor, John, 6:327

Dinsmoor, Martha McKeen, 6:327

Dinsmoor (Dinsmore), Silas, 6:327

Dinwiddie, Robert (illus., 1:119), 1:34, 132, 140, 141, 156, 160, 178, 184, 318, 3:138, 226; GW visits, 1:34, 37, 114; appoints GW adjutant, 1:34, 118; commissions GW to carry letter to French commandant, 1:114, 126, 127, 128, 130; id., 1:118; GW offers services to, 1:119; Ohio Company member, 1:120, 121; appoints Indian commissioners, 1: 121; correspondence regarding French threat, 1:123, 126; receives warning of French occupation, 1:123; correspondence

concerning ordering of French from Ohio, 1:127, 130, 148, 151, 158; relations with Indians, 1: 139, 140, 154, 178, 181, 182, 183, 190, 192, 202, 203, 204, 205, 209; GW delivers French reply to, 1:155, 160; orders publication of GW's journal, 1:160; expedition against French, 1:162, 165, 166, 174, 181, 182, 187, 188, 189; relations with burgesses, 1:163, 164; and Proclamation of 1754, 1:163, 2:256, 257; commissions GW lt. col., 1:174; GW sends news of surrender to, 1:180; attends Indian council, 1:193, 196, 200; appoints GW to command Va. Regiment, 1:200

Dismal Swamp, 1:274, 319-26, 2:102; GW at, 1:319-26, 2:4

Dismal Swamp Company, 1:319; 4: 131, 133, 134, 199

Dives, "Captn.," 1:222

Dix, John, 6:156

Dix, William, 6:156

Dixon, John, 2:107, 249, 257; 3:96, 97, 142, 200

Dixon & Littledale, 1:249; 2:110

Dixon, John, & Isaac Littledale. *See* Dixon & Littledale

Dix's ferry, 6:155, 156

Dobbs, William, 3:393, 396

Dobbs Ferry, N.Y., 3:389

Dobson, William, 6:154

Dobson, Mrs. William, 6:154

Dobson's tavern, 6:154

Dogs, 4:247, 5:444; hounds, 2:31, 32, 33, 34, 61, 116, 120, 128, 136, 207, 3:77, 99-101, 157, 159, 160, 162, 167, 220-21, 4:184, 242-44, 248, 252, 254-55, 259, 262-63, 267, 273; breeding, 2:43, 50, 67, 73, 91, 98, 105, 126, 139, 157, 164, 173, 232, 233, 259, 260, 275, 335, 4:199, 277; illness of, 2:98, 171, 173, 5:73, 6:263; French hounds, 4:186, 195, 199, 242-44, 248

Dogue Run (Creek), 1:211; 2:30, 31, 50, 57, 204, 218, 221, 222, 331; 3:4, 12; 4:84

Dohrman (ship owner), 5:448

Index

Index

Fairlie, James, 4:246, 247

Fairmount Park, 3:335

Fairweathers plantation, 2:37

Fallen Timbers, 6:179

Falls Church, 2:52, 77

Falls of the Great Kanawha River. *See* Great Kanawha River, Falls of

Falls of the Ohio. *See* Ohio River, Falls of

Fanny (brig), 4:349

Fantasque (ship), 3:384, 385

Farley, Francis, 1:325, 326

Farm equipment (illus., 1:xxxii, 278, 2:22, 4:227), 1:304, 4:261; plows, 1:xxix, xxxiii, 250, 255, 263, 4:304-9, 311, 314, 316, 320, 325-27, 329-33, 344, 353, 5:16, 62, 101, 107, 111, 135-36, 138-39, 145-47, 205-6, 208, 210, 219, 225, 333, 350-51, 355, 372-73, 380, 387-88, 391, 6:67; threshers, 1:xxxii, xxxiii, 6:12; weather effects use of, 1:248-49, 254, 265, 2:267, 268, 4:115, 293, 295, 299, 307, 309, 319-20, 331-32, 337-40, 344, 5:12-13, 30-31, 36, 38-39, 51, 73, 94, 105, 107-8, 111, 116, 118, 121, 124, 135, 216, 218, 222, 227-28, 273, 275-76, 280, 283, 286-87, 289-90, 303-5, 307, 311, 318, 332, 353, 358-59, 361, 368; wheelbarrows, 1:254; harrows, 1:266-67, 269, 291, 4:120, 127-28, 166, 307-8, 311, 314-15, 319, 332, 353, 5:16, 35, 37, 42, 109-11, 123, 126-27, 132-33, 136, 140-41, 143, 145-46, 192, 201, 289, 291, 300, 309-10, 321, 323, 333, 348, 350-51, 353-55, 392, 403; rollers, 1:268, 4:121, 124, 307, 314-15, 319-21, 5:16, 127, 132, 136, 146, 203, 291, 304, 306, 333; wagons and carts, 2:23, 4:97, 253, 294, 330, 5:17, 127, 293, 309, 311-12, 371-76, 379-82, 391-95, 397, 400, 403-4, 406; hoes, 4:315, 341, 345-46, 348, 5:330; rakes, 5:4; scythes, 5:192, 383, 403

Farmer, Mr. (of New York City), 3:181

"Farmer." *See* Bloxham, James

Farmer (*Anne and Elizabeth, Fairfax;* brig or brigantine), 3:120, 226, 240, 241, 304, 320, 321, 322, 323

Farmer's Compleat Guide through All Articles of His Profession, The (book), 3:50

Farmington, Conn.: GW at, 3:368, 371

Farquahar, George, 2:94; 3:3

Farrand, Max, 1:xlix

Farrel, John, & Co. *See* John Farrell & Co.

Fauchet, Jean Antoine Joseph, 6:208, 215

Fauquier, Francis (illus., 1:273), 1:118, 175, 272, 273, 280, 295, 318; 2:29, 106, 293

Fauquier County, 3:239

Fayetteville (Campbelltown), N.C., 6:119, 120

Fayetteville (James McHenry's estate), 5:154

Federal City, 4:149; plans and surveys, 6:103-4, 105-6, 164-66; authorized by Congress, 6:104; sites for, 6:104-5, 169; land negotiations for, 6:164, 165; GW at, 6:200, 248, 261, 281, 297, 316, 319, 327, 350, 375; commissioners of, 6:205; speculation in, 6:205; foreign embassies in, 6:265; description of, 6:281

Federal City, commissioners of. *See* Stuart, David; Johnson, Thomas, Jr.; Carroll, Daniel, of Frederick County, Md.; Scott, Gustavus; Thornton, William; White, Alexander

Federal Convention. *See* Constitutional Convention

Federalist (ship), 5:339, 366

Feild, Alexander, 6:304

Feild, Richard, 6:304

Fences and fencing, 1:xxxi, xxxii, 248, 265, 296, 2:36, 287, 4:117, 145, 285, 5:60, 332; bottom rails laid out, 1:243-44, 246; fences blown down, 1:268, 5:116, 360; cutting and gathering lumber

Index

Index

Gray (lives on French's land), 5:119, 121

Gray, George (founder of Gray's Ferry), 5:155, 156, 158, 176

Gray, George (1725-1800), 5:246

Gray, Robert, 6:60

Graydon, Alexander, 3:180

Graydon, Rachel Marks, 3:180

Gray's Ferry, 5:155, 156

Gray's Ferry Gardens, 5:158, 159, 176

Grayson, Benjamin, 2:110; 4:206

Grayson, Eleanor Smallwood, 4:107

Grayson, Spence, 4:206, 207

Grayson, Susannah Monroe, 2:110

Grayson, William (c.1736-1790), 2: 110, 181, 228; 3:75, 221, 309; 4: 77, 107, 139, 163, 169, 206, 268; 6:69, 260

Grayson, William (1766-1806), 5:408

Great Beaver Creek, 1:144

Great Bend of the Ohio, 2:283

Great Bridge, 1:325, 326

Great Britain, 1:119-29, 162-66. *See also* Foreign Affairs, Great Britain

Great Crossing of the Youghiogheny, 2:280; 4:18

Great Falls (of the Potomac; illus., 4:171), 4:172-73, 196, 208; GW at, 4:171-73, 196-97, 207-8, 269-70, 287-89, 347, 5:3, 47-48, 335

Great Glades, 4:7

Great Hockhocking River (Hocking River), 2:283

Great Hunting Creek. *See* Hunting Creek

Great Kanawha River, 2:307, 308; 4:50

Great Kanawha River, Falls of, 2: 306; 4:48, 49, 50

Great Meadows, 1:192; GW at, 1:192-93

Great Meadows tract, 4:20, 33

Great Miami River, 2:319, 321; 4:59, 69

Great Run. *See* Beaver Dam Creek

Great Salt Lick (Big Buffalo Lick, Salt Lick Creek, Licking River), 2:319, 321

Green, Ashbell, 6:296

Green, Charles, 1:215, 231, 236, 237, 245, 255, 258, 268, 315; 2:182, 236; 3:157

Green, Lewis, 6:156

Green, Margaret. *See* Savage, Margaret Green

Green, Peter, 1:338

Green, Sarah ("Sally") Bishop, 4:249

Green, Thomas, 4:249; 5:37, 86, 233, 332, 333

Greenbrier River, 4:8

Greenbury Point, 6:100; GW at, 6: 100

Greencastle, Pa., 6:190, 191; GW at, 6:190

Greene, Catherine Littlefield, 5:448, 450, 451, 500, 502, 504; 6:53, 135, 136, 139

Greene, Christopher, 3:364, 365

Greene, Nathanael (illus., 6:139), 3:380, 4:97, 5:64, 160, 6:123, 135; and military affairs, 3:358, 359, 380, 381, 388, 391, 401, 402, 424, 433, 436, 6:148, 149, 150, 154, 155; provides introduction, 4: 151; id., 5:451; Greenville, N.C., named in his honor, 6:115; his plantation described, 6:136

Greene, William, 3:377, 407

Greenfield, 1:297

Green Hill plantation, 3:103

Greenhow, James, 6:328

Greenleaf, James, 6:238

Green Spring (James City County), 5:236; GW at, 1:114

Green Spring (Md.), 3:307

Greensville County, 6:114; GW at, 6:113

Greenview, 3:235

Greenville (Martinsborough), N.C., 6:115; GW at, 6:115

Greenway Court (illus., 1:10), 1: xxiii, 1, 7, 245; 2:92, 134; 3:12

Greenwich, Conn. *See* Horseneck, Conn.

Greg (slave), 1:232, 234

Gregory, Mildred Washington. *See* Washington, Mildred (aunt of GW)

Gregory, Roger, 2:30

Gregory, Stephen, 5:359, 386, 387

Mason (tavern keeper of Charlotte, N.C.), 6:150

Mason, "Colo." (of Fayette), 6:193

Mason, Mr. (at Colchester), 4:241

Mason, Ann Eilbeck (d. 1773; illus., 3:174), 3:174, 175, 290

Mason, Ann Eilbeck (1755-1814), 3:74, 75; 5:310

Mason, Ann Stuart. *See* Stuart, Ann ("Nancy")

Mason, Benjamin, 3:59

Mason, Elizabeth Mary Ann Barnes Hooe. *See* Graham, Elizabeth Mary Ann Barnes Hooe Mason

Mason, George (of Gunston Hall; illus., 1:318), 1:252, 2:150, 189, 3:298, 4:101, 105, 108, 5:61, 6:310; agricultural exchanges with GW, 1:xxii, 295, 315, 317-18, 327-28, 337, 3:319, 4:246; and Ohio Company, 1:120; and Gunston Hall plantation, 1:222, 237, 2:46, 142, 4:81, 107, 109, 247, 248, 264, 5:103, 112, 141, 234, 257, 355, 423; land transactions, 1:241, 248, 2:142, 189; id., 1:317; and John Posey's debt, 2:30, 189; at Mount Vernon, 2:111, 114, 142, 159, 189, 219, 221, 3:108, 198, 199, 204, 205, 245, 261, 303, 321, 4:107, 109, 5:135; and family, 2:111, 254, 3:71, 74, 137, 175, 220, 245, 290, 4:100, 139, 242, 5:135, 310, 6:260, 267, 310; development of New Pohick Church, 2:132, 3:39, 113, 233; legal duties of, 2:167, 3:204, 4:206; and neighborhood dancing school, 2:219, 229; and Virginia nonimportation association, 2:256; arbitrates legal disputes, 2:264, 331, 332, 3:3, 8, 16, 24, 29, 125; executor of Daniel French's will, 3:39, 233; hunting with GW, 3:71; GW visits, 3:71, 178, 4:100, 101; political activities, 3:260, 4:312, 5:135; drafting Fairfax Resolves, 3:261; and Continental Congress, 3:271-72; visitors to, 3:305, 5:279; and Virginia Convention, 3:322; and

Mount Vernon Convention, 4:105, 106, 107, 108; and Constitutional Convention, 5:158, 185, 237, 247; business affairs, 5:347

Mason, George (of Lexington; illus., 4:242), 2:189; 3:220, 290, 303, 321; 4:108, 242, 5:135, 158, 209, 255, 417, 418; 6:310

Mason, George (of Pohick), 3:220; 4:100

Mason, John, 5:347; 6:280, 281

Mason, Sarah Brent, 6:310

Mason, Sarah McCarty Chichester, 5:103; 6:266, 267, 336

Mason, Thomson (1733-1785; of Raspberry Plain; illus., 1:252), 1:252, 255, 258, 260, 281, 282; 2:69; 3:8, 100

Mason, Thomson (1759-1820), 1:248; 4:100, 267; 5:103, 124, 235; 6:263, 266, 267, 286, 336, 348

Mason, William, 4:139; 5:135

Mason's Hall (Blandford), 6:112

Mason's Neck, 1:216; 2:28

Mason's tavern, 6:150

Massey, Mrs. —— Burwell (wife of Lee Massey), 2:236

Massey, Dade, Jr., 2:99

Massey, Elizabeth Bronaugh, 2:236, 254

Massey, Lee, 2:235, 236, 254; 3:132, 188; 5:142, 143, 298

Massey, Mary Johnston, 2:235

Massey, Parthenia Alexander. *See* Dade, Parthenia Alexander Massey

Massey, Peggy, 2:254, 255

Mathers, James, 6:53, 54

Mathews ("Brig[adie]r"), 6:193

Mathews, Mr. (Matthews; Mount Vernon visitor), 5:36, 395

Mathews, George, 6:7, 8, 48, 49

Mathias Neck, 1:275

Mathias Point, 1:274

Mathis, "Captn.," 3:178

Matildaville, 4:269, 270

Matoax, 5:44

Mattaponi River, 1:272

Mattawoman (Charles County, Md.), 5:135

Mattawoman Creek, 1:256

Odell house, 3:390

Oden (Odem, Odum; of S.C.), 6: 144-45

"Ode to Columbia's Favorite Son; Great Washington, the Hero's Come—", 5:475

O'Donnell, John (1715-1780), 6:343

O'Donnell, John (died c.1805), 6:343

O'Flynn, Patrick, 5:155; 6:237

O'Flynn's tavern. *See* Sign of the Ship (O'Flynn's tavern)

Ogden, Euphemia Morris, 5:180

Ogden, John Cosens, 5:488

Ogden, Samuel, 5:180, 244

Ogdensburg, N.Y. *See* Oswegatchie, N.Y.

Ogle, Benjamin, 3:208; 4:184

Ogle, Samuel, 3:208

O'Hara, Charles, 3:432, 433

O'Higgins, Thomas, 6:338

Ohio, Forks of, 1:121, 158, 162, 164, 177, 178, 180, 181, 182, 184, 188, 199, 200; GW at, 1:132, 133

Ohio Company of Virginia, 1:123; supporters and members of, 1:12, 118, 120, 194, 247, 317; early history of, 1:120-21; Christopher Gist explores for, 1:130; constructs storehouses and forts, 1:132, 162, 180, 182, 184; conflict with Grand Ohio Company, 2: 287-88

Ohiopyle, Pa. *See* Youghiogheny River, Falls of

Ohio River, Falls of, 2:317, 320

Ohio River, Great Bend of, 2:283

Ohio River, Long Bottom of, 2:304, 305

Ohio River, Long Reach of, 2:283

Ohio Valley, 2:51, 256, 261; GW at, 1:126-61, 162-210, 2:277-84, 286-326

O'Kelly (lawyer; Mount Vernon visitor), 5:409

O'Kelly, John B., 5:152, 216, 217, 235, 236, 409

Old Church. *See* Indian Town Church

Old Farm, 3:216, 251

Old House (S.C.), 6:135

Old Orchard Point, 1:300, 301

Old Quarter (Custis plantation), 3:26

Old Shingle House, the (tavern), 6:118

Old Town, Md., 4:14; GW at, 2:324; 4:12

Oldtown Creek, 2:305, 307

Oliffe, Anne Knight, 3:61

Oliffe, John, 3:61

Oliver, Mr. (Mount Vernon visitor), 6:343

Oliver (slave, Muddy Hole), 5:381

Oliver (tavern keeper), 6:112, 113

Oliver, John, 6:343

Oliver, Robert, 6:343

Oliver's tavern, 6:112

Onderdonck (Onderdonk), Andrew, 6:67

Onderdonck (Onderdonk), Hendrick, 6:66, 67

Oneida Lake, 4:65, 70

Oneida River, 4:70

O'Neill, Bernard, 4:170

Onondaga River. *See* Oswego River

Opequon Creek, 2:134, 135

Opossum Creek. *See* Broken Timber Creek

Orangeburg, S.C., 3:380

Orange County Court House, 4:56

Orapeake (Corapeake) Swamp, 1: 321

Orchard Point, 1:300

Order and Discipline of the Troops of the United States, 3:358

D'Orleans, Louis Philippe, duc, 6:265, 266

Orme, Archibald, 4:172, 173

Orr, Benjamin Grayson, 4:268

Orr, John (b. 1726), 4:268

Orr, John (clerk), 2:114

Osborne (of near Petersburg), 6:111

Osborne, Jeremiah, 1:18

Osgood, Maria Bowne Franklin, 5:448, 449; 6:36

Osgood, Samuel, 5:448, 449, 504; 6:9, 26, 36

Ossian Hall, 4:72

Ossining, N.Y. *See* Singsing, N.Y.

Oster (Ouster), Martin, 5:53

Index

Index

Swan, James, 5:95, 97, 98
Swann, Thomas, 6:344
Swan Point, 2:92
Swanwick, John, 5:28, 180, 244; 6:317
Swanwick, Mrs. John, 6:317, 372
Swearingen, Andrew, 4:31
Swearingen, Thomas, 4:6, 8
Swearingen, Capt. Van (of S.C.), 6:145
Swearingen, Van (of Va.), 4:29, 31, 36
Sweet Hall, 2:54, 148
Sweet Springs, 4:6, 7, 8
Swett, Hannah, 5:484
Swett, Joseph, 5:484
Swift, Ann Roberdeau, 4:78
Swift, Foster, 4:236
Swift, Jonathan, 4:78, 79, 236; 5:71
Swift (brig), 2:272
Swift Run Gap, 4:56
Swingate, Benedict. *See* Calvert, Benedict
Sycamore Island, 4:197
Sydebotham, William, 2:140
Syme, John, 3:188
Symonds, Thomas, 3:432

T. Eden & Co., 3:179
Tables of distances. *See* Maps and tables of distances
Taft, Mercy ("Patty"), 5:494
Taft, Polly, 5:494
Taft, Samuel, 5:493, 494
Taft's tavern, 5:494
Talbott, Richard, 2:233, 244
Tallmadge, Benjamin (alias John Bolton), 3:357, 374, 375
Taneytown, Md., 6:167
Tappahannock. *See* Hobbs Hole
Tarboro, N.C., 6:114; GW at, 6:114, 115
Tarleton, Banastre, 3:387, 388, 402, 424, 429, 433; 4:82; 6:45
Tarrant, Leonard, 3:302
Tar River, 6:114, 115
Tarte, Mr. (Tart; Mount Vernon visitor), 4:199
Tasker, Benjamin, 1:246, 258, 299
Tate, Mr. (of England), 5:361
Taverns
    Connecticut: Brigham's (Coventry),

5:496; Brown's (New Haven), 5:466, 467; Bull's (Hartford), 5:468; Carrington's (Wallingford), 5:467, 468; Cogswell's (Washington), 3:371; Marvin's (Westport-Norwalk), 5:497; Morgan's (Washington), 3:367, 368; Perkin's (Ashford), 5:494, 495; Sheldon's (Litchfield), 3:368, 371; Stanton's (Kilbourn House; Litchfield), 3:371; Stillman's (Wethersfield), 3:368; Webb's (Stamford), 5:462, 463; Woodbridge's (Hartford County), 5:496; Woodruff's, 5:465
    Delaware: Buck Tavern (William Carson's; New Castle County), 3:274, 287, 6:99; Christiana Ferry (Christiana Bridge), 3:274, 418; O'Flin's (Sign of the Ship; Wilmington), 5:154, 155, 6:237; Red Lion (Red Lion, Del.), 6:99
    Georgia: Brown's (Savannah), 6:135, 137; Garnet's (Effingham County), 6:140; Lambert's, 6:140; Pearce's (Pierce's; Effingham County), 6:140; Russell's, 6:140; Skinner's, 6:140; Spencer's, 6:139
    Maryland: Annapolis Coffeehouse, 3:55, 56, 136, 178; Ball's (Spurrier's; Waterloo), 5:186, 247, 6:205, 213, 238, 322, 327; Barney's (Havre de Grace), 6:204, 209, 327; Black Horse Tavern (Sutton's; Harford County), 3:186; Brothers's (Frederick), 6:166; Cookerly's (New Midway), 6:167; Down's (Kent County), 3:274, 287; Fountain Inn (Daniel Grant's; Baltimore), 3:327, 328, 419, 5:153, 154, 6:237, 238; Golden's, 6:191; Gwin's (Gwyn's, Gwynne's), 4:16, 17, 19; Heil's ("Dutch man's"), 4:173, 175; Hodges's (Rock Hall), 3:274; Hollingsworth's (Elkton), 5:154, 155, 6:237; Laidler's

[526]

Index

Thompson, Israel, 4:3
Thompson, James, 6:36
Thompson, John, 3:8
Thompson, Jonah, 5:71
Thompson, Mary Gardiner, 6:65
Thompson, Richard, 3:208, 209, 290
Thompson, Sarah Bradnor, 6:65
Thompson, Sarah Carter, 3:8
Thompson, Thomas (or William), 1:305
Thompson, William (of Colchester), 3:321, 322; 4:283; 5:63, 340, 440
Thompson, William (of Fauquier County), 3:161
Thompson, William (of Stafford County), 3:8, 9
Thompson, Joseph & Co. *See* Joseph Thompson & Co.
Thompson, Conn., 5:494
Thomson, Charles (illus., 5:445), 3:275, 329; 5:445, 447
Thomson, George, 5:382, 383
Thomson, Hannah Harrison (wife of Charles Thomson; illus., 5:445)
Thomson, James (minister), 4:200
Thomson, James (poet), 5:176
Thomson, Thomas, 5:382, 383
Thornhill, Dowding, 1:27
Thornton, Miss (daughter of John Thornton), 6:254, 256
Thornton, Mr. (Mount Vernon visitor), 6:312
Thornton, Mrs. (Mount Vernon visitor), 6:312
Thornton, Anna Maria Brodeau, 6:303, 306
Thornton, Anthony, 6:381
Thornton, Charlotte Belson, 5:50
Thornton, Elizabeth, 6:349, 350
Thornton, Francis (died c.1795), 2:166, 167
Thornton, Francis (d. 1784; of King George County), 3:170; 6:254, 350
Thornton, Col. Francis (Spotsylvania County), 1:251; 2:166
Thornton, George, 2:175
Thornton, Jane Washington, 6:254
Thornton, John, 3:170; 6:254

Thornton, Mildred. *See* Washington, Mildred Thornton
Thornton, Presley (1721-1769), 1:280, 281; 5:50; 6:381
Thornton, Presley (1760-1807), 5:50; 6:319, 320, 349, 350
Thornton, Robert, 4:42
Thornton, Sarah Fitzhugh, 3:170; 6:350
Thornton, Col. William, 1:120
Thornton, Dr. William (1759-1828; illus., 6:305), 6:205, 305, 306, 319, 327, 330, 333, 344, 348, 356, 365, 375
Thornton, William (son of Francis Thornton of King George County, d. 1784), 3:170
Thornton, Winifred Presley, 6:381
Three Brothers, the (Eureka, Broadback, and Willow islands), 2:301-2
Throckmorton, Albion, 4:350
Throckmorton, John, 4:350
Throckmorton, Mildred Washington, 2:101; 3:119, 120; 4:350
Throckmorton (Throgmorton), Robert, 4:12
Throck's (Throg's) Neck. *See* Frog's Neck
Thruston, Ann Alexander, 2:173
Thruston, Charles Mynn, 2:38, 39, 173, 176, 207
Thruston, Mary Buckner, 2:38
Tilghman, Anna Francis, 3:276
Tilghman, James, Jr., 3:277; id., 3:103; at Mount Vernon, 3:103, 114, 115, 118, 119, 146, 147, 149, 154, 160, 162, 173, 174, 175, 178, 187, 190, 193, 194, 200, 204, 209, 245, 246, 248, 249, 320; visits and travels of, 3:119, 190, 194, 209, 245; correspondence with GW, 3:167, 245
Tilghman, James, Sr., 3:103, 276, 277, 331, 334
Tilghman, Tench (illus., 4:347), 3:277, 376, 432; 4:87, 291, 292, 307; 5:163, 164
Tillotson, Margaret Livingston, 4:146
Tillotson, Thomas, 4:146

Index

Venango (Franklin), Pa., 1:136, 144, 177; GW at, 1:143, 144, 154, 4:59, 69

Vergennes, Charles Gravier, comte de, 3:372, 373

Verling, David, 2:58, 95

Verling's Virginia Company, 2:95

Vernon, Edward (illus., 1:216), 1:24

Verplanck, Gulian, 6:55

Vestal, John, 1:176, 276, 277; 4:5

Vestal, William, 1:277

Vestal's ferry. *See* Key's (Keyes') ferry

Viaggio negli Stati Uniti dell' America Settentrionale, 4:256

Vicars, William, 1:251

Vidler, Edward, 4:114

Ville de Paris (ship), 3:420, 421, 426, 433

Villeon, M. de la (French naval officer), 3:425, 426

Villiers, Louis Coulon de, 1:166, 169, 170, 171, 172

Vincennes. *See* Wabash Post

Vining, John, 6:45, 71, 89

Violette, Edward, 1:289, 296, 307

Vioménil, Antoine Charles du Houx, baron de, 3:427, 428

Virgin (slave, Home House), 5:355, 356

Virginia Convention, first (1774): called, 3:252; Fairfax County Resolves, 3:260-62; meeting of, 3:266-69; authorizes second convention, 3:309

Virginia Convention, second (1775), 3:309, 314-16

Virginia Convention, third, 3:322

Virginia Cross Creek. *See* Cross Creeks

Virginia Regiment: GW receives commission in, 1:174; disbanded, 1:295; bounty lands, 2:256, 261, 276, 277, 278, 3:12-13, 61, 63, 67-68, 138, 141-42, 144, 146, 200, 210, 226, 228, 4:39; disabled veterans, 3:94-95, 99

Virginia Short Creek. *See* Cross Creeks

Virginia Yazoo Company, 6:69, 108

Vobe, Jane, 2:193; 3:25, 68, 141, 142

Vobe's tavern, 2:193; 3:25

Wabash Post (Ouabache Post, Vincennes), 2:318, 320

Wabash (Ouabache) River, 2:319, 321

Waddell (Waddill), Edmund, 4:273, 274

Wade, Eleanor, 2:1, 57, 227, 331

Wade, Robert H., 6:341

Wade, Sarah, 2:1, 57, 227, 331

Wade, Valinda (daughter of Zephaniah Wade), 1:241, 242; 2:1, 57, 227, 331; 3:3, 14; 4:75

Wade, Valinda (wife of Zephaniah Wade), 2:1, 57, 4:321

Wade, Zephaniah, 2:1, 57

Wadsworth, Jeremiah (illus., 5:106), 3:368; 5:105, 106, 468, 469; 6:7, 45

Wagener, Miss (daughter of Peter Wagener), 5:407, 408

Wagener, Mr. (Mount Vernon visitor), 3:236, 307

Wagener (Wagoner, Wagner), Andrew, 3:228

Wagener, Ann, 5:408

Wagener, Mary Elizabeth, 5:408

Wagener, Peter (1717-1774), 2:121, 142, 167, 227, 255; 3:20, 33, 83, 171, 249

Wagener, Peter (1742-1798), 2:120, 121, 181, 182, 256; 3:9, 11, 31, 114, 147, 313; 4:116; 5:408

Wagener, Sarah ("Sally"), 5:408

Wagener, Sinah, 5:408

Wagener (Wagoner, Wagner), Smith, 3:228

Waggoner, Thomas, 1:195, 209, 210

Waite, Thomas, 1:237

Waite, William, 3:259

Wakefield, 2:63; 4:210

Waker, Mr. (midshipman), 2:253

Walden, Frederick von, 4:199

Wales, Andrew, 2:77; 5:423

Walke, Anthony (1692-1768), 1:305, 307

Walke, Anthony (1726-1782), 1:305

Walke, Anthony III, 5:333, 334

Walker, Ann Alton, 5:26

[535]

Washington, George (*cont.*)
gational clergy (New Haven, Conn.), 5:464; committee of Connecticut legislature, 5:464, 465; Hartford, Conn., mayor, aldermen, and common council, 5:469; Societies of the Cincinnati, 5:477, 478, 6:76, 137, 234; Boston citizens, 5:477, 478; Massachusetts executive, 5:477, 478; Harvard College, 5:477, 478; Salem, Mass., citizens, 5:483; Marblehead, Mass., citizens, 5:483, 489, 490; Massachusetts and New Hampshire Presbyterian clergy, 5:489, 490; Portsmouth, Mass., citizens, 5:489, 490; New Hampshire executive; 5:490, 491; Dartmouth College, 5:497; New Jersey legislature, 5:504; Virginia legislature, 5:510, 6:68; Congress, 6:6-7, 197; Roman Catholic clergy and laity, 6:46, 47; state of Georgia, 6:46, 47; intendant and wardens of Charleston, S.C., 6:47, 48, 129, 133; legislature of Georgia, 6:48, 49; faculty of St. John's College, 6:102; corporation of Fredericksburg, Va., 6:107, 108; city of Richmond, Va., 6:109; city of Petersburg, Va., 6:112; freemasons of St. John's Lodge No. 2 (New Bern, N.C.), 6:117; freemasons of King Solomon's Lodge (Trenton, N.C.), 6:118; inhabitants of Wilmington, N.C., 6:120; inhabitants of Fayetteville, N.C., 6:121; Masonic brethren of Prince George's Lodge No. 16 (Georgetown, S.C.), 6:125; inhabitants of Georgetown, S.C., 6:125; merchants of Charleston, S.C., 6:129; Grand Lodge of the State of South Carolina Ancient York Masons (Charleston), 6:130; people of Prince William's Parish (S.C.),

6:134, 135; freemasons of Georgia, 6:137; Congregational Church and Society of Midway, Ga., 6:137; mayor and aldermen of Savannah, Ga., 6:137; German congregation of Ebenezer, Ga., 6:137; citizens of Savannah, Ga., 6:137-38; citizens of Augusta, Ga., 6:141, 142; Gov. Telfair of Georgia, 6:143; citizens of Columbia and Granby, S.C., 6:147; citizens of Camden, S.C., 6:147; inhabitants of Salisbury, N.C., 6:152; United Brethren of Wachovia (N.C.), 6:153; inhabitants of Frederick, Md., 6:167; inhabitants of York, Pa., 6:168, 169; inhabitants of Lancaster, Pa., 6:169; inhabitants of Harrisburg, Pa., 6:181; inhabitants of Carlisle, Pa., 6:187; farewell address to army, 6:195-96; French minister (Adet), 6:215; Pennsylvania governor and legislature, 6:234; officers of the army, 6:234; council of Baltimore, 6:237-38

amusements: theater, 1:33, 81, 2:94, 95, 239, 247, 248, 3:3, 25, 41, 56, 63, 64, 67, 68, 95, 96, 97, 99, 100, 136, 137, 5:175, 176, 242, 243, 500-1, 502, 6:229, 230, 232, 233, 235; barbecues, 2:154, 261, 3:203, 204, 248, 271; sleight of hand, 2:181; concerts, 3:100, 5:163-64, 169, 239, 240, 477, 478; 6:131, 139, 153, 235-36; wax works, 3:143; puppet show, 3:143; boat race, 3:248, 249; fireworks, 3:255, 6:132, 139; turtle feast, 4:235; Gray's Ferry Gardens, 5:158, 159, 176, 183, 186, 238, 241, 246; Bartram's Botanical Gardens, 5:166, 168, 240; Chovet's Anatomical Museum, 5:174, 242; exhibition at Alexandria Academy, 5:210-11, 256; ratification celebration in Alex-

<cite></cite>

Index

Washington, Mildred (aunt of GW), 2:30; 5:340; 6:68
Washington, Mildred (daughter of John Augustine Washington), 2:215; 4:209, 210, 211
Washington, Mildred (daughter of Lawrence and Ann Fairfax Washington), 1:24
Washington, Mildred (daughter of Warner Washington). *See* Throckmorton, Mildred Washington
Washington, Mildred (sister of Warner Washington, Sr.). *See* Bushrod, Mildred Washington
Washington, Mildred Berry, 4:290
Washington, Mildred Thornton (wife of Charles Washington), 1:251; 2:166; 6:257, 260
Washington, Mildred Thornton (wife of Samuel Washington), 2:269
Washington, Mildred Warner, 2:63
Washington, Needham (Nedham) Langhorne, 5:436; 6:358
Washington, Richard, 3:297, 298, 302
Washington, Robert (d. 1765), 3:187
Washington, Robert (Lund Washington's brother), 4:168, 169, 218, 219, 283; 5:63
Washington, Samuel (brother of GW; illus., 2:268), 1:xxiv, 224, 2:167, 222, 278, 287, 326, 3:44, 204, 325, 4:93, 253, 5:19, 405, 406, 6:314; with GW in neighborhood, 1:224, 2:64, 271; id., 1:225, 270, 2:269; GW visits, 1:270, 2:63, 64, 87, 92, 278, 286, 324, 326, 3:13, 112, 239; vestryman for St. Paul's Church, 2:64; at Mount Vernon, 2:215, 218, 268, 269, 271, 3:162, 165, 204, 205; and land, 2:280, 286, 290; possibility of being inoculated, 3:63; finances, 3:155, 4:93
Washington, Samuel (son of Charles Washington), 2:167; 6:194, 256, 257
Washington, Sarah ("Sally"). *See* Bolling, Sarah ("Sally") Washington

Washington, Sarah ("Sally") Washington Harper, 1:118; 4:169
Washington, Susannah, 6:334
Washington, Susannah Perrin Holding (Holden), 5:405, 406
Washington, Thacker, 2:153
Washington, Thomas (nephew of Lund Washington), 4:168, 169
Washington, Thornton, 2:268, 269; 3:204; 4:290
Washington, Townshend, 2:37
Washington, Warner, Jr. (1751-1829), 2:101, 176; 5:50
Washington, Warner, Sr. (1722-1790), 2:129, 141, 153, 3:293, 4:4, 36, 52, 147, 350; at Fredericksburg, 2:101; id., 2:101, 173; fox hunting, 2:129; at Mount Vernon, 2:129, 132, 136, 141, 142, 157, 207, 236, 273, 276, 3:69, 70, 119, 120, 162, 165, 174, 175, 245; accompanies GW, 2:154, 276, 3:112; GW visits, 2:173, 180, 3:13, 110, 112, 292, 5:336; at Belvoir, 2:207; home of, 3:292
Washington, Whiting, 6:367, 378
Washington, William (1752-1810; illus., 6:133), 4:139, 153, 321; 6:98, 124, 133, 318, 359, 360, 364
Washington, William (1785-1830), 6:124, 134, 359, 360
Washington, William Augustine (1757-1810; illus., 4:209), 2:63; 3:188; 4:141, 142, 168, 209, 210, 211, 286; 6:311
Washington, William ("Billy") Augustine (1767-1785), 3:188, 322
Washington (ship), 6:60
Washington and Lee University (Liberty Hall Academy), 4:140
Washington, D.C. *See* Federal City
Washington District (N.C.), 6:43, 44
Washington District (Va.), 6:44
Washington Hotel (Carrington's tavern), 5:467, 468
Washington's Bottom, 2:290; 4:1, 2, 15, 16, 20, 21, 24, 33; 5:74; GW at, 4:18-25, 31, 32
Washington's Run, 4:21
Waterbury, David, 3:386, 387, 389, 398, 404

[546]

Index